CASSANDRA EASON'S
COMPLETE BOOK OF

Natural
Magick

CASSANDRA EASON'S

COMPLETE BOOK OF

Natural Magick

quantum

LONDON • NEW YORK • TORONTO • SYDNEY

quantum

An imprint of W. Foulsham and Co. Ltd
The Publishing House, Bennetts Close, Cippenham, Slough,
Berkshire, SL1 5AP, England

Foulsham books can be found in all good bookshops or direct from
www.foulsham,com

ISBN 0-572-03170-X

Copyright © 2006 Cassandra Eason

Cover illustration by Jurgen Ziewe

A CIP record for this book is available from the British Library

Printed in Great Britain by Creative Print and Design (Wales), Ebbw Vale

CONTENTS

INTRODUCTION

Natural magick is the oldest form of magick in the world. It is portrayed on the walls of Palaeolithic caves and on talismans of the hunt found etched on mammoth tusks, the earliest dating from 32,000 BCE.

From 35,000 BCE, Cro-Magnon man, the first recognisable human society, emerged. After this time until about 10,000 years ago, communities created hidden worlds in caves by drawing, painting and engraving animals and humans in animal masks dancing in rituals on the walls.

These animal images were not just representations of what the hunters saw. By drawing parallels with still-existing hunter gatherer societies and their rituals we can understand the magickal significance. Painting antelopes galloping across the cave walls, with some fallen and pierced with spears, was believed to call real antelopes to the hunting grounds and to guide the huntsman to where the animals would be. The finest examples come from the caves of Lascaux near Montignak in the Dordogne in France. The caves were discovered by four boys in 1940 and date back to the Palaeolithic age. They contain more than 2,000 pictures of horses, bison, deer and bulls. Because they follow the contour of the rocks, they appear three-dimensional and full of life. Against this backdrop, cave dwellers could not only invoke a successful hunt, but carry out rituals to increase animal and human fertility, the latter necessary for the survival of the tribe in hazardous times of incredibly high mortality

The practice of cave art has continued in hunter gatherer societies and there are many fine examples of more recent African and Australian rock sculptures (see pages 225 and 313).

The mother of all

The worship of the earth mother evolved within a few millennia of the emergence of modern humans, as people began to understand and marvel at female fertility. They developed the concept of a great earth mother who gave life in the form of human children and animal and bird young and brought the annual seasonal growth of plants. In her womb, the soil, the dead were buried and it was imagined returned to be reborn like the blossoming plant life. Ecologically the view is sound because the minerals restored to the soil by the decay of dead animals (and humans) is vital for a healthy crop of plants to feed and give life to herbivores who in turn are eaten by carnivores, who themselves die and return to the soil.

Before too long the link between the female cycle and that of the moon (see pages 431–35) was also made, and in societies where there is no artificial light women still menstruate by the moon. What is more, the greater cycle for all humans of birth, maturity and fertility, decline, death and even rebirth were mirrored in the sky in the phases of the moon.

Pregnant and at first featureless, mother goddess stone statuettes were probably the first fertility symbols, invoking the fecundity of earth and humankind. These statuettes have been found worldwide between 28,000 and 20,000 years ago, with prominent breasts and hips and have been named Venus figurines. In later periods they were carved with a girdle and necklaces and wore a headdress or had coiled hair like the earlier forms. They are frequently stained by smoke, suggesting that they were worshipped by the hearth as household gods.

The earliest known fertility figurine was found in Willendorf in Austria. She dates from 24,000 to around 22,000 BCE or perhaps even earlier. She is made of limestone tinted with red ochre. The first moon mother, the goddess of Laussel, was unearthed in the entrance to an Ice Age cave in the Dordogne region in central France. She dates from around 23,000 BCE. She holds in her right hand a bison horn, shaped like the crescent moon. The horn is divided with 13 marks probably representing the 13 moons in a lunar year. Her other hand is positioned over her womb.

The hunter and corn deities

A more evolved form of the earth mother became the mistress or lady of wild things among the nomadic hunter gatherer peoples. Because it was believed that the mother goddess gave birth to all forms of life, so she was entreated with the most precious parts of offerings from the first animal killed and in ritual dance and ceremony to release the herds into the hunting grounds. These goddesses exist today, for example Zonget, a Siberian mistress of the herds. Zonget rules all birds, animals and the people who hunt them. Birds and animals would allow themselves to be trapped if she ordained it and so shamans of the hunting peoples still have to make sure she is given offerings and that the creatures are treated with reverence or food supplies would cease. Zonget is said to appear to mortals in the form of a grey Arctic bird.

Even sophisticated Swedish city dwellers during the moose-hunting season leave the liver of the slain moose on a rock in the forest.

The lord of the hunt, the son or consort of the mistress of wild things, represented by the male shaman of the tribe, became an important figure from early on. One of the earliest recorded examples of magickal ritual is the Dancing Sorcerer. Painted in black and found on the cave walls of Les Trois Frères in the French Pyrenees, this shamanic figure that may portray a specific man dressed in animal skins and mask, dates from about 14,000 BCE and stands high above the animals that throng the walls. Only his feet are human and he possesses the large round eyes of an owl or lion, the antlers and ears of a stag, the front paws of a lion or bear, the genitals of a feline and the tail of a horse or wolf. Similar costumes can be seen in African seasonal and rites of passage ceremonies today.

In Neolithic times, as farming began from around 6,000 BCE, the lady of the wild things became in more settled communities the corn or barley mother, and the corn god replaced the lord of the hunt as the willing (or in some myths unwilling) annual sacrifice for the land. In different cultures these deities were given individual names and myths to explain reasons for the changing seasons (see pages 441–63).

In ancient Sumeria, the earth father was called Dumuzi, a mortal shepherd who gained immortality through his marriage to the fertility goddess Innana. The marriage brought fertility to the land, both crops and animals. However, Innana became angry and allowed the demons of the underworld to take Dumuzi away, whereupon barrenness fell on the earth. So she persuaded her sister Ereshkigal, goddess of the underworld, to allow Dumuzi's sister to replace him for half the year in the underworld. Therefore when Dumuzi was in the underworld the plants died. The subsequent re-enactment between high priestess and king of the sacred marriage at the year's turn ensured the coming of spring and the renewal of crop and animal life

The relevance of natural magick today

Early peoples and indeed people right through to the times of the Industrial Revolution recognised not only the importance of nature for their survival, but their own need to share ritually in the cycles of the seasons. The old nature goddesses were incorporated into the saints and the Virgin Mary and the corn god sacrifice was overwritten by the death and resurrection of Jesus Christ and by folk customs. Indeed the May queen and the annual cutting down and rebirth of the green man, ancient lord of vegetation, in modern May Day ceremonies are reminders of these older connections. In the 21st century the wheel of the year and our own personal life cycles continue to revolve.

Does it matter? I believe it does more than ever. The natural cycles of the sun and the moon, the seasons and the weather offer an accessible and instant source of energy and spiritual renewal in our daily lives, outside the window and off the freeways.

Though we may no longer as a society physically see the link between rituals for a good harvest and the food that appears in the supermarket trolley at the wave of a credit card, nevertheless nature still governs harvests and the weather. More than a third of the world's population is hungry while obesity and the disposal of food packaging are serious problems in westernised countries. Humankind's interventions or neglect of these natural cycles have contributed to ecological disasters on an unparalleled scale and the speeding up of natural processes like global warming so that Gaia, mother earth, is struggling to keep the balance within her creation.

The modern hyperactive lifestyle has, with 24-hour-a-day heating and lighting and processed food, beyond doubt accelerated our own frantic patterns of living. Twenty-four-hour-a-day shopping and television as well as zapping games consoles and bleeping text messages have, I am sure, increased stress-related illnesses, Attention Deficit Disorders and hyperactivity among children and adults.

Consumer spending has hit an all time high and yet a number of those people who apparently have everything feel alienated from modern life and lonely even when surrounded by family or living in the centre of a city. People spend a small fortune on ever more gut-churning simulated rides in Florida theme parks and adventure holidays, whereas they could go camping in wild places or take children to a woodland chalet or caravan by the sea for a fraction of the price.

But this is not an entirely gloomy picture. Forests are being replanted in the UK, for example Sherwood near Nottingham, and polluted waters cleaned up. Wild otters, after being threatened with extinction during the 1980s even in remote countryside by industrial pollution and destruction of their habitats, have returned to rivers and canals in the UK during the last five years. What is more, they are being seen right in the centre of towns from where they disappeared hundreds of years ago, for example along canal and river banks in the centre of Leeds, Bristol, Norwich, Doncaster, Newcastle and Glasgow.

Going back to nature

In the modern world, it is doubly valuable to those who live in towns or work in artificially lit and heated workplaces to reclaim natural energies for personal power, protection and healing. Country dwellers too may get caught up in the technological jungle. White witch and Druidess I may be, with the sea less than ten minutes down the road and the Downs five minutes from my front door, but I realise a week has gone by and apart from going into the garden to feed the birds and in the car to the supermarket or a radio broadcast, I have chained myself to my computer and barely even looked out of the window.

This book is about everyday living quite as much as magick. For if we can bring our bodies and minds back into harmony with the natural world we automatically open ourselves to the vast magickal powerhouse all around us, and can experience the ebbs and flows of energy that prevent burnout.

For more experienced witches I have developed the natural themes through rituals and suggestions for enriching more formal magickal practices and restoring the instinctive surge of spontaneous outdoor spell casting that needs very little in the way of tools or set formulas.

The book will begin with a brief overview on natural spellcasting and magick for newcomers, and in the following sections will draw on the practices of many cultures and ages. Though it is intended as a companion guide for my *Complete Book of Spells* (see Further reading, page 516), my *Complete Book of Natural Magick* is entirely self-contained. If you are more experienced you may wish to begin with Part 2. However, you may be interested in some newer techniques that I have developed since writing *Complete Book of Spells* while teaching witchcraft in Sweden. These are included in Part I.

PART I

ALL ABOUT MAGICK

INTRODUCTION

Natural magick is, as I said in the introduction to the book, spontaneous and dynamic. However, it still follows the basic laws of all magick and is indeed the oldest form of magick, going back to the last Ice Age when humans first sought to influence their lives by tapping into natural powers to seek the blessings of mother earth.

Essentially it is the easiest form of spellcasting for you have the energies all around you ready mixed, in the weather, the moon and the sun as well as trees, herbs, flowers, colours and fragrances. These will carry your wishes from your thoughts into actuality.

It is the magick of outdoors, whether a balcony in south London, the snowy pine forests of a Scandinavian winter, the Australian bush land, the shimmering quartz sands of Andalusia, an ancient stone dolmen on the Russian steppes or the desert and rocks of Arizona in the blazing heat of summer.

People have from time immemorial adapted their spells and rituals to the climate. However, in the modern world where we can fly from winter to summer in less than a day, we can work our magick in olive and orange groves or in cool deep mysterious woodlands in central Europe.

Above all we can visualise and call the powers of nature to us as we work so that our spells are filled with the vitality of the life force itself.

In the first part of the book I write about casting magickal squares and circles in the ground, adapting different kinds of magick to natural settings and creating symbols from natural materials. I explore the elements not as formal abstract magickal stages, but as real places and the natural substances that hold and will release their powers. I also write about the nature deities from many cultures that embody the different elemental energies. Above all I suggest ways you can not only structure your spells and rituals to tap into the store house of mother nature, but gain personal energy, health and happiness as you weave spells for others.

Though I have tried to cram in a lot of basic knowledge and some new perspectives that I have gained, this is a practical hands-on section where you can adapt my suggestions to your own needs and inspiration. Even if you are new to magick you can cast natural spells almost instantly.

Natural magick is like a quest. The following is a version of a Native North American legend that has been changed many times in the telling. I can't even remember the first time I heard it but for me it summarises what this part of the book and indeed the book itself is trying to say:

When the world was quite new, the Wise Creators decided that unlike the other creatures, humankind needed a Quest to discover the purpose of this earth journey. The other creatures, winged and four-footed, trees and stones, knew with their essence the purpose of their being, but humankind was more and yet less clever.
'Let us hide the answer at the bottom of the ocean,' said the whale, Lord of the Swimming Creatures.
'No, they will fish the oceans dry,' the others replied.
'Let's put it on the moon,' the owl, Guardian of the Creatures of the Night suggested.
'No, they will reach that and before long desecrate it,' the others said.
The little mouse, Lady of the Timid Creatures, who understood secrecy best of all, whispered, 'Let's put it inside of them; they will never look there.'

And so, for all but the true seekers, the answer is never discovered. Happy spellcasting.

WHAT IS NATURAL MAGICK?

Magick is a constantly flowing stream of energy. It is a concentrated and channelled form of the life force that flows through all animate life forms: people, animals, birds, insects and plants of all kinds. The life force is also present in rocks and crystals, in some cultures regarded as living energies, in rain, sunshine, the moon, winds, storms, the rainfall and the rivers and seas. In *Charge of the Goddess*, written by the late Doreen Valiente who revised much of Gerald Gardner's *Book of Shadows*, the high priestess speaks as the goddess:

> *I who am the beauty of the green earth, the white moon among the stars, and the mystery of the waters call unto thy soul; I am the soul of nature.*

This is a good summary of the powers of all magick, but especially natural magick that lies at its heart.

We receive and give out the life force in its spontaneous form through our aura, our psychic energy field that extends about an outstretched arm span around us. It also passes to and from our bodies through our chakras or psychic energy centres. These energy centres filter the aura energy and receive power from the earth beneath and the sky above us, from what we eat and drink and breathe and from those with whom we interact.

When you stand in the shallows of the sea and feel the waves pushing your toes, that sensation is the life force and the force behind magick. If you stand on a windy hillside and are tugged by the wind, that also is the life energy and the power behind magick. When you bury your feet in earth or press your soles against grass barefoot you are taking in the pure power.

Magick involves channelling and directing the life force by tapping into those energies in ritual and in spells and using the directed and concentrated flow to transfer thoughts and wishes (if positive) into actuality. This occurs in the same way that a strong wind can buffet you off course or the tide can lift you unexpectedly off your feet. It can be exciting occasionally to surrender yourself to the unchannelled might of nature and see where it carries you.

In spells and ritual, however, you structure words, images and actions to collect the power, and channel it into a named purpose. You can then amplify and release the concentrated strength into the specific purpose or area of the spell or ritual. In the release your wishes and focused thoughts make the transition through the psychic sound or light barrier so you have the impetus to make these desired possibilities come true.

What is the difference between a spell and a ritual?

In practice the terms 'spell' and 'ritual' are used interchangeably in magick and throughout this book as umbrella terms for magickal workings.

A spell tends to be a less formal kind of magick, usually cast for a specific purpose or need, for example to protect a named traveller (maybe yourself or a family member) on a particular journey or trip for a specified length of time. The energies are raised and then released so they will bounce back to activate the purpose of the spell which has been represented by a symbol of that journey. This physical focus of the spell might in natural magick be a feather or some chopped fennel herbs to symbolise travel.

In contrast a ritual is usually based on a more general or long-lasting focus. A ritual may be carried out at specified times, for example the first day of spring or to celebrate the birth of a baby. A ritual, even in natural magick, follows a more structured format.

What is more, whereas a spell builds up to a climax and release of energy, the ritual may release energy more evenly throughout the weeks and months ahead.

How is natural magick different?

Sometimes you might put on a lovely dress and dance in a ballroom following taught steps so that you and partner move in harmony. On other occasions you might dance spontaneously, moving freely alone on a moonlit seashore or at a friend's party to fast exciting music. Both are dancing, in the same way that formal magick and natural magick are both ways of performing magick. Neither is better, nor are they mutually exclusive.

Formal magick uses traditional rituals and beautifully made tools to control magickal energy, while natural magick uses tools made from natural materials: wood, clay, herbs, beeswax or crystal. Usually they are very simple because they are secondary to the setting of the spell or ritual. For where possible natural magick is performed outdoors, winter or summer, rain or shine, whether in woodland, on the seashore or in your garden. You can, in really bad weather or if it would not be safe or feasible to cast spells outdoors, practise natural magick inside your home by bringing in flowers, herbs or berries and by linking your magick to what is happening outside the window.

Sometimes on a seasonal festival or personal rite like a handfasting (pagan wedding) you may carry out quite an elaborate outdoor ritual and of course ritual magickal practitioners and covens do work outdoors where possible.

So natural magick involves a difference of emphasis and location, but adheres to all the traditional rules of magick that follow.

Natural magick in your life

The natural world is a power house of magickal energy that can be used to amplify our personal psychic powers and daily lives even if we don't have the time or inclination for a spell. We all possess these abilities but they can get blunted by modern life. Working with nature rapidly restores the instinctive connection with our own inner self and you find as a bonus that you are more intuitive and aware of hidden factors in your everyday decision-making. At specific times we can tap into the ever-changing energies of the sun, the moon, the seas, lakes and rivers and the weather and into the magickal qualities manifest in different flowers, herbs, trees and crystals. All these I will describe in the following chapters, so that you can tune into the best times and places, moon phases and days of the week to carry out your rituals – or to bring your daily life more into harmony.

There is nothing strange about our magickal powers; they are part of our right-hemisphere brain functions which include imagination and creativity. Working with symbols and images, the ability that underpins much magick is also located in the right-hand side of the brain. With practice we can expand possibilities first in our minds and then during rituals to transform the stored energies and magickal meanings contained in even everyday symbols and images into magickal power. For example, if we were working with a wax butterfly we had made, it would represent a new beginning because that is the meaning given to butterflies throughout the ages. The 16th-century mystic Teresa of Avila described the spirit leaving the body after death as a butterfly emerging from a cocoon. You might not be aware consciously of such symbolism (though much of this symbol code is stored in our genes to be awakened in magick), but you would instinctively know that by choosing a butterfly as a symbol in your spell, it would be a joy-bringing focus. Magick is the sister of psychology, and good magick operates on sound psychological principles.

Adapting natural magick to different traditions

Natural magick is an important part of coven work, and the spells and rituals I describe in this book can be easily adapted for a coven or for any group of friends or family who would divide the words and actions among them. I do write mainly for the solitary practitioner for that is the way I practise, and lone witches often do not have the support or teaching materials available to more organised groups.

In natural magick my training as a Druidess or nature priestess in the Celtic revival tradition fits perfectly into my beliefs as a white witch. The real difference is that Druidry emphasises solar aspects where witchcraft is more lunar based. In this book I have tried to give a mixture of both solar and lunar emphases.

Druidry uses a circle of trees for its sacred space. Many Druids and Druidesses do not cast circles before ritual, believing that all space is already sanctified. However, I recognise the need to mark out a protected area for magick that also provides a concentrated centre of power. I therefore find circle casting a necessary part of more structured rituals as opposed to a quick spell (though even here you can visualise a circle of light surrounding you). I have written more about this in the next chapter.

The directional quarters in natural magick are opened and closed in longer rituals. However you may prefer to picture the devas of the quarters (see page 483) more as wise higher nature spirits guarding them rather than the more stately lords and ladies of the watchtowers.

Equally I think it is important if working outdoors or with plants indoors to welcome nature essences into your circle and, if you wish, your wise ancestors who centuries ago may have lived in country places.

In the various chapters I have introduced relevant nature deity forms for you to use as you wish. However, you may choose to call on the generic earth mother and sky father, the moon mother and sun father, the mistress and lord of the animals or the corn goddess and barley god or open yourself to less differentiated benign and divine light of the universe or your own supreme goddess/god form. In witchcraft the goddess takes precedence, but the god figure is a necessary power to keep the dynamic balance. Aradia, daughter of the Graeco-Roman Diana, who was taught all magickal wisdom by her mother and Cernunnos the Celtic horned god, are popular pairings in modern witchcraft although they originate from different eras and cultures. Feel free to mix and match your deities. Isis, the Ancient Egyptian mother goddess and mistress of enchantment, is sometimes invoked in both her aspects. Isis Unveiled is the goddess of nature and the mysterious Isis Veiled is lady of the stars and the moon.

White magick

Like any spiritual force, magick is neutral, whatever its form. In the past, and even today in some parts of the world, formal religion can be used to justify all kinds of cruelty and intolerance. Magick used for dark purposes is really about power and sometimes people do hide behind the name and practices of witchcraft to abuse the vulnerable, whether physically, sexually or psychologically.

Usually these folks aren't really devil worshippers as they claim, but have watched some nasty inaccurate horror film about satanism and get themselves into all kinds of psychological as well as psychic minefields, not to mention the dreadful harm they do to others – and to the good name of witchcraft.

Almost as harmful in terms of misinformation and causing psychological damage, though not intentionally, are witch cult films that glorify special effect spells with fire, sulphur and blood sacrifice, ritual sex and mediaeval demons unleashed to grant their wishes.

I get a lot of e-mails to my website from distressed teenagers who have called up ancient demons from an on-line grimoire or adults who have gone along for a private initiation at the invitation of some self-styled magus or high priestess they met in a pub.

To real witches all life is sacred even that of the smallest insect. If you're looking for wild sex, forget witchcraft. You're more likely to get a list of herbs to learn or the altar silver to polish at your local coven than an invitation to attend a moorland orgy.

White or positive magickal practice, the kind recommended in this and other books by responsible witches and organisations such as The Children of Artemis, probably the best on- and off-line resource, is a highly moral and responsible code (www.witchcraft.org). Common sense is the key and covens are like gold dust to find. You can be sure if you are offered instant initiation in some lonely place or after a few private lessons; you should drink up and leave fast. It recently happened to me!

Natural magick is by its simplicity naturally protective and reassuring. However, in case we do get intoxicated by our own powers, floods, whirlwinds, volcanoes and earth tremors are a sharp reminder that we work with and do not control mother nature.

The rules of white magick

The rules of white magick are very moral. Some witches do practise magick while actively following a religious faith, because there is no need to compromise. You need integrity of the highest order when practising witchcraft. I do get letters to my website from Christians who are afraid they will be damned in hell because they are attracted to magick. The main misconception is that witches worship the devil. In fact the old horned god was a hunting god and witches do not believe in a devil as such.

Witches believe we choose to do wrong and so are accountable for any wrong words or actions. We can't blame a devil for tempting us, only our inner desires. Witchcraft accepts polarity in the expression of both goddess and god energies. It also recognises that evil is a fact as much as good and can't be eradicated once and for all. However, we should all work to increase goodness in the world and to contain and minimise the effects of those who choose to do harm.

The same polarity is described in Oriental philosophy as yang and yin, each of which contains the seed of the other, god and goddess, male and female, light and darkness, action and receptivity, hot and cold, summer and winter, dry and wet. Neither is better than the other but when one reaches its limits or extremes it must give way to the other, just as day follows night and night day. At the spring equinox (around 21 March in the northern hemisphere, six months later in the southern) light and darkness are equal. Thereafter light increases till the summer solstice around 21 June, after which darkness begins to multiply till the balance is restored on the autumn equinox, around 22 September in the northern hemisphere. The darkest nights and shortest days last until 21 December, the midwinter solstice, after which light slowly increases once more. In the magickal wheel of the year this dynamic struggle represents our own inner changes and dynamics.

In magick, therefore, you are accountable for your actions and can't just say sorry and three Hail Marys and be absolved. We have to try to put it right or carry the bad deed or karma (another Eastern Buddhist and Hindu concept) with us. This leads us to the first of the rules of magick, as explained below.

The first rule of magick:
You are free to do as you choose as long as you harm no one

This rule sounds deceptively simple to keep. However, scientifically it has been shown that a butterfly fluttering its wings subtly alters the energies of the universe. Therefore any decision, act or spell must affect others. We should never use magick to interfere with the free will of others, though there are binding spells that can restrict the effects of a person's negative behaviour (see page 24).

Of course in order to survive emotionally and sometimes to survive at all, you cannot always avoid hurting others in everyday life or in magick. So magick does involve a lot of careful thought and evaluation and usually relates to what is happening in our everyday lives.

Supposing you needed more money each month to pay the bills. You know a senior colleague at work is holding a comfortable, well-paid position under false pretences. She is leaving you to do her work and taking the credit. However justifiable your resentment you should not do a spell to get her fired. If you were subsequently offered her job (and it might be given to someone else just as nasty from outside the firm) you would never be happy in it because you got it by negative magick. You could instead do spells to raise your own positive profile at work so you do get offered promotion and also to take earthly steps to limit your colleague's plagiarism. You could, in addition, cast spells so that you would find a better-paid job where you were appreciated. Usually such free-loaders are noticed by higher management and may get moved on naturally.

The second rule of magick: What you send out comes back threefold

This is a great incentive to do magick to help others and for the environment.

If you use magick to send healing, love or abundance to other people, the same qualities will come into your own life unexpectedly in ways you need them, with three times the intensity.

Equally, if you send out negative thoughts or wishes in a spell to a nasty gossiping neighbour, you may well succeed in making the target of your spells unhappy. But this may make her gossip even more. What is more, similar unhappiness or nastiness will come back into your own life three times as powerfully – even if the person you are sending bad thoughts to deserves them. Bitterness and anger are natural emotions, best shared with a loving friend or relative or relieved by an hour digging the garden and not amplified in a magickal way to pollute the cosmos.

You know yourself that if you wake in a happy mood, you smile and everyone responds positively to you because your energy field is radiating happiness and so attracting it back. Think of the cosmos as a giant aura or energy field (more of this in rule 4) and do your share of Mary Poppins-style magick.

The third rule of magick:
You can ask for enough for your needs and a little more

Magick can be used for any area of your life where you need power, money, healing or protection. There is nothing wrong in asking for the resolution of an urgent problem. After all, you can't be drawing down lunar energies or healing rainforests successfully if you are worried sick about the bald tyre on your car and you've got to drive your grandma to hospital for her annual check-up the next day.

Witchcraft is and always has been about real people and their daily needs. As the Christian Lord's Prayer says, 'Give us this day our daily bread'. The religion of witchcraft is no less caring.

Our ancestors' seasonal and domestic rituals were based on the need for enough food, shelter and clothing. These were days when the harvest or the hunt was crucial to survival. The necessity of enough rain and sunshine for the growth of the seeds and animals formed the focus of seasonal rites. In societies that still depend on hunting, fishing or the harvest, these seasonal rituals have maintained their urgency and central position in the religious life of the community.

As long as your needs are realistic, you can usually obtain the resources you asked for, plus maybe an unexpected free upgrade, by doing even a simple spell. Be sure that your heart is in it and that you suspend logic – at least while casting the spell.

You can ask for love, health, healing, career success, fertility, concentration and an improved memory to pass an examination or take a test. As long you do put in the necessary hours of studying or earthly effort to bring your wishes to fruition, magick can give you the extra boost and the confidence to succeed.

The fourth rule of magick:
There must be cosmic balance

Though it is important, this rule is sometimes forgotten.

As I mentioned earlier, even the fluttering of a butterfly wing affects the energies of the universe. So when you take from the cosmos at a time of need, you must redress the balance by a practical gift at another time when you are able to give. This need not be financial giving but should involve positive effort. There isn't a time limit and if you are surviving on two hours' sleep with a teething baby, the cosmos won't charge interest on unpaid debts.

Sometimes you can pay back into the same area from which you took the energies. For example, if you used the power of the sea or a river in your spell to launch a venture, you could in the everyday world join a campaign for clean water in the Third World, help a harassed new mother with her washing and ironing or plan to feed the local ducks in winter when no one else bothers.

Occasionally perform an open-ended ritual to send out good vibes or healing to wherever it is most needed or to say thank you for your life, even if it is not perfect right now (it may suddenly and dramatically improve after the ritual).

Equally when you blow out your altar candles try to send the light to people who are being cantankerous or spiteful in the hope that it will brighten their aura. It may take a whole lot of butterflies to shift negativity but it is possible (and then you have some credit in the cosmic pot).

A Book of Shadows

If you practise magick mainly alone, your Book of Shadows will be among your most valued tools. I have seen Books of Shadows of all kinds, from dark leatherbound volumes with pentagrams engraved in gold leaf on the front to equally effective ones scribbled in old school notebooks.

Many magickal practitioners have a large book of unlined paper in which they record spells they have created themselves, any particularly beautiful chants they write or speak and personal associations for different herbs, flowers and crystals. They may also record the names of those who need healing and the dates when healing was sent.

Other sections describe seasonal celebrations, wisdom received during full-moon meditation and other times of power. Some practitioners will create lists of protective angels and pre-Christian deities whose qualities form a focus for different strengths and qualities.

It can be incredibly useful to have to hand details of a particular incense mix created when you threw lots of ingredients into your mortar and it smelled fabulous.

There may be a chant you created one morning at a sacred site high on the moorlands when the sky was blue and you had the place almost to yourself (if you don't count the children and the dog).

I once created a very spiritual walking chant in a huge turf labyrinth that linked my footsteps into the spiralling energies. But I didn't write it down and I have never been able to recall the sequence in its entirety. Even if you do buy a leather bound book, as your Book of Shadows, keep a notebook for your en route scribbles (in a waterproof bag with a waterproof pen for days when the sky is not so blue).

Keep a back-up of any charts or lists you develop on computer and a back-up CD in case you ever lose your book – for the contents are more precious even than the book itself.

Make time at least weekly to update it and express your insights, while you are waiting for a candle or incense to burn through at the end of a spell. At such a time you will find that you are especially open to prophetic abilities, and the most down-to-earth among us may write beautiful chants when inspired by a particular ritual or spell.

Keep your Book of Shadows safe and only share its insights with those who will respect your tradition. One day it will become an heirloom of great spiritual worth.

The name 'Book of Shadows' is also given to the formal handwritten reference book that is held by the High Priestess of a coven. Gerald Gardner, who founded the Gardnerian tradition, believed that the Book of Shadows, or grimoire, should be hand-copied from teacher to student, and some covens still adhere to this practice.

Different kinds of magick

Though I give numerous examples of spells and rituals in this book, the main purpose here is that you be able to create and cast your own natural spells and rituals. You can refer and add to or alter the lists of useful incenses, colours, etc. I give throughout the book, much as you would adapt and annotate a general recipe book rather than creating a set menu from it.

There are different kinds of magickal energies you can direct through spells and rituals. In more complex spells or those for life changes, you can combine two or more kinds of magickal power, for example first banishing sorrow or pain and then attracting new opportunities or health.

Attracting or sympathetic magick

Attracting magick is sometimes called sympathetic magick because a focus is used to represent a person or need and then magickal actions are carried out upon that focus to endow it with the necessary power. The accumulated power will then be transferred in the release of energy at the climax of the spell into the actual person or need represented by the symbol.

In natural magick it is more effective to choose or make a symbol of a natural material or something which is living: flowers for love, a small wooden toy house for a home move (my children's wooden Brio train sets have been appropriated for many magick spells), a feather for travel, seeds for the growth of a venture or prosperity and nuts for fertility.

Alternatively you can make wax symbols or figures by softening pieces of beeswax or a child's modelling clay, for example a small baby in a cradle if you wish to conceive a child. You are not creating the much-feared wax images in which pins were stuck. In fact, most wax dolls with pins displayed in museums were actually used as an early westernised form of acupuncture or the ends of the pins were tipped with a healing oil (to symbolise healing entering the person). After the spell has run its course, you can roll the wax back into a ball and bury it with the words: 'Return to your own element, with thanks.'

Equally every herb and crystal has magickal meanings and so can be a focus for a spell. A green aventurine crystal will when empowered in a spell bring you good luck and money, especially in matters of speculation.

Some spells are best repeated over several nights to build up the attracting powers. If you wanted a new love relationship to develop (with the proviso that it is right to be, the cosmic opt-out clause) you might move two beeswax candles, one pink and one green, closer on each of the three nights before the full moon for increasing energies. Finally, you would join the flames together on the fourth night of full moon power (more of lunar energies on pages 421–37).

Contagious magick is very similar but involves using something personal that the person has used or trodden over. For example an Eastern European marriage spell involves a woman scooping up the earth in which a lover's footstep is imprinted and planting marigolds, a love and marriage flower, in the soil. As the flowers grow, so it is said will the love, leading to marriage. Presumably in modern times there could be a role reversal.

Binding magick

Binding magick is sometimes considered a difficult area for white witches because of the issues of the infringement of free will. It is an area where careful and honest heart searching is needed to be sure your magick is for the highest cause and with the purest intent.

Some binding magick is straightforward. If you were going on a long journey, you could legitimately bind a small child to you temporarily so that he or she would not get lost or wander off, as the child is not old enough to take responsibility for him- or herself.

But what if you know a drug dealer is peddling in a place your teenager insists on visiting in spite of your warnings. Can you morally bind the drug pusher from harming your child without overriding their free will or that of your teenager? Some witches would argue the drug pusher is potentially threatening a lot of teenagers and not just your own and so could not be left to spread his poison.

It is possible with care to carry out positive and protective spells to bind such adverse behaviour, so that the drug peddler is not able to approach your child with the intent of doing harm.

You could bind your teenager, who after all is still young and vulnerable, from buying substances that will cause harm. You could add an attracting spell for your teenager to find new friends who spend their time in less dangerous settings and also to strengthen your teenager's natural moral standards.

Binding spells often involve the use of images or figures, such as dolls or ones made from beeswax or clay that you bind up with ribbons or cord (of course you do not harm the image). You would then gently wrap the figure in soft cloth and put it in a safe place until the specified time for the binding spell is through.

If there is not a set time, binding spells generally have to be recast monthly with new figures. The old doll should be returned to its element: to the earth if made of an earth substance; clay or wax should be rolled into a ball.

Since the drug pusher and teenager need to be kept apart you could put the drug pusher figure with blessings into the freezer compartment and wrap your child's image in a drawer. You could also, if you felt it morally right, create another figure to represent other unspecified teenagers in danger and wrap that separately but safely with your child's figure well away from the drug pusher doll.

Banishing magick

Banishing magick removes or returns any negativity, psychic attack or physical threats to you, your home or loved ones. It can be the next stage on from binding magick and may sometimes be necessary if a wrongdoer continues to pose a threat even after binding. So, for example, if binding the drug pusher didn't work and teenagers were still being dragged into the drug pusher's web, banishing might be the next stage.

As with binding, though you can't banish a person, you can banish their bad influence from your life or that of a loved one, so you might put a dead branch on top of a hill and for each dead leaf say:

May his harmful influence be banished from the lives of these young (or indeed all vulnerable) people.

Leave the branch and as the wind strips the leaves away so the influence would hopefully decline.

In fact, this is a real case. Being a nasty character, the drug pusher was not affected by the binding, though the particular teenager involved, whose mother I helped, did inexplicably, she said, suddenly stop going to the club.

A week after the banishing spell the drug pusher was forced to leave the neighbourhood as he had fallen foul of a local gang for selling them impure drugs. No one has taken his place at the club.

Because banishing magick in the protective context is stronger than binding magick and you are tackling what may be bad vibes head on, it should be used sparingly on both people and situations.

However, it can be used very positively. You can cast banishing spells to get rid of sorrow, sadness, pain and sickness, bad habits or the negative effects of people who make you unhappy.

Banishing magick can also help you to end in your own mind the ties of a destructive relationship, especially if you have been betrayed or badly treated but blame yourself or cannot let go. Sometimes we need the impetus of a spell if we are to walk away or get over the old sad scenes that run round and round in our heads and stop us from moving on.

For this kind of banishing, place a beeswax candle on a metal tray. Then hold a natural fabric cord or a long reed grass taut, an end in each hand, over the flame. As you burn the centre of the cord till it breaks, say:

*I cut the cords that bind me (or another person you are doing the spell for) to (name
the destructive person or bad habit, for example smoking or binge eating).*

You may need to repeat this spell many times using shorter cords or reeds. Bury the burned cords or reeds when they are no longer required.

You can also use banishing magick to protect yourself from harm by returning any ill wishes, spite, malice, gossip, curses or hexes to the sender without adding any bad feelings of your own. Under the threefold law, what ill wishers send out they get back three times as strongly. Simply say:

I return what is yours. Send it not again.

As you speak, hold your hand palm outwards, fingers splayed into the wind.

2

SPELLCASTING

Spellcasting involves following a format that provides the structure to channel, amplify and release energies to bring into actuality the fulfilment of a wish, a need or desire. In this chapter I will provide the background knowledge you need for successful spellcasting and rituals and for generally using magickal energies in your daily life.

Spellcasting can bring results fast if you really are in a crisis situation, perhaps because you endow the spell with the urgency and emotion. Mel, a 25-year-old store manager living in a historic town in the south of England, desperately needed a home to rent and had been to every agency in the town with no results. A couple of days before she was due to move out of her present flat, Mel did a simple spell to find her a comfortable, affordable home as soon as possible. She took the symbol she had empowered, in fact a written one, to work having slept with it under her pillow.

The next morning her mobile rang. It was a man to say he and his wife had a home to rent and she could go to see it that evening. When Mel got there the house was perfect and affordable but the couple had no idea where they got her number because she hadn't given it out and they had not even got round to advertising the house, so it had not come though an agent. The couple said they would let her know, but just as Mel was driving off disappointed, the man ran after her and said the house was hers and she could move in the next day. The couple didn't know anyone to whom Mel might have mentioned the house problem. Mel moved into the house soon afterwards and was very happy there.

The energies of someone wanting to rent out a property and Mel's urgent need must have telepathically been drawn together (more of the mechanics of this process later in the chapter).

Of course most spells aren't as instant and may involve more earthly leg work. However, spells do get the energies moving and usually bring into your sphere, through unexpected opportunities or seemingly chance meetings, what it is you need – at the time you need it. Under the rules of cosmic exchange you need to be willing to reciprocate by passing on information or surplus items when you hear through a friend of a friend of a need, even if this involves a lot of effort or you are busy at the time.

Sometimes the stages of a spell are clearly defined as set out in the next chapter where I will run through a checklist of the step-by-step mechanics. On other occasions spells evolve more subtly and stages become combined.

Rituals also follow similar stages beginning with a statement of the purpose, adding elemental powers and ending with the desired result. This would, for example, be the rebirth of light at the December midwinter solstice, celebrating the return of the sun after the shortest day – and, as importantly, acknowledging or bringing your own rebirth or renewal of hope.

The power of words in spellcasting

We already know, words have the power to heal, to express love, to praise and to comfort and negatively to hurt or criticise.

In magick, words spoken deliberately and rhythmically are one of the most significant ways to build up the energies in a spell and I have written about chants in detail in the section on sound magick (see page 291).

In Ancient Egyptian magick, the basis for modern magick, one of the major creation myths tells how Ptah the creator god, *thought* the world in his mind and then created it by speaking magickal words or *hekau*. The generative power he used was called Heka, which is also the name of the god of magick. This power is equivalent to the concentrated life force I described in the previous chapter. In some versions of the myth it is Heka himself who speaks the words that give form to the thoughts of Ptah.

The Ancient Egyptians believed that this creative power animated every spell as it did at the first creation. So to the Ancient Egyptians every act of magick was a recreation of that first act of world creation, using words to bring thoughts into actuality.

Amplifying the power of your words in magick

A funerary spell from a Middle Kingdom sarcophagus (coffin) may be found in a corner of Cairo Museum, a museum where it is said to take many months to see every exhibit. Here is a rough translation of the spell. By reciting the words you absorb magickal power into yourself or in more modern terms awaken your own inner higher spiritual and magickal mind power.

To become the god Heka
I am Heka, the one who was made by the Lord of All before anything, the son of he who gave
form to the universe. I am the protector of what the Lord of all has ordained to be.

Reciting this in your mind can be a good way to empower yourself at those times when you are scared or anxious or the odds are totally against you – or to open a spell or ritual when you have a particularly important issue to tackle. In this way you can assume the power of a specific deity of nature and channel this into your spellcasting and indeed your everyday life.

For example, the Celtic Epona, the white horse mother goddess who was worshipped even by the Romans, is wonderful for women travelling alone as well as for evoking fertility (see page 218).

In coven work the High Priestess, sometimes assisted by the High Priest, draws the power of the goddess within herself for the duration of the rite.

If you work alone you can ask for specific deity powers to strengthen you for particular ventures. I have listed deities in the various chapters and also in the elemental correspondences later in this chapter (see page 31).

This is not blasphemous or presumptuous. You are using the inner divine spark we all possess and plugging into an amplified version of that power, as contained within the archetype or ideal of a particular divinity. It is only if you still think you are Isis, who can stop the sun, while you are in the supermarket queue that you need a bit more earthly input in your life and maybe a short break from magick.

Internalising natural magick

In natural magick you can borrow elemental qualities, taking into yourself spiritually the power of the elemental forces – for example the power of the wind when you add the air element to the symbol in a spell (see also pages 328–31 on air magick).

For example, you might say the following as you add incense power to your symbol that represents the purpose of the spell.

I am that mighty wind that blows through time and takes away inertia. And so I empower _____ and myself to bring change.

You can use the crashing of the sea, the wind in the trees or the falling rain on your tent to amplify and give your words rhythm. You may find it helpful to hold a symbol as a focus while you speak.

It is quite possible to carry out a spell or indeed a ritual just by using words. Taking it one stage further, the ritual or spell can be visualised, using both words and actions in your mind. In order to stimulate your psychic senses you may choose to carry out this visualised spell while sitting on the seashore or in a glade. Once you are experienced at visualisation, you can bring that glade on to a crowded train or into an airless office as you weave your spell.

The beauty of inner spells and rituals is that there are no limits. Your air element really can be shooting stars, your water element a sparkling waterfall or tropical blue ocean. Then next time you carry out a spell externally you will still be able to feel and see those shooting stars or that sparkling water, and so your work is enriched and more powerful.

Even if you are quite experienced in magick these spoken or internalised spells are a very good way of aligning your mind with powerful external forces and thus bringing them together in your rites. They are also useful if you are in a special place but circumstances mean that you are not able to start chanting or dancing. You may be in a sacred place or one of outstanding beauty, but accompanied by a tourist party or your in-laws.

By working on this astral or spiritual plane, as you speak the words in your mind you can carry the purpose of the spell through the barrier on to the earth plane of actuality.

Working with the four elements

In all magick and most powerfully in natural magick the four ancient elements earth, air, fire and water form the building blocks of magickal power and can be used formally and informally in spells to endow a symbol with power and to build up that power.

The combination of the four elements creates a fifth element, ether or akasha, or quintessence, pure spirit, the energy and also the substance that transforms thoughts and desires to actuality.

This is the symbol of spirit. This is the energy released at the climax of a spell that shoots your wish into the cosmos – and then bounces back into actuality.

We all contain these four elements within our personalities in different proportions. The psychotherapist Jung talked about earth equating with sensations (practical functioning), air with thought (logic), fire with intuition (inspiration) and water with feelings (empathy and emotions). We can call upon these strengths as contained within elemental substances and in nature both in spells and in our lives to bring their powers into play.

The inner powers of the elements, for example the practical stability of earth or the inspiration of fire, can be brought into the actual world for the fulfilment of your spell. This happens first when you visualise the elements, for example a beautiful golden ploughed field for earth or a tall bonfire for fire, and then in the words you use when calling the power of the element, for example by making a chant about all the different ways you imagine the earth. This transfers the powers of the elements into your mind. Then, on the physical level, you work with, say, salt for earth and a candle flame for fire, and this together with your visualisation and words joins the powers of the elements on the thought and actual levels. The energy created is the key to successful spellcasting as the intangible thoughts and the actual substances come together.

Sometimes you will put the emphasis on one or two particular elements, for example earth and air to speed up a house sale and/or purchase.

In this case you could choose a setting, for example a woodland on a windy day or the rough grass on a hill top. You would use a combination of earth- and air-related symbols, for example a feather tied to a white stone to represent your new home (you could draw a house on the stone). You could then release the feather at the end of the spell.

In a pure water ritual, for example to send healing to a particularly polluted body of water where your children would like to swim, or to ask for clean drinking water for those who do not have it, you could light blue candles at each of the four quarters and perhaps have a cauldron or dish of water in the centre. You could symbolically purify this water with a few drops of flower essence such as Dr Bach's Five Flower Rescue Remedy or pour one of your magickal waters (see pages 124–37) into the earth. (See pages 280–90 for more suggestions of flower remedies.)

Of course the other elements would be present. Incense (air) would empower, activate and help the need to be communicated to those who can help resolve it. Fire (candle) would inspire and give the necessary force to make actions and not just words happen in the real world. Earth (salt) would sort out the practicalities such as who will pay for clean water. Then you can create the necessary magickal rocket of power in the fusion of the four elements. When these four meet, they become a fifth element called quintessence, ether or akasha. This collective energy fills the physical symbols with the psychically generated power.

Elemental mixing and matching

Most of the associations in the following lists, such as the places, seasons, times of day, deities, animals and birds are intended to give you ideas when you are creating your own spells. These may inspire chants and empowerments or suggest natural settings for your spells.

In some spells you might focus on the animals associated with the four elements or, in another, the different crystals. You might call on different elemental deities or draw together a number of associations in your chants and your visualisations as you add the physical elemental substances to your spell.

Essentially the elements provide the driving force and the substance of your spellcasting and ritual work and, in their combination or by emphasising certain elements, you can create the power necessary to synthesise the energies in Spirit where conscious limitations on possibility no longer exist.

Sometimes this all happens spontaneously. On the summer solstice last year I splashed through the first path of sunlight (fire) in the shallows of the sea (water), holding my dish of herbs and flowers (earth) upwards to the sky (air). I didn't really need to say or do very much to feel the elements combining to make Spirit and add power to the energies of that special morning. Some of these energies were then drawn back into myself and into the herbs and flowers as I used them over the following days.

You will no doubt want to add to the elemental deity lists as you read more of the book and indeed to incorporate those you already know and love. You can, as I said, pair across any tradition of elements.

If you associate herbs or crystals with different elements to those shown on the following page, feel free to change them as there are no definitive associations, only those that different people have sometimes agreed work best.

Earth

Direction: north

Time: midnight

Season: winter

Colours: green, brown

Qualities: stability, common sense, practical abilities, caretaking of the earth, protectiveness, upholding of tradition, love of beauty, patience, perseverance, generosity, acceptance of others, nurturance

Rules over: abundance and prosperity, fertility (also fire for fertility), finance, law and order, institutions, authority, motherhood, the physical body, food, home and family, animals, the land, agriculture, horticulture, environmentalism

Animals: badger, bear, bee, bull, serpent, snake, spider

Archangel: Uriel, the archangel of transformation, whose name means fire of god, the archangel who brought alchemy to humankind.

Uriel brings warmth to the winter season and to cold or unhappy periods in our life. He melts the snows with his flaming sword or torch. Ecologically he works at conserving resources, protecting rainforests, wildlife habitats and endangered species.

Visualise him in rich burnished gold and ruby red with the brightest flame-like halo and fiery sword, like a bonfire blazing in the darkness.

Crystals: amazonite, aventurine, banded brown agates, emerald, fossils, jet, malachite, moss agate, petrified wood, rose quartz, tree agate, all yellow brown and mottled jaspers like Dalmatian jasper, rutilated quartz, smoky quartz, tiger's eye and all stones with holes in the centre

Elemental creatures: gnomes (see page 501)

Goddesses: Cerridwen, the Celtic Great mother, keeper of the cauldron of inspiration and rebirth

Gaia, the Ancient Greek earth mother, whose name has been given in modern times to the earth

Hecate, wise crone goddess of the Ancient Greek tradition who also rules magick, good fortune and the waning moon

Isis Unveiled, from the Ancient Egyptian tradition, as mother of nature and protectress of all

Mati Syra-Zemlya, or Moist mother earth, the Slavic goddess, who spins the web of life and death

Nerthus, the Ancient Viking earth mother, associated with the fertility of the crops and her successor, Frigg, wife of Odin and patroness of women and childbirth

The Virgin Mary

Gods: Cernunnos, Horned god of the Celts, who is also called Herne from the Anglo Saxon

Frey or Ingvi, Viking and Anglo Saxon names for the god associated with the fertility of the earth

Geb, the Ancient Egyptian earth god and consort of Nut the sky goddess, associated with the sacred goose who laid the egg from which the world emerged

The green man, the ageless god of vegetation, still recalled in May-time celebrations

Osiris, son of Geb and consort of Isis, who after his murder by his brother became the embodiment of the annual growth of the corn, watered by the tears of Isis at the Nile flood

Herbs and incenses: bistort, cypress, fern, geranium, heather, hibiscus, honesty, honeysuckle, knotweed, magnolia, mugwort, oak moss, oats, oleander, patchouli, primrose, sagebrush, sorrel (wood), sweetgrass, tulip, vervain, vetivert

Places: caves, the crypts of churches and cathedrals, forests, gardens, grass, groves, homes, ley or psychic power lines in the earth, megaliths, ploughed fields, rocky places, snow- or ice-covered lands and glaciers, sand (see also fire), stone circles, temples

Sacred substance: salt (also soil and clay)

Zodiacal signs: Taurus, Virgo, Capricorn

Air

Direction: east

Time: dawn

Season: spring

Colours: yellow, grey

Qualities: logic, clear focus, an enquiring and analytical mind, the ability to communicate clearly,  concentration, versatility, adaptability, quest for truth, commercial and technological acumen, healing powers through channelling higher energies

Rules over: new beginnings, change, health and conventional healing, teaching, travel, house or career moves, knowledge, examinations, the media, science, ideas, ideals and money-spinning

Animals: all birds of prey (especially the eagle and hawk), butterfly, moth, white dove

Archangel: Raphael, the healer archangel and travellers' guide. He is the angel who offers healing to the planet and to humankind and all creatures on the face of the earth, in the skies and waters, especially effective against technological and chemical pollution and the adverse effects of modern living. He is depicted with a pilgrim's stick, a wallet and a fish.

Visualise him in the colours of early morning sunlight, with a beautiful green healing ray emanating from his halo.

Crystals: amethyst, citrine, clear crystal quartz, diamond, lapis lazuli, sapphire, sodalite, sugilite, turquoise

Elemental creatures: sylphs (see page 505)

Goddesses: all moon and sky deities (moon goddesses also rule water)

Arianrhod, the Welsh goddess of the full moon, time and destiny, who turns the wheel of the stars

Diana, goddess of the witches, the moon and huntress goddess of the Ancient Greeks and Romans. Her daughter Aradia came to earth to teach her mother's wisdom (Aradia arguably is an earth, air, fire and water goddess)

Myesytsa, the Russian moon maiden who was the consort of Dazhbog the sun god and became mother of the stars

Nut, the Ancient Egyptian sky goddess whose body arches over the earth, covered in stars and into whose womb Ra the sun god enters to be reborn each night

Pavati (or Parvati), wife of Shiva, the father god in Hinduism, the beautiful young goddess of the mountains, who is the catalyst and power source without which Shiva would be impotent

Gods: Hermes, the winged Ancient Greek messenger and healer god who, like Mercury, his Roman counterpart, is also god of medicine, money lenders and thieves

Horus, the Ancient Egyptian sky god, represented as a falcon or a falcon-headed man. His eyes were the sun and moon and his wings could extend across the entire heavens

Jupiter the supreme Roman sky god whose Greek counterpart was Zeus, who cast thunderbolts upon the unrighteous

Myesyats, the Slavic moon god, who represented the three stages of the life cycle as a youthful, a mature and then an old man

Odin, the Norse god (the Anglo Saxon Woden), known as all-father, god of inspiration, wisdom and poetry as well as war

Herbs and incenses: acacia, agrimony, almond, anise, benzoin, bergamot, borage, caraway, clover, dill, elecampane, eyebright, fennel, fenugreek, lavender, lemongrass, lemon verbena, lily of the valley, linden, marjoram, meadowsweet, mulberry, Nag Champa, palm, papyrus flower, peppermint, sage, star anise

Places: balconies, cliffs, hills, mountain tops, open plains, planes (looking out of the window at banks of cloud), pyramids, roof gardens, the sky, steeples and spires of churches and cathedrals, tall buildings, towers, open windows, anywhere by moon or starlight

Sacred substance: incense

Zodiacal signs: Aquarius, Gemini, Libra

Fire

Direction: south

Time: noon

Season: summer

Colours: red, orange, gold

Qualities: fertility in all aspects of life, creativity, light-bringing power, passion, joy, initiating, transformation, courage, mysticism, clairvoyance, prophecy

Rules over: ambition, achievement, illumination, inspiration, all creative and artistic ventures, poetry, art, sculpture, writing, music, dance, religion and spirituality, psychic powers especially higher ones such as channelling, innovation, sexuality. It is also potent for destruction of what is now no longer needed, for binding and banishing rituals and so for protection

Animals: dragonfly, firefly, fox, lion, lizard, stag, tiger

Archangel: Michael, archangel of the sun and light and the warrior angel.

Michael is the angel of power and of illumination and brings in the summer season and fertility, growth and energy into our lives and to the land, to animals and the crops. He is also potent, for reviving barren land despoiled by industrialisation and for cleansing air pollution.

Visualise him resplendent in scarlet and gold with a huge sword, golden scales in his other hand and often a dragon crushed beneath his feet.

Crystals: amber, bloodstone, boji stones, carnelian, garnet, hematite, iron pyrites, lava, mookaite, obsidian, red jasper, ruby, sunstone, topaz

Elemental creatures: salamanders (see page 507)

Goddesses: Amaterasu Omigami, the Japanese sun goddess whose name means 'great August spirit shining in heaven'

Brighid, the Celtic triple (three sisters) goddess of fire and of the hearth, patroness of healers, poets and smiths

Gabija, the Lithuanian goddess of the hearth fire, who was honoured by throwing salt on the fire each evening after the main meal

Pele, goddess of volcanoes, fire and magick, who is still revered in Hawaii by those who claim descent from her and who still set up altars near lava streams

Saule, Baltic queen of the heavens and earth, dressed and crowned with gold who drove her golden chariot across the skies, and danced with her daughters the planets on the festival of St Lucia, the light maiden, just before the midwinter solstice

Sekhmet, the Ancient Egyptian lion-headed solar goddess of fire and healing who is the patroness of modern businesswomen

Vesta, the Roman goddess of sacred fire whose Virgins tended the sacred fire in Rome

Gods: Agni, the Hindu god of fire, who is said to be manifest as the vital spark in mankind, birds, animals, plants and life itself

Apollo, the Graeco-Roman sun god, who was twin brother of Artemis, the moon goddess, and was patron of the arts, especially music, beauty and harmony

Helios of the Greeks, known to the Romans as Sol, who was regarded as the sun himself. He ascended the heavens in a chariot drawn by winged snow-white horses to give light, and in the evening descended into the ocean

Lugh (Llew in Wales), the ancient Irish god of light and the cycle of the year, born at the midwinter solstice, made king at the summer solstice and willingly sacrificed at Lughnassadh at the beginning of August in order to maintain the fertility of the land and ensure the success of the harvest

Ra or Re, the Ancient Egyptian sun god who sailed the sun boat across the heavens during the day

Herbs and incenses: allspice, angelica, basil, bay, cactus, carnation, cedarwood, chamomile, chrysanthemum, cinnamon, cloves, copal, dragon's blood, frankincense, galangal, garlic, juniper, lime, marigold, nutmeg, olive, orange, pennyroyal, rosemary, snapdragon, sunflower, tangerine, thistle holy, thistle milk, witch hazel

Places: bonfires, all conflagrations, deserts, hearths, hilltop beacons, lightning, sacred festival fires, solar eclipses, thunder, volcanoes, at the height of noon or at a blazing sunrise or sunset, plains shimmering in the heat, any sunny place, sandy shores on hot days, near banks of yellow or golden flowers

Sacred substance: candle

Zodiacal signs: Aries, Leo, Sagittarius

Water

Direction: west

Time: dusk

Season: autumn

Colours: blue, from dark inky or grey blue to brilliant Mediterranean turquoise; silver

Qualities: intuition, empathy, sympathy, healing powers, inner harmony, peacemaking, unconscious wisdom, divinatory powers especially connected with water scrying, ability to merge and interconnect with nature, the cycles of the seasons and the life cycle

Rules over: love, relationships, friendship, dreams, the cycle of birth, death and rebirth, purification rites, alternative healing, using the powers of nature, especially crystals and sacred water, all water and sea magick, moon magick, travel by sea

Animals: albatross, dolphin, frog, heron, seagull, seal, shark, toad, whale, all fish, especially salmon, fish of the summer on the native North American Medicine Wheel and of wisdom in the Celtic tradition

Archangel: Gabriel, archangel of the moon, who represents the fruits of the harvest, the rewards of our successes and the need to let go of our failures and regrets.

Gabriel protects fish stocks, those who travel across water and against inclement weather. He cleanses polluted seas, lakes and rivers.

Visualise him in robes of silver and midnight blue with stars interwoven on the crescent moon in his halo.

Crystals: aquamarine, blue and pink chalcedony calcite, coral, fluorite, jade, moonstone, ocean or orbicular jasper, opal, pearl, tourmaline

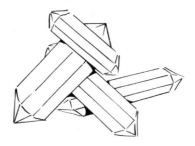

Elemental creatures: naiads (see page 510)

Goddesses: all moon and water deities

Coventina, indigenous British water goddess of sacred springs; also revered at sacred wells in Spain and Gaul

Ganga, the Hindu healing water goddess who is manifest as the sacred river Ganges and was daughter of the Himalayas

Heket or Heqet, the frog-headed Ancient Egyptian goddess who breathed life into the clay figures that her husband Knum the potter god made; a goddess of fertility and creativity

Mama Cocha or Mother Sea, the Peruvian whale goddess

Ran, the Norse sea goddess who loves gold more than anything else; a goddess of protection

Sedna the ancient sea mother of the Inuit people who releases the seals and shoals of fish for hunting

Stella Maris, patroness of sailors, fishermen and travellers by sea, once identified with Isis and now associated with the Virgin Mary who is depicted in this role with a crown of stars

Gods: Hapy or Hapi, the god of the Nile flood, who wears flowing papyrus and lotus flowers on his head, carrying a loaded offering dish with wine, food and lotus blossoms, as a symbol of his fecundity

Mannanan or Manannan mac Lir, Lord of the Otherworld Isles of the Blest which include the Isle of Man and Arran; he casts magickal mists around them to keep away danger

Poseidon, Greek god of the sea, who carried a trident, became Neptune in the Roman tradition and was said to have drowned Atlantis (or some blame Zeus) because of the corruption of this Golden Race

Tlaloc, the Aztec god of rain, whose eyes and nose were formed of intertwined serpents and who was entreated in annual ceremonies to bring rain to fertilise the crops

Herbs and incenses: apple blossom, apricot, Balm of Gilead, camellia, catnip, coconut, coltsfoot, cowslip, cyclamen, eucalyptus, feverfew, hyacinth, iris, jasmine, lemon, lemon balm, lilac, lily, lotus, lucky hand, myrrh, orchid, passionflower, peach, sandalwood (sometimes under air), strawberry, sweet pea, tansy, thyme, valerian, vanilla, violet, yarrow

Places: flooded land, flood plains, fountains, lakes, marshland, the ocean, ponds, pools, rainy days, rivers, sacred wells and streams, water features

Sacred substance: water

Zodiacal signs: Cancer, Scorpio, Pisces

Psychic protection

Finally comes the all-important issue of protecting yourself psychically while you cast spells or carry out rituals.

Casting a circle and/or a magickal square (see page 57) offers you a great deal of psychic protection as does the process of grounding yourself after a spell (see page 52).

Also doing spells only for positive purposes and with good intent is in itself protective. There is no point in standing within circles, squares or triangles if you are summoning up dark forces or playing about creating elemental thought forms. If what you are doing makes you uneasy or you couldn't tell your best friend, mother or sister (if they are generally sympathetic towards magick) what you are up to, don't. That is the basic rule. The following may also help.

* Set an earth crystal, an air crystal, a fire crystal and a water crystal (see lists on the previous pages) that you have sprinkled with a sacred water mix (see page 124) at the main direction points around a room or an area where you are working. As you set each one, ask for the protection of light and goodness (or dedicate each to a special deity).
* Alternatively, use an ordinary round dark brown stone for the north, a white one for the east, a reddish one for the south and a pinkish grey for the west. The north and west stones should be round or diamond shape and the others pointed.
* Wash the crystals or stones in running water after the spell or ritual.
* Read the chapter on angel magick (pages 469–82) for information on using angelic protection.
* You can designate the four traditional archangels to the four watchtowers, external direction points around the room, your outdoor circle or your altar (see pages 473–78 for the archangel of each element and his candle colours and crystals, etc.).
* Light four angel candles (see previous pages for colours or use natural beeswax) and place them halfway along each actual or visualised line of a magick square or round your circle at four main direction points.
* Even if you don't cast a circle for a simple spell you can picture the four angels or substitute angels of nature for the four archangels. Though the conventional elemental archangels do have ecological foci, you may prefer to choose a nature angel for each element especially for outdoor magick and use his herbs, crystals and candle colour to complete your protection. Four especially suitable nature angels now follow.

Nature angels

Zuphlas

Angel of the forests and of trees

Picture him in pine green, with a halo entwined with laurel and pine, his wings wreathed in leaves and carrying a golden axe and a staff from which are sprouting small branches, leaves and blossoms.

Direction: North

Colour: Soft moss green or autumnal orange

Incenses: Apple or orange blossom, cedar, eucalyptus, pine, tea tree

Herbs: Basil, bay, thyme

Crystals: Green jasper, jet, petrified wood, rutilated quartz, tree agate

For more on Zuphlas, see page 478.

Rampel

Angel of the mountains and the high places

Picture him wearing deep purple, his wings perpetually shrouded in silver mist. He is very tall and slender.

Direction: East

Colour: Dark blue or indigo

Incenses: Frankincense, heather, hibiscus, hyacinth

Herbs: Hyssop, marjoram, sagebrush

Crystals: Blue chalcedony, clear crystal quartz, lapis lazuli, malachite, sugilite

For more on Rampel, see page 476.

Rismuch

The angel of agriculture and cultivated farm or grazing land

Though not a sun angel as such, Rismuch is associated with the ripening crops and the harvest and with fertility. Picture him in every shade of brown, with tawny wings and halo, carrying a scythe and a hoe as symbols that he is conserver of the land and the crops.

Direction: South

Colour: Natural beeswax or pale yellow

Incenses: Chamomile, mimosa, rosewood, sandalwood

Herbs: Dill, parsley, yarrow

Crystals: Banded agate, brown jasper, flint, fossils, yellow jasper

For more on Rismuch, see page 477.

Rahab

Angel of the sea

Picture Rahab in deep blues and greens, carrying a trident, and striding over the white-foamed waves with his billowing white wings like sails.

Direction: West

Colour: Turquoise or red

Incenses: Anise, copal, dragon's blood, kelp

Herbs: Agrimony, cinnamon, ginger

Crystals: Aqua aura, aquamarine, aventurine, coral, ocean or orbicular jasper

For more on Rahab, see page 476.

3

CASTING A SPELL OR SETTING UP A RITUAL

In the same way that every party has the same underlying structure, whether it is a party for child's birthday, having a few friends round for drinks or a formal dance event to raise funds for the local community, your spellcasting will follow the same basic format, whether you are casting a short impromptu spell or setting up a more open-ended ritual.

If you work from a basic magickal format, you can devise anything from a five-minute spell to call a friend's missing cat home to a full-scale welcoming the spring for a hundred people on a local hillside.

What is more, once you have decided how the different components fit together you can change the order round to suit your needs. There is a huge variation in practice across the witchcraft community. Sometimes even experienced witches follow an order or way of doing things they were taught or read about that doesn't fit with their own natural rhythms. Even if you are doing it right by the book, your magickal energies won't be as powerful as if you were following the flow of the occasion. So, for more experienced practitioners, I am describing my practices for solo and group events so that you can re-examine your own structure – and then maybe decide it was right for you all along (or that you are turning the whole ritual format on its head and creating an entirely new and exciting system).

For newcomer or established witch, coven member or solitary practitioner, once you have internalised a structure that suits you, you can create your own spells and rites, complex or simple, instinctively without needing to check that you are on track.

You will discover as you read this book that some spells do not use the altar but are focused on the setting and everyday items. In these the structure is compressed but still effective. Don't feel you have to go through all these stages of altar casting, etc. for a simple spell. You can adapt my suggestions to either working alone or in a group.

The preliminaries

As when organising a party, it is important to spend a little time planning your spellcasting. Think about the precise purpose of the spell, the best time, most appropriate setting and for whom the spell is being cast. For a ritual you need to consider the underlying as well as the obvious focus of the ritual. Do you need to change the emphasis of a tried and tested format? Even a seasonal rite will have a theme, for example the May eve/Day celebrations have traditionally been associated with fertility (see Seasonal magick, pages 438–63). This fertility applies in whatever way it is needed, whether personally, ecologically or globally. Therefore you and the guests or participant should decide in advance precisely what you are working towards and carry out rituals to take advantage of the prevailing energies.

Location is important even for a quickie spell. You wouldn't set a child's birthday party in the same place you would your great-aunt's golden wedding. With open air spells or rituals you need a wet weather or sheltered location plan just in case a force 8 gale blows up. Some spells can be planned in advance for a day out or weekend away, but others will be spontaneous, when you happen to come across a perfect location while on your way to somewhere else. There are also urgent occasions when you will have to imagine that crashing sea while stood by the local canal at lunchtime.

The timing of a spell is also vital. See pages 54–57 for the best times of day, moon phases, etc.

Before you cast the spell you also need to decide how long you want the effects of the spell to last and how quickly you need results. Do you want an immediate infusion of power within the 24 hours following the spell? Will the effects take longer – before the next full moon, within three months? You should build this time frame into the spell and declare it in the purpose of the spell.

Should it be a single spell or one carried out, for example, every Friday for a month or on the three days before the full moon in order to build up the powers?

Then you need to decide on the symbol or symbols that will act as the focus for the spell energies (you can't dance and chant round a would-be lover in the office).

Do you need to emphasise any one element in the spell? Is the spell mainly fire based for power or is there a fairly evenly spread elemental mix, for example to resolve a long-term justice or court matter.

You need to think about any special props, magickal tools or substances that are required. After all, you wouldn't use the same china or serve the same food at your teenager's post-exam party as you would if the boss was coming to dinner. Do you want a full altar (see pages 72–80) or will it be mainly a word- or personal-movement-based spell? If on a beach or in a wood, can you use what you find there as tools and symbols?

Finally, who are you inviting to your spell or rite? The friend who has lost the animal you are casting the spell for? Your sister to help you with a love spell? Are you organising a welcome-into-the-world party for your family, to celebrate the birth of a baby to a family member who lives in another country? Are you entrusted with the organisation of your magick group or coven's autumn thanksgiving?

If you work alone, as many witches including myself do most of the time, you're still not a magickal Billy or Betty No Mates. You won't be short of spiritual company. You can welcome the guardians of the four quarters even in a relatively simple spell; invite the wise ancestors to celebrations such as Samhain or Hallowe'en or New Year.

As for the nature essences, whenever you work outdoors or even indoors in a circle of pot plants (my favourite setting on a really foul day) they will be curious. So invite them in and benefit from their energies.

Preparations

You need to get yourself and the area or altar ready for the spell.

Clear the space you intend to use either psychically or physically. This could involve lighting cleansing incense like pine or lemongrass or having a quick smudge round the room or outdoor area where you will be working (see page 108). For a more formal ceremony, sweep and asperge the area (sprinkle it with water; see page 124).

Use a compass to ascertain the four directions or calculate these from known places.

Set up any psychic protection that is required around the area you will be working in. You can concentrate this protection around the edges of what will be your magick circle, whether this is positioned in your mind or symbolised by the candles of the four main archangels or angels of nature. In these positions, they could act as the guardians of the four quarters instead of the nature devas (see page 483 for more on nature devas).

However, if you have more time available, you may prefer to set up a protective square (see page 57) to act as psychic boundary within which to cast your circle. You could also position your archangels at the edges of your garden or working area, or empower four large marker trees, bushes or stones. You should thank them and bid them farewell once the circle has been uncast (in stage 5).

If you are creating an external physical circle made, for example, of branches, stones or shells this is a good time to set it up, with the help of anyone who is sharing the occasion. The standard diameter for this circle is 2.7 m/9 ft (see page 60 for more information), although this can be altered if you are working in a confined space alone or if a number of people are attending and you want to move around.

Set up the basic altar and put everything in its place (for a more formal spell you can dedicate the altar now or at the beginning of the rite; see page 74). I suggest you read pages 72–80 on setting up different kinds of outdoor and indoor nature altars if you are not yet experienced in magick.

Basically, a bowl of salt goes in the north, incense goes in the east, a candle in the south and a water bowl in the west.

If you are making a sacred salt and water mix, you will be tipping the salt into the water so remember either to save a little in the bowl for the earth empowerment in stage 2 or have some spare salt in a second small dish at the side of the altar that you can use in stage 2.

If you are incorporating a cakes and ale part into a longer ceremony or spell (a formal dedication of honey cakes and wine, beer or juice to give thanks to the earth mother and sky father for sustenance and all good things in our lives) set the cakes ready on a plate to the north of the altar The drink will be put in a goblet or chalice (ceramic, glass or metal) to the west of the altar. Since this won't be part of everyday spellcasting, I haven't included the chalice or goblet in the tools used on your normal indoor nature or outdoor altar.

As this is natural magick you should aim for organic products, barley wine or beer, or organic juice, and organic cakes with honey in the recipe if possible. You may well not have the time (or in my case expertise) to make your own.

If you are having a garden ceremony, you can have a bath beforehand in water to which you have added rose or lavender oil, and put on something comfortable. If you are holding your ceremony on a windy beach, thick sweaters and jeans may be the order of the day. However, you can still cleanse yourself psychically. Anoint your hairline, centre of your brow, throat and both wrists with one of your special waters to open your higher chakras or energy centres (see page 269). Or use an essential oil in lotus, lavender or rose. Below is a full-blown ceremony containing everything. Mix and match and cut out any stages that don't fit a particular occasion. For example, you'll only have the cakes and ale on special occasions and sometimes you'll want just a simple circle cast while following only the basic spellcasting steps.

Starting the ceremony

* Light any altar candles. If it is a very simple altar and you are putting directional candles on the actual altar, the southern altar candle will serve as the elemental candle as well, so don't light this one yet.
* If others are present, stand in the centre of your visualised or maybe stone-constructed circle and face your guests. Otherwise stand in the centre of your visualised circle. Make a short spontaneous call for blessing on all present or on yourself if carrying out the ritual alone. Hold your wand or a pointed quartz crystal in your power hand, circling it clockwise as you speak.
* In a simple outdoor spell this opening blessing will serve as casting the circle if you picture light beams emanating from your wand to make a light circle round you and your altar space which rises into the sky and sinks down into the ground.
* My own favourite greeting blessing is adapted from an old Celtic blessing. You can find many on-line or in my *Complete Book of Spells*, the companion guide to this book (see Further reading, page 516). I say:

Circle this place / hillside / garden / woodland / seashore, Mother / Father. Keep harm without, keep peace within. Circle this place, Father / Mother. Bless all who gather here this day.

The 'all' will, if you are working alone, include the nature essences and elemental guardians of the four quarters of the circle.

* Generally you will now want to cast a full circle of magickal power round the group, or round yourself and the altar if working alone.
* Cast the circle with your wand, crystal point or the index finger of your power hand (the hand you write with). Always do this clockwise, starting in the north (my preference) or east. This draws earth and sky energy into you. (See page 62 for information on circle casting by walking round the area.)
* If you want a more elaborate circle (you need not and can go straight on to opening the four quarters) make a triple circle to empower the magickal one you created.
* If you were making these three circles, this would be the point at which you would light the candle of the south and any incense. Pre-heat the charcoal for loose incense as it takes about ten minutes; a stick is instant. If you are using a sacred salt and water mix in the ritual or the circle casting, empower the mix now (see page 124). You can use your wand to stir the salt and water together. For a

special ritual, you would set the salt and water dishes on your pentacle (see page 90) for more on this.

* Make the triple circles with three clockwise circles, one over the other or extending inwards, the first with the sacred salt and water mix (or just salt), the second with incense and the third with the directional candle of the south. If not using the salt water mix, substitute magickal water droplets for the candle to make the third circle. If there are others present, three of you can walk round in a complete circle, one following the other, or make a single triple-empowered circle starting in the northeast.

* Put the wand in the south of the altar (some use the east as they regard the wand as an air tool).

* If you are inviting the guardians of the directions you should now visit the four quarters moving in a clockwise direction. (See page 58 for suggestions of methods for opening the quarters.) Greet each one in turn and ask for their appropriate power and protection. Again, I start in the north but many practitioners work from the east.

* Otherwise you and anyone present can simply face that direction and raise both arms in greeting (palms flat and uppermost). Visualise the elemental forces as they are in nature entering the circle. You would still be greeting the guardians as you faced the different directions, just not actually be visiting the four quarters.

* You can do elemental greetings even with just a small travelling or outdoor altar by picking up each of the elemental substances in turn and inviting the guardian of the element into your altar and your spell. Reverse the actions at the end of the ritual and thank them.

* If you aren't opening the quarters, light any directional candles now and then add some incense to the charcoal if you didn't use incense to cast the triple circle.

* If using an incense stick, light this now from the nearest candle (again, if not used for the circle casting).

* If you want to, you can now invite the ancestors or a particular one who acts as your guardian spirit by facing the west and calling them in. Some people strike the ground with their staff at this point (see page 86 for making or buying a staff).

* Now invite the fey beings into the circle (turning to all four directions as you call them). I do this in every outdoor spell.

* Finally, if you want to make your ritual really special, face south, open your arms wide and ask if any deities (you can name them) would bless your ritual.

The five stages of spellcasting

Every five-minute spell or hour-long ritual incorporates the following five stages, though of course in really quick spells you may not use the elemental substances so formally.

Stage 1: Formally defining the purpose of the spell

* Take your symbol that should be made of natural material, natural fabric, crystal, beeswax, dough, clay, flowers, herbs, twigs or metals.
* Set the symbol in a dish or flat plate in the centre of the altar (you can use a pentacle dish if you wish). I have described the uses of pentacles on page 90.
* Raising the symbol dish in the centre of the altar as you face north, name the purpose of the spell and the time scale, for example 'by the time the leaves are on the trees', 'by the next full moon' or 'within seven days'.
* At the same time, define the person for whom you are casting the spell – this could be yourself.
* If you wish, you can now, while you are speaking, pass the symbol on its dish slowly in turn over all four elemental substances, beginning in the north or east.
* You may now, speaking slowly and confidently, ask for any god or goddess or maybe an angelic power that could be helpful.
* Put the symbol back in the centre. Touch the symbol with your wand or with a crystal point or the outstretched tip of your index finger to make the connection between the symbol and the energies to be raised. Say:

  Be filled with powers and blessings that _____ (name) may be / have / do _____.

* In a ritual you would announce the purpose of the gathering and draw everyone together in an initial chant or action during this first stage.

Stage 2: Setting the energies in motion

You are now ready to begin endowing the symbol and spoken intention of the spell with power. Here you will use words, actions and visualisation to build up this power within the physical symbol.

One of the most common methods of empowering the symbol is to pass it round or through the four elements in turn, so that the power builds up within it. This process is described on pages 93–94 but is given here briefly in order to set the scene.

Some practitioners start in the east with the incense. It does not matter as long as you are consistent. It depends whether you want to add your stability (north) at the beginning or end. I prefer to start with stability and to end with the flowing waters of the west.

* Begin with the salt in the north and make three clockwise circles of salt round the symbol, moving the circles outwards.
* State again the purpose of the spell and then create an earth power chant, which should be spoken three times, visualising at the same time what seem to be

relevant earth powers (see page 31). Visualise the power of the element in its natural form and then see that power entering you and meeting your own inner elemental power (like two rivers meeting). You can plan your chants in advance or just let them come spontaneously; they don't have to rhyme. You can speak the chant as you make the circle, or afterwards for each of the four elements.

* Next surround the symbol on the dish with three clockwise circles of incense smoke. Create an incense chant as you make the smoke circles over the salt ones. Afterwards you can also write the purpose of the spell in smoke over the symbol if you wish.
* Repeat the process for fire with the candle or, if easier, circle the symbol on its dish clockwise over the candle of the south three times. Create a fire chant and again recite it three times.
* Finally you are going to fill the symbol with the power of water in the same way. Make sure the water droplets are over the circles of salt and incense smoke (approximately). Again create a simple water power chant to be recited three times as you make the three water circles.

Stage 3: Raising or increasing the power

This is the most active and powerful part of the spell, and involves building up the speed and intensity of the action you started in stage 2.

Raising the power is especially easy out of doors as you connect, especially if barefoot or wearing thin-soled shoes, with the natural spiralling energies or straighter ley flows beneath the earth.

Grass or sand near a river or seashore is also energised by the water flow, especially around the week of the new and full moons (see page 432). On a safe beach you can dance though the shallows (see Sea magick on pages 355–66).

There are many ways of raising power, limited only by your imagination. When working alone and in a potent natural setting, perhaps at a power time like sunrise (see page 409), you will sing, sway or move quite without prompting or run along the beach or through long grass round in circles or spirals like a dog let off the leash. Watch children playing for inspiration.

Most effective is a combination of words or sound and movement in such a way that your conscious mind is carried along by the power, like riding a carousel when everything blurs except for the music. The purpose of this stage is not only to empower the symbol but also to empower yourself, since you are the vehicle to carry the magickal energies from the thought (mental) and spiritual (astral) planes to actuality (earth). This is the same process used by shamans to trigger their out-of-body or out-of-everyday consciousness (see page 214).

* Enchant the symbol with a pair of lighted incense sticks, one held in each hand, a few centimetres/an inch above the symbol. Move the right one clockwise and the left one anticlockwise. Move them faster and faster and chant faster and faster in order to draw in all four elemental powers.
* Increase the speed and intensity so the incense sticks cross and uncross over the symbol. As you move the sticks rhythmically, recite your elemental chant continuously.
* Alternatively you can move your wand clockwise in flourishes or a spiral, a smudge stick in your power hand in huge circles allowing it to dictate its own

pathway and shapes. You can move the other hand anticlockwise in rhythm if you want.

* A very simple chant is:

Air, water, fire, earth,
Bring, I ask, this wish to birth.

* You can continue over and over again at increasing intensity and speed, adding variants or weaving your own simple four- or five-word chants, around the natural surroundings and the elemental associations.
* Other spell chants include goddess names, the most popular being Isis, Astarte (Ass tart–ay), Diana, Hecate (Hekarr tay), Demeter (Dem eat-er), Kali (Karly) and Innana (In–arn-a).
* Isis is the Ancient Egyptian mother goddess; Astarte is the supreme female divinity of the Phoenicians, goddess of love and fertility, associated with the moon and all nature; Diana, the Graeco-Roman goddess of the moon and hunt and queen of the witches; Hecate, the Ancient Greek crone goddess of the underworld and waning moon; Demeter, the Ancient Greek Corn mother; Kali, the Hindu creatrix/destroyer goddess and Innana, the Sumerian fertility Queen of Heaven and earth goddess in the Middle East area of modern Iraq. Feel free to substitute your own goddesses/gods.
* You could instead move round and round the altar or circle, chanting and clapping, while stepping, stamping or whirling and twirling. Sufi spiritual whirling dancing has been eagerly adopted by the New Age as a way of altering consciousness. Trust your feet to follow the spirals of the earth energies.
* You can add the beat of a hand drum using your hand or a striker or use a tambourine. We can all play these, without training or a natural ear for more formal music. Just let your hands and feet set the beat and if you chant along they all harmonise. The simpler and more repetitive words and actions, the better.
* Move and chant until you feel that the power has reached its height, like revving a car with the hand brake on or a plane whose wheels are starting to lift off the tarmac.
* Through visualisation, individuals and groups can create a cone of power with the circle as the base, picturing a mass of stars or swirls of rainbow light collecting as a light cone above you. Imagine the cone getting higher and brighter as the apex gets taller and the cone denser with rainbow light. As you swirl you may even see it.
* When this psychic power peaks in intensity it is released through the apex as shooting stars. Imagine yourself standing in the middle of a firework display.

Stage 4: Release of power

This stage will blur and merge naturally into the previous one if you trust yourself.

* When the moment is right, raise the incense sticks and hold them upright and above you, calling for the release. Then plunge the incense sticks simultaneously into a bowl of sand. Do the same if you're using the smudge, with a final spiralling above your head (pretend you are using a lasso).
* If you are just using your hands or a wand, raise your arms high either side of your head, then swing them down, one behind you and one in front of you to waist height in a slashing movement.
* Picture yourself releasing the pressure within the cone and lighting the touch paper on the entire firework display. Picture that cone of stars cascading into the night.
* End the song with a final shout, the dance with a final clap, and a leap. Then call out 'The power is free', 'The wish is mine' or 'The spell is done', whatever feels right to express the culmination of the spell.
* See spiralling rainbows of light shooting upwards like rockets or hundreds of white doves, coloured balloons or butterflies being released at the same moment into the air.

> If working as a group, one person should be responsible for calling 'Now' or the drummer could give a huge bang. In practice the synchronised energies will bring the climax into synchronicity. But it really doesn't matter if some psychic fireworks go off a few seconds after the other; it just prolongs the joyous tension.

An alternative stage 4

If you are carrying out a healing spell or one for gentle love or letting go of sorrow, setting off psychic fireworks may seem a bit over the top.

Instead you may choose to infuse a healing herb mix with the power to relieve pain or exhaustion or infuse a dish of crystals so that they can afterwards be buried for peace in four directions. Gently directed power can be used to steer away in a psychic way someone who is making you unhappy.

> In a group celebration you may likewise not want to have everybody jumping up and down (it could certainly scare a baby at a blessing ceremony and a few elderly relatives at a hand fasting). You need instead to use the accumulated power and direct it into sanctity, whether that be the vows of a couple or of godparents. Or you might each make reflective wishes for the year ahead after the shouting of Happy New Year and banging of saucepan lids and blowing of whistles at a turning-of-the-year rite.

Though the technique is straightforward, it is like learning to do a hill start in a car – getting the clutch and accelerator in perfect balance so you can stay ready but motionless for as long as necessary.

* When the power in your spell has built up to almost a climax, instead of releasing it, hold it for a moment, keeping your movements and your voice steady and then begin to recite the words more slowly and more softly until your words fade through a whisper to silence and make your movements slower and gentler

until your feet become still. The incense sticks, your hands or wand will likewise become still.

* Point downwards with smudge, incense sticks, wand or your hands towards the symbol at a 45-degree angle (slightly away if necessary so no ash falls on the symbol, herbs or crystals).
* Push very gently, psychically holding your hands or sticks motionless, using words to make the power and light flow into the symbol. You may detect a rainbow aura or green light round the symbol.
* When you feel the power ebbing, stand motionless and silent for a moment and then replace the wand, smudge or incense sticks in their place or holders or put your hands in front of you pointing downwards so any residual power can flow into the symbol or be used to heal the earth.
* Leave the incense to burn through and whisper:

May you be blessed.

In a ritual this would be a good time for everyone to make personal offerings or quietly pass the symbol round and make low soft promises of practical ways you all personally will help to bring peace or work for the good of others. At a midwinter ceremony you would quietly, after the cry 'The sun is born again', light your candles one by one round the circle and make your own perhaps silent resolutions for bringing light back into your life and the world.

Stage 5: Moving to a conclusion – grounding or internalising the power

* If you would like to incorporate cakes and ale into a spell or ritual, this would be the point at which you would first take the cakes on the dish. When you are working alone, this is a lovely part of a spell or ritual to help to connect you with the love all round you.
* Raise the cakes on their plate (one for you and one for the birds if working alone) skywards away from the altar.
* Then lower them to waist height in front of you, saying:

May the abundance of the Mother and the bountifulness of the Father bless and nourish, sustain and protect me / you / us all my / your / our days.

* You can, if more than one person is present, choose one to hold the dish and another to bless the cakes by making either a pentagram (see page 90) or a cross over the dish as the words are spoken. You can, of course, do this alone with your power hand.
* Put the plate in the centre of the altar.
* Now take the chalice or goblet in your receptive hand and your wand in your power hand and gently lower the tip of the wand so it almost touches the surface of the wine or juice. Say:

As male to female, god to goddess, so in this wine/juice is joined power and love, strength and compassion, striving and acceptance.

* Return it to the centre of the altar.
* If more than one person is present, one can bless the cakes and another can bless the wine. The same people are usually chosen to carry out the blessings, but you may prefer to share the duties. Often the wand is held by a female and the cup by a male for the crossing of energies, but two women or men can carry out the ceremony.
* You should then take the cakes, scatter a few crumbs on the ground (or in a dish indoors) and say:

I return this gift to the earth mother in thanks for blessings received. Blessings be.

After the ceremony feed the rest of this cake to the birds.
* At this point if there were two people involved, you can offer each other a cake and then pass them round to anyone else present. Each person can say:

Blessed be

or add a blessing before eating.
* You should then return the plate to the altar and take the wine, pouring a little on the ground and thanking mother earth again for her blessings. (Pour this offering into a dish if indoors and you can put the crumbs and liquid outside after the ceremony.)
* Now drink or offer the drink to the other person who blessed the chalice. He or she will take a sip and offer it to you and to the other person who carried out the blessing, saying:

Blessings be.

* If others are present, pass the cup round so each can take a sip, saying:

Blessings be

and perhaps adding a blessing before passing it on.

Stage 5 continued: Parting company

* Next you need to say goodbye to your spiritual and any human guests.
* If you are having cakes and ale, you should close the quarters now.
* If you did not have cakes and ale, say goodbye after a few brief moments of stillness following stage 4.
* For a simple spell you would go on to the uncasting of any circle and the final blessing after stage 4, but again give yourself a few quiet moments sitting or standing to ground yourself.
* In closing the directions first face south and say goodbye and thank you to your invited deity energies if this was part of the opening.
* Face west and bid any ancestors farewell and thanks, closing in reverse order of opening. If you wish, you can make a banishing pentagram (see page 92). Anyone present can face the same direction and do likewise.

* Then move slowly to the south, the east and the north, extinguishing any directional candles as you go.
* Some people close in the same direction that they opened, from north or east clockwise, and you can do this straight after the ancestors if you prefer. Again extinguish directional candles as you go.
* The fey folk will want to stay as long as possible.
* Next uncast the circle. I walk round anticlockwise from north back to north, but others might prefer to uncast clockwise, some starting from the east.
* This is the point at which in a simple spell where I haven't used quarters or even a formal circle, I repeat the opening circle blessing, but say:

Circle this place, Mother, Father,
Keep harm without and peace within.
May I carry in my heart and in my life
your blessings until I return to/we meet in this place again?
Blessings be on you and your kin.
Take care, you people of the fey and I promise to care for your land/sea/riverbank till we meet again.

* If you haven't done so already, extinguish any directional candles. Leave the altar candles burning till you leave the site and then extinguish in either order, sending the light to whoever needs it.

Stage 5 conclusion: Tidying away the magick

* Before you go back to the real world you may like to sit in the still sacred place and carry out some simple natural scrying. This may involve looking at the moon in a bowl of water or cauldron, casting herbs on water and making images, looking at the clouds or listening to the messages in the waves or the wind in the trees, just allowing images to come and go in your mind.
* Don't be in too much of a hurry to get back to the world, it will turn for another five minutes without your intervention. Even the shortest spell with virtually no ceremony should provide a space away from the mundane.
* You have already released the energy from the circle as you uncast it (see page 64 for suggestions on clearing the circle away if you wish).
* A final walk around the area following where the circle line was, first anticlockwise and then clockwise, is a good way of grounding yourself and allowing the power to settle.
* If you do this, you will not need formal grounding.
* However, if you do still feel buzzing, to bring yourself back to earth, sit on the ground and press down with your hands and feet on to the earth to let excess unfocused energy drain out.
* Alternatively stand with your feet apart and your hands by your side, fingers pointing downwards and feel yourself gradually slowing down and your body and mind relaxing.
* Afterwards, clear and wash any tools and go for a walk or eat a light picnic or tend plants in the garden, while making plans for your first practical steps towards fulfilment of the spell.
* You can use the empowered symbol as a talisman or, if wax, dough or clay, roll it into a ball and bury it.

4

DEVELOPING
SPELLCASTING

he timing of spells and rituals is crucial. You can draw on the prevailing energies of the moon, the sun and the seasons and also factors like weather to amplify the power of your spells. To flow with the energies of the natural world is like walking or cycling with the wind or swimming with the tide as opposed to against it.

Much of the information on the moon, sun, seasons, the sea tides and weather is contained within different sections of the book, so in this chapter I have offered an overview. However, successful timings are ultimately about trusting your innate instincts. A number of experienced practitioners can feel if the moon is right or sense a rising tide even before they reach the shore.

This is not so easy initially for city dwellers or for people who like me grew up in the centre of towns. The more time we spend close to nature, the more this instinctive awareness returns, for we all carry it in our genes from our distant ancestors, though it may be deeply buried.

You can help to reinstate this awareness by rising and sleeping according to natural light patterns. This is easiest done on holidays or weekends especially on natural camping grounds where there is no electric light. Watching the moon in the sky without light pollution is a good way of connecting with natural rhythms and timings, especially if you note down your feelings as the moon changes each night. You may find a particular moon day evokes the same emotions each month.

I still have a tendency to think I should switch on the heater on a grey day even if it is muggy but I am getting better at listening to my body and not my logical mind.

I have also described circle casting in more detail in this chapter. Again, successful circle casting is less a matter of accurate measurement and knowledge of correct procedure than a feeling the pulse of the land you are working with and allowing your instincts to help you create an empowered and protective area for magick.

I have also written about the older magickal square from the Viking tradition that retained its popularity in folk magick in Europe until agriculture ceased to be such a driving force with the coming of industry in early Victorian times.

The best times to carry out spells and rituals

If a need is urgent then you can work at any time and picture the full moon or rising dawn whose energies you need, even at a different time of the month or at darkest midnight.

Sometimes the nature of the ritual will dictate the timing. For example, a new beginning spell can be launched on any new date: the first day of the month, the first day of the year, any Sunday, the first day of the week, the first hour after dawn or at the crescent moon when it first appears in the sky. Best of all is the first hour after dawn on a Sunday, which is ruled by the Sun, and so offers a double dose of power for that new beginning.

Working by the moon

Moon time is the oldest measurement of time used by humans and it accords with our natural rhythms in the lives of men as well as women. In magick we primarily look to the moon for timings.

The waxing or increasing moon from the crescent to the night before the full moon is potent for all forms of attracting magick, for the gradual increase of money, love, happiness or health and for fertility spells. These powers will grow daily as the physical moon size increases, to reach their height on the full moon.

The full moon represents a surge of power that can be plugged into for fertility, the consummation of love or commitment, a major money gain or for launching a creative venture. Also, because the full moon is unstable, this day and night is good for initiating change.

The waning moon helps us to let go of what we no longer need or wish for in our lives and can banish pain, sorrow or a destructive influence; a perfect phase for starting diet spells. As the moon decreases in size so the pull that holds negative people or factors in your life likewise weakens.

On pages 431–35 I have listed the moon phases as these are easy to follow by the actual movement of the moon in the sky and are a valuable source of power for natural spells as indeed for all magick.

Working by the sun

As the alter ego of the moon, the sun offers a significant source of energy for natural magick, and solar energies often offer power for more instant magickal results. I have written in detail about solar phases on pages 412–20.

Dawn is best for new opportunities, beginnings and people entering your life; noon for a burst of instant power, energy, success and prosperity. Dusk is for reconciliation or letting go. Midnight assists healing magick, psychic protection and in accepting what cannot be changed.

You can combine lunar and solar energies for a quick solar fix and the slower continuous lunar consolidation of the initial solar results in your life. Noon spells on the day of the full moon will get things off the starting block and keep up the impetus through the month. Often the moon and sun are in the sky at the same time (check your moon diary or weather section of the newspaper, or just look) and combine the energies accordingly.

Working by the tides

The tides are another power source if you are anywhere near the sea, an estuary or a tidal river. The incoming tide or flow will attract and bring fulfilment of wishes or dreams; the ebb tide will take away negativity and also protect those who travel, especially those who work at sea. The slack tide between flow and ebb, which can last for up to an hour, is excellent for building up power before the surge and moment of release at tide turn.

Working by the days of the week

Each day is ruled by a planet, whose influence takes on great importance in natural magick spells. This is therefore the most straightforward way of organising the times at which to practise magick.

The following guide is a summary of the strengths of individual days and the associations that work well in natural magick.

Sunday is ruled by the sun ☉

Archangel: Michael

Candle colour: gold

Incenses: frankincense or orange

Crystals: amber or clear quartz

Use Sundays for spells for new beginnings, for worldly success, to achieve ambitions, and to reverse bad luck, especially financial and for health.

Where possible, use an open space in sunlight for sun spells, such as a sunny beach or shimmering plain.

Monday is ruled by the moon ☾

Archangel: Gabriel

Candle colour: silver

Incenses: jasmine or myrrh

Crystals: moonstone or opal

Use Mondays for spells for fertility, protection especially while travelling, for home and family and to increase psychic and healing powers.

Where possible, work close to any water and, as a bonus, by moonlight.

Tuesday is ruled by Mars ♂

Archangel: Samael

Candle colour: red

Incenses: dragon's blood or cinnamon

Crystals: jasper or garnet

Use Tuesdays for spells for courage, change, independence in home or business life, for overcoming seemingly impossible odds and for passion.

Where possible, work near a fire or bonfire or with a huge red beeswax candle as a focus; alternatively work next to a flowerbed or large vase of red, orange and/or yellow flowers.

Wednesday is ruled by Mercury ☿

Archangel: Raphael

Candle colour: yellow

Incenses: lavender or fennel

Crystals: citrine or yellow calcite

Use Wednesdays for spells for money-making ventures, learning new things, passing examinations and tests, house moves and travel, overcoming debt, and repelling envy, malice and deceit.

Where possible, work in a windy place or when the clouds are moving fast across the sky.

Thursday is ruled by Jupiter ♃

Archangel: Sachiel

Candle colour: blue

Incenses: sandalwood or sage

Crystals: lapis lazuli or turquoise

Use Thursdays for spells for career, justice, prosperity, leadership, creativity, marriage and all partnerships, whether love or business, and for male potency.

Where possible, work on a hillside, moorland or near a natural sacred site.

Friday is ruled by Venus ♀

Archangel: Anael

Candle colour: green or pink

Incenses: rose or geranium

Crystals: jade or rose quartz

Use Fridays for spells for love, fidelity, healing, for anything to do with beauty, the arts and crafts and for all spells concerning the environment.

Where possible, work in any enclosed beautiful place outdoors, for example a botanical garden, a field, park or your own garden – or even in a circle of plants indoors.

Saturday is ruled by Saturn ♄

Archangel: Cassiel

Candle colour: purple or brown

Incenses: patchouli or mimosa

Crystals: jet or banded agate

Use Saturdays for spells to do with property, security and long-term financial matters, for closing doors on the past, for psychic protection and for locating lost objects (as well as animals and people).

Where possible, work in woodland, near rocks and stones or on animal or bird reserves.

Magickal squares and circles in natural magick

Magickal squares and circles date back to prehistory. Megalithic stone circles were created from around 3,500 BCE and set out according to precise geometric and astronomical measurements. They were used for rituals of all kinds by the Neolithic tribes especially on the seasonal change points to invoke the ancestors for fertility of crops, animals and people and continued to provide the setting for magickal gatherings throughout the millennia.

In Sweden and Norway the sacred square grid has formed a magickal device for more than three thousand years. It was used originally on the great seasonal fire festivals, at midwinter, midsummer and harvest. Nine turf squares were etched in the earth and eight removed, leaving the middle one to form the centre of the ritual fire.

The magick circle and square also have their place in modern natural magick. Both shapes occur naturally in forest clearings and can be drawn in sand, earth or snow, or formed out of twigs, branches, shells, flowers or even crystals.

Both act as markers for the main directions, the circle as though on a clock face and the square halfway along each side, both giving equal segments for the elements.

The magick square

Squares have a strong folk magick tradition; a magickal square would be marked in a field with hoes, rakes or other agricultural implements. In times of persecution squares could be consecrated as a magickal space, but were much easier to disguise as magickal workings than circles. Some were undoubtedly used to mark as sacred land where a former sacred Roman temple stood, just as a circle of stones or tree stumps beneath a church or cathedral might mark a former sacred Druidic grove.

In Scandinavia, the magickal square formed the outline for a grid of nine squares, three by three. These were made by the seiör, the witch seers of the Norse world who channelled wisdom from the spirit world, specifically from Helheim where the crone goddess Hel cared for the deceased. The seiör sat on raised thrones within the grids and travelled astrally to Helheim to talk to the ancestors and receive advice for the living. Only later did the goddess Hel become demonised, and in recent years there has been a revival of seiör craft.

The water witches of the West Midlands also used a magickal square, or mill as they called it, for magick. They were people who came from the Netherlands to live and work on the Midland canals in the 1800s. They practised an ancient form of folk magick that did not die out till the mid-1900s and there are still a few practitioners remaining. Rituals were practised by these canal people on a square of land adjacent to the canal bank within a triple magickal square. Each square was joined by four lines and constructed from wood and was known as the Mil. Only women entered the sacred area under the leadership of a senior female water witch, though the chief male, known as the master, standing at the edge, summoned a spirit entity to assist in the ritual.

In modern Iceland, the Landvaetir or Land guardians often have particularly sacred square fields that cannot be built on, where offerings are left in order to bring protection to the homes and farms around.

In the following chapters I have used the square not just for protection but as an alternative to a circle for casting spells for defence or security.

Casting a square

The square is a very powerful symbol of protection. Even if you work within a circle you can still designate an outer square as an additional protective enclosure. If you can't have a permanent altar outdoors, your magick square can designate the smaller space where you regularly set up your magickal tools.

It is also very protective of the home, even more so than a circle, and is an easier shape to cast in many gardens than the circle. I draw one around my caravan with small stone markers if the site is very quiet or if I have to leave the caravan unoccupied for a while.

It is effective also for keeping children or animals temporarily off lawns or flower beds you are trying to grow.

You can visualise a protective square of any size, from a small one around a precious artefact to one around a sacred site where you have organised a seasonal ritual.

They are very protective around natural circles such as groves where you would not draw a circle.

Indeed, you can create a temporary square if you are working in a public spot and don't want your magick area invaded by dogs and curious coach parties. In modern times where working in isolated places may be less safe, you can visualise one around the beach or forest while you are working or around yourself (as well as your protective circle) on a deserted station platform or taxi rank.

* Stand in the centre of your designated square, which may also be the centre of your projected magick circle.
* Hold out your arm as far as you can with your palm upright and outwards and say:

Enough and no more. I draw my square of protection. Preserve this space as sacred.

* Picture a line of light forming the top horizontal (west to east). Keep turning, making next the vertical north–south line along the right east side as you face north. Speak and visualise till you have all four lines in place and can see a shimmering outline to your square of light.
* You can also walk your square from the furthest away top left-hand corner, moving clockwise and ending at the nearest, bottom left corner. Use your wand in front of you and put a small dark stone at each corner and one halfway along each line. You can align with a compass or estimate north in the middle of the top line furthest from you as you face north.
* You can assign your midpoints, the main directions, to archangels or to the lofty Landvaetir, the tall brown guardians who in Iceland, Finland, Sweden, Norway, Germany and eastern parts of the UK are recognised as protecting land and all

who live on it. You can further protect the corners with the traditional taller dark stones if you are setting up a permanent magickal square.

❋ Bless your square as you would a circle the first time you create it.

Empowering the square

❋ Use smudge and proceed clockwise round the square from the top north-west corner (as you face north) until you end at the same place. If possible empower at sunset, and as close to the three days after the full moon as you can.

❋ Make a swirl at each corner with the smudge and ask for blessings and protection from the benign lesser earth spirits who will, if you are fortunate, take up position there (especially if you have taller rocks on which for them to make a home).

❋ Greet each of the loftier mid-point guardians, however you picture them, by raising your smudge to the sky and then downwards to the earth. Greet each of the guardians on the first occasion with a small rounded black stone offering (you can use jet or tourmaline if you want to use a crystal but not the fiery obsidian).

❋ Unlike archangels, a land wight may not reveal his specific name so greet him as 'sacred or noble land wight of the northern land' and so on round the four directions.

❋ You can if you wish refer to the northern direction guardian as Tiwaz the Viking spirit warrior who represents the Pole Star, the east as Odin the Viking father god, the south as Thor the mighty thunder and blacksmith god and the west as Ingvi or Ingwaz, the ancient fertility god who, according to the old sagas or legends, went anticlockwise, against the sun, that is westwards.

❋ You can empower a temporary or large visualised square by standing in the centre and pointing your smudge in the same order as you walked: north-west corner, north centre, north-east corner, etc. and repeating the words as you turn the smudge clockwise and anticlockwise.

❋ If you are making a protective square of light around yourself in a dangerous place, picture staves of light rising vertically at all eight points.

❋ Magick squares don't need to be uncast as their energies will flow back and forth from the soil.

❋ Re-empower a permanent magick square monthly at sunset, on any day during the three days after the full moon.

Circle casting in spells and rituals

Long before circles were adopted by ceremonial magicians, they have appeared in folk tradition as people for thousands of years have danced in circles around a festival fire. They offer power as well as protection.

In essence you can cast a circle anywhere for any kind of spell or ritual (a visualised one using your index finger takes seconds). If someone is being spiteful at work, you can swivel round in a circle in your chair casting a circle close to your aura (about an extended arm span all round) so that nasty words bounce off or are diverted back to the speaker.

I have repeated some information from the previous chapter to fill in gaps.

Any circle you create should enclose yourself, your altar and tools, if you are using them, and anyone working with you to create an enclosed protected place of concentrated power. Even if you are carrying out a whole spell with words or in your mind you can cast a visualised circle of light.

What size is your circle?

Traditionally circles are 2.7 m/9 ft in diameter; created with a 2.7-m/9-ft cord looped over and pulled taut at a central stake in the ground (the cord should be a bit longer to allow for the loop). Obviously it is easier to do this with two people so you can swing the taut cord round the projected circle and put ground pegs in at the four quarters (or at eight point to include the midpoints, south-east, etc.). You'll need a compass to identify magnetic north unless you are using known places for an approximation.

If you are working alone, or if you are short of time, you can always make an approximation of diameter (the distance across the circle through the centre). A tallish man is 1.8 m/6 ft so imagine one lying down across the centre of the circle and add another half of him in your mind. Picture the lying man in advance if you are casting a visualised circle of light from the centre or walking round a spiritual circle as you create it. You can also set four smaller stones in advance around the circumference at the main directions to guide you.

You may need a smaller circle if you are working alone, are using your miniature travelling altar or are in a confined space. A larger circle will be needed if you are inviting lots of people. You can estimate in multiples or divisions of three, your required diameter from the 2.7-m/9-ft concept.

As a general rule, to preserve connection for a larger number people, you should imagine everyone holding hands and try to envisage whether there would still be room to move round the altar/open quarters. Then estimate the space as if they were standing a step or two apart just inside and round the circle. Obviously, even with a smaller number, the more active the ritual, dancing, drumming, etc., the more space you will need. Size is a question of preference and practice, watching other people's circles and experimenting for different spells and rituals.

A physical circle

Your circle can be of various forms or sizes and can be created either before or as a part of the spell or ritual. A physically marked circle can be a good idea if you are a very visual person or are inviting people who maybe are unfamiliar with magick and need a tangible focus.

Some people create a permanent circle in their garden of stones and shells and then empower it at the beginning of each spell or ritual. This sort of circle retains positive energies and is regularly empowered by the weather, the moon, the sun and the seasons.

The materials you use to give an outline of your circle don't have to join up and their size will depend on the size of the circle. Small shells, stones, glass nuggets or crystals can easily be set up round a travelling altar to create a circle just before a spell.

White stones are generally used for circles, but you can also make a large temporary physical circle with fallen leafy branches, herbs or flowers set clockwise around your altar area. You can even weave branches together to make the circle.

Flower circles are lovely at personal, family or seasonal celebrations, and a young guest can help to form a flower circle either just before or as part of the ceremony if at a baby blessing or handfasting.

If it is windy, use masses of herbs and petals in the formation so it doesn't matter if some blow away. In fact, once you have empowered the circle, the flowers are no longer necessary and can carry energies as they fly.

You can also add a petal circle as the first or third of your triple circles.

For a large or small temporary circle, make a circle of tea lights and light them clockwise from inside the circle at the start of the ceremony.

You could alternatively put a larger green candle in the north for earth, a yellow one in the east for air, a red one in the south for fire and a blue one in the west for water and light these when you open the watchtowers or early in the spell to open the circle and create tangible markers (see page 58). You would cast a spiritual or invisible circle first to enclose them.

If the setting allows, you can use a natural existing outdoor circle, such as a grove of trees or a ring of flowers or toadstools. Always ask permission of the natural essences of the place. You do not need to cast or uncast this kind of circle as the natural energies will hold the power and protection, but always leave an offering.

Alternatively, you can draw a clockwise circle in earth, snow or sand with a stick, or your staff (see page 86 for making or buying one). Try to do it in a single sweep.

If you are organising a group rite, you can make a circle of people united in good will. After the blessing (see page 43) you can lead your guests in joining hands, ideally left palm up, right palm down, though it doesn't really matter if someone does it differently.

You then have the option of casting a spiritual physical or invisible circle behind the group.

I prefer to ask the group to cast the circle themselves, starting with the person in the north of the circle and moving clockwise from person to person. Ask each in turn to pass visualised light from hand to hand saying just their name slowly and deliberately, 'Birgitta, Susan, Helen...'

Alternatively you could pass an actual light in a secure holder from person to person (they would then not hold hands).

Either way, you will psychically see the light circle spreading and rising above and down to the ground.

Be part of the group for the casting (maybe start it yourself in the north). Afterwards you can all chant:

> *We are the circle; we are the circle,*
> *with no beginning and with no ending.*
> *Blessed be.*

You can drop hands at any time, but the circle remains.

Some practitioners light any candles/incense before the circle casting, but you may prefer to light them near the beginning of the ritual after this first circle is cast.

You can give additional power to a physical circle with any of the methods below.

Symbolic circle casting

The most popular magick circle is a symbolic one, physically cast by walking round the visualised circle area clockwise. It is visible psychically as a circle of light but not seen externally except by those with evolved clairvoyant light – and children.

You can make a symbolic circle before a simple outdoor spell and it is a good way of connecting with the earth energies.

Form the psychic light circle in the air, about waist or knee high, whichever feels more natural, with a pointed crystal or wand held in your power hand (or your index finger). Direct the point at about 45 degrees, casting the circle in front of you so you step into the emerging light and become empowered.

If you wish, you can make a circle-casting chant that you repeat either aloud or in your mind as you walk, for example:

> *May the circle be cast and so remain unbroken,*
> *May the love of the goddess be forever in our hearts.*
> *Blessings be.*

If working in a group, some practitioners like to cast a symbolic clockwise circle straight after the introductory blessing and then welcome other members of the group into it, drawing the psychic circle over head height at the planned entry point (north-west for a north-beginning circle or north-east for an east-initiated one). The guests enter at this psychic gateway and you can then finish off the circle when they have entered.

Personally I prefer to make the circle round the people once they have entered. You can then enter the circle where you began casting it through a visualised doorway, sealing it afterwards.

I think unless it is a real emergency people shouldn't leave the circle during a ritual as this involves a lot of sealing and unsealing and psychic disturbance.

Strengthening the circle

A circle of light or a physical circle can be strengthened by casting three elemental circles just inside it.

Some practitioners aim to put the triple circle on top of the light one but I prefer radiating circles, albeit close together.

If using empowered salt and water as one of your elemental circles, you would empower this mix first before the elemental casting.

The three clockwise circles, either positioned one over the other or extending inwards, should be made with salt and water, or just salt (the first), with incense (the second) and with the directional candle of the south or a central one (the third). If you use salt for circle one (and not the salt and water mix), use incense for number two and magical water droplets for the third circle.

Create simple elemental casting chants according to the substances you are using and the nature of the spell or ritual.

With a group, before the triple circle casting invite them to walk the triple circle in line after you as you cast it. As I said earlier, you can use three people to make thr triple circle by having them each carry a substance around it. You need not use words for this unless you wish. With a group it is easier to make the three circles over one another just inside the original light circle.

You can end the triple element casting by sprinkling each person with a few drops of either the saltwater or the water alone saying:

You are blessed.

If you are working alone, end the triple circle casting by taking the water and sprinkling yourself, saying:

May the lord and lady god and goddess bless me and my spell/ritual.

Visualising the circle

At certain times it is more appropriate to visualise a circle, for example when you want a quick spell or if you are in a place where it would be awkward to walk round in a circle (maybe you are in a park or on a beach and other people are around not connected with you). This can also be effective in a relatively confined space such as a small garden or indoors or in your office, or in a lonely place where you feel vulnerable.

* Stand in the centre of your area facing where you think north is (or east if you prefer).
* Holding your pointed quartz crystal or wand or subtly extending the index finger of your power hand, at waist height, turn your body and feet slowly in a circle, while remaining in the centre spot.
* Picture light flowing outwards and then into a circle round you at the required distance. As you make one sweeping continuous movement of your hand, visualise the circle as gold, white, silver or blue light.
* If necessary, you can also visualise a circle emerging just by turning with your hands in front of you, fingers horizontal and palms down. Picture the light

flowing upwards from the earth and downwards from the sky joining to form a reddish gold light circle of the required circumference.

Uncasting the circle

The reason for uncasting an outdoor psychic light circle is to release any remaining energies after a ritual so that any animal or bird won't get tangled up in the energies, and anyone entering the space will not pick up any vibes, however pleasant, that do not belong to them. This should also be carried out for a physical circle.

I uncast circles anticlockwise – I always have. Some practitioners say that is wrong, but moonwise or anticlockwise seems to me the completion of what was set up sunwise or clockwise and goes with the natural flow. I do not believe that by moving anticlockwise I am undoing the spell or reversing the energies. I do, however, respect the traditions of those who uncast clockwise.

Some people close the watchtowers and blow out the candles clockwise, starting from the east or north. Again, with watchtowers, I go anticlockwise, starting where I ended in the opening. This farewell and extinguishing of the lights is sometimes considered adequate uncasting, but being a logical soul I like to finish the job and uncast the circle (any triple circles will have merged by now).

To uncast, walk round anticlockwise from north back to north (or east to east) with the source, finger, crystal or wand behind this time, picturing the light returning to the source, finger, crystal or wand. Say a closing chant like:

May the circle that is open yet remain unbroken in our hearts and in our lives. Blessings be.

Alternatively, stand in the centre, facing north (or east) and turn anticlockwise on the spot, drawing the light back into the source, crystal, wand or finger or picturing it sinking into the ground. This is a nice ending to a simple personal spell or ritual.

If you used tea lights, blow out any that are still alight in reverse order of lighting, sending a final blessing with each light. If you used a natural substance like herbs or flowers, leave them to blow away.

Uncast the spiritual circle round a more solid, permanent circle in order to release the energies. If the circle is quite solid, make a physical gateway by removing a few stones to allow the energies to blow in and out at will. The energies will soon dissipate and you can replace the stones after 24 hours.

A circle made of stones or shells collected on a beach can be dismantled after the ritual. A circle drawn in the sand or the earth can be rubbed out or left for the tide or rain to erase. Make a hole in the line if you are leaving a circle to the elements.

If you cast a circle round a group of people, lead them out in a spiral with an uncasting chant, such as:

We leave this place willingly, we joyfully uncast, the circle that we made. Within us the enchantment, inside us dwells the sanctity, the circle lives forever, safe in our hearts.

In any uncasting, even after a quickie spell, finish with a closing blessing to carry the magick into the everyday world.

PART 2

YOUR REFERENCE SOURCE FOR NATURAL MAGICK

INTRODUCTION

This is the most extensive and probably vital section in the book, since it describes the basic tools of natural magick and the methods for making incense, amulets, talismans and magickal waters. I also describe how to make an outdoor altar, one for travel and how to bring nature into your indoor magickal place so that you can practise outdoor magick even if you live in an apartment in the centre of a city.

If you have read some of my earlier books, you will notice I have evolved both magickally and practically. I hope in this book I have improved or expanded (and hopefully explained more clearly) my earlier techniques. This is a result of learning from others I meet at witchfests and festivals or who write to me – and above all from trusting myself more than I used to. I have also recorded some of the tips and short cuts for relatively new practitioners that I wish someone had explained to me so that I could have saved myself a lot of burned and cut fingers – and tears.

However, essentially natural magick isn't the kind you do with book in hand, not even the Book of Shadows (see page 22) and so this section is just a template to set the scene and lay out a few of the necessary props.

For in natural magick the script and rules are written by mother nature herself to be passed on through the messages of the wind in the trees or in cloud images overhead. A lot of what I write, even if you are new to natural magick, you will know instinctively or recall from some distant genetic memory. This is a witch's greatest gift, to connect with the well of wisdom – so don't doubt yourself.

Given time and trust in your own powers, you will develop your own style of this most powerful, yet least formal, style of magick. For those who are expert in ritual magick, natural magick can give back some of the spontaneity and excitement we all felt when we first discovered the Craft.

I am aware that this huge section is by no means comprehensive and that even in this most unstructured of magickal environments other traditions will have their own valid ground rules. A number of practitioners, for example, feel you should only make wands from hazel trees that are a year old and cull the wood on a Wednesday at sunrise. Others have different ideas and priorities. In the wand-making section I have suggested a number of alternatives. However, if you see a beautiful fallen branch and it is not the kind you were looking for and sunlight is shimmering on it, follow your heart and not the instructions and you will have a truly powerful wand. You may choose to buy one that is no less special and you can soon, by working with it outdoors, make it your own.

With the boundless power of nature anything can become magickal by your own joyous rituals as you connect with the earth, the waters and the sky, whether in the wilderness or in your local park.

For the tools of natural magick are not like those of ritual magick, elaborately carved with magickal symbols. I believe that in natural magick we do not need the same adornments to inspire us. Therefore even the altars I suggest are quite basic, but set beneath the temple of the stars or in the centre of a flower-filled grove, they are glorious and majestic.

Sometimes the reality will be rain dripping down your face while you are trying to set up your travelling altar at a fabulous ancient site you have waited years to visit. Go with the day and use your hands, your voice and the falling rain to weave your spells. You can light the candles and incense when you get home, but the fresh-mown grass and the pine needles in freshly flowing torrents will connect you with the real mystery and wildness. Afterwards, when you've dried out, you will remember the day and place as enchanted.

So enjoy this section and take what is of use. Adapt any relevant parts to your own lifestyle and your personal magickal needs or those of your coven or friends with whom you work informally.

Replace those suggestions that do not seem right for you with what may be some new angle on your previous learning. Or you may now know for sure that your way of doing things is right for you.

The resources and sources of natural magick are infinite and we never stop learning. After nearly 20 years of active solitary practice, I am finding that my 18-year-old daughter Miranda makes better incense than I do, though I am just about ahead on the theories. Her prowess delights me and I would be pleased to hear from any of you via my website (see Further reading, page 517) if you know better ways of making magickal waters, smudge and amulets. I will include them and credit you in future books.

But first I will describe finding a magickal place of your own outdoors. Here nature reveals her own sacred energies and we can touch spiritual heights as surely as we would in the most ornate indoor temple.

I

YOUR NATURAL MAGICKAL PLACE

Natural magick is very spontaneous. On days out, weekends away and holidays you will sometimes come across a perfect setting for a ritual, usually when you least expect it. On a seashore or in a woodland you will suddenly find an abundant supply of tools and material for your spells. What can be more potent than to stand in the wind on a beach, drawing your magickal circle or labyrinth in the sand? Use a driftwood stick stripped and bleached by the waves for your magickal sea wand and make shell wishes or offerings.

However, there are times when you will want to draw those spontaneous energies into a more organised ritual with tools you carry with you in the back of your car or in a backpack.

In this chapter I describe what you need for a portable natural magick altar. Some magickal practitioners already have a miniature travelling kit for indoor use when they are away from home. Occasionally a smoke alarm going off in the hotel at a magickal conference will indicate someone (not me of course – well hardly ever!) who has inadvertently set off a smoke alarm by lighting incense in a non-smoking room. I also talk in this chapter about creating a permanent outdoor altar in your garden or on your patio and how to adapt a traditional indoor altar for natural magick if you don't have any outdoor space at home. But let's look at discovering a special outdoor place, a repository for power, that you can visit regularly in order to be uplifted and restored.

Finding the place for you

You may already have discovered your sanctuary which gives you the feeling of coming home and which you are reluctant to leave even in less clement weather. It might be a beautiful stone circle you visit every month or so or on seasonal change points. It could be a rose garden in a local botanical garden, a grove of trees in an arboretum or forest or a particular seashore. I know I have written before about the grove of trees opposite my old caravan where I go to work away from the phone and e-mail. I have been working at least once a week in the grove in sun and moonlight, rain and wind for six years now. Though the grove is situated on an immaculately lawned site (except for my pitch near the hedgerow), it is filled with wildlife and flowers. See pages 485–87 in deva magick for a lot more on visiting sacred places.

Select somewhere you can visit at least every month or six weeks, or more when you need extra energy or harmony. It need not be exotic, but should be quiet for at least part of the day. It would be a bonus to be able to visit this place at different times of the day or night, but, especially in cities, and sadly, for safety considerations in the modern world, this may not always be possible. You may, however, find somewhere you can camp regularly and so be able to enjoy your site by moon- and/or starlight.

Once you have found your special place,

* You need do nothing except connect with the place by sitting or walking quietly, touching any stones or special trees with the palms of your hands to make a connection.

* Allow the guardians of the place to accept you and spend your first proper visit walking the site, if possible barefoot, so that your sensitive sole chakras can also directly connect with the energies. Otherwise, wear thin-soled shoes or sandals, for example, with rope soles.

* When you sense it is time to leave on this first visit, make an appropriate crystal offering, leave a flower or tie a ribbon to a tree. If it is an open site, such as a shore or forest, take home with you in your crane bag a stone, shell or small branch that seems to have a form or face. I talk about crane bags on the next page.

* If you are at a sacred site, pick a small stone from outside the designated boundaries as the energies will be almost the same as within the boundary.

* On subsequent visits, stand in the centre of the site and picture a circle or square of light enclosing the area. Hold your wand (see page 82) outwards in your fully extended power hand and, starting by facing the approximate north, slowly turn clockwise in a circle.

* Visualise the rays of light forming a huge enclosure round the whole site. You can create a smaller circle round your immediate working place if you are doing a ritual and maybe wish to move to a more private spot on the site (see page 60 for circle casting).

* Then carry out any ritual that seems appropriate, not necessarily asking for something, not even for the environment, but sometimes sending blessings and thanks to the place and its guardian spirits.

* When you have finished, hold your wand in your power hand again and as you turn slowly (still clockwise for this process) picture the light and the energies sinking back into the ground, firstly from your large and finally from your miniature circle.

* Don't be in a hurry to leave. If you can camp, try to have four small rituals on one of the days over a weekend or holiday.

* Make the first one early in the morning (or when you wake) to correspond with the dawn energies and to greet the morning. The next should be in the middle of the day to correspond with the noon energies when you align your own power with that of the height of the day.

* The ritual at dusk can be carried out when you are closing your day and is ideal for letting go of anything you do not wish to keep emotionally in your life. The final ritual should be carried out when you go to bed to correspond with the midnight tide and to send healing to yourself and others. You can weave your own words and actions or read the section on sun magick (see pages 412–20) for my suggestions.

* Alternatively, if your special place is on the seashore, work with the three tides: incoming, high, slack and ebbing (see pages 358–62). Slack tides occur between the high and low points of the tide cycle.

* Also experiment with the different energies in your chosen place during different moon phases (during the day if necessary), on different days of the week and in different seasons, to experience the rich energy variations.
* If appropriate you can begin a small cairn or stone pile and, each time you go, add a stone and a blessing. You may start a trend, as at St Nectan's Glen, near Boscastle in Cornwall. Here, near the base of the waterfall, is a small cave filled with stone cairns dedicated to the pre-Christian lady of the waterfall.

The crane bag

As a practising Druidess, I carry on outdoor forays what is called in Druidry, the sister nature religion to witchcraft, a crane bag.

The crane bag is so named after the bag created by Mannanann Mac Lir, Celtic lord of the sea, from the skin of a sacred crane. He used it to carry the natural treasures of Ireland (and according to legend, his shirt) and so it signifies wisdom. (There is more of the strange origins of the crane bag in my *Modern Day Druidess* handbook – see Further reading, page 514 – and on my website.)

Your crane bag can be of any natural fabric, hessian, cotton or silk with a long broad strap to wear over your shoulder. You can also adapt a basic backpack, duffle bag, drawstring bag or a satchel-type bag.

Mine is a big, embroidered hessian bag with a single long broad handle. I bought it from an ethnic store in Oxfordshire and it has a solid base. Some people prefer leather obtained from a reputable source. You can find crane bags for sale on the internet and locally. Most markets have a stall selling bags of all kinds and one with compartments can be useful.

Within the crane bag you can have individual smaller crane bags or pouches for separating smaller items. In one you can keep small treasures from nature you find on outings or after outdoor rituals: a special stone glinting with quartz, shells picked at full moonlight on the shore, an acorn from a sacred oak indicated by the mistletoe growing on it, seeds, blossoms or berries that have fallen from a magickal tree such as one of the Glastonbury Thorns that bloom in winter, a fossil, some herbs or flower petals you have dried that were picked on a seasonal festival (see pages 440–63). These treasures can be used in spells or as sacred offerings in outdoor rituals or placed on an indoor altar to transfer their natural power.

You can also carry in your crane bag the altar artefacts listed on the next page, so that everything is ready when you sense the energies are right for a spell or you want to celebrate the beauty of nature and of the day.

Making a mini altar

Whether in your special place or on days or weekends away, you can take a mini travelling altar set for more complex rituals or to celebrate a moon phase or seasonal change. First you will need a bag for transporting your magickal tools. You will not want to take anything cumbersome or heavy, especially if you are walking to the top of a hill or over rough terrain or are out for the day without a car.

For your mini altar you will need

* A small pillar-type stone or crystal to represent the earth in the north. Alternatively you can keep a little clean soil in a screw-top jar in case there isn't any available in situ.
* A feather for air in the east. It is best to find one or buy one from a bird sanctuary where you know the feathers were obtained without harming the bird. This symbol is excellent when you cannot safely or easily light incense or smudge. You can also cleanse an area or even draw a circle by holding a feather instead of smudge or incense.
* A gold earring or other small item of jewellery or a gold-coloured coin to signify the fire and south when you cannot light a candle.
* A small bottle or flask of sacred water. You can buy bottled waters from sacred wells or from a source where there are healing springs, such as Buxton or Malvern. In a small unglazed bowl, this represents the water element. It can also be used to sprinkle water droplets for casting an outdoor circle or as an offering poured on the ground for the earth mother. You can also add a few drops to bird drinking dishes outdoors as a more practical offering. If containers are attractive enough, you can use them on your open-air altar.
* A small screw-top container full of dried nuts and mixed seeds of different kinds both to use as a focus in a growth/increase/new beginnings spell and as an offering in an open space for the birds. Take another container full of dried herbs such as sage, lavender or rosemary to serve as a focus for healing rituals.
* You can usually find a dead branch, petals or leaves to represent what is redundant or destructive for banishing spells. You can carry a few dried petals in another small container to scatter in water or bury. These are also good for healing rituals.
* A tiny smudge stick in sage, cedar, rosemary or pine for rituals where it is safe to use fire, to serve as incense and to represent the east and air. Use smudge also for ritually cleansing an area or artefacts, for protective and cleansing magick and for raising power while swirling it both clockwise and anticlockwise and chanting. Take a small screw-top jar of sand along to douse the smudge after use.
* For those occasions where there is a rock large and flat enough for an altar, you can take a tea light or small natural beeswax candle slotted into a special lidded ceramic container. Do be careful near grass. Some houseware stores sell candles in a small tin that are ideal for carrying and storage. This can be used for the fire/south element and for endowing a symbol with power by passing the symbol over the flame.
* A small piece of natural beeswax bought as a sheet or taken from an old candle that has become discoloured. Wrap it in greaseproof paper for making images as

symbols for outdoor rituals. You can soften it by rolling it in your hands or hold over a tea light.

* A small twig wand (see page 82) or a pointed clear quartz crystal for marking out a circle and directing power.

* Very small crystals such as moss or tree agate for offerings after earth rituals, citrine or blue lace agate for offerings for air rituals, carnelian or clear quartz crystal for fire rituals and fluorite or amethyst for water. You can also use one of each kind to mark the four directions for an instant magick elemental circle (see page 76 on making more permanent indoor altars). Individual crystals are also useful for empowerment or healing rituals and can be carried afterwards as a charm or sent to a sick person.

* A round, flat dish, either ceramic or wooden, or a small piece of slate (engraved with a magickal pentacle symbol if you wish; see page 90) wrapped in cloth or in a small bag. This will hold your beeswax symbol, or any crystals or herbs you are empowering for healing, and should be placed in the centre of your impromptu altar.

* One or two biodegradable ribbons to hang on trees near sacred sites, such as wells, especially after healing spells.

* A sturdy square cloth in a natural fabric to put your items on as an instant altar (and a plastic sheet underneath if damp) if there is not a suitable flat rock.

* A compass if you want to be accurate about directions (you may prefer to use four significant horizon points in the approximate directions).

* A notebook and pen in a waterproof pouch for a travelling Book of Shadows.

* A number of utility items: water-resistant safety matches or a tiny lighter, a crystal pendulum that can be used for all kinds of work from decision-making to tracing ley or psychic energy lines beneath the earth, a large paper bag to collect debris after a ritual, an electric torch in case it suddenly gets dark. The torch also becomes an instant symbol of fire/light for after-dark rituals when you can't use natural fire.

* Unless you are taking a car you will only include some of these in your travel kit, depending on where you are going. Keep your bag topped up for unexpected rituals and, in the back of the car, a supplementary bag or box for the bulkier items.

Dedicating the altar

As you are working outdoors you need do little cleansing, but you can empower your mini altar before casting a circle of light round it the first time you use it (and subsequently as part of a ritual).

* Begin by passing your hands, palms down, a few centimetres/an inch above the altar rock/cloth, moving the right hand clockwise and the left hand anticlockwise at the same time saying:

May only light and goodness enter here and may the gentle powers of mother nature bless and protect this altar and my rituals.

* Continue speaking and moving your hands until you feel the altar connecting with the positive energies of the place in which you are working. You may sense nature spirits or devas nearby.
* Before you set each artefact in its place clockwise (the central dish last), hold each item so that your palms make contact with it through the sensitive chakra or psychic energy points within them. Say three times for each artefact:

May this ____ be used only for the greatest good and the purest intent. Blessings be.

Set it down in its place.

* After the dedication ritual, end by passing your twig wand three times clockwise round the impromptu altar and saying:

Let the light return to the sky and the power into the ground to the mother.

* Clear the site and leave an appropriate offering, for example a moss agate near a stone circle, or a flower.

Making an outdoor altar

You need only a small area for this. If you can create a permanent altar space in your garden or on a balcony, it will increase in potency over the weeks. Just by going there and lighting a candle or smudge, you will also feel empowered and harmonised when you are feeling stressed or dispirited. Try to find a spot that is relatively sheltered so you don't get too buffeted in inclement weather. Gazebos are good for wet-day outdoor rituals.

* First you need a small table to serve as your altar. Choose natural wood (you can weatherproof it) in a circular or square shape. Neither metal nor plastic is suitable.
* Alternatively use a large piece of slate raised on bricks. In Viking magick, a stone altar called a harrow was always used.
* You do not need a cloth, but a small piece of slate in the centre is useful for positioning your symbol dish and other small pieces under your candle and incense.

* You may wish to have a god or goddess statue or both, the goddess to the left and the god to the right. I would recommend trying to find one or two small branches of wood or rock with a face or the shape of deities naturally etched within it. It may take you a time to find the right pieces. Alternatively you can carve out a rough shape from two pieces of wood or make your own pottery representations. You can buy clay that does not need firing.

* A large shell for the goddess and a bone horn for the male is also a typical representation as is a pointed jet crystal for the god and rounded amber sphere for the goddess. Some witches wear amber and jet necklaces for this reason. In some traditions amber represents the god energies, but jet seems to work best for me. However, some people prefer not to have representations of any kind on outdoor altars and to substitute altar candles indoors for the polarity energies.

* In the north for earth put a pillar-shaped stone of medium height. A dish of dried herbs or a small bowl of sea salt or soil can be added for rituals.

* Mark the east with a feather. Cover it when the altar is not in use (upturned glass bowls are ideal as dome covers). For rituals you can add a large smudge stick in sagebrush or cedar or the larger, firmer kinds of incense stick or an incense burner and charcoal if you want to burn non-combustible or loose incense (see page 97 for incense making). I have recently seen some mini blow gas torches not bigger than an ordinary lighter that are good for starting off charcoal discs or blocks outdoors in damp conditions. You can use an ordinary lighter or long match.

* Mark the south with an item in gold colour or brass – you may find an ornament portraying the sun. Try to track down an old horse brass or use a dish of gold-coloured coins or a long, golden-coloured pendant or neck chain. Again, cover well. These will need to be cleaned regularly to avoid tarnishing, though it does not matter if the gold colour burnishes.

* For rituals use an undyed beeswax candle for fire. In the south quadrant too will be your wand, though you will not want to leave it out in all weathers (see page 82 for making one).

* Finally, in the west you will need something silver, maybe a moon ornament or a silver necklace or silver-coloured coins in a dish for the west, and water. Again, cover when not in use. If gold or silver coins get tarnished you can bury them beneath a strong tree to attract prosperity and replace them with new ones.

* For rituals, use an unglazed ceramic bowl to contain rain or mineral water for the water element.

Marking the altar

Outdoors tangible marking of a permanent ritual area is useful and helps to build up the power.

I like to mark out the area round the outdoor altar, however small, in an actual protective square, the agricultural forerunner of the circle and very potent for outdoor work.

Traditionally you would mark this area with hoes and rakes at the four corners, but you can plant (in tubs if necessary) four bushes to mark the four directions. With the simplest of compasses you can set the altar so that the altar is in the north of the ritual area, horizontal to the horizon. Some people paint the four directions as a cross in the centre of the altar. Keep a growing plant in a pot in the centre of the altar to keep the energies fresh. You can vary the species according to the seasons.

Dedicating the altar

The first time you set up the altar and before any ritual you should sweep the area in anticlockwise circles with your besom or broom. You should then asperge the area by dipping some twigs that you have tied together in rain or tap water and then sprinkling the water over the area.

Actual empowerment and cleansing need only be very light as the physical elements manifested in rain, wind, the sun and the moon are very powerful in purifying an outdoor altar.

* Set up the artefacts on the altar in the morning as the day becomes brighter. Stand in front of the altar facing north (with your back to the south). The altar should be about a third of the way inside your visualised boundaries in the northern part of the area.
* Hold your wand directly upwards to the sky and then down to the ground, then extend it horizontally so the tip of the wand is over the centre of the altar.
* In this position, pass the wand clockwise in a circle round the whole altar without moving your feet, picturing light flowing and radiating like the beams of the sun when it suddenly appears from behind a cloud.
* Say three times:

> *May you be blessed by the light of the sun and the beauty of the morning. May only light and goodness enter this altar.*

* Move away from the altar so you have room to turn in a circle. First look towards the northern perimeter of your magickal area (the northernmost bush or pot plant), then in turn face all the directions with your wand pointing horizontally ahead.
* Say in each direction:

> *So grows light in the north, the east, the south and west. Blessed be you guardians who stand watch at the four quarters. I offer you honour and give reverence to all that is created in sky, sea, flowing waters and that lives above and within the earth.*

* You should re-empower your altar about every three months and at the change of season, when possible.

Making an indoor altar

You can incorporate nature into an existing personal altar if you don't have room for an outdoor altar. If this is your first altar, this and the following chapter will help you to create the kind of personal space that will enable you to keep in touch with nature's powers even on the top floor of a city apartment.

In natural magick even indoors it is more customary to use your wooden wand rather than an Athame or black-handled ritual knife for casting circles, empowering water, etc. If you do want an Athame in your rituals and on your altar, stand it in the east of the altar as an air tool. The wand is fire in a number of traditions.

- It is often easier to site an indoor altar in the centre of the room, rather than the north, so that you can move all round it.
- Crystals, herbs and fragrances are the best ways to keep natural energies flowing into your altar and your life. In the section on aroma magick I describe the properties of different perfumed oils (see pages 282–90).
- Use a natural wooden table – it does not have to be smart. You may choose an altar cloth made of a natural material such as silk or cotton to cover the table. There are many different designs available: moon, suns, zodiac signs, images of nature. Alternatively buy a large scarf or hem your own fabric square. You may like to change the colour of the cloth according to the season (see Seasonal magick on pages 438–63).
- Align the direction of the altar with a compass or, if this just won't fit your room, use approximations. We are not performing high or ceremonial magick and so directional accuracy is not vital as long as you always keep to the same directional names. Indeed, in magick, north is magnetic rather than true north.
- In the north set a small bowl of sea salt.
- In front of it place an earth crystal such as red jasper, tiger's eye or red tiger's eye, moss or tree agate or garnet.
- To the left of the dish of salt place a dish of herbs. Earth herbs and flowers include cypress, fern, geranium, heather, hibiscus, honeysuckle, magnolia, oak moss, patchouli, sagebrush, sweet grass, vervain and vetivert. Use one herb or a mix.
- In the east set your incense and holder, whether for an incense stick or loose incense. You can use air fragrances or ceremonial incense like sandalwood, dragon's blood or frankincense. You may be able to buy a combustible incense stick or cone that has been made with a sandalwood powder rather than saltpetre, but this is more expensive.
- For your air crystal choose angelite, blue lace agate, citrine, lapis lazuli or sodalite to stand in front of the incense.
- To the left of the incense place your small dish of air herbs or petals that may include almond blossom, anise, benzoin, bergamot, dill, fennel, lavender, lemongrass, lemon verbena, lily of the valley, marjoram, meadowsweet, peppermint or sage.
- To the south for fire position a natural beeswax candle (or use a red or orange candle if you prefer). If you can't get beeswax try to use a candle in which the colour goes all the way through. It need only be small. Use a deep holder to catch any wax. To the right of the candle is your wand (even if you have an Athame in the east).
- In front of this, where wax will not fall, is your fire crystal, which could be amber, aragonite, citrine, clear crystal quartz , obsidian or sun stone. Crystal quartz is also associated with the air element.
- To the left of the candle set your dish of fire herbs or flower petals that could include allspice, angelica, basil, bay, carnation, chamomile, cinnamon, cloves, copal, dragon's blood, frankincense, heliotrope, juniper, marigold, nutmeg, orange blossom, rosemary or tangerine.

- Finally, in the west place a bowl of plain still mineral water or rainwater that has not touched the ground (from a barrel or bowl on a low roof). In front of the water will be your water crystal: amethyst, aquamarine, crystal, fluorite, jade, rose quartz or tourmaline. Amethyst can also be linked with air.
- To the left of the water bowl set your water herbs or petals that could include apple blossom, apricot, coconut, eucalyptus, feverfew, heather, hyacinth, jasmine, lemon, lemon balm, lilac, lily, myrrh, orchid, passionflower, peach, strawberry, sweet pea, thyme, valerian, vanilla or violet.
- In the centre are your altar candles: goddess to the left and god to the right (or yin and yang, anima and animus, female and male energies, if you prefer to think of them in a more abstract way). You can of course choose a goddess statue or a god/goddess paring from your favourite culture or follow the suggestions for the outdoor altar. I still use the candles.
- In each direction set a candle, either natural beeswax or white in all four directions or green or brown in the north, yellow or grey in the east, orange, red or natural in the south and blue or purple in the west. The traditional silver for the west and gold for the south are used more for moon and sun work in natural magick. In a water ritual you could use all blue and in a fire ritual all red and so on.
- In the centre of the altar place your symbol in a dish, unglazed if possible. Some practitioners use a dish decorated with a pentagram or a pentacle (see page 90). You can also have a pentacle flat dish in the north for more formal spells.
- You can also have a pottery offerings bowl in the west to hold any bread or wine that outdoors you would pour directly on to the ground.

Dedicating the altar

This dedication can form the core for other rituals.
- Work in the morning when you wake. Set everything up the night before and use all six candles: the goddess, the god and the four elemental ones.
- You will not want to sweep an indoor area with a besom but you could use a soft brush, sprinkle lavender on the floor and sweep that up to cleanse the area.
- A circle is better suited to an indoor altar than a square, so start by visualising a light circle extending round the whole room.
- Stand just south of the altar, facing north.
- Begin the dedication by lighting the two altar candles, first the left goddess candle and from that the right god candle. Then, in your own words, make a promise to work for others and to conserve the natural world and ask that in return you may receive abundance if it is right to be.
- You are now going to incorporate the powers of the guardians at the four directions, asking that each will grant its special blessing. You can ask for the stability of the north, the clarity of the east, the inspiration of the south and the gentleness of the west to be reflected in your magick and your life (see page 496 for a full list of elemental qualities). At each direction, you should also explain aloud how you will use each of the qualities for the good of others and the earth.
- Light the north candle from the goddess candle and greet the northern guardians of the earth. Ask for their particular protection and strength and to bring you wisdom as you work with your altar and the sacred area round it. Make your promise of what you will do in return for the earth.

- Light the candle of the east from the candle of the north (using a taper or the actual candle). Ask for the protection of the guardians of the east.
- Light the south candle from the candle of the east and the west candle from the candle of the south, again calling on the guardians.
- Next you are going to bless the altar itself. Take the salt in your left hand and with your right hand put three small pinches into the bowl of water. Stir the water with your wand clockwise three times. If you have a crystal in the end of the wand, the crystal can just touch the water, otherwise let the tip almost touch the water and swirl the bowl round three times to mix the salt. Alternatively, set the salt bowl on the pentacle dish in the north and follow the method of making sacred water (see page 124). Generally this second method is used for more formal rituals.
- Say three times as you stir:

Earth mother (or name your goddess), bless and make sacred this water that it may sanctify my altar and my work.

- Sprinkle drops of the now sacred water in each of the four directions of the altar near the edges, beginning in the north and saying:

So may all be holy and of worth.

- You can extend this ritual by incorporating the dedication of your tools (see page 93).
- Finally, you should make the invoking or opening pentagram of power, which symbolises the connection of your own power amplified through the altar. To do this, face north while standing to the south of the altar, and hold your wand in front of you just higher than your head. Follow the diagram below to make the pentagram.

- Raise your arms above your head in a V to allow the power to merge with that of the sky and flow down through your feet, which you should set apart to prevent excessive buzzing.
- Leave the candles and incense to burn through as you quietly sit in front of your altar meditating, writing chants or future rituals in your Book of Shadows or reading a special magickal book. If you wish play soft, magickal or Gregorian chants in the background.

* When all is burned through, use your wand to make the banishing or closing pentagram in front of you and say:

> *The dedication is complete. Blessings be on this place and on all I love.*

(This includes you.)
* Dispose of used wax, etc. in an environmentally friendly way and set the altar ready for the next ritual. This is a good way of grounding or settling yourself.
* On other occasions you can make the invoking pentagram in a formal ritual at each of the quarters as a way of opening their energies. You could also use the banishing or closing pentagram, which is drawn in the opposite way, to close the quarters of your circle (in reverse).

Making natural magick anywhere

Natural magick can be practised anywhere – even in the workplace or in a hotel room. Sometimes you won't even be able to set up a mini altar, but with your four elemental crystals or four elemental herbs (if necessary in four tiny purses) you can make a dedicated place wherever you choose.

You could, for example, make your circle with four elemental crystals on your desk or set four growing herb plants in the four main directions of a room.

All you need then is a pointed crystal quartz to act as a wand to cast the circle, either on your desk or round the whole room. This will help to deal with any bad vibes and will also energise you (sharp end pointing inwards towards you on your desk during the day) or protect you (sharp edge outwards towards any potentially hostile person or situation that may approach you).

Wash the crystals regularly and make sure the plants are well tended and you will soon notice the positive changes in energies.

You can also celebrate the four pointers of your day: arrival, lunch, tea break or going home and arriving home with empowerments or small personal rituals (see Sun magick on page 412 for suggestions).

2

TOOLS OF MAGICK

The essence of natural magick is spontaneity. Unlike formal ritual magick you do not need lots of tools. If you want to read more about the use of ceremonial tools such as the bell, the Athame and the chalice there is detailed information in my book *The Practical Guide to Witchcraft and Magick Spells* (see Further reading, page 516). Of course, many formal rituals are carried out in the open air, but natural magick taps directly into the power source of nature herself and so the tools need only be simple.

Tuning into the energies

Ultimately, in any form of magick you are the only essential magickal tool necessary. You have your hands to cast circles and direct power, and your feet, hands and voice to raise and release it into the cosmos or into the earth.

The Ancient Egyptians believed the power of words was the mightiest magickal force of all and was central to all rituals.

As I said in the previous chapter, you will often find natural tools in the forest or on the seashore. You can make a magickal symbol from woven dried grasses or sticks as our ancestors did or you can scratch a wish or banishment on bark or a stone to serve as a focus for your spells.

But many practitioners do find that simple tools made of natural fabrics or fibres help them to build up and direct magickal energies more easily and effectively. Many can be created even by those, like me, with little aptitude for crafts. Equally, you can, on outings to different places, look in antique stores, car boot sales and garden centres and suddenly find your ideal tool in the most unexpected place.

So this chapter is about the pleasure of finding the right wand or staff, whether at a country fair, a New Age store or festival or on-line, or of painting a pentacle, the five-pointed star within a circle, on clay bowls and dishes you have made or bought to set on your altar. How you empower and use your tools is the key to successful natural magick as to all magick.

The wand

Primary element: Fire

The wand is the single most valuable all-purpose tool in natural magick. It is usually regarded as a fire element tool. The instructions for making a wand and information about the different woods that are suitable should also be of use if you decide you would rather buy a wand. Some people have different wands for different needs and a special one for major outdoor ceremonies or for a boost of power. You can also find or buy a small twig wand for travel. My miniature one is less than 30 cm/12 in long. You can use any small smooth branch as a temporary wand by asking the blessings of the forest where you find it.

Using your wand

* Making ever-increasing clockwise circles with your wand will attract whatever or whoever is needed in your life; making decreasing anticlockwise circles will banish sorrow, illness, bad luck and anything negative.
* Circling your wand clockwise in small regular circles (using the power hand) will enchant any symbol that represents a need. At the same you should move your other hand in similar-sized circles, anticlockwise, all the while softly chanting the purpose of the spell. By association you are sending power to whomever or whatever is represented by the symbol. You can empower herbs or crystals by the same method.
* Bring your magickal intentions to reality by writing them in the air with your wand. Do this faster and faster until you reach a peak of power, when you should raise your wand to the air vertically and then bring it down behind you and back up again to waist height to release the power. This can also be done with any secret magickal names that you use to draw power into you and the aura, the psychic energy field surrounding you.
* Casting a small circle of protection about an arm span all around yourself in the morning before work or in the evening when you get home will afford you protection when you feel afraid, unwell or under attack.
* In order to banish, albeit temporarily, anxiety, pain or physical weakness, hold the wand in front of your face while speaking banishing words. You can hold your other hand upright palm outwards at the same time.
* Direct power generated through magickal words towards a place or person by holding the wand horizontally in the right direction, whatever the distance, and reciting the place name nine times, saying:

May it be healed/restored/ saved.

* Draw a circle of power and light within which to carry out magick by walking round the visualised circle, pointing your wand diagonally downwards from waist height in front of you. See the light coming from the wand to protect above and below in the circle (see page 60 for circle casting).
* Your wand can be used to close a circle in the same way (see page 64 for circle uncasting).
* You can use your wand to open the four directions of your circle by drawing,

attracting or invoking pentagrams in the air as you welcome the four guardians. You can likewise, in reverse order of opening, close the circle with banishing pentagrams drawn in the air in the four directions.

* Draw down the moon or sun by holding the wand in a sharp angle to the sky and turning in rapid clockwise circles for the sun and the reverse for the moon. This should create the psychic sensation of the heavenly body rushing towards you (see pages 408 and 429).
* Use the crystal tip of your wand to mix in salt and make sacred water.
* Filling the wand with power by leaving it on the outdoor altar for brief periods during storms for courage, rain for healing or banishing, under a rainbow for granting wishes and in winds for change. Hold it soon afterwards and feel the energies passing through it to you, topping up your own energies and determination.
* When your wand becomes weathered, you can keep it near the altar until it splinters and finally rots; empower a new one meanwhile as the old one's work is done.
* Use your wand as a personal power channeller, amplifying your own power to give you daily strength. Hold it at 45 degrees from your body, facing the morning sky, noon, dusk and midnight, filling you with cosmic and earthly power.

Choosing the wood

Wands can be straight, slightly curved, tapered to a point or twisted like corkscrews. If you find one of these twisted pieces of wood, you will find that it needs hardly any empowerment or improving to make it effective.

Look for a relatively straight branch, about the width of your forefinger that tapers slightly. Some traditions insist a wand should be 53 cm/21 in long, but if you find a piece that is right but shorter, go with that. (I find 53 cm/21 in too long.) Others recommend cutting the branch so that it is the same length as the distance from your elbow to the tip of your middle finger. The ideal is to find a freshly fallen branch that does not need cutting.

Driftwood

This is surprisingly effective since it is already smooth, the bark has been worn away and, as long as it is still firm, it has all the power of the sea.

Tree branches

* You may find fresh branches on the ground if there has been pollarding, tree felling or a high wind.
* You can cut a small branch from a growing tree. You must ask the permission of the Dryad of the tree (as well as an earthly owners, where necessary). If you feel a cold breeze or sense resistance, try another tree or wait until another day.
* If you wish, you can use a pendulum and ask it to lead you by its positive swing to the right tree. (A pendulum will respond to the movement of your hand directed by your mind, a psychic process called psychokinesis. Practise by thinking of something happy and the pendulum will move spontaneously as you hold it loosely to give its positive response – often a circling clockwise.)
* Traditionally wands are cut on Wednesday, the day of Mercury, or on the full

moon, but you may choose a day that has personal significance. It is up to you how elaborate or simple the cutting ceremony is and whether you want to cast a circle round the tree.

* Use a small hacksaw, as this is easier and kinder to the tree than breaking off a branch. Cut slightly diagonally to give you a firm end to hold. You may need a stepladder unless you are a regular tree climber. The wood should be dry, with leaves growing on it. If it has been lying a while, check it is not too damp or has not started to rot inside.

* If you want to be really formal, use a boline, a ritual white-handled knife for cutting. Bert, a local environmentalist who made me a special wand and has taught me a great deal of natural lore, says you should cut the required length of branch at five 45-degree angles, giving the remaining branch a five-sided point for regrowth. Other wand experts have confirmed this. However, some insist it should be cut with a single stroke.

* Remember to thank the tree and leave an offering, closing the circle if you cast one. Crumble a few biscuits near the roots for wildlife.

Magickal wood for wands

Wands can be made of almost any wood (though not elder unless you find it on the ground, as it is a magickal tree that should not be cut or burned). The following meanings also hold true if you are making or choosing a staff.

Alder: The wood of stability and so brings magickal desires and energies into the here and now.

Apple wood: Very fertile and will help to spread abundance and creativity; also used traditionally for casting circles and in love magick.

Ash: The world tree that formed the axis between earth and heaven. It is also a healing tree and the tree of travel and travellers and so is good for portable altars; good for your special wand.

Cedar: The tree of truth, integrity and purity and so demands high standards of the user.

Elder: Associated with faerie and nature spirit magick (see page 501) and is good for any visualisation work. Only suitable if you find a fallen branch – do not cut an elder tree.

Hazel: The traditional tree of wisdom, knowledge and justice and so grounds magick in a secure foundation. It is linked with the magick of the sun. The wand should be cut from a tree that has not yet borne fruit. It is another good choice for a ceremonial wand.

Oak: A tree of great strength and wisdom and will help you to develop your inner understanding of the deeper significance behind even simple rituals. It is also ideal for those who wish to progress further in magick and are prepared to accept the extra responsibilities. Some practitioners will only work with fallen branches of oak.

Pine: Brings courage and inspiration to your work; a good wand for mothers and wise women.

Rowan: Both magickal and protective; ideal if you work mainly in an area where there are security problems or extremes of weather or if you are new to magick.

Willow: The moon tree, is wonderful for moon magick, for women and younger witches and will develop your divinatory powers.

Making your wand

* You should remove any leaves and twigs as soon as you cut or find your wand.
* In more formal practice the wand is left for a year and a day in a dry, safe, airy place, but this may not be practical for a first wand. I have seen some beautiful wands, made from fallen branches, that were found only a day or two previously. Do at least try to leave it in a warm, airy place for a few days until the wood is dry.
* Each wand will retain some of the essence of the tree spirit. I am always very wary of buying a wand or staff whose maker declares it to contain a tree spirit per se (and usually charges you a great deal extra for the resident).
* Strip off the bark if you wish. Some people leave as least some of it on as, especially with twisted wands, this looks beautiful and means no extra adornment is needed.
* Sand or rub it smooth.
* I believe that unadorned polished wands are the most magickal. However, you can if you wish bind the handle, and add cords, crystals or charms.
* You may choose to inscribe your wand with a natural magickal symbol from one of the natural alphabets such as runes or Ogham (Celtic staves). You can find these on-line or in my *Complete Guide to Divination* (see Further reading, page 516).
* Carve either with a pyrographic tool or a very fine awl, pocket knife or screwdriver that has been held over a camping gas cooker or an ordinary gas cooker flame. Do take care when working with these hot tools.
* If your preference is for an unadorned wand, you can use incense stick smoke to write your power names and magickal wishes in the air above the wand to represent the different energies you want for it. Do this after polishing the wand. Ritual magick symbols are, I think, rather heavy for natural magick.
* Sometimes the wood will already be marked with a distinctive spiral or eye which can be accentuated with a thin brush and a subtle brown wood paint.
* Buy sealing oils for the wood from a DIY store. Try to use natural ones such as linseed oil.
* You can give your wand a crystal point. You need to make a split in the top of the wand with a pocket knife so the crystal will slide in and remain firm (have a couple of spare identical crystals in case one falls out). You can use glue if you wish.
* While making your wand, it is a good idea to make a simple, small, unadorned wand for your travelling altar set.

Caring for your wand

Whether or not you treat your wand with preservative or varnish or buy one that has been treated, you should polish your wand before and after each use with a soft cloth kept specially for the purpose. It is also a good idea to have a pouch to keep the wand in.

Once a week, use furniture polish, ideally the old-fashioned lavender or beeswax polish in a tin. This cleanses the wand psychically and increases its power.

If you haven't used the wand during the week, spend a few minutes holding your wand and picturing light beams and sparks flowing in and out. When possible, leave it out under the full moon.

The staff

Primary element: Air

The staff is a tool purely of natural and not ceremonial magick and also of Druidry, a nature-based religion with primary emphasis on the sun and tuning in with nature rather than casting spells as in more lunar-based witchcraft. The staff is longer than the wand, usually the same height as the user or to the height of their heart. Some practitioners prefer a shoulder-height staff: tall enough for support but manageable. It is carried in the power hand and is used vertically. Staves is the plural form.

Using your staff

* Your staff can be used to mark the centre of a visualised circle and to hang a lantern on if it is dark or during midwinter celebrations (see page 46).
* Set to the direct north just outside a visualised or actual circle with an empowerment, a staff will act as guardian or watcher and keep away all harm. In earlier times of persecution, there would be an actual watcher who stood on high ground, looking for any who might intrude or be hostile to a gathering.
* Knocking your staff on the ground three times in the centre of a magickal circle will draw upwards the power of the earth. It can also be used to ask for the presence of the wise ancestors and the nature essences in a ritual or when you are carrying out personal meditation or past-life work. Face south to call the ancestors.
* Mark out a physical, as opposed to visualised, circle in earth or sand. Afterwards the markings can be rubbed out with the end of the staff.
* Direct healing sky energies into the earth with a downwards movement of the staff.
* As a psychic as well as a physical strengthener as you walk up hills or over rough terrain – for those times when you really think you cannot walk another step up a steep muddy track even to find the most beautiful and sacred site in the known world.
* To set behind your bedroom or house door at night with a night-time blessing and request to invoke the protection of the protective land guardians.
* As a representation of the world tree axis that was supposed to link earth with heaven. As such, it naturally conducts power between earth and the skies when

set in the ground. You will be energised by the union of power when you take your staff up again even if you were just having a rest or a picnic.

Making or buying your staff

Staves are widely available in country stores, gift shops at animal and bird sanctuaries and at all kinds of rural fairs and gatherings. The staff may have an animal or bird head and is often elaborately carved and polished. You can choose one that represents your personal power animal.

Fortunately, the art of woodcarving is returning and a local craftsperson may make one to order. Traditionally staffs or staves are made of yew, ash or hazel, but it is your choice.

You can make you own staff. Note that the end you hold is usually cleft on a homemade staff so you can hang a lantern or your crane bag from it when it is set upright in the earth or grass. You will need sturdy tools to cut and smooth it.

* Find a long, slender branch (ideally about the width of a broomstick and tapering slightly at the end) about 1.5 m/5 ft long, though you may prefer a longer one or shorter one.
* Rub the bark until it is quite smooth and then engrave on it any symbols that are personal to you or perhaps an image of your power creature. Then use clear wood varnish.
* You may choose to have a number of staffs made of different woods and may even make special ones for the family to go walking together.

Cauldron

Primary element: Water

The three-legged iron cauldron really comes into its own as an outdoor natural magickal tool. If you have a small one, it can also fit in your altar room to the north-west of the altar as it is a tool of earth and water (and also of fire, if a candle is set in it). I have four cauldrons of various sizes, one small enough to stand in the west for the water element on a tabletop altar.

The cauldron is a symbol of Cerridwen, the Celtic mother goddess, whose cauldron brought rebirth and transformation. It was originally a household cooking pot hung over black ranges and open fires in many lands and so is a reassuring and stable tool.

Using your cauldron

* In the centre of a ritual area (with or without an altar) the cauldron can be used to receive offerings, such as flowers, fruits, crystals, etc. in a seasonal celebration or abundance ritual.
* Half-fill your cauldron with water on the full moon so that you and anyone present can look into the silvery water and scry (look for images). You can interpret these images as you would dreams to answer questions or to receive wisdom from the moon mother and your wise inner self (see Moon magick on pages 421–37).
* Scry also in bright sunlight or by candlelight by dropping a handful of dried, chopped cooking herbs on to the water to give you moving images to answer questions.
* If your cauldron is cast iron and not a replica, you can put a heatproof fire basket or metal liner inside and light a small fire. Alternatively, fill the cauldron with sand and embed a candle in the centre. In this you can burn wishes, or scatter herbs or incense.
* Burn incense in the cauldron either as charcoal or as sticks or cones embedded in sand.
* Dance and chant around the cauldron.
* Fill the cauldron with water, then cast petals or herbs on to the surface as you circle the cauldron to symbolise healing energies flowing. Alternatively, as a banishing ritual you could ritually tip away the water and, for example, dead leaves you threw into the water symbolising what is unwanted. Best of all, tip it back into the earth or a water source.
* Fill the cauldron with earth and, during a ceremony, plant herbs and flowers, and bury coins or crystals. This indicates prosperity, love or healing growing as the plants grow. You can transplant the whole lot after the ceremony or use an old or spare cauldron for this ceremony so that the rite can be ongoing (maybe from spring equinox to autumn equinox).

Choosing your cauldron

A cast-iron cauldron is by far the best if you intend to use it for any fire work. These are for sale in some garden centres as well as New Age stores. You can sometimes discover an authentic cauldron in an antique shop as I did, or in street or flea markets, especially in the countryside. It may be an original iron cooking pot. You can clean it up with a gentle wire brushing and a little grate polish. Alternatively, adapt a round coal scuttle.

Fire dish

Primary element: Fire

Another favourite tool of mine for outdoor magick is a fire dish. Though you can burn a small fire in a cauldron, having a fire in a special bowl or dish is one of the most magickal experiences, particularly under star- or moonlight. You can carry it with you in the back of the car for rituals on beaches. Some stone circles, such as the Rollright stones in Oxfordshire, have a fire dish in situ to borrow for ceremonies under supervision of the warden.

Ideally, you would use the cauldron for water and the dish for fire: a perfect elemental balance.

Using your fire dish

* A fire dish is ideal for any seasonal or personal rite of passage for which traditionally a bonfire was lit. Sometimes you can have a bonfire or remove turf and make a fire pit with bricks, but this is not always possible, especially near sacred ground.
* A fire dish is wonderful for unifying those sharing a rite, whether a coven, friends or family.
* When you are not travelling, keep your fire dish to the south of the outdoor altar as a powerful representation of the fire element and to attract fire spirits and faeries (see pages 507–8). You can cover it when not in use or during inclement weather.
* Sprinkle incense or herbs directly on to the burning wood to make personal empowerments and to raise or release power during a spell.
* Burn wishes scratched on the inside of bark with a small knife or burn dead leaves and twigs to represent banishing what is redundant in your life.
* Use your fire dish as a focus for chanting and dancing and as an added bonus for supplying light and warmth during a ritual.
* Make sure the fire dish is not too full to avoid the danger of tipping over or getting too hot. Keep water nearby to extinguish an over-zealous fire.
* Some woods like juniper and cedar spit; ash and pine are excellent as is oak although some people will not burn the latter. Sandalwood smells fabulous if you can get it; you can sometimes buy small sandalwood logs in bags from a hardware store. You can mix the woods.
* Practise before your first ritual with your fire dish so you know how to light a good but not ferocious fire. When everyone had an open fire in the living room, this was daily practice. Nowadays, unless you were a Scout or Girl Guide or belong to a coven, you may not have been taught the art. Follow the instructions on a pack of firelighters or ask an older relative for a lesson.

Choosing your fire dish

I have seen beautiful copper fire dishes on metal legs for sale in garden centres, which are not expensive and need no adaptation.

Alternatively, you can use any large fireproof metal dish either with metal legs or raised off the ground on heat-resistant bricks to avoid scorching. This can be a very large cast iron wok or the bottom half of a domed iron barbecue, again the kind with legs.

A chimenea is also a good alternative and these are widely obtainable, as is the less exotic incinerator base.

Pentacles

Primary element: Earth

A pentacle is a pentagram enclosed by a circle. Though pentagrams are now associated with ceremonial magick, pentacles made of clay or beeswax or etched or painted on slate are an excellent tool for natural magick.

The pentagram emblem is found naturally inside apples and watermelons and represents the four natural elements combining to make the fifth element, ether, akasha or spirit, on the uppermost point.

The pentacle, like the pentagram, has been a magickal sign for thousands of years. The five-pointed star is a sacred symbol of Isis, and modern witches often associated the single top point as representing the union of the triple goddess aspects. It is the original and constant symbol of the divine feminine in spirituality.

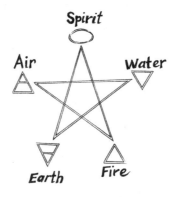

Using pentacles

✳ A flat circular plate decorated with a pentagram, the points of which touch the edge, or a plate or dish with the design of the encircled pentagram in the centre, can be placed in the centre of the altar for holding the symbol of the ritual. You can pass the symbol on the pentacle through the four elements on the altar for amplified power or round a circle of assembled participants for each to empower with a wish or blessing.

✳ As a magickal tool of the north, the pentacle, when set flat on the altar, will hold herbs, crystals or just bring the earth stability of the north to the altar. You can also on an indoor altar use small flat pentacle dishes at each quarter to contain the elemental crystals and herbs (see pages 385–98).

* A huge pentacle painted, chalked or drawn on a paved area or floor or, more temporarily, in earth or on sand, can be large enough to walk round in the order of drawing. You would greet the elements as in the normal circle, but would add spirit whose colour is dazzling white (see page 258).
* You can also walk the large pentacle continuously while chanting alone or as a group to raise the power. When it comes to releasing the power, stand on spirit if you are alone, or with one of you on each point if there are enough of you.
* As a personal protective charm made from beeswax and empowered in a spell, a pentacle can be carried round with you (see page 139 for making charm bags). The pentacle can also serve to keep your other tools safe when they are in your travelling bag.
* Set an upright free-standing pentacle in the north on your indoor altar as protection (or a weatherproofed wooden one likewise on your outdoor altar).
* A free-standing pentacle positioned upright on a base in the north of the altar during a ceremony will ground the spell, balance the energies and keep out all but benign energies.
* You can also use pentacles, flat or free-standing, to charge other tools or substances with power by placing or balancing a tip of the tool or substance against the pentacle. Then make an invoking pentagram over the tool and pentacle to seal the power. For larger items, hold the pentacle face down over the artefact and visualise a pentacle of fire descending into the artefact (the fire dish should be unlit, of course).
* Set pentacles over doors and propped up against windows or buy pentacle ornaments in glass to hang at windows to keep your home safe.
* Decorate cakes with pentacles for part of celebratory feasts (use icing or dough). You can use an especially large pentacle dish to pass them round from person to person at the end of a celebration. Each can make a blessing to honour the bounty of the earth mother. You can also serve pentacle biscuits and cakes at home for tea to family and to more liberal visitors to bring abundance.
* Paint pentacles in the bowls that you use to hold salt and water in your rituals.

Making or choosing a pentacle

Pentacle plates and dishes and upright free-standing pentacles can be bought from New Age stores or on the Internet. Dishes are usually ceramic or wood and free-standing pentacles are made of brass, silver, copper, bronze or wood or any metal that can be engraved.

Pentacles are traditionally made on or around the night of the full moon.

Making a clay pentacle

* Use a wooden rolling pin to roll the soft clay out into a thick circle, the size you need for your pentacle. Unless you have access to a kiln, use self-hardening clay.
* Draw a pentagram on a circle of thin or tracing paper cut to precisely the same size as your clay. Draw an invoking or attracting pentagram (see next page) so that the five points touch the edges of the paper circle. Practise drawing pentagrams and use a ruler if necessary to get the lines straight. You can enlarge/shrink the images in this chapter as a template if you prefer.

- If you used tracing paper, place it over the clay and re-draw over the outline with a broad-tipped pencil so that it presses through and appears on the clay.
- If you used thicker paper, place it over the clay circle and use a sharp pencil, toothpick or thin-bladed paper knife to make dots along the outline, piercing the paper and creating a dot pentagram on the clay below. Remove the paper and join up the dots on the clay with a modelling tool or pencil and make into a smooth or slightly raised line.
- Leave to harden.

Making a wax pentacle

- A wax pentacle is traditionally supposed to hold its power until the wax crumbles. They are firm enough to act as a dish for symbols or as a talisman to guard you or tools.
- Use a large beeswax pillar candle (see page 242 for making your own, or buy one) and stand it on a large, flat, metal holder. Secure the candle by lighting it and dripping wax on to the holder where the candle will stand. Alternatively, roll out a sheet of beeswax, warmed over a candle, draw your pentacle and cut out the shape carefully with a sharp knife. Put greaseproof paper underneath so the wax does not stick.
- Enchant the candle by moving your hands on either side of the burning flame (without getting too close) as though your hands were snakes dancing in unison.
- Endow the candle with whatever you seek (the earth security aspect is inbuilt).
- Build the chant to a crescendo and then release the power by making an arch with your arms over the candle, then crossing your hands over it and finally bringing your arms earthwards so your hands end either side of the candle, level with the base.
- Leave the candle to burn through and when the wax is still molten mark a circle in the wax with a fine-tipped screwdriver, thin-bladed paper knife or a special art engraving tool.
- Within the circle, draw the pentagram so that it touches the edges. Again this can be an invoking pentagram unless you are specifically making a protective charm in which case draw a banishing pentagram (see below for a reminder of both).
- Finally just before the wax hardens, redefine the outline circle with your knife so the pentacle separates from the remaining wax. Ease with a spatula on to greaseproof paper on a tray and leave until hard.

Dedicating your tools

You will probably obtain or make your tools separately, but you can cleanse and empower more than one or indeed all of them in the same ritual.

You can slot this in to your altar dedication if you wish and dedicate the major tools one by one with their own element, having cleansed them before the ritual. Here I will give a separate cleansing and empowering rite.

First you want to cleanse your new tool, even if you made it yourself so that it contains only its own innate natural energies and not those of the people who made the wood stain, etc.

Cleansing

Fire and smoke (incense) are the most effective methods of purification.

* Light a candle and incense or smudge stick and also the altar candles if you are working indoors. Work after dark when the moon is visible in the sky.
* If you are working outdoors, use moonlight if possible. The full moon is excellent or any of the days leading up to it or the two days afterwards when the moon is still bright. You can supplement the moonlight, if it is cloudy, with a circle of small candles or tea lights in jars.
* Set smaller artefacts on the altar and larger ones where they would naturally stand: a fire dish, for example, to the south of the altar. Do not fill the fire dish or cauldron yet.
* Cleanse your tools by circling the artefact/s nine times anticlockwise with the smoke of a lighted smudge or an incense stick.
* Alternatively, you can pass the tool/s above a flame nine times anticlockwise (not wax, which will melt).
* Whichever method you choose, move with the candle or smudge rhythmically. Use a broad-based, heat-resistant candle holder and a heatproof incense container so as not to burn yourself (see page 97 for making and lighting incense).
* Say nine times slowly as you equally slowly pass smoke or candle flame nine times anticlockwise over or round the artefact:

Three by three, three by three,
Mother earth I call on thee.
May this (name tool) be purified by mother earth,
she by whom all is given birth.
Be cleansed likewise by mother moon,
who takes all back into her starry womb.
Three by three, cleansed and blessed be.

Empowering

Now after cleansing you need to empower and dedicate each tool separately for positive purpose, again using its own elemental power (see page 31). So for the wand you need fire, the staff air and so on. If you are dedicating more than one tool, work through them in order: earth tools first, then air, then fire and finally water.

* For earth tools you can use sea salt (make nine clockwise circles of salt round it).
* For air tools use incense (weave nine smoke spirals round it – stand the staff upright in the ground).
* For fire tools pass a candle either round the artefact or vice versa in nine clockwise circles.
* For water tools use water from a sacred source or in which nine tiny clear quartz crystals have been soaked for eight hours from first light or when you wake, whichever is sooner. Make nine clockwise circles of water droplets.
* You can fill the fire dish but do not light it, and put water in the cauldron. Say nine times over each:

> *So shall it be three by three,*
> *empowered by creative light of the father,*
> *lord of the animals, lord of the skies,*
> *three by three, empowered be,*
> *by _____ (name your element), your power rise*
> *to star filled skies,*
> *so might it be!*

* Now you can light your fire dish, raise power with your wand or lift your pentacle to the skies. Weave your own rite of power round each or all of the dedicated tools, so that you begin by releasing energy, not for any particular purpose but to add to the positivity of the universe.
* You can re-dedicate your tools at any time with your wand, which you can keep empowered from the pentacle, and vice versa. These are your two ongoing power sources. Place the tool so it touches the pentacle and tap it nine times with the wand.
* If either of these becomes low in power, recharge them in following way. For the pentacle, sprinkle three circles of salt round it and repeat the empowerment chant above. For the wand, pass it over a candle flame nine times repeating the empowerment chant.
* You can cleanse your tools at any time using the original method and words, followed by the full empowerment, but once a month or after a major ceremony is usually enough.
* Some people do not like other people to touch their special tools. However, if you do invite friends or family to share celebrations, contact is inevitable and not at all harmful. You can cleanse and re-dedicate your tools afterwards so that they are once more personal to you.

3

MAGICKAL INCENSES

Making, empowering and burning magickal incenses on charcoal or an open fire is a very ancient form of natural magick. We know that the Aztecs burned copal and floral incenses in huge human-shaped obsidian censers on top of the pyramids of the sun and the moon and the pyramid of Quetzalcoatl, the feathered serpent god. The incense rituals on the feathered serpent pyramid were performed to call rain and sunshine for the crops to grow.

In Ancient Egypt, Greece and Rome ordinary people, as well as the priests and priestesses, cast the first blossoms on to ritual fires or on censers on family altars so that the deities might be pleased by the fragrance and bring abundance to the home.

Incense is said to carry our wishes and dreams into the cosmos on the smoke, whether it is burned ceremonially in a marble temple or rises against a sunset in your back garden.

Incense magick can be as complex or as simple as you choose. You can grow the herbs and flowers yourself or buy them at a market or from a garden centre or supermarket. You can dry them, crush them into powder with a mortar and pestle as you empower them with your spoken hopes and desires and then burn the charged incense on charcoal. This kind of incense is called non-combustible.

Combustible incense requires no charcoal as the fuel is contained within the incense stick, cone or loop. The combustible material may, in more natural incenses, be a wood powder such as pine or sandalwood. There are many pure herbal commercial incense sticks as well as the loose kind that can be bought as granules, beads or powder.

It really doesn't matter if you don't have time to make incense. However, of all the DIY activities, incense-making is probably the most fun and satisfying, as well as very therapeutic. Though my garden is not large, it is filled with herbs, flowers and small trees, which my daughter Miranda and I use to make our own incense.

When I was researching my Ancient Egyptian magick book in Cairo, I visited an incense stall in a bazaar. Because my Egyptian guide knew the owner, I was lucky enough to see and handle some of the more precious incenses and brought back a big bag of frankincense granules, probably the best resin that you can mix with dried herbs or flowers for incense-making at home.

What is herbal incense?

Incense is made by combining roots, bark, leaves and flower heads, mixed together with a gum resin such as frankincense, dragon's blood, copal or the traditional gum Arabic (acacia gum). A drop or two of essential oil is sometimes added to improve the fragrance, but if you use fragrant herbs or flowers this is not necessary.

Incense should be ground very finely if it is to be burned on charcoal. The finer the grains, the better it burns.

Combustible incense is quite complicated to make. I have suggested an excellent book on the subject by the late Scott Cunningham in Further reading (page 514) if you would like to try.

Using incense

* Combine different energies within a single incense mix. Each herb, flower and tree has its own significance (see pages 176–83, 162–65 and 188–90 for these).
* By burning different herbs you amplify and empower their innate energies and release them into the cosmos.
* Use incense, especially large, firm sticks, to cast a magickal circle for a spell, for protection round yourself before going out, or round artefacts or your home.
* Incense can be used as the air element in magickal rituals to add focus and clarity to the purpose of the spell and to initiate change or movement from thought to actuality.
* Use incense to create personal, empowered incense rituals for any purpose (see page 104).
* Prolong happy memories by making incense from flowers dried from a wedding bouquet, one sent for a birthday or anniversary, on Mother's Day or by a lover. You can, if the rest of the family doesn't mind, take a few favourite flowers from a loved one's funeral wreaths to preserve as incense.
* Incense sticks can be used to write your private power names in the air or over a crystal or charm to empower it.
* Use incense to create a meditative state and enhance psychic powers.
* Write wishes or needs in the air with incense stick smoke, so that they may be carried upwards and transformed.
* Incense can be used as a background mood enhancer or relaxant, for example lavender releases gentle energies, rosemary brings positive but clear communication.
* On hearth fires or bonfires, incense brings blessings to the home and family or those gathered.

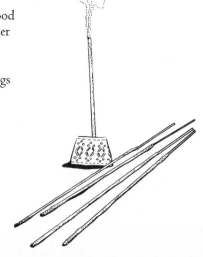

Making and empowering incense

* Use a mortar and pestle, a large one so you can mix more easily. There really is no substitute for this tool and they are widely obtainable in cookware stores (usually at half the price of those in New Age stores). You can buy ceramic, marble or wooden (though wood can stain).

* You can use a mixture of home-dried herbs and flowers or buy them ready dried. Cooking herbs and spices from kitchen jars are an excellent addition to a home mix and in an emergency you can mix these with a resin such as frankincense for an almost instant home brew.

* You will need resins and do need to buy these. Look for a supplier that sells sensible quantities, as it is prohibitively expensive to buy the small packets.

* You can also buy ready-dried flower petals, heads and chopped dried herbs from an herbalist, health store or old-fashioned grocers. As a rough proportion, aim for about one-third resin to two-thirds other ingredients or more for easier burning.

* Dried and grated orange or lemon peel gives freshness.

* Though I have suggested some mixes that my daughter Miranda and I regularly make, do experiment with your own creations. I haven't given proportions as these will vary according to the significance of the incense. For example, in a love mix you might add more lavender if you wanted the love to be gentle, more rosemary for passion or bay leaves if fidelity was your main concern. Experiment to get the fragrance you like.

* I have given the magickal meanings of the resins on page 102.

* Spend a little time devising what you want to put in. Incenses are very good-tempered and it is hard to make a foul-smelling brew if you use fragrances.

* Aim to have at least two fragrant substances.

* Lavender, rose petals, lemon balm and verbena, bay leaves, jasmine, mimosa, most of the fruit blossoms, mint, sage, rosemary and chamomile are all very fragrant. Have a sniff round a garden centre and see which herbs, flowers and trees are especially fragrant and match your particular need. Sometimes even within a species such as sage or thyme there is a huge variation in scent.

* Rose petals, chamomile, rosemary and lavender heads are all-purpose incense materials and can be added to any mix as they bring gentleness and love as well as prosperity, health, happiness and healing.

* Collect and dry pine needles, cedar bark chippings and juniper berries, which are excellent additions to incense and, in the case of bark and chippings, aid burning. You may be able to buy sandalwood chips.

* Because you need to pound and grind herbs and flowers for your incense mix, you can empower the incense as you mix. I have found that it takes about as long for charcoal to heat as it does to mix incense and so you can combine the two at the beginning of a spell. However, you can make incense in advance and just add it as part of any spell.

* Concentrate on the magickal intentions of your ingredients and recite a chant slowly and mesmerically as you mix.

* First pound any leaves and petals. Chop roots beforehand very finely and crumble bark. Mix them all against the sides until you have a fine or grainy powder, and then add the resin beads or granules.

* Pound and mix these well into the powder as the smoother the incense, the better it will burn. You can add all the ingredients together before mixing, but this method seems to give a good-quality blend. Discard any stems that are sticking in the mix.
* You can add a drop or two of essential oil mid-way through the mixing, but if you do, be sure to use it sparingly so that the moisture is absorbed quickly by the mix. Personally, I don't use oils but I give suggestions for oils to use on pages 282–90.
* Add just a few dried nettles to any protective mix. Though they do not have a very distinctive smell this will give a powerful defence to any spell.
* Mix the incense faster and faster for any dynamic purpose, saying for example for a travel mix of fennel, frankincense (as resin), lavender and lemongrass:

Far across the ocean, far across the sea, to (name your chosen place) incense carry me.

* Continue to chant even faster and with a final pound release the power into the mix, saying in this case:

Travel come to me.

For a healing or gentle love or happiness mix such as lavender, chamomile, sage, myrrh (resin) and rose petals, endow softer energies by chanting faster and mixing faster until you can feel the power ready to fly. Then chant and mix more slowly and quietly and end with a final mixing and whisper as you push the power into the herb with a final smooth, slow, downward movement of the pestle.

Batches of incense can be mixed and stored in sealed jars for future rituals. You can make up basic core mixes for love (jasmine, lavender, rose and myrrh) or prosperity (basil, frankincense, sage and mimosa) and then add individual ingredients for specific spells.

Keep meticulous notes in your Book of Shadows of your different mixes and rough proportions that work for you so that you have a database for future mixes.

If you buy loose, powdered incenses, mix these in a mortar and pestle, while chanting, before use as if they were homemade. Of course, you need not be so vigorous or prolonged in the mixing.

You can also empower your incense sticks or cones by placing them in the container in which you are going to burn them and chanting over the container. As you do this, turn the container nine times clockwise or pass your wand clockwise nine times or you hands clockwise (power hand) and anticlockwise (receptive hand). Again, you can mix fragrances in the proportion you need, perhaps two frankincense sticks and one thyme for focusing on success in a test the night before or vice versa if you are starting to study.

Put a few spoons of any fragrant mix into a little plastic sachet and then into a pretty drawstring bag. These make excellent presents and some people keep them as herb bags rather than burning them.

Drying herbs for incense

You can buy ready-dried bags of herbs or flowers such as lavender or rose. However, drying your own, having picked them just after the full moon, if possible, does add even more of your personal essence and good intentions to spells.

In the following chapter (pages 108–22) I have described the process of smudging, which comes from the Native North American tradition. This involves burning certain broad-leafed dried herbs in a bowl without charcoal. You can dry and store the herbs for smudge in exactly the same way I describe here.

There are various methods of drying herbs (I describe three here), but once you have successfully dried a few bunches it becomes second nature. Gradually you instinctively know the different drying times in your own area and specific drying place. If I am picking herbs, leaves and flowers for drying, I always bring a few indoors to put in a vase in the hearth as a way of appreciating the fresh growth.

Keep an eye on the garden to see when a bloom has peaked or a herb bush is mature and full enough to take leaves and stems without harming future growth. A flat-based basket is good for collecting and secateurs or a boline (white handled knife) for cutting. Some practitioners believe you should never cut herbs with metal, but rather pick them with your hands. The Druids use golden sickles to harvest mistletoes from the sacred oak, but these are not very practical and rather expensive. After harvesting, herbs take a little time tending the garden as a way of saying thank you.

Hanging up to dry

This is the method that our ancestors used – and the easiest. There are many old folk customs surrounding this method, for example hanging a bunch of dill inside the entrance to repel harm. Once dry, the herbs could then be burned or stored for cooking, thus bringing continuing defence to the home.

* I tie the stalks firmly together with twine and hang bunches of herbs and flowers upside down on hooks from the glass-covered yard area outside my back door. They stay dry but also have the air circulating round them. Any dry, well-ventilated and warm area indoors or out (not in direct sunlight) is perfect.
* Some people prefer cool conditions but these take longer.
* Make sure the herbs are still fresh and moist but not soggy when you hang them.
* To test for readiness, take a leaf or flower between your fingers. If it crumbles like burned paper when you squeeze it gently, it is perfect. The herb should still be fragrant and not be left to wither.
* You can make a cord washing line and attach the bunches with string or use clothes pegs as fasteners for small bunches of light or single herbs.
* The drying process may take about two to three weeks depending on the weather and the kind of plant you are drying.
* You don't need to make the incense straight away but can store the dried sprigs in sealed jars – glass cookware jars with lids or stoppers are excellent. Store away from direct sunlight unless you use darkened glass.
* Remove any long stems after drying. A little orris root powder mixed in will help with preservation.
* Remember to label the jars, as if you are drying a lot of herbs and flowers it is all too easy to get them muddled.

Drying flat

An old wooden clothes dryer or a flat mesh board (the kind used for windows) is ideal as a drying rack. The key is that air must be able to circulate all round in order to prevent the herbs from going mouldy. You can position your rack in an outbuilding, but it must be moisture-free and not hot. Utility rooms with tumble dryers are not suitable. This method ensures quicker drying than the hanging method, but it is more time-consuming as you have to spread the herbs out individually. Again, test your herbs regularly.

Traditionally, metal was not used for drying herbs because of the dislike nature essences have for iron but, in practice, the mesh boards are very effective and metal cake cooling trays are excellent for drying small batches of herbs .

Using artificial heat

Herbs can be dried in an oven or microwave if you separate out the leaves and put them on a flat dish. However, the quality of the dried herbs will not be nearly as good as those obtained by natural methods, so use this as a last resort. Thirty seconds is about long enough in the microwave and about five minutes in a pre-warmed but not hot oven.

One word of warning: Wait for the herbs to cool before using them and don't use the same container you microwaved or heated them in as this will have absorbed moisture and the mix will not blend.

Burning herbs or herbal incense on charcoal

Charcoal is considered a gift from mother earth and was used frequently in the Native North American world. Its colour is a natural absorber of negative energies and as it forms ash so the redundant negativity is transformed into fire energy. Bamboo charcoal is totally saltpetre-free, and totally natural charcoal is also available, but these are much slower burning and quite hard to light.

The easiest charcoal to work with initially is an individual disk about the size of a very large coin, which will fit on any incense dish. This will have an indentation in the centre on which you can scatter your petals or herbs.

You can also sprinkle a little incense on barbecue coals or any open fire, though not while cooking.

I know that many of you will already use charcoal regularly, but for those who do not here are a few tips that I would have appreciated when I began using loose incense. They should help you to avoid burned fingers – and tears.

Using charcoal is not much harder and infinitely more satisfying than lighting commercially made sticks. As I said, it takes about the same length of time to mix incense from dried herbs and flowers as it does for your charcoal brick to heat up.

* The secret of lighting charcoal is really long matches or one of those mini extra-power gas lighters. The latter are excellent outdoors in damp conditions and are sold in various gadget shops and on-line stores as mini pocket blow lamps. Do be sure to take extreme care.

* Charcoal disks, both large and small, can be obtained from New Age stores, on the Internet and from some hardware stores. Buy in bulk so that you never run out. They come in foil packets and you should make sure that you always keep them sealed and dry. When working outdoors, wrap the charcoal in plastic until you need to take it out. Charcoal briquettes can be bought from camping shops and are suitable when you need to burn a larger quantity of incense.

* For smudge or incense, choose a flat, open dish around which the air can circulate. Choose a dish with a heatproof rim or handle if you will be carrying it.

* I find a flat dish is better than a censer (an enclosed incense dish) as it is simpler to top up and the air circulates more freely. You can put sand or salt in the bottom of the dish to absorb the heat.

* If working outdoors, you could put your burning incense in the bottom of a cauldron. Do use a suitable metal tray or a thick layer of sand inside the cauldron – either underneath the charcoal or to hold incense sticks.

* Charcoal burns for ages so will usually last the length of a ritual. You can light two disks on the same dish, one a minute or two after the other, for longer-lasting smoke.

* Either hold the side of your charcoal disc between your fingers (with extreme care) or between small, broad metal tongs. Smaller disks will slip out of barbecue tongs.

* Hold the lit match in the other hand at about 45 degrees (it burns longer like this). Unless someone is helping you, it takes practice to light the match (this is where a lighter or mini blow torch is easier).

* Hold the match against the side of the disk. You may need two or three matches to get it going. If a match goes out, go back to the same spot on the disk, where it is already warm.

* When the disk sparks and one or two patches glow red, blow on them so that the red spreads. Then put the charcoal on the dish and blow it occasionally if you want faster results. At first it may not look alight, but don't poke it as you may well burn yourself (as I have found in the past).

* When the disk is white, you can add the herbs or incense mix, a small spoon at a time. Old-fashioned sugar spoons (smaller than teaspoons) are ideal – you may get one at a car boot sale.

* Add more incense as necessary, periodically adding an empowerment as you fuel the charcoal up.

* Scrape the ash off the disk with the back of the spoon or blow gently if the charcoal seems to be losing its heat.

* Do not add too much incense at a time. You can add more as it burns as part of the ritual.

* At the end of the ritual, collect the ash in a container so that you can scatter it to the four winds or bury it for a banishment.

Magickal resins and their properties

Each of the resins has its own significance that can add depth and meaning to the mix. You can burn resins alone, especially copal, frankincense and myrrh for occasions when you want to have a rush of power, but often non-resins (ordinary herbs, flower petals, etc.) give the mix a softness and subtlety. At least a third of your mix should be resin, but you may choose to add more if the magickal meaning accords strongly with the overall purpose of the spell. You can also add more than one resin but do beware of overwhelming the mix.

Benzoin

Properties: Money; increasing mental powers and concentration
Uses: for the increase of prosperity, for abundance, for success in career or learning, for all examinations and tests, for speculation and good luck, for new opportunities and for unexpected help in times of need

Copal

Properties: Protection, purification, especially good for cleansing crystals
Uses: for special occasions, for spiritual purposes and for all times when you, your property or home need protection; also for overcoming bad atmospheres and quarrels and the removal of unwanted influences or addictions

Dragon's blood

Properties: Love, protection and passion, male potency
Uses: when you need the power or protection of the dragon in your incense and your life, for a sudden burst of power, for passionate and enduring love, for success materially and for overcoming seemingly impossible odds or opposition; also for reversing bad luck, especially financial

Frankincense

Properties: Courage, joy, strength and success
Uses: for travel, for expanding your horizons or for house moves; for prosperity rituals, for happiness, increased self-confidence, creative ventures, good luck, health and for leadership qualities
  Frankincense is an all-purpose resin and can be added to any mix.

Gum Arabic (acacia)

Properties: Secret love, optimism, making friends
Uses: for attracting new love, for family matters, and for love under difficulty; for good communication socially and at work; for the increase of happiness and well-being; also for keeping secrets and for finding what has been lost or taken

Myrrh

Properties: Healing, peace, protection and inner harmony
Uses: in healing incenses, for rituals for gentle love and reconciliation, for inner

peace and peace with others, for environmental concerns, mothers and children, animals, and for increased psychic powers

Myrrh is an all-purpose resin and can be added to any mix.

Pine (pinon or collophony)

Properties: Healing, fertility, purification, protection, money; returns hostility to its sender

Uses: for new beginnings and in rituals for conceiving a child; for increased inflow of money, for cleansing homes psychically and for strong defence against any hostility from troublesome neighbours or from psychic attack

Herbs to treat with caution

It is important to use the utmost caution during pregnancy. Some pregnant women avoid smudging and incense work except outdoors.

There are, in addition, medical conditions that warrant care. For example, avoid herbal inhalations if you suffer from asthma or any chest or lung problems, angelica if you have diabetes, ginger if you have high blood pressure, and rosemary if you have epilepsy or heart disease. These are just a few recommended precautions, so if you do have a medical problem, be sure to check with a doctor or pharmacist.

Avoid using incense in the presence of children or animals.

Choosing incense for ritual

In some traditions three, seven or nine different herbs and flowers make up a mix. In practice, however, you may find that you need five or six separate ingredients. You can buy mixes with names like rain mix or protection mix, but check the contents to make sure that the energies are the ones you need.

Feel free to add to a ready-prepared mix. Indeed, I believe that where possible you should add a secret ingredient to your personal mixes, especially when you are making them for a particular person or event. Be sure to note this in your Book of Shadows in case you need to make more of a particular mix at a later occasion.

This extra ingredient need not be anything exotic and could be a herb or flower that you associate with the person or occasion. Add this ingredient last, while making a special silent blessing.

To recap, the mix should be made up of:

* dried flowers and herbs, at least two of which should be fragrant, chosen and in proportions according to your magickal intention,
* a suitable resin, making up at least a third of the total mix (frankincense and myrrh are suitable for any purpose),
* a few dried nettles for protection (optional),
* your extra ingredient (optional).

Suggested incense mixes

The following are mixes Miranda and I have used. These are given without the individualised extra and if you don't want to add anything they are effective as they are. You can, of course, create your own empowerments to repeat as you mix your incense; mine are just examples. Experiment to get the proportions right for your need and for what smells right for you. Use a little of each at first and add to it, smelling the mix as you work. If there are any ingredients you don't like, leave them out or substitute one with a similar magickal meaning. There aren't any rights and wrongs; just do what feels right.

A protective incense for driving away harm

This incence can be used to dispel negativity from you and your home, workplace and belongings.

Resin: Myrrh

Herbs: Angelica, basil, juniper berries (squashed), lavender, myrrh, nettles, rosemary, sage

Empowerment: *Winds of the mountains, breeze from the sea, blow away danger; drive away harm, leave only calm*

This basic format can form the basis of incense rituals for many other purposes, using a different symbol as necessary to represent the desire. This symbol can be empowered by lighting the charged-up incense and filling the symbol with its power.

Light the charcoal just before you begin to empower and mix (about five minutes before with bought incense as this needs less empowering). You can change the chants to fit the theme of the incense and ritual.

* Light a candle if you wish or strike a singing bowl (see page 293) with its wooden or leather stick to mark the beginning of the ritual.
* If you are using incense sticks you will need to choose the three most representative of the purpose. Empower these in their container (use a holder that will contain all three).
* Empower as you mix the incense, using a chant to focus the energies and bringing the chant either to a climax of power or slowly and gently infusing the incense with quiet power according to the nature of the ritual (see page 45). In this protective mix, use the slower, quieter method.
* When the incense is ready, begin by holding your hands palms uppermost and flat with your arms extended upwards on either side of your body. Face north or in the direction of a distant place, person or anima to be protected if the focus of the spell is absent.
* Name the purpose of the ritual and, addressing a favourite archangel, god or goddess or calling upon an all-inclusive power of goodness and light, say:

  I ask _____ to bring protection from _____ (name the main danger or anxiety).

* When the charcoal is ready, add the first spoon of incense and say:

Purify.

If using incense sticks, then light the first stick.

* Carry the incense clockwise round the place or pass it nine times around pictures or the written name of the people or place to be protected. If you are seeking protection for yourself, walk nine times clockwise round the incense. Do this in silence while focusing on the purpose.
* Add to the incense, saying:

Sanctify.

and repeat the actions. If using sticks, light a second stick.

* Finally add a little more incense saying:

Bless and protect.

If using sticks, light the third one.

* Repeat the actions for the third time and end facing north, saying:

So may it be. The rite is done.

* Leave the incense to burn through and scatter the ashes either on a garden or to the winds. You can, for ongoing protection, bury the ashes beneath a gentle plant such as lavender.

A love-me-forever incense mix

Resin: Dragon's blood

Herbs: Bay leaves, ginger or cinnamon, lavender, lilac, rosemary, rose petals, sandalwood chips or sage

Empowerment: *May love find me, may love bind me, inflame and bring fidelity throughout eternity*

* Use a picture of your lover and adapt the protective ritual format and words.
* You could have two candles, one pink for you and one green for your love. Move them closer each time you top up the incense (twice as in the above ritual). Blow them out together.
* If you haven't met your love, use a symbol such as a silver or wax heart, a pink rosebud or two white ribbons tied together with three knots.
* If the symbol is small enough, you can pass it through the incense smoke nine times clockwise at each stage of the spell, three times in total (see the protective ritual above).

A money–happiness mix

My daughter Miranda's creation is this gentle incense for ensuring more money gradually flows in than goes out. It also attracts money for purposes that will spread happiness, something special like a holiday, a party, a wedding or launching a project. You can also use this for fund-raising ventures for charities.

Resin: Frankincense

Herbs: Apple blossom, basil, mimosa, mint, thyme

Empowerment: *May money flow to spread abundance and with it the joy to share good fortune*

* Make the candle green and fill a dish with gold coloured coins and small pieces of gold-coloured jewellery as the focus.

A major financial-and-fortune improvement mix

This is a more powerful and fast-acting blend, for financial crises or at times when Lady Luck seems to have run out and you are really struggling. For this reason, I have used two resins.

Resins: Frankincense and dragon's blood

Herbs: Cedar chips or saffron, cinnamon, honeysuckle, mint, orange blossom or finely chopped orange rind, rosemary

Empowerment: *Flow and grow, grow and flow that the tide may turn and luck be bountiful once more*

* Use a beeswax candle and tie any unpaid bills or demands three times with red ribbon as a focus.

A moon mix for increased psychic awareness

Miranda devised this incense for use during divination with Tarot cards, a crystal ball or any other psychic tools. It can be used monthly on the new moon (before it is visible in the sky) to enhance psychic powers and especially clairvoyance. It is also a good incense for the night of the full moon for divination on this most magickal of nights.

Resin: Copal or myrrh

Herbs: Jasmine, lemon balm, linden blossom, rose, stocks or mimosa

Empowerment: *Maiden, mother, grandmother moon, awaken my vision of the hidden mysteries*

* Use a dish of moonstones as a focus and a pure white candle; also any of your divinatory tools.
* You can circle them all with the incense or walk round the incense carrying your tools. You can keep the empowered moonstones with you in a protective circle when you next read the cards or gaze into your crystal ball.

A sun mix for success and confidence

This is good incense before interviews, for all creative ventures and when you need to shine in your career or studies.

Resin: Benzoin

Herbs: Bay, chamomile, cinnamon (one pinch only), lemongrass, pine, rosemary, sage

Empowerment: *Shine, sun, with golden radiance and lead me on the pathway to fulfilment*

* Use a natural beeswax candle and a small dish of sun crystals (amber, carnelian, clear quartz) as the focus.
* Afterwards, carry the crystals in a drawstring bag to interviews or set them round any creative project as you work on it.

A health-and-happiness mix

Use this for domestic happiness as well as for personal pleasure and happy social events. It is good for overcoming depression, debilitating conditions and low self-esteem.

Resins: Frankincense and myrrh

Herbs: Chamomile, cherry blossom or any fragrant blossom, hibiscus, lavender, lilac, rose

Empowerment: *Bring blessings into my life that I may be filled with joy and so share blessings*

* Light a beeswax candle near the centre of your home.
* Carry the incense round your home and keep small dishes of empowered incense in different rooms so you can top it up as necessary.
* Make a blessing on home and family for each spoon of incense added. You may need more than three if you have a big house and possibly a second charcoal disc ready.

A wishes-and-meditation mix

Resin: Myrrh

Herbs: Hyacinth, jasmine, lemon balm, lemon verbena, mimosa, mugwort or rose, violet leaf

Empowerment: *May I walk the pathways of mystery and remembrance of the old ways to wisdom?*

* Light a beeswax candle and circle it with your incense as in the protection ritual (see page 104), softly chanting your wishes or the psychic powers you seek to gain.

4

HERBS FOR SMUDGING

Dried herbal smoke sticks or bundles, known as smudge, are one of the most straightforward and purest sources of natural power. They can be bought or made quite easily from fresh herbs.

Smudge is essentially a wand made of herbs, and therefore, in its burning, the magickal elements of fire and air unite. As the wand burns away so its powers travel, amplified, into the cosmos. This transformative process generates power, blessings or protection according to the purpose of the ritual and the herb of which the stick is made.

Smudge sticks also serve as the tool of the east in outdoor magickal ceremonies. Smudge sticks have entered westernised magick from the Native North American tradition. However, burning herbs without the addition of resin almost certainly was common in eastern and western Europe and Scandinavia not only at seasonal festivals but on hearth fires and bonfires. We know that on New Year's Day, Scottish people closed the doors and windows of their home and burned juniper berries, presumably in bowls, to cleanse away the bad luck of the previous year.

If you feel incense is too formal for natural magick, smudging, the less ornate but equally potent sister, may suit you better for both indoor and outdoor rites.

What is smudge?

Smudge sticks are tied dried bundles of herbs that are lit at one end. The ensuing smoke is then directed towards whatever is to be empowered, cleansed or released into the cosmos. Large dried leaves can also be burned without charcoal in an abalone shell with holes in the base or in a flat clay dish.

Smudge sticks do not burn for as long as herbs on charcoal, but this can be ideal for a shorter spell. Strictly, incense contains resin and is usually burned on charcoal. In practice the overlap between incense and smudge is considerable and incense can be cast on fires and some pure smudging herbs do need charcoal to burn.

The following herbs are good for smudging, whether you buy the sticks or leaves ready prepared or make your own sticks or leaf mix. Evergreen trees and bushy herbs are popularly used; rosebuds and lavender can be added to the centre of a smudge stick, but generally smudge is not floral.

Check out the lists on page 170 for the herbs with which you need to take care during pregnancy or if you suffer from a medical condition. As with incense, avoid using smudge in the presence of children or animals.

Using smudge

* Personal spiritual cleansing and empowerment are often part of a smudging ritual. Anticlockwise spirals up and down the body with the smoking smudge stick are used to remove negativity, followed by clockwise smoke spirals to restore energy and bring power. Two people can do this, each with their own smudge stick, by standing and facing each other and moving in rhythm as though dancing. The crown is sealed with a clockwise circle and the feet likewise, followed by a final clockwise crown circle.

* Mark boundaries around your home against bad neighbours or potential intruders by creating a psychic defence wall with alternate anticlockwise and clockwise spirals of smoke. Chant as you smudge:

May goodness and those with good intent enter here and only peace remain.

* Purify a home or individual rooms of negativity, whether from a hostile visitor, quarrels or an unfriendly ghost, by using anticlockwise spirals.

* Purify and empower artefacts, such as items you have bought, been given or inherited, especially jewellery, to make it your own. Pass objects or crystals through the smoke nine times anticlockwise to purify them, followed by nine circles clockwise. The words you speak and the fragrance you use will direct the purpose and attract the appropriate energies.

* Cleanse and empower magickal tools and your indoor and outdoor altar (see page 93).

* Open the four main directions in a ritual. With practice you can make an invoking earth pentagram with the smoke from a small smudge stick (see page 92).

* Unite the six directions: east, north, south and west (the order of honouring the universe in smudge rituals), then earth (downwards) and sky (upwards).

* Use for planetary healing or peace rituals.

* Heal people, animals and places where there has been a human or naturally created disaster. Direct the smoke towards an absent person or animal, or a place or swirl it in huge spirals in all the directions. Chant the purpose continuously until you reach a powerful speed and intensity of words and movement with the smoke. Then lower your voice and smudge more slowly until you end with a gentle final thrust and a whispered:

May _____ be healed.

* Smudge round the outline of a drawn plan of your workplace, anticlockwise and then clockwise, to bring positivity to the office. (Smudging the office itself might set off smoke alarms.)

* In wish magick, use a chant to call what it is you desire while writing the wish in the air with a smudge stick. End with three deliberate spirals of smoke directed directly upwards (with hand or fan).

* Induce a state of meditation or, before divination, use a fragrance like juniper, mugwort, pine, sage, yarrow or sweetgrass (see herbal properties on the pages

following) to amplify psychic powers.

* Cleanse and heal the human aura, the rainbow-coloured energy field that extends an outstretched arm span all round us in an ellipse. Move anticlockwise to remove impurities and clear blockages in the energy flow and clockwise to fill the aura with light and energy.

* Create a sacred circle or strengthen one already made with salt and water and/or a candle flame. Casting a smoke circle around you gives protection during magickal work or divination and concentrates power.

* Use smudge in personal dedication ceremonies when you declare intentions and transform the energies around you to galvanise the transformation.

* Connect with benign guardian spirits, wise ancestors and angels.

* Smudge can act as the east/air element instead of incense in outdoor rituals and on your outdoor altar.

Herbs for smudging

In theory you can make a smudge stick by combining any tall, firm, full-leafed herbs. Some burn better than others. My list contains herbs that are traditionally made into Native North American smudge sticks and others used for both commercial and personally prepared smudge sticks. Smudge sticks are made with fresh herbs, and the whole bundle is dried together after formation.

I have also noted those herbs whose leaves, generally broad, full ones, can be effectively dried and then burned in bowls (see page 99 for how to dry individual herbs).

Accepting the broader definition of smudge as herbs that are burned without resin, I have also noted where a herb does burn better on charcoal.

Smudge herbs do tend to be single or dual herbs rather than a mix as in incense and are, on the whole, characterised less by sweetness than earthiness.

I have also given the magickal meanings of the main smudging herbs so you can choose or make the right ones for specific rituals. For more information on smudging and sample ceremonies see my *Smudging and Incense Burning Guide* (see Further reading, page 515).

If you need to use charcoal, drop just one or two drops of lavender or rose essential oil on to the hot charcoal to add fragrance before you begin to burn the herbs. This is effective, especially if you are smudging indoors.

For homemade smudge, try to choose herbs that grow in your region. Look on the Internet for dried varieties to burn in a bowl or ready-prepared less common smudge sticks. Also try to choose organically produced herbs.

Bay/laurel

Powers: Attracting health and fidelity

Drives away nightmares and bad luck. A natural health-bringer, bay heals sorrow and purifies all forms of pollution and negativity. Use therefore to heal the planet or endangered areas and species as well as for personal psychic protection and defence of home, family and pets.

In marriage or a settled relationship, bay encourages fidelity and trust.

As smudge: Found in many gardens and parks, bay comes in numerous varieties including the culinary kind. With its firm leaves, it can be used in smudge sticks. However, it does burn quite fiercely so if making your own smudge sticks, mix with slower-burning leaves like cedar or sage.

The pre-dried leaves (available in supermarkets) burn best on charcoal but if you choose large leaves and ensure they are bone dry, bay will burn in a bowl without fuel. Bay mixes well with mugwort to enhance psychic awareness.

Bergamot

Powers: Attracting money and love

Fast acting for the improvement of finances, for house moves, buying, selling and renting. As a healer, bergamot reduce fears, panic, free-floating anxieties, addictions and the hold of destructive relationships. Bergamot will also attract new love, especially after a period of being alone or after heartbreak.

As smudge: Can be made into a smudge stick; good alone with its distinctive citrus-like, fresh tang.

Cedar

Powers: Cleansing and attracting prosperity

For removing negativity from situations, homes and artefacts and therefore good for cleansing magickal tools. Burn cedar when you move to a new home to ensure you will be happy there. A bringer of abundance and financial good fortune, cedar relieves worries about debt by generating money-attracting energies.

A good herb for the home and for protecting special artefacts from theft or damage. Cedar reduces emotional and physical pain and grief and if burned regularly is said to keep away sickness from the home and family. Burn to connect with guardian spirits and angels.

As smudge: One of the herbs used in commercial sage sticks from Native North America and more recently from Australia. The cedar used in smudging is usually Western Red Cedar or California Incense Cedar. Thuja, the generic name for cedar, means sacrifice.

Cedar has a more subtle scent than sagebrush, but it is sometimes difficult to keep alight if your stick is even slightly damp. Sagebrush is much better tempered in all situations and weathers.

Most cedars are excellent as smudge sticks; also the loose tips or needles can be burned in a bowl, if dried first. By needles, I mean the long green brush of leaves and not, as I used to think, the tiny needles of the kind that are shed by Christmas trees. The wood chips may need charcoal.

Copal

Powers: Healing and positive energies

Strictly a resin and incense, copal is nevertheless also included as a smudge because it was used for thousands of years in Central and South America in smudging rituals. Copal was burned on hot coals or charcoal by ordinary people because it was naturally and easily obtainable and therefore cheap. Copal banishes all negativity, replacing it with light and loving energies. It is traditionally lit before and during healing to drive away pain and sorrow, as a mood enhancer and for making easier meditation and divination (see also page 102 for more of its magickal uses).

As smudge: Its rich aromatic fragrance is good on charcoal as pure smudge as well as mixed into incense.

Fennel

Powers: Travel and positive change

Fennel brings courage, hastens desired house moves, and brings protection to homes and to children and animals. (Do not smudge in the presence of young children or animals; rather use a picture or speak their name as a focus as you work.) Smudge over maps or pictures of desired locations to hasten travel; also round job applications to aid employment. Also good for healing and purification.

As smudge: Use firm, full, feathery stalks or mix with mugwort, rosemary or cedar leaves to make smudge sticks.

Juniper

Powers: Cleansing and new beginnings

Juniper is a wonderful space clearer, whether of negativity after a quarrel or of a critical visitor or to bless a new home. It is protective before a trip against accidents, sickness, road rage or violence (particularly valuable as journeys become more hazardous in the modern world). Smudge around luggage before a journey to prevent loss and round children's school bags as an antidote to bullying. Juniper also increases psychic awareness when used in a smudge stick.

As smudge: Make smudge sticks with juniper leaf sprigs. The greenery is sometimes substituted for cedar in smudge bundles or bowls with sagebrush and sweetgrass.

The berries are best squashed on charcoal, though I have known them to burn whole if very dry.

Lavender

Powers: Peace and reconciliation

Use lavender alone or mixed with other healing herbs to induce peace in a turbulent situation or in a home or workplace where strong personalities vie for centre stage. Lavender is personally effective for restoring trust and harmony and for increasing self-love and self-esteem after any abuse. Lavender smudge attracts loving energies and benign guardian spirits and angels. Use in any peace rituals and those to stop cruelty towards other people, animals and birds. Lavender is, in addition, used for sending wishes into the cosmos.

As smudge: Lavender is quite fine and so needs to be very bulkily packed with numerous twined stems, leaves and heads. However, it works especially well in the middle of bulkier herbs in a smudge stick. The dried flower heads can be burned separately on charcoal.

Mugwort

Powers: Psychic awareness and prophetic dreams

One of the most popular smudge materials on both side of the Atlantic, mugwort aids all kinds of psychic and spiritual work, including seeing guardian spirits and angels and inducing a meditative state. Mugwort can also bring spontaneous recall of past lives. Mugwort smudge can be used in all kinds of healing rituals, before divination and prophecy and in small quantities before bedtime to induce peaceful sleep. Use with caution as some people find it to be slightly mind-altering; avoid before driving.

As smudge: Make sure the leaves are firm for smudge sticks. It can also be burned in bowls with sagebrush.

Orris root

Powers: Psychic ability and protection

Orris root increases psychic gifts. It aids focus and concentration for intellectual as well as psychic purposes, especially when celery seeds are added.

Alone, or even more powerfully with sage or sagebrush, orris protects against physical, psychological and psychic malevolence and turns back harm upon the sender.

As smudge: From the Florentine iris, the powdered root smells like violets. Burn it finely chopped and then powdered in a bowl with celery seeds (you may need charcoal but try it without). Smudge with the leaves as the inner part of a smudge stick combined with sage or sagebrush.

Pine, fir and spruce

Powers: Purification and new beginnings

These are cleansers and purifiers of people and places and are potent for hastening a new beginning. Traditionally, Celtic midwives whirled a burning pine torch three times clockwise around a mother and infant to endow them with the protection of earth, sea and sky.

Burned before divination, pine ensures that a reading will be accurate. Pine also brings courage to continue on a difficult but necessary path or to cut your losses if you are in no-win situation. It also encourages integrity even if it means you have to stand against popular opinion.

Very protective, pine returns negativity to the sender; doubly effective for any purpose if gathered at midsummer and made into smudge sticks.

As smudge: Burn the needles in a bowl if very dry and piled thickly (see cedar, page 111). I have made successful smudge sticks from the fallen pine in the grove opposite my caravan. However, more usually, pine is combined in smudge sticks with other herbs, especially juniper as it will enhance its effects.

Pinon pine is especially resinous and needs to be burned on charcoal, though you can still make smudge sticks with the leaves (see page 103 in the incense chapter).

Rosemary

Powers: Love/passion and healing

A multi-purpose smudge that can be used for attracting love, fidelity and passion or for the revival of passion in a long-standing relationship. It is also effective for any form of healing spell, especially for absent healing (when the focus of the ritual is not present) whether of a person, an animal or a place.

Smudging with rosemary improves memory, focuses thoughts and increases energy levels. It will help to heal destructive or confrontational relationships as well as protecting against illness. It is good for mending quarrels and for purification, and also attracts abundance and fertility.

As smudge: Rosemary is often included in commercially produced smudge sticks with other herbs like sagebrush, cedar or lavender. I have also burned rosemary alone as a smudge stick, but you do need to make a thick smudge stick packed very tight to avoid it falling apart on lighting.

Rosemary, like other finer- or feathery-leafed herbs, should be made with profusely leafy sprigs with minimum twig It can also be burned dried in a bowl. The powdered dried culinary herb can be combined with the other three traditionally prophetic herbs (parsley, sage and thyme) and burned on charcoal before divination.

Sagebrush/sage

Powers: Health and wealth

An all-purpose herb that can be substituted for almost any other smudging herb, sagebrush is used in commercially prepared Native North American smudge sticks and is the kind you are most likely to buy.

Good for all transformation and empowerment rituals, sagebrush and sage itself, in all its forms, brings long life, prosperity, good health, wisdom and protection, and speeds justice towards a positive resolution. It grants wishes, improves memory, and aids success in career, examinations and tests.

Sagebrush and sage drive away negative energies, carrying them upwards on the smoke and transforming them into positive feelings and actions.

Smudging a house with sagebrush makes a lasting positive change in energy patterns and therefore affects all who live and visit there for at least a week afterwards, even if they were not present at the smudging.

Sagebrush and sage will energise where there is stagnation or exhaustion. Above all it is the herb of healing and may, when used in a smudge ritual, trigger the innate power of the body, mind and soul for regeneration.

White sagebrush is also good for cleansing and empowering the human aura and for cleansing and empowering crystals before and after use.

Sagebrush leaves and branches are traditionally wrapped around sacred objects to keep them from harmful influences and from losing power.

As smudge: California White or Desert Sage (*Salvia apiana*) and Western Grey Sage (*Artemisia tridentata*) have broad leaves and so are easy to burn loose in a bowl without charcoal. Their most usual form is as a smudge stick and you can buy very large ones for a longer festival rite. It lights easily and remains alight even in windy or damp conditions. I would recommend a sagebrush if you are new to smudging. The Desert Sage has a stronger fragrance than the Western Grey Sage.

Later in the chapter I have suggested a way of cleansing/empowering bought smudge sticks in order to imprint them with your personal energies before burning.

There are a wide variety of sagebrushes that grow in different regions of America and Canada and similar herbs are now found in the desert regions of Australia. These are all very widely obtainable as smudge sticks, and the market is growing.

You can make smudge sticks of the culinary sage if you choose the broad-leafed variety and make sure it is paper dry before lighting. However, I have heard some people complain that culinary sage does make them cough and is less successful spiritually than sagebrush. I have had no problems personally.

For a failsafe method, burn powdered dried sage (the kind you buy in jars in the supermarket) on charcoal.

Sweetgrass

Powers: Positive energies, gentleness and healing

This is my personal favourite and the gentlest of the traditional Native North American smudging herbs. Its sweetness is loved by children and is safer for them and those who may find sage overpowering.

Sweetgrass is called the hair of the earth mother, holy seneca or vanilla grass and contains very concentrated earth energies.

Good for all women's spirituality and magickal work, sweetgrass is also a gentle purifier of grief, sorrow and abuse for men and women. Sweetgrass brings healing, reconciliation and hope in difficult times; it is a giver of abundance of good things, not just money, and the promise of better luck.

Ask for whatever it is you need, while smudging first over your head, then your heart, followed by your navel and finally the womb or genital area. This is especially potent if you can sit outdoors in sunshine, being careful not to allow sparks to fall on dry grass.

You can also ask for beauty and blessings to enter your life if you sit with your dish of smoking sweetgrass by candle- or moonlight. You can visualise the smoke being transformed into silver light and inhale this very gently through your nose, exhaling darkness through your mouth equally slowly and gently.

Sweetgrass is also protective, and unburned sweetgrass braids or bundles can be hung over doorways and entrances. Unburned sweetgrass can also be wrapped around special objects when they are not in use.

Some practitioners find that grey sage serves similar functions.

As smudge: Sweetgrass is frequently braided in the fields as it is picked.

Light one end of your sweetgrass braid and gently waft it by holding the other end part-way down. Alternatively, place the braid in a flat heatproof dish. It may look as if it is not alight, because it smoulders very slowly.

Unpick a braid or buy the loose strands and burn this in a bowl for more smoke. Make sure you keep sweetgrass in dry conditions as it can be difficult to keep alight.

Tansy (also called wormwort)

Powers: Health and protection

A bringer of fertility, tansy promises health and long life to those living in homes where it is smudged. Another valuable property is its ability to lower one's psychic profile before times of danger or potential confrontation. Smudge it round a representative map of a workplace at times of uncertainty, conflict, takeovers or potential redundancy. Waft the smoke round yourself, your mobile phone and your luggage before travelling to deter muggings or personal attack. A good smudge around the boundaries of a home deters burglars and vandals.

As smudge: This feathery herb can be used to make smudge sticks if the leaves and stems are thick and are tightly bound or included with other firmer smudge materials.

Thyme

Powers: Good luck and health

Thyme has numerous powers and is one of the strongest transmitters of positive earth power. It brings health, healing and prophetic dreams, overcomes misfortune, restores good luck and improves career opportunities by raising your personal profile. It increases psychic powers, improves memory and is good for courage, passing tests and examinations, and encourages long-term prosperity. Thyme drives away fear and danger and is good for cleansing a room after psychic work.

As smudge: Use firm, larger leaves rather than one of the very fine thymes. There are numerous varieties so look for a broad-leafed kind with a fragrance that appeals. You can also burn very dry, large-leafed thyme in a bowl without charcoal. I once bought some from the cooking section of a French supermarket, and it burned for ages.

Yarrow

Powers: Fidelity and psychic awareness

The herb of marriage and committed love, yarrow can be burned at a handfasting or a renewal of vows; to encourage fidelity in a relationship if this is an issue or if one partner is becoming less than attentive.

Burn yarrow also during divination, meditation or while working with past lives or clairvoyance to enhance psychic awareness and melt the barriers between the dimensions.

As smudge: Make smudge sticks from firm yarrow sprigs or combine it with other herbs (it is good as an outer leaf). Alternatively, burn it in a bowl.

Yerba santa

Powers: Increasing beauty in self and in the environment

Burn yerba santa to enhance the aura of radiance around yourself. Environmentally, it is an ecological healer and can be used to smudge round pictures of natural or human disasters such as oil slicks, war zones, tidal waves and earthquakes; also smudge pictures of endangered species. Yerba santa will protect boundaries of homes and draw those who live within into closer harmony. Combined with rosemary or lavender, yerba santa encourages glimpses of the ancestors, with ancient wisdom and the rhythms of the moon and seasons.

As smudge: Burn separately as a smudge stick or add to sage or rosemary smudge sticks. The latter will attract love. Burn it also in a bowl, with charcoal if you add rosemary or lavender (another love enhancer).

Making a smudge stick

With a little practice, making a smudge stick is remarkably easy, though you may prefer to buy them ready made. The secret is to pack and entwine your herbs really tightly so that they will not fall apart when you light them. There are many different methods and the following is just a series of tips I have found useful.

- You can use sprigs of fresh herbs from your garden or garden centre for taller smudge sticks or use packs from a supermarket (either ready cut or still growing in a pot) for smaller smudge sticks.
- Before making your bundle of herbs, test the twine you intend to use by burning a little in your flat dish. Does it flare up or smell foul? Try cotton without any synthetic additions, as synthetic fibres will break. Experiment with undyed natural twines or those where vegetable colouring has been used; you will find one that works well for you. Horsetail is the best, but is not easy to obtain.
- Use thick sprigs (about seven or eight in total) of the fresh herbs with plenty of greenery no more than 30 cm/12 in long. The ideal length for your finished smudge stick is 17–23 cm/7–9 in, so use the longer herbs in order that you can trim the bottoms and tops off to give a smooth finish.
- Use a very sturdy herb to act as anchor at the centre of the smudge stick. Some people use a dry stick as a base around which to twine the stems to give the bundle substance. Taper the stick at one end so that the woody part you hold is slightly narrower. Broader smudge sticks tend to work better than narrow ones.
- Lay the herbs flat on a surface on smooth fabric, leather or newspaper. First wrap the thread around the bottom of the herb wand four or five times.
- Then, with the separate ends either side of the herbs, begin to criss-cross from the bottom at about 2.5 cm/1 in intervals. Leave the top third to a quarter unbound. You can if you wish knot every other cross. Tie very tightly, pressing and weaving the herbs together as you work.
- Turn the stick over and, from the top, repeat crossing or knotting again at about 1 cm/0.5 in intervals so the whole stick is now tied at 1-cm/0.5-in intervals.
- When you get back to the bottom, make two or three wraps, tie the ends together and cut off the excess.
- Trim the bottom of the bunch below the tie.
- You may also trim any straggly herbs and trim the top.
- Trim the bottom or top off after binding.

An alternative method

* For this you will need much taller herbs, about three times the length of the finished smudge stick you want to make. You will also need fewer herbs since you are folding them over to three times the original thickness. You will need very pliant herbs that will not snap. Aim for a 17–20-cm/6–7-in finished smudge stick.
* Again work on a flat surface. You will need a large piece of newspaper, fabric or soft leather for this method. Hold the herbs tightly together and turn the top third of the herbs over the middle third, so the herbs are now double over the top part of the stick. Do this carefully so they don't break. Secure with twine and a firm knot.
* Now bend the bottom third up so the stick is three times its original thickness, and tie again with a knot to include all three levels. The stick should now be a third of the original height, but very chubby like a cigar.
* With slightly smaller herbs you can bend the herbs just once.
* Before binding the stick, roll the newspaper, fabric or soft leather round it at an angle as tightly as possible. Tie the paper very securely and leave for about 8 hours, with the top and bottom of the newspaper just open to let in air.
* Now unbind the newspaper and tie the compressed herbs tightly with twine. Starting from the stem end, bind them in a criss-cross pattern as before, tying them again very tightly about every 1 cm/0.5 in along. Leave the herbs to dry for two or three weeks.

Drying the smudge stick

* Hang your smudge bundles upside down using a knot in the twine so that the air can circulate. Ensure the area you keep them is warm and not damp, and not exposed to direct sunlight.
* Leave the smudge sticks to dry for about two weeks. They are ready when they are dry but not completely moisture-free. Watch out for mould.

Equipment you will need for smudging
A smudging fan

The purpose of a fan is to spread and direct the smoke from a smudge stick or bowl of herbs around the person, object or place to be cleansed. If you prefer, you can use your hand or a leaf brush made, for example, of pine needles. Use your hand only if you are writing in smoke with your stick.

Feathers and wing fans are traditional and are believed to assist in cleansing the human aura or psychic energy field as well as adding the qualities of the particular bird to the magick.

You can buy feather fans or use a single large feather you have bought or found.

Bowls

For burning pre-dried herbs without charcoal you need a heatproof dish as the heat is very fierce. It should be flat enough to allow the air to circulate. You can put a layer of sand or dry soil in the bottom as insulation. In the Native North American

Indian tradition an abalone shell is used. This has natural perforations to let out the heat and ensure that the air is distributed evenly all round to give a regular streams of smoke. Shells are symbolic of the mother goddess.

My own favourite smudging bowl is ceramic, broad and quite flat with a shallow rim and wide lip that remains cool even when herbs are heated and broad feet so that it can be placed on a table or on the floor without the risk of scorching. You could make your own bowl, thus endowing it with your personal energies.

My bowl has raised spirals inside, a symbol that from Palaeolithic times and in all cultures has represented the earth mother.

You also need a deep bowl for sand or earth in which you can extinguish smudge sticks when you want to end a ritual and they have not gone out naturally. You can also catch the ash or any sparks from your smudge stick in the bowl. Some people extinguish a smudge stick by tapping it on the edge of the bowl. Water is not used, except in an emergency.

Lighting smudge

* Use long matches or a candle but do not get wax on the smudge.
* Light the tip of the smudge.
* Let the flame die down and then blow the stick until the end glows red and smoke begins to curl upwards. Take time to get it really smoking well, especially outdoors on damp days.
* If you are using candles at the quarters of a circle in ritual, you can briefly hold the smudge into each flame in turn as you address the quarters.
* Keep a fire source like a candle in a safe holder near where you are smudging. If the stick goes out, you can relight it at any time during the ritual, adding a blessing at the same time.

Charging a smudge stick or herbs

Whether you make your own smudge stick, use a prepared one or are planning to burn herbs in a bowl, you can endow them with power.

If you are using a smudge stick, hold it between your hands. If you are using a bowl, place your herbs in the bowl and hold this during the ritual.

In this ritual, we will use the six directions recognised by the Native North Americans: the four main compass points, then downwards and finally upwards. Begin in the east, important to Native North Americans as the direction of dawn. Indeed a number of western practitioners start traditional magickal rituals by facing the east and opening the watchtowers here. I start with the north for security (see page 31). If indoors, ventilate the room well.

* Stand so that there is space round you.
* Light a circle of red or natural beeswax candles in deep holders, one at each main direction and one in the centre to ignite the smudge. If this is part of a ritual outdoors, you can visualise a ring of fire and omit the candles except for the one used to light the smudge. If you do light directional candles, light the central candle and then the candle of the east, south and so on. During the ritual you can move and stand by each, facing outwards in the appropriate direction of you wish.

* Light the smudge from the central candle. Standing in the centre of your fire wheel, face first the east, the direction of dawn and spring. Raise your stick or bowl and say:

> *I greet the freshness of dawn and brightness of the new morning. Fill, I ask,*
> *these my sacred herbs with new life and swiftness of purpose.*

* Turn next to the south, direction of noon and summer. Lift your smudge stick or bowl upwards and say:

> *I greet the brilliance of noon and its radiant fire. Fill, I ask, these my sacred herbs*
> *with inspiration, integrity and courage.*

* Face the west, direction of dusk and autumn and once more raise your smudge tools, saying:

> *I greet the deepening skies and the first star of evening.*
> *Fill, I ask, these my sacred herbs with love and healing.*

* Face the north, direction of midnight and winter. Lift your stick or bowl, saying:

> *I welcome the darkness and the time of quiet repose. Fill these sacred herbs with acceptance of what*
> *cannot be changed and with the wisdom of the ancestors.*

* Standing still in the centre of your actual or visualised fire circle, next to the central candle, lower the smudge towards the earth and say:

> *Kind mother earth, bless your own sacred herbs and absorb all that is not worthy of*
> *beauty in this wand of herbs and in my intentions.*

* Finally, lift your stick or bowl high in the air, saying:

> *Father sky, bless these sacred herbs that my wishes and prayers may rise and*
> *be transformed into whatever is right and of worth.*

* Some practitioners end with mother earth, or you can vary it according to the nature of the ritual.
* As well as charging your herbs with power, you can create a complete ritual by facing and invoking the six directions with your smudge and then smudging yourself (see page 109) as a means of empowerment or protection. Alternatively, you can empower a symbol by carrying it to each of the four directions in turn and smudging it while declaring the purpose of the ritual.
* You can end by lowering it to the earth and smudging it there, and finally raising it upwards and releasing the energies in the smudge skywards.

A smudge ritual to send blessings to the earth or a particular cause – and to yourself

In magick the good wishes and blessings you send out will return to you threefold in ways that you most need in your life (see page 20).

The following ritual is an extension of the empowerment smudge ritual above and can be combined to empower your commercially obtained or homemade smudge stick or herbs at the same time.

* Having empowered the smudge stick or herbs with the six directions, face east or if you have lit directional candles return to the east, facing outwards. Make three clockwise circles of smoke, saying:

Bring change.

* Name an ecological change that is needed and also an area of your life where you seek change.
* Next, in the south or facing south, make three more clockwise smoke circles and say:

Bring power.

* Name an ecological problem where power (whether governmental or that of pressure groups) is needed to solve an injustice or corruption. Name also an area of your life where you need power either to fulfil a dream or to right an injustice.
* Next, facing west or in the west, make three clockwise circles of smoke and say:

Heal.

* Name a species, place or disaster that needs healing and also an area that needs healing in your own life.
* Finally face or go to the north and, making three clockwise smoke circles, say:

Protect.

* Name where protection is most needed both ecologically and in your life.
* Return or remain in the centre and, pointing downwards, make three anticlockwise circles of smoke, saying:

Take away.

* Name a hazard, pollution, corruption or disease that should be removed from the face of the earth and also something or someone you would like to leave behind.
* Finally spiral your smoke circles upwards in a straight line and say:

Send.

* Ask for a blessing on the earth and on yourself.
* Say:

I give thanks to the guardian spirits, the earth mother and sky father.

* The ritual is now ended. Blow out any candles in reverse order of lighting. Leave the smudge in a deep container in the centre of the actual or visualised circle until it is burned through.
* Spend time in contemplation, gardening or writing in your Book of Shadows.
* Finally, bury any remaining herbs and those that have been burned or dispose of them in an environmentally friendly way.

5

MAGICKAL WATERS

I have already mentioned making sacred water by adding sea salt to water. There is, however, a more formal method of making sacred water that you can use for special rituals and when you need stronger sacred water for protection against unfriendly ghosts at home or against psychic attack. There are also a number of other forms of magickal water that can be substituted for traditional sacred waters in healing and magick. They can be used in everyday life to bring calm or confidence, according to the properties with which they are imbued. For water can be filled with many natural powers: crystalline, sun, moon, rain, melted snow and the power of the storm and winds.

What about water?

I was teaching a workshop in Scotland recently and describing how it was a good idea after healing to cleanse a crystal pendulum under running water. Certain crystals and gems like pearl or opal should not be washed, but one person at the workshop said that she had been told it was not safe to use tap water for this purpose because it was filled with chemicals.

Pollution and additives are problems facing all modern witches and healers, but we cannot exclude the vital fourth element of water, nor can we always use bottled or filtered water. Of course, in earlier times when magickal rules were set down, drinking water from wells was not always pure and still is not in many parts of the world. This was perhaps one reason why salt was added to ceremonial water.

Rainwater collected before it touches the ground, in water tubs or in bowls on a low roof or outdoor table, is also a traditional source of magick water, though with the increase in acid rain again there is need for caution.

It is vital that we do campaign for safe water, but I think we can still use tap water for cleansing purposes in magick, for making magickal waters in larger quantities and for washing away symbolic sadness or what is redundant in our lives.

For drinking-in spells or anointing, you may decide to stick to filtered or bottled water. A number of bottled waters on the market do come from healing springs but occasionally controversy will break out over one of these.

To cleanse water spiritually, pass a pendulum over it anticlockwise and then clockwise to remove impurities. Alternatively, add a few drops of true sacred water from wells such as the Chalice Well in Glastonbury to the water you use in spells. You can add a pinch of sea salt to a glass of water prior to plunging your pendulum or crystals into it for cleansing (see also Flowing and still water magick, pages 343–54).

Ultimately, if you use water from as pure a source as possible (and many of us do have safe tap water) to make magickal waters then we shouldn't become over-concerned and let anxiety spoil our spells.

I have listed under each different kind of water the magickal and healing purposes for which it can be used.

Using sacred water

* As the water element in a ritual.
* To create a circle of water droplets around a circle that has been psychically drawn with a wand.
* For purifying rooms and homes where there is a bad atmosphere, blocked subterranean earth energies (see page 492) or paranormal activity that is disturbing.
* For anointing the chakras or bodily energy centres or in a ritual or for psychic protection. Oil is also used as a form of chakra protection (see page 274).
* Sprinkle over your hairline and round your head if someone negative or psychically draining has been troubling you.
* To cleanse and empower magickal tools or personal artefacts by sprinkling a few drops over them and asking for the blessing of the god or goddess, archangel or your favourite deities.
* For marking a protective line in a binding spell, for example across a threshold, over which harmful influences or intruders cannot cross.
* Add a pinch of pepper as well as salt to warm water for a powerful floor wash if you are experiencing a run of bad luck, spiralling debt or are afraid in the house at night.
* In a ritual for empowering a symbol with one or two of the elemental powers: earth (salt) and water. The others are air (incense) and fire (the candle flame).

Making sacred water

You can begin more formal spells by first empowering the water with this ritual – after casting the initial circle with your wand.

* On your outdoor altar (or indoors if the weather is really bad) set two bowls side by side in the centre of the altar: one of sea salt on the left (or if you prefer in the north); one half-filled with the water to the right (or in the west).
* You can use still mineral water or filtered water or be really traditional and use a bowl of rainwater. Don't use rainwater if you will be drinking it or adding it to your bath.
* Only use a small amount of salt in the bowl (a few pinches).
* Set your pentacle in the north of the altar, a candle in the south and incense or a small smudge stick in the east.
* Finally put your wand in the south for fire (or east for air if you follow that tradition).
* Light the incense and the candle in the south (you won't need altar candles unless you are carrying out a full ritual).
* Place the bowl of salt on top of the pentacle and put the tip of the wand, held in your power hand, so it just touches the salt. Say:

Bless this salt, mother, father of all, that it may be purified and used only for pure intent.

* Return the bowl of salt to its place.
* Next take the bowl of water and place that on top of the pentacle.
* Touch the surface of the water with the tip of your wand if you have a crystal tip or if not hold the wand 0.5 cm/^{1}/$_4$ in above the surface of the water and picture light rays entering the water. Say:

Bless this water, father, mother of all, that it may likewise be purified and used only for pure intent.

* Put the wand back in the south (or east).
* Taking the bowl of salt in your power hand, tip the contents into the bowl of water that is still on the pentacle.
* Put the empty bowl back in the north and, taking the bowl of salt water in your power hand, swirl it round three times clockwise and say:

By earth (one swirl), by sea (second swirl) and sky (third swirl) be blessed and so bring blessings.

* Set it back on the pentacle and pass the incense three times round it, moving clockwise, repeating the chant.
* Finally, pass the candle round it, saying:

By fire be filled with power, by sun and moon and stars and so give power and healing to wherever it is most needed.

* The water is now ready for use.
* You can make some magickal salt water specifically to bottle for purification of the home, etc. and keep it for about two weeks in a cool place.
* Tip away any that is unused once its purpose is complete (such as cleansing the home). Either tip it into the earth or into flowing water (even under a tap). Remember that salt water is bad for grass and growing plants.

Sun water

One way of imbibing the healing and energising powers of the sun is by making sun water. This can be stored in yellow, gold-coloured or clear glass bottles in a fridge or cool place.

Using sun water

* Add a few drops to your bath in the morning to energise you and fill you with optimism for the day.
* Drink the water. A few drops can be added to sparkling mineral water, orange juice or to water with which you make hot or cold drinks. This will fill you or family members with confidence and help you to express yourself clearly and with authority. It also helps if you are feeling spaced out or alternatively enervated and unable to relax.

- Splash a little in the centre of your hairline (for your crown chakra or psychic energy centre that opens you to cosmic influences), the centre of your brow (your third eye or psychic energy centre), on your Adam's apple to energise the throat chakra (that enables you to speak clearly and wisely and often to say the things deep in your heart that you might not otherwise find the words to express). Finally, anoint the inside of each wrist to activate your heart chakra and love for your family, friends and all humanity. These four higher energy centres enable you to connect earthly goals and achievements with your higher spiritual potential. For more information about chakras see my *Chakra Power* (see Further reading, page 514).
- Use sun water for the water element in rituals for success, travel, courage, health, new beginnings, confidence and prosperity.
- Use sun water sprinkled over plants that are wilting to revive them.
- Put some in animal or bird drinking bowls if a creature is exhausted, very old or sick and to keep your outdoor birds well, especially during the breeding season.
- If you know a person well and they are present, you can open the bottle in sunlight and anoint their brow with a few drops. You can create your own healing words, based on love and caring.
- For healing, if the person or animal is absent, pour the water into a small glass bowl. Look on to its surface and visualise the face of the person, the animal or indeed a threatened place. Picture the water changing and them restored to vibrance. Whisper:

May _____ be healed and restored. Blessings be.

- You can send the rest of the bottle of sun water to the sick person, with a small citrine as a gift, saying that it comes with your love, and explaining how and why you made the sun water.
- Rub some on your brow or that of a person with a headache and picture a golden light spreading through the head and then downwards through the whole body. This should make the energy field round the body shine.
- Use in a doorstep wash to attract good luck, health and money to your home.
- Make a circle of sun water droplets round a picture of anyone who is exhausted or a place where nature has been destroyed. Light a beeswax candle to shine on it (without shedding wax on the image) or leave it in bright sunlight.
- If the damaged place is local or you can visit it, sprinkle the water on the ground or in a polluted water source.
- Sprinkle nine drops of sun water on a charm or talisman to empower it while reciting the purpose of the charm nine times.
- Use sun water to empower magickal tools or crystals.
- Pour sun water to which you have added one or two drops of a orange essential oil into a plant spray. Use this to spray the water round any dark gloomy rooms to lift the atmosphere, at work before an important meeting and round your desk at work so that only those coming with praise or positivity will approach (see page 272 for more on aroma oils).

Making sun water

Sun water is at its most potent when made on the morning of the longest day, the summer solstice, around 21 June (21 December in the southern hemisphere), and during a partial solar eclipse or — if you are lucky enough to have one in your region — a total eclipse of the sun. However, you can also make sun water on any day when the sun is shining or the light is clear. You can put a fine mesh on top to stop any particles or insects falling in.

* Outdoors, half-fill with still mineral water (or tap water) a brass or gold-coloured bowl or one made of clear crystal (the kind used as old-fashioned fruit bowls). Surround the bowl with freshly picked sunshine-yellow flowers or a circle of small citrine, carnelian or clear quartz crystals, especially if it is winter.
* Before beginning, stir the water three times clockwise with a clear crystal pendulum or pointed clear quartz crystal and ask that the sun fills the water with power and healing. Name any special purpose for which you are making the water.
* Leave the water from dawn until noon or when the sun is directly overhead in your time zone, in a place that catches the morning sunlight. You can put the bowl out overnight if you do not wish to get up early. In winter, when dawn is later and solar energies are weaker, allow eight hours from first light or as much daylight as there is. In climates where there is not much light, leave for two days.
* When this time is up and ideally when the sun is shining on the water, stir the water again three times clockwise with your clear crystal pendulum or pointed quartz crystal and ask that the sun water brings power and healing.
* Again, name the focus and the purpose of the water, if there is one.
* Using a clear glass jug and a filter, bottle the water in small clear, yellow or gold-coloured glass bottles with stoppers or screw-top lids. Antique and craft fairs are a good source of these. Alternatively, save clear glass medicine bottles that have been well washed out.
* Sun water will keep its power for about four weeks in a fridge or a cool place.

Moon water

Moon water can be made during a full moon ceremony or by leaving the water out on the night of the full moon. Gentler than sun water, moon water is both magickal and healing and can be used in any spell as the moon is the natural friend of the witch.

Using moon water

* In any magickal ritual for the water element, especially those concerned with love, fertility and the increase of psychic powers, or for healing chronic conditions and reducing pain.
* Increase prophetic powers during divination by sprinkling moon water around the table where you are working and your Tarot pack. This also gives you protection while you work.
* Add to a bath to attract love or a particular lover.
* Drink a few drops daily for a month starting on the morning after the full moon to bring yourself in touch with your own bodily rhythms and cycle of energy ebbs and flows (suitable for men and women).
* Use in drinks to soften angry words, slow hyperactivity and to make gatherings peaceful and harmonious.
* Use in a soothing hot drink at night to relieve insomnia.
* Moving in a moonwise (anticlockwise) direction, sprinkle the water round the bed of a child or adult who suffers bad dreams, asking the moon mother for quiet sleep.
* To heal women and children who are present, anoint the psychic third eye in the centre of the brow with the water and rub the water in moonwise (anticlockwise), saying:

Dear grandmother moon, take away pain/relieve (name the problem). Restore with tomorrow's moonrise energy/health/happiness once more.

For absent healing, make a small wax figure and anoint with moon water on the head, the brow and both arms, left then right, asking for the healing that is required and stating the time scale.

* Empower protective amulets on the night after the full moon by sprinkling a moonstone, selenite/satin spar, jade, amethyst or rose quartz nine times with moon water and stating the protection needed and for whom the amulet is being made. The same can be done with jewellery.
* Give moon water to plants that that are neglected or abused (for example, being used as an ash tray in the reception area of an office). I use moon water on garden-centre reject plants that I buy because I am sorry for them, including the last wilted Christmas tree at a DIY store that four years later is now green.
* Add moon water to the drinking water of pregnant animals and birds or those who have been abused.

Using moon water to assist fertility

* Assist innate fertility in a woman who wishes to conceive a child by helping her to get in tune with her natural cycles. Moon water helps the body to become more receptive in cases where anxiety is blocking or making a physical problem worse (suitable even for IVF or artificial insemination).
* The woman should make or buy a tiny cradle and make a small wax or modelling-clay doll or buy a small fabric one. Sprinkle the doll and the cradle with three

drops of moon water each every evening before bed, saying:

Maiden, mother, wise woman moon, bring me a child if it is right to be.

(See page 422 for an explanation of the three moon goddesses who represent the three phases of the moon.)

* On the night of the next full moon sprinkle nine drops of water around the marital bed, repeating the words:

Maiden, mother, wise woman moon, bring me a child if it is right to be.

* Set the doll's cradle by the bed. Make love, even if it is not the correct time according to the ovulation chart (unless this is medically inadvisable). Repeat monthly.

Making moon water

Moon water is at its most potent when made on the night of the full moon or during a partial or total lunar eclipse. You can also make it in the two or three days before the full moon if the skies are clear and the moon is shining brightly.

* On the night of the full moon (it rises around sunset) set a silver-coloured or clear crystal bowl outdoors where the moonlight can shine on it.
* Half-fill it with still mineral water, if possible from a sacred source, and, if you have any, add a few drops of water from a holy well. You can substitute bubbling tap water.
* Surround the bowl with pure white flowers or blossoms or small moonstones.
* If you have a small silver bell, ring it three times, saying for each ring:

First the maiden, now the mother, then the wise grandmother.

* Alternatively, raise your arms on either side of your head, your hands facing upwards flat with palm uppermost and repeat the same words three times.
* Stir the water nine times moonwise (anticlockwise) with a silver-coloured paper knife (silver being the colour and metal of the moon) or an amethyst crystal point. Ask the moon mother to bless the water and those who use it.
* If you are not carrying out a moon ceremony, leave the bowl in position, covered with fine mesh, overnight.
* Ring the bell three more times before leaving and say:

Blessings be.

* If you don't have a bell, kneel and put your hand round the bowl, saying:

Blessings be.

* Using a glass jug and filter, pour the water, if possible, into small blue, silver or frosted glass bottles that you can seal and keep in your fridge or a cool place until

the next full moon night. If you use a plain bottle, label it so you don't mistake it for another kind of magickal water.

* Any water left at the end of the moon period should be poured into the ground before moonrise on the next full moon night.

Storm and wind water

The weather in its wilder forms provides a great deal of spontaneous power that can be absorbed by water and therefore stored for when you need a sudden burst of energy or determination.

Using storm and wind water

* Drink this water when you need courage or are proposing a major change in your life.
* Pour storm and wind water into your bath for defining your own identity and to resist bullying or abuse in any form.
* Use this water as the water element in positive spells to bind or banish if the opposition is very strong or ruthless.
* Add a few drops to a protective charm bottle that you bury or hide outside your home to guard against burglars, vandals and damage to your property by storm or wind.
* Use as a doorstep wash if you live in a dangerous area.
* Scatter over boundary plants to give added protection to your home and land and to help them hold firm in bad weather.
* Splash the water on the inside of your ankles or the soles of your feet (access points for your root or base chakra, the seat of your physical energy and survival instincts). This will give you instant power, stamina and determination.
* Sprinkle round a timid child or adolescent's school bag to give them courage when starting a new school or if they are being teased or bullied.
* Pour into a washing machine to give protection to an adult whose clothes you are washing if they are about to enter a risky or potentially frightening situation and you cannot be with them. This is particularly good for protecting wayward or impulsive teenagers.
* Sprinkle the water as droplets in a clockwise direction round a picture of a land where people are living under a cruel or very oppressive regime to give those persecuted the strength to come through the situation.
* Sprinkle clockwise round symbols, images or photographs of animals or birds that are poached or hunted almost to extinction to galvanise their instinctive awareness to evade capture.

Making storm and wind water

* You will need a large wide-necked glass jar with a lid (cookware jars are ideal) so that the jar will not become overfilled if it rains.
* In advance dig a hole in the earth deep enough to hold the jar securely or find a sheltered corner outdoors where it will not blow over.
* Half-fill with water and when a storm or high winds begin, swirl the sealed jar three times clockwise, followed by three times anticlockwise, saying six times:

Fierce the winds blow, wild the storm rages, within keep vigil, to guard and defend.

* When the storm or high winds die down, hold the jar and reverse the order of shaking, but recite the same words.
* Use a filter to bottle the water in dark-coloured bottles. The water will last about a week in a cool place. Any left over should be cast to the winds with thanks, saying:

Return to your element.

Rainwater

In spite of the problems with acid rain especially in some areas, rainwater is still important in magick and for planetary healing rituals.

Using rainwater

* Use rainwater as the water element in outdoor rituals where the water will not be drunk.
* Use in rituals to bring rain after a period of drought (or to drought-affected lands). Scatter rainwater drops over a bowl of dry soil or sand or outdoors on any patch of dry earth. As you do so, name where the rain is needed and invoke the angels of rain by chanting their names continuously nine times:

Mathariel, Ridya, Zalbesael; Mathariel, Ridya, Zalbesael.

* Conversely, to relieve flooding, reverse the order of the names in the chant, reciting the angel names as you dig a hole and pour the water into it, covering up the hole with earth.
* For banishing magick, stand in the pouring rain and tip a bottle of your water into the falling rain, saying:

Return to your own and wash away (name the sorrow/illness/destructive person or addiction) that I may henceforward be free. It is gone. It is done, to trouble me no more.

Using rainwater for reconciliation

* In rituals of reconciliation, tip a bottle of your rainwater off a bridge into flowing water from upstream so it flows under the bridge. As you do so, say:

Water under the bridge, time to let go of what cannot be resolved or undone.

* When you have emptied the bottle, speak words of reconciliation in your mind or aloud, picturing the person from whom you are estranged in the hope of mending the quarrel.
* Afterwards, make an actual, non-confrontational gesture of peace.
* Then if the quarrel or estrangement cannot be mended, repeat the ritual twice more.

- If there is still no positive reaction, you have done your best. You can let the bitterness or regrets flow away on a final fourth ritual and be free. This is also a good ritual if the dilemma concerns a lover who may or may not return.

Using rainwater to attract increase into your life

- Plant a basil, thyme or sage seedling or small plant. Place in turn a copper-/bronze-, silver- and gold-coloured coin at the roots.
- For the bronze/copper-coloured coin (copper is the metal of Venus), drop rainwater on it as it lies in the ground, name an area where you need increased love or, if alone, call love, and say:

May love grow in my life.

- For the silver coin (metal of the moon), drop rainwater on it in the soil, name an area of your life where you need fertility or a creative solution, and say:

May fertility grow in my life.

- Finally plant the gold coin (for the sun) and drop rainwater on it in the ground, name an area of your life where you need one of these blessings to grow, and say:

May prosperity/abundance/success grow in my life.

- Cover the coins and roots with soil and tip the rest of the water round the basil, thyme or sage plant, saying:

May good things grow as the gentle rain falls and nourishes my life and my endeavours.
Blessings be.

- You can plant the herb in a pot indoors or use another herb of increase (see pages 176–83) if you prefer.

Making rainwater

This is the easiest of waters to make since all you need do is collect it, either in a rain butt or a bowl on a low roof or outdoor table.

You can leave it in the container until you need it and fill small bottles with it for the rituals listed above or any others when you want energy to flow into or out of your life.

Snow water

Snow water is obviously seasonal, though in parts of northern and eastern Europe, the Baltic and parts of Scandinavia there may be several months of snow each year. If you live in a country where there is no snow, you can allow the snowy kind of ice from round your freezer shelves to melt naturally or use ice cubes.

But if there is even a day of snow, then drop everything and gather your bowl of snow as this is perhaps the most magickal water of all. Because snow water was once solid (an earth element) you have the power of earth and water combined. If the snow is then gently melted over heat, fire and air (steam) are also added, thus synthesising all four elements.

Using snow water

* For any urgent need, heat a bowl of snow in an old saucepan over a gas burner (outdoors, if possible) and stir it with a wooden spoon as the steam begins to rise. Chant continuously and steadily as you stir until the water is almost boiled away, saying:

  Earth, air, water, fire, bring the love/health/job/success/prosperity I desire.

* When only a little water is left, carry it while it is still hot and tip it back in the place where you took the snow, saying:

  Return your own. Bring (name/wish) to me within (state the time frame).

* You can use the same method by writing in snow the name of a person you wish to be reconciled with or wish to forget. Pour warmed snow water over the name, either calling the person to you if it is right to be or banishing them in peace from your thoughts and life.

* If you use ice water in non-snowy conditions, you can perform the last two rituals by writing your need or the wish in chalk on a board or on a paved area and then pouring the water on top of it.

* Make a tiny snowman or draw one in soft snowy ice from the freezer to represent a fear you have or someone who is bullying you or holding you against your will by emotional blackmail. Stand the snow figure in a deep bowl in a warm place and let it melt naturally. When it has melted, pour the water away down a flowing water source (a drain will do), saying:

So dissolves my fear and your power over me. Flow in peace and be transformed into gentleness.

* Tread in newly fallen snow, scoop up your footprints and place the snow they imprinted in a bowl to melt naturally. When the snow is melted, water a plant of love such as a rosebush or lavender with it. As the plant grows, so will love or new love will come to you. You can also use a lover's footprints in snow, melted, to speed up passion and commitment.

Using snow water to melt coldness and increase commitment

* In love magick, snow water can be used to melt coldness or indifference and to increase commitment or fidelity in a relationship.
* Allow the snow to melt naturally. While it is still pure snow, turn the bowl slowly anticlockwise using both hands, saying six times (the number of Venus and love):

(Name), soften your heart as this snow likewise softens, and look to me with affection/kindliness/love/fidelity.

* Repeat the movement when the snow is half-melted but this time say:

(Name), warm your heart to me as this snow likewise warms and look to me with affection/kindliness/love/fidelity.

* When the snow is melted, turn the bowl clockwise and say six times:

(Name), the coldness in your heart is melted as this snow likewise has melted. Come now to me with affection/kindliness/love/fidelity. So shall it be.

Making snow water

Whether you use actual snow or ice from a freezer, you will need a metal bowl (stainless steel is ideal) if you are going to allow the snow to melt naturally. Use it immediately as ice water rapidly loses its power.

Any old saucepan will do for heating snow and you should tip out the water as fast as possible after melting.

Crystalline waters

Waters in which crystals have been soaked are one of the oldest and most potent forms of magickal water, both in ritual and in personal empowerment, protection and healing. The Celts used to boil nine small clear quartz crystals in water and drink the cooled water over nine days to infuse themselves with health.

Using crystalline waters

You can mix more than one kind of crystalline water to combine different strengths, either by adding two different crystals to the water or by pouring two or even more waters together after they have been made.

* For any rituals or personal empowerment/healing where you would use a magickal water. Crystalline waters add the particular qualities of the crystals with which they are made (see pages 385–98 for a list of magickal and healing meanings).
* In magick spells as the water element to strengthen the focus of the ritual, for example, tiger's eye or lapis lazuli water in a prosperity ritual and jade or green aventurine water to attract good luck in a personal empowerment spell.
* Add to drinks to alter mood both subtly and positively, for example amber water when you need to radiate confidence or talk your way to promotion, sodalite water to stop you panicking while flying, or amethyst water while on a diet to minimise food cravings. Amethyst water and blue lace agate water are good in party drinks or punch to keep partygoers happy but not confrontational and, in the case of teenage events, to prevent those present getting out of hand.
* Add to baths to infuse yourself with the power of the crystals (better than adding the actual crystals to the water as they can get clogged up and discoloured with bath foam/soap). If you were going on an important date, you might use moonstone water to make you appear mysterious and alluring or jade or rose quartz water for gentle love, maybe if you had been let down previously.
* Use waters made with environmentally healing crystals to heal specific places or to encourage your garden or indoor plants to grow. Moss agate water is excellent for herbs and flowers, and tree agate for reviving individual trees and regenerating woodland. Crystalline water is also cheaper than planting the actual crystals and can be used regularly to top up the energies. A little crystalline water added to water in dry periods keeps plants fresher than would be expected. Crystalline water made with a warm crystal like red jasper or garnet, and used round the roots, helps in winter to limit frost damage, especially for more delicate plants.
* Pour environmental crystalline waters on to earth and name a place or creature that needs healing or protection.
* Pour crystalline waters such as clear quartz water into polluted rivers and seas and any of the brown agate waters on to a litter-strewn beauty spot or wasteland to cleanse the earth.
* Crystalline waters can bring healing and maintain health in all kinds of ways, including jade water to energise an old or sick animal and fluorite water for calming the mind and relieving anxieties and phobias. Angelite water, when sprinkled on a symbol or in an actual location, will bring angelic blessings to

unlovely places and situations. More practically, it will help protect your children from bullying when added to their lunchbox drinks.

Making crystalline waters

* You need only small crystals to make crystalline water. See the list below and chapter on crystal magick on page 381.
* Obtain a variety of glass containers and stoppered or screw-top bottles in which to store your crystalline waters. If you are going to make waters directly in the bottles, you need ones with necks that are sufficiently wide. Glass mineral water or juice bottles or small wine bottles (250 ml/0.25 pint) with screw-top lids are better than plastic. However, there are times when you have to compromise, even though plastic and natural magick are not easy bedfellows. Car boots sales and holidays abroad in areas such as Greece, Egypt or Turkey will provide an array of coloured glass bottles and you can, for added power, use a colour that is the same as the crystal (see Colour magick on pages 255–7).
* Use filtered or still mineral water where possible. If you use tap water, run it for a minute or so to get the energies flowing.
* Use rounded crystals and wash them well before use. Avoid malachite as it can be slightly toxic when soaked in water.
* Add the appropriate number of crystals to the quantity of water: one crystal about the size of a one-pence piece to 250 ml/0.25 pint of water.
* Leave for eight hours. Sparkling crystals like clear quartz or citrine love sunlight at least for part of the time and amethyst or rose quartz love moonlight
* Surround the bottle with growing greenery such as pot plants to add the life force.
* Remove the crystal/s or filter the water into smaller bottles. Crystalline waters will last about three or four weeks, but as they are so easy to make you can prepare them almost daily according to your needs and energy levels.

Ten of my favourite crystals for making crystalline waters

Amethyst: Purple and transparent or glowing. Healing; for reducing the power of addictions or destructive behaviour in people; for all forms of protection: physical, emotional and psychic; and for enhancing psychic powers.

Blue lace agate: Soft blue, gleaming or opaque. For defusing unkind words or criticism; good for making drinks at work, at meetings and family gatherings; for bringing personal harmony and stillness; calms the hyperactive and workaholic; soothing in the drinking water of aggressive or noisy animals and birds.

Carnelian: Orange and glowing. For courage, confidence, self-esteem, fertility and creativity; for independence and self-employment and for any dealings with the media.

Citrine: Yellow and sparkling. For logic, learning, tests and examinations, clear communication and for any risk taking, speculation or money-making ventures.

Clear quartz crystal: Brilliant and clear. All-purpose; for new beginnings, energy, health, optimism and happiness.

Jade: Soft to dark green, transparent to opaque. For love, fidelity and friendship; for healing, long life and health; for attracting gradual wealth and good luck; for healing the environment and for maintaining the well-being of animals and birds.

Red jasper: Red and opaque. For strength, both physical and emotional; for stamina and endurance; for excitement and passion; for protection from attack; for bringing positive change, overcoming stagnation and inertia in self and others; for action and expanding horizons; for overcoming exhaustion or debilitating illness.

Rose quartz: Pink and softly transparent or translucent. For all forms of healing, especially in children, women and animals; for patience, peace, reconciliation and quiet sleep, family happiness and happy homes; also for first love, young love, secrets and love after betrayal.

Sodalite: Deep blue, indigo and purple. For safe travel, especially by plane; for harmonious house moves, employment and career advancement; for psychic protection and justice; for calming panic, especially fears of flying.

Tiger's eye: Gleaming gold and brown. For courage and overcoming obstacles; for prosperity and unexpected opportunities; for successful property matters, the home, successful dealings with officialdom, security and stability.

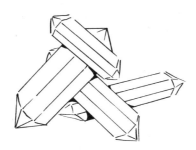

6

NATURAL SPELL BAGS, AMULETS AND TALISMANS

From ancient times, people have crafted amulets and talismans to protect themselves from harm and to attract abundance into their lives. The original protective amulets were animal parts or representations of animals made on tusks or bones. They were linked with the success of hunting expeditions and were designed to attract good fortune.

For example, a human figure with the head of a lion, probably intended to endow the user with courage, was carved from mammoth ivory 32,000 years ago and was found at the Hohlenstein–Staddel Grave at Asselfingen in Germany.

Another hunting charm about 12,500 years old showed a wounded bison on stone, engraved during the Upper Palaeolithic Age. It was found at Tarn et Garonne in France and has diagonal lines of red ochre on the animal's side to represent the blood. Spears are pictured as wavy lines.

Talismanic painted pebbles were discovered in mountain caves in Northern Canada dating from the late Upper Paleolithic Age. Similarly dated ones, found in caves in Le Mas d'Azil Ariege in the French Pyrenees are estimated to be 11,000 years old. The grey pebbles are painted with red ochre with a variety of patterns formed by dots and lines that may have stood for particular ideas.

Charm bags made of skin and filled with bones, wings, herbs and seeds have not survived from these very early times. However, we can speculate their existence from the practices of remaining hunter-gatherer societies from the Sami Reindeer people in Lapland to the rainforest peoples of the Amazon and Africa. Their ways have been unchanged for thousands of years. There are also traditional Native North American medicine bundles that were used to attract abundance, to lead the women to plenteous edible plants and to bring fertility and health to the nations.

Minerals and meteorites were also prized for their protective value.

Animal wings or feet were believed to transfer the strength of the creature to the person carrying them. This may be seen today in the lucky rabbit's foot.

Amulets, talismans and spell bags

In practice, the terms 'amulet' and 'talisman' are interchangeable. An amulet is primarily protective. It could be an unmarked crystal worn as jewellery, or carried in a drawstring bag. It could consist of several herbs in a tied cloth, each with the magickal strengths you need. It could also be a wax, clay, metal or ceramic animal or bird whose actual form might offer power or protection. Amulets may also be kept around the home, at work, in the glove compartment of a car or buried in front of a property. They slowly release their energies into your life.

The amulet is empowered by a ritual, during which the person or place for which it is intended, the time frame and the purpose are written over it in magickal smoke.

A lucky charm is an empowered object in the shape of something that represents luck, for example a small lucky horseshoe in silver (a lucky metal). The charm stores good fortune and becomes luckier the more it is used. In this book I focus on lucky roots (see next page) that can be carried as lucky charms or form part of a charm or spell bag.

A talisman is an image or words engraved or marked on bone, stone, crystal, wax or clay (like the prehistoric buffalo image). It portrays a symbol of what it is intended to attract into your life (by sympathetic magick). For example, an engraved or painted acorn might be etched in a wax or clay tablet, so that your business will grow as the oak grows from the acorn (a sort of magickal shorthand).

As I said in the first part of the book, images are very effective conductors of magickal power, one reason why the Egyptian pictorial hieroglyphs are themselves said to hold power and not just be symbols.

The talisman is empowered before use with its purpose, which tends to be quite specific, for example an owl engraved on to clay (symbol of wisdom) 'to help Louisa study for and pass her examinations in six weeks' time.

In nature magick, a charm or spell bag is a collection of items, such as herbs, roots, crystals, stones and feathers, rather than manufactured items, such as money. They are charmed or enchanted using a spell to empower them during the making. They last either for a specified time or until any fragrance fades.

Charm or spell bags

I will begin with these spell or charm bags (the name is interchangeable). Many of their contents have already been described in the sections on drying and preparing or buying herbs or roots.

Charm bags are made with three, five, seven or nine natural items. These may include herbs, flowers, tree leaves, berries, nuts, seeds, crystals or stones of the kind and proportion you need for particular strengths.

You can make and empower them for any purpose and I give an example of making an employment charm bag later in the chapter.

You could hang a charm bag in a garden on a tree (non-toxic herbs only) to release protection against a short-term problem such as a difficult visitor who is staying a few days or a cat who is ruining your plants that you only want to deter rather than harm.

Where possible, you should add a lucky root or plant to your charm bags or empower and carry a lucky root as a natural lucky charm.

Spells bags are slow- but generally long-acting, unless hung outdoors when the flow of air round them makes them work faster, but also makes them deteriorate faster. Make them on any of the three or four days before the full moon and after dusk to attract good things; or on any of the three days after the full moon for protection and to banish pain, illness, bad luck, debt, etc. The evening of the summer solstice (around 21 June) is best of all of for making these bags, and also amulets and talismans, regardless of the moon phase. The bags can be empowered by the light of the new solstice morning. Make a special solstice bag for success in the following weeks. Trefoil, vervain, St John's wort and dill are popular midsummer herbs.

Roots and plants for your charm bag

The following roots, plants and berries that can be bought from good herbalists or by mail order are popular additions to charm bags or may be used alone as lucky charms. You can enfold one in melted beeswax to preserve it if carried alone, engraving the outside of the wax to make it talismanic.

I have given the names you will usually buy them under and any alternative names by which they are known.

Adam and Eve roots

Power: Love, fidelity

These are usually sold in pairs. The long, pointed one is called the Adam root and the round one, Eve, for obvious reasons. They are like many more exotic roots from the orchid family.

Use them in charm bags or the two alone in a bag to attract love or a marriage proposal. Sometimes they are made into twin love bags and, after commitment, the man carries the Eve root in his charm bag and his partner the Adam root. The two bags are empowered together for fidelity.

Archangel root (angelica/masterwort)

Power: Protection of the home/healing

Use the root in a charm bag for happiness and protection in the home, in healing spell bags or alone as a charm to bring angelic influences into your life. The root also brings psychic awareness and luck in speculation and money matters where there is a risk.

Black snake root (black cohosh)

Power: Courage, passion

Use the root in charm bags or separately to bring courage, for male potency and for passion in both sexes; also a natural money attracter.

Clover or trefoil (shamrock)

Power: Good luck

The three-leaved clover or shamrock is the emblem of Ireland and brings good luck and protection to the wearer or bearer.

The rarer four-leaf clover brings treasure of all kinds. According to a Sussex rhyme:

The first leaf is for fame, the second for wealth, the third a glorious lover and the fourth for health.

Any variety of clover can be added to charm bags or carried for good luck. Substitute the two-leafed variety for love, the five-leafed for money.

Devil's shoestring

Power: Protection, employment

A pointed cleft root, good in charm bags to get a job, especially in hard times or after a period of unemployment; to attract money; for good luck in any area of your life; for money and to protect against physical harm.

Heather

Power: Wishes, lasting love

White heather brings good luck and the granting of wishes (especially if found growing wild). Purple heather brings the promise of eternal love.

Modern gypsies have substituted rosemary in bloom for heather as a luck- and love-bringer and you can do the same.

Hawthorn berries

Power: Fertility, banishing harm

Use in a pink bag for fertility, marriage and general happiness and, maybe surprisingly, in a yellow bag to bring luck to fishermen.

Good in charm bags generally for banishing fear or danger and for protection of property against bad weather, especially storms; also for an increased awareness of nature essences and in any fey magick or wishes.

High John the Conqueror

Power: Money, success

This brown, nut-like root is poisonous, so if you have children in the house, substitute Low John. It is good for success, money, and to bring protection against psychic attack or ill-wishers. Place in a healing bag for protection against depression.

Job's tears

Power: Healing, granting wishes

These tear-like seeds are protection against any sorrow and are said to absorb pain or sickness. Three in a bag bring good luck and seven will grant wishes made when the bag is sealed. They also help to prevent accidents befalling the individual who carries them in a charm bag, and household accidents if kept indoors near the stairs or kitchen.

Lotus root

Power: New opportunities, long life

An Ancient Egyptian charm, lotus root brings blessings in whatever area they are sought: protection, love, long life and the ability to open any doors to career aspirations or opportunities for expansion. It also brings good luck whether carried in a bag or separately.

Low John the Conqueror, galangal

Power: Justice, success in all official matters

Protects against injustice. Good in a bag to resolve legal matters, to help with examinations and to increase passion, good fortune and family happiness. Carry in your pocket separately to a court case, tribunal or enquiry for a speedy and satisfactory resolution. You can substitute ginger root.

Lucky hand root

Power: Employment, games of chance

Another rare type of orchid with a spicy smell, usually shaped like a hand and the size of an average button. Good for all career matters and also for travel, winning competitions, gambling and financial risks. Carry separately if you are entering a contest, acting, singing or dancing in public.

Saw palmetto

Power: Power and energy

Berries can be added to a charm bag for health and vitality, for passion (in a red bag) and romance (in a pink one); use a green bag for money and good luck.

Tonka beans

Power: Courage and good luck

These are poisonous, so do not have them around children. They are said to make any wishes come true, keep illness from the home (when used in a house sachet), bring luck and money and to bring courage to overcome any obstacles.

Making the mix

* Decide which quality you need most in your bag and therefore the appropriate herb. This can then be your main ingredient as well as the focal root – or you might choose two or three strengths in equal measure.
* Take your time writing the formula, calculating approximately the proportions of herbs you will need, according to the emphasis you wish for the bag. Your dried spice or cooking herbs rack will be full of inspiration. The ingredients need not be exotic.
* You can also use your incense mixes in spell bags though generally herbs and roots are not powdered for this purpose, but left whole or chopped to a size to fit.
* Make sure that whatever you use is really dry to avoid your spell bag going mouldy. See pages 99–101 for information on drying herbs.

* As with incense, aim for two fragrant items per bag. You then know that when the bag loses its fragrance it is time to replace it.
* You can add a shell, a stone you have found in a special place, a crystal or some other small item like a feather from your crane bag.
* Generally, sparkling or gleaming crystals like clear quartz crystal, citrine or golden tiger's eye, bring energy, focus and attract money; strongly coloured opaque crystals like red jasper, lapis lazuli or turquoise bring courage, power and success; soft transparent or pastel opaque crystals such as rose quartz, amethyst or jade bring love or healing.
* Darker crystals like smoke quartz or Apache tear (obsidian that you can see through) bring protection; gleaming dark crystals like hematite or obsidian are fiercely defensive. Any banded or mottled stones like moss or brown agate or Dalmatian jasper (spotted like the dog) bring security, stability and gentle growth. All agates are good for animals and protect property. See pages 385–98 for a full list of the crystal meanings.
* Lodestones (magnetic iron), either single or in pairs, are ideal for charm bags. Two that attract (one pointed and one round) will attract love or can be put in separate love bags like the Adam and Eve roots to be carried by a couple who are temporarily parted. A single pointed lodestone attracts money.
* Meteorites are protective of homes and travellers, and bring health and good luck in unexpected areas.
* Lava or pumice (lava with holes) protect the home from natural disasters and intruders, and attract good luck.
* The final ingredient is usually an essential oil. You can use general ones, for example patchouli for all financial matters or career; orange for fertility, marriage, happiness or abundance; pine for purification, prosperity, beginnings, anti-theft and psychic protection; or rose absolute for love, healing, good luck and protection of the family and home. Alternatively, I have listed 47 different kinds of oils on pages 282–90.
* If you don't add oil, have an extra or one less ingredient to make the odd number.

The employment mix

This is my version of an employment mix, made for Susan, a 50-year-old friend of mine, who was made redundant and was told she was too old to get another job. She carried the blue employment bag I made, tied with orange cord, for a month while applying for everything that was vaguely suitable. On the thirtieth day she was offered an interview with her former senior manager who was setting up her own firm. Two years later Susan is a partner.
* Start with a basic focus, an employment lucky root if possible, such as lucky hand root or devil's shoestring. One root or a few berries are enough per bag. If you can't get the lucky hand root or devil's shoestring, substitute another herb or tree of employment, such as clover or chestnut leaves.

- Then add a sprig of dried ash or oak tree leaves for courage.
- Dried chamomile flowers or leaves will restore confidence – necessary in an area of high unemployment and when age is an issue.
- Rosemary or sage keep the mind focused and sharp for writing job applications and attending interviews.
- Add a little ginger or allspice for added vitality to overcome feelings of tiredness. These will also bring the ability to communicate clearly during an interview.
- Thyme is good for clear communication and promotion in the future.
- Dried marigold petals should ensure that the job is well paid.
- A lapis lazuli crystal brings success.
- Finally, add a drop of essential oil – I chose frankincense for authority.

Making the bag

- Start by deciding the size of bag you want. Most spell bags are pocket sized, though for a household protection charm bag you could make one the size of a small evening bag. Some bags are tiny, designed to hold a single crystal or root.
- Next decide what you want to make your bag from. Natural undyed fabric or brown leather is fine for making a bag for any purpose (though some practitioners do not like using leather, even from a reliable source). You can also use different coloured natural fabric according to the purpose of the bag (see below for a summary of colour meanings and pages 258–65 for a full list). Add further meaning by adding a different coloured cord for a secondary strength.
- You can either gather the cloth up and tie it round the top once the bag is filled or make holes round the edge of the cloth to take a drawstring.
- Alternatively, you can use a ready-made drawstring bag or fabric purse.

Blue: Employment, career, justice, long-term and distance travel and house moves, leadership, prosperity. Dark blue can be used for protection of self and property

Brown: Animals, property and officialdom, protection of all kinds, money matters and older people

Green: Love, fidelity, gradual increase of money, health and love, healing, environmental matters, good luck

Grey: Banishing and binding magick, secret matters, secret love and lowering one's profile in times of danger

Orange: Fertility, creativity, independence, self-confidence, communication and personal happiness

Pink: First or gentle love and romance, home and family, mothers and children, mending quarrels

Purple: Wishes, psychic powers, healing the mind and emotions, psychic protection

Red: Action, courage, passion, overcoming obstacles, change and binding magick (if much power is needed)

White: New beginnings, health, originality, energy, power and all attracting magick

Yellow: Examinations, tests, financial speculation, gambling, communication, short-term or distance travel and house moves

Assembling and empowering the bag

* You will need a white or natural beeswax candle and two incense sticks such as rose, lavender, myrrh or chamomile for a gentle purpose, or ceremonial ones like frankincense, dragon's blood or sandalwood for more powerful urgent needs or protection. See pages 176–83 for other options and feel free to mix the fragrances.
* Work outdoors if possible and add a tea light for extra illumination, if needed.
* Set out all your ingredients in advance separately in small dishes on a table or flat surface, including separate holders for each incense fragrance.
* Spread out the cloth or open the bag you will use as the spell or charm bag.
* Begin by lighting the candle and then the two incense sticks while naming three times the purpose of the bag, who it is for and the time scale, for example:

May it be so. May Susan get a new career within a month and a day that will make her fulfilled and lead her to the success she deserves.

* Add each ingredient separately in the order that feels right, naming each one and its purpose, for example:

May this sage enable Susan to sell her talent persuasively on her new CV, as her old one was too self-effacing. So shall it be.

* When you have added the herbs and roots, put the crystal inside and name its purpose, for example:

May this lapis lazuli enable Susan to regain her management status and gain the promotion she merits before too long. So shall it be.

* If you wish, you can add a single drop of essential oil, again with an empowerment, for example:

I add frankincense in order that Susan regains the respect and authority she deserves in her new career. And it shall be.

* Close or tie the bag and set it in the centre of the table. Taking an incense stick in each hand, write in smoke with the one in your power hand the purpose of the spell bag, the name of the person and the time scale, plus a secret message of power.
* Then with the power-hand incense stick moving clockwise and the other one anticlockwise about 2.5 cm/1 in over the bag, recite an empowerment or protection chant continuously. Be careful not to drop ash on the bag. Mine for Susan was:

Bring success and prosperity, for it is right to be, before the moon is past, so the spell I cast, will come to fruition.

* The chant and movement of the sticks needs to get faster and faster in order to build up the power in the spell bag. This is necessary even for protection or healing bags.
* When you can chant or move the sticks no faster, join the sticks for a second in the candle flame and say:

Flame and flare as I count three,
One, two, three.

* Extinguish the candle by blowing it out on three. Return the incense to the holders, saying:

So power continue until the spell is done.

* Leave the incense to burn through.
* You can use a similar empowerment for your amulet (see below).

Keeping the bag

* Once sealed, your bag should not be opened. Unless the bag is a personalised or expensive one, I would be inclined to throw the whole lot away after the allotted time span or when the bag loses its fragrance (three months is about maximum).
* If you have made the bag for someone else, give it to them as soon as possible after the spell.
* It will not spoil the magick if the bag is seen, but it is better if you or the owner can keep it where it will not be touched. You can carry it at crucial times, but keep it otherwise somewhere safe: with your personal things in your bedroom, in a private drawer or locker at work or hidden in a high place in the home. You can make very small bags to carry with you in a bag or pocket or to keep in the glove compartment of a car or in luggage. Susan kept hers with her in her desk drawer in her living room where she wrote letters on her computer, and only took it out on the day of the interview.
* Since all herbs could be dangerous if eaten by small children and some animals, keep charm bags well out of children's and pets' reach. Do not use poisonous roots if there are children in the home, unless under very controlled conditions.
* You can make spell or charm bags for friends or family for any purpose. Perhaps create one for a new baby or for a teenager who is going away travelling or to college.
* If you think that the person you have made the bag for may not like it, you can keep it, with a photograph of the person, in a drawer for the specified time. There is no harm in this if the bag was made for a positive purpose.

Making amulets and talismans

Make amulets on the waning moon, on any of the three or four days after full moon and talismans in any of the three or four days before the full moon, both after dusk.

You can make amulets or talismans for any purpose for yourself or other people. If you have a friend or family member who needs protection or a particular strength or healing, but you know they would not like to have the talisman or amulet personally, you can keep it, with a photograph of the person, as long as its purpose is not an infringement of free will.

For example, you could make a talisman for someone who has an addiction. You should, however, send the person strength or courage rather than trying to get rid of the addiction, which would not work if the time was not right. Equally you could make an amulet for self-love and courage or to give protection from cruelty if someone was in an abusive or what seemed to you a destructive relationship.

Clay and wax are the two best materials for personalised amulets and talismans, unless you are skilled with wood or metal. But crystals are also a traditional material and are innately protective and empowering.

Crystal amulets and talismans

You can use a single crystal in a small drawstring bag or up to seven to signify the particular protection or powers you need or wish to send to someone else (see page 385).

If using more than one crystal, make sure they are smooth so they do not scratch one another. You can also empower a crystal pendant or necklace as an amulet.

Witches often wear a necklace of alternate jet and amber beads for the god and goddess energies. I assign the god power to jet and the goddess power to amber (called the tears of Freyja, the fertility goddess in Scandinavia). However, a number of non-Scandinavian traditions do reverse these.

A crystal can be endowed with power as an amulet. If you are very dexterous, you can make the crystal into a talisman by drawing on an image with glass or acrylic paint.

Wax amulets and talismans

Wax amulets or talismans are especially potent because they come from bees, which are recognised as sacred creatures in all cultures (see page 240). What is more, if you make one from a melted candle or indeed by warming wax, your amulet or talisman will have been created from the four ancient elements: earth (the candle), air (the smoke), fire (the flame) and water (the melting wax). The union is said to create a fifth element, spirit, ether or akasha, that is captured in the wax tablet.

The designs you create are limited only by your imagination. You could even create an animal-shape amulet by cutting it out of the wax and thus endowing it with the protection and strengths of the chosen animal.

You can use the colour meanings given for the bags to enable you to draw extra strengths into your amulet or talisman.

Method 1

* For this easier of the two methods, you use a sheet of beeswax. Beeswax comes in numerous colours as well as natural. If possible, choose one coloured with natural dyes.
* Take a piece of wax about two or three times the diameter or length of the amulet/talisman. This enables you to make a thicker amulet/talisman, which is less likely to break than a thinner one.

- Melt the wax gently over a candle for a minute to soften the wax (you can use a hairdryer if you prefer). Then you can press or mould the wax either flat or into any shape, and cut round it or better still just press into shape.
- If you are going to engrave the wax, put it on a tray or flat plate covered with greaseproof paper so it will not stick.
- Use one of the symbols on pages 150–54 on your talisman or your own favourite natural symbol.

Method 2

- This method involves melting a good-quality candle. Do not use the dipped kind that is white inside or church candles that do not leave a pool of wax. Try burning a candle first on different surfaces and holders and see how the wax falls. Personally, I like to use a large, squat beeswax or natural wax candle (tall, thin ones don't work).
- Secure the candle on a circular metal tray by dripping melted wax from the candle on to the tray. Sometimes you will end up with strange wax shapes but these are ideal for crafting and engraving.
- Alternatively, large holders with spikes are good as you can fill in the indentation while the wax is still molten or place a cord through the hole with three knots when the design is finished. (If robust enough, you could hang the amulet/talisman for a short-term purpose.)
- You can create circular amulets in a cake tray with a number of separate deep compartments (the kind you use for making small pies or cakes). Stand different coloured candles in the individual compartments in order to create pools of wax. In this way you can make several different amulets at once, perhaps one for each family member.
- Alternatively, if you want a specific shape such as a circle (potential), square (stability) or triangle (increase), drip the molten wax from the lit candle to create the shape you want. Use a metal tray or very strong greaseproof paper on the tray for easy removal (or use a wooden spatula).
- Light the candle and state the purpose of the amulet or talisman and for whom you are making it. Repeat in your mind nine times secret words of power and protection.
- While the wax is still soft, engrave any talismanic symbols using a small screwdriver, a paper knife, wooden skewer or a metal nail.
- When the wax is set, ease it from the tray with a wooden spatula or very gently with a knife.

Clay amulets and talismans

There are a number of self-drying clays that can be rolled and formed into different shapes. You can buy clay-molding tools very cheaply and can use one of these or a silver-coloured paper knife or screwdriver to mark your talismanic images.

Dedicating amulets and talismans

You can use this method for dedicating crystal amulets as well as wax or clay.

* When it is hard, set your amulet or talisman on a small square of fresh white cloth on your indoor or outdoor altar and enclose it with a square of white or beeswax candles at the four main directional points.
* Facing north, light each candle in turn beginning in the north and naming for each, the person, purpose and time scale of the amulet or talisman (the time scale can be 'until the wax crumbles'). Say:

May the amulet / talisman and the cause be blessed.

* Now take two incense sticks as you did for empowering the charm bag, one either side of the white cloth and light the left-hand one from the candle of the north and the right-hand one from the candle of the south, repeating the dedication for each.
* As you did when empowering the charm bag, move your right hand clockwise and left hand anticlockwise at the same time, creating a power or protection chant about your amulet or talisman.
* When you have raised the power and can chant or move the sticks no faster, hold both sticks first in the west candle and then move to the east candle very fast and hold the sticks in that for a second. At both say:

Flame and flare, enter here in glory and in triumph.

* Still holding the sticks, blow all four candles out in rapid succession. Raise the sticks, saying:

So shall it be as I count three,
Three, two, one,
The spell is done.

* Return the incense sticks to their holders and allow them to burn through.
* When it is done, wrap the amulet or talisman in fabric ready to place where you will keep it safely, or find a safe place to display it where it will not be touched except by you or the person for whom it is intended.

Keeping amulets and talismans

Amulets and talismans should be touched gently every day and the purpose repeated. Crystal are the easiest talismans to keep since they don't crumble. Keep your crystal talisman in a tiny purse or a drawer, wrapped in fabric for the specified time.

If you need the talisman for a long-term matter, rededicate it every three months by repeating the ceremony. You may need to repaint the image.

Wax and clay will crumble and are better for shorter-lasting needs. However, you can make a new one for the same purpose at any time and bury pieces of one that is showing cracks before it breaks.

If you do drop your amulet or talisman, you haven't lost the luck. Make a new one (in an emergency you can work after dusk at any time of the month) and wrap a small piece of the old one with it to transfer the luck. Bury the rest under a healthy plant or tree.

Talismanic images

The following are images associated with natural magick, but you can use your favourite power animal or bird or any magickal symbols, such as the pentagram (see page 90). With pentagrams, the key is how they are drawn: invoking to attract good things, banishing for protection or to banish unwanted things.

The horned god

Representing courage and power

The male principle of the ancient lord of animals, the hunt and the winter, consort of the earth/moon goddess. Use for courage, passion, power, potency, travel, fathers and fatherhood, for change, overcoming obstacles and protection. He has nothing to do with satan or the devil. Indeed, it was Christianity that misunderstood this powerful and protective god of nature (see page 211 for more on this).

The fire sign

Representing creative ventures, ambitions

The ancient alchemical fire sign is good for ultimate success, dreams come true, power and creative fulfilment, fame and recognition; also for living in sunny places.

The mother goddess

Representing fertility and abundance

The female principle. Use for fertility, pregnancy and birth, healing, abundance, mothers and children, a safe and happy home, protection of the vulnerable.

The triple moon

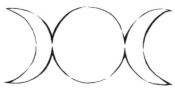

Representing fertility, protection against
emotional vampires
Protective and empowering for women; good
for conceiving children, for safe pregnancy
and childbirth, also for young women and
those experiencing the menopause; also guards
against emotional blackmail and con artists; protective for travel, especially across
water.

The Ankh

Representing good luck, new beginnings
The Ancient Egyptian hieroglyph and symbol of good fortune.
Use for new beginnings, health and long life. It was carried by
the gods and goddesses as a protective symbol.

The feather of Ma'at

Representing justice and truth
The hieroglyph for the feather of Ma'at (the Ancient Egyptian
goddess of truth and justice) against which the hearts of the
deceased were weighed.

The entwined staff of Hermes

Representing healing, balance
The entwined, healing caduceus or staff of Hermes (in the
Ancient Greek tradition), Thoth (in Ancient Egypt) or
Mercury (in Roman tradition) is a symbol of health and healing.
It is also good for balancing emotions or different demands
on your time and at any time when you have two equally
demanding priorities.

Shen

Representing long-term happiness and fidelity forever
Shen, the Ancient Egyptian hieroglyph represents the
sun rising over the horizon and says that happiness
and love will last as long as the sun rises over the horizon
each day. This is good therefore for business ventures.

The sign for water

Representing love, reconciliation
The ancient alchemical sign for water signifies love,
healing, fertility, the mending of quarrels, growth
and natural healing.

The sun

Representing prosperity, career success
This is the symbol of the sun and so of all potential
and making wishes come true.

Or

Representing the power needed to be single-minded
and to focus all your energies for a short burst of
time on one matter
    The Ancient Egyptian sign for the sun, Aten.

The earth symbol

Representing property, financial security
The ancient alchemical Earth symbol also brings success
to business and those who are self-employed; and protection,
keeping family, the home, animals and property safe.

The Eye of Horus

Representing protection, banishes all ill intent and spite
The ultimate protective symbol from Ancient Egypt.
The moon eye of the sky god Horus was originally used,
and still is in some Middle Eastern lands, to protect against
the evil eye; good against bullying, envy and gossips.

The splayed hand

Representing psychic defence, protection of home and loved ones
The splayed hand, here shown from the Jain religious tradition,
repeals all harm, spite, theft, manipulation and evil. You can
draw just the hand if you wish.

Ancient Egyptian Scarab beetle

Representing good luck, new beginnings
The beetle restores luck after a run of bad luck and offers
a new start after difficulty; good if there are unemployment
or money worries.

Nefer

Representing harmony, the mending of quarrels
Nefer, the hieroglyph for the oud, the Ancient Egyptian guitar,
is the hieroglyph of harmony. It brings happiness within self,
to the home and especially in love. It is also good for world peace.

The air symbol

Representing travel and learning
The ancient alchemical air symbol signifies success in all
tests or examinations, conventional healing, travel,
successful house and job moves, employment and
career advancement.

PART 3

MAGICK OF THE PLANT WORLD

INTRODUCTION

This section forms one of the core parts of the book. This is partly because it contains a great deal of information and magickal associations that will enable you to create magickal incense spell bags and weave your own rituals.

The plant world is also the most accessible form of natural magick, whether we live in deep countryside or in the centre of a city. We can all grow plants, whether indoors in pots or in a garden, to bring different planetary energies into our lives. By working with our plants both practically and for magick, our personal energies and harmony are spontaneously enhanced.

Though it is depressing to hear about the destruction of rainforests and it remains a serious problem for all of us, in towns and cities new wildlife gardens are springing up; forests with native trees are likewise being replanted on land abandoned by industry or buildings on the outskirts of major towns. This then should be a source of hope.

Flowers span all ages and cultures and can be used in spells and also to energise and inspire us by their beauty and fragrance. As we explore the traditions, the myths and the magick of flowers, trees and herbs, so we can not only inspire ourselves and draw strength and healing from them, but give back to nature by our efforts to preserve and protect it.

What is more, as we take our children and grandchildren or friends' children to botanical gardens, arboretums and naturally growing wild places so we are passing on a reverence for and wonder at nature's beauties. As a Malaysian proverb says, we don't inherit the earth from our ancestors but borrow it from future generations. So the more we learn ourselves, often by direct contact with plants, the more we can teach and inspire a younger generation weary of games consoles and simulated experiences.

Though I do give spells in these chapters, most of all I hope to offer resources to enable your own creativity and innate connection with nature to blossom. In this way, you can ritually, and in your everyday life, exchange energies with trees, plants and herbs for mutual advantage.

FLOWER MAGICK

Flowers have been used in magick and spellcasting for thousands of years because of their beauty, colour and fragrance. The Ancient Egyptians believed that the spirit or essence of plants contained magickal healing powers given by the deities. This power was transmitted through the fragrance of the flowers and in the petals.

Actual flowers, as well as sacred oils extracted from them, were placed in the tomb to empower the spirit on its journey through the afterlife. When the British Egyptologist Howard Carter opened the tomb of Tutankhamen in the Valley of the Kings on 4 November 1922, the air was rich with scents that had survived for almost three thousand years since the young king's burial around 1,322 BCE. In the antechamber were two huge wreaths of the blue lotus, hibiscus and narcissus, which, although desiccated, were still recognisable.

Flowers are not only used in healing magick, but for empowerment and bringing joy, prosperity, good luck and love.

Deities of flowers

Growing flowers are absolutely bursting with the life force. This is reflected in the number of flower gods in the Ancient Egyptian, Russian and Aztec traditions who are concerned with new life and regeneration. You can use these deities as a focus for the rituals or empowerments you carry out with flowers. I have created a flower deity chant to restore beauty to the world and to your life in the way you most need it, using some of the deities' names. You are, of course, free to substitute your own favourite flower gods and goddesses.

Flower goddesses

Antheia

Qualities: Young or new love, love for friends

Antheia was Greek goddess of new or young love. Her name means blooming or blossoming, and because she was so gentle she was called the friend of flowers. She was a daughter of the mother goddess Hera, wife of Zeus and had a temple at Argos. She is portrayed as a young girl and, in Crete, was also associated with vegetation, blossoms, gardens and the flourishing earth.

Aphrodite or Venus

Qualities: Lasting love, fidelity, beauty, self-esteem

Aphrodite, or Venus as she is known in the Roman tradition, is the ultimate goddess of love and beauty, and was also a goddess of flowers. Her special flowers are pink and red roses, symbolising blossoming love and fidelity. Pansies or violets were also flowers of Venus, especially for young lovers or secret love. Venus love posies were tied with pink or green ribbons.

Blodeuwedd, Blodwin, Blancheflor

Qualities: Love under difficulty, secret love, overcoming lost love or love ending with kindness

Blodeuwedd is the much misunderstood and maligned Welsh maiden goddess of May Day, of the moon and of the blossoming earth. In her most ancient form she is called the ninefold goddess of the Isles of the Blest.

She was created from nine different flowers as a bride for Llew, god of the waxing year or increasing light, and he was her one true love.

Later she was turned into an owl for her infidelity with Llew's twin, Gornwy, the god of the waning year or decreasing light. This union led to the death of Llew. Blodeuwedd, of course, had to play her part in the changing of the seasons so that winter could follow summer. This meant she had to mate with the god of the waning year – and so be unfaithful to Llew, her true love. He had to die in order that his child might be born at the midwinter solstice around 21 December and become the new sun king who would defeat his uncle on the spring equinox on 21 March and so restore light to the world in the never-ending cycle.

Flora

Qualities: Joy, fertility, love of family, love for the planet

Flowers are named after this Roman goddess of flowers whose festival, Floralia, lasted from 26 April until 3 May. This was a major fertility festival throughout Eastern and Western Europe (see Seasonal magick, pages 448–51). She was called Khloris in the Ancient Greek tradition and was the wife of Zephyros, god of the west wind. The flowers came from her mouth and were scattered by the wind.

Xochiquetzal

Qualities: Passion, creativity, animals, birds and insects, love in later life

Flowers were greatly prized by the Aztecs and grown for rituals in great quantities in chinampas, man-made fields at the edge of the city.

Xochiquetzal (pronounce the beginning of her name as a Z), whose name means flower feather, is the goddess of vegetation, artists and erotic love. In some legends she was taken to the underworld by the god Xolotl where she ate forbidden fruit, but returned to earth with the growth of the flowers. Others recall that she married the rain god Tlaloc who fertilised the flowers. Wherever she walks, she is attended by butterflies and birds. Every eight years the Aztecs had a huge flower festival where participants wore flower and animal masks.

Flower gods

Nefertum or Nefertem

Qualities: Perfection, harmony, healing

Ancient Egyptian young god of the lotus flower, Nefertum represents the first sunrise when the first lotus opened on the waters at creation. He is lord of the lotus, of all perfumes and oils. His name is linked with the hieroglyph Nefer, the Ancient Egyptian oud or guitar, the musical instrument that symbolises harmony.

Nefertum is depicted either as a beautiful head rising from a lotus flower, a child with a side lock sucking his thumb and sitting inside the lotus or as a youth with a lotus headdress.

Xochipilli

Qualities: New beginnings, regeneration and abundance

Xochipilli (pronounce the beginning of his name as a Z) is the Aztec Prince of Flowers and was also called Macuilxochitl, which means five flowers. He is the twin brother of the flower goddess Xochiquetzal and also the god of rebirth, maize, love, games, singing, poetry and dance. His statues show him sitting cross-legged on a throne that was adorned with flowers for rituals. Flowers were painted or tattooed on his arms and he wore a necklace of the skin of a jaguar head.

Yarilo

Qualities: Abundance, power, love of animals and nature, justice and rewards

Yarilo is the young, handsome, fair-haired Russian and Baltic god of the spring and of erotic love. He is depicted wearing a wildflower crown and a white cloak when he comes to earth each year to bring the spring and the first flowers. He remains on earth until the harvest. Wherever he walks or glances, flowers and crops will spring up before his feet.

Making your flower deity chant

Chants are considered very powerful in magick. As far back as the time of the Ancient Egyptians it was believed that to speak magickal words was to give life to the words and bring wishes and desires into actuality. Indeed, in one Egyptian creation myth, Heka, the god of magick, spoke the words that brought the world into being.

Flower deities are a good focus for all chants for growth in your life, love, abundance and fertility, or just to bring joy to your daily world.

* Plan in advance the qualities you need from the lists given with the deities above and select two or three deities who seem to symbolise your needs. Mixing cultures is fine. Flower deities don't just bring love in the sense of a couple's devotion, but also love between family, friends and animals, and altruistic love or love for new beginnings or abundance in any aspect of life.
* Weave a repetitive chant around the chosen names. Then recite this rhythmically or sing on a pentatonic, five-note rising and falling scale .

You can find one example of the pentatonic scale by playing only the black notes on the piano. The simple chanting tune given here is in the pentatonic scale (the numbers correspond to the marked piano notes).

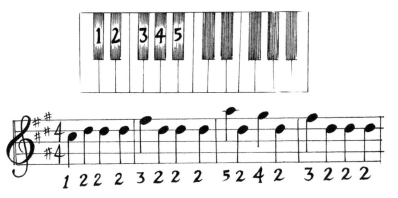

* Allow the words and sounds to become faster and faster until they are entirely spontaneous and then create a regular rhythm, perhaps of three or four words that can be repeated, alternating with the deity names.
* When your chant is ready, try to find a flower-filled place or make a circle of flowering plants.
* Hold a bowl of petals to scatter as you chant.
* Turn clockwise three times, followed by anticlockwise three times, then clockwise three times, etc.
* First chant slowly, softly and rhythmically, then gradually increase the speed and volume, building the chant to a height, then reduce the speed and volume until your words fall into silence.
* Remember, simplicity is the key.

A flower deity chant for restoring abundance, beauty and fertility to a place that has been spoiled

I created this chant after builders had destroyed my garden while dealing with subsidence. Two years later, the garden is a mass of flowers and flowering herbs again. The chant gave me the incentive and impetus to start again. It is also good if someone has been cruel or abusive, to restore your belief in life and for any despoiled areas, whether local or global, such as rainforests.

Flora, Venus, Nefer-tum, Flora, Venus, Nefer-tum, restore, bring beauty and fertility, Flora, Venus, Nefer-tum, Flora, Venus, Nefer-tum, etc.

It is simple and yet these chants are channels of great power. The sound releases the energies into the cosmos where it is amplified and enters the focus of the chant.

I scattered a bowl of flower seeds instead of petals on the sea of mud and many have since grown.

Flower spells

Every flower has a magickal meaning and a message, so you can create a spell with different flowers to make a living wish.

You can empower the flowers and then send or take them to the person for whom you made the spell. If this is not appropriate or the spell was for you, keep the posy in your home, releasing the energies for continuing power or protection as long as the flowers last.

You can just use one or two different kinds of flower or build up a complex spell with six or seven.

You don't need to buy expensive flowers because humble wildflowers or those from an indoor or outdoor garden are equally filled with the life force. You can often get cheap flowers from market stalls especially towards the end of the market day.

Flower spells are wonderful for healing and, what is more, the flowers can be sent to the sick person after the spell has been cast. You can also dry the flowers before the spell and that way they will last much longer if results are anticipated to take a while. Alternatively, repeat the spell weekly or monthly.

You can also make planetary spell posies or more elaborate bouquets by referring to the associations in the chapters on gardening (see pages 199–201). There are some discrepancies between associations given in different chapters, due each system having a different emphasis and source. Use whichever you prefer for astrological posy spells.

The properties of flowers

The language of flowers was popularised in Victorian times, but was formalised as a system of communication, especially between lovers, in the early eighteenth century when Lady Mary Wortley Montagu, living in Turkey at the time with her ambassador husband, discovered the hidden meanings that could be concealed in a bouquet of flowers.

However, the language of flowers was used by the Ancient Egyptians, the Chinese, Indians and Ancient Greeks. During the time of Elizabeth I in England, flower meanings appeared in verse and Shakespearean plays, gillyflowers as symbols of gentleness, cowslips of wise counsel, pansies for thoughts, flowering rosemary for remembrance and marigolds for married love.

Use the following to build up your own wishes or messages and then turn to page 166 to find how to empower your wish flowers.

Acacia: Secret love, optimism, making friends

Alyssum: Increasing what is of worth, whether love, money or fulfilment

Amaranth: Faithful love, beauty

Amaryllis: Achievements, especially in writing and all creative arts

Anemone: Calling a lost love back

Apple blossom: Fertility, good fortune

Aster: Delicate matters or negotiations

Azalea: Moderation, freedom from addiction

Bee-orchid: Putting right misunderstandings

Begonia: Protection against gossip; love that faces opposition; psychic protection; guarding against accidents

Bluebell: Constancy and faithfulness

Buttercup: increasing wealth; sharing resources

Camellia: Courage; desire

Campion: Hidden passion, forbidden love

Carnation (pink): Being made welcome; acceptance into a family or work environment

Carnation (red): Passion; also calling a love that is absent

Carnation (white): Maternal love, love in later years, truth

Carnation (yellow): Anti-spite and criticism

Celandine: Future happiness, gentle pleasures and holidays

Chrysanthemum (brown): Ending a relationship with kindness; healing animals

Chrysanthemum (red): Passion; also marriage

Chrysanthemum (white): Truth and integrity

Chrysanthemum (yellow): Banishing gently an unwanted lover or a love gone cold

Cornflower: Protecting the vulnerable

Cowslip: Learning and examinations; wise advice

Crocus: Children and young people; joy

Cyclamen: Protection, especially psychic defence; endings leading to beginnings

Daffodil: Forgiveness; finding one true love

Dahlia: Change, travel

Daisy (field): First love

Daisy (Michaelmas): Seeking justice, anything to do with autumn

Dandelion: Wishes for the future, courage

Delphinium: Getting the job you want

Edelweiss: Adventures, fun

Evening primrose: Overcoming jealousy

Forget-me-not: Calling a lover

Gardenia: Increasing beauty and radiance

Geranium (pink): Overcoming uncertainty

Geranium (red): Commitment in love

Gillyflower: Family joy, gentleness

Gladiolus: Strength, especially of character

Guelder Rose: Older people, winter matters

Harebell: Hope, restoration of trust

Heather (pink): Good luck

Heather (purple): Faithfulness forever; also money and gambling

Heather (white): Good fortune, wishes coming true

Hibiscus: Gentleness and healing

Hollyhock: Fertility

Hollyhock (white): Ambitions

Honesty: Integrity, financial advantage

Honeysuckle: Commitment in love; babies

Hyacinth: Regaining lost love.

Hydrangea: Changing career; overcoming obstacles to success and happiness

Iris: Clear communication; receiving long-awaited news

Jasmine: Making dreams come true; discovering the identity of a secret admirer

Jonquil: Encouraging mutual love; justice, especially personal; clearing up uncertainty

Lavender: Gentle love; healing

Lilac: Domestic happiness; permanent relationships

Lily: Spiritual matters, marriage, mothers

Lily, Tiger: Wealth, achievements

Lily of the valley: Return of happiness, pregnancy, sweetness of nature

Lupin: Grace, beauty, dignity

Magnolia: Beauty, sensuality, nobility, love of nature

Marigold: Marriage, money, employment, summer matters

Mimosa: Riches, increasing beauty

Narcissus: Self-esteem, self-confidence

Nasturtium: Victory, success, generosity; also maternal devotion

Oleander: Wise caution, especially with money

Orange blossom: Marriage, fertility, abundance, health

Orchid: Abundance, prosperity

Pansy: Togetherness; people from the past returning; kind thoughts

Passion flower: Finding a twin soul

Peony: Forgiveness

Periwinkle: Early love

Petunia: Overcoming despair, debts or fear; bringing calm

Poinsettia: Unexpected gifts or offers

Polyanthus: Riches

Poppy: Peace, pleasure, increasing imaginative gifts; quiet sleep

Primrose: New love; also spring matters, new beginnings

Rose (pink): First love; also healing

Rose (red): Love forever; also health

Rose (white): Secret love and all secrets

Rose (wild or dog): identifying a secret admirer

Rose (yellow): Repelling jealousy; an older lover or love in later years

Snapdragon: Overcoming rejection and loss; the revelation of truth

Snowdrop: New beginnings; all matters concerning the spring

Stock: Becoming beautiful in the eyes of a particular person

Sunflower: A wealthy lover; also fulfilment of ambitions; splendid opportunities

Sweet pea: Partings; also passion fulfilled

Tulip (pink or white): Finding the perfect lover

Tulip (red): Love acknowledged

Tulip (yellow): Unrequited love

Violet: Trust, modesty; keeping secrets

Wallflower: Happiness after misfortune

Wisteria: Breaking possessiveness that is holding you back

Woodbine: Family love, especially between siblings

A bouquet or posy spell using flower meanings

As an example, I will describe a three-flower spell I made for Jenny for overcoming spite towards her and her children on her remarriage to Phil. Her new in-laws were being very unpleasant (they had a strong bond with their previous daughter-in-law though she was persistently unfaithful to their son).

Jenny is anxious for the sake of her children, Andrew aged six and Penny aged four, to keep the peace, especially as she and Phil are hoping to have more children together.

Like Jenny, you will need to do a little preparation in advance to decide on the flowers you will be using for your spell. Choose as many or as few as you wish.

I would suggest you buy a good flower book with illustrations or visit a website, so that if you can't obtain the flower you want, you can substitute one of a similar colour and kind. In spring you might decide to use local wildflowers, but otherwise you can get hold of most flowers, most of the year round.

Timing: Flower spells are daylight spells, and are especially good in the morning. Unless you are an early riser, choose your flowers the night before and leave them in water overnight. Best of all, if there are suitable garden flowers, pick them just before the spell.

You will need: The chosen flowers, several of each kind if you want to make a nice bouquet to send or keep. Jenny chose pink carnations for being made welcome and for acceptance into Phil's family, yellow carnations to get rid of spite and what was unfair criticism, and finally cream-coloured lilies for marriage and mothers because it was Phil's mother who was being really nasty and trying to break the marriage. If one need is predominant, you can increase the proportion of those flowers to the rest. You can, of course, use only one kind of flower if you wish.

A vase of water for the flowers during the spell.

* Jenny took the flowers outdoors in the vase (you can work indoors if you wish) and first picked out a single yellow carnation.
* Jenny held the flower so that it rested in the palms of her hands. In this way energy could be transmitted via the psychic energy centres or small chakras in her hands into and from the plant. In this way the flower energy will fill you with the power you need and your own good will/love/power/whatever you are transmitting from within you, passes into the flower as a two-way exchange.
* Jenny first spoke words based on the yellow carnation energies to soften the spite. You can create words linked to the flowers you choose and your needs. The more specific you are with names, etc., the more focused the spell:

Gentle carnation, shield myself, my husband, Phil, and my children, Andrew and Penny, from the hurtful words and unkind actions of Brenda and Sean, my in-laws. May they replace anger with gentleness, malice with kindliness. As I count three, two, one, the spite is gone.

* She took next the pink carnation and rested it in her hands, touching the yellow carnation. Jenny touched both flowers and said:

Welcoming flower, make me likewise welcome in my in-laws' home and lives, and my children, that Phil may likewise feel at home once more. As I count three, two, one, may harmony come.

* Finally she added a tall cream lily and said as she touched all three flowers:

Lily of love, Brenda is a mother. I a mother am. We both love Phil. My marriage is precious and under threat. As I count three, two, one, the danger's gone. My spell is done. Let there be peace between our households. Blessings be on all.

* Jenny tied the flowers into a small bouquet and took them to her mother-in-law's house, leaving them on the doorstep with a friendly message. Words from the heart are as effective as the finest poetry in a spell.
* There were no miracles, but during the weekend visit, Brenda thanked Jenny for the flowers that she said were her favourite. Her husband Sean had got out and repainted Phil's childhood swing and climbing frame for the children.
* Jenny repeated the spell weekly, alternately keeping and sending the flowers to Brenda. Slowly the atmosphere is melting.

The Scandinavian seven-flower wreath dream spell

This is a traditional and much older variation of the bouquet or posy spells above. If you wish, you can use the list above to add extra meanings to this spell.

There are a number of versions of this ritual that was traditionally carried out on the eve of the summer solstice or longest day (usually the evening of 20 June). From mediaeval times, summer solstice rites became grafted on to the Christianised calendar, at midsummer or St John's Day on 24 June. However, you can use this spell any time you want to call a lover, known or unknown, to your life or to your side.

Timing: Traditionally either the eve of the summer solstice or midsummer's eve,

23 June or, if you prefer, the night of the festival day itself. Alternatively, any evening just before dusk when you want to call love.

You will need: Seven different kinds of flowers from your garden, three or four of each kind if you are making a flower wreath. (Even if you live in the middle of a town in a high-rise apartment, you can buy a bunch of flowers containing seven different kinds of flower, as supermarkets stock these all year round. Alternatively, grow indoors small flowering pots as a source.) You can have seven colours if you wish – red, blue, purple, pale yellow, pink, white and golden yellow (gold) – but this is not necessary.

A small wire circlet or, if you are clever, you can weave one from pliant wood or cane.

* Pick your flowers before sunset in silence and weave them with the twine on to the circlet.
* As you do so, call in your mind your lover, whether known or as yet unknown, to come into your life and dance with you in your dreams.
* When you are finished, hang your circlet of flowers over your bed.
* Before sleep, say softly seven times:

> *With seven flowers sweet do I call thee, love. Come dance with me in my dreams and, on the morrow, lead me round the midsummer tree and again on our wedding day.*

* Picture, as you drift into sleep, a known or unknown figure leading you to dance round a green flower-decked tree (traditionally woven from branches for midsummer's day celebrations in Scandinavia). Alternatively, picture any favourite tree.
* You may dream of dancing with your love, but if not, visualise the scene in your mind when first you open your eyes. You may have a glimpse of the identity of your lover in this mind's vision or may even connect telepathically with your would-be lover. He or she may phone or text you early, even before you get up.
* When you get up, hang your garland on a tree or bush in your garden. If there is no convenient tree, hang it on a nail or hook on a door that faces outdoors or an indoor ornamental bush.
* Contact your lover if you have one (if he or she hasn't phoned already) and suggest a day out or at least lunch together. Then make plans for the evening.
* Pick one of each of the flowers and take them with you in a small purse when you meet your lover. Scatter them to the winds at the end of the day.
* If you have not yet met the love of your life or he or she cannot be with you on this day, leave the wreath on the wall or tree. If unknown to you, he or she should come before the flowers are faded.

2

HERB MAGICK

Herbal healing remedies are becoming increasingly popular in the modern world as it is discovered that some hold the key to curing modern ills; generally too they are gentler and less toxic than drugs created artificially. This knowledge has been around in some cases for hundreds or even thousands of years, but became disregarded or forgotten and is now being incorporated further into modern medicine.

Herb magick, the topic of this chapter, is an equally ancient tradition, one that does not need elaborate tools or complex rituals. However, there is a great overlap between herb healing and magick, for herb rituals too can trigger the body's own self-healing system because of their abundant life force.

Almost all magickal herbs have healing properties and you can find details of these in any good herb book. I have suggested some books I use regularly in Further reading on page 515. Herbs can also be used for spiritual healing; see pages 253–57 on the natural senses we possess.

Though herb magick is simple, it is also very potent. As well as using spells, you can draw on their strengths in a number of ways in your daily life.

I recently visited the National Herb Centre near Banbury in Oxfordshire and the whole place buzzed with the energies of so many different herbs gathered in one place. I filled the back of my car with pots of species that I had previously only ever seen pictures of or bought dried. I'm surprised that the air didn't glow as my daughter Miranda and I drove back down the A34.

My daughter has used our recent acquisitions to create a new herb terrace in my long but small garden. The day after it was finished, for the first time in nearly twenty years, a heron landed in my small garden close to the new herb bed. He was obviously not going to be well fed, as my two tiny ponds contain mainly weeds and algae, but I took it as a blessing since the heron is my favourite bird.

Herb magick in daily life

If you have never grown herbs in your garden, in pots indoors or on window ledges, you may be surprised how easy they are to care for and how fragrant, flowering at different times during the year. See pages 97–101 for information on how to make your own herbal and floral incenses by drying your garden or kitchen herbs and flowers.

In every supermarket you will find shelves of dried cooking herbs in jars. These can be stored in the kitchen for ages and are perfect for magick with the simplest of empowerments. Herb magick does not require elaborate magickal tools or rituals, but can be absorbed in traditional style during your everyday life.

* Sit close to growing herbs and slowly and regularly breathe in their fragrance. With non-perfumed herbs, visualise green herbal light or the colour of the flowering heads surrounding you and flowing within you. This can be both empowering and healing. Since each herb has a different strength, you can choose ones whose powers you need (see pages 176–83 for a list of herb meanings). Lavender (that you will find also in the chapter on flowers) eases emotional pain and heals both mental and physical abuse, while feathery green fennel that flowers yellow in summer gives you courage and confidence.

* Add herbs to cooking or to make herbal teas. If you don't have time to make your own teas from fresh or dried herbs, there is a huge range of herbal teas and tea bags on the market.

* Most supermarkets sell ready-washed herb salads. Try fresh fennel and mint in a homemade salad; the former will further travel plans and the latter give you the money to pay for the tickets; as a bonus, this combination of herbs will do wonders for your digestive system.

* Before cooking with herbs or making a herbal tea (even with a tea bag), you can whisper words of empowerment as you stir the herbs, or enchant your herbs or the tea bags by passing your hands over them, the right clockwise and the left anticlockwise at the same time while softly chanting your needs.

* Use natural herbal bath products or make your own with flowering herbs and leaves in a tied muslin bag suspended in bath water. Many flowers count as herbs both in magickal and medicinal terms and I have given a number of meanings in the flower and tree chapters (see pages 162–65 and 188–90).

* Knotted stockings or tights make an excellent makeshift bag to put in your bath water or suspend from the taps. You can add to your herb bag carnation petals, catnip (small quantity only), chamomile flowers, elecampane, elder flowers, eucalyptus (surprisingly relaxing), fennel seeds, hop flowers, hyssop, jasmine flowers, lavender, lemon balm, lemon verbena, lilac, linden blossoms, marjoram (sweet), olive blossoms, orange blossoms, dried orange peel, passionflower, peppermint, rosemary, rose petals, skullcap leaves, slippery elm bark and valerian root.

* Commercially prepared mixtures tend to be a good guide to what works. You can read much more on this in my *Fragrant Magic* book (see Further reading, page 516).

* For protection of the home, hang bunches of dried herbs around the house or place cut, fresh flowering herbs into vases. Dill hung over doorways, above infants' cradles or scattered around the boundaries of a home, traditionally protects against malice and envy.

* Have protective herb pots or dishes of dried herbs such as sage, basil, rosemary and thyme or dried chopped nettles in a dish on your desk at work, or sprinkle them across thresholds to keep out harm.

* For quiet sleep, you can buy or make herbal dream pillows (many contain rose petals, lavender and chamomile). Again you can read about these in *Fragrant Magic* if you want to make your own.

A word of caution

Though you are using herbs for magick rather than healing, you still need to take care when handling them, eating them or adding them to baths.

A few generations ago we would have been taught which plants were safe to eat and touch by our great grandmothers. Those few peoples that still live undisturbed in rainforests can identify in dense forest a plant that has medicinal or culinary value – and one looking remarkably similar that is toxic.

With the fracturing of extended families that began with the Industrial Revolution and was finally sealed for many people with the new mobility of labour after the Second World War, knowledge of the old ways has become diluted. Because we can buy a huge range of herbs and spices from many parts of the world all the year round in supermarkets and health stores, we no longer work with a smaller number of familiar local herbs.

We have also lost an instinctive awareness passed through our genes of potential danger. In the wild, animals naturally eat herbs that are good for specific disorders. Bears and monkeys are especially gifted in this area. Because we have lost this innate herb wisdom we don't know which herbs are safe to eat or use medicinally or what would be a sensible dose.

Therefore, though I have given a list of a number of herbs that should not be taken internally or burned close to pregnant women, you do have to be cautious. Herbs should be kept away from small children, as any dosage could be toxic.

If in doubt, use culinary herbs in small quantities and check in a good herb book or with a pharmacy about suitability and dosage.

Hopefully, as we do grow and use herbs more, so future generations will become more knowledgeable and able to recognise growing herbs and know their properties, both healing and magickal.

Herbs to avoid in pregnancy

This is not a comprehensive list but does mention herbs I haven't used in this book. Avoid: Aloe vera, angelica, autumn crocus, barberry, basil, caraway, cayenne, cedarwood, clary sage, fennel, feverfew, golden seal, hyssop, juniper, male fern, mandrake, marjoram, myrrh, parsley, penny royal, poke root, rosemary, rue, sage, southernwood, tansy, tarragon, thuja, thyme, wintergreen, wormwood, yarrow.

Other conditions such as heart problems, raised blood pressure, diabetes and weak kidneys make it unwise to use some herbs internally. So check with a herbalist or good book if you intend to use herbs medicinally or handle them for prolonged periods and have a chronic medical or serious condition.

The history of herbs

Herbs have been used medicinally and for magick in many different cultures and ages. Indeed, the two functions ran parallel until the 17th century and in the modern world are moving closer again. The first evidence of herbs being used for magickal purposes was discovered by an American anthropologist in 1960 at a 60,000-year-old Neanderthal burial site in a cave in the Zagros Mountains of Iraq. Analysis of the soil in the grave around the human bones revealed large quantities of eight species of plant pollen, including yarrow and groundsel. It seems likely that the body was buried with herbs to protect and empower the person after death.

Healing herbs have been used for at least 4,500 years in China, and in Ancient Egypt, herbal remedies and magickal rituals in administering them went hand in hand.

Herbalism has always primarily been the medicine and magick of ordinary people, the lore passed down orally through village wise women to their apprentices and by grandmothers to their own families. In Western Europe and Scandinavia, the witch burnings from the 15th to the 17th centuries, meant that many village wise women died with the resulting loss of what had been mainly an oral herbal tradition. However, in remote areas of Wales, Ireland and Brittany, secret remedies have survived and are still handed down through the generations (some suggest they go back as far as ancient Druidic magickal lore).

The most famous herbal book on sale today is still *Culpeper's Complete Herbal,* written by Nicholas Culpeper, the 17th-century astrologer, physician and parliamentarian. It contains effective magickal, herbal remedies, as well as planetary associations.

The deities of herbs

Being a more homely art, herbalism has not attracted many deities. Those I have discovered are female and all are regarded as powerful magicians. In Ancient Egypt the mother goddess, Isis the goddess of enchantment was believed to endow all medicinal knowledge, based on herb lore.

The Celtic goddess Airmid was the Irish healing goddess of medicinal plants. The daughter of the god of medicine, Diancecht, Airmid cared for the grave of her brother Miach and on this all the herbs of the world grew. As she cut them, each described its healing properties. Myths tell how her father destroyed this knowledge and many of the herbs, and this may be a symbolic reference to the appropriation of healing by male physicians in more patriarchal times.

Folklore from Brittany and Wales tells of the magickal cauldron of the crone goddess Cerridwen in which she brewed magickal herbal elixirs that granted immortality and rebirth. We know also from legend that nine young Druidesses created special initiatory brews in a cauldron at the ancient Pentre Ifan cromlech (a gigantic stone table over a long barrow used for ceremonial burials) near Tenby in Wales. Here Druidic initiations involved being reborn from the tomb beneath the great stone table. The initiates took three drops of the liquid and the rest was cast on the ground.

In the Slavic tradition, Kupula was goddess of water, sorcery and herbal lore. Her followers would cast offerings of flowers on water as they invoked her powers; since they were also healers, they helped to develop and preserve knowledge of magickal plants and herbs today.

Many herbs were dedicated in Christian times to the Virgin Mary. These were often once linked with pagan goddesses whose worship the Virgin Mary replaced. For example, in Iceland a wispy plant once called Freyja's hair after the Norse goddess of love and beauty became known after Christianisation of the land as our lady's hair. Mullein is called in many places including the UK, our lady's candles, because once its stem was dried, tipped into tallow and lit. White-spotted leaves such as lady's milk thistle or holy thistle are said to have been created as the Virgin's maternal milk fell on them. In Germany, lungwort, often called elsewhere Bethlehem sage, is called our lady's milkwort, with its green and white-spotted milky leaves whose flowers change from blue to pink as they blossom.

Using enchanted herb salt

Salt is naturally protective and can be sprinkled over thresholds or used in floor washes to keep you and your home safe. It is also associated with prosperity and good health rituals (see my *Complete Book of Spells* in Further reading).

However, salt into which herbs have been blended gives both the salt and the herbs additional potency. Blended empowered salt amplifies both the properties of the salt and the herbs to give a concentrated burst of power and/or protection.

You can buy ready-made herb salts, notably garlic, onion (a herb of Mars), parsley, caraway and celery seeds. If you empower herb salt jars or indeed any jars of herbs in your kitchen before use (see the next page), the energies will spread throughout the home – and as a bonus make mealtimes more harmonious.

You needn't be limited to the herb salts you would use in cooking, though you should of course keep only the culinary-friendly ones where people will add them to food. You can make a whole range of empowered salts, clearly labelled for different needs. Empty dried herb and spice jars are excellent for storage.

Empowered herb salt can be used in a number of ways in rituals or in everyday life.

* Use different herb salts to represent the earth element on your altar in order to focus specific spells (for example, a mint or basil salt made for a prosperity spell and a rosemary salt for passion).
* Add a pinch of herb salt to spell bags to kick-start the predominant quality (see page 139), for example sage salt as well as ordinary sage mixed with other herbs for abundance.
* Use the culinary-friendly herb salts in cooking. As you add the salt and stir the dish or turn cooking meat, chant the purpose for which you are using the herb; for example, garlic salt if the family is undergoing a crisis or one member is facing an external threat.
* Leave very finely ground empowered salt in a cruet on the table at mealtimes to draw the family or friends together
* Sprinkle a few empowered grains of herb salt into a beeswax candle (you can buy beeswax candles naturally dyed in many different colours, see Colour and Insect

magick, pages 258–65 and 241–43). As you do so, name what it is you desire to increase in or to cleanse from your life. For example, thyme salt is a natural luck- and health-bringer and a purifier of fears and all harm. The flame will sparkle and spit. When you blow out the flame, the herbs will settle in the melted wax and make your candle fragrant next time it is lit. Be careful not to use too much salt and avoid garlic as this smells horrible when burned.

* Add just a pinch of sage or basil herb salt to a make a protective floor/doorstep wash with any domestic cleaner (traditionally a pinch of pepper is added as well). Use very hot water to dissolve it and stir nine times clockwise defining the protection your home needs. A lemon-, eucalyptus- or pine-based product is excellent (or you can add a few drops of essential oils to plain hot water). Sage and basil will attract prosperity to your home as well.

* Carry a twist of empowered basil or mint herb salt in silver foil or greaseproof paper in the glove compartment of your car to avoid accidents and road rage against you, especially if you are travelling (mint herb salt is good with lamb or in salad dressing if you don't overdo the mint). Tarragon salt twists can be put in your office desk or briefcase to help your career or job hunting; twists of basil salt are also good for fidelity, so slip one in a tiny waterproof bag in your partner's wash bag when he or she is going away (this is not suitable for international journeys as customs may be unsympathetic).

* Finally, salt with very finely chopped dried nettles (you can often buy powdered or finely chopped dried nettles from health stores) is perhaps the most protective mix of all. Sprinkle some outside doors and under outside window ledges when you go away to deter intruders or at night if you are alone in the house and are nervous. As you sprinkle it, you can recite one of the traditional protective rhymes or make your own. My favourite is:

Drive away harm, keep away danger,
Make my home safe from false friend and stranger.

Making empowered herb salt

Timing: After dusk, especially near the beginning of the waxing or increasing moon cycle.

You will need: 350 g/12 oz/one small cup of the best quality sea salt you can get; 2 teaspoons of very finely chopped fresh herbs (you can use more than one) or 1 teaspoon of chosen dried herbs (see list on pages 176–83). Fresh is best but not essential.

A mortar and pestle. These are on sale everywhere in supermarkets and cookware shops. You can alternatively use a ceramic or wooden bowl and wooden or ceramic round spoon (like a Chinese soup spoon). You can use an old coffee grinder if you want a really smooth herb salt (and chant as you do it), but the mixing by hand is a powerful part of the spell. It is best to make the salt with a particular need in mind, about a week ahead. You can store the rest for future use and over the weeks you can build up your collection.

* Chop fresh herbs in advance or make this the beginning of the spell, reciting softly and continuously the purpose of the herb, for example:

Tarragon, tarragon, herb of dragons, give me courage.

* If using dried herbs you can, if you wish, use a small separate bowl and mix them in the same way first.
* Add the salt to the bowl, saying:

Salt of abundance, salt of protection, salt of healing, empower and protect, bless and bring harmony.

* Add the herbs, stating the purpose of the herb salt, for example:

I ask that this parsley will take bad luck away.

* Then grind the herbs and salt together thoroughly, reciting as a soft chant; for example, for parsley salt:

Take away misfortune and restore abundance.

* Chant and mix so that your words increase in speed and intensity and then fall away softly until you are silent. When you have finished say:

It is done.

* Now with the empowered salt still in the bowl, enchant it by holding your hands palms down flat over the bowl about 2.5 cm/1 in above it. You may be able to feel your hands tingling in anticipation.
* Move the right hand clockwise and at the same time the left hand anticlockwise (practise and you will soon get the rhythm) while reciting softly and mesmerically:

Be for me magickally, be for me powerfully, harmoniously and lastingly.

* When you feel the herb salt is filled with light and power, state in a few words why you have made the salt and end with:

Blessings be.

* Finally, press the salt down into a jar, seal it (make sure it is airtight as salt absorbs water) and leave the salt for about a week to settle. You can use it straight away if you need to, as, in a magickal sense, it is ready.
* Empower commercially prepared jars of herb salt in the same way. If you have several kinds, you can set them in a small circle and enchant them at the same time.

Making herb wishing powder

These are from a very old tradition common to both Eastern Europe and Mediterranean regions. The recipes travelled, with colonists, to America, Australia, New Zealand and South Africa, where indigenous herbs grew alongside those carried on ships from former homelands and were then planted as a symbol of home.

Jars of dried herbs are good for storing wishing powders. You only need a very small quantity of herbs as you can't save wish powders and should make them fresh every time you make the wish. Keep a note of the proportions in your nature journal.

Timing: If you are an early riser, this is a bonus as you should make the powder as early as possible in the day. Any day in the waxing moon cycle is ideal; the closer to the full moon, the more immediate the effect will be. Don't use the full moon itself or the dark of the moon, the two to three days at the beginning of the cycle when the moon is not visible.

If you are making a wish to get rid of something, such as excess weight or a relationship that holds you back, go for the waning moon and make your powder after dusk.

You will need: Two, three or more finely powdered dried herbs, spices or roots.

One or two drops of an essential oil: orange for abundance, marriage or fidelity; ylang ylang for love and passion; pine or juniper for new beginnings; frankincense for career, travel or success; myrrh for healing and protection or sandalwood which is multi-purpose. (See also the chapter on aroma magick on page 272 and the herb meanings on the following pages, as a number of these can be bought as essential oils.)

* First decide upon your wish and choose the herbs, spices or roots that meet the need. Use proportions according to the nature of the wish so that you have twice the amount of the major herb component compared with the total amount of the other herbs.
* Empower the herbs by mixing them thoroughly as you did your herb salt in a mortar and pestle; this time say the wish over and over again as you mix. Remember Dorothy in the *Wizard of Oz* wishing to go home, saying, 'There's no place like home' over and over again? That's the technique.
* Add just a drop or two of the essential oil so the mix is still quite dry, and repeat the wish nine times as you stir nine times clockwise.
* Use anticlockwise stirring for both herbs and oil if it is a wish to banish something negative or for protection.
* Place the mix into a small container with a lid.
* Because you will be scattering them in various ways, make sure that you use only pure herbs.
* When you have mixed and empowered your wishing powder, go outdoors. Or you can make the wish powder outdoors if the weather is fine.
* Scatter a pinch or two on to grass or soil for the power of the earth to make your wish happen in your daily life. Recite your wish.
* Toss a small handful into the air, so that the power of the air element will give movement to bring your wish from the thought plane. Recite your wish again.

* Drop just a few grains into either a candle flame (find a sheltered spot and place a metal tray beneath the candle holder) or on to an open fire, lighted barbecue or fire dish or bonfire. This provides the energy of the fire element to bring your wish to life. Recite the wish for the third time.
* Finally, sprinkle a pinch or two into water. You can use an outdoor tap or a bowl or bucket of water that you afterwards tip down a drain. This allows the energies and necessary opportunities to flow into your life by the power of the water element. Recite your wish for the last time.
* End the spell by saying:

The power is free by earth, air, fire and water. So may it be.

* You can repeat the wish weekly or monthly, on the same day of the week if possible (make new powder).
* Because you are using an earth power, you should also do something positive for the earth, like picking up litter or feeding the birds, to preserve the balance.

The properties of herbs

Below is an extensive list of the most traditional properties of different herbs. The only limits on herbal spellcasting are your imagination.

* You can use these in your spell bags as I described on pages 139–43, in wish powder or empowered salt (see above), in smudge sticks (see page 108) in herbal incenses (see page 96) or in your daily life as described at the beginning of this chapter.
* You can also substitute a particular herb for salt as the earth element in any spell or weave your own spells using fresh herbs.
* Growing herbs can be used as a focus for spells. For example you could plant coins in the earth round a growing money herb such as basil and burn a green or natural beeswax candle until it melts so the light shines on the growing plant.
* For travel, you could place a postcard or brochure of a place you would like to visit beneath a fennel plant in a pot in full moonlight to further travel plans (see Moon magick, page 433); then put the picture or brochure in a drawer until the next full moon, but water the fennel every day with water to which you have added a few drops of water you left out in the full moonlight. Each time you water the plant, name your chosen destination and ask that it may be possible for you to visit it.

Aconite: Healing, astral projection, invisibility to those who would do harm

Adder's tongue: All forms of healing, dream and moon magick; protection from spite

Agrimony: Protection, peaceful sleep; returns negativity to sender

Alfalfa: Prosperity, abundance, money

Allspice: Money, luck, healing, passion, fertility

Aloes, Wood: Love, spirituality, health, protection, good luck

Althea: Protects against negativity; draws spirit guides closer

Angelica: Banishes hostility from others; protection, especially for children and against attacks on the home; healing; brings energy, health and long life

Anise: Reduces fears of attack and anxiety about ageing and infirmity

Balm, Lemon: Love, success, healing, creative dreams, optimism, harmony

Balm of Gilead: Love, carried as love amulet; also for visions of other dimensions; protection, healing

Basil: Love; protection against intruders, accidents and attack; brings courage, wealth, fidelity, fertility, astral flying; conquers fear of flying in the real world; good against road rage

Bay leaves: Protection, psychic powers, healing, purification, strength and endurance, marriage, fertility, prosperity

Bergamot, Orange: Money, property; reduces addictions, fears and the hold of destructive relationships; brings new love

Betony/wood: Protection, purification, love

Bistort, also called snakeweed or dragon's wort: Fertility; deters malice in others and increases natural intuitive and divinatory powers (good for overcoming spiritual or psychic blockages)

Bladderwrack/kelp: Protection against accidents or illness, especially at sea; good for sea rituals and wind rituals; action; attracts money to the home; psychic powers

Blessed or Holy Thistle: Spirituality; protection against psychic attack and all dangers; good for women and babies

Bodhi: Fertility, protection, wisdom, meditation

Borage: Courage, psychic awareness

Bracken/broom: Healing, prophetic dreams, female fertility, rain-making among Native North Americans, unexpected money

Bryony: Money, protection, women and mothers

Buchu: Psychic powers, prophetic dreams

Buckthorn: Protection, exorcism, wishes, legal matters

Buffalo herb: Ambition, courage, promotion, power

Burdock: Protection against negativity; healing; good for love and sex magick; good luck

Cactus: Protection, purity, overcoming difficulties

Camphor: Purity, fidelity, health, divination

Caraway: Protection, passion, health, anti-theft, improves mental powers

Carob: Protection, health

Cascara sagrada: Legal matters, money, protection

Catnip: Love, beauty, happiness in home, fertility; good for cat magick

Cedar: Healing, purification, money, the home; for protecting tools and special artefacts

Celery seeds: Potency, money, protection, travel

Chamomile: Money, quiet sleep, affection, children and babies, gentle love and family, fertility; healing, increases self-love, especially after abuse; restores confidence after bad luck

Chicory: Removing obstacles, invisibility in hostile situations, receiving favours, melts frigidity both physical and mental

Cinnamon: Spirituality, success, healing, powers, psychic powers, money, love and passion

Cinquefoil: Money; protection; prophetic dreams, especially about love; peaceful sleep; good health

Cloth of gold: Telepathic communication with animals; wealth; self-confidence

Clove: Protection, banishing negativity, love, money, healing

Clover: Protection, money, love, fidelity, banishing negativity, success, good luck, employment

Cohosh, black and blue: Love; courage; protection; potency; restoring natural cycles and harmony to stressed modern lives especially for older women; fertility

Coltsfoot: Love, visions, peace and tranquillity, protects horses

Columbine: Courage, love, retrieves lost love

Comfrey: Safety during travel; money, health

Coriander: Love, health, healing; protects property; passion; ensures clarity of thought and creativity and relieves a troubled mind by promoting optimism. Traditionally, pregnant women ate coriander to ensure their unborn children were quick-witted and creative in life.

Cotton: Luck, healing, protection, rain-making, abundance, good for fishing magick

Cumin: Protection, especially of homes, property and cars; fidelity, exorcism

Curry: Protection, passion, ingenuity

Deer's tongue: Passion, psychic powers, escaping hazards

Devil's shoestring: Protection, gambling, luck, power, employment

Dill: Protection, keeping home safe from enemies and those who have envy in their hearts; also for money, passion, luck

Dittany of Crete: Contact with other dimensions, astral projection, leadership

Dock: Healing, fertility, draws money to home and customers to business

Dodder: Love, divination, knot divination

Dogwood: Wishes, protection, good for animal safety

Dragon's blood: Love magick, protection, dispels negativity, increases male potency; courage, confidence

Dulse: Passion, harmony and reconciliation

Eau de cologne mint: Protecting babies and children, enhances beauty

Echinacea: Strengthening, healing; enhancing personal intuitive powers; resisting pressures

Endive: Passion, love, house moves

Eryngo: Travelling luck and safety, peace, passion, love

Eyebright: Improves mental powers, psychic awareness, perception; unexpected career opportunities; known as the herb of truth; an important cleanser of illusion and less-than-honest influences; removes indecision

Fennel: Travel, courage, house moves, protection, healing, purification; especially protects animals

Fenugreek: Increased prosperity over a period of time, not only in resources but in health and strength; healing

Fern: Rain-making, protection, luck, riches, finding hidden treasure, youthfulness, good health

Feverfew: Protection, healing, calming addictions and anxiety; guards travellers and all who must go to unfamiliar or hostile environments

Flax: Money, protection, beauty, psychic powers, healing

Fleabane: Banishing negativity, protection, purity

Galangal: Protection, passion, health, money, psychic powers, dispelling hostility

Garlic: Psychic protection, healing, banishing negativity, passion, security from thieves; money

Gentian: Love, gentleness, power, secrets

Ginger: Love, passion, money, success, power

Ginseng: Love, wishes, healing, beauty, protection, passion, increases male sexual potency

Goldenrod: Money, divination, finding buried treasure, charm against rheumatism

Golden seal: Healing, money, self-confidence, leadership; creativity

Gotu kola: Meditation, wisdom, learning

Grass, Sweet: Protection, wisdom, purification, psychic awareness, all women's matters

Groundsel: Health, healing, kindness

Heliotrope: Banishing negativity, prophetic dreams, healing, wealth, invisibility in potentially threatening situations

Hops: Healing, peaceful sleep, money

Horseradish: Purification, banishing negativity, winning competitions

Horsetail: Repels spite and gossip, brings fertility and expansion of opportunity

Hyssop: Purification, protection, removing negative influences from property, precious artefacts and people

Irish moss: Money, luck, protection

Ivy: Protection, healing, marriage, fidelity, breaking possessiveness

Juniper: Banishes negativity, increases male potency, new beginnings, money, luck; used to purify homes and to protect against accidents, thieves and all forms of illness

Kava-kava: Psychic visions, protection, luck, magickal powers, especially highly regarded as magickal token in its native Hawaii and Polynesia

Knotweed: Binding, lovers or friends, for keeping promises; health

Lavender: Love, protection, especially of children; quiet sleep, long life, purification, happiness and peace, gentleness, mending quarrels, money and luck; banishes guilt

Lemongrass: Repels spite, protection against snakes; passion, increases psychic awareness, moves of all kinds; removes what is redundant in your life

Lemon verbena: Purification, love, family, gentleness, healing, friendship

Lettuce: Purity, protection, love, divination, sleep

Liquorice: Love, passion, fidelity, ambition, success, gambling

Liverwort: Protection, love, learning

Lovage: Love, luck, career, secrets

Lucky hand root: Employment, luck, protection, money, safe travel, gambling

Mace: Increases psychic awareness and mental powers; luck, money

Maidenhair: Beauty, love, mothers and babies

Male fern: Luck, love, potency

Mallow: Love, protection, exorcism of fear and psychic attack

Marigold: Protection, prophetic dreams, legal matters, increases psychic powers; growing love, marriage, money

Marjoram: Protection, love, happiness, health, money

Master wort: Strength, courage, protection, success

Mastic: Increases psychic awareness, visions of other dimensions, passion

Meadowsweet: Lasting love, happiness, reconciliation; increases peace within the self, between warring factions and globally

Milk thistle: Fertility, pregnancy, mothers and children, healing, care of animals

Mint: Money, love, increasing sexual desire, healing, banishing malevolence, protection (especially while travelling) against road rage and accident

Moonwort: Money, love; associated with phases of the moon

Mugwort: Strength, psychic powers, prophetic dreams, healing, astral projection; drives away danger and increases fertility; helps shape shifting and is protective on journeys of all kinds, especially from predators, human and otherwise.

Mulberry: Protection, strength, fertility, home

Mullein: Courage, protection, health, love and love divination, banishes nightmares and malevolence

Mustard: Fertility, protection, increases mental powers

Myrrh: Protection, banishing negativity, healing, spirituality

Myrtle: Love, fertility, preserving youthfulness, fidelity, marriage, peace, money

Nettle: Banishing negativity, protection, healing, passion

Oats: Money, security, stability

Oregon grape: Money, prosperity

Onion: Luck, money, love choices, health, protection

Orris: Love, protection, divination, positive change, prosperity; preserving what is of worth

Parsley: Love, protection, divination, passion, purification, abundance, good luck, takes away bad luck

Pennyroyal: Strength, protection, peace, banishes debt

Pepper: Protection, banishing malevolence, overcomes inertia and gives focus, positive focus for change

Peppermint: Purification, energy, love, healing, increases psychic powers

Pimpernel: Protection, maintains good health, young or new love, fertility

Pine: Healing, fertility, purification, money, new beginnings, returns hostility to sender; drives away all harm, both to the home and family and especially to newborn infants; good also to resist emotional blackmail, double-dealing and psychic attack

Purslane: Sleep, love, luck, protection, happiness

Quince: Protection, love, happiness

Ragweed: Courage, overcoming obstacles

Ragwort: Protection; good for fairie magick and the ability to see faeries

Rattlesnake root: Protection, money, good fortune for gambling

Rose: Love, enchantment; increases psychic powers; healing, especially babies, children and all who have been abused; love and love divination; good luck; protection

Rosemary: Love, passion, increases mental powers, improves memory and concentration, banishes negativity and depression, nightmares; also for purification, healing, quiet sleep; preserves youthfulness; tests and examinations

Rue: Healing, protects against illnesses of all kinds and speeds recovery from surgery or wounds, increases mental powers, love, enchantment; banishes regrets and redundant guilt or anger

Rye: Love, fidelity, prosperity, property

Saffron: Love, healing, happiness, raising the winds, passion, strength, increases psychic powers and offers second sight

Scullcap/skullcap: Money, employment, business partnerships and investment, unexpected gifts, love, fidelity, peace

Sage: Long life, good health, wisdom, protection, grants wishes, improves memory; justice, prosperity, career success, healing; examinations and tests

Sagebrush: Purification, banishing negativity, leadership, success, prosperity

St John's wort: Health, power, protection, invincibility, courage, banishes malevolence, earthly and otherwise from the home, strength, love and fertility, divination, happiness

Sandalwood: Protection, healing, banishes negativity, spirituality, contact with guardian angels, Higher Self, passion, wealth, an all-purpose herb

Sarsaparilla: Love, money, excitement, fun, spontaneity

Sassafras: Health, money, travel, creative ventures

Sesame: Money, passion, job opportunities

Slippery elm: Prevents gossip and malice; brings truth and integrity

Snakeroot: Luck, money, gambling, speculation; good against spite

Solomon's seal: Protection, banishes all negativity and hostility; wisdom, leadership, success, power

Sorrel wood: Healing, preserves good health; nature magick, secrets

Spanish moss: Protection, fertility, growth in any area of life, overcoming injustice

Star anise: Increases psychic awareness; luck, wishes

Tansy: Health, long life, conception and pregnancy, invisibility against potential danger

Tarragon: Associated with dragons and serpent goddesses; courage; new beginnings; shedding the redundant; career; prosperity; regeneration in any and every aspect of living; helps the user to focus on new targets

Thistle: Strength; protection against thieves, prolonged sadness and active hostility of thought or deed; speeds healing

Thyme: Health; healing; prophetic dreams; overcomes misfortune and brings luck, career opportunities; increased psychic powers; improves memory, love, purification, courage; long-term prosperity; connection with earth power; drives away fear and danger; good for tests and examinations

Turmeric: Purification, good luck, energy

Uva ursa: Psychic rituals, divination, female power, truth

Valerian: Love and love divination; quiet sleep; purification; protection against outer hostility, inner fears and despair; reconciliation; reuniting those parted by anger or circumstance

Vanilla: Love, passion, increases mental powers, fidelity, money, well-being, health and harmony, preserving youthfulness

Vervain: Love, transforms enemies into friends; purification, peace, money, prophecy, preserves youthfulness, peaceful sleep, healing; protects the home, attracting the blessings of nature spirits and wights who guard the land on which even urban homes are built

Vetivert: Love, breaks a run of bad luck; money, anti-theft, protects against all negativity

Vitex/chaste tree: Fertility of new ideas as well as for birth of child; purity and integrity

Wintergreen: Protection, healing, deflects hostility; reduces debts

Witch hazel: Mends broken hearts and relationships, finds buried treasure and underground streams; protection

Wolf's bane: Protection, invisibility against hostility; courage; loyalty, especially to family

Woodruff: Victory, protection, money; good news from afar or from people from the past

Yarrow: Courage, love, psychic powers, divination, banishes negativity; protection against illness and domestic strife; symbol of lasting marital happiness

Yellow evening primrose: Finding what is lost; healing, women, self-love and esteem

Yerba santa: Beauty, healing, increasing psychic awareness, protection.

3

TREE MAGICK

Sacred and magickal trees are found in the religions and mythology of almost every culture. Trees form the link between earth and sky, because they have their roots in soil and their branches in the air and were originally regarded as a creative form of the earth mother.

In early forms of religion, people believed that trees were themselves deities, a belief that gradually gave way to the idea that the spirits of deities or nature essences lived within the tree. In Japan, temples have been built around sacred trees for more than two thousand years. Here it is believed that Mononoke, the magickal life force, is concentrated in trees and rocks. The Japanese cryptomeria and the evergreen sakaki trees are especially rich in this force and are often used for building sacred shrines. The tree itself is incorporated into the central pillar so the indwelling power of the nature deity might bless the site.

In parts of Sweden until quite recently, a guardian tree, often elm, ash or lime, was planted close to farms or small settlements and it was forbidden to take even a leaf from this tree. Pregnant women used to embrace the tree to ensure an easy delivery.

Trees have also been associated from Africa to Eastern Europe with the spirits of fertility, who regulated rain, sunshine and good harvests. In Germany and France, in some agricultural areas, a large leafy branch or even a whole tree, decorated with corn ears or the last corn sheaf, adorns the last wagon of the harvest. It was traditionally set on the roof of the farmhouse or barn for a year to ensure future good harvests.

In India, sacred trees are still visited in order to ask for blessings, especially for fertility, from the indwelling spirit or deity; food and flowers are left at the tree shrine and offering ribbons are tied to the tree.

The Celtic Druids worshipped not in temples, but in groves of trees. These natural sites may have predated the Celts by thousands of years; and still in Wales, Brittany and Cornwall the trees are hung with ribbons, trinkets and petitions for healing and blessings.

Trees and creation

In the Norse tradition, Yggdrassil, the world tree, supported the nine realms of existence. At the top was Asgard, the home of the Aesir, the principle deities, led by Odin and his consort Frigg. This level also contained Vanaheim, the kingdom of the wind, fertility and sea gods, with whom the Aesir fashioned an uneasy peace, and Alfheim, home of the light elves. On the middle level was Midgard, the land of the humans. They shared this level with Jotunheim, the land of the frost giants and Nidavellir, the realm of the dwarves, who guarded their treasure and made artefacts for the deities. The lowest realm was divided between Niflheim and Hel, realms of the dead and Svartalafheim, home of the dark elves.

In Eastern Europe as well as in Asia the mythological world tree was considered the axis of the world with the pole star at the top. Shamans, the magickal priests or healers of indigenous peoples worldwide, climb this tree in a trance to reach other realms. Look up through the branches of a very tall tree on a starry night and you will see how this belief came into being.

The tree appears in numerous creation myths. In one Maori legend, the tree was the first thing to appear at creation and on it grew countless buds that contained all created life. A number of Native North American creation myths tell how the first humans climbed pine or fir trees from the underworld and broke through on to the earth. In Viking myth the first man was fashioned by Odin and his brothers from an ash (Aesc) and the first woman from an elm tree (Embla). The gods found the trees while walking on the seashore.

Creating a magickal tree

You can create your own, albeit more modest but nevertheless magickal, world tree in your garden.

Although I only have a small garden, in the centre I have a magickal tree that I use to circle round for spells and rituals and as a focus of power. It changes its energies according to the seasons and I sit close to it in sun, moon and starlight (see Magick of the spheres and seasons, pages 403–37) to absorb their different powers.

You can use any tree or a large bush as long as it has plenty of branches. Indoors, you can use a large ornamental tree or bush. Alternatively, use large, stripped-wood branches indoors or set them in soil. Wherever it is located, your magickal tree acts as a protective force to repel harm from your property.

You can start the tree with just one or two items. You will need some of the following:

✴ A witch ball or coloured-glass fishing float that reflects the garden and shines in sunlight. These are both protective and empowering. Witch balls resemble huge

Christmas baubles and come from the American folk tradition. You can make one by painting a glass sphere with metallic paint or buy one from a New Age shop or website. You can also find them sold as disco balls in gift stores.

* Fishing floats made of transparent glass are on sale in antique stores or garage sales, but increasingly in gift shops and houseware stores. Hang two or three of these from the tree. I have a rope with three fishing floats, each of a different coloured glass on my tree.

* Mirrors. These need only be small to reflect the flow of the life force round the garden and repel all harm. You can use ordinary round mirrors or Chinese lucky Bagua mirrors that display the old Chinese symbols for eight natural forces that together energise the universe and our lives. Convex ones that curve outwards are especially protective.

* Outdoors, nets of seeds and nuts or fat balls bring wild birds to the tree. This is especially important if the tree itself is not living.

* Symbols of fertility and prosperity. Fill small raffia baskets with long handles with coins, sparkling crystals like yellow citrine and clear crystal quartz or dried herbs like sage, rosemary and thyme that bring abundance to the garden and your home. You can often buy ornamental baskets set with wooden or ceramic fruits and flowers. Look in ethnic stores. I have a Chilean fertility basket given to me by Adela, a dear friend who now lives in Scotland.

* Small metal birds (you can sometimes buy them made of recycled metal). They will gleam in the light and encourage the circulation of positivity.

* Feathers on cords to encourage positive change and the free-flowing life force.

* Seasonal flowers, again especially important if the tree itself is not living. These can be weaved into circlets (see Flower magic, pages 162–65) or used as garlands secured with twine. You can use the magickal meanings given in the flower magick chapter, for added significance. Keep these fresh and replace regularly.

* Sun catchers, crystals or polished glass stones on chains.

* Ribbons tied on the tree for different wishes. Secure the ribbon with three knots on to the tree and make your wish. Use ribbons that are not synthetic.

* Use the following list when choosing the colours of items to put on to your magical tree:

Blue: Justice, career, travel and house moves

Brown: Animals, property, finances and officialdom

Green: Love and fidelity, for gradual increase in health, alternative healing, prosperity and to heal the planet

Orange: Creativity and fertility

Pink: Children, new or first love, peace, peaceful dreams and reconciliation

Purple: Psychic awareness, peace, alternative healing and for protection

Red: Passion and change

Yellow: Learning and anything that needs to happen fast or temporarily in your life; also for conventional healing

Making the tree a place of power

Outdoors, your tree will be naturally cleansed and empowered by the weather, and if some of the items get battered, don't worry. However, you may wish initially to cleanse and empower the tree and any artefacts on it at the first full moon after it has been created. You can do this by smudging round the tree with a smudge stick made of a bundle of tied and dried herb sticks (see pages 117–19). I summarise the basic technique here:

* Light one end of the smudge stick and let the flames die down, then gently blow on the end until it glows red and you have a stream of smoke. You can use your other hand to fan the smoke. Smudge sticks are generally held in your power hand.
* If indoors, be careful about sparks and ventilate the room. Also try to stand where you can see the moon or at least the sky through the window. Indoors, you can substitute a sage or pine incense stick if you wish.
* To cleanse and empower the tree, stand facing the tree at about five paces distance. Raise your smudge stick upwards to the sky and downwards to the earth.
* Walk nine times clockwise round the tree, making alternate clockwise and anticlockwise spirals of smoke, high and low, stamping your feet as you move and chant.
* Relax and enjoy the experience. Let your feet carry you, often in a spontaneous spiralling step movement, as you connect with earth energies and your hand weaves smoke patterns. Work barefoot if possible as you have sensitive energy centres or chakras in the soles of your feet.
* Say continuously until you have made nine circuits:

Empowering tree, be for me, strength and healing. Keep away harm, guard what is dear, and keep love near.

* You can repeat this ritual whenever you add something new to the tree or before using it as the focus for a personal spell or chant. Re-empower every third full moon (see also how to combine this ceremony with drawing down the moon, page 429).

Trees and magick

Each tree species carries strength and healing, though obviously longer standing trees with deep roots and spreading branches have greater repositories of energy. Each kind of tree also has its own unique powers. These you may associate with the kind of nature essence dwelling in that species or more abstractly with the qualities filtered through different kinds of wood.

Hold a crystal pendulum close to different trees and you will feel in your hands and body, amplified by the crystal, the differing tree strengths. For example, a redwood may make you feel confident and a willow, dreamy and intuitive. Note these feelings in your nature journal along with any images or words that come into your mind.

There are variations in intensity even with different trees within the same species. Take time to explore these energies and to visit forests (children love them) to get yourself attuned.

An arboretum or botanical garden is a good place to start if you are not familiar with trees. Buy a small tree book to carry with you so you can identify trees wherever you go, even in cities.

Using the magick

* You can use trees in magick in countless ways, the most basic by touching a tree with both hands, palms flat against the trunk and asking for its particular powers to enter you (see the tree spell for strength and courage, page 192). This is another way of tuning into the different strengths of various trees.
* Collect twigs from different trees or small hand-carved items made of the different woods and use them as charms to bring the powers you need into your life.
* You can empower these with salt, incense, candle flame or water if you wish, though the natural wood is already intrinsically powerful.
* Craft fairs are an excellent source of small hand-carved items, as are ethnic stores that give a fair price to crafts people.
* Carry a different wood when you need its particular strength.
* You can also burn incenses and oils made from different trees (where possible, use natural plant products) and state aloud nine times the power you seek from the tree fragrance as you write your need in the air with the smoke from an incense stick.
* You can eat seeds, nuts and fruits from different trees or use products made from the blossoms in your bath to absorb the magickal strengths into your life. Natural tree, as well as flower and herbal, products used in the kitchen give your home protection and harmony — and are much better for the environment than many of the alternatives.
* Finally you can burn two or three of the woods in a fire dish, barbecue or open fire to release the qualities you need. Create chants or a simple phrase or two incorporating the names of the chosen trees and what you seek from them.

The properties of trees

Below is an extensive list of the properties of different trees. See pages 190–92 for information on how to use these properties in spells.

Alder: Prosperity, security, stability, house moves

Almond: Abundance, prosperity, fertility and love without limits

Apple: Fertility, health, love and long life

Ash: Expansion of horizons; travel, especially by sea; courage, healing, strength prosperity

Aspen: Clear communication, good news from afar, eloquence, protection against theft, healing

Avocado: Increasing the desire of someone for you, growth of beauty in self or environment

Bamboo: Protection, especially of household boundaries and against the negative thoughts of others; good luck, especially in money matters

Banana: Fertility, male potency, prosperity

Banyan: Good luck and optimism

Bay: Fidelity, marriage, preservation of family, home, pleasant dreams, abundance

Beech: Knowledge, formal learning, positive change

Birch: Cleansing, health, new beginnings, protection of young children and animals

Boxwood: Discovering hidden treasure, new sources of income, developing forgotten talents, unexpected good fortune

Cedar: Good luck, fidelity in love, mature relationships

Cherry: New love, increasing divinatory abilities, fertility

Chestnut: Abundance, expansion of opportunity, employment

Chestnut, Horse: Money, healing, courage

Coconut: Fertility, motherhood, the flow of new life and energies; gives protection against all negativity, especially psychic attack

Cypress: Long life, healing and comfort in sorrow

Dogwood: Clear focus and determination, tests and examinations

Elder: Increases clairvoyance; overcomes negative feelings; healing; good for older women

Elm: Tree of quiet sleep, of family love and giving and receiving in equal measure

Eucalyptus: Cleansing, healing, clarity of thought, overcoming obstacles and misunderstandings.

Fig: Wisdom, creativity, fertility, harmony and balance

Fir: Birth and rebirth, new beginnings, cleansing, unexpected gifts and money

Hawthorn: Courage, marking boundaries, purification, protection, male potency, cleansing and protection

Hazel: Wisdom, justice, good luck, fertility, knowledge and inspiration, psychic powers.

Holly: Protection, especially of the home against all negativity and harm; overcoming impossible odds, persistence; also a tree for money and material gain

Ivy: Fidelity, married love, committed relationships, restoring lost love

Juniper: Protection against all negative forces, purification, prosperity, new beginnings, justice

Larch: Protection, especially against thieves; optimism

Laurel: Protection from illness; success and realisation of ambition; winning through in spite of difficulty

Lime/linden: Justice, co-operation with others, partnerships of all kind, dealing with officialdom

Mango: Health, permanence, lasting happiness

Maple: Long life, health of children, fertility, riches of all kinds, pleasure

Myrtle: Stable relationships, married love, fertility, matters concerning young people; also preserving youthfulness; peace, money

Norfolk Island pine: Assurance that you and your family will never go without the necessities of life

Oak: Knowledge, power, independence, confidence, success, courage, prosperity and potency

Olive: Peace, mending of quarrels; forgiveness, especially of our own mistakes; abundance, healing and fertility

Orange: Love, abundance, fertility, marriage, passion, luck and money

Palm: Fertility, potency, energy, starting again, rejuvenation

Pear: New life, health, girls' and women's needs, fertility

Peach: Marriage, pregnancy and birth, abundance, happiness, fertility, wishes and long life

Pine: Ending destructive relationships or habits; cleansing negativity; friendship in adversity, knowledge, protection from all harm, money

Redwood: Ambitions, limitless potential, success, spiritual growth, focus, courage, strength, concentration and increased mental acuity

Rowan/mountain ash: Protection of the home, intuition, increasing psychic powers, healing

Silver banksias: Protection of all kinds, allowing one to let go of sorrow, grief and destructive habits or relationships

Sycamore: Protection and the granting of wishes; increasing influence over others and situations

Tamarind: Love, especially new love and the rebuilding of trust

Vine: Rebirth and renewal, joy, ecstasy, passion, good luck in games of chance

Walnut: Prophetic powers, prosperity, health, increase of mental powers, fertility, granting of wishes

Willow: Intuition, moon magick, healing, prophetic dreams, making wishes come true, increasing psychic energies, understanding the emotions of others

White mangrove: Nurturing self and others, being sensitive, intuitive, caring, balanced and in touch with the life force

Yew: Endings, of new and good things coming out of the old, of permanence, aims that are slow to come to fruition, enduring strength, what is of worth, union between two people after difficulty

Tree spells

Tree spells are among the oldest in existence because tree spirits and deities formed the earliest kinds of worship. The tree also represents slow but sure growth from the smallest beginnings, fertility, strength and endurance, shelter from wind and rain (and so protection) and permanence – all qualities that humans have always wanted in their lives.

A tree spell for protection of self and the home

There are a number of variations of this traditional ritual. Especially in Scandinavia and Germany, red is a colour of protection and was the colour of Thor/Thunor, the thunder god whose magickal tree was the oak.

Trees are believed to stand guardian over homes. If you don't have one near your house, if you live in a potentially dangerous area or live alone and feel vulnerable indoors, you can use leaves to transfer tree power and as a portable symbol of protection. This spell is very effective for creating a psychic shield round yourself and your home.

Since the spell uses red leaves, it is easiest in autumn, but copper beech and red maple are just two trees with naturally red leaves. If you walk round an arboretum or ornamental garden, you will find a number of different species.

Timing: As the sky reddens at sunset

You will need: Three red leaves. Always remember to thank the tree even for a few leaves and do something small for nature, when you have time, in return for the power given. If you can't find any red leaves, use three sprigs of any tree (oak is very effective) with a few leaves still on each stem. Tie the stems together with red wool or thread in three knots before you begin.

Any single tree essential or fragrance oil such as birch, cedarwood, cypress, laurel, pine or sandalwood.

A small red scarf or circle of fabric.

* Work in the open air, if possible close to the tree from which you take the leaves or if not where you can see the sunset. If you need to be indoors, light a red candle.
* Pick the red leaves, if possible close to or at the beginning of the spell.
* Set them on the red cloth and very carefully anoint each leaf or sprig with a drop of oil, saying as you do so, over each leaf:

> *Leaves three,*
> *Grant to me*
> *Protection this night*
> *That from thy sight*
> *Harm and malice,*
> *Darkness and danger*
> *Fears and intruding stranger*
> *May flee.*

* Fold the scarf or cloth round the leaves and knot the top three times to make a bag. Repeat the chant three more times as you make the bag.
* Hang the bag on the back of the main house door or your bedroom door if you sleep alone and are anxious.
* Repeat the spell when the leaves have crumbled or every three months, whichever is sooner.

A tree spell for strength and courage

You can carry out this spell with an oak, ash or redwood, which are traditionally associated with courage and strength. But all trees are intrinsically powerful and so if you have a favourite grove of trees or piece of woodland, you can choose any tree you especially like. You could also use your magick tree.

By adapting the words you could, alternatively, use the tree spell to heal yourself, especially if you have a debilitating or chronic condition or suffer a lot of pain.

There are lots of ways we can return strength to trees, for example by picking up litter in woodlands, planting saplings in memory of loved ones in local woodlands on tree-planting days or campaigning for the preservation and regeneration of forests.

Timing: If possible, as sunlight filters through the leaves, but any bright morning

You will need: A chosen tree. If you carry out the spell in an unfamiliar place, touch a number of trees and feel which one seems receptive to your energies.

A red (for strength and courage) or pink (for healing) biodegradable ribbon – not synthetic.

* Touch your chosen tree with both hands at about waist height so that you can comfortably place your upright outstretched palms against the tree to create a circuit. Loop the ribbon round your power hand.
* Your power hand will send your energy into the tree and it will flow out through your other hand, through your body and in again.
* Stand for a few moments and allow the connection to flow.
* Then say softly:

You are strong. Give me strength/courage/healing if it is right to be.

* You may be rewarded by a gentle breeze through the trees, a sudden shaft of sunlight, a pleasant buzzing vibration through your hands or a sense of peace and rightness. If the tree feels unresponsive, thank the tree nevertheless and try another one.
* When you feel the connection, press your hands more firmly against the trunk and allow the power to flow. Your whole body will feel more alive and energetic, and you will be filled with confidence, certainty and maybe even joy and harmony.
* When you sense the power ebbing slowly, remove the pressure until your palms are just lightly resting against the trunk.
* Thank the tree for its gifts and tie the ribbon round an accessible branch.
* Spend a few moments sitting against the tree looking up through the leaves. When you can, return the favour to nature.

4

GARDEN MAGICK

ardening dates back thousands of years to the first farming communities in Neolithic times, beginning in Europe and the Mediterranean around 6,000 BCE. About this time plants were first cultivated for food, and people began to grow vegetables.

In the Near East, farming began as early as 10,000 BCE. Because people were able to stay in one area, as opposed to the earlier hunter-gatherer way of life, they grew not only crops but herbs for medicines and spices. Wealthier people, and temple and palace gardens, had areas for flowers and recreation as well as ornamental ponds containing fish.

In Ancient Egypt from about 3,000 BCE, flowers from the temple and palace gardens were regularly used in ritual processions, as offerings to the deities and ancestors, and were offered to guests at festivities. They were also buried in tombs that their fragrance might animate the Ba, the hawk-headed spirit within the mummy.

To the Romans, their gardens were as important as their houses and formed the focus of social events, even in cooler climates like Britain. The *hortus rustica;*, or the kitchen garden, was next to the living quarters, which were often built around an ornamental courtyard with a square of open patios called the atrium. In the garden typically there was also a large pool lined with stone and tiles. Bedding trenches first devised by Pliny the Elder were dug for growing roses and other ornamental flowers such as lilies. Flowering trees were entwined around timber framework just as in modern gardens, while topiaries were made in the shapes of animals.

Once Christianity was established in Europe and the Mediterranean, monastery gardens appeared from around CE 500 and flourished through the ages. Indeed many of these medicine gardens can still be seen even where the abbey or monastery is in ruins throughout Europe and Scandinavia. Bishops' palaces from the Middle Ages, like the one in Canterbury, have survived in almost original form today and have elaborate flower and water gardens to aid, it was said, contemplation of paradise.

Gardens of paradise

The word 'paradise' means garden and is derived from the Persian *pairidaeza*. Heaven is described as a wonderful garden and those who experience near-death encounters, children as well as adults, frequently describe flower-filled gardens with fountains and wonderful fragrances.

The Bible tells that humanity was created in the Garden of Eden, which has recently been identified at Qurnah, near the southern borders of Iraq at the delta of the Tigris and Euphrates. It still contains Adam's tree.

Another garden became one of the seven wonders of the world: the hanging gardens of Babylon, famous for its huge waterfalls and stones columns, fabulous plants and flowers. The date of its creation has been estimated around 600 BCE. It was green all the year even in such an arid region because the water from the River Euphrates was transported in special pumps that could carry water to great heights. The gardens were created by King Nebuchadnezzar for his wife, Amyitis, who missed the green mountainous land where she had grown up. We know of the gardens from the Greek writer and geographer Strabo who was writing in the first century BCE.

Oriental sacred gardens

To the Chinese, the wider natural landscape in miniature, for example the garden of a house, offered escape from the bureaucratic, ordered world in which people even hundreds of years ago were forced to live.

Most popular were tiny gardens in basins that were kept in offices and indoors. It was believed that rocks and mountain pines in miniature held the essence of actual mountains and tree-covered crags.

The miniature gardens, like their larger counterparts, represented to the Chinese a temporary glimpse of paradise. The miniature gardens were often made of crystals, notably jade, itself a stone associated with immortality.

For Taoists, followers of one of the early Chinese religions, perfection and harmony existed within the natural world. For others, such heavenly bliss resided in alternative worlds, like the real one but without defects, disease and decay. In both cases the garden and the miniature garden offered the possibility of seeing such paradise while still on earth.

In China and Japan today, gardening is still an expression of divinity and a way of connecting with divine power, both through the creation and care of a garden and by spending time looking at it. In Japan, *tsukiyama*, or hill gardens, contain water, including ponds and streams, balanced by artificial hills, bridges and paths with carefully landscaped flowers and trees to re-create in miniature a natural landscape. *Karesansui*, or dry gardens, use rocks, gravelly sand and sometimes moss to symbolise a scene of mountains, seas and islands.

Zen or contemplation gardens, first created in China in the sixth century, came to Japan from China with the spread of Buddhism and have greatly influenced karesansui. They have been recreated in cities in America and Europe as well as in their original lands, as a counter to modern urban pressures.

Miniature Zen gardens, called *bonseki*, are created in dishes. In these tiny gardens too, stones and sand or gravel are used to represent respectively mountains and water. You can buy these tiny gardens in garden centres, sometimes with air plants and ceramic Oriental figures, but you can easily make rock and gravel areas in your own garden or a miniature one in a large, flattish dish.

Making a dry garden

A dry garden should include some of the following elements:

* Sand or gravel areas, rippled to represent the sea or bodies of water, such as lakes. You can make undulating pathways for rivers. Use gravel rather than sandpit sand.
* Single, pointed rocks for mountains, rounder ones for hills.
* Bridges over the sand/gravel water to connect the areas and act as a bridge between dimensions.
* Stepping stones in groups of five to form a pathway to divinity and slow down walkers or the eye if you are sitting outside looking in.
* Five stone balls or cylinders (you can often pick these up at garden centres) to represent earth, air, fire, water and the heavenly realms.
* Five islands made of flat, oddly shaped rocks to signify the Isles of the Blessed or immortality. Traditionally, one is crane-shaped and one turtle-shaped.
* If you feel that this is too sparse for you, add areas of bamboo, small bushes, well-shaped small trees or clumps of small, pastel-coloured flowers if you wish. In your miniature version, bonsai trees are excellent. Add also jade crystals (pointed ones traditionally signify mountains) or one of the purple, blue or green fluorites.
* You need only make a small area that you can either walk in or sit and look at from outside.
* If you are walking in the garden, have a flat stone near the entrance where you can make offerings of seeds for the birds, or position a dish of jade crystals or small pots of flowers.
* At the entrance to the garden there is often a rippled sand and rock area representing a lake, but you can mark the entrance by a real small water feature, so combining the two kinds of garden.
* Use your garden to walk the pathways, either actually or in your mind. You can use tiny Chinese lanterns or candles and, on a warm evening, sit with half-closed eyes and look at your magickal land. Go there at sunset or in the stillness before a storm.
* What should you do? What should you say? Nothing. Just breathe gently and in time your miniature indoor or outdoor garden will change into some well-loved actual landscape of mountains and water or an ideal you may have glimpsed in dreams or meditation. Inside magick, when the change in us comes spontaneously as we allow ourselves to be still and do nothing, say nothing and think nothing, is the hardest magick of all. But when you can do it, then more active magick also has greater meaning, as the external building of power mingles with the stillness within.

Creating magick in your own garden

Garden magick enables you to interact with nature within a contained area, so concentrating the natural forces and also combining the different energies of the plants you choose.

Plants are linked with cosmic forces and not only can you plant flower or herb beds or trees associated with different planets, but you can ensure better growth by planting and cultivating according to the moon phase and moon sign most favourable to the individual species. This knowledge has been known for thousands of years and still forms a core of modern gardening lore and also applies to harvesting.

It is believed by many gardeners that nothing happens by accident, even in a seemingly ordinary garden. If you are given a plant or ornamental tree by a friend or find that your mail order contains bulbs or shoots you were not expecting, these will give your garden unexpected colours or unusual foliage. These incomers will emit a lot of good energy when you weed near them, and may have healing properties that you or a family member need (see Herb magick, page 168).

When you go to a garden centre, walk around and you may notice either a species or particular plant that attracts you. Even though you walk away from it several times and the label says it could not grow in your kind of soil, you are drawn back. Buy it and, against all odds, it will thrive and prove to be just what you needed to fill an empty corner. If you don't buy it, you'll see the plant growing everywhere you go – until eventually you give in – and, as I have found, usually pay far more than the original price.

Pollen-rich flowers attract butterflies as well as bees and these are linked with nature essences. Dragonflies too are considered spirit forms, and even a small natural pond will draw them and their luck-bringing qualities to your garden.

As with Japanese Zen gardens, you can create a miniature garden with indoor planters in wood or ceramic in your office. In this way, you do not have pots of unconnected individual plants but rather an area where the energies flow together. Bottle gardens are excellent if space is limited, and candles can be set round it in the evening to create a mystical glow within.

Working with garden energies

* Whether you garden is well stocked, you are starting with very little or you are creating an indoor garden, you need to empower it. For empowering gardens, I am not keen on using candles or incense unless they are pure beeswax candles or incense made from just plant materials with no saltpetre.
* Smudge sticks, dried and tied bundles of sagebrush, cedar, pine or rosemary are excellent outdoors and offer both flame when lit and smoke, so combining fire and air elements. You can make your own (see page 117) or you can buy them ready made.
* If you have back and front gardens, you can empower both if you wish. If using a large indoor planter, set it if possible where full moon as well as sunlight will shine on it through a window or part-glass door to keep cosmic powers topped up.
* Prepare your water in advance by soaking one of the gardening crystals for eight hours in a bowl of rainwater left from dawn to noon. Do this in summer or for the eight lightest hours later or earlier in the year. This adds the element of earth to the water. Gardener's crystals include moss and tree agate, jade, green jasper, green, blue or purple fluorite, green calcite and rutilated quartz. Remove the crystal from the water and keep it safe for future empowering.

* Empower your garden either in sunlight before noon or in moonlight (any of the days leading up to the full moon during the second quarter of the moon) when you can see the moon in the sky. After a rain shower is ideal, but not essential.
* Set your smudge stick, with lighting materials, in a dish of sand so you can safely extinguish it. Also, prepare a bowl of the empowered water.
* First mark the corners of your garden or indoor area. In each corner bury a gardener's crystal, which need only be small, proceeding clockwise. As you do this, ask the nature essences living there to protect and bring life and growth to your garden.
* Next you need to honour the four directions and mark your boundaries. For an indoor or yard area, miniature trees and bushes are excellent and you only need one per side in the four main compass positions (use a compass or approximations).
* You can use any protective and luck-bringing plant for your area, such as bay (laurel), lemon trees, bushy sage, olive, hawthorn, conifers, lilac, palms, eucalyptus, orange trees, rosemary, sage, thyme or cactus. Green leafy bamboo is increasingly grown in European gardens and brings good fortune as well as guarding your home from physical, psychological and psychic harm.
* If you have an established garden, you can use smaller plants to slot in between the existing plants.
* Position each plant close to where the gardener's crystal is buried and for each, say:

May you be blessed and bring blessings.

* For each plant touch the earth and say:

By earth.

* Then sprinkle three drops of crystal water from the bowl on the plant and say:

By water.

* Finally, reach upwards with your index finger of your extended power hand and say:

By sky be blessed.

* Now light one end of the smudge and when the flame dies down blow gently until you see red sparks in the smudge and a stream of smoke begins. You can fan the smoke with your other hand (hold it in your power hand). Smudge round the perimeter of the garden or indoor plant area with the lighted smudge (or indoors with a natural incense stick in sage or pine).
* Move the smudge naturally with clockwise spirals downwards towards the earth and upwards to the sky, then downwards to the earth and so on. If you relax you'll get into the rhythm.

* Say continuously as a slow chant:

Powers of earth, our mother, powers of sky, our mother, enclose this place and make it sanctuary.

* Extinguish the smudge in the sand and spend time in your garden, enjoying it and doing little tasks that give you pleasure.
* Once a week, make garden crystal water and sprinkle your boundaries clockwise, saying:

May you be blessed and bring blessings.

Tapping into the power of the garden

Garden energies can be channelled to and from a garden. You can draw strength and healing from plants and also give these to a wilting or lifeless plant.

With a round, clear quartz crystal in each hand, you can energise any plants or trees that are not thriving. Keep two crystals in a dish outdoors or resting in the soil of your indoor planter for this purpose.

* Hold each crystal between two fingers and picture rays of gentle white light, like early morning sunlight, pouring downwards via the chakras or energy centres in the palms of your hands, on to the plant. For trees, hold the crystals so they lightly touch the trunk.
* Continue for a minute or two and wash the crystals afterwards under running water. Hold them up to natural light to dry.
* To receive energy from a healthy plant or tree, either hold your hands flat, palms downwards over a healthy plant about 2.5 cm/1 in away or press them upright against the bark of a tree.
* Leave your hands in place for two or three minutes, close your eyes and you will feel calmer but also full of life and hope.
* Thank the plant or tree. You may find a particular plant or tree becomes yours (see also the spell to find your guardian of the garden, page 202).
* In return, leave food out for the birds, hedgehogs or other small garden creatures. And make sure you have a small wild area for them, if possible.

Making a planetary garden

Even with a very small garden or a patio or indoor area you can create a planetary garden with different flowers, trees and herbs that will enable you at any time to draw upon the strengths of the planets. I list the various plants for each planet, but you need only use one or two plants for each. The associations I have given are traditional ones that work for me, but inevitably different practitioners regard the energies of a specific plant in different ways. So if, for example, heather is a plant of Mars rather than the sun for you, then go with what feels right. Indeed, I have changed some of the associations over the years as I have gained more experience and worked with different people who have shared their ideas.

In flower beds you can divide the different areas with small bricks, tiles or stones. I have used the seven traditional planets, but you can of course add Uranus, Neptune and Pluto if you wish and find the associations in books (see the Further reading section or the Internet). I've included, in common with modern gardening trends, lots of what were formerly called wildflowers, some of which are flowering herbs, as these are especially rich in natural powers. If you can't find the planetary association for a specific flower or plant, as a general rule you can go by colours.

The sun ☉

Use your sun plants for a pure injection of the life force, for improving or maintaining health, for good luck, for new beginnings of all kinds, for personal fulfilment, wishes and power, for self-confidence, for inventions and innovations and for any creative ventures.

Sun plants include: Acacia, angelica, ash, bay, buttercup, carnation, celandine, chamomile, forsythia, heather, juniper, lotus, marigold, Michaelmas daisies, mistletoe, olive tree, orange tree, palm, peony, rosemary, rue, St John's wort, sunflower, vine plants and any orange or golden yellow flowers

The moon ☽

Use your moon plants for matters concerning the home and family, mothers, children and animals, for fertility and for worries about ageing, for healing powers and for alternative healing methods, protection of all kinds, for increasing psychic powers and for keeping secrets.

Moon plants include: Bamboo, banana, black and blue cohosh, burdock, clary sage, coconut, dahlia, dog rose, eucalyptus, gardenia, jasmine, knotweed, lemon, lemon balm, lotus, marsh marigold, moonflower, orchid, pinks, poppy, saxifrage, snowdrop, stocks, water lilies, willow, wintergreen, any white or ivory-coloured flowers, especially small ones

Mercury ☿

Use your Mercury plants for money-making ventures and reducing debts, for taking examinations and tests, for conventional medicine and surgery, to receive expected good news, for all forms of communication, for improving memory and concentration, for selling or media work, for short-distance travel and house moves, for gambling and speculation, to guard against gossip and against those who steal your ideas or possessions.

Mercury plants include: Almond, caraway, cumin, daffodil, dill, eglantine or sweet briar, fennel, fenugreek, fern, fuchsia, iris, lavender, lemongrass, liquorice, lily of the valley, myrtle, narcissus, parsley, pomegranate tree, rosemary, tarragon, trefoil, valerian and any yellow flowers, especially small ones

Venus ♀

Use your Venus plants for attracting new love, deepening love and affection and for fidelity in long-term relationships, for increasing your inner radiance, for developing gifts and expertise in the arts, crafts and music, for mending quarrels and the slow but sure growth of prosperity or improvement in health. Also for fertility (like the moon), for women's health and for all matters concerning wildlife and the environment.

Venus plants include: Apple blossom, birch, bluebell, camellia, catnip, cherry blossom, coltsfoot, crocus, elder, elecampane, feverfew, forget-me-not, geranium, lilac, lily, magnolia, peach, periwinkle, pinks, rose, sorrel, star of Bethlehem, strawberry, sweet pea, tamarind, vanilla, vervain, violet, yarrow and any pink flowers

Mars ♂

Use your Mars plants for courage, assertiveness, positive competitiveness, initiating change and taking the initiative, for working towards independence or self-employment, for passion and the consummation of love and for physical strength.

Mars plants include: Anemones, barberry, basil, blessed thistle, borage, chives, coriander, cypress, dragon's blood, garlic, gentian, ginger, hibiscus, hollyhock, lupin, all mints, ornamental grasses, passionflower, pine, thistle, thyme, sweet tobacco, tulip and any red flowers

Jupiter ♃

Use Jupiter plants for gradual increase and expansion of opportunity, good luck, career prospects or obtaining promotion, for long-distance travel or house moves, for justice and legal matters, for partnerships of all kind, leadership, for honest dealings, long-term learning, wisdom and altruism.

Jupiter plants include: Anise, cedar, chervil, chestnut, chrysanthemum, cinquefoil, cloves, cornflower, dandelion, delphinium, dock, echinacea (purple cornflower), fig tree, fir and pine tree, honeysuckle, hydrangea, hyssop, lime tree/linden blossom, meadowsweet, moss, maple, narcissus, oak, polyanthus, rhododendron, sage, walnut and any blue flowers

Saturn ♄

Use Saturn plants for unfinished business, endings that lead to beginnings, all slow-moving matters and for accepting limitations, as well as for overcoming obstacles; also for addictions, compulsions and cutting destructive ties; property and financial matters; dealing with officialdom, slowing the outward flow of money and to encourage those who owe you favours or money to repay.

Saturn plants include: Bistort, comfrey, cypress, foxglove (be careful around children), gladioli, harebell, hibiscus, holly, hyacinth, ivy, lemon verbena, mimosa, mugwort, mullein, pansy, patchouli, black and white poplar, saffron/safflower, sloe bush, Solomon's seal, star flower, vetivert, wallflower and any purple flowers

Using your planetary garden

* You can dry the herbs and flowers from your planetary garden to make planetary incense (see page 106). You can mix planetary energies in proportion, for example two parts of the courage of Mars to one of the optimism of the sun and one of Saturn for strength. You can take a few of each kind, tie with string and hang upside down in a cool place (I use my covered glass patio). When they are dry but still fragrant (two or three weeks or less according to the plant, take off the flower or herb top and discard stalks. For an ever-ready supply, keep in a labelled dark glass jar with a teaspoon of orris root, if you wish, as preservative.
* Fill a small drawstring bag with dried planetary herbs and flowers and carry it as a talisman until the fragrance is gone.
* You can also have a small display of freshly cut planetary plants around your home or even on your desk. For example, you might pick a small bunch of Venus flowers or herbs when a difficult relative is calling in order to make the encounter gentle and loving. You could just choose one kind of plant, such as tulips for courage or a Mars selection to give yourself confidence. You can, of course, buy small pots or bunches of different planetary flowers for the same purpose (most are available all year round from florists or supermarkets).
* Alternatively, you can breathe in and absorb the energies of the different planets by touching a single flower, herb or tree to make the link. Picture the green light or flower colours entering your body as you gently inhale and sigh out through your mouth, your doubts, fears or exhaustion pictured as grey mist on the out breath.
* For balance, pick one flower or herb of each planet and keep them close to where you work or socialise in order to ensure a free flow of joy and harmony through your home and workplace.

A spell to restore health and energy

This spell is based on the ancient principle of exchange, that we offer a token gift to nature and in return can draw on her abundance. The seeds are scattered without conditions and so mother earth will use them as she sees best. Trusting her is vital, as then we can trust that she will help us.

You will need: Two or three packets of seeds that will grow into sunflowers or any bright yellow flower. A yellow or white dish for the seeds.

Timing: Any time during the waxing or increasing moon cycle as close to noon as possible. Sunday, the day of the sun, is a good choice. A sunny day, if possible.

* Stand as near to the centre of the garden as you can, preferably on soil. Alternatively, find a garden area in a park (not a really formal garden as the owners may object to you scattering seeds).
* Tip your seeds into the dish and face the direction of the sun or, if it is overhead, approximate south.

* Turn three slow clockwise circles, scattering half your seeds with your power hand, and saying:

So do I scatter new life and growth to be received by the earth, carried by birds or eaten by small creatures. I make this offering willingly. Do as you will, mother earth, with the seeds of life.

* Pause and face the sun or south again. Put down the dish and open your arms as high and wide as you can and say:

So do I ask for health and strength and life from mother earth as fair exchange and, as my pledge, I make my further offering.

* Repeat the actions and words as given in the two bullet points above.
* End by stating:

Blessings be.

* Look around for a small token from the earth, a feather, a white or smooth brown stone, a blossom or flower blown by the wind, but do not pick anything. If no gift is obvious, walk round the garden until you see something appropriate. Keep this in your crane or nature treasure bag (see page 71). Return it to the place you found it if you need to repeat the ritual, which you can do weekly if necessary.
* Spend some time in the open air after the spell and, if you feel strong enough, go for a short walk.

A spell to find your personal garden guardian spirit

Even the smallest garden or indoor plant area has a number of nature essences. In neglected gardens or public ones that are litter-filled they work very hard. Each outdoor area, even the humblest suburban plot, also has a guardian of the land who has chosen that garden to be its home. All nature is precious and the guardian of your garden cares as much about your plot as if he were lord of some stately palace garden.

You may even be lucky enough, if you created the garden out of a building site or it is a very old, established garden, to have a deva or higher nature essence (see page 483) present.

The garden's guardian spirit may be detected most strongly in a clump of herbs or flowers or in a bush, though the energy pervades the whole garden. Once you have identified the spirit's sanctuary, it may be the area to which you instinctively go to draw energy when you are tired or dispirited. What is more, you can strengthen the positive energies by making a small offerings table here.

Don't think of nature essences as friends (see Faerie magick, page 499) because they are primarily concerned with the plants and are made of natural forces and so are unpredictable. But if you care for your garden and nature generally, you will receive strength and healing – if not cosy chats.

First you must seek to make the connection.

You will need: A glass or crystal jug of garden crystal water (see page 198).

Timing: Twilight or as dawn is breaking

✱ Walk round the garden in silence three times in a clockwise direction, sprinkling water droplets over the plants. As you do so, say in your mind continuously:

> *Guardian of this land, I seek to know you. I pledge to care for this place and would make you tribute.*

✱ After the last circuit or when you have said the chant nine times, return to the centre of the garden and face the dawn or the dying light. Put down the jug and open your hands palms uppermost, arms bent and just above waist height, saying:

> *I ask now for a sign of your presence and your blessing.*

✱ You may be lucky and detect a sudden movement or a flash of light in one area of the garden, a bird call, or a bird that swoops down, a brilliant butterfly that appears and hovers or, at night, a huge moth. Occasionally you may hear a soft voice on a sudden breeze. The connection may be experienced as a vibration in your hands and feet so that you instinctively know where the guardian's special place is.

✱ If you experience nothing, be patient. We cannot summon nature essences at will and you should leave the spell a week before repeating. In that time, do what you can to make the garden extra beautiful, especially doing boring but necessary garden chores.

✱ When you do find the guardian's place, make a small, flat, stone altar, with two small bricks or squat stones supporting a small elongated stone, no bigger than an average tea tray.

✱ Whenever you pick flowers or herbs, leave one in a dish for the guardian. Keep a very large unpolished green calcite crystal or a smaller round jade that will be washed by the rain, and perhaps a tiny beautiful nature essence statue, a seashell or fossil.

✱ Keep the stone swept and tidy and it will form the heart of your garden.

PART 4

MAGICK OF THE ANIMAL KINGDOM

INTRODUCTION

Acording to Native North American belief, all life is the manifestation of the Great Spirit. And as the most recent creation, humankind has much to learn from the older and wiser forms of life. The spirits of animals and birds can act as guardians endowing those who seek to invoke their protection in magick or as power icons with their unique strengths and wisdom.

In creation myths from indigenous societies from Siberia to Polynesia, swimming animals and water birds assisted in forming the world – or as in Australian Aboriginal mythology, acted as the creating mother. Animals, birds, sea creatures and insects were not just made for the food and sustenance of humans as in Judaeo-Christian creation myths.

In tribes across North America, for example, it is told that the beaver helped the Great Spirit to build the land from the seas. He and the Great Spirit brought up all the mud they could carry from the primal waters to create caves and canyons, hills and tall mountains, where birds could fly freely. The Ancient Finnish creation myth of the exploding egg is similar to the more recent 'big bang' theory.

In Australian Aboriginal lore, the rainbow serpent, the mother of all, who existed before any other form of life, sacrificed herself to bring forth life. She asked the kingfishers, one of the first tribes, to come forth and to shoot an arrow at her head in order to allow the rest of creation to be freed. The rainbow serpent is still actively present in her creation, for as her rainbow scales flew into the air to become the colourful lorikeet tribe, the reflection of the colours became the rainbow in the sky as a continuing reminder that all life has a common source.

Another Australian Aboriginal creating mother is Eingana, whose sacred animal is the kangaroo. She is also described as a snake. Her children grew inside her but, though she swelled, she had no means of giving birth to them until the god Barraiya pitied her pain and threw a spear at her, enabling life to pour forth.

However, she survived the birth and still exists in the magickal dreamtime, a state like the astral plane, where all potential life exists and sends forth new species from time to time. She also brings death to her children. She holds a sinew of life joined to each creature and person, and when she lets it fall, they die.

Birds, animals and insects are therefore a rich source, not only for magickal spells, but for renewing our own connection with other species and the creating earth.

Some of the ideas in this chapter date back to 5,000 BCE, the date of a bird goddess statue that was excavated in Spain (see page 225), but they are equally relevant to modern life. For we have much to learn from the animal kingdom both spiritually and in terms of magick.

Above all, in a world weary of simulated experience, we can still marvel at a spider's web jewelled after rain or the first rainbow butterfly of summer as a promise of hope.

See Sea magick (pages 355–66) for information about sea creatures.

ANIMAL MAGICK

Animals have always been associated with magick because the first rituals were carried out by cave dwellers to attract animals to their hunting grounds and also to guide hunters telepathically to the creatures.

Among the Innu people and others in the far north of Canada and America who depend on the caribou (deer) migration for survival, ceremonies are held to seek the abundance of the caribou master of the animals. Before the hunt, the leaders dream of the route the herds will take. In preparation for the pre-hunt ceremonies, the wives of the hunters decorate caribou skin coats with the dream route. In this way the psychic connection between hunter and hunted continues.

Native North American people who still live primarily off the land pray to the migrating fish, birds and mammals to ensure that they return each year. These ceremonies may date back 40,000 years to the earliest inhabitants of the Americas who hunted now-extinct species of mammoth, bison and horse.

Like the caribou master, the first deities, the mistress of the herds and the horned hunter, provided rules for the wise hunters and leaders by means of instructions given in dreams or telepathically. These ensured the forest or land would not be over-hunted and that respect for the animals was maintained. Some of these laws were practical, such as not killing breeding females, while others had moral overtones. Even in later civilisations like the Ancient Greeks, Artemis, goddess of the hunt, threatened any who killed pregnant or nursing animals with death by her silver arrows.

In my earlier book *Cassandra Eason's Complete Book of Spells* (see Further reading, page 516), I have suggested numerous spells for working with your pets to heal them and help them cope with daily life.

As the emphasis of this book is on nature, I will focus in this chapter on techniques of drawing the different animal strengths into you in empowerments and enhanced visualisations and chanting.

You can, of course, absorb these energies directly from your pets and from local wildlife, as well as more exotic creatures, through ritual and visualisation/chanting (see pages 212–14).

Mistresses of the herds and goddesses of the hunt

One of the earliest forms of the earth goddess was the mistress or lady of wild things among the nomadic hunter-gatherer peoples. Because it was believed that the mother goddess gave birth to all forms of life, so she was revered with either the most precious parts of offerings from the first animal killed in the hunt or in ritual dance and ceremony.

The priests and priestesses of these fierce goddesses were the first shamans. Shamanism is a natural religion practised for thousands of years from Siberia through to sub-Saharan Africa, Australia and New Zealand. The shamans are the magickal priest healers who travel astrally (in their spirit bodies) to entreat the mistresses of the animals, the birds and the sea to release the creatures to be hunted and to ensure their fertility and health, and that of the people the shaman represented.

Archaeological evidence from the Baltic suggests that women were, from early times, regarded as magicians in the tribe, because of their ability to bring forth new life like the earth mother herself.

Arduinna or Ardwinna

Gallic goddess of the wild wood and the boar goddess, she demanded an offering for every animal she allowed to be hunted, and rode on a wild boar.

Bugady Musun

Siberian mother goddess of the animals, she was an old, but very physically powerful, goddess who sometimes assumed the form of a huge elk or a reindeer. She controlled all food supplies and even today is offered the finest part of the first animal killed.

Devana or Debena

Czechoslovakian goddess of the forest and of the hunt, she is called Dziewanna in Poland. A beautiful young virgin, she rode accompanied by her maidens and hounds and like the Graeco-Roman Diana was also a moon goddess. Devana heralded in the spring and also controlled the weather.

Flidais

The ancient Irish hunt goddess who could shape shift into any of her creatures, Flidais rode in a chariot pulled by stags and possessed a cow who could give milk to thirty people at a time.

Cailleach

In Scotland, where she is also called Scotia, this powerful sorceress is pictured with the teeth of a wild bear and boar's tusks. The generic name Cailleach means 'the veiled one'. This name is pronounced Kailey in parts of Scotland.

As the Scottish Cailleach Bhuer, the blue hag, she manifested herself as an old woman wearing black or dark blue rags with a crow on her left shoulder and a holly staff that could kill a mortal with a touch. She cared for the moorland animals in winter.

In Ireland, she was linked with the crone huntress goddess, Garbh Ogh, and was said to hunt the mountain deer with a pack of seventy dogs, all of whom had the names of different birds.

The lords of the hunt and wild animal gods

Cernunnos

This was a generic term, meaning 'horned one', and was given to the various horned gods of the Celtic tradition. He dates back to the early Shamanic cave images (see page 150).

Cernunnos was lord of winter, the hunt, animals, death, male fertility and the underworld. In some myths he dies at the end of summer or around the autumn equinox – a time that still signals the beginning of the hunting season in many Scandinavian countries – and is reborn in the spring.

Cernunnos' importance is in his continuing role as the male principle in witchcraft through the ages, in modern wicca and in other neo-pagan faiths.

Herne the hunter

Herne the hunter is another ancient form of the antlered god from the Germanic and Anglo Saxon world that has survived in the folk tradition of England, especially in the area around Maidenhead and also in Windsor Great Park. It is said his ghost is seen when there is a national emergency as a sign that he is protecting his people still.

Pan

Pan was the Ancient Greek herdsman's god of forests, flocks and fields. He was portrayed as half-goat, with goat horns, legs and feet. Too wild to be allowed on Mount Olympus with the other deities, he roamed the groves of Arcadia, playing his magickal pipes. In the secret magickal traditions of the early twentieth century esoteric societies, the invocation of Pan, the goat god summoned his wildness back into the over-sophisticated modern world.

Svantovit

This Slavic horned god was, in folklore, a protector of the fields and was also invoked for the success of the harvest. Portrayed with four heads and holding a horn of wine, his totem or power animal is the white horse. In times of war, a white horse would be led across a row of wooden posts. If the horse led with the right hoof, then Svantovit was indicating that all would be well.

Rediscovering wildness

Wildness is at the centre of natural magick. Contact with these ancient deity energies is a good way of rekindling our own inner spontaneity and joy in nature and also a sharpness and determination to strive and seek. This is the other side of the meditative letting-go approach and is just as vital.

Ecstasy and heightened power featured in the shamanic traditions as a way of releasing the shaman from the world for soul flight. Modern shamanism avoids the use of hallucinogenic drugs because not only are they bad for you and illegal, but they prevent exploration of your own spiritual heights. This method may involve scheduling a weekend away, but it is well worth it to bring out a side of yourself that is not easily expressed in modern, synthetic life. These out-of-town sessions are valuable for all kinds of natural magick.

The idea is to have a magick weekend, with a few friends, three or four times a year. It's cheaper than a health farm or consciousness-raising workshop, and far more effective, because you just plug into what is around you and let it happen.

* Go out into the wild countryside, whether a forest, a hillside or wilderness where you can camp or stay in a chalet or caravan.
* If this is not possible, choose a windy, rainy day and go out to a park or other place that will be quiet or even into your garden when the wind is blowing sufficiently hard to shut out traffic noise.
* On a winter's day, visit the seaside and, when you have the place to yourself, run along the beach and let the crashing waves blot out the sound of chanting for anyone who does come dog walking.

- You might also find an urban deer park where you can park the car and walk. Stately homes often have deer and wild areas as do large conservation parks, where you can walk for hours over muddy tracks that are built for animals rather than visitors. Richmond Park is very near central London, but there are wild deer everywhere and many areas where you can find clearings and wild land. Take along a friend and work together.
- Work in the early morning or just before dusk, if possible barefoot. If it is windy, chilly or damp, so much the better as you can feel the weather.
- Choose a male and female wild deity as your focus. You need not use one of the ones I have suggested but may find others on the Internet or you could create your own and give it a name, if you prefer.
- Create your chant when you are in your wild place rather than beforehand.
- You can use a drum, tambour or tambourine to help raise the power. Chant the names and simple repetitive words in a regular beat, for example:

Ardwinna, Ardwinna, horned one Herne, come to me, be with me, set me free.

- Continue to chant and gradually start to move, faster and faster, still chanting, allowing your feet to link into the earth spirals beneath the ground.
- Keep moving and whirling and chanting your wild deity names, adding:

Come to me, be with me, set me free, be in me, come with me, free shall I be.

- Build the chant round the same words or keep it simple.
- When your head is spinning and you have merged with nature, call your deity names once more with a final:

Come to me. Be in me. Free I shall be.

- Sink down fast to the ground and press your hands and feet downwards. You may feel the beat of hooves and may be rewarded by the sight of an animal in the distance.
- Close you eyes, recite your chant over and over, slowly and softly.
- Picture your deities rushing through the forest. Recall the sensations of the grass or sand as you moved and etch the smells and sounds of this moment into your memory.
- In this way you can recall the wild mother and father whenever you need their strength or daily life becomes arid.

Deities in animal form

To the Ancient Egyptians, the powers of the deities were mirrored in animals and birds. For this reason, sacred animals were kept at the temples of those gods and goddesses with whom they were associated. It was believed that after death a spirit could assume the form of an animal or bird and temporarily return to this world. It was taught too that the deities likewise could take on bird or animal forms, sometimes choosing one particular sacred animal.

Animal associations were a good way for ordinary people to understand the different characteristics of the deities, whether through a creature they feared but admired, such as the desert lion in Sekhmet or one who was famed for nurturing mothering qualities such as the cow imagery of Hathor.

Of course, no one actually worshipped Hathor as a cow. Rather it was a strong metaphor to express that just as a cow provided milk for its calf and for humans, so Hathor would eternally suckle humankind in death as well as in life.

In the same way, you can take within you the positive strengths of the creatures with whom you feel affinity.

Assuming animal powers

According to shamanic beliefs from Siberia to sub-Saharan Africa and Oceania, all living creatures have spirit counterparts which frequent water, rapids, mountains and caves. Shamans in Central and Southern America might become aligned with the spirit of a supernatural jaguar and thereby assume the power of this nocturnal and feared predator. It is these spiritual or idealised powers that you will connect with when working with power animals.

In Russia, Siberia and Native North America a number of shamans claim direct descent from a bear that has died naturally or been killed at the time the shaman undergoes a ritual death. The new shaman is thus empowered with the spirit of the reborn bear.

Shamanic stools among the Paliu of the north-eastern Amazon and the Upper Xingu of the southern Amazon are carved with powerful predators and raptorial birds. Their spirit doubles are believed to carry the shaman in soul flight. As the shaman mounts the stool, the jaguar or black panther acts not only as steed to carry them, but as protection in other spirit realms.

Amulets made from the claw, beak or teeth of one of these creatures were and still are worn or carried to endow the wearer with the protection of the creature. When empowered as talismans by chanting or ritual, they attract the strength or qualities of the creature.

In the modern world, animal charms and amulets can be empowered by magick to endow us with those animal qualities that will bring power and success. This is an easy way to carry with you the strengths of your creature (see pages 146–50 for making these).

Working with power creatures

We all have affinities with particular creatures — either specifically, perhaps with your cat or your horse, or with a species you see regularly, like a rabbit or a tiger at a local conservation park.

You may even find you are linked psychically with a particular creature of the kind within the enclosure.

Though ideally all creatures should live in a natural habitat, tigers, for example, have been hunted almost to extinction in some areas. Therefore, as a short-term measure in the hope some day that all creatures can live freely, it is vital that we support those conservation parks that are trying to keep species breeding. I have discovered that sometimes if a place is less than ideal but it is obvious that the owners and staff are trying to do everything they can, help with fundraising, sponsorships of animals or campaigning for grants can really turn a park around.

* Choose two animals, one an aloof, nocturnal, shy or gentler creature and one fiercer or more active or a creature of the sun. Both are ecologically necessary and, if you are naturally soft and gentle, you may find a more dynamic alter-ego animal will help you to develop the other equally valuable side of your nature.

* What is more, our fierce animal ego helps us to give off an aura of confidence that spontaneously reduces bullying or manipulation by others — and even seems to keep away drunks on late-night trains. Bear in mind that this list is not comprehensive.

* When you choose an animal, whether or not it is on the list, find out about the mythology behind it that may hold the key to its true nature.

* Look also through the lists of birds and sea and water creatures on pages 230–37 and 362–65 as these can be included too.

* Study the feeding, sleeping and movement patterns of your chosen creature. There are some excellent wildlife programmes on television and DVD, though nothing substitutes for actual contact.

* Local naturalist societies organise nocturnal badger- or bat-watches and conservation parks may have 'meet the animal' sessions.

* Holidays are excellent for encountering less usual wildlife. There are wolf parks in central France not far from Limoges and near Santander in northern Spain, just two of many where the visitors are the captives as they walk or drive through tracts of land where the animals live free.

I have listed a broad spectrum of creatures with which I am familiar. However, if you do have indigenous wildlife crocodiles or alligators (strictly reptiles, like the snake), wallabies, dingoes, possums, opossums or monkeys then you may want to work with these. I highly recommend Ted Andrews' *Animal Speak* (see Further reading) for a huge database of options worldwide.

Bat

Intuition, secrets, developing our hidden self

The bat is one of the most magickal and misunderstood creatures of the night because of its legendary association with the mythical vampire. Because some bats roost during the daytime in caves and ruined buildings, they have come to symbolise the spirit world. African legend tells that it was the bat that first brought darkness into the world.

Bear

Protection, healing and connection with the wise ancestors

Bear shrines and bear skulls and bones have been discovered, buried with human remains of Neanderthal man.

Because bears hibernate in caves (the womb of the goddess) and the female bear nurtures her young for many years, they possess strong maternal qualities expressed as fierceness, especially in protecting the young. In Ancient Greece and Rome, bears were sacred to the moon goddesses Artemis and to Diana.

Boar

Courage, single-mindedness and persistence

A sacred animal to the Celts, appearing as an emblem on their banners, shields and helmets. It represented the pugnacious courage and the willingness to fight to the death that Celtic warriors themselves displayed for a worthwhile cause.

Buffalo (bison)

Generosity of spirit, gentle power, unity, a bringer of abundance

To the North American Indian nations, the buffalo was the source of everything needed for survival: flesh for food; bones for cooking implements, weapons and tools; skin for clothes and covering.

Even though the buffalo herds were almost wiped out by the settlers, a recently born white buffalo calf has become a symbol of hope for peace and unity returning to the world. The buffalo has become a power animal of women who feel affinity to the Native North American world.

Bull

Animus power, potency and survival instincts

The bull appears in early Neolithic art as the son or consort of the earth mother. In Ancient Egypt, the Bull of Apis was considered a manifestation of the creator god Ptah on earth and was used as an oracle at Memphis.

Cat

Mystery, independence, magick powers
Bastet, the Egyptian cat goddess who accompanied Ra, the sun god in his solar boat and protected him from the serpent Apep, was mistress of love, fertility, joy and protectress of women and children.

In northern Europe and Scandinavia, the black cat was the power creature of Freyja the goddess of beauty, magick and fertility, who led Odin's Valkyries or swan maidens on to the battlefields to choose the noblest of the slain (see Bird magick, page 226).

In some Tibetan temples, the sacred temple cats are believed to be the reincarnation of particularly wise priests and teachers and so are given great respect.

Cow

Abundance, motherhood, nourishment
In Scandinavian legend, Audumla the primal cow sprang from the melting ice at the creation and licked a block of salt to release and then nourish the first hero god, Buri.

The cow is a sacred creature to the Hindus, and milk is offered to the gods in temples to represent both the nourishing earth mother and the lunar goddess.

Deer

Fidelity, enchantment, swiftness of response
In the north of Scotland and in the Scottish Isles especially, there is a long tradition of deer goddesses and faeries in the form of deer. These date back to the hunter tribes who worshipped the mother goddess as mistress of the herds.

Faeries, it was said, would frequently assume the form of a deer to escape pursuit.

A white hind is said to indicate the presence of an otherworldly being or an entrance to the otherworld.

Dog

Loyalty, friendship, protection, justice
Dogs have been 'man's best friend' for thousands of years and all domestic dogs are believed to descend from three founding wolves in China 15,000 years ago.

The Celtic hound was so valued and respected that its name became a title of honour given to chiefs, warriors, heroes and champions. These swift hounds not only kept food on the table in the form of small game but also served as protectors of the home, family and clan.

Elephant

Wisdom, stability, strength, intelligence

The Ancient Greek philosopher Aristotle credited the elephant with great wisdom and intelligence, traits echoed in Hinduism where elephant-headed Ganesh is god of wisdom and is always invoked at the beginning of any journey or before any important enterprise. The Roman historian Pliny believed that the elephant had religious feelings and worshipped the ancient deities of the moon and stars.

Fox

Survival instincts, inventiveness, creativity

The fox was the great trickster and questioner of the status quo in the American Indian world. In China the fox is believed to become a human when he reaches the age of 50 and will thereafter seek revenge on those who tried to hunt him. He is said to lead the way into magickal realms and, to Choctaw Indians, was the sign of unity in the family.

Goat

Spontaneity, potency, passion, instinctive power

The goat is the symbol of Pan, the Ancient Greek god of forests, flocks and fields. The ram is also the symbol of the first astrological sign Aries and was linked with Amun the Ancient Egyptian creator god.

Hare/rabbit

New beginnings, fertility, hope, increase in all things

The hare is a symbol of new beginnings and fertility. It is especially associated with spring and was the sacred animal of Ostara, Viking goddess of spring, and of Oestre, Anglo Saxon goddess of spring, whose name gives us 'Easter'.

Brer rabbit featured as the ingenious survivor in African folk myth and passed into the American folk tradition. In Buddhist and Hindu myth the hare lives in the moon.

Horse

Stamina, travel, harmony with a significant other, fertility

Pegasus was the magickal winged horse in Ancient Greek tradition of the hero Perseus, created from the blood of the slain serpent and former mother goddess Medusa.

Epona was the Celtic horse goddess, known as Macha to the Irish and Rhiannon in Wales. She was frequently depicted riding a mare or as a mare herself with a foal, and was a powerful fertility goddess as well as a goddess of death and rebirth and a protector of warriors.

Jaguar/leopard

Unbridled power, night magick, self-reliance and the unexpected

To the Mayans, the Jaguar god was very protective and guarded villages from harm at night. He was called the earth father, lord of all the forest.

In South America it is told that the jaguar taught humans to use bows and arrows and gave them cooked meat from his own fire. But men stole the fire and killed his wife and so he lives alone in deep forests and is now their enemy.

The most powerful predator in Mexico, the jaguar was associated with the omnipotent Aztec god Tezcatlipoca and was the form the sun took on its nightly journey.

Lion

Courage and nobility, leadership, authority
In western mythology, the lion is the king of the beasts. He represents the power of the sun and was associated with the sun gods and later with kings.

The lion was sacred to the Egyptians, who decorated their doors with gaping lions' mouths because the Nile, source of water and prosperity, began to rise when the sun was in Leo.

In China, stone lions protected the courts of justice and were believed to come to life at night to keep away all harm.

Lioness

Female power, passion, protection against abuse or prejudice
Lion goddesses were important in Ancient Egypt and the Middle East. Astarte, the Phoenician moon goddess and goddess of war, is depicted with a lioness' head, as is the fierce leonine sun goddess Sekhmet in Egypt.

Sekhmet was a powerful magician and healer, associated with fire and the hot desert wind and much loved by those whom she protected. Juno, wife of the Roman god Jupiter, had a chariot drawn by lions.

Mouse

Keeping a low profile, for overcoming impossible odds, for keeping secrets, for starting small and working your way up
Legends abound of how a tiny mouse saved a huge creature and thereafter enjoyed protection. In *Aesop's Fables* a mouse nibbled the cords tying a lion. In Ancient Egyptian magick, the shrew mouse was the hidden night aspect, the vital subterranean alter ego of the hawk of light, associated with the sky god Horus.

Otter/beaver

Versatility, adaptability, moving forward
In the American Indian tradition, the beaver was one of the wise creatures who taught the people how to adapt to new situations In Viking lore, beavers were among the few creatures to survive Ragnarok, the end of the old world, and to carry the new world into being. Caer is the Celtic otter goddess, a creature regarded with wonder as it is equally at home on land or in the water.

Pig

Prosperity, good luck, happiness
Pigs are symbols of good fortune and prosperity in many cultures. In Chile and

Peru, the three-legged lucky pig would be made from a lemon, sprinkled with salt and burned to attract money and good luck.

Piggy banks, with a slot for coins, are a symbol of accumulated wealth.

Snake

Wisdom, new beginnings, female spiritual power, birth

The snake is a symbol of wisdom and of the mother goddess from time immemorial. In a number of African and Australian Aboriginal myths, the rainbow snake mother gave birth to animals, plants, birds and humans. The serpent goddess was also important in the Minoan culture of Crete, perhaps as early as 6,000 BCE, and certainly surviving at least until 1,600 BCE. Here, Ariadne the fertility mother was depicted wreathed in snakes.

The snake sheds its skin in spring and so is a symbol of the ability to start again.

Sow

Fertility, fierceness, abundance

Cerridwen was called the white sow goddess of the Celts because the sow was a symbol of divine fertility and she was a symbol of rebirth.

Ardwinna was also the Gallic sow goddess, entreated for abundance at the beginning of the annual boar hunt. Sows are symbols of nourishment and were sometimes buried in Celtic times with the great to feed them in the afterlife.

Squirrel

Conserving energy and resources, for overcoming debt (in the modern world), paying attention to detail

In Viking mythology, Ratatosk the squirrel carried messages up and down Yggdrassil the world tree between the realm of the deities and the realm of mortals. In Native North American myth, the squirrel was once huge but was so quarrelsome towards humans that the Great Spirit stroked the squirrel until he was no bigger than a human hand.

Stag/moose/elk

Potency, the hunter, invincibility and nobility

The stag is the power animal symbol of the horned god who was the son or consort of the Neolithic earth goddess. He also signifies the sun. This ultimate power creature was, like the deer, associated with an entrance to the otherworld. The antlers or horns, which form a Viking power rune symbol, represent virility and masculine strength.

Tiger

Fierceness, courage, regeneration.

The tiger is the king of beasts in Eastern mythology. In China, it is given the title of lord of the land animals.

Amber contains the souls of tigers and so is a crystal of courage.

In Japan, the tiger is believed to live for a thousand years. Malaysian legend tells that tigers contain the souls of sorcerers and therefore their name must be used with care, for fear of attracting bad magick.

Wolf

Altruism, defender of others, loyalty and kinship
Legends abound of mother wolves suckling human children (and there are one or two reported actual cases in Asia). Lupa was the Roman goddess she-wolf who suckled the infants Romulus and Remus, founders of Rome. It is said the female wolf is the fiercest of all creatures in defence of her young and her pack.

Magickal shape shifting with power animals

You may already have a personal power animal or bird that perhaps has appeared in your dreams or by which you have been fascinated since childhood.

If your usual power animal roams in daylight, you may find it helpful to connect with a nocturnal creature as well, especially if you are nervous of darkness, if you frequently work or travel in darkness or if you need reserves of power at a critical time in your life.

The easiest way to internalise the power of your creatures is to shape shift into them.

Shape shifting is a shamanic technique from many lands. The Celtic Druids and Druidesses were great shape shifters (see more on this in my *Modern Day Druidess*, see Further reading section).

Shape shifting in the Western tradition has become associated with experienced witches. However, by channelling the all-powerful imagination and generating energy through movement, chanting or drumming, anyone can shape shift to absorb and store animal strengths and wisdom. Of course, the more you practise, the more significant the experiences will become.

Once you have chosen your two power animals (birds or sea creatures), you just need to internalise the power to make it instantly accessible at any place and at any time.

Though you will work primarily with your power creatures, you can adopt different powers from other creatures in addition to your main animal source when you need other resources or encounter a new life situation.

Preparations for shape shifting

1 Vision/visualisation

* Sit quietly, if you have the chance, and look directly at your creature, perhaps while it is resting in its enclosure. The magickal household cat is an ideal power creature with which to practise even if she is not your main power animal.
* Memorise the details of your chosen creature so that you can see it while your eyes are closed. Alternatively or additionally, memorise a picture of your creature on the move so that when you close your eyes in the open air the creature is still

there before you. Practise recalling the details with your eyes closed so that you can instantly call up a vision of your creature sitting, sleeping, running and eating.

2 Sound/clairaudience or psychic hearing

* Does your creature have a distinctive call? Does this vary? A cat on the tiles yowling sounds very different from a contented cat purring by the fireside.
* How does your creature breathe? You may get sound bites of both breathing and animal calls on the internet or use your imagination to hear how your animal might pant if running.
* What natural sounds or music do you associate with your creature: rainforest or jungle sounds, drumbeat or natural tones, wolf (or dolphin call), roars of other background animals at night, birdsong, rain, wind, storm? There are many excellent nature CDs available.
* Work with actual sounds as often as possible so that you can hear them in your mind at any time.
* Now put these stages together and sit in silence outdoors, picturing and hearing your creature.

3 Smell/clairsentience or psychic senses

* Go to any zoo, stable or farmyard and you will know that animals aren't fragrant. Wolf enclosures maintain their distinct pungency even if no animals are in sight. Tomcats double well for wolves in terms of scent.
* For some creatures you may smell pine forests or musk (incense can help here) or damp grass after rain.
* Again, absorb the smells and then add these to your internal images and sounds. Practise calling these up in the open air where there are no animal smells.
* Clairsentience or psychic senses is as much about impressions as psychic smells and will draw together all the impressions of your creature.

4 Touch/psychometry

* You are unlikely to get to touch a tiger, but there are many animals with smooth or rough coats, from goats to horses to cats, so you can fill in the psychic gaps. Looking at the creature and relating it to one you can stroke will help you to build up the complete picture.
* Leather or skins from different creatures (from a source where the animal was killed humanely and not for the sole purpose of its skin) or synthetic furs can breach the gap.
* Cats' fur is related to that of tigers and jaguars. Lions have more in common with smooth-skinned horses. Elephants are rough and quite hairy.
* Imagine the coat or hide enveloping you and add this to the other senses.

Shape shifting for real

* Now all you have to do is to let your spirit step out of you and into the animal in order to merge with its energies. Work on separate occasions to internalise

your creatures as they will have different rhythms at different times of the year or times of day and night. An ancient African saying says that if we can talk we can sing, and if we can walk we can dance. The inhibitions come from living in societies where we do not move spontaneously and where dancing is subject to strict rules and fashions instead of being regarded as a natural expression of joy or power or as a release of anger.

* Work outdoors, either by moon or sunlight, if possible in a forest setting or near a tree or big bush in a garden or park for a jungle or woodland creature and in an open space for a free-roaming one.
* The easiest way is to dance into your power creature's energy field. If it is a quiet, gentle creature, move slowly, and if it is tiny, visualise it as just larger than you (and therefore easier to fit into).
* Picture your creature in front of you, poised but still, and allow your body to twist round it, allowing your arms and legs to move in their own way.
* Rattles are a powerful shamanic method of connecting with higher vibrations. You can buy these cheaply from music or craft shops or can make your own using beads, beans or rice inside a sealed container. Best of all is a gourd with a wooden handle attached with a nail.
* If you work with a friend, one can use a drum and the other a rattle. You can each focus on your own creatures.
* As you start to move, allow the personal call to come. When spoken in your mind, this call will always bring your power creature into your sphere. It can be a few words, such as 'wolf mother defend', or a more complex recitation.
* Recite the words over and over as you move and, through half-closed eyes, see your creature.
* Whether a gentle steady chant or a fierce beat, let the power build up until you feel you are merging with your animal. Then call out once:

We are as one. I claim the power with gratitude and with reverence.

* Now sit motionless with your eyes closed and either see through your creature's eyes, breathe their breath and feel the floor beneath you or run with your creature through the thicket, leap from a rock or burrow into your sett in the earth.
* When you are ready, thank the creature and start to breathe normally and feel your own outline emerging.
* Slowly open your eyes and feel the power as part of you.
* Each morning and each night, as you lie in bed, allow your animal to come into your mind. In time it will appear spontaneously whenever you need its power and recite its chant.

It is said that once a new shaman finds her or his helper spirit in the form of a creature it will act as a guide to otherworldly journeys. Your own power creature may begin to work through your dreams, showing you exotic places or other centuries, leading the way but remaining close and protective.

2

BIRD MAGICK

Birds, like bees, have long been regarded as the messengers of the deities, and many gods and goddesses had their own sacred birds. For Zeus, the Greek father god, and the Roman Jupiter, it was the eagle. The Celtic hero god Bran called upon his ravens. They still guard the Tower of London, beneath which his head is said to be buried.

Celtic Rhiannon's blackbirds sang so sweetly at the entrance to the otherworld that all were glad to enter. The Irish Cliodna of the golden hair possessed rainbow-coloured birds that could heal any sickness or sorrow. Doves were sacred to the Greek love goddess, Aphrodite, and her Roman counterpart, Venus; peacocks to Hera, the Greek goddess consort of Zeus and her Roman equivalent, Juno; while wise Athena adopted the owl. Crone goddesses in the Celtic tradition frequently assumed the form of owls.

Some gods used their ability to shape shift or change into birds for less than noble purposes. Zeus disguised himself as a wounded dove, which was comforted by the earth goddess Hera, whom he subsequently raped and then married as his consort but not equal.

In terms of magick, birds offer powerful totems or power icons in the same way as animals in the previous chapter. They are a symbol of rebirth, being a form taken by newly freed souls in cultures such as that of Ancient Egypt, to fly to the heavens. In Finnish mythology it was believed that birds were servants of Sielulintu, the soul bird. On his behalf they carried human souls into their bodies at birth and took them back when the person died. For this reason, in modern folk custom a wooden bird is placed at the bedside to prevent the soul flying off during sleep.

Bird creation myths

There are a number of legends in different cultures about bird goddesses and gods, usually associated with water birds, laying the egg of the world. Water was the first matter of creation and the water fowl was believed to dive down and bring up the seeds of new life (see also the Hungarian Magyar legend on page 227).

In Siberia, myth tells that the earth was once covered with water. Two water birds, the diving loon and the golden-eyed duck continued to dive until they had brought up enough mud to form the first land.

In India, according to one creation myth, a swan laid the golden cosmic egg from which Brahma, Hindu creator of the universe, emerged.

According to the mythology of Finland, the world was created from an egg that broke into thousands of pieces to form the land, the trees, the hills and all the creatures of the earth. Lintukoto, the land of birds, lay at the edge of the world and was a warm place to which they migrated in the winter. They travelled along the Milky Way to this land.

In one Ancient Egyptian creation legend, Geb, the earth god, in the form of a goose, laid the egg of the world from which Ra the sun god emerged to bring light into the world as the first sunrise.

In Japanese folk tradition, the wagtail assisted with the creation of the earth, which was believed to be a huge marsh in its original form. The creator sent wagtails to beat the land with their wings and tails until the hills formed so that the water could drain away and humankind could cultivate the soil.

The Tlingit people of Alaska credit the raven as creator of people, animals, the sun, the moon and the stars.

Bird goddesses

Ancient bird goddesses

We learn of these from archaeological evidence.

A well-known statue that gives clues to the early forms of the bird goddess is the Spanish Neolithic bird goddess. She was worshipped around 5,000 BCE and was an icon of fertility and rebirth. She is depicted with bee eyes and antennae as well as lines across her wings indicating that she is flying.

Another early bird goddess statue made of terracotta dates from 4,000 BCE and was found in Vinca in the east Balkans.

More graceful and more human-like is the pre-dynastic fertility goddess with a bird's head and wings like dancer's arms extended in an arch over her head. She was made from ancient Nile mud. Pre-dynastic is prior to 3,000 BCE; she may, however, be much older in her mythology.

Dynastic Ancient Egyptian bird goddesses

The goddess Isis was sometimes called the mother vulture.

The vulture hieroglyph shown here represents the protection and power of mother Isis and was used as an amulet of protection for the deceased, with the ankh, for life, engraved on each talon.

Isis is often portrayed as a golden goddess with wings outstretched shielding Osiris and the pharaohs (see also Selkit and the other winged protective goddesses in Insect magick, page 250). The four protective goddesses of Egypt: Isis, Selkit, Nehythys (goddess of the twilight and sister of Isis) and Neither, the fate goddess, can be seen guarding the shrine of Tutankhamen, in which the canopic jars containing his body organs were contained.

Nekhbet was another Egyptian vulture goddess who was said to give her maternal milk to the pharaoh. Her image also was worn on the nemes, the pharaoh's headdress, along with the uraeus, the cobra serpent's head.

Celtic bird goddesses

Most famous of the Celtic bird goddesses were the three raven sisters: Morrigan, Macha or Nass and Badbh or Nemhain. They were called the Morrigu. Macha, the mother form of the Morrigu, flew over the battlefields as a huge crow or raven, accompanied by a flock of ravens, warning of the enemy's approach and encouraging her chosen tribe to victory.

Badbh, the crone goddess, carried the souls of the slain to the otherworld for healing and rebirth. She chose who should live and who should die.

Viking bird goddesses

The Valkyries, the battle goddess maidens whose name means, in Old Norse, choosers of the slain, were in early times called the raven maidens. They swooped over the battlefields like birds. In this form they also prophesied who would win the battle.

From around the seventh century, the Valkyries became depicted on protective battle amulets and in pictures on memorial stones as beautiful women, with blonde hair and blue eyes wearing red robes or armour and a cloak of swan feathers, carrying shields and spears.

Freyja, goddess of love and beauty but also death and battle, was head of the Valkyries and wore a magnificent cloak made from feathers from all the birds in the known world. Her maidens chose those who were worthy to enter the father god Odin's halls of Valhalla or, in earlier legends, Freyja's own hall.

In Valhalla, the Valkyries dressed in white, tended the warriors who feasted by night and re-enacted great battles during the day. They prepared for the great final battle of Ragnarok in which the gods of Asgard (the realm of the high gods) would be threatened by the forces of evil.

Bird gods

Ancient Egyptian bird gods

In Ancient Egypt the Ba, part of the soul to survive death, was pictured as a hawk-headed spirit that could fly upwards to the blessed field of reeds in the Milky Way where the celestial Nile flowed.

Horus was the sky god, son of Osiris, the vegetation god, who was murdered by his brother Set. Horus is depicted either as a falcon wearing the double crown of Egypt or in his falcon-headed form with a crown. He protected the pharaohs who were considered an embodiment of Horus on earth. He was worshipped by ordinary people and was a god of healing and protection as well as of the rising sun in later myths.

Sometimes regarded as the first of the deities present at creation, Thoth was the ibis-headed god of law, writing, medicine, mathematics and the spoken word.

Thoth possessed command over all magickal knowledge and dictated, it is said, the first magickal treatise: the emerald tablet. He rode in the solar boat with Ra. In this function, he ordered the measurement of time.

Thoth as an elder god taught Isis the magickal incantations to restore life to the body of Osiris. He is depicted in ibis or ibis-headed form with the pen and tablet of a scribe.

Hindu bird gods

Garuda is the Hindu god or king of the birds, who can fly faster than light. He acts as steed for the preserver god Vishnu. Portrayed with the head, wings, talons and beak of an eagle and the body and limbs of a man, his body is gold. Though of mortal parents, his light rivals that of the fire god Agni and so he is greatly revered.

The Hungarian tradition

Magyar was the Hungarian sun god whose parents were the original god and goddess. He is described as a youth with sunbeam hair who transformed himself into a golden diving bird. He descended to the bottom of the ocean and brought up the seeds to create the first humans, that they would be his people.

Discovering soul flight

Some shamans wear feathered headdresses and cloaks with feathered wings to indicate their ability to fly through the dimensions. They might sit beneath and climb a tall tree (either in their minds or, more hazardously, actually while in a trance). This tree signifies the axis of the world tree, above which shone the pole star, the gateway to the stars.

Soul or astral flight is an important magickal technique that can be learned by anyone. It enables you to experience a temporary spiritual freedom as the energy is released at the climax of a spell or ritual.

You can use the same method either while sitting outdoors looking up at the stars or indeed as you lie in bed at night or make love, gazing directly into each others' eyes so that you and your partner can ascend spiritually together.

The flight takes place either in your mind or, some believe, in the spirit or etheric rainbow body that is a more perfect form of our physical body. Its energies can be perceived radiating from within us as the aura or psychic energy field that surrounds the body. Some prefer to picture this astral travelling on the back of a huge bird.

In soul flight you can travel wherever you wish, to past worlds to other lands or to the mythological worlds on the astral or spirit plane where you can encounter the bird gods and goddesses or the mistresses and lords of the animals.

To achieve soul flight I have suggested a spell, but you can equally use the drumming, dancing, rattling and chanting techniques I have described on pages 45–49. Meditation or counting from nought to ten slowly as you gaze at a high light or into a candle flame in a dark room are other common methods (see my book *Discover your Past Lives* in Further reading).

A spell to fly

The bonus of this spell is that you can release a dream, a wish or something that is holding you back, into the cosmos by calling it aloud as you launch yourself astrally. Initially, work in the open air on a starry night and then you can visualise the setting when you are in bed or in a less spiritual setting whenever you feel the need to move beyond the immediate.

If the idea of astral travel spooks you, think of it as happening within your mind, in the same way that your mind can vividly recreate an event from the past or another place as though you were actually there. (This is intense daydreaming, of which astral travel is an enhanced form.)

You will need: A sagebrush smudge stick; a feather or feather fan; a container of sand or soil; and a single small lantern, either a battery one or the enclosed safety kind that holds a single tea light and will go out if you knock it over. Your body is the symbol that is going to be empowered.

Timing: Star- or moonlight, looking up through a tall tree with branches mainly high up, like a Douglas fir, a pine, a redwood or a cedar of Lebanon. If there is not one of these available, plant your staff in the ground and use that as your *axis mundi*, your axis of the world. Visualise it as extending to the sky with a profusion of gold or silver leaves.

* Switch on or light your lantern close to the chosen tree.
* Light the smudge and use the feather to fan the smoke upwards.
* Look into the light through the smudge for a minute or two and whisper:

> *I am the soul bird, bird of flight. I am the soul bird. I rise though the skies to the stars.*

* Begin to circle the tree, making spirals of smoke above and all round you as you move and chant your soul-bird empowerment. Picture yourself with feathered wings (it may help to wear a cloak).
* Try to keep a flowing, gentle rhythm as you move faster so that you become

entranced or enchanted and your feet feel as though they are hardly touching the ground.

* When you feel light-headed, stop, look up through the branches of the tree and pick a particular star. It need not be the pole star.
* Sit on the ground, close to your lantern, gazing up through the branches, still swirling your smudge gently round you, chanting and swaying, very rhythmically but increasingly fast so that you are lulled into a light trance state.
* Now slow your movements so you are sitting motionless fanning the smoke directly upwards.
* Begin to chant even faster and more intensely so the sound builds up in your body and you feel you are beginning to float.
* This splitting between intense sound and no movement is a way of focusing all the power within you. Gradually your spirit form may seem to be rising from the physical, conscious sense of self and you may sense a luminosity around you.
* When you have reached an intensity of chanting, plunge the smudge into the container of sand and grip the feather between both hands.
* Focus on the star and propel your mind towards it as you did with the cone of stars in your spellcasting (see page 47), calling out the chant a final time, followed by:

Wings, carry me.

* Once you are free in your mind (or spirit body) you can travel anywhere. Feel your cloak as feather-like wings, carrying you through the still night air.
* When you are ready to return, focus on the light of your lamp getting larger and closer until you are sitting close to the tree (or your staff) again. You may feel a gentle bump or buzzing as your body and spirit reintegrate.
* Sit quietly and recall the place you visited and any wise helpers you met, especially birds or animals. Write about the experience in your Book of Shadows.
* If you find that this doesn't work, try two or three more times when you are relaxed and sleepy.
* Failing this, visit a planetarium and wear headphones to muffle any commentary. Carry out the spell in your mind without moving or using smudge but creating an imaginary pathway through the stars to a particular planet or a bright star that you can visualise as a special world. By your second visit I can almost guarantee you will be the soul bird.

Birds as messengers

The dawn chorus is quite magickal, but whenever you hear bird call, your psychic mind can translate the sounds into a message for you. It helps if you watch birds circling, through half-closed eyes. Focus on the patterns of silver and blue made by their collective energy fields or auras. In this way, you can learn to merge with the essence of the birds and so be able to obtain psychic as well as physical impressions more easily.

Finding your power bird

As with power animals, birds signify different strengths. They are very easy to work with, whether you attract birds to your garden or balcony with a feeder or visit bird parks, especially ones with walk-through aviaries. On holiday you may see different kinds of birds in their natural habitats or in botanical gardens.

Whatever power bird you choose, the more you sit and watch any birds flying free or settling and feeding, the more you will connect with their air power, their lack of boundaries and their openness to all experience.

If you are in a restrictive period of your life, birds can help you to feel less trapped, and sometimes give you the impetus to move on.

You may choose to have one animal and one bird totem or power icon. However, you can if you prefer have power birds as well as power animals.

If you are adopting two bird icons, make one a local species or one in a local bird park. In this way you can, over time, identify an individual bird with distinct markings. I currently have a blackbird that comes up to the back door and eats the cat food while the three cats watch in amazement.

The second can display greater potential to travel far or reach great heights, such as an eagle or swan or a more exotic hummingbird that offers different energies.

You can connect with birds in the same way you did with animals (there are many bird song CDs). I also suggest a spell that you can adapt to animals or sea creatures (see Sea magick for sea creature power icons, pages 362–65).

There are, of course, numerous bird species that I don't mention here. You will need to do some research and read about their myths as well as their habits in order to get inside their psyche.

Bird of paradise

Representing transformation, the life force, radiance
Real birds of paradise are now under conservation in New Guinea and its neighbouring islands. Female birds are dull but the males have brilliant plumage.

It may have been these birds or a similarly rainbow-plumed creature that inspired stories of the legendary bird of paradise, which perched in the tree of life in various cultures, especially in the Far East.

Blackbird

Representing a bringer of joy, cheerfulness under difficulty, defensive of their territory and family against bullies
An especially magickal bird. These were the birds of the goddess Rhiannon who sang on the tree at the entrance to the Celtic otherworld. A blackbird was also one of the creatures that rescued the Mabon the divine sun child of Celtic myth from his imprisonment in the otherworld so that he could take his rightful place as the son of light.

Cockerel

Representing protection, wise warnings, wakefulness
The cockerel was a sacrificial animal in many cultures and was buried under the foundations of ancient buildings as a guardian.

In Viking myth there are two cockerels. Vithafmir was the golden cockerel perched at the top of Yggdrassil, the world tree, as a guardian against evil. Fralar, cockerel of the underworld, lived in Valhalla, abode of the slain warriors to waken the heroes for the final battle.

Crane

Representing knowledge, wisdom, lasting health

Associated with long life, a legendary crane on the island of Innis Kea, in County Mayo, Ireland, was said to have existed since the beginning of the world.

The crane is a sacred bird in Japan, a symbol of health and long life. It is called the honourable lord crane and, according to both Japanese and Chinese myth, lives for a thousand years and more.

In China, too, white cranes are especially sacred and live on the Islands of the Blest, the Chinese earthly paradise.

Crow

Representing traditional wisdom, magickal powers, rebirth

Crows are sacred to Athena, Greek goddess of wisdom, although she would not allow crows to perch on the Acropolis in Athens since this was regarded as a bad omen. They are also the birds of the Crone goddesses, for example Hecate in the Ancient Greek traditions and the Celtic Cailleach Bhuer, the blue hag (see page 378). In this role they carry the souls of the deceased or fatally sick into rebirth.

In Amerindian lore the crow is a teacher of magick.

Dove

Representing peace, love, gentleness

A far more powerful totem than it appears, the dove features in the flood stories of the Babylonians, Hebrews, Chaldeans and Greeks as a symbol of peace and reconciliation. It is an emblem of Aphrodite/Venus, representing faithful and committed love and is also sacred to wise Athena and the symbol of Sophia, goddess of wisdom, and links her with the concept of the female holy spirit.

The cooing of sacred pigeons or doves in the oracular groves dedicated to Zeus at Dodona were used for prophecy by the priestesses.

The dove bearing the olive branch back to Noah's ark has become an international sign of peace.

Eagle

Representing vision, leadership and limitless potential

The eagle is king of the birds. In Amerindian lore, the feathers of the eagle carry the prayers of the people to the father sun. It was said that the eagle was the creature that could fly closest to the sun and not be burned. It could also, according to legend, look into the noonday sun and not be blinded.

Eagle feathers are a symbol of healing wisdom.

Falcon or kestrel

Representing vigilance, communication and focus
Symbol of Horus the Ancient Egyptian sky god, and so a sign of focused power.

The bush falcon, found in the Antipodes, was regarded as a messenger from the earth to the heavens and was used in establishing whether a location for a new Maori ceremonial house was favourable to the gods and ancestors. It was imprisoned by its flight feathers on the ridge pole, which was then put in its position on the front post of the new building. If the falcon flew free, it was seen as returning to the gods and ancestors who had sent it. However, if it remained trapped, the ceremonial house would not be used.

Goose

Representing family togetherness, home-building and alertness
In Ancient Egypt the goose, like the swan in other cultures, laid the great cosmic egg from which the sun came (see Bird gods, page 225).

The goose was also linked in the Classical world with Hera/Juno in their roles as wife and mother, and became the symbol of domestic happiness.

Cackling geese alerted the Romans when the Gauls were making a silent raid on the Capitol, and geese were kept thereafter to warn of danger. The cackling of geese became a sign of hidden enemies.

Hawk

Representing enlightenment, memory and great ambition
In Egyptian mythology the hawk, like the eagle, was a bird of the sun and could also soar towards the sun and look into its brilliant face without being blinded.
Sacred to Horus, the sky god, the hawk was the symbol of the return of light after darkness and so of joy after sorrow.

In the Classical world, the hawk was the special emissary of Apollo, the god of light. Gayatri, the hawk of Indian legend, brought soma from the heavens, a juice that induced sleep and prophetic visions.

In Polynesia, the hawk is both prophet and healer, while among the Australian Aborigines the hawk is a powerful totem creature for great leaders.

Heron

Representing rebirth and self-belief
The heron is identified with the Ancient Egyptian Benu bird, the original mythical phoenix that perched on the first mound and represented the first sunrise. Herons returned to Egypt at the time of the annual flood that fertilised the land and so became linked to rebirth. The Benu was said to be consumed by flames every five hundred years. The young bird then rose, carrying the ashes of its parent that it buried beneath the sacred mound.

Hummingbird

Representing truth, harmony and spontaneity
The hummingbird was one of the birds that helped to carry back fire to the North

American Indians, according to the legends of the Wintu tribe. The hummingbird always speaks the truth.

Bird of the gods, he is a bringer of harmony and happiness to all who see or hear him. Because the hummingbird is skilled in hovering and flying backwards, his feathers are used in the modern world as charms for safe plane journeys.

The hummingbird was the creature of the feathered serpent, Quetzalcoatl, the sky and sun god of the Mayans and Aztecs, who wore hummingbird feathers.

Ibis

Representing learning, writing and healing
The white and black ibis was sacred to Thoth (see page 227).

The ibis was also associated with Hermes, Greek god of wisdom, medicine and the written arts. Hermes assumed the shape of an ibis in his flight to escape from Typhon, the hundred-headed monster who was killed by Zeus's thunderbolt.

Kingfisher

Representing harmony, tranquillity and unexpected blessings
A kingfisher or any bright blue bird promises a tranquil period for fourteen days after it is seen. It is often called the halcyon bird, hence the expression 'halcyon days'.

The origin of these halcyon days comes from Greek myth. Alcyone, daughter of Aeolus, king of the winds, threw herself into the sea, overcome with grief at the death of her husband. The gods transformed her into a kingfisher and Aeolus said that henceforward the winds would not stir up the sea during the halcyon days. These fourteen calm days, often located around the midwinter solstice, last from the hatching of eggs to when the young birds are able to fly.

Magpie

Representing good luck, unexpected news or opportunities, prosperity
Magpies are divinatory birds. One magpie alone is traditionally considered a bad omen and unless a second follows rapidly, you should take off your hat and bow, saying, 'Good morning (or afternoon or evening), Mr Magpie and how are you today?' This ensures any news you receive that day will be good.

In the Far East, the magpie's arrival is welcomed for the bird is a symbol of happiness and prosperity.

Its chattering, according to modern usage, heralds unexpected but very welcome visitors.

Nightingale

Representing musical gifts, faithful love, reconciliation
The nightingale is a truly magickal bird whose song can be heard in the stillness of the night.

One myth tells that on a wintry night a nightingale soothed the baby Jesus to sleep with her singing. As a result Mary blessed the bird and declared its singing should be the sweetest of all birds.

Another legend says that the first lily of the valley loved the nightingale. But because she was so shy, she hid in the long grass to listen to his song. The nightingale became lonely and at last said he would no longer sing, unless the lily of the valley bloomed every May for all to see. Now, when the moonlight shines upon the delicate white bells, the nightingale sings his sweetest and the returning song of her tiny bells can be heard in the stillness.

Ostrich

Representing justice, integrity, staying in touch with reality
Although it does not fly, the ostrich runs very fast and so represents the power to stay in touch with the earth while moving forward.

In Ancient Egypt an ostrich feather was worn by Ma'at, goddess of wisdom and justice, and was used to balance the heart of a dead person on the scales of justice. The ostrich is also important in African magick as a symbol of perpetual light and motion and its eggs have magickal significance as symbols of fertility and new life. Contrary to myth, the ostrich doesn't bury its head in the sand when there is trouble, but runs!

Owl

Representing wisdom, the power of the night and our alter ego
The owl is called night eagle in Amerindian lore, being the lady of the night and moon as the eagle is lord of the day and the sun. In the Classical world, the owl was the special bird of the Greek Athena and her counterpart Minerva, goddess of wisdom.

The darker connotations of the owl originated in Rome where the deaths of several Roman emperors were foretold by an owl landing on the roof of the palace and hooting. The association with death also came from Celtic lore where the owl was regarded as a form of the crone goddesses who heralded death, but also rebirth.

Parrot

Representing communication, fame and artistry
Among the Amahuaca of eastern Peru, fire was stolen by a parrot from the giant Yowashiko who refused to share his gift with humankind. Though Yowashiko tried to drown the parrot with rainstorms, larger birds shielded him with their wings and kept the gift safe.

The parrot is the news bringer and revealer of secrets in Afro-Caribbean lore.

Peacock

Representing self-esteem, lasting happiness, star qualities
The peacock was the bird of Juno, Roman mother goddess who was goddess of joy and marriage. If a peacock spreads its tail feathers before your eyes, lasting happiness in love, happiness and prosperity will follow.

Because its flesh was said never to decay and it was associated with the deities, the peacock became a symbol of immortality in Rome and was adopted by both emperor and empress as their luck-bringing icon. However, as the old pagan gods and goddesses became discredited with the spread of Christianity, the eyes on the tail feathers were unfairly regarded as the evil eye (though they are protective against it and malice). They should not be brought indoors.

The peacock is a weather prophet, its dance foretelling rain and storms.

Pelican

Representing devotion, nurturing and altruism

The pelican is famed for her maternal instinct. People once believed that the mother pelican, reaching in her pouch for food, was ripping open her breast to feed her young on its own blood. Legends grew up that the pelican could revive dead infant birds by feeding them her life blood.

This image was adopted after a vision by St Gertrude as representing the sacrifice of Christ. The pelican with her brood also became a heraldic symbol of piety.

Quail

Representing fertility, passion, courage against difficult odds

The quail is associated with passion and fertility for it is a bird of fire. Its eggs are traditionally eaten at the time of the full moon to ensure fertility.

According to the country in which it lives, it is associated with the coming of spring or summer. It also symbolised victory and valour in battle for the Romans. Pliny reported that, on migration, quails displayed great intelligence and organisational powers and dropped stones as they flew in darkness to establish whether they were over water.

In Russian tradition, the quail lived in the sun and the hare in the moon.

Raven

Representing finding what is lost, magickal powers and hidden potential

Ravens are the birds of Odin, the Norse all-father. His two ravens, Hugin and Mugin (mind and memory), sat on his shoulders, and the Vikings carried Odin's raven banners into battle. These banners could be made only by the virgin daughters of Viking hero-warriors.

The raven is the teacher of magick, seen both as the great trickster and creator in Native North American lore. He is sometimes called the big grandfather or raven man and, like the hawk, was one of the creatures who re-created the world after the flood. The raven is also a messenger of the Great Spirit.

The raven is likewise the sacred bird of Bran, the Celtic god-king. Ravens are still kept at the Tower of London because legend says that if they should leave their sacred place, the Tower and London itself would be destroyed.

Unlike the jackdaw, the raven is a finder of lost property. If you lose something, ask a raven for its location and a picture will form in your mind of its whereabouts.

Robin

Representing compassion, the granting of wishes

Several legends explain why the robin has a red breast. One says that he burned it in the fires of hell bringing water to lost souls. Others claim it was stained with the blood of Christ as the robin pulled the thorns from Christ's crown. A third version says that as the robin was covering the body of Christ with leaves as he was taken from the cross, the robin was touched by His blood.

In Native North American tradition the raven, in his creator role, made the robin to bring joy with his warbling.

The robin can also grant wishes, especially the first robin of spring.

Seagull

Representing travel, the desire for adventure, the return of people from our past
Seagulls are said to be the souls of dead sailors and so should never be shot.

Storm petrels, known as Mother Carey's chickens, are especially protected by sailors. If a gull settles on any part of a ship in which a person is travelling, it is said the voyage will be a happy one.

Stork

Representing life-bringer, fertility and enduring love
Storks are believed to carry unborn babies from the salt marshes where they grow to waiting parents. The strong association with birth came about because the stork represented woman as the bringer of life in the form of the Classical mother goddesses Hera and Juno.

Because the stork was also sacred to Venus, a nesting pair of storks on or near a home was considered a blessing from this goddess and a promise of enduring love.

The stork got its name, according to Scandinavian myth, at the crucifixion. A stork flew round the cross, uttering cries of distress, 'styrka, styrka', which means 'strengthen'.

Swallow and martin

Representing rebirth, renewal of hope and consolation
The swallow was sacred to Isis and also to Venus and Aphrodite. It has been regarded as a symbol of awakening after winter and of the renewal of life since early times.

To see a swallow in early spring is a promise of a happy summer. If swallows build in the eaves of a house, success and happiness are promised to all who live there.

Like the stork, in Swedish tradition, the swallow flew over the cross, calling 'svala, svala', which means 'console'.

Swan

Representing grace, beauty, creative talents
Swans were a form taken by faerie women and goddesses in both the Celtic and Viking traditions.

In Celtic myth, swan goddesses or faeries were famed for their wonderful voices and healing powers and were identifiable from other swans by gold and silver chains around their necks. Because of the belief in fairie swan maidens, for many years it was forbidden to kill a swan in Ireland.

The black swans of Australia are, in some areas, considered the manifestation of the mother/sister female counterpart of Balame, the Aboriginal all-father.

A swan was said to carry Saraswati, Hindu goddess of wisdom and music and the wife of Brahma, whenever she travelled.

In Native North American tradition, the great white swan calls up the four winds. Swans also contain the souls of great poets, writers and musicians, since Apollo's soul also took the form of a swan.

Turkey

Representing care of others, altruism and idealism

Turkeys, known as the jewelled fowl, were sacrificial creatures in Mesoamerican society and so, on the American continent, became a symbol of noble self-sacrifice.

The turkey was central to the tribal new-fire ceremonies and became the focus of Thanksgiving Day in North America on the fourth Thursday in November. This festival commemorates the first harvest feast of the Pilgrim Fathers in 1621 when four wild turkeys were eaten.

Wagtail

Representing love, creativity, prophecy

The water-wagtail is a love bird in Japanese myth and its feathers are highly prized as love tokens.

In India, the wagtail is the chief divinatory bird. Predictions were made by the direction of its flight and where it landed. For example if it perched near a lotus, elephant or the sacred cow, good fortune was promised to any who saw it.

Wren

Ingenuity, ambition, psychic gifts

The wren once temporarily gained the title of king of the birds from the eagle by an ingenious plan. According to Norse myth there was a contest between all the birds. Whoever flew nearest the sun would be king. The eagle soared highest but the wren hid in his feathers and, as the eagle approached the sun, the wren perched on his head.

The wren was also the Celtic king of the birds and was used for prophecy.

The wren is said to be blessed because she carried moss to the stable on Christmas Eve to line baby Jesus' manger.

In Japanese folklore, the bird is greeted as the small god who brought fire from heaven to humankind.

Power bird spells for aiming high

Whatever your dream or ambition, bird spells have from Ancient Egyptian times formed a focus for soaring intellectually, spiritually or creatively.

You don't have to work only with your own power bird but can choose any whose qualities you need at a particular time. You can also carry out bird power spells for family, a partner or friends.

Before casting the spell for a particular purpose, try to make a connection with your chosen bird. This can be done by listening to its song (there are some excellent audio nature sites on the Internet; key the name in of your chosen bird) or by seeing the bird itself. You could visit a bird-of-prey conservancy centre where you could watch birds in flight or even book a lesson to fly one. Otherwise, try local wild bird conservation areas or bird parks. A well-stocked bird table in your garden will bring many species, especially at times of migration.

Above all, use the greatest tool in magick: your imagination. Picture your chosen bird focus at rest, feeding or flying.

The spell below is an extract from a longer spell, but will demonstrate the concept. It comes from the great Egyptologist Wallis Budge's translation of the *Book of the Dead* (see Further reading).

This formula was given in the papyrus of the scribe Ani so that after death his deceased spirit or Ba might recite it and assume the form of a swallow at will:

> *The Osiris Ani, whose word is truth, saith: 'I am a swallow, I am a swallow. Hail, O ye gods whose odour is sweet ~ I am like Horus. Let me pass on and deliver my message.'*

There are various other spells in the *Book of the Dead*, for example one to become a hawk of gold. These spells were not just used in the afterlife but to empower the living to strive for their dreams.

As I explained earlier, words in Ancient Egypt were believed to have great power. As you recite your own bird spell, picture the most magnificent of the species with the sweetest song, feathers golden against the sun or tinged silver against the full moon if it is a night bird. The spell will carry your wishes to the sun or moon.

A power bird spell for any ambition, dream or powerful need

You will need: Five feathers from any bird, but ideally five different birds. When you visit a bird conservancy or park, stock up on feathers for spells. Undyed feathers are often for sale at reasonable prices in the shops attached to these places. Also keep an eye out on seashores, in parks or near a dovecote.

A small piece of wax, dough or clay to make a bird. You can find a flat stone in situ to make it on.

Fennel, fern or any of the air incenses on page 33 (loose incense or a stick).

Timing: For a bird of the sun in sunlight or the brightest part of the day. For a night bird, moon or starlight.

* Sit in the open air away from trees or near an open window.
* Light the incense and for a few moments watch the smoke rise.
* Don't pre-plan.
* When you feel ready, take your wax or clay and shape a bird with its wings outstretched on a flat stone or rock. You don't need to be an artist, but as you work, picture a real bird preparing for flight, either as part of a flock or, if alone, silhouetted against the sun or moon.
* When you have finished, set your five feathers round the bird on the stone to create a wing or fan shape.
* Leave the bird on the stone and, holding your hands fingers down about 2.5 cm/ I in above it so that your own energy enters the model, weave your spell words.
* Start with:

I am.

or, if for someone else, for example:

Tony is _____.

* Say these first words aloud. I am provides a terrific statement of power and determination, especially if you feel your identity or talents are currently stifled.
* Next name your chosen bird and describe it, for example, 'a hawk of pure gold'. Now say the first and second parts:

I am a hawk of pure gold.

* Or you might be a nightingale pouring out its heart in love or the courageous blackbird whistling in spite of the odds against it.
* Next consider, what does your bird do? Rise almost vertically upwards, circle, swoop and dive to bring up new life from the bottom of the ocean? Add this new information to the existing words:

I am a hawk of pure gold. I soar towards the sun without fear of its brilliance.

* What does your bird carry with it: a dream of writing your great novel; a desire for freedom; a need for recognition? Add the earlier statements to your growing empowerment.
* Where must your bird carry these things on your behalf? Across the ocean where your lover is? To the United Nations for peace? To the office of the firm you want to employ you? To the little French market town where you would like to spend the rest of your days? Keep building the empowerment, reciting it aloud in its fuller growing version at each new stage.
* When do you need fulfilment or freedom? Add your time scale.
* Now recite the full empowerment nine times, each one more confidently as you pass the incense nine times clockwise round the bird and the feathers.
* Replace the incense.
* Hold the first feather in the smoke and recite the words even more confidently. Now say:

I take the first step to _____.

Name this step and release your feather into the wind.
* Repeat with new steps until all the feathers are gone.
* End by saying slowly but with certainty:

I have soared high, as have my wishes. So shall all be fulfilled if it is right to be.

* Roll the bird back into a ball and bury the wax or clay. If indoors, bury it in a dish of soil or sand that you can put outside later.
* Let the incense burn through and know that your desires will be fulfilled because you now have the will power and determination to reach those heights in your everyday life.

3

INSECT MAGICK

I nsects have always been a source of fascination to humans for they are the most ancient of creatures. Spiders' webs, shimmering in sunshine after rain, must have transfixed our distant ancestors who found them outside their caves, as they do now when we see them hanging from an unlovely city doorway or from a bush in the garden.

A caterpillar, being reborn from the cocoon as a fabulous butterfly, became a symbol of rebirth certainly by Neolithic times and was described by the sixteenth-century mystic Teresa of Avila as like the spirit emerging from the body after death.

The honey bee predates humanity like many insects and, for people in different ages and lands, provided not only food, but a preservative and healing substance for everything from sore throats and coughs to burns.

Beeswax could be formed easily into lights and, though prized and precious because it was not widely available to ordinary people, was much more fragrant and pure than lights made from animal fat.

All these mysterious creatures, tiny yet with what seemed wondrous powers, were used as symbols of the goddess by Neolithic people. Legends abound that humans learned weaving and net-making techniques from insect goddesses who, like the spider, wove the web of human life and, like the bee, gave abundance.

In this chapter I mainly focus on the bee, butterfly and spider and show how today they can be a focus for spells as they have through the ages.

There are, however, other crawling or flying insects, especially nocturnal ones, who were feared as being part of the unknown world of the spirits and these also remain significant. These are covered at the end of the chapter.

Bees

From early times the queen bee was used as an image to represent the mother goddess, and the hive was likened to the womb of the great mother, with her devotees, the worker bees. The most famous icon, depicting the goddess with the head of a bee and the feet of a bird, was found in a cave painting in southern Spain and dates from Neolithic times (see right).

Bees, like butterflies, another early mother goddess representation, were and still are etched or painted on protective charms, especially for children, babies, pregnant women, mothers, and very old or sick people, and to guard against loss, rejection, loneliness and grief.

Over the millennia, bees have been adopted as the icon of Rhea, the Greek earth mother, Demeter the Ancient Greek grain mother, Cybele, originally an Anatolian earth and mountain goddess whose worship spread throughout the Ancient Greek world and Roman Empire, Artemis the huntress and her Roman counterpart Diana, and Aphrodite, goddess of love.

In Celtic myth, bees were regarded as sources of great wisdom and as messengers between the dimensions, and in Christianity as emissaries of the Virgin Mary. For this reason they were kept informed of any major changes in their owners' lives as it was thought they would otherwise leave the hive. It is still considered unlucky to kill a bee that goes into a house as she is bringing blessings to the home.

In the Slavic folk tradition the bee is linked with the immaculate conception. On 26 July, the feast of St Anna, mother of Mary, whose birth also resulted from an immaculate conception, is the time when beekeepers pray for the conception of new healthy bees. In the Ukraine, bees are the tears of our lady, and the queen bee of any hive is called Queen Tsarina, a name associated with Mary, queen of heaven.

The magick of honey

Because honey was, apart from salt, the main preservative for thousands of years, it was treated as a magickal substance and has traditionally been used in folk rituals. Both the Egyptian papyrus *Ebers*, a medical treatise that was written about 1,500 BCE, and the Jewish Talmud cite honey as a healer for many external and internal illnesses. In the African tradition, the Yoruba mother goddess Oshun heals humankind with her sacred honey through her medicine men and women. There are several honey spells in my *Complete Book of Spells* (see Further reading).

Throughout Eastern Europe, Mary is protectress of bees and beekeepers, and consecrated honey is offered on altars on the feast of the assumption of the Virgin Mary on 15 August, the date linked with her ascension into heaven.

A food altar

Honey is usually placed in the south of a circle in magick and also acts as a focus for abundance, fertility, health and wealth in less formal spells.

In this altar formation, bread or vegetables are in the north, seeds in the east and nuts or fruit in the west (see Earth magick on pages 316–18).

Try this in a spell for abundance or arrange an informal supper at home with the table laid out in this way. Butter and cheese can also go in the south.

Magickal beeswax

Beeswax has for thousands of years been used in magick, both for making symbols in spells (see pages 147–48) and as the fire element in the form of candles. It is the purest and most natural candle substance and releases energy to attract positive results in its subtle fragrance and bright flame.

Whatever your spell or ritual, when you do have time, it can be very satisfying to roll your own beeswax candles. In the three or four minutes it takes to make a single candle, you can experience a transition from your hectic daily world. You can endow the candle with the purpose for which you are making it or, if it is to be a present, with your good wishes for the recipient.

I suggest a very basic form of beeswax candle-making, but once you start work it is self-explanatory. You can have candle-making sessions with friends and family, before a party or family gathering (children love making them), designing simple or elaborate creations which, as they burn, will release happiness and harmony.

You can store candles you have stockpiled in large plastic food containers to keep them dry and fresh and likewise keep any supplies of beeswax and lengths of wick.

In Sweden, beeswax sheets and candles are available in every supermarket. With the revival in interest in natural crafts, you can buy supplies from any craft store (there are craft supermarkets in some out-of-town retail parks). Country farm shops, farmers' markets, local honey suppliers and the Internet offer ready access to these materials as well as various appliqués for decorating candles with symbols, initials, zodiac signs, etc.

When shopping on-line, buy a small quantity from a site that sells naturally dyed beeswax and then test their reliability and quality for yourself.

If you buy ready-made beeswax candles, empower them before lighting. One tip is to stock up with candles at country markets or local fairs where they will be much cheaper than in New Age stores.

Making and empowering beeswax candles

There are many sites on the Internet that teach you how to make different kinds of beeswax candles, but essentially it is question of experimenting and having fun doing so. It is also a good idea to look at candles on sale commercially, especially those of traditional candle-makers at fairs, for ideas.

* Buy beeswax in ready-cut sheets. The standard sheet will make a candle without the need for cutting.
* Use the thicker wicks, called square braid, that is usually sold in long strands. You will need a length that extends 1 cm/0.5 in above the top of the candle and just before the bottom of the candle when formed. However, it is easier in practice to cut the wick a bit longer than this and trim afterwards when the wax is in place.
* Beeswax sheets roll well at normal room temperature or on a sunny day outdoors at about 20°C/70°F plus a bit. If it is cold, then a 30-second blast on low with a hair dryer will make the sheet pliable. If you are making the candle as part of

a spell, you can warm the wax gently with another candle flame.

* If it is too cold, the wax will crack as you roll it. If it is too hot, it will melt and the mottled pattern will fade. An awareness of the correct temperature soon becomes second nature. Enjoyment is the key to letting your candle absorb your happy vibes and it's hard to go wrong, even for a craft-inept person like myself.

* Work on a flat surface (you can put greaseproof paper down if you wish) or a ceramic or wood chopping or cheese board.

* For tall, thin candles, place the wick vertically on to the longer side of the beeswax sheet; for thicker more squat ones (my favourite) place it on the shorter side. The wick should be about 3 mm/^{1}/$_8$ in from the edge of the wax.

* Crease the edge of the sheet over the wick and press firmly so that it is well sealed. Make the first roll very tight to avoid trapping air between the wax and the wick.

* Spread your fingers across the length of the candle so it rolls smoothly, making sure that top and bottom are level.

* When you have finished, press the outer edge of the candle gently to seal the candle and stop it coming apart when lit. Alternatively, either use the flat blade of a warmed knife (the kind used for butter), or a spatula warmed for a few seconds by the flame of another candle (a 30-second blast with your hair dryer is faster). I would not do the latter if making the candle at the beginning of a spell but it is fine for candle-making sessions.

* The tighter you roll the candle, the longer it will burn. Conversely, if you are melting the candle to make an amulet, then a looser one will give quicker results.

* You can make beeswax candles of any size by cutting the wax on a firm surface using a sharp knife and a ruler (in half for pairs of matching candles).

* When making smaller candles, cut the end of the beeswax diagonally for a snugger fit.

* Empower your candle by chanting or saying in your mind the purpose of the spell continuously as you roll. When you seal it you can say:

Thus is the purpose and intent (named if you wish) sealed within the wax and it shall be.

* For general-use candles, you can empower them for peace, happiness, health or love and then be more specific when you light them for a spell.

* You can also endow candles for a party, for example:

Grant Alison a happy 21st birthday party and bring her luck and love in the following days.

This will be activated as the candles are lit.

* You can use different coloured waxes for different purposes (see pages 258–65).

* Hold bought candles briefly before you set them in a holder, whether for home use or a spell. State the purpose for which you are lighting them nine times (this might be something simple like reducing family quarrels), then revolve the candle nine time clockwise and say nine times:

May those who see this light be blessed.

A beeswax candle spell to bring abundance and wealth into your life in the way you need it most or for someone who has a pressing need

This is not a mercenary spell, though as I said earlier in the book, individuals and communities have from time immemorial used ritual to attract a good harvest or enough food and shelter. Under the cosmic rule you should then give practical help to someone in need when you can.

You may be seeking abundance in a different form, such as a happier home, fertility for yourself or a family member, good fortune for someone who has lost confidence or a good holiday or family gathering. You can more precisely define your own focus as you light the candles and it will work as well with candles you have bought.

Even if you carry out the spell for others, as a bonus, abundance will flow into your life in the way you most need it.

You will need: Four natural beeswax candles you have made or bought (they need only be small ones).

A dish or pot of honey and a spoon (you can often buy lidded bee-design pots with spoons at car boot sales).

A small slice of bread or a biscuit on a plate next to the honey.

Timing: The afternoon on any waxing or increasing moon day. Thursdays are good. For ongoing abundance cast the spell on four consecutive Thursdays.

❋ Set the four candles in a square around the honey dish and spoon and put the bread on its plate next to the honey.

❋ Light the south candle, for the direction of fire (and honey) and say:

*I light this candle that the lady mother, wise honey bee, will grant abundance to/for _____
(state how it is needed and by whom).*

❋ Repeat for the west, the north and the east candles.

❋ Touch the plate holding the bread and say:

I ask four wishes, if it is right to be, of the honey mother.

❋ Take the first small spoon of honey, just a drop, and put it on the bread, saying:

I seek abundance and ask the blessing of _____ from you, lady mother, wise honey bee.

❋ Put the spoon back and hold the bread with the single drop of honey, on the plate over the candle of the south, saying:

So I receive your abundance and blessings with thanks.

❋ Repeat and then hold the bread with the two drops of honey over the west candle, then three drops to the north and finally, to the east, four drops, using the same words and actions.

* Return the plate to the centre, eat the bread slowly and then say:

As I have received your abundance, so shall I give in return.

* If asking for abundance for yourself, name one small thing you can do to share your new abundance, maybe asking a difficult relative to a family gathering or a lonely colleague out to lunch.
* If you have asked for abundance for someone else, describe a way you can practically help or encourage them to maximize the gift, for example by looking after their pets or by keeping an eye on a teenager while they have the much-needed holiday you have asked for in the spell. You could also research cheap, last-minute weekends on the Internet on their behalf if money is the problem.
* Blow out the candles in reverse order of lighting, saying;

Lady mother, wise honey bee, I leave all to your care and offer thanks.

* You can repeat the spell on up to three more occasions at weekly intervals, if necessary.

Butterflies

The butterfly goddess was another Neolithic icon and reflected the powers of the mother goddess to bring new life and to offer spiritual transformation, hope and joy

The butterfly goddess icon appeared as the crowned butterfly goddess around 4,000 BCE in Minoan Crete, a centre of bull worship. She is depicted rising from the horns of the sacred bull, as a promise of fertility and regeneration.

Hina from the Polynesian tradition of the Pacific Islands is another traditional butterfly goddess. Hina is called the creatrix of the world, lady of the moon, and her spirit is said to be contained in every woman, for she was the first woman. Now Hina lives in the moon, having travelled there on a rainbow pathway. Every butterfly is a reminder to enjoy every moment of happiness.

Butterfly spells

Butterfly spells are easy in the summer and in warmer climes when butterflies are plentiful. Butterfly centres or farms attached to garden centres or in tourist resorts are also a natural setting for your butterfly spells.

But if it is the dark of winter, buy yourself a huge butterfly mobile or make one using natural materials rather than plastic or perspex. Hang it where the breeze will catch it and add one or two small silver bells.

It is said that today is the tomorrow you worried about yesterday. I am aware I fritter away a great deal of energy and sometimes spoil a happy occasion for myself by worrying about what I cannot change or something that may not happen anyway.

Equally, I have discovered as a mother that childhood doesn't last for ever.

What my now almost grown-up children recall are the picnics, sometimes in howling gales, or the after-school trips to the local country park, with the M4 providing background music and not the fact that they never took homemade cakes to school fetes and that the unmatched sock mountain rivalled Everest. In fact, my youngest, Bill, added cynically that what he can recall most is sleeping in a hotel wardrobe in Brittany when we ran out of beds!

The butterfly is a reminder that if the sun is shining to leave the chores or the work you brought home for the weekend, spend just a few hours outdoors – and look for butterflies.

Or, if it is cold and wet, find your nearest butterfly farm or visualise rainbow butterflies everywhere. This can be especially encouraging if life is hitting a down and you can't ever imagine how things could get better (not easy but, as I have found, psychically and psychologically more energising than sitting huddled by the heater eating a packet of chocolate biscuits and hexing uncaring humanity).

A butterfly spell for not worrying about the future or for finding the energy to start again after a setback

You will need: Butterflies, preferably fluttering free, but if not a paper butterfly mobile that you can reach as you stretch up.

Timing: Daylight, ideally a warm sunny day but usually when you need this spell it's pouring down and you've got the fire on. In such circumstances, visualisation is a real bonus and seems to get the serotonin flowing again.

* Unusually, do not consciously define your purpose in detail as butterfly energy is by its nature spontaneous and very mobile.
* If working with a butterfly mobile (paint it before the spell to get yourself in the mood), have bright flowers, preferably fragranced or fragrant herbs around you.
* Start by standing in the centre of the room, garden or butterfly area.
* Turn round three times clockwise, three times anticlockwise and three times clockwise, saying aloud or in your mind if there are people around (just after opening you might get a butterfly farm to yourself):

I chase butterflies. I seek – what do I seek? Butterfly goddess, lady of joy, what should I seek? Butterfly lady, open your heart that I may open mine likewise in joy.

* If in a place where there are butterflies, reach out each time you see a butterfly settle so that you almost touch it without disturbing it.
* Indoors, reach up and set your butterfly mobile in motion. Each time it stops, start it again. Keep picturing the most beautiful rainbow butterflies all round the room.
* Each time you contact a butterfly, open your arms wide and say, for the first butterfly or swing:

I chase butterflies. Butterfly lady, I seek to shed ____.

Let words come into your mind of what you wish to lose.

✴ For the second butterfly or swing of your indoor butterfly, say:

Butterfly lady, I seek to gain ____.

Let what you seek to gain come spontaneously into words. It may surprise you but will be an illumination. Begin each butterfly contact with:

I chase butterflies. Lady butterfly I ____.

✴ Continue for the third:

I banish the fear/worry (let it come).

✴ For the fourth:

I gain the hope.

✴ For the fifth:

I forgive.

✴ For the sixth:

I ask forgiveness for_____.

✴ For the seventh:

I lose the desire for _____.

✴ For the eighth:

I anticipate the pleasure of _____.

✴ For the ninth butterfly let a spontaneous wish emerge.
✴ You can continue as long as you want, chasing the butterflies and pairing what you seek to lose with what you seek to gain.
✴ When there are no more wishes or you are tired, enjoy the butterflies a while longer or swing your butterfly to and fro and fill your room with imaginary butterflies.
✴ End the ritual by sitting quietly and letting the energies settle.
✴ Hang your paper butterfly outdoors where it will be carried away by the wind.

Spiders

The most powerful Spider goddess in mythology is probably the Native North American Grandmother Spider Woman. She is the creatrix goddess who wove the web of the world and peopled it with figures from the earth made from four different clays: red, white, yellow and brown. Tawa, or Grandfather Sun, breathed life into them.

After creation, the sun returned to the sky, but grandmother spider has returned many times to teach and guide in many guises. She has taught many crafts: how to cultivate food, the power of herbs, how to smudge, ways of healing and how to weave dreamcatchers to stop bad nightmares, especially for children.

In the Ancient Greek tradition, Arachne was called the spider goddess. She was once a skilled mortal weaver who challenged the great goddess Athena, herself a weaver of fate, to a contest. The contest did not go well for Arachne, as Athena tore up her tapestry. Arachne killed herself in sorrow, but was restored by the juice of aconite. In some versions, Arachne now weaves the weather and the seasons as a goddess in the skies. In others, Athena turned Arachne into a spider and declared that henceforward Arachne and her descendants should hang forever from threads as they wove their webs.

In the African tradition, Anansi, the spider man could climb higher than any other mortal. He ascended (or wove) the celestial web into the heavens. He returned to earth after meeting Nyambe, the supreme god, with the gift of stories for humans and the knowledge of farming. In return, Anansi gave Nyambe the sun.

Spider spells are very potent for all creative ventures and for weaving together families, colleagues, different groups of people and even to work for peace.

Candle webs are increasingly popular. These involve people in different places lighting candles at the same time or at staggered intervals so that candles are kept burning to remember a particular incident or cause. After the 11 September disaster an Internet site passed e-mails around so that candles are and still may be kept continuously burning in memory. I have written about this and other candle webs in my *Complete Book of Spells*.

Webs in magick

Webs are about connections, and web magick will draw people together psychically and emotionally.

Beeswax candle webs are lovely if you have a common event or aim, perhaps a family birthday, an anniversary or family gathering in the garden at home (or indoors). You could also invite friends who have not met for a while to drive to a central place for a picnic or barbecue and bring a candle each.

Each person can then light their candle and makes a greeting to the others or a wish for the person for whom the occasion is being held.

You can also send healing through a candle web, gathered with well-wishers in one place, perhaps to a relative who is having an operation, a family member who can't get home for Christmas or to mend a breach caused by an acrimonious divorce where grandparents cannot so easily see beloved grandchildren.

You can set up candle web events for World Peace Day or for a summer or winter solstice when everyone lights a candle as dusk falls or dawn breaks wherever they are. If you work by dawn or dusk lighting you can circumvent time-zone differences. However, I would suggest everyone lit the candle, say, at 10pm, the healing hour, so that the energies flowed over a longer period through different time zones. Otherwise you can synchronise a suitable shared time frame.

A private web spell for overcoming a very personal or secret fear or obstacle

You will need: A natural spider's web, preferably outdoors where it is lit by sun- or moonlight. If you find one indoors, light a beeswax candle. If you are scared of spiders use an abandoned web. Otherwise hang up a small, unadorned dreamcatcher where it swings free outdoors but is low enough for you to be level with the web.

A small bowl of sacred water (see page 124) or, for speed, three pinches of salt mixed into still mineral water.

Timing: By natural light, if possible.

* Face the spider's web about three paces from it and put the bowl down on the ground or a low table.
* Raise your arms and pretend you are weaving a web, so your hands are moving in and out in patterns. Do not touch the actual web.
* As you weave, say:

> *Grandmother spider, help me weave a better web, one stronger, one made of love and laughter. Untangle this fear.*

Name the fear and, as you do so, undo an imaginary knot in the air.

* If you want to, talk quietly about your fear or the insurmountable mountain you have to climb.
* When you have finished, take the bowl and scatter drops to weave a web between you and the actual web or dreamcatcher, Finally, sprinkle the centre of your hair line, your brow and left and right wrists, all in silence.
* End by turning, still carrying the water bowl, and say:

> *Blessings be, grandmother. Bless me.*

* Tip any water on to the ground.

Nocturnal insects

Insects of the night have sometimes been a source of uncertainty because they fly in the night and so have strong links with the spirit world. So, likewise, have strange creatures like the centipede.

The mysterious moth, the scorpion and the centipede provoked both terror and reverence in the fierce Aztec warriors. The Aztecs dedicated altars to these feared creatures, carving their images on to the altars and making offerings to propitiate them. The night owl, the scorpion, the bat and the spider were associated with the Aztec Mictlantecutl, lord of death and so were protected species.

To the Aztecs even the spiders were scary. Spiders hanging down from a thread were equated with the Tzitzimime, spirits who gathered at crossroads. Since these were supposed to encourage men to commit adultery, those with partners with wandering eyes might do well to keep cobwebs out of the bedroom.

The centipede was associated with the earth, night and the powers of darkness. Night was the time when the sun crossed the underworld and so was to be feared.

Grasshoppers, however, were welcomed and carnelian models have been found of them. The grasshopper signified abundance in the fields after the rainy season, which he heralded.

In Ancient Egypt, Selkit or Serqet was a beautiful scorpion goddess, one of the four protective goddesses of the pharaohs and later of ordinary people. The others were Isis, Nephythys, her shadowy sister of the twilight, and Neith, the weaver goddess. Selkit holds the dual function of protector and attacker. Fiercely vengeful for those who are unworthy or destructive, she nevertheless cures the innocent who are wounded by the spite and malice of others. In Egypt she guarded against or was entreated for healing of scorpion stings.

Moths

As a species that has existed for about 60 million years the moth is, not surprisingly, also a symbol of immortality. Like butterflies, moths are primarily a symbol of reincarnation and regeneration, because of their metamorphosis from egg to caterpillar to moth.

The concept of moths as souls in transit is found in a number of cultures including the Australian Aboriginies and the Chinese. The attraction of moths to the light is regarded as an attempt to make the transition to the spirit world.

Whenever you see a moth indoors, you should try to guide it to an open window or door and in return you can ask for light to come into your life in any way you need it.

Outdoors, moths at twilight are, like butterflies, a way of sending away your fears of the night and insomnia and for letting go of what you must set free. Whisper to the moth as it settles your worries and it will carry them to be transformed, leaving you to sleep peacefully.

PART 5

MAGICK OF THE SENSES

Introduction

Our physical senses are the channel through which we observe and interact with the natural world. They also provide a doorway to our extended psychic senses that are activated in spellcasting and rituals. The meeting of physical and psychic senses opens up the rich resources of the magickal meanings behind colours, oils and sounds in nature. These storehouses of knowledge collected over thousands of years enable us to move beyond the everyday fixed realms into the worlds of possibility and the expansion of our horizons. Some of this you know instinctively, as well as through your learning and experiences, because they are our collective cultural heritage. This inheritance, I believe, can be accessed and recalled through our genes once we start on this road of exploration and is at least partly activated through magickal work.

Too often in the modern world we may barely hear natural sounds over the canned music, the disharmony of a thousand mobile ring tones and the constant announcements over tannoys on trains, in shopping malls and in supermarkets.

We are visually bombarded by simulated images on hundreds of television channels, at theme parks, in cinemas and in museums. The latter are very valuable for bringing history alive, but have meant that many children now don't even stop to wonder at an ancient carved image on a mammoth rib and consider an otter in a sanctuary far less exciting than a dinosaur show.

So too have strong chemically produced perfumes and household products eliminated unwanted odours from our sanitised universe, promising to emulate the freshness of a spring day or ocean breezes in the living room or tumble dryer.

But outside the box of the reconstructed reality, we can still smell the real spring in the air, the salty tang of a seaside town, burning wood smoke and fields of lavender that are sprouting up on the outside of cities as natural lavender makes a comeback. Even DIY superstores have their fragrant herb section.

As we reconnect with real outdoor nature through our physical senses, so we spontaneously plug into the life force, and our psychic senses are likewise reawakened.

We can add chanting or Tibetan bell vibrations to give rhythm to our spellcasting, use the variety of colour meanings as yet another of nature's zip files to open up our magickal horizons through the use of flowers, fruits and crystals in our spells. We can eat the magick in red apples or purple grapes that we have empowered.

As we mix our oils with magickal meanings or make floral oil waters to enhance our words and actions in ritual we may dimly recall what our ancestors knew, the symbolic folk meanings attached to fresh pine, lemon or cedar wood.

What is more, all this information enriches our daily lives, making colours seem richer, sounds more harmonious, fragrances stronger and more uplifting as we move closer to harmony and a sense of connection with the natural world.

This is inevitably a labour-intensive part of the book for me and for the reader. I have introduced a lot of the background information that I have collected over nearly 20 years and am constantly updating as I learn more. These keys to meaning offer the tools to weave our very own magick.

Each new spell is a learning experience for me (and hopefully for you) and a revelation of nature's wonders.

COLOUR MAGICK

olours enhance both magick and healing. Each colour is like a zip file on a computer whereby you open up a whole world of magickal associations and powers contained within it.

The colours of nature and the cosmos offer different life-force qualities in flowers, crystals, gems, fruits, plants and trees, the sky, the sun, the moon and stars. Potent also are colours animated by fire in candles.

The three primary colours, red, blue and yellow, from which all other colours can be derived, hold the seeds of colour energy, as does pure white, the synthesis of all the rainbow colours. The Ancient Egyptians believed that red, yellow and blue corresponded to the mind, body and spirit, respectively.

All colours vibrate at different frequencies and affect us physically as well as psychologically: healing and energising white light, dynamic and warming red, cooling and calming blue, growth-inducing green and soothing pink to name a few. At the higher spiritual and magickal level the qualities and strengths represented by each colour amplify similar yet sometimes hidden or undeveloped strengths within us.

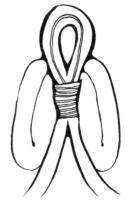

Ancient Egyptian amulets and charms, as well as statues, were made from particular coloured crystals or metals or painted in a certain colour to indicate and release the magickal power. For example, Osiris, the god of rebirth and regeneration who was associated with the annual growth of plants, was painted green. Red was almost always the colour of the amulet of the Tjet, called the girdle of Isis. This image was associated with Isis in her role as mother and so with female power and magickal menstrual blood. It would be engraved in or on carnelian or red jasper. The magick spell spoken over it to bring fertility began with the words:

The power of Isis and the blood of Isis and the words of Isis . . .

and through the spell the red raw energy was released.

What is colour?

Each beam of coloured light has its own wavelength and is absorbed by the body through the skin and the optic nerves. This triggers complex biochemical changes. People who spend prolonged periods in darkness suffer from vitamin deficiencies, hormonal disorders and disturbances of the normal body cycles, including irregular sleep patterns, metabolic imbalances and depression. SAD, Seasonal Affective Disorder, is caused by a lack of sunlight, and can trigger depression and lethargy during long, grey winter months.

Each of the seven primary wavelengths or vibrations of light visible to the human eye focuses on a different part of the body, evoking in each both a physiological and psychological response.

Red is the longest wavelength of visible colour and violet the shortest. The colours that we can see make up only a very small segment of the electromagnetic spectrum and lie between the infrared and ultraviolet rays.

White, the combination of all seven colours, was first associated by the Pythagoreans with the godhead and purity.

Black, the absence of colour, is associated with negativity, though not in Ancient Egypt where it symbolised the fertile Nile mud and so brought new life after the dry arid season.

Colours in magick

Colour can be used in spells as well as empowered in our everyday lives to infuse us with those aspects of the life force we most need.

By absorbing the energies of natural sources of colour in a variety of ways, we can almost instantly fill ourselves with confidence and vitality or calm any inner turmoil or panic. Natural colour is released spontaneously by flowers, trees, fruits, the sky and sea in all their moods, the grass, the red, orange or gold sun, the silver moon and the ever-changing shades of brown, red and gold of the earth.

In spellcasting we can both amplify and focus the colour power and ensure it continues to filter into our lives through the rush of colour entering us or by means of a symbol that can be carried as a charm.

Naturally dyed pure wax candles, when lit, release a very active stream of colour. By using specific candle or crystal colours we can give particular weight to those qualities or strengths we seek to evoke in the spell. For example, you might use blue candles in all four directions on your altar for a spell to obtain justice in the days before a court case or tribunal.

You can, of course, mix your colours in magick as in painting in order to get a particular colour balance. For example, orange and blue, if predominant in a spell, would ensure enthusiasm and creativity for a project, but at the same time longer-term focus and authority, so your ideas will be accepted and others will co-operate if you are the initiator.

Adding colour to spells

* Keep a selection of different coloured altar cloths for specific kinds of magick. These need not be expensive and can be made from off-cuts of fabric or be bought in sales. A pink cloth would be used for healing or family spells, blue for a career improvement, justice or legal matter and gold for the achievement of a major ambition. You can buy natural fabrics such as linen or silk and tie dye or print your own designs.
* Use different coloured purses or drawstring bags, again in natural fabrics, to hold symbols, herbs and crystals and for spell bags (see page 139).
* Burn the candle colour most relevant to your spell as the candle in the south of your altar. Engrave the candle using a long pin or small screwdriver with its planetary symbol and, if you wish, the appropriate zodiacal sun sign glyph (see page 152).
* Use different coloured dried flower petals or herbs instead of salt for the earth element.
* Ring the symbol and the dish with a circle of appropriately coloured crystals, for example, small orange carnelians or glass nuggets if you want to increase your self-confidence.
* Empower the elemental water in the west with a crystal of the colour of the qualities you need. Leave the crystal in the water overnight before the spell and take it out just before the spellcasting.
* Use fresh flowers of the colour or colours whose strengths you are invoking near the centre of your altar.
* Before beginning the spell, breathe in visualised coloured light from the flowers or any source of colour in the setting where you are casting the spell (for example a green forest). Very softly inhale each in-breath. Pause momentarily and then gently push the out-breath through your mouth as a sigh so that the light is spread around the altar and will infuse the symbol and tools. Pause momentarily again and take another slow in-breath, establishing a slow, regular rhythm until the altar and you feel infused with the colours.
* Use different colours of fruits, vegetables or unprocessed foods (lightly cooked where necessary) as your focus in personal spells. Once it is empowered the food can be eaten after the spell to absorb the charged colour.
* Make wax amulets in particular colours, or engrave talismans and charms with the colour's ruling planetary glyph.
* Carry out spells entirely with one colour for candles, crystals and flowers.
* Stage-manage a spell so that the whole scene is bathed, for example, in silver moonlight or have golden brown earth, blue or grey sky, a green tree and maybe some red flowers to create the colour mix you need.

Colour meanings in magick

The following are the most popular associations for the colours. White has two entries because you have the dazzling white brilliance of bright sunlight and the softer white glow of moonlight. Each shade has different properties.

You can weave magickal spells to activate the strengths inherent in the colours, using the deity names, the ruling planet, the archangel, the crystals, the elements and even the day of the week associated with each colour. Some of the associations you will find are linked with the days of the week and include deities you have met earlier in the book. Gradually magickal associations come together to form an intertwining web of power, so each spell or ritual becomes infused with symbolic significance.

White, bright

Use bright white in spells for fulfilling potential, for increased energy, optimism and enthusiasm, the free-flowing life force, originality, new beginnings and for innovations of all kinds

It is potent also for bringing or restoring prosperity when fortunes are low, for breaking a run of bad luck, and for all matters concerning fathers; also good health, vitality, for spiritual development and contact with one's higher self and angels, spirit guides and divinity; also for purity, cleansing and for mind, body and spirit healing. In magick, white can be used as a substitute for any other colour

Planetary ruler: ☉ the sun

Day of the week: Sunday

Deities: Dagaz, the Norse god of the dawn who rode his chariot drawn by a white steed, Skjin-faxi (shining mane). Brilliant beams of light radiated from its mane in all directions, scattering the night

Sopdet or Sophis, the Ancient Egyptian star goddess of Sirius, the brightest star in the sky, whose rising heralded the Nile flood. She was depicted with a star on her head

Grainne, the Celtic sun goddess who woke the fertility of the earth every spring after the long winter and to whom hilltop fires and processions led in midsummer and at the harvest

Archangel: Michael, archangel of the sun

Element: Air

Gems and crystals: Aragonite, clear crystal quartz, clear fluorite, diamond, Herkimer diamond, opal aura, rainbow quartz, white sapphire, white topaz, zircon

Sun sign: Leo, the lion (23 July–23 August)

White, soft or cloudy

Use soft or cloudy white for protection against negativity, for pregnancy, mothers and for babies and small children, for restoring hope, for success in writing and poetry, for gradual new beginnings after loss, for intuitive awareness, for the granting of wishes and fulfilment of dreams, for recovering from illness, depression or exhaustion, for discovering secrets (see also grey) and for calling someone from afar

Planetary ruler: ☽ the moon

Day of the week: Monday

Deities: the White Goddess of the Celtic peoples who inspired writers and poets

Selene, the Greek goddess specially associated with the full moon, sometimes forming a triplicity with Dana and Hecate. She rises from the sea in her chariot drawn by white horses at night

Berkano, the beautiful silver birch tree goddess, whose ancient worship is still recalled in folk custom in lands as far north as Russia at the old whitsun when the birch maiden is made from a young birch tree and adorned with flowers

Archangel: Gabriel, archangel of the moon

Element: Water

Gems and crystals: Calcite, howlite, milky opal, milky quartz, moonstone, pearl, selenite, snow quartz

Sun sign: Pisces, the fish (19 February–20 March)

Red

Use red in spells for action, courage, assertiveness, power, determination, stamina and strength, sexual passion, potency, sensual pleasures and the consummation of love; for the impetus for positive change and for taking the initiative, it also represents competitiveness, standing out against injustice and protecting the vulnerable and loved ones under threat; for survival and for overcoming seemingly impossible odds

Planetary ruler: ♂ Mars

Day of the week: Tuesday

Deities: Mars the Roman god of both agriculture and war, who represented the ideal Roman as farmer, protector and wise ruler and then as conqueror

Bellona, the Roman goddess of war, the female counterpart of Mars whose chariot she drove into battle

Sekhmet, the Ancient Egyptian lion-headed goddess of fire who sent out her obsidian arrows against her enemies but used them protectively to defend the sick and vulnerable

Archangel: Samael, archangel of cleansing fire

Element: Fire

Gems and crystals: Blood agate, bloodstone/heliotrope, fire opal, garnet, jasper, red tiger's eye, ruby

Sun sign: Aries, the ram (21 March–20 April)

Orange

Use orange in spells for self-esteem and confidence, strengthening identity and establishing personal boundaries between self and others and for independence; for balance and negotiations, for the media, for music, for fertility, both physical and mental, for creativity and all creative and artistic ventures and for abundance of all kinds

Planetary ruler: ☉ sun

Day of the week: Sunday

Deities: Apollo, the god of light and most glorious of the gods, who inspired musicians and artists

Ana or Danu, ancient mother goddess of Ireland and the old gods. She was the original owner of the cauldron of rebirth called Annwyn that was filled with pearls and guarded by nine maidens

Heket or Heqet, the Ancient Egyptian frog-headed goddess who assisted in childbirth and breathed life into the clay figures created by her husband Knum the potter god

Archangel: Metatron, archangel of light and the heavenly scribe

Gems and crystals: Amber, aragonite, beryl, calcite, carnelian, celestine, jasper, mookaite and sunstone

Element: Fire

Sun sign: Sagittarius, the archer (23 November–21 December)

Yellow

Use yellow in spells for logic, focus, improving memory and concentration, for learning, for passing examinations and tests, for mastering new technology, for clear communication; good also for job changes and overcoming money problems; for all money-making ventures and speculation; for persuasion, adaptability and versatility; for short-distance or short-duration breaks; for recovery through conventional methods of healing, especially surgery. It is also potent for repelling envy, malice and spite and to protect against those who would deceive

Planetary ruler: ☿ Mercury

Day of the week: Wednesday

Deities: Mercury, the Roman winged messenger and healer god (the Greek Hermes) and son of Jupiter. Carrying a healing rod entwined with two serpents that could induce sleep, he travelled between the heavens, earth and the underworld

Aesculapius, the healer son of Apollo and the mortal Corona, who became a god after Zeus killed him with a thunderbolt for raising the dead. The first shrine dedicated to Aesculapius was built in Athens in the fifth century BCE by Sophocles

Iduna, the Viking goddess of eternal youthfulness, health and long life, who possessed a store of golden apples that endowed immortality to all she favoured

Archangel: Raphael, archangel of healing and travellers

Gems and crystals: Calcite (yellow and honey calcite), chrysoberyl, citrine, jasper, lemon chrysoprase, rutilated quartz, topaz

Element: Air

Sun sign: Gemini, the heavenly twins (22 May–21 June)

Green

Use green in spells for love, fidelity and commitment; to bring beauty into your life; for the acquisition of beautiful possessions; for harmony, for horticulture and the environment; also for healing people through natural methods such as herbs and crystals and for healing the planet, especially the land and forests. Because of its association with growth, green can be used for the gradual increase of all energies, especially health, wealth and resources as well as good luck

Planetary ruler: ♀ Venus

Day of the week: Friday

Deities: Aphrodite, the Cretan and Greek goddess of love and beauty, born of the foam, associated with the sea, as well as with passionate love

Innana, a Sumerian goddess, queen of heaven, goddess of beauty, abundance, fertility and passion, famed for her loveliness and her lapis lazuli necklaces formed from the stars. She was the first goddess of the morning and evening star, a legacy that has passed via Innana and Astarte to Aphrodite and Venus

Venus, as the goddess of love, fertility and beauty is the Roman form of Aphrodite. By her liaison with Mercury she gives birth to the young god of love, Cupid

Archangel: Anael, archangel of love

Element: Earth and water

Gems and crystals: Amazonite, aventurine, chrysoprase, emerald, fluorite, jade, malachite, moss agate and tourmaline

Sun sign: Virgo, the maiden (24 August–22 September)

Blue

Use blue for matters of justice, for career and employment, especially promotion, for acquiring traditional knowledge, for leadership opportunities, for authority and power used wisely, for long-distance or long-term travel and house moves; for marriage and partnerships of all kinds, for expansion of business and financial improvement based on past efforts, for idealism, for drawing down healing powers from higher sources and to heal air pollution and the seas

Planetary ruler: ♃ Jupiter

Day of the week: Thursday

Deities: Dazhbog, the sun and father god who is called grandfather of Russia. He travels in a chariot across the sky, bringing with him the morning light, justice and abundance. The seven planets act as judges for him

Odin, the Norse father god, known as the all-father, god of inspiration, wisdom and poetry, as well as war

Ma'at the Ancient Egyptian goddess of truth, against whose feathered headdress, the hearts of the deceased were weighed to test their worthiness

Archangel: Sachiel, archangel of abundance and the harvest

Element: Air

Gems and crystals: Angelite, aqua aura, blue chalcedony, blue lace agate, blue quartz, celestite/celestine, cobalt aura, iolite, kyanite, lapis lazuli, sapphire, topaz and turquoise

Sun sign: Libra, the scales (23 September–23 October)

Purple

Use purple for spiritual knowledge and increasing psychic powers, for finding answers through dreams, for any form of teaching or counselling work, for banishing what lies in the past but is still troublesome, for diminishing pain, for healing all addictions and neuroses and for contacting friends and family members with whom you have lost touch or who live far away; for spells concerning older people and for protection physically, mentally, emotionally and psychically

Planetary ruler: ♃ Jupiter

Day of the week: Thursday

Deities: Osiris, father and underworld god of the Ancient Egyptians, who assured for all, not just pharaohs and nobles, immortality if their hearts were pure

Saga, Norse goddess of wisdom and prophecy, who gave the gift of storytelling to the world and encouraged the people to transmit their wisdom in verse

Athena or Athene, Greek goddess of wisdom, born from the head of her father; the goddess of wise counsel, both in peace and war, of intelligence, reason, negotiation and all forms of the arts and literature

Archangel: Raziel, archangel of mysteries

Element: Air

Gems and crystals: Amethyst, ametrine, charoite (looks like purple lapis lazuli), fluorite, lepidolite, sodalite, sugilite, super seven, titanium aura

Sun sign: Aquarius, the water carrier (21 January–18 February)

Pink

Use pink for reconciliation and the mending of quarrels or coldness, for happy family relationships, for friendship, gentleness and kindness, for very gentle binding magick; for all matters concerning children and teenagers, for girls entering puberty and women entering the menopause, for young or new love and the growth of love and trust after betrayal or a setback; good also for healing stress-related illnesses, psychological trauma and abuse, especially left from childhood, and to bring quiet sleep

Planetary ruler: ♀ Venus

Day of the week: Friday

Deities: Frigg, or Frigga the Norse mother goddess and patroness of women, who had the gift of prophecy and knew what even Odin her husband could not see, but would never reveal her secrets

Parvati, the benign and gentle Hindu mother goddess, consort of the god Shiva

Madrones, the three mother goddesses of the Celts and Romans who protected children and mothers and ensured enough food for the people

Archangel: Zadkiel, archangel of gentleness and integrity (also archangel of Thursday in his abundance role)

Element: Earth

Gems and crystals: Kunzite, mangano or pink calcite, morganite, pink chalcedony, rose quartz and tourmaline

Sun sign: Taurus, the bull (21 April–21 May)

Brown

Use brown in spells for all practical matters, security, the gradual accumulation of money, for self-employment and learning new skills, especially in later years; for the home, property, institutions such as banking, for animals and for conservation of old places and traditions. Brown is good also for absorbing pain and panic, for finding what is lost or stolen and for increasing strength after an illness or in later years; good for healing animals

Planetary ruler: ♄ Saturn

Day of the week: Saturday

Deities: Ingwaz, the ancient Norse fertility god who brought new life to the land each spring and then retreated to allow his efforts to come to fruition

Tellus Mater, the Roman mother earth in whose name oaths were sworn

Mata Syra Zjemlja, Mokosh or Matka, the Slavic earth mother whose name means Moist mother earth. She is the goddess of fertility, birth and midwives. A fate goddess, she spins the web of life and ordains when the individual threads shall be cut

Archangel: Cassiel, archangel of compassion and wise silence

Element: Earth

Gems and crystals: Banded agate, brown zircon, desert rose, fossils, fossilised or petrified wood, leopardskin jasper, rutilated quartz, and all the sand-coloured and brown mottled jaspers, smoky quartz and tiger's eye

Sun sign: Capricorn, the goat (22 December–20 January)

Grey

Use grey in spells for casting invisibility around yourself to create a low profile in times of danger or unwelcome confrontation, for neutralising unfriendly energies and feelings, for compromise, for peace-making, keeping secrets and to repel psychic attack

Planetary ruler: ☿ Mercury (sometimes called hidden Mercury)

Day of the week: Wednesday

Deities: Isis veiled, the hidden mysterious aspect of the Ancient Egyptian goddess Isis

Tiwaz, the spirit warrior of the Norse gods who symbolised the pole star

Persephone or Kore, the Greek maiden goddess who was abducted by Hades, god of the underworld, and became queen of the underworld for the winter months, returning to the world as the light-bringer in spring

Archangel: Sandalphon, archangel of carers and what is yet to be revealed

Element: Air

Gems and crystals: Apache tear (obsidian), banded agate, laboradite, lodestone, meteorite, smoky quartz

Sun sign: Gemini, the heavenly twins (22 May–21 June)

Gold

Use gold in spells for attaining perfection, fulfilling a great dream or ambition, for all sun magick, for an urgent or large infusion of money and resources; for a long and happy life, for a major leap forward, for discovering your unique potential, for recognition and fame, to recover after a huge setback, for contacting angels and for healing when the prognosis is not good or a patient is not responding to conventional treatment

Planetary ruler: ☉ the sun

Day of the week: Sunday

Deities: Aine, another Celtic sun goddess, sister of Grainne, goddess of the sun and moon; goddess of cattle and corn and the harvest

Svarozhich, the Slavic fire god who gave power to the winter sun and lit fires at the harvest to dry the gathered crops before they were ground into grain

Ra or Re, the Ancient Egyptian sun god who was portrayed as the sun at its full power and depicted by the symbol of the sun and also in his solar boat. Ra is shown variously as a man or a hawk-headed man, crowned with the sun disk

Archangel: Uriel, archangel of transformation and alchemy

Element: Fire

Gems and crystals: Boji stones, clear quartz crystal, cuprite (copper nugget), diamond, gold, polished iron pyrites, tiger eye, topaz

Sun sign: Leo, the lion (23 July–23 August)

Silver

Use silver in spells for establishing natural cycles for fertility, for all moon, star and night magick, for increased financial good fortune, for bringing the unexpected into your life, for discovering the truth about a matter, for increased intuition and for women's magick of all kinds

Planetary ruler: ☽ the moon

Day of the week: Monday

Deities: Arianrhod, Welsh goddess of the full moon, time and destiny. Her mystical fountain of wine offered eternal health and youth for those who chose to spend their immortality in the afterlife

Britomaris, the Cretan moon goddess who was adopted by the Greek invaders as protectress of all who sailed the seas. She was also a prophetess and is linked with

Ariadne, the fate and fertility goddess of the Minoans

Khonsu or Knensu, the Ancient Egyptian moon god, whose name means to cross, because he crossed the heavens every night in his lunar boat. He is depicted in human form with a crescent moon supporting the full moon disk

Archangel: Ofaniel, the archangel who rules the individual days of the moon cycle and their angels

Element: Water

Gems and crystals: Haematite, moonstone, pearl, rainbow moonstone, rainbow obsidian, selenite, silver, white opal

Sun sign: Cancer, the crab (22 June–22 July)

Black

Use black in spells for endings; for banishing sorrow, guilt, destructive influences and for acceptance of what cannot be changed; for working within limitations and restrictions, for mourning, for rebirth and for reducing chronic pain; also for blocking a negative or harmful force

Planetary ruler: ♄ Saturn

Day of the week: Saturday

Deities: Saturn, the Roman form of Cronus, god of time, Jupiter's father who was deposed by his son. Saturn was sent to Italy where he taught the farmers agriculture and engineering and established a golden age of peace and plenty

Badbh, the Irish Morrigu crow, raven or vulture goddess who also assumed the form of a wolf or a bear. Vulture goddesses picked clean the bones of the deceased so they might be reborn

Chamunda, the eight-armed Hindu goddess, who wears a necklace of skulls but promises, to those who can look her in the face, rebirth in a new, more perfect form – and to her devotees, protection and relief from suffering

Archangel: Raguel, archangel of ice and snow, who protects against their ill effects

Element: Water

Gems and crystals: Black opal, black pearl, jet, obsidian, onyx, snowflake obsidian, tektite and tourmaline (schorl)

Sun sign: Virgo, the maiden (24 August–22 September)

A four-colour spell to bring new and lasting love

You will need: Four freshly picked flowers: one pink, one red, one white and one blue; a metal or heatproof ceramic dish for the petals.

Rose water, either bought or a bowl of water in which you have floated a single rose in moonlight from dusk to dawn (for making your own flower waters see my *Fragrant Magic* book in Further reading). You can buy ready-made rose water from garden centres, pharmacies and herbalists.

Four small candles (natural beeswax is best): pink, red, white and blue.

Timing: At the beginning of a week or month

- Set the candles in a row, left to right as you face them: pink, red, white and blue.
- Place the flowers in front of their corresponding candle.
- Put the bowl of rose water to the left of the pink candle and the petal dish to the right of the blue candle.
- Light the pink candle and say:

That I may find new love / love again.

- Light the red candle and say:

That desire may flame between us.

- Light the white candle and say:

That we may be together.

- Light the blue candle and say:

And stay so forever.

- Take the pink flower and pluck a single petal. Say:

That I may find new love / love again.

- Hold it in the flame of the pink candle and repeat the words.
- When it just singes, drop it in the dish.
- Do the same with petals from the other three flowers, repeating the earlier colour refrains for each.
- Return the dish to its place to the right of the blue candle.
- Finally sprinkle rose water droplets clockwise in a circle to enclose all the candles, the flowers and the dish with the four petals on it.
- Recite the pink, red, white and blue refrains one after the other as you make the circle.
- Now blow out the candles in the order of lighting, saying:

Love

- Blow out the pink.

Come

- Blow out the red.

To

- Blow out the white.

Me.

* Blow out the blue.
* Put the four flowers in a vase at a window facing the road and bury the four singed petals beneath a flourishing plant.
* Repeat the spell as necessary at the beginning of each new week or month.

Collecting colours

To supplement the lists given in this chapter start your own colour section in your Book of Shadows.

* Dedicate a set of pages to each colour so that they can act both as a resource and a stimulation to your psyche at times when, for example, in the middle of winter you crave the positive impetus of a field of scarlet poppies waving in the breeze.
* List particular varieties of flowers that grow in your garden and region at different times of the year and dry petals of the fragrant ones so you can recapture the colour power throughout the year and use them in colour spells.
* Note down crystals that represent different shades of a colour, from the watery green fluorite for gentle love and reconciliation, the apple green chrysoprase of growing love and peace to the vibrant malachite for tough love or the survival of love under difficulty.
* Collect small crystals in different shades for spellcasting. Carry one empowered by any spells you cast, as a good luck charm and a reminder of the power you generated in the spell. You can leave the crystals in the centre of the altar during any spell to absorb the spell energies, even if you are using another symbol, like a wax image or flower as the main focus.
* List herbs and evergreens that grow in your garden, local park or woodland. Dry the flowering heads or different coloured leaves when at their most fragrant or mature to store for when you need instant colour power. There are different shades of green, mauve, red, silver and grey in the most common of herbs. Look in a garden centre for inspiration.
* Write also names of places you can easily travel to where natural colour is vibrant. These you can use as a backdrop for colour magick. They might include green hillsides, red sandstone rocks, areas of almost black soil, a sea that always sparkles blue in sunlight or one that, like my local one on the Isle of Wight, the site of fossils and dinosaur footprints, foams brownish red all year because of the high clay content of the beach.
* Note also with approximate dates of flowering and seasonal sources of colour: a carpet of bluebells in the late spring in a local botanical garden or woodland, a field of cornflowers that appear every year near a favourite picnic spot, ripening corn or expanses of brilliant yellow rape seeds, bright red apples at harvest time on emerald green trees.
* Note also any beach or open space where the later stages of the waxing moon and the full moon regularly bathe the spot in silver light or one which has spectacular sunsets.
* Describe in your Book of Shadows your feelings and sensations as you stand in your chosen places, for example the bluebell woods, so if you need the energy of a particular colour you can in the future invoke its power by recalling the image of the bluebell woods and the mass of blue.

Chakra colour energies and magick

Colours flow in and out of our psychic energy field or aura and the colours you use in a spell will, as a bonus, energise or harmonise your energy field as well as empowering the focus of the spell. The chakras are our inner colour power source and link with external colours in nature, amplifying the colours we use in spellcasting.

Each of our seven main energy centres or chakras is associated with one of the rainbow colours and these same colours radiate in the aura.

These colours cannot be physically seen, except as a faint glow, but can be perceived by the clairvoyant eye or by children, whose clairvoyant and physical sight is not really differentiated.

The chakra colours released and generated within you during spellcasting act as supplementary colour power and help you to internalise the benefits of the spell. The individual colours strengthen the areas of your mind, body or spirit as listed below and help you to activate and merge with the spell power, allowing it to remain within you long after the spell is completed. They also illuminate and strengthen your aura colours so that you create a positive impression with others and spontaneously attract the love, success and recognition you need.

Red and brown: Linked with the root or base chakra located in the perineum and also with the chakras in the soles of the feet. The root chakra is associated with our survival instincts and five senses. It draws energy from the earth. These are good energies in any spell to give a practical foundation to wishes and the stamina to see them through in the everyday world; good for earth spells.

Orange and sometimes silver: Linked with the sacral chakra energies. This chakra is located below the navel in the abdomen, around the womb or genitals. It controls our desires, needs, feelings and self-esteem. Orange or silver are good for fuelling a spell with the necessary emotion to activate your psychic powers; good for water spells.

Yellow: The colour emitted by the solar plexus chakra. This is found around the upper stomach area. It is linked with will power, determination, focus and confidence to project our talents in the world. Yellow therefore focuses and directs the spell energies; good for air spells.

Green and pink: The colours radiating from the heart chakra, which extends from the centre of the chest and down the arms to the sensitive energy centres in the palms of the hand. It reflects love, altruism and healing energies. It draws energy from the life force from nature and from nature spirits. Pink and green are excellent for all healing and environmental spells and to encourage the flow of feeling; good for earth and water spells.

Blue: The colour emanating from the throat chakra, which radiates around the Adam's apple, through the neck into the passages leading to the ears and the nose. Blue assists communication, creativity, ideas and idealism and integrates thought and emotion; helps in chanting and in creating spells.

Indigo merging into other shades of purple: The colour of the brow or third eye chakra, which is located between and just above the eyes and eyebrows, radiating into the central cavity of the brain. Indigo and purple aid insight, psychic

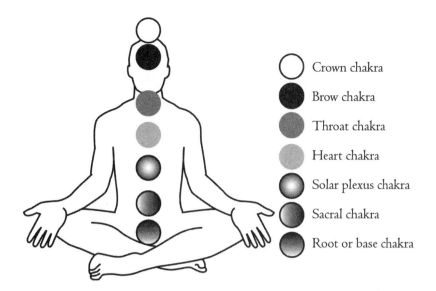

Crown chakra

Brow chakra

Throat chakra

Heart chakra

Solar plexus chakra

Sacral chakra

Root or base chakra

functioning and especially clairvoyance. As integrator of the inner and outer world and other dimensions, these chakra colours offer contact with angelic or spirit guides and the higher self. Indigo is good for visualisation in spellcasting, angel spells and astral and shamanic travel, such as in bird, soul or animal flight.

Violet, merging to white with tinges of gold: The colour of the crown chakra, which is located at the top of the head, the pivot axis point of the skull, where the different parts of the skull intersect. This is the chakra of integration, of mind, body and spirit, of the union of elemental powers within us and the fusion of sky and earth powers. Its function is to allow the merging of the individual with cosmic consciousness. In spellcasting, violet or white and the crown chakra bring together the different elements and components of the spell to create the fifth element as power is released.

Chakra colours in a spell

You won't always want to emphasise chakra power consciously in spellcasting. It will, as I said, automatically amplify colour spell casting as your inner colours are spontaneously activated in the spell.

If spellcasting is proving difficult at any time, focusing on your inner chakra colours can be an effective way of releasing your own innate powers to create magick. They are also very good if you feel tired or out of sorts as they will energise your body and harmonise any out-of-balance area during the spell.

* You can wear chakra crystals on a pendant or a bracelet (on your receptive hand) and as you move your hand or body, so you activate the inner colours. For suggested crystals see the colour list (page 258), Crystal magick (page 385), or my *Chakra Power* (see Further reading).
* Alternatively, create a circle of seven chakra crystals round the altar with the root or base crystal (1) in the north; solar plexus (2) and throat (3) in the east; the crown (4) in the south; the sacral (5), heart (6) and brow (7) in the west.

* The numbers refer to the order of setting a chakra colour circle. This can be done before any other circle casting. Arrange the crystals at regular intervals (the west will have most crystals).
* In an informal spell you can use this method to create a circle on a small altar, setting and sweeping your hand or wand clockwise over the crystal circle afterwards to activate the light.
* You can make a chakra crystal circle round your travelling altar if you carry small crystals in small drawstring purse.
* Take a minute or two before a spell, especially if you are feeling rushed or fraught, to hold each crystal in order of the ascending chakras: root, sacral, solar plexus, heart, throat, brow and crown.
* Picture each crystal activating and opening its own chakra and, before making the circle, set them in an ascending row of chakras (as given in the diagram) on your altar.
* When you have the row, set the crystals in the circle, starting with the root and ending with the brow, naming each colour you are calling. You can vary the qualities you ask for according to whether you need, for example, dynamic red at the root or base (north) or a more stable golden brown.
* To uncast the circle after the spell, sweep the hand or wand anticlockwise and then remove the crystals one by one anticlockwise, setting them in their place in the chakra row, this time in descending order, on your altar.
* Then hold each again this time in order from crown to root or base, closing the energy centres in your body as you do so.
* Afterwards, wash the crystals.
* Alternatively or in addition, you can light chakra candles in the circle order given to create a circle of colour to empower spells and rituals. Candles are an instant way of releasing the colour energies into your life and spells. Again, as you light the candles name the power you are seeking (or indeed healing).

A chakra candle and crystal spell for restoring (or maintaining) balance and stability in your life

This is a good all-purpose spell if you feel out of sorts, irritable or have been shaken by bad news or an unprovoked verbal attack or bullying. It gives your whole energy system a tone up and removes any blockages or knots in the energy field that can be caused by stress, noise, pollution, anxiety or exhaustion.

It can also be used to right an imbalance in one particular area of your life if you light an extra chakra colour candle in the centre of your circle (see magick meanings on page 258).

You will need: Seven crystals and seven candles in the colours of the chakras (see list on page 268 or choose your own favourites — if you use indigo/violet for the brow and crown, you can substitute natural beeswax for the solar plexus which it also empowers and opens). Use pure wax colour candles or dyed beeswax. The candles need only be small.

An extra, taller central candle, either white or beeswax, for general balancing to synthesise all the colours or a different colour, for example red for courage or yellow for logic if that is the overall strength you need.

Timing: Any evening at or after dusk so that the energies can continue to work during the night. As a harmonious spell it won't keep you awake.

* Pre-set the candles in the positions listed for the circle (see page 61) beginning with the red/brown candle in the north for the root moving clockwise to the brow in the north-west as you face the altar.
* Put your eighth candle in the centre to act as a focus.
* Set the chakra crystals out in a row in ascending order: root/base, sacral, solar plexus, heart, throat, brow and crown. Picture each energy centre awakening as you touch the related crystal.
* Then put the root crystal in the north, saying:

I awaken red/brown in my life to (name a red/brown strength that you need).

* Continue to position the crystals in a circle, holding each in turn and naming the strength you need from its colour. Take time to learn the chakra crystal circle order in advance.
* Light the root candle and say:

I release red/brown into my life to (call again on the strength you need).

* When you have been round the circle lighting the candles and calling the energies, light the final eighth candle and say either:

I release (the colour you have chosen and the strength you need, repeated from earlier in the spell).

or if you have used a white candle:

I release white for harmony, for unifying all the disparate elements in my life and for peace and stability after this period of change/turmoil/opportunity/ to maintain balance in my life (if you are in a stable period and want to keep it that way).

* End the spell by blowing out each candle in turn in reverse order of lighting, repeating each strength as a single word as you progress. Leave the central candle burning.
* Take the crystal circle apart anticlockwise to re-create the crystal row in descending order on your altar.
* Hold each crystal in turn, picturing the energy centre closing.
* Leave the central candle to burn through.
* If you sought a particular strength, carry its crystal with you in a small bag.

2

Aroma Magick

Essential or aromatic oils belong as much to the magickal tradition as to the therapeutic one, though aroma magick does have beneficial effects on health and well-being at physical and emotional levels as well as spiritually. I shall focus on in the magickal aspects in this chapter as this is an area I have researched and worked with a great deal since first writing about aromas in *The Practical Guide to Witchcraft and Magick Spells* (see Further reading, page 516).

Essential oils work not only through the olfactory system as we inhale the scent but also by being absorbed through the skin and glands into the bloodstream in baths or anointing rituals. Some oils, such as lavender, sweet marjoram, clary sage, sandalwood, frankincense and ylang ylang, stimulate the production of serotonin, which promotes a sense of well-being. This then makes it easier for us to fulfil our dreams and desires in day-to-day life.

Aromatic oils have an established tradition. The Chinese write of the use of infused oils as early as 2,650 BCE. Perfume magick was one of the early forms of magick practised by the Ancient Egyptians, who believed that fragrances came from the gods and that therefore mortals might become more perfect by absorbing the scent. The true and very expensive Egyptian perfumes are still entirely oil based and do not contain alcohol like many modern-day westernised perfumes.

Working with essential oils

In the modern world there is a huge range of essential oils available to be used in magick and they are a very versatile form of natural fragrance.

Synthetic oils are much cheaper and some are sold purely for burning. For natural magick it is better, if possible, to use the more expensive natural essential oils but to dilute them in a cheaper carrier oil so that they stretch further. You can ask for the more expensive ones like a beautiful rose, jasmine or lemon balm as presents.

Some are multi-purpose or core oils and these I have marked with an asterisk. Try to build up a small collection over time.

Often a herbalist, pharmacist or a garden centre will offer a reasonably priced, but still pure, selection of oils, at a better price than a New Age outlet.

Here I describe different kinds of aroma magick along with a list of those I find most useful.

Few people extract their own oils as it is very expensive and time-consuming.

Using essential oils safely

The difference between ordinary aromatherapy and aroma magick is that magick involves empowering the oils as you mix or use them in spells or add them to an oil burner.

If you are using an oil for anointing or massaging, do check the label or a good aromatherapy book like those written by Joan Radford (see Further reading, page 515) for details, as some oils are irritants on delicate skins. Citronella and juniper, for example, should only be used sparingly in a mix. If in doubt, use more than the recommended amount of carrier or mixing oil (60–70 ml/2.5 fl oz instead of 50 ml/2 fl oz per 15–20 drops). Carry out a patch test if you have sensitive skin. I have indicated which oils should be diluted well, as they are known to be possible irritants, but it does vary from person to person.

If necessary, one of the good-tempered oils like lavender, rose or chamomile can be added or substituted if you have delicate skin. These have various properties. Citrus oils, such as lemon and lime, are photo toxic and should not be used immediately after you have been in sunlight. You should also not go out in bright sunlight for six hours after using them on your skin (even if used in a bath).

For safety, avoid all oils during the first twelve weeks of pregnancy. See page 170 for those that should be avoided altogether in pregnancy and for a list of medical conditions that preclude skin contact with certain oils. Check with your physician before using any oils if you have a chronic condition.

Oil mixing magick

Both carrier and essential oils have magickal properties so you can mix and match your own for spells and to rub in while reciting an empowerment or protective words before an important meeting, journey or date.

Empowering an oil mix for anointing or massage magick:

* Choose up to four essential oils, plus a carrier oil that best suit your magickal purpose. The carrier oil is used to dilute the essential oils to a safe strength (see list on pages 289–90). You should also pre-plan the proportions of essential oils that you will use.
* As an example, for a sweet dreams love mix to anoint or massage yourself and a lover before sleep, you could use rose, jasmine, ylang ylang and chamomile in sweet almond carrier oil. You could add first five drops of rose oil to induce spiritual lovemaking, then five drops of ylang ylang for passion, two drops of jasmine for magickal dreams of each other and finally three drops of chamomile for peace and to ensure any earlier quarrels are forgotten. You could change the proportions if you were just massaging yourself to dream of your lover and call him telepathically in sleep.
* The mix will keep for two to three days or you can make it at the beginning of the ritual or just before the magickal use, for example to anoint your pulse points, brow and hairline if you need courage (frankincense) or to radiate charisma (rose).

- Essential oils are generally sold with a single dropper in the lid of the bottle; alternatively you can use an eye dropper. You will also need a ceramic measuring spoon or tiny glass jug for the carrier oil.
- Pour the required quantity of carrier oil into a mixing bowl. Generally 25 ml/1 fl oz of carrier will do a single person massage. Use 50 ml/2 fl oz of carrier oil to 15–20 drops of essential oil.
- Name the purpose of the spell and the particular magickal strength of the chosen carrier oil you are invoking, for example apricot for abundance and fertility.
- Swirl the bowl nine times clockwise as you speak. (Swirling is more magickal than using a spoon.)
- Then add the first essential oil, naming the power of the oil and repeating the overall purpose of the spell as you swirl the bowl nine times clockwise.
- Do the same for each oil that you add.
- After you have added and swirled the last oil, enchant the mix by holding both hands, palms down, about 2.5 cm/1 in above the bowl. Move your power hand clockwise and the other hand anticlockwise at the same time. Create a short chant, for example, for your love sleep mix:

Come to me in love, stay with me in passion and afterwards shall we sleep as one.

- For this mix, raise the speed and intensity and then reduce the sound and intensity (see page 47) and finally, as you become silent, hold your fingers downwards over the bowl and push the love gently into the mix.
- For more active mixes you may wish to raise and release the power by creating an arch with your hands over your head after enchanting the bowl and bringing both of your palms down to cover the bowl, saying:

So shall it be.

You would repeat the enchantment words in your mind nine times softly as you began the massage and as your lover began to massage you. Then allow images of the flowers and the natural setting of the origins of your oils in sun, moon or starlight to flow through your mind to amplify the fragrance power.

Chakra oil anointing magick

Anointing your main chakra or energy points in turn with an oil mix is a simple but very powerful way of absorbing the magickal powers inherent in fragrances that are associated with the different chakras. This empowers you from within and, if part of a spell, will combine with the released energies.

You can anoint your seven chakras while empowering them with words to draw all your energies together for a single purpose. If any chakra or chakras seem to have particular importance in a spell, for example the throat chakra for clear communication to succeed at a job interview or court case, you would anoint that chakra with an extra drop of oil and repeat that chakra chant.

You can also use an oil anointing ritual at any time for energising yourself (work root to crown) or calming (crown down to root).

You can alternatively use four oil flower waters for anointing. I describe how to make these on page 280. Lavender or rose can be used for all the chakras.

You might like to remind yourself at this stage of the different chakras, their roles and positions.

To locate your own chakras, hold the palm of your power hand in turn around the areas shown in the image on page 269; you may feel a swirling in a slightly different place that indicates the centre of your own chakra positions.

Chakras and their properties and related fragrances

The root or base chakra

For stability, survival, strength and practical achievement

Colour of the energies: Red or golden brown

Element: Earth

Part of the body to anoint: The soles of the feet or ankle bones

Main base/root fragrance: Mimosa

Other base/root oils: Cedarwood, evening primrose (carrier), patchouli, rosewood, vetivert

The sacral chakra

For needs, desire and dreams and the ability to flow with any situation

Colour of the energies: Orange or silver

Element: Moon

Part of the body to anoint: Centre of the lower abdomen, around the top of the womb or just above the genitals

Main sacral fragrance: Jasmine

Other sacral oils: Apricot (carrier), eucalyptus, lemon, lemongrass and myrrh. Dilute lemon or lemongrass with extra carrier oil or use just apricot as this area is very sensitive.

The solar plexus chakra

For will power, determination and self-confidence

Colour of the energies: Yellow

Element: Fire

Part of the body to anoint: The centre of the body, above the navel around the central stomach area

Main solar plexus fragrance: Chamomile

Other solar plexus oils: Frankincense, grapeseed (carrier), neroli, olive, orange blossom and peppermint. Dilute peppermint with extra carrier oil.

The heart chakra

For love, empathy, altruism, caring and personal charisma

Colour of the energies: Pink or green

Element: Winds

Part of the body to anoint: The centre of the chest or breasts or the centres of the palms of the hands

Main heart fragrance: Rose

Other heart oils: Sweet almond (carrier), geranium, melissa or lemon balm (also for the solar plexus) and any floral oil

The throat chakra

For clear communication, creativity, ideas and idealism

Colour of the energies: Blue

Element: Sound

Part of the body to anoint: The centre of the throat close to the Adam's apple or the nape of the neck

Main throat fragrance: Lavender

Other throat oils: Avocado (carrier), clary sage, passion flower, pine and tea tree. Dilute clary sage with extra carrier oil as it can be an irritant.

The brow chakra

For awareness of hidden factors, for intuition, psychic awareness, people-reading skills and for a little extra magickal help

Colour of the energies: Indigo and pale purples

Element: Light

Part of the body to anoint: The centre of the brow just above the bridge of the nose

Main brow fragrance: Sandalwood

Other brow oils: Aloe vera (carrier), bergamot, lime, sweet marjoram and wheatgerm (carrier). Dilute bergamot and lime extra well and make sure none gets anywhere near the eyes. Be extra careful with any oils used on the face.

The crown chakra

For integration of abilities and mind, body and spirit; a global view; good luck and boundless potential energy

Colour of the energies: Violet or pure white light merging into gold

Element: Akasha or spirit, all the other elements combined

Part of the body to anoint: The centre of the hairline

Main crown fragrance: Frankincense

Other crown oils: Chamomile (also solar plexus), orange, peach (carrier), rosemary and sunflower (carrier). Dilute orange very well to avoid irritation and avoid eyes.

Some people find frankincense a skin irritant so dilute with extra carrier if necessary.

A chakra oil anointing spell on the night before an important job interview

If you have time, the mixing process (see page 273) could be incorporated into the beginning of the spell. If not, the oil mixes should be kept in small dark or amber glass bottles. The mixing of each oil should be accompanied by an empowering chant, created according to the oil selected for the chakra and the overall purpose of the spell. These chants will be repeated as you anoint the chakras in the spell.

For lavender, you might use the following chant:

> *May the power of the throat chakra and this lavender enable me to answer questions coherently and communicate my talents well.*

Alternatively, you can anoint each chakra with just a rose or lavender mix or an oil mix, the meaning of which is close to the subject of the spell.

✻ Before the ritual, pour each mixed chakra oil into a small separate bowl and say:

> *May you be blessed and bring blessings.*

✻ As you pour each oil into its bowl, set it in a circle in the centre of your altar so you have a circle of tiny bowls. Egg cups or tea light holders are ideal. Start with the root fragrance in the north, and continue in an anticlockwise direction until you position the crown fragrance almost in the north-east to the right of the first bowl you set.
✻ To avoid confusion if you are using seven different oils, put a coloured circle or crystal next to each one to remind you of the chakra it represents.
✻ Once you have set up your fragrances, have a bath in plain water and put on a loose robe that unfastens down the front.
✻ Work by candlelight in the evening when you can be alone and quiet.
✻ If you wish, begin the actual spell by anointing each direction of the altar by sprinkling a little elemental oil flower water (see page 280), saying:

> *I work in light and love and for the highest purpose and greatest good.*

✻ Say each chakra chant in turn as you anoint the chakra with a single drop of its own oil mix. For empowerment work root to crown, and for protection work crown to root.
✻ Use different fingers for each fragrance, beginning with the index finger on your power hand and ending with the ring finger on the other hand (do not use the thumbs).
✻ Picture the rainbow colours and fragrances swirling together and merging as they move upwards to form white light and downwards to be absorbed in rich red connecting with the earth.
✻ Visualise the individual fragrance as you use it, for example for the solar plexus see fields of golden flowers.

- When you have anointed all the chakras, say:

May all come to pass as I ask, if it is right to be.

- Sit quietly picturing the successful outcome of the spell and, when you are ready, blow out the candles.
- You can use this anointing ritual with a partner, naming a love commitment or promise associated with each chakra fragrance.

Using candles

- To anoint candles to be used in a specific spell, dilute one or two drops of an appropriate essential oil in a small quantity of virgin olive or pure sunflower oil.
- Small medicine dose caps are ideal to hold the oil.
- Rub the oil into the candle using small circular movements. Work upwards from the bottom of the candle to the centre and downwards from the top to the centre. Avoid the area around the wick.
- As you work, picture the successful completion of the purpose for which you will light the candle.
- Do remember that anointed candles are more flammable.
- Alternatively, drop one or two drops of essential oil into the melted wax round a lighted candle, while asking for its powers to be released. The oil power will be reactivated every time you light the candle.
- You can add even more power to the ritual by using candles of an appropriate colour (see page 258).

Oil and water magick

Using a burner is an effective method of releasing the fragrance of an essential oil. Burners can be ceramic, toughened glass or metal and have a tea-light holder at the bottom below a bowl in which the water and oil is heated.

Pour water into the bowl until it is about a third full and then add 6–10 drops of essential oil. If the fragrance fades during the ritual or spell, you can always add more drops of oil, speaking an additional empowerment as you do so. Similarly, if the bowl starts to dry out, you can add more water during the spell (warm water is a good idea).

- The oil burner can be positioned in the west of your altar as the water element. Pass the symbol through the rising fragrance. This complements the dry fragrance of the incense in the east and the fragrances of the two will meet over the symbol in the centre.
- Light the tea light under the burner at the same time as the altar candles and make a small blessing, saying:

May the power of the fire and the air and the water carry this _____ to birth/from my life.

- You can then add the oil or oils, one at a time in the proportion you need, naming the powers you seek, so the fragrance will be ready when you need to use the substance of the west as part of the spell.

* Alternatively, you can make the burner the focus of a spell and speak an empowerment as you put the water in the bowl, as you light the tea light, and as you drop the oil or oils in the water. Oil burning is very good for word-based spells or for absent healing.
* Begin, as you light the candle, by saying, for example:

I kindle this flame to release the power of (name the oil or oils) that I may find love again.

* As you drop in the single oils in turn, 1 or 2 drops of each, state the oil name and its own strength and how this applies to the spell. For example:

May this lavender heal the harsh words spoken and the unkindness of the betrayal that I may move forward to new love. So shall it be.

* You can empower the spell symbol or a charm or amulet by holding it in the fragrance and asking that the particular powers or protection of the oils enter the symbol, charm or amulet. Build up the power by adding different components of the wish or different steps to attaining the goal each time you hold the symbol in the fragrance above the burner or pass it in and out as if weaving the fragrance into the charm.
* You can also pass the symbol anticlockwise for a banishment, describing as you do so the hold of the destructive habit, person or situation lessening. Afterwards bury the symbol or throw it away.
* You can end by blowing out the tea light and calling out the purpose of the spell to release it or remove it from your life.
* The oil does remain hot for some time, which can be an advantage as the residual fragrance provides an easy transition between psychic work and a gentle return to the everyday world.

Magickal oil baths

You can also dilute the empowered oils in a magickal bath, adding them one by one after you have run the bath.

* Add a tablespoon of carrier oil or a cup of full-fat milk to the bath and mix well so that the oils will be absorbed when they are added.
* Use 6–10 drops of essential oil per bath for a healthy adult; reduce if the person is sick. Use only a drop or two of astringent oils and mix with some gentler ones (see the list on pages 282–90).
* Add up to four oils in the proportions you need them.
* Name what you seek from each oil as you add it.
* Sit or lie in the bath and let the oils bring the magick to you.
* Swirl the oil pools or the milky water to draw the energies into yourself and make wishes.

- If you light scented candles the light will shine on the water and you can draw the fragrant light pools towards you, moving them in clockwise circles.
- For cleansing and banishing spells, push the oil light pools gently away from you in anticlockwise circles, describing softly what you wish to leave behind, when and how, and picturing a happy outcome.
- After the bath, dry yourself and swirl the water as it runs away down the plug hole saying a variation of:

> *Fear and sorrow flow from me, from the rivers to the sea, leaving only harmony.*

or for a wish:

> *Love and laughter come to me, from the rivers and the sea, and joyous once again will be.*

Oil and water power and protection

- Add cleansing oils like pine, tea tree or lemon to floor washes (10–20 drops per bucket of warm water or just one or two drops if using a commercial cleaner) to protect doorsteps and scrub away negativity. Work in anticlockwise movements and tip the water down an outside drain afterwards.
- For an instant burst of power or protection, drop three or four drops of neat oil into a bowl of steaming water as you name the power or protection you need.
- Add three or four drops of any empowered protective essential oil to a saucer of warm water on your desk at work or in a strange hotel room, especially late at night, to keep you safe from malice and intrusion. Top up regularly and re-empower as you add fresh oils.

Making oil flower waters

- Prepare flower waters by adding three or four drops (more if you want a stronger fragrance) of a flower oil to 200 ml/7 fl oz of still mineral water in a lidded or screw-top bottle. Some people use amber-coloured bottles.
- Good flower water fragrances include bergamot, chamomile, geranium, lavender, lemon, mint, orange or neroli (orange blossom), rose and ylang ylang.
- Make general flower waters for love, money, healing or protection. Name the general purpose of the water as you pour it into the bottle.
- Swirl the water three times clockwise.
- Shake the bottle several times while repeating the purpose of the water.
- Label the bottle and then store it in a cool place away from direct sunlight.
- Continue to shake the bottle three times every day (when you wake, in the middle of the day or when you come home from work and at bedtime), repeating the empowerment. After about ten days it will be ready for use.
- You can mix general fragrances and keep a supply of small bottles for rituals.
- Re-empower and link the water with a specific spell by chanting the words with which you originally empowered it plus what you are hoping to gain from the spell as you make your preparations. You can also make wedding- or birth-blessing waters and waters for seasonal change points.

Using oil flower waters

* You can make essential oil flower waters for spraying in a small plant-watering spray to lift negativity in the home or workplace and to create a mood of harmony and co-operation if sprayed in a room ten minutes before a gathering or meeting.
* Use different oil flower waters to act as the water element in a spell (see page 35) and to give different emphases.
* Anoint the four directions of the altar with the flower water or their elemental oils (see page 72) after casting the circle to add power to a spell or ritual.
* Set the elemental flower waters ready in four small dishes. I suggest patchouli or mimosa for the north/earth, lavender or sandalwood for the east/air, chamomile or frankincense for the south/fire and rose or jasmine for the west/water.
* You can also make a combined earth, air, fire and water fragrance by adding one of each of the above oils or others from the elemental lists in a single water. This mix can then be sprinkled at each of the four quarters to open and close them. You can add extra oil if one element is most important – for example, double the rose for love.
* Make seasonal flower water mixes (see pages 162–65 for lists of seasonal flowers) for using in seasonal rituals by using their aroma oils.
* You can add your empowered flower waters to your bath or splash them on pulse points. Repeat the purpose for which you empowered them each time you use them.

Using undiluted oils

* You can inhale gentler essential oils such as lavender, chamomile, sweet marjoram, sandalwood or rose, during spells in order to take in their qualities as you breathe. Visualise the power as you breathe. Only do this for a second or two as the oils are all very strong when used in this way.
* Afterwards, state aloud the power or protection you now possess and every time you panic or are afraid, breathe and visualise the scent or put a little on a tissue to carry with you.
* In a spell, set mild elemental oil at each direction and name the quality you are absorbing (see pages 31–36). I would suggest mimosa for earth, lavender for air, chamomile for fire and rose for water. Breathe in the elemental power.
* Alternatively, drop lavender, chamomile or rose on to pillows as part of a quiet sleep ritual. Be careful not to put any where it could get into your eyes.
* Before using neat oil in a spell or for any magickal purpose, however simple, write over the sealed bottle with a lighted incense stick, your name or the person for whom the ritual is being carried out. Write also in smoke the name of the oil and the particular magickal property you are seeking to awaken, the time scale (if relevant) and the purpose of the spell. Do take care that no sparks fall on to the oil. Leave the incense to burn through.

Magickal oils for every purpose

I list here 35 of the most popular oils for using in magick, though there are many other oils you can use. I have included the Latin names but you may find variations in these, so ask when buying and check labels about purity.

I have suggested oils that mix well together, but feel free to experiment.

Bergamot, chamomile, frankincense, geranium, jasmine, lavender, neroli, rose, sandalwood and ylang ylang are the best mixers.

Lavender and rose will mix with anything and are fortunately all-purpose magickal oils.

I have stated which oils should not be used in pregnancy.

I have indicated where certain powerful oils (like ginger and citronella) should be diluted well and be used sparingly (just one drop in a mix or an extra 10–20 ml of carrier oil per mix). These oils can burn the skin.

* indicates a good oil to have in your collection.

** indicates an oil that can be used for a number of purposes; therefore if you are only buying very few, these should be your first choices

*** indicates an oil that can be substituted for any other oil. Just name the purpose of the spell. These oils are also excellent for sensitive skins.

Basil, Ocimum basilicum

The oil of prosperity and uplifting the spirits

Deters negativity, attracts money, increases harmony, fidelity, promotes optimism and sharpens the senses, including psychically; brings good luck to new homes or for home moves.

Not in pregnancy and should be extra well diluted for personal use.

Mixes with eucalyptus, bergamot and pine.

Benzoin, Styrax tonkinensis

The oil of personal power and confidence

Purifies negativity and bad atmospheres, attracts riches and business success, personal power, confidence and a sense of well-being; good for promotion or career rituals.

Should be very well diluted for personal use.

Mixes well with rose, pine and lavender (smells like vanilla).

Bergamot, Citrus bergamia

The oil of communication and opportunity

Amplifies opportunities in the area you most need them, whether for attaining love, prosperity, success or true happiness; good for all forms of communication, increases radiance, charisma and persuasiveness; encourages returns on investment and attracts fast money.

Avoid sunlight when using citrus oil; dilute bergamot very well for delicate skin.

Mixes well with frankincense and ylang ylang.

Cedarwood, Cedrus atlantica

The oil of spiritual development and long-term achievements

A symbol of long life, increases sexual desire, especially after a bad experience or a period of celibacy; increases self-esteem,; protective especially of property and effective for gentle binding; good to initiate or speed a long-term plan or ambition.

Avoid in pregnancy. Should be very well diluted for personal use.

Mixes especially well with cypress, juniper and rosemary.

Chamomile, German or blue, Matricaria recutitao and Roman, Chamaemelum nobile

The oil of peace and mending quarrels **

Good for all spells for children, babies and families; for family happiness, mending quarrels , for protection against anger and malice; preventing nightmares and sleep disturbances; for attracting money and winning it or prizes; for lessening obsessions and addictions and healing sorrow or abuse; also attracts money.

Mixes well with ylang-ylang, geranium, lavender and lemon.

Citronella, Nardus cymbopogon

The oil of independence and repelling intrusion and intruders

Magickally draws boundaries around the self and home against intrusion, spite, gossip or attack and unwanted visitors – human, insect and paranormal; increases energy, mental alertness and determination; good for uncovering secrets and in banishing spells; an oil for going it alone, whether self-employment or moving into your own home.

Do not use if pregnant and dilute very well.

Mixes well with lavender and jasmine.

Clary Sage, Salvia slarea

The oil of positive thoughts and hope in difficult times *

Overcomes, fears, nightmares and repels danger from ill-wishers; encourages optimism and self-belief as well as the strength to go on; restores balance, calm and harmony after stress or a setback; unblocks frozen emotions; good for all gentle spells of healing and for children and happy family spells; reverses bad luck.

Avoid in pregnancy.

Mixes well with ylang ylang, rosemary and lavender.

Cypress, Cupressus sempervirens

The oil of comfort after loss and healing

Reduces the pain of loss and injustice; good for gentle banishing and binding spells; for moving forwards after a period of stagnation, for blessing rituals and for all forms of protection. Use also for restoring what has been lost or stolen and for connecting with people from the past.

Do not use if you have high blood pressure or during pregnancy. Always dilute well.

Mixes well with geranium, juniper and lemon.

Eucalyptus, Eucalyptus globules

The oil of clearing stagnant energies and for new beginnings *

Cleanses and banishes all negativity and anger and offers physical, psychological and psychic protection; moves long-standing problems towards resolution (so good for court cases and official matters or neighbourhood disputes); good for passing tests and examinations, for health and for healing spells; also for job opportunities and travel.

Do not use if you have an epileptic condition or high blood pressure.

Mixes well with cedarwood, clary sage and peppermint.

Fennel, Foeniculum vulgare

The oil of courage and travel

Brings together people or situations that are pulling in opposite directions; provides personal balance, courage, strength and perseverance to win through whatever the obstacles; use in travel or relocation spells; drives away malevolence, diminishes jealousy and possessiveness and disarms hidden enemies.

Do not use if you have epilepsy or during pregnancy. Dilute well.

Mixes well with chamomile and eucalyptus.

Frankincense, Boswellia carteri

The oil of leadership and success **

A ceremonial oil; use for ambition, authority, expansion of business interests, travel and confidence; also for creative ventures, leadership, promotion, employment, prosperity and contact with other dimensions.

Do not use during pregnancy.

Mixes well with cypress, sandalwood and myrrh. Can be an irritant, so check and dilute well if necessary.

Geranium, Pelargonium graveolens

The oil of harmony and happiness *

An oil of happiness, friendship, the growth of love, gentle love, bringing or restoring harmony to the home or workplace, and healing coldness and indifference; diminishes self-doubt, fear of failure or inadequacy, guilt trips and over-critical people as well as deterring intruders; brings fertility and good health; use also to attract good news and welcome visitors.

Dilute well for sensitive skins.

Mixes well with lavender, rose or ylang ylang, cedarwood and chamomile.

Ginger, Zingibere officinale

The oil of exploration and speculation *

The energiser and fire oil; adds or renews passion to love; good for all money-making enterprises, especially speculative, and to reverse the outflow of finances; for travel, new ventures and enterprises, for originality and innovation when a new, bold approach is needed.

Dilute well.

Mixes well with bergamot, cedarwood and jasmine.

Jasmine, Jasminum officinale or grandiflorum

The oil of night magick and fertility

Attracts love and increases passion; enhances male potency and female fertility; use for all night and moon rituals; also for peace and for enhanced psychic powers; deflects potential hostility and unwanted influences and emotional vampires or those who drain finances; increases self-love, personal radiance and melts emotional blockages and fears.

Expensive, but a nice oil to have in your collection.

Mixes with most other oils, especially rose and ylang ylang.

Juniper, Juniperus communis

The oil of new opportunities and for removing negative influences

For all psychic protection and for the banishing of hostility, old sorrows, bad habits or destructive people and guilt; guards homes and property against theft, damage and accidents; removes bad luck and ill wishes; increases male potency; good for new beginnings and attracting new opportunities; opens doors that previously have been closed.

Do not use in pregnancy and dilute well.

Mixes well with rosemary, frankincense and cypress.

Lavender, Lavandula angustifolia

The oil of family, kindness and romance ***

Attracts new love and romance, encourages kindness and gentleness in love and lasting faithful love; also for family happiness; for peaceful sleep; for animal spells, deterring bullies, attracting friendship and romance, healing quarrels and sorrow; use in all healing and health spells; will slowly improve finances.

Mixes well with almost every oil, especially geranium, chamomile, marjoram and ylang ylang.

Lemon, Citrus limon

The oil of clarity of thought and logic *

A good moon oil for night magick, an energiser and cleanser; brings new beginnings and overcomes obstacles; removes addictions and destructive ties from the past; also for good luck and prosperity, travel and house moves.

A citrus oil and an irritant – dilute very well.

Mixes well with chamomile, eucalyptus, lavender and myrrh.

Lemongrass, Cymbopogon citrates

The oil for removing what is redundant from your life and for repelling negativity

A very protective and cleansing oil, used to clear away old resentments especially in families, or spite and gossip in workplaces; also for banishing sad memories and past failures that hold back present and future achievements; increases sexual desire, blows away stagnation and attracts unexpected money or resources.

Use very well diluted.

Mixes well with frankincense and geranium.

Lime, Citrus limetta

The oil of justice and innovation

An oil to get things going in your life; for new beginnings, new places and people, fresh investment and original ideas; also repels spite, jealousy, nasty neighbours or colleagues who take credit for your ideas; use in justice spells and where there has been unfair treatment.

A citrus oil – use very well diluted.

Mixes well with eucalyptus and lavender.

Marjoram, sweet, Majorana hortensis

The oil of connection with others and unity *

Drives away loneliness, alienation and fears of separation or abandonment; good for increasing family loyalty, resolving divided loyalties and encouraging compromise; also for increasing commitment in love and money flow; good for all joint ventures.

Always use in moderation. Do not use during pregnancy.

Mixes well with lavender and rosemary.

Melissa, Melissa officinalis, sweet or lemon balm

The oil of abundance and long life *

Increases abundance and all good things in your life; reverses bad luck and grants wishes; good for long life and for drawing love; for all healing magick and for psychic dreaming; for psychic development, especially past-life work.

Expensive, but worth buying when you can.

Do not use during pregnancy and dilute well for general use.

Mixes well with rose and lavender.

Mimosa, Acacia dealbata

The oil of tranquillity and love without limits

Attracts and increases love, from new or first love through to love in later life; helps older lovers; helps those who have lost a partner to love again; sustains love in bad times; also for connection with absent lovers and for grieving for loved ones who have died or left us forever.

An oil of the night; use for keeping secrets and secret trysts; also for reducing panic attacks, phobias or free-floating anxiety and for acceptance of what cannot be changed.

Mixes well with bergamot and chamomile.

Myrrh, Commiphora myrrha

The oil of regeneration and healing **

Another ceremonial oil; use to begin again after difficulty or loss; excellent for post-redundancy and retirement spells; for all who would or already work in alternative therapies; for all healing rituals; for meditation, visualisation and enhanced psychic awareness, especially of past lives; good for spells against prejudice and war; for all blessings, especially of the home.

Do not use during pregnancy.

Mixes well with mandarin, pine and patchouli.

Neroli, Citrus aurantium

The oil of fertility and abundance

Better known as orange blossom (from the bitter orange tree), a flower given by the Roman sky god Jupiter to his bride Juno on their marriage, and carried by brides to calm their nerves. A gentler substitute for orange. The oil of marriage and fidelity; for creating calm and lessening panics or addictions; a natural enhancer of confidence and self-esteem and for restoring happiness and good fortune.

Very expensive in its pure state, but a special oil. One of the gentler citrus oils.

Take care to store it in a cool, dry place.

Mixes well with geranium and jasmine.

Orange, Citrus sinensis

The oil of happiness and good fortune *

An oil of the sun; brings abundance and prosperity, happiness and health; good for developing creative talents, for personal fulfilment and for good luck and success; also very calming and associated, like neroli, with marriage, fertility and fidelity; use in solar rituals.

A citrus oil – needs to be diluted very well.

Mixes well with frankincense, lavender and ylang ylang.

Patchouli, Pogostemon cablina or patchouli

The oil of prosperity and environmental protection *

An oil associated with the earth and earth energies; good for attracting money and money-making opportunities; good for healing the environment; brings stability for business ventures and for property matters; also for spells for sacred or committed sexual relationships and for physical strength.

Mixes well with geranium, myrrh and pine.

Peppermint, Mentha piperita

The oil of protection and for money *

Good for cleansing and for stirring of fresh energies; for protection, especially during travel; for banishing spells and for attracting good fortune; brings money, increases passion and also improves mental acuity; use to see through con artists and illusion.

Dilute well. Mixes well with eucalyptus.

Pine, Pinus sylvestris

The oil of truth and illumination *

Purifies just about everything and everybody, especially homes; good against tricksters, emotional vampires, liars and psychic attack; use to discover the truth about a matter; associated with birth, baby blessings and new beginnings, inspiration and illumination and so is good for increasing fame and getting creative projects off the ground; also for courage and prosperity.

Dilute very well for sensitive skin.

Mixes well with juniper, lemon and marjoram.

Rose, Rosa, Otto or Damascena

The oil of love and fidelity ***

An expensive but all-purpose oil (you actually need to use very little); brings lasting joy and fertility; fidelity and family joy; burned for all forms of love magick and to increase personal desirability; for all healing rituals, especially of abuse; also for all spells concerning children and babies, animals and the old or vulnerable; offers psychic protection.

Mixes well with almost every other oil and can be substituted for almost any other oil for magick.

Rosemary, Rosmarinus officinalis

The oil of memory and intellect

For passing tests and examinations, for improving memory and for learning anything new; for justice, and career success; also a major love oil especially for attracting love and for passion; encourages money to flow into your life.

Do not use in pregnancy or if you have high blood pressure or epilepsy.

Mixes well with cedarwood, frankincense and geranium.

Rosewood, Aniba rosaeodora

The oil of reconciliation and for slowing life down *

Banishes conflict at work or home; counteracts the hyperactivity of modern life; good in crystal, herb and flower spells for quiet sleep, forgiveness of the frailties of the self and others and letting the past go; reduces family histrionics and dramas of all ages and stages.

Mixes well with jasmine, neroli and geranium and helps to give depth to other fragrances.

Sandalwood, Santalum album

The oil of ceremony and for sensuality **

Another sacred oil for special rituals to increase spirituality; also enhances sexual magnetism and commitment in love; helps to deflect anger, unfair criticism and spiteful words; for healing, to enhance self-esteem and a positive body image.

Mixes well with many other oils, especially chamomile, lemon, patchouli and rosemary.

Tea tree oil, Melaleuca alternifolia

The oil of healing and for cleansing negativity

For all healing; effective for absent-healing spells, especially for blocked energies; protects the home and workplace, drives away fear, danger and negativity; increases courage, generates money, heralds overdue change and encourages independence and travel.

Mixes with lavender and sandalwood.

Vetivert, Vetiveria zizanoides

The oil of money-making and good luck

For wish magick and to attract good luck or to break a run of bad fortune; good in gambling and speculation; good for finding new or self-employment; also for all practical ventures, crafts and hands-on skills.

Mixes well with patchouli, orange and cypress.

Ylang ylang, Cananga odorata

The oil of sensuality and creativity

The oil of poets and writers, for artistic or creative ventures; for love and passion and increased self-esteem and image; enhances personal radiance and sexual magnetism; encourages success within realistic limits.

Mixes well with clary sage, geranium, lemon and chamomile.

Carrier oils

These are used to dilute essential oils and are health-giving substances in their own right, containing important vitamins and minerals as well as magickal properties. Carrier oils are considered safe for all skin types, but people with highly sensitive complexions can develop an allergic reaction, so test each carrier oil on a small area. If in doubt, dilute with a little baby oil.

Almond

The oil of fertility

Brings fertility and abundance in every way. Odourless; can be used on its own or blended with grape seed, jojoba or sunflower oil.

Aloe vera

The oil of balance

Calms and brings stability; good as a base if anointing the brow or face.

Avocado

The oil of prosperity

Promotes well-being on all levels and attracts money; also excellent for the face; expensive and quite heavy, but can be blended with other oils such as almond.

Evening primrose

The oil of regeneration

Naturally healing and restorative; good for women's spells. A sticky, concentrated oil, easiest to use when diluted with lighter oil, such as grape seed.

Grape seed

The oil of pure joy

Light, easily absorbed, inexpensive oil, for personal and family happiness Gentle and odourless, ideal for oils with distinctive fragrances, which it enhances. Suits all skin types. Can be used undiluted.

Hazelnut

The oil of wisdom

A fertility oil, also traditionally associated with wisdom and with getting justice. Can be used undiluted or diluted with grape seed or sunflower oil. Mixes especially well with sandalwood, rosewood and ylang ylang. Once open, store in the fridge.

Jojoba

The oil of versatility

More of a wax than an oil as it is solid at room temperature. Good for all skin types (very light) and for facial oil blends; slightly dilute it with another carrier.

Olive oil

The oil of peace and plenty

Use for abundance, cleansing, healing and reconciliation spells; use only 100 per cent extra virgin cold-pressed olive oil; slightly dilute for personal use. Excellent used on its own for candle anointing.

Passion flower

The oil of love

Promotes self-love; attracts and keeps the love of others; good for the face and for a love massage spell mixed with ylang ylang, jasmine, rose or geranium.

Peach/apricot kernel

The oil of wishes

Relatively odourless but filled with abundance and fertility energies and the power to grant wishes; also attracts love.

Sunflower

The oil of confidence

A sun oil, bringing confidence, courage, health and energy; light in texture, inexpensive and can be blended with the more exotic oils. Use only unrefined sunflower oil that still retains its nutrients. Store in the refrigerator; good for candle anointing.

Wheatgerm

The oil of completeness

Brings fulfilment and the successful completion of projects; a good mixer oil; use with other oils as it is too thick and sticky to use on its own.

3

Sound Magick

Music, chanting and playing simple repetitive sounds on instruments provide, in both religion and magick, a gateway to higher levels of consciousness and to spiritual realms. They induce in the player, singer and/or listener light trance states, enabling us to become part of the spell or ritual and so link directly with the released energies. They can also provide the structure and tempo for rituals, whether a dreamy otherworld healing spell or an upbeat empowerment for a successful business.

Harmonious sounds have from Ancient Greek times been regarded as a microcosm or earthly expression of the harmony of the heavenly bodies. The 'music of the spheres' was the term used by the Greek philosopher and mathematician Pythagoras to express the harmony of the different levels of cosmic existence. Each planet, he believed, had a specific numerical vibration or note that, when combined with those of the other planets, gave the cosmic form of earthly music.

Since only a small proportion of the vibrations of the universe could be heard by the human ear, the purpose of chant and song was to attune the spirit of the chanter or musician to the more subtle sounds on higher levels. In doing so, the soul might move closer to harmony and finally unity with the cosmic rhythms – and the ultimate perfect silence at the heart of sound and of the cosmos.

Think of that silence as the moment after the last vibrations of a truly great orchestra have faded away and before applause begins; the silence between two waves as the poet T S Eliot called it or the total stillness of night in deep countryside. After a spell our voices fade into silence, our movements still, but we can sense the released energies vibrating in the air and, most importantly, radiating into and out of our aura.

Sound, whether chanting, drumbeat, pan pipes, the vibration of a Tibetan singing bowl or a didgeridoo will attune even simple spells. This attunement synthesises the disparate elements and energies of the spell to create ether, spirit or akasha. This is the state in which the ultimate silence and stillness resides. It is also the perfect balance of creative matter and impetus in which our wishes are held beyond measured time, filled with power and bounced back into actuality. This is sometimes called the still point of the turning cosmos and, as such, is not subject to ordinary laws or limits of possibility.

The power of sound

According to the Book of Genesis, it was sound that brought the world into being:

In the beginning was the Word. And the Word was with God and the Word was God.

In the Hindu tradition, *OM* or *AUM* is the first, the primal or sacred sound that brought the whole universe into being. The name Nada Brahma, that of the Hindu creator god, is the word form for both 'He who creates all' and 'Sound'.

In the Ancient Egyptian tradition, the power of Heka, the god of magick, was used by the creator god Ptah to speak the words to create the vibrations that caused the first mound to rise from the waters.

Nepalese shamans can shatter huge rocks with their long horn-like trumpets, while in the Bible the power of sound brought down an entire city. According to Joshua 6, God instructed Joshua to circle round the city of Jericho with seven priests with ram horns. On the seventh day He commanded that they should blow the trumpets at the same time as Joshua's followers and army should send forth a resounding call. This they did, and the walls of Jericho came tumbling down.

During the 1930s, Hans Jenny, a Swiss researcher, demonstrated that sound could not only cause matter to move, but create specific forms and shapes from it. By vibrating sand, powders and liquids on metal disks or drumheads at certain audible frequencies or playing the violin, Jenny caused the substances to form complex geometric shapes that are found in nature, for example snowflakes, honeycombs or the markings such as those on a tortoise's shell.

As higher sound frequencies were introduced, the forms became more ethereal in form. Complex tones increased the complexity of shapes, and specific frequencies produced the same patterns on every occasion when the particular sound was made. If the sound frequencies stopped, so did the movement.

Jenny also investigated sacred sounds. When he chanted *OM* into a device called a tonoscope, it produced first a circle and then a mandala pattern, a sacred geometrical symbol in Eastern religions, which signifies sacred sound itself.

Creating natural balance with sound

In the music of a number of indigenous societies, the organisation of sounds into harmonious patterns is used to help regulate ebbs and flows of the seasons. In the Andes of South America the Indian peoples, descendants of the Incas, live and farm in accordance with the energy flows of Pachamama, the earth mother.

The Andean mountain climate has alternate dry and wet seasons. The intense cold of the nights and the sunny days of the dry season cause the drying of the earth. So, while waiting for the wet season and in order to generate new life, these people carry out rituals to coax water from the underground world of the ancestors, to flow through the landscape as springs, rivers and lakes, fed by the natural cycle of rainwater and snowmelt high in the mountains. Music is integral to these ceremonies.

Disequilibrium, which is strongest at the transition of the seasons, is also necessary to generate this flow.

At the beginning of the seasons there is a ritual dance in which the pan pipes are played in a zigzag dance that mimics the movement of a snake, with a small boy at the tail and a full-grown man at the front. This represents growth from childhood to adulthood and the corresponding growth, flow and balance that are central to the well-being of land, animals and people.

Afterwards more soothing music is necessary in order to restore equilibrium. Pairs of pan pipes are used, with each player harmonising the melody to Pachamama to play in the new seasons, but also to prevent climatic excesses.

Musical intervention continues during the agricultural year. Farmers play pinkula or ornamental flutes during the growing season to attract the rain and encourage the crops to grow.

Once the cold, dry season begins, julajula pan pipes are used instead of the pinkullas to maintain the new balance.

Ritual music to the Andeans is likewise linked to individual harmony. If the individual flow of animu (soul flow) and suerte (good fortune) were blocked, it might lead to illness or lack of fertility. Human growth and flourishing is an integral part of the ceremonies for the success of the crops.

Music in magick

There are many CDs of pan pipes, flutes, ocarinas and didgeridoos as well as drumming tracks. You can use these as background to spells, rituals and empowerments.

However, by playing even a few pure chords yourself you are aligning your personal energies with that of the instrument. You don't need to be musical and there are lessons available on-line as well as on CD and DVD that will help you to master the basics.

Go out into woodlands or on to the seashore to practise what you have learned, and the natural sounds around you will help you to tune into natural harmonies.

You may find that you become sufficiently proficient to experiment with your own basic melodies and this will become an additional tool in your spellcasting.

Tibetan singing bowls

Though associated primarily with meditation and healing, a singing bowl is a perfect way to start and end a ritual so that the sound vibrations are raised and the spell is carried into the cosmos on the sound. The singing bowl vibrations last long after each touch or strike. You can learn the basic technique within a few minutes and yet connect into profoundly spiritual and healing sounds.

You can harmonise a chant to be released at the climax of the spell at the same time as the final singing bowl sound fades into cosmic silence, leaving your aura positively buzzing. Holding the singing bowl, as it vibrates, over the focus of your spell will fill it with energy and healing – particularly useful if you will be using the focus as a talisman after the spell.

Singing bowls originated in the pre-Buddhist, shamanic Bon Po culture of the Himalayas. They are made in Bhutan, Nepal, India and Tibet. They have been used by Buddhists for more than 2,000 years. The tone of a good quality singing bowl is said to be the sacred *AUM* or *OM* and so recreates the energies in miniature of the first act of creation.

Some singing bowls are made of crystal, which transmits thought forms and so is effective for spellcasting. However, I would recommend for purity of sound you choose initially a traditional metal alloy bowl created from an amalgam of at least three or four of the seven planetary metals: gold, silver, copper, mercury, tin, iron and lead.

If possible, buy a singing bowl personally as they do all vary greatly and this is the best way to find the one that is right for you. Start with a small bowl as these are easier to hold. Different proportions of each metal in the alloy will vary the sound and the most expensive won't necessarily be the best for you.

The rounded wooden striker (puja) or wand resembles a mixing pestle and sometimes has a padded or leather striking end. The striker is usually sold with the bowl. Some bowls have a mallet as well, purely for striking the side of the bowl.

You can substitute an ordinary metal bell or the kind with a striker for some of the singing bowl functions.

A singing bowl spell

This is an incredibly harmonious way of spellcasting and after ten minutes' practice with your bowl you are ready to make music. The singing bowl can aid any spell but especially those cast for love, healing, the relief of pain, peace, the mending of quarrels, letting go of sorrow or what you wish to lose from your life.

* Hold the singing bowl flat on the palm of your left hand. Smaller bowls can be supported on your lightly cupped fingertips.
* The key to success is to relax totally and let the sound happen.
* Grasp the puja firmly in the right hand, about halfway down the handle, with all your fingertips pointing downwards and touching the wood.
* Hold it vertically like a pen.
* Keep your palm downwards and gently but firmly tap against the side of the bowl once. Use the sound as a background as you state the purpose of the spell.
* Next you are going to chant an empowerment softly three times. As you do so, with an even pressure, rub the puja clockwise around the outside edge of the rim of the bowl, maintaining contact all the time.
* Move your arm and not just the wrist, and keep the striker vertical. Gradually increase the speed as the bowl begins to vibrate. It will continue to vibrate after you have stopped the contact.
* Continue to alternate words and vibrations so you have a seamless increase in intensity and power.
* With practice your words will cease as the vibration takes over and as the vibration fades into silence you can chant softly again.
* When the time is right and the air is buzzing, tap the side of the bowl once more and let your voice be carried on the sound as you release the spell.

Drums

I have already suggested drumming as an aid to chanting and to moving into a state of personal magickal awareness in which possibility expands.

* For accompanying rituals and chants or raising and releasing power you may like to use a hand-held tambour-type drum so that you can beat time with a stick.
* However, for more intense drumming for personal empowerments and shamanic work, such as power bird flight (see page 228), try hand contact, using the thumbs and the side of the hand until you have a steady rhythm.
* Increase the rhythm until you can feel it in every part of your body. You may find that you are swaying as you drum and you may start to move naturally.
* Combine the drumming and the chanting and feel the energy flooding through you.
* If you are using a drum alone to raise power or merge with your spell energies, practise until you can achieve about a steady 240 drumbeats a minute or four beats a second.
* At first use either a metronome or watch the second hand of a clock, beating one hand in time to the passing seconds while beating four beats with the other hand. This rhythm aids the lower vibrations of the ear and is considered the single most effective tool for raising consciousness and allowing healing to take place. In a short time you won't need to count beats but will be able to allow the spell to carry you along.

Didgeridoo

The long trunk-like wooden tube of the Australian Aboriginal didgeridoo or Yakadi has been played for more than 40,000 years, it has been estimated, in ceremonies to call the rains, as a powerful connection with the earth and earth mother and for rites of passage and for healing.

It is sacred to such earth goddesses as the Australian Aboriginal creator woman Warramurrungundjui. She emerged from the sea and gave birth to the first people. She carried a digging stick and a bag of food plants, medicinal plants and flowers. Having planted them, she went on to dig water holes and then, leaving her children to enjoy the fruits of her work, she turned herself into a rock.

The first didgeridoos were naturally formed from eucalyptus trunks hollowed out by ants. Eucalyptus is still highly prized as having the purest earth sound. Like many of these natural instruments, the didgeridoo was perhaps originally inspired by the wind blowing through a hollow trunk.

A didgeridoo earth power ritual

This is an open-ended ritual in that you are not asking for anything, but are making a connection with the earth and using the sounds to stabilise and reassure you.

* You only need to blow a single pure sound for this ritual.
* To draw up the earth power, stand barefoot on soil, sand or grass with your feet apart.
* Blow just once deeply and slowly into the didgeridoo, sloping it downwards towards the earth.

* As you do so, say slowly and rhythmically in your mind over and over until the sound fades:

> Mother I call you, Mother I reach out to you. Hear my voice.

* As the sound fades, take your lips away and stamp three times slowly with your right foot (if you are right-handed). Say aloud:

> Mother I call to you. Mother I reach out to you. Hear my voice and be my strength and my consolation in good times and bad.

* Blow downwards once again into the didgeridoo, repeating the words in your mind until the sound fades.
* Now listen to the vibrating silence and hear the words of the wise mother.
* Afterwards thank her as you blow downwards for the third time and repeat the full chant once more in your mind.
* Sit on the ground with your didgeridoo at your side receiving pure vibrating earth power through your hands and feet and the small of your back as they connect with the ground. If you can't get the hang of the didgeridoo, softly sing the note into the tube.

Ocarinas

These potato-shaped, holed instruments have been played for magickal purposes since Palaeolithic times and have appeared independently in Asia, South America, Europe and Africa. They are regarded as a gift from the earth or water spirits who are said to manifest if the ocarina is played at dawn or sunset in a forest or near flowing water.

We know that the Mayans used ocarinas for fertility festivals, and that their mournful notes were used in hunting festivals to call game and water birds to the hunters (some hunters became skilful at imitating the actual calls).

Ocarinas have been found made of wood, bone, antlers and pottery, often brightly coloured and in the form of birds, turtles or animals. Ocarinas are easy to play and come with a rudimentary instruction leaflet. A number of schools in the UK are teaching the ocarina to young children as an alternative to the recorder.

Pan pipes

In the same way as the ocarinas, pan pipes are considered to be closely connected with nature essences as well as with the flow of water through the earth.

Pan pipes are the instrument of the goat god Pan (see page 212) and have become very popular not just in the spiritual and magick world.

The pipes were played not just in Ancient Greece, at the earliest around 2,500 BCE, but lands from China to the Americas and Oceania to Africa. They may have been played in the Middle East as early as 7,000 BCE. Though primarily made of bamboo or reeds, pan pipes have been cast from precious metals – probably for formal ceremonial use.

A pan pipe nature essence ritual

* To connect with faeries, nature spirits or devas, work either in the early morning or just before dusk. You can also carry out this ritual with an ocarina.

* Play a few pan pipe chords softly while sitting in the centre of a circle of trees, where there is long grass, by a river or in the middle of your garden. Nature essences will not be impressed with a CD recording, so persevere with the leaflet or buy a teach-yourself book. If all else fails, play a five-note scale up and down on a recorder.

* Light a small smudge stick and still sitting, holding your pipes now in your receptive hand, use the smoke and the pipes to weave spirals of energies, moving softly and rhythmically.

* Meanwhile, whisper a few words, asking if you may become aware of the fey people who are most certainly drawn by the sounds.

* Place the smudge in a holder where sparks will not ignite the grass.

* Blow the pipes once more and you may be rewarded by a whispering in the grass or shimmers of light.

* Sit quietly until the smudge has burned through, perhaps sketching impressions of the darting figures suggested by the shimmers of light in your Book of Shadows or allowing the essences to speak to you as sudden wind in the trees or through the grass.

* If you are by water, look into it and you may glimpse a fast-moving shape that swoops and darts like a small dragonfly.

* You may see an actual dragonfly, beautiful moth or butterfly depending on the time of day.

* End the ritual by playing the pipes softly once more to seal the rite and to thank the nature essences.

Other ways to use sound in spellcasting

* At the beginning of a ritual or spell, strike or ring a bell, small gong or singing bowl once. This marks the division between the everyday world and the transition into a magickal time frame in the same way that casting the circle creates a separate empowered space. Alternatively, use Tibetan bells.

* You can also cast your circle with sound by using the striker to create long notes on a singing bowl as you walk clockwise round the circle to form a vibrating wall of power. A slow, regular drumbeat as you walk the circle will have the same effect.

* Uncast the circle with slower, softer notes or beats while moving moonwise (anticlockwise).

* You can greet the four quarters with a bell or Tibetan singing bowl, with a single drumbeat or the same notes played on an ocarina or pan pipes at each quarter. As the sound fades, greet the guardians so that your words flow after the sound at the same pace and rhythm.

* Use the drum, singing bowl or a single bell between words in an empowerment to send the words into the cosmos.

* For psychic protection and physical safety at home, strike a singing bowl while facing closed doors and windows at night. As you move from room to room, say:

Harm and danger enter not here. This wall of sound enfolds and holds safe me/my family and home until morning light. Blessings be.

❋ Play the pan pipes or ocarina in a room before members of the family come home if they are being quarrelsome or when expecting difficult visitors. This will fill the room with harmony. This is one occasion when it is acceptable to use a CD of the music.

❋ If you see an interfering neighbour crossing the road, take your pan pipes or ocarina and blow three times. In between each chord say softly:

Faeries away, guide her/him to some happy place where s/he will experience tranquillity and not trouble me.

Chanting magick

Chanting, the art of saying or singing repetitive words or phrases rhythmically, has been used in religious and mystical ceremonies and in magick for thousands of years. Earlier in the book I quoted an African saying in relation to the universal ability to dance. The beginning was a reminder that if we can talk, we can sing.

You should relax yourself while chanting, and focus on power not performance. You can either chant as a way of building power or accompany your chanting with dancing or drumming, which both stir the air and so increase harmony.

A good chant and drumming session not only has magickal properties, but will also get the serotonin and the metabolic system flowing at a time when maybe nothing else is moving positively in your life.

The Navajos have many ceremonies of hatal, a word that literally translated means 'sings'. These elaborate songs and chants are an essential part of the rituals for healing, to herald the changing seasons or to bring an abundant harvest.

If a person is taken ill, a rite is chosen by the diviner, and a singer, who will be expert in the precise order and detail of the chants, will be appointed. The hogan or home of the sick person is swept and cleansed, and healing herbs and necessary materials for the ritual will be brought in. The chantway, hailway and waterway chants treat illnesses caused by cold or rain, while the shooting chant is used to cure burns from lightning, and injuries caused by arrows or snake-bites.

The night chant or yeibichai is a major ceremony, lasts for nine days and is carried out only between the first frost and first thunderstorm. It is a ritual of winter renewal and rebirth and is held in a ceremonial hogan.

How chanting works

You can of course chant entirely in your mind. Mantras that originate in the Hindu and Buddhist traditions involve chanting sacred words or phrases either aloud or in the mind. These mantras can be perfected by adepts as a means of developing and channelling psychic energies for healing, for positive power or for astral travel.

When chanting is part of a ritual in which a number of voices are joined together, great spiritual and psychic power can be generated and a collective energy greater than the individuals' separate output is created.

However, you can chant effectively alone and there is the bonus that you can improvise and experiment in a way that you cannot in a group. You can in addition draw collective power from the nature essences that are attracted by the rhythm.

Chanting also kicks into play a different thought mode. This is not the logical left brain, our conscious thoughtfulness, analysing and categorising in words. Nor is it quite like the right-brain clairvoyance or enhanced visualisation where we work primarily through images and conjure up the rushing rivers and mountain peaks of our elemental chants. Chanting, at its most powerful, synthesises left and right brain to evoke a spiritual out-of-body state that may seem to last for an hour or more, though the chant may only be for five minutes.

You will know this is happening when, as you picture the rushing rivers to generate power, you are suddenly sailing on or swimming in the water, feeling the splashing, cool sensation on your face and tasting the purity (cosmic rivers are never polluted).

Creating your own chants

Most of us are inherently poetical, but our enthusiasm and confidence is often stifled.

Chants can be inherently simple, a single phrase, two or three interwoven phrases or lines with an added refrain. By keeping the words to a minimum you will avoid the struggle to recall the next line, which would stem the flow of harmony.

You may for some occasions choose to write a longer poem, for example for a solstice celebration, a memorable family occasion or a personal milestone. You can copy the words into your Book of Shadows and read it by candlelight or in bright sunlight as part of or as a simple ceremony.

* There are existing beautiful calls to power such as the late Doreen Valiente's 'Charge of the Goddess' or 'Drawing the Moon'. These you can find on the Internet or in ritual magick books like Janet and Stewart Farrar's *A Witches' Bible* (see Further reading, page 516). Look on the Internet too for translations of the 'Hymn to the Sun', spoken to the supreme sun god Aten at each sunrise.
* You can as easily write your own chant or praise poems and in *The Practical Guide to Witchcraft and Magick Spells* (see Further reading). I have given alternative versions as a basis for your own charges to the goddess and god.
* Compose chants to the moon, the sun and the stars, to the winds, the trees and the ocean.
* Weave chants round the elements (see pages 31–37 for ideas). The more natural energies you can call into your chants, the more you activate the energies of the actual forces around you. Sometimes you will just want a few simple words and to let nature be the backdrop.
* Use train journeys, pre-flight times at airports, sitting in the car waiting to collect a child or partner and all those minutes at the end of spells when you are inspired but need to wait for a candle or incense to burn away.

Thirteen steps to chant writing

The following is a very basic format. Thirteen is, of course, the number of the goddess and of the moons per year, so you don't need to sing with your fingers crossed behind your back.

1. What is the chant for? Is it for a particular spell or ritual? Is it just an open-ended hymn of praise or thanks?
2. Is there an existing chant given in a book if you are following a particular spell? Or is it better to insert your own words? If so, can you allow the words to come spontaneously or would you prefer to write them before performing the ritual?
3. Should the chant be simple, a few words or several lines? Are the words going to be easy to remember when you are out in the countryside and don't want to refer to bits of paper? Or is this a special occasion when you would like to read some more complex praise or entreaty? If so, is it a chant you will use often and so should memorise?
4. Do you need more than one chant in the spell or ritual, or can you adapt the same one throughout? It is in many ways easier to stick to a root chant and perhaps build it up during the spell.
5. Who is the chant dedicated to? It may be you, a person, animal, place or situation, or the spell may be for an abstract quality.
6. Is there a suitable nature deity focus as well or instead of a personal dedication? Do you need a god and goddess or just a god or goddess? Or do you want a list of related deities, for example different mistresses and lords of the hunt?
7. Will the setting for the spell be integral to the chant? If you are carrying out your spell by the sea then sea powers are the obvious energies to weave words around. However, you may want to include the other elements, for example earth (sand) or fire (a fire made on the beach to be carried away by the sea after the spell). Will you include the wind power for the air element? Picture your setting beforehand and be prepared to adapt a pre-written spell chant if the weather changes.
8. What time will the spell or ritual be? Is it a sunrise or a moonrise spell? If a lunar spell, what phase will it be? Is this timing integral enough to be included in the chant, for example as lady moon or will this be reflected in the deity names?
9. Are the seasons involved and if so what aspect: the dark days, the winter snows? Are these integral to a more complex chant?
10. Who will say or sing the chants: you, your friends or your coven? If more than one person is involved, will it be a collective chant or will you take it in turns in the early part of the ritual and maybe join chant energies as you rise to a crescendo?
11. If you are working alone, will the words need to build up to a final call or will they softly fade into the sound of silence or into the herbs, crystals or symbol that you are empowering?
12. Are you planning any accompaniment, using a drum or a singing bowl? If so, will the two sound mediums work in tandem or will one succeed the other in subsequent waves?
13. Do you need to repeat the chant daily or weekly or when you feel afraid late at night? If so, should you endow a symbol such as a crystal with the chant energy?

PART 6

MAGICK OF THE ELEMENTS AND CRYSTALS

INTRODUCTION

This section is devoted to working with the elements in their natural forms, with the winds, the waters, clay and soil and the changing forces of different weather conditions from the gentle hope-inspiring rainbow to enveloping snow.

We can appreciate and absorb the essential magickal qualities of the elements best in these natural settings. In modern urban society we may be more insulated from the extremes of weather by central heating and electric light that turns night into day at a flick of the switch. However, it only takes a sudden snowstorm or gales to bring that ordered world to a temporary standstill.

Even in the centre of a town we can still connect with the elements, for example by working with clay or by going outdoors on a rainy day or in windy weather. Fire too can empower and inspire us as explored in the section on fire magick. Air magick offers both spiritual and physical benefits, which can be attained through the use of feather rituals.

Finally I have drawn together different strands of crystal lore that have appeared throughout the book. Crystals are a very portable, instant and yet long-lasting source of elemental power. The chosen crystal can be carried as an amulet or empowered charm, cast into the sea as an offering in return for the granting of a wish or focused as an amplifier of personal strengths or potential life-enhancing qualities in an empowerment or protection spell.

Above all, this part of the book, like the following one, is concerned with the cycles and rhythm of nature, the ebbs and flows of the tides and the different qualities of the four winds. All of these can help to carry our spells and rituals naturally towards their stated purpose and to then bring back to us the fulfilment of our wishes and needs on those natural energy waves.

And where are we in this pattern of nature? We are in the centre of these powers, and by drawing strength from them and amplifying thereby our own innate coping strategies, we can meet our own needs and spread positive influence throughout our lives.

EARTH MAGICK

The physical soil and clay of the earth has from Palaeolithic times been regarded as the womb of all creation and also the tomb in a never-ending cycle of rebirth, death and new creation.

Earth magick is an instinctive response to living close to the earth. The statues of the first pregnant goddesses, small enough to be clasped in the hand and dating from around 24,000 BCE, were formed from stone or bone marked with red ochre, the natural earth pigment to signify life-giving blood.

More than 200 of these figures have been excavated from sites occupied by Ice Age or Upper Palaeolithic peoples (35,000–9,000 BCE) extending from the Pyrenees to lake Baikal in central Siberia The earliest burials from the same period in every culture were directly into the earth or in clay urns. These urns contained either cremated remains or more usually the body smeared with red ochre, in the foetal position, to await rebirth like the plants and the slain animals.

We know soil is composed from rocks that have crumbled or eroded or been cast up from the sea bed; from volcanic ash, from rotting vegetation, animal and human faeces and bones whose minerals feed the richness of the soil in a continuing cycle.

Therefore, even in this technological age, we still depend upon the earth and eat plants and animals for nourishment; likewise we return to her, our mortal remains creating the earth for future generations (plus, regrettably, millions of tons of plastic and toxic waste).

The creating earth

The later version of the Genesis creation story refers to God creating man and woman from the dust of the ground.

In Ancient Egyptian mythology, Khnum was the creator god, who made men and women from Nile clay on his potter's wheel. He was the husband of Heket, the frog-headed goddess, who assisted him in creation. The finished human, complete with ka or soul, was set in the mother's womb at conception. Significantly, Khnum was also the god who released the fertilising waters of the Nile each year.

A number of indigenous legends also tell how the first humans came from the earth or from clay.

The Wichita nations recount how the first woman lay naked on her back in the sun and sank slowly into the earth until her body was absorbed. As a result, trees, plants and all creatures, including humans, came from the newly fertilised earth.

In the chapter on insect magick I describe how, in Native North American myth, Grandmother Spider Woman used clay to fashion animals, birds, insects and finally man and woman (see page 248).

In a number of Australian Aboriginal legends, the earth was once a dark, vast, empty plain and the ancestors, along with the sun, the moon, and the stars, slept beneath the earth. At last the ancestors woke themselves and broke through the earth and assumed different life forms. Two of them, the Ungambikula, carved humans out of the half-formed animal and plant matter.

In African myth, the ancestors still live beneath the earth, continuing their lives much as they did on earth, and are consulted by the living through earth oracles, using flour, stones or bones, on matters such as the advisability of a journey.

Magickal soil

Black soil, found in land at the confluence of the Rio Negro and mainstream Amazon, once a large permanent settlement, is highly prized by modern-day farmers as a gift from the past to the future because it is so fertile for the crops. The skulls and bones of the ancestors were once buried directly, deep within the rich black earth, and this is said to endow it with its magickal fertility.

Soil has always been regarded as protective and even today people take with them a pot of earth when they leave their native land to preserve the link with home in a new country. Mothers throughout the ages have thrown a handful of earth as their children leave the safety of the home, to endow them symbolically with the protection of mother earth.

Using soil in magick

* You can use soil as the earth element in outdoor magick.
* Draw circles in the earth using your staff or a small branch you have found and uncast them by rubbing out the circle anticlockwise. Earth circles are very protective and stable.
* Use footstep magick to imprint your impression in the earth. This is potent for any success or determination ritual. You stamp in your plan of action, speaking one word for each stamp, and moving in progressively smaller circles or spirals (see also the labyrinth ritual on the next page).
* You can use some of the foot-printed soil to plant a flowering plant or herb, so that as it grows it will mirror and strengthen your own personal or financial growth over the months ahead.
* Burying rituals are a universal form of banishing magick. In unplanted soil, the buried symbol will just decay away. Planting your symbol beneath a plant or tree symbolises bringing new life from the old. Use a biodegradable symbol, dead leaves or petals or decaying fruit or vegetables.
* You can etch a word or symbol on a potato skin, an apple, a root vegetable or a fruit with a stone. In this way, once the symbol has decayed the new life will grow.
* Walk barefoot over soil and allow the energy to flow upwards through your sensitive sole chakras. As you do so, draw from the earth powers of stability and common sense, and a connection with your home and family.

* When you lack inspiration, feel stressed or need to ask a question with no obvious answer, use a tray of soil and, with a stick, draw circles, labyrinths, squares, and landscapes. Add a little water. Make miniature houses and towns as you did when you were a child. Joy and creativity will return, along with the answer that will suddenly seem so simple.

Earth labyrinths

Labyrinths are sacred spiral forms found in almost every land. They first appeared during the Bronze Age (around 3,500 BCE) in cultures in which there was no geographical or trade connection and were originally a mother goddess icon. However, the basic labyrinth motif itself was discovered on a figure in the Ukraine and may date back to 15,000 BCE or even earlier.

Labyrinths, etched directly into soil or drawn on a sandy shore with a firm stick or your staff, are one of the most concentrated forms of earth power. As you slowly walk in and out continuously of a small one with a few coils or in once and then out again of a huge labyrinth with seventeen coils, you spontaneously become entranced, entering a light trance state. Walk barefoot and you soon reach that wonderful stage of not thinking or anticipating but just being and accepting.

The original labyrinths were drawn on grass or were made with stones laid on the earth. Only later did they become ornate tiled creations within cathedrals. The new revival of interest in labyrinths has seen a trend towards open-air earth-based ones (see my *Complete Guide to Labyrinths* in Further reading, page 514).

Simple or complex, labyrinths have between three and 17 coils (occasionally more). You walk along the unicursal pathway that leads to the centre, though in larger ones you may constantly feel you are being taken outwards again.

You have to trust your feet to follow the pathways, which is part of the surrendering to the labyrinth process. In the centre you have a time of contemplation or acceptance.

Walking out involves the reintegration of the new information or state as you get nearer the everyday world.

* Work at different times, by moon, sun or starlight, at sunrise or sunset and in different seasons.
* Make your labyrinths in different places, facing the sea, in a forest clearing, in your garden.
* Sometimes just walk the coils in silence and sit in the centre (take a cushion or rug), letting your inner stillness be restored.
* In a small labyrinth do two or three in and out circuits and when you feel light-headed go to the centre and sit down.
* As you sit in the centre you may want to talk to the earth mother whose energies are powerful but supportive. You may yell out frustrations as you walk in and then make positive affirmations on the way out.
* Making and walking a larger labyrinth is a good exercise in family or group unity (draw the coils in turn or get younger members to mark the coils with small stones or shells).
* Use a diagram to construct the labyrinth (see page 308).

* Draw and walk a labyrinth whenever you feel alienated or spaced out or can't settle to life.
* Ask a question on the way in. Don't think about it and you will have the answer on the way out.
* Dance, sing or drum a labyrinth or walk it with your singing bowl, making a new vibration as you enter each coil (see page 293 for more on singing bowls).
* Labyrinths are wonderful to walk with a lover. One of you should begin about half a minute after the other. You can join hands as you pass in the coils and exchange words of love or reconciliation. If in a secluded place, make love in the centre and take advantage of the wonderful fertility energies.
* Carry out magickal rituals and spells in the labyrinth coils and centre, setting your mini altar in the centre beforehand. Try experimenting by using a labyrinth instead of a circle.
* Labyrinths need no extra protection because of their shape (spirals naturally keep out negativity).
* Light the coils with candles at night and place your friends, family or coven in different coils or walk together in a long, slow line, step in front of step, in and out, joining hands in the centre and making positive affirmations of unity or for joint concerns.
* Work on the seasonal change points and leave offerings in the centre.
* Bury what you need to leave behind in the mother's womb, the centre, or plant a few seeds here for future growth.
* Make your labyrinth on the shore line and let the tide wash it away or walk out as the waters begin to lap round your feet.
* After a ritual you don't need to rub a labyrinth out like a circle. The energies will rapidly flow down into the earth as you close your ritual quarters. Leave it for children to enjoy.
* If you can't find a large enough area to make a walkable labyrinth, draw a miniature one in earth or sand on a tray and walk it with your fingers and in your mind. You can set a tea light in each coil after dark.
* There may well be a turf open-air labyrinth near you. The most ancient turf labyrinth in England is at Saffron Walden in Essex. It is one of the largest in the world, with seventeen rings and a diameter of 40 m/132 ft, which means a walk of about 1.6 km/1 mile to the centre. It is well worth the effort. The paths are lined with bricks and are very wide, and there is a large grass mound in the centre. It is on the village green and was once used for fertility dances and games. There are four bastions that carry the walker outwards and inwards until he or she is truly amazed.
* Turf labyrinths are also found in France, Germany, the Netherlands, Denmark and the US (where there are a large number of new ones). In the early morning or winter they may be deserted and a number are, like Saffron Walden, open all day and all night.
* Occasionally, when on soil, grass or sand, walk a labyrinth without drawing one, letting the earth energies guide you. (Children and dogs running in circles often follow spiral patterns spontaneously.)

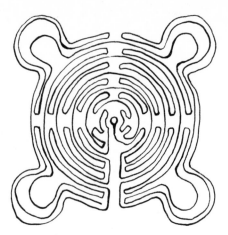

The Saffron Walden labyrinth

How to draw labyrinths
(five to 17 coils)

This is an easy method for drawing a labyrinth.

1 Begin with a shepherd's crook shape. The bow of the crook forms the heart of
   the labyrinth.

2 Next draw a broken circle around the inner circle right to left with the broken
   side on the left. This forms the last circuit, which will lead to the heart of the
   labyrinth.

3   Draw another broken circle around the second, this time left to right, leaving the gap on the right side.

4   Draw another circle, again broken on the opposite side. By now a pattern may be appearing.

5   You should be into the swing of this by now – draw another broken circle.

6   Now we'll close the pattern with a final broken circle.

This is a very simple design and you can adapt it to produce as many coils as you require.

Just keep adding the broken circles and extending the vertical line of the shepherd's crook where necessary.

You can carry on right up to the massive 17-coil version, which will serve the most complex of rituals or meditative work. The beach is perhaps the best place to make a labyrinth of this size.

A soil labyrinth ritual for uncovering your true path

Labyrinth rituals are different from conventional spells, because the speed and intensity of words and movements decrease gradually as you walk towards the centre, and stop in the centre as you connect with the earth mother (even altar work here will have a slow, dreamy quality). The speed and intensity then increase again as you move out of the labyrinth, so you begin and end outside with the same momentum.

Instead of cosmic release as experienced after many spells, at the end of a labyrinth spell you will almost certainly feel a warm satisfying fire in your belly as if after a good meal or being hugged by someone you love. This will occur even in a small labyrinth as you walk in and out several times. You may also experience a strong sense of spiritual transformation.

This ritual is for uncovering your true path. Bear in mind that this may in fact be the path that you are already on.

You will need: A dish of edible bird seeds; a rug or cushion; earth or soil from near the labyrinth site in a deep wooden or ceramic bowl; a small brown or yellow opaque crystal, such as one of the banded agates or sandy mottled jasper.

Timing: Early morning or late afternoon, so that you walk towards the sunrise or sunset as you face the entrance

* Put the dish of seeds in the centre of the labyrinth before the ritual. Put a rug or cushion also in the centre so you will be comfortable.
* Put your earth crystal in the centre of the bowl of earth. You will carry this on your labyrinth walk.
* Face the entrance, holding the bowl and walk slowly, not thinking about the direction your feet will take. Just keep following the coils and you'll get there.
* As you walk, drop the earth bit by bit, saying softly and slowly each time you change direction:

> *Mother, I return your own, earth to earth. Let me return to my true self and find the right pathway to my future.*

* When you reach the centre (of a labyrinth of seven coils or more), sit down, put the bowl beside you on the ground and let any remaining soil trickle silently through your fingers.
* When only the crystal is left, cup it in your hands and speak to the earth mother. You could choose a goddess from the list for earth on page 31, but you may prefer to allow your own image of her to appear in your mind.
* Explain your current life path and anything that worries you or does not seem clear.
* Speak softly and slowly, either aloud or in your mind.
* When you have finished, say:

> *Mother, I leave all in your care. When the time is right show me the pathway that is right for me.*

* Bury the crystal at your feet and sit, breathing in the air and allowing any worries, anxieties or restlessness to flow out on each out breath.
* When the time is right to leave, which may be a minute or two or half an hour later, pick up the dish of seeds and say:

Until we meet again, wise mother, in vision or in dream or in the labyrinth, I leave in thankfulness. Send, I ask, a sign when the time is right.

* You will know when to go as you will feel a sudden breeze, see a flock of birds overhead or more subtly sense the energies withdrawing.
* Scatter the seeds as you walk slowly out of the coils, increasing in momentum as you go. Walk in silence as images, words or positive impressions of how things could be may come into your mind.
* At the entrance turn to face the centre once more and picture the energies descending into the ground as autumnal colours, whatever the time of year, and the mother also fading (or gathering her robes round her as she prepares to depart).
* Turn outwards and circle outside the labyrinth once, saying:

I go forward with joy and with certainty to whatever lies ahead.

* Scatter any remaining seeds around the perimeter as you walk.
* With a small labyrinth, sprinkle the soil in the coils on your final walk in before sitting in the centre, and scatter the seeds on the way out after you have been sitting in the centre.
* Spend the rest of the day or evening, if possible, in the open air. You may see a sign, an unusual butterfly or a bird that settles nearby or flowers growing out of season. You will know in your mind your direction or perhaps that your feet were on the correct path all along.

Clay and fertility

Few crafts are as satisfying as working with clay even if you are not even remotely artistically inclined. When my children were young, we used to go down to a local beach and pick lumps of clay off the beach. It was very messy but very therapeutic and calming both for me and my youngest son who was suffering bullying and getting very stressed at the time.

Clay in Africa is associated with the fertility of the earth and especially with female fertility. Women make the majority of clay pots. This action has great magickal significance since it symbolises the great mother creating humans and all life from the clay of the earth. Each time a pot is made the creative power of the potter rekindles the first creative energy in herself and the recipient of the pot.

Pottery is the regarded as the most ancient creative art on earth and itself gave birth to metalworking that was discovered during the firing process. In the sub-Saharan continent the wives of smiths are generally potters.

In West Africa, the senior female potter in a village is generally also the midwife, and is often married to the blacksmith who will combine this role with that of undertaker. Because of the powers this couple hold over life and death, their clay pots and images are regarded as containing great supernatural power. Among other African peoples too an older female potter will be the village healer.

At weddings, new pots would be made for the bride, while at funerals pots would be broken to symbolise the severing of life. Other vessels would contain offerings linking the everyday and spirit worlds thus creating a safe location for the spirits of the dead. Sometimes a ground-up pot belonging to a deceased person would be incorporated into a new pot.

Using clay in magick

Make your own fertility and abundance jars to attract good things into your life.
  If you do not have a kiln, self-drying clay is very useful.

* Work in sunlight or the brightest part of the day. It can be a good unifying ritual to make pots with friends and families, and provides an opportunity to talk about joint plans and dreams.
* If working alone, endow your pot with lovely thoughts of sunny places, abundance and your own future happiness, even if it seems a while away.
* Push away negative thoughts and free-floating anxieties and roll into your creation daydreams and visions or memories of happy times.
* Don't worry at all about the end product. Rather recall the pleasure you experienced as a child while mixing and rolling clay.
* Use rolled coils of clay to form the jar, then smooth out the sides.
* Keep your fertility jar unglazed and add adornments in clay or by drawing designs with modelling tools of bees, butterflies, birds, zigzags, lozenges, spirals and other goddess images (see page 150 for other symbol ideas). You can also use a thin brush and red pigment paint. Or leave it totally unadorned.
* The triple spiral, the first form of labyrinth, represents the three aspects of the goddess: maiden, mother and wise woman. The triple spiral can be found on the Newgrange passage Grave near Dublin that dates from 3,100 BCE.

* Every day add three pinches of sea salt (the sacred substance of the earth) to your jar. As you do so, say:

First for the maiden goddess that I may be filled with hope.
Second for the mother that my wish/desire/need for _____ may come to fruition.
Third and greatest for the wise one for the power of the healing earth to bring the wisdom to use the blessing I seek wisely.

On the night of the crescent moon, tip your jar of salt into flowing water that it may bring fertility and abundance into your daily life or that of a loved one.

* Alternatively, make a small abundance pot with a lid to hold coins. Add a coin each day. When the pot is full, use the coins to bring happiness, reserving one for the next money collection in the pot.
* Make your own pentagram dishes for your altar (see page 90).
* Make one of the ancient goddesses, like the Palaeolithic Venus of Willendorf (see below) who will bring fertility and abundance into your life.
* You could create an earth spirit (see page 501 for ideas).
* Create a power animal or a bird figure (see pages 216 and 230) for your altar. They can be quite abstract.
* Roll your clay to make a giant spiral or circle and draw a labyrinth on it to walk in your mind.
* Set your creation in a warm, dry place and empower it by sprinkling salt round it in three concentric circles, moving outwards, saying:

From conception, through creation and with blessings, I charge you, be a symbol of my fertility and let me likewise bring abundance into my life or _____'s life. (Name a person or place that needs abundance.)

* If your creation crumbles or cracks (or if you drop a pottery artefact), it does not mean that your luck is lost, merely that it is time to reaffirm your creativity.
* Make or buy a new pot, adding a small piece (not sharp) from the broken object inside the new one for continuity.
* Create for yourself a secret power sign, perhaps your initials or those of any secret magickal names interwoven with a spiral or another magickal shape. Paint or etch this in clay on the bottom of any pottery you buy or make.

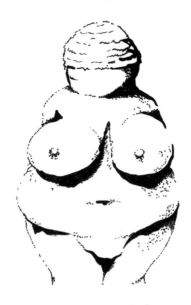

The Venus of Willendorf

Buying pottery for use in magick

* Visit a pottery where they still craft clay by hand and choose a fired but unglazed jar, a lidded pot and perhaps a small animal statue.
* Smudge them before use with clockwise and anticlockwise spirals of sagebrush or a pine or sage incense. This will not take out the love of the potter but will overwrite your personal essence.
* Decorate your pottery with red-ochre-type paint. Enquire at the craft or DIY store about its suitability for unglazed pots; usually ceramic-type paints work well.
* As you draw your zigzags or lozenges or maybe small goddess outlines like those on pages 150–54 of the bird, butterfly and bee goddesses, again endow the pot with your dreams and any special hopes for fertility and abundance in your life.
* Empower the pot in the same way as for those made yourself.

Using clay to release the power of the ancestors

In Ancient Egypt what were called pottery dream letters existed right from the Old Kingdom through to the Late Period. These letters were written in hieratic, a less complex script than hieroglyphics, around the outer rim of a pottery bowl. The words were a request to the wise ancestors or a local deity.

Most of these clay letters ask for assistance and guidance in matters that concerned the family (and so were of personal interest to the ancestor). Petitions might be for a baby for a beloved daughter who was having difficulty conceiving, to resolve a problem about inheritance or property, or for intervention in the case of an injustice.

Sometimes the words written round the offerings bowl might remind the deceased of a kindness done for them in life by the petitioner. On one such bowl dating from the first millennia BCE, a dutiful son reminded his late mother how he had hunted diligently for seven quail she had wanted to eat.

The bowls were filled with offerings and set on the ancestral or deity altar with a request that the matter might be resolved favourably as soon as possible. It was also requested that the chosen ancestor would appear in a dream with a solution and that they would continue to give support.

I'm certainly not suggesting that you summon spirits or ghosts, but rather that you draw positive energies from the past that are still available to us in a family affection that does not die whatever your theories of the afterlife. Dreams are the most efficient way for higher or unconscious wisdom to be given at a time when the conscious mind is least active.

In modern psychological as well as psychic terms, creating your magickal bowl allows you to tune into your own inner strengths and ingenuity, inherited from those ancestors, to make the necessary changes, seize an opportunity or overcome what seems an almost insurmountable obstacle.

Your clay letter request can be for anything concerned with security, stability, abundance and fertility, from money to relationship issues or the success of creative adventures.

You may have a particular ancestor on whom you wish to focus, perhaps a family hero or heroine who turned the family fortunes around, one you know who faced a similar situation to your own generations ago or a deceased great grandparent who was supportive to you during his or her lifetime.

As a bonus you will dream creatively whether of the ancestor or of a scenario that will offer you positive guidance and when you wake, you will feel energised and ready for anything.

A bowl spell for abundance or fulfilment

You will need: An unglazed pottery bowl, bought or made; an incense stick in a ceremonial fragrance such as sandalwood, frankincense or myrrh; a dish of suitable offerings to put in the bowl, such as dried flower petals, herbs, crystals or nuts and seeds. You can match the offering to the purpose of the spell, for example, nuts and seeds for fertility, small green aventurine crystals if you need good luck (see suitable crystals on page 385) or bay leaves and basil for an increase in family funds.

Timing: In the late evening by candlelight so that you can drift into sleep soon afterwards and dream creatively or as the Ancient Egyptians called it 'dream true'

* Place the bowl in the centre of the altar with another smaller dish to the north of it containing the offerings and the incense in a holder to the east.
* Light a candle in the south, the direction for the Egyptians of the sun's most blazing heat and also the source of the Nile. Say:

May wisdom come and blessings and with them abundance.

* Light the incense from the candle, while repeating the words.
* Take the empty bowl in your receptive hand and write your request in incense smoke clockwise around the rim. Do not speak your petition aloud, but let the words flow in the smoke, as many times as you wish.
* When you have finished, return the incense to its holder.
* Add the offering to the bowl and say:

I make these offerings freely and thank the wise ancestors for all they have taught me. I ask that I may remember and draw strength from their lives and their experiences. I recall especially _____ (name the particular ancestor who is the focus) and give thanks for his/her life and inspiration.

* Set the bowl in the centre of the altar and leave the incense and the candle to burn through.
* This would be a good time to read some of your Book of Shadows or create a new poem or chant about the wise ancestors.
* When the candle and incense are done, dispose of the ash and any wax and go to bed to dream and to be filled with inspiration.

Getting rid of negativity

* Normally I am very against any destructive magick and so, except to commemorate the freeing of a person's spirit in death, would not deliberately use magick to break a pot (though in my fierier days I did hurl one or two non-magickal ones at walls in temper).

* However, if there is something or a situation in your life that you are having trouble banishing, create an image in clay to represent the situation, for example a scorpion for spite, a cake if you are having problems losing weight that you need to shed for health reasons, a pile of clay cards to represent credit card debt, a monster to signify bullying or fears or a small clay house for one that just won't sell.

* As you make the image, name what you wish to banish, adding:

Not to harm, not to hurt, not to diminish or endanger, but to loosen the hold / remove the barriers and set myself free. I send only good thoughts and kind words at the moment of parting.

* Hold the finished form and speak over it anything you wish to say as closure. Then roll the clay back into a ball to create something new in the future.

Food magick

Food magick is a particularly effective form of earth power since you absorb the energies you have raised during a spell by eating the food.

Gradually as the Ice Age retreated it became possible for people to settle, to capture and breed animals and for women to develop their existing knowledge of plants to cultivate wheat and grain. Farming began around 8,000 BCE and the earth mother became the goddess of the barley or corn, like the Roman Ceres from whom we get the word 'cereal'. The consorts of the various earth goddesses, for example Dumuzi the Sumerian shepherd god consort of Innana, or in the case of Ceres, her daughter Prosperpina (Demeter and Persephone in the Ancient Greek tradition), was the spirit of the corn, cut down in autumn (or abducted to the underworld) to sprout again in the spring.

In Ancient Egypt, an annual ceremonial was held to bury the Grain Osiris. This was a small flat hollow clay model of the Osiris mummy or of the Osiris himself (the slain father god). It either had a compartment filled with grain, or the grain was set directly into the clay. These Grain Osiris models were also placed in tombs to bring rebirth. The Ashmolean Museum in Oxford has an extensive fine collection of them.

Many indigenous peoples like North Americans have corn goddesses, such as Corn Woman.

Cherokee creation myths tell of Selu and her husband Kanati who are ruled by mother sun. Selu is the corn mother from whose body comes corn and beans. The corn mother's symbol is a perfect ear of corn without a single missing or misshapen kernel. One of these is often placed in a healing medicine bundle, especially those of medicine women, and represents fertility as well as the powers of regeneration.

Feasts at seasonal celebrations have from time immemorial been a way of attracting enough food and resources to the community and to individuals throughout the year. The finest of the harvest was always given to the earth mother or the corn deities of the culture.

A food altar

You can use unprocessed food as the magickal substances on your altar (see page 244 for a honey ritual). Position them as follows:

* Bread, oat or rye biscuits, herbs and spices, meat or vegetables in the north
* Seeds or eggs in the east
* Honey, butter or cheese in the south
* Nuts, milk, cereals or fresh or dried fruit in the west (a jug of milk – the drink of the Celtic maiden goddess Brigid – or fruit juice can also be set in the west). You can pre-cook any of these, if necessary, to eat during or after the spell.
* Bless each of the foodstuffs in turn, naming the powers you seek from each and in turn eat or drink a little of each (starting in the north).
* You might say, for example for the fire element:

I take power from this cheese that I may be inspired to finish my novel by Christmas.

* You can include a quality for each power and use yourself directly as the symbol absorbing the powers as you eat them.
* Alternatively, make a family meal into an altar by setting the foods (more than one if you like for each element) in the four directions on the table or preparing a platter with one of each of the foods to place in the centre of the table.
* Before the meal, pass your hands clockwise and anticlockwise together above the table or directly in front of you as you sit in the south facing north, making a blessing on the food and those who eat it.
* See my *Complete Book of Spells* (in Further reading) for more meal and abundance blessings.
* Make pastry, cakes, biscuits or bread to represent fertility and abundance. Endow them as you make them with the blessings you need, and repeat the blessing before you eat them.
* Make ordinary cakes for the purpose of bringing peace by decorating them with a pastry olive branch or dove and then taking them to a family party; endow a birthday or Christmas cake with special wishes; make a love cake adding rose essence; make little cakes for a special seasonal ceremony or prepare protective rolls for a child's lunch box.

A food spell to bring what you most desire

You can cast this spell for yourself or for others.

You will need: Ingredients for pastry, biscuits or bread (either basic ingredients or a mix if you are in a hurry); a bowl; a wooden spoon and flat wooden platter; one of each of the elemental foods or liquids that can easily be added to the mix, for example seeds, egg, honey, nuts, dried fruit and spice. You can substitute the flour for the north element if you don't want to add a spice.

Timing: Early afternoon, especially on a Friday or Sunday

* Pre-heat the oven.
* Begin with the basic ingredients in the bowl and name what you aim to produce, for example a small pastry boat for travel or a pastry house for a new home.
* Endow the mix with each of the elements in turn, naming the elemental strength you seek (see page 31 for these). Do this by adding a small quantity of each to the mix and stirring it in nine times clockwise as you speak, for example:

I add spice for earth that I may find an evening job to finance my trip (practical application) and seeds for air that the travel plans may gain impetus by my contacting/finding the right person in Adelaide who would like to exchange apartments for six months.

* Mix the ingredients thoroughly with your hands, endowing them with any strengths or creative qualities you need in your life right now, such as courage, initiative, concentration, fertility (whether physical or in bringing a project into being).
* Recite a chant or mantra over and over again as you work, something as simple as:

Creating mother, may courage empower me.

* As you work, picture the dough or pastry being filled with light.
* Make a ball of the mix and finally shape it into whatever you want. End by saying:

This I have created. I will take in the power and walk on the pathway to fulfilment/love/travel.

* Set your creation on a baking tray and put it in the oven.
* While it is cooking, stay focused by making plans or writing in your Book of Shadows.
* Once it is cooked and cooled, hold your creation, name what you have produced and repeat:

This I have created. I will take in the power and walk on the pathway to fulfilment/love/travel.

* The spell is done and you are ready for the first steps in actuality.

2

AIR MAGICK

Air magick is centred on movement, initiating positive change, connecting with sky and spiritual energies, the opening of horizons, the expansion of possibilities and new beginnings. Its sacred substances, feathers and incense are set in the east of the altar and the eastern gateway in the circle is sometimes opened by the guardian of the four winds. See pages 95–107 for more about incenses. In this chapter I focus on the magick of feathers and the magick of the winds.

Feather magick

Feather magick, symbolising the wondrous ability of birds to fly, spans different cultures and ages. To the Huichol Indians of Mexico, Tacutsi Aramara, mother eagle, is the mother goddess and wife of Ireeku, the Sun father. She is called mother of the sky and queen of the heavens. Though the eagle is her special bird, all birds are considered messengers to the Huichol deities. Feathers are attributed with magickal powers, especially those of the eagle and wild turkey who are considered birds of the sun. Healing arrows, with hawk or eagle feathers suspended from the shaft, are fired directly upwards to carry prayers for healing and abundance to the deities.

I have already mentioned the feathered cloaks worn by shamans, the magickal priest healers of different lands for astral or spirit travel (see page 227). Feathered cloaks (often made with mallard feathers) were, according to mediaeval Irish literature, also worn by Celtic Druidic bards and later Irish poets. Stories abound of high-ranking Druids who at ceremonies and for prophecy wore feathered headdresses, along with the prophetic white bull skin from bulls sacrificed on the midwinter solstice.

Shamanic rattles across the globe are decorated with feathers to connect the shaman with his spirit bird helpers who assist him in his astral travel (often he will sit on the back of a huge bird in his trance state). They are also believed to bring healing.

To the Indians of the rainforests of South America, feathers are an important feature of birth and funeral ceremonies, symbolising the entry to and exit from this world of the human spirit through flight.

Modern magick and feathers

Feathers are used in spells and rituals to carry wishes, blessings and intentions and also for protection and healing. Any feathers can be used to signify air.

The more feathers from different species you collect, the more varied will be the qualities you can invoke in your feather spells (see pages 230–37 for a list of bird qualities). However, if all you have to work with are seagull feathers (travel) and pigeon feathers (like the dove, symbols of peace and messages) you can empower any feather for any magickal purpose by naming the intention and writing it over the feather with the smoke of a miniature smudge stick or incense stick.

Though in most cultures birds of prey like the eagle or hawk are especially prized for magick, song-bird feathers naturally obtained are also of great value in assisting creativity, communication and for healing in the spellcaster (or wearer).

The feathers of nurturing birds such as turkeys and geese are also traditionally considered of great worth, especially in the Americas where they are valued for their protective qualities towards home and family and also for financial security, fertility and abundance.

Collecting and caring for feathers

You may already be using a feather or feather fan in your smudging.

* If you do decide to build up a varied collection of feathers, take a digicam image or a photo of each feather with a label of its species.
* You can put these pictures in your Book of Shadows with information about the birds and, more importantly, the feelings you have about the feathers and the messages you receive as you hold them.
* Ideally you would only use feathers you have found, but in modern urban environments it is not always possible to get a variety of clean ones. Certainly it is good to work with feathers from local birds and you can build up a collection of indigenous species over months, supplementing it with feathers you find on holiday.
* However, many bird conservation parks, bird of prey conservancies and wild bird reserves do sell feathers that have been found. You can be assured that the birds in these places are treated with respect You may be able to buy brightly coloured parrot feathers that are beloved of the South American rainforest peoples who sometimes keep tame parrots in their villages.
* When not in use, keep your feather collection wrapped in natural cloth or in a long fabric pouch.
* If you haven't used your feathers recently, once a month you should stand them in a tall container and smudge them. If you choose the night of the full moon, you can afterwards leave them on a window ledge to be bathed in full moonlight.

Native North American feather magick, the guardian birds

Feather magick is practised all over the world but many of our modern traditions come from Native North America.

There are four main feathers associated with Native North American feather magick that symbolise the four guardian birds of the four cardinal directions. These are the wisest of the birds and will act as psychic markers in your spell circles and in your life as they do on some medicine or power wheels. You may be able to get these feathers from bird conservancies. Buy two or three of each so that you have spares in case one gets torn. Do this even if using a substitute to the recommended feather. In this way you also build up the energies of the specific feathers.

Regardless of your personal power animals and birds, these four guardians offer strength and guidance in your magickal undertakings, and their messages are always significant, if not necessarily comfortable.

The difference between the guardian birds and our personal power birds and animals is one of degree. These are the wise clan chiefs rather than a personal friend and guide, in the same way that an archangel offers us spiritual power while our personal angels offer comfort. They are four challenging and powerful birds, but to fly with them occasionally can move you forward personally and in your magickal work.

* An eagle feather in the east represents spring and dawn. You can substitute a falcon or kestrel feather or any grey feather.
* A hawk feather in the south represents noon and summer. You can substitute a golden brown or tawny feather.
* A raven feather in the west represents dusk and autumn. You can substitute any black feather.
* An owl feather in the north represents midnight and winter. You can substitute any white feather.

Encountering the guardian birds

I have listed some of the strengths associated with the following four birds. These strengths can be absorbed as you hold, breathe on or work in a spell with the feathers.

* Start a page in your Book of Shadows for each.
* Hold each representative feather in turn about 5 cm/2 in away from your lips at different times of the day, moon phase and seasons and picture the four guiding birds sitting motionless before you. As I am writing this, a small yellow kestrel is perched on the post outside my caravan.
* If necessary, visit a conservancy to help you focus and find, for example, a snowy owl or an eagle owl that seems to signify for you the archetypal owl.
* Let each bird speak to you and at these different times convey any messages it has for you. Still your mind and wait – like the bird, relaxed but always ready.

The eagle

Tribal chief of all birds, the eagle soars high in the sky, yet sees everything below. He is said to carry the prayers of the people to father Sun. He is associated with the mythical thunder bird, the rain-bringer with a lake of water on his back, whose flashing eyes are lightning and flapping wings bring thunder.

The eagle is the bird that can help you to soar in your life in whatever way is right for you. He will offer you the strength to keep to your principles and your own unique world view and to rise above any pettiness or spite. He also offers the vision to see the whole picture and your future path so that you can make wise choices.

Leadership and idealism are the strengths of the eagle.

Unrealistic expectations and dogmatism are the weaknesses highlighted by the eagle that he can help you overcome.

The hawk

The messenger of spirit, the hawk has the power of healing and its feathers are used in healing ceremonies. Amerindian nations used hawk feathers to bring rain in times of drought. Sometimes, like the eagle, the hawk is associated with the thunder bird and the power of the sun. Pueblo Indians call red-tailed hawks, red eagles.

He is the bird that can offer focus to decide your priorities and avoid frittering your energies and talents. He brings courage in times of anxiety and uncertainty and the inspiration and fire to create whatever is of beauty and worth for you or to turn adversity into opportunity.

Courage and creativity are the strengths of the hawk.

Impatience and intolerance are the weaknesses highlighted by the hawk that he can help you to overcome.

The raven

Regarded both as the Great Trickster and Creator, the raven is the teacher of magick. He is sometimes called the Big Grandfather or Raven Man, and like the hawk was one of the creatures in Amerindian lore that re-created the world after the flood.

It was said the raven stole the sun, a reference to his love of bright things and his desire always to understand how and why things happen and if they can be done better.

He is also is messenger of the Great Spirit.

The raven is the bird to offer help when you need to be quick-witted or when you fear being out-manoeuvred verbally by others.

He is the great communicator and can make

bridges between people and disparate parts of your life, but also challenges and questions at every stage so that there is constant progress and self-awareness.

Intuition and adaptability are the strengths of the raven.

Deviousness and distractibility are the weaknesses of the raven that he can help you to overcome.

The owl

Sometimes called the night eagle, the owl is the bird of the night and the moon in the same way that the eagle rules the day and the sun. To the woodland people of south-east America, the owl is chief of the night and a sacred protector of all who must travel or work in darkness.

He is the bird that reveals the wise counsel of your inner voice and connects you with your inner stillness when your emotions or life become unstable.

The owl also teaches that there is a time and season for everything and that by kicking against fate we sometimes hurt only ourselves. He can also warn you when you need to protect yourself and those you love.

Perseverance and patience are the strengths of the owl.

Pessimism and inertia are the weaknesses of the owl that he can help you to overcome.

Using the four feathers in magick

* For any spells with an air focus such as travel, healing, learning or career, position the feathers at the four directions of your altar.
* As well as or instead of passing your symbol through the sacred substances associated with the four directions (see pages 31–37), in turn, hold your feather in the power hand and waft it over the symbol of your spell.
* Move it in clockwise spirals, naming the particular strengths of each guardian and how these strengths can aid your venture.
* For example, if you were casting a promotion spell, in the north you might say:

I call on the wise owl of the north to help me to persevere, even though I am tired after work, to study to pass the assessment that will gain me the promotion I desire.

* Alternatively, work with just one feather in a less formal setting. Choose the guardian bird that most closely matches a particular need.
* Hold the feather in your receptive hand and weave it through the smoke of a sagebrush smudge or a sage or cedar incense stick, stating the strengths you need from that guardian.
* Then hold the feather close to your lips and breathe gently, picturing the energies of the bird entering your energy field.
* Sometimes you may need more than one guardian strength, in which case hold two or more of the feathers like a fan and breathe in the energies you need.
* For balancing your personal energies either at an important stage or before a

significant event in your life, or if you feel irritable and tired but unable to rest, set the feathers at their own directions on your outdoor altar.

* Begin in the east for air power and smudge over each feather in turn, holding the smudge in your power hand and the feather in your receptive hand.
* Weave the smoke over each feather in turn and then around your own head and shoulders lightly, saying:

I take into myself the power of _____ (choosing the aspect of each guardian you most need to steady you).

* To discover which guardian will help you most on a significant or potentially difficult day, first thing in the morning put all four feathers in a tall container and close your eyes. Turn the container round nine times clockwise and then the same anticlockwise and ask for the particular bird guardian who will act as your mentor during the day ahead to speak.
* Let your hand guide you to pick the feather you need and, as you hold it close to your lips and breathe quietly, let the bird guardian speak to you in your mind the message it has for the day or task ahead.
* If you don't trust your own psychic powers to choose, have a spare set of three or four of each feather just for divination so that you select from 12 or 16. But you will choose the right one even out of four if you relax and listen in your mind.
* Over time you may develop most kinship with one of the guardian birds and find you pick their feather more than any other, even if you are using a whole selection of the feathers of different birds.

Feather spells

You can work with any number of kinds of feathers, the more the better, but always include those of the guardians.

Spend time holding the different feathers, if possible as soon as you acquire each new one, recording over time the messages and the strengths you detect in each, in your Book of Shadows.

You can choose particular feathers for different magickal needs, as the focus for spells and also to signify the element of air, for example a dove or pigeon feather in a reconciliation spell or one for love.

Even if you only have feathers from one or two species, the following spells are effective since they are not specific to certain species.

* Use feathers to send messages whether to a lover known or unknown, to potential employers or a family member far away with whom you have lost touch. Speak the message as you hold the feather in a high place or on a windy day and then release it.
* You can use just one feather to send wishes or love, or four of the same kind of feather for the four winds and directions. If, for example, the matter is one of overcoming obstacles from a position of weakness and remaining cheerful in the face of adversity, four blackbird feathers would be ideal (see page 230 for more ideas of bird qualities).

* Stand in an open or high place holding the four feathers in your power hand.
* Face the east first and say:

> *Fly swift and free fly to where _____ (name the person)/love/employment lies waiting*
> *and carry this message for me.*

* Say what you wish to say in as few or many words as you wish and, when you have finished, blow on the feather three times and release it.
* Repeat for the other three directions and release a feather at each of these, blowing on the feather three times.
* End the spell by turning in all four directions and picture your message being received and the desired results winging their way towards you.

Prayer sticks

Prayer sticks, flags or trees are feathers attached to a stick, a branch or a tree to release petitions, entreaties or blessings as the feathers blow. They are found in cultures from Tibet to Native North America and in more recent years have become a focus for collective peace rituals in which everybody plants their feather stick into the ground with a blessing or ties a feather to a tree.

We cannot and should not try to re-create the ceremonies of other cultures as our own backgrounds are very different. However, I do believe it is valid to use concepts from different cultures in a way that feels right, as long as we are acting with good intent. If you do want to use prayer sticks or flags in a more authentic manner, there are a number of excellent Native North American websites giving information in this area.

Magick with prayer sticks

* Individual prayer sticks can vary in size from between the length of an average finger to the measurement from elbow to fingertips.
* The stick itself is the prayer whether or not you speak it aloud or say it in your mind as you prepare your stick.
* The feather is the means by which the archetypal or spirit bird energies of your chosen species carry the prayer or wish that is made.
* Traditionally prayer sticks or flags in Native North America are made of willow or cedar with the bark stripped off.
* Some people choose the stick according to the kind of tree in which the chosen bird perches or nests. This is quite possible if you use garden trees or bushes and the feather of birds that regularly visit.
* In a home I visited in central Sweden last year, I saw a small prayer stick set in tiny turquoise chippings in a bowl to hold the stick upright. Turquoise is an air crystal. The feather was of a buzzard-type bird that could be found around the lakes in the area. Ingrid, whose home it was, said the idea was American but that her late grandmother, who lived in the far north in a community that still relied on hunting, used to hang hawk feathers from the midsummer tree to bring sunny days and plenty to the community. Her grandmother continued to do this when she moved down to Stockholm to be with her children when she was very old.

* I have also seen feathers attached to wind chimes in a modern hotel in northern France.

Making and using a prayer stick

* Find or cut a forked or a straight stick of the length you want. Use a personal measurement such as your elbow to fingertip length, to make the stick your own.
* Strip the bark and smooth the stick. If you wish, you can also etch or paint a design in a natural pigment.
* As you work, endow the stick silently with blessings for the purpose of the creation.
* Add a feather to the stick of a kind that seems appropriate to the purpose. Tie it rather than glue it.
* You can, with a forked stick, use a pair of feathers from the same species to balance your energies or use two different feathers for contrasting bird qualities that you wish to blend in the prayer. You can dedicate your prayer stick to a cause or to a particular person, animal or place that needs blessings.
* Plant the prayer stick outdoors directly in the earth in an open place. The feather will fly physically in its own time or will gently decay. In the meantime it will continue to release your message spiritually to the cosmos as it flutters in the breeze.
* Some people buy or make a permanent prayer stick for ceremonies. This is smudged before each use. You could have individual prayer sticks for different family members and keep them in the heart of the home even when the family members are away. Add new ones for additions to the family and bless the sticks of any people who are away, renewing the feathers as necessary.
* Keep all the sticks upright in a large bowl of crystal chippings or with a balance of amethyst and small pointed clear crystal quartzes for energy and harmony.
* Have a small family or home prayer stick in the heart of the home, in a bowl of soil or crystals, to protect the home and to fill the room with positive powers. Smudge it monthly on the full moon and then set it where moonlight can shine on it.
* Make yourself an altar prayer stick with all four guardian feathers attached (obtain spares). Secure this in crystals or soil and set it in the centre of your outdoor altar. You can touch each feather in turn during a spell and call its strengths or just those relevant to the particular spell. Alternatively, use feathers from four different birds that for you signify the energies of the four directions.
* Use a prayer or petition stick as the focus for a spell. Empower it with the four elemental substances. When you have built up the power in the spell, reduce the intensity and speed to silence and stillness. Leave the prayer stick in place to transmit your needs, slowly and continuously, to the cosmos.
* You can, at seasonal, family celebrations or any collective cause, invite people to bring along individual prayer sticks they have created. Once the circle has been cast, each person can sit within the circle with their prayer stick in the earth or resting in their hands in front of them.
* In turn, clockwise round the circle, each person makes a blessing for the occasion or need, as they gently touch their own prayer stick. They end by saying:

I pass the power of the feather on.

* The final person to speak should add:

The circle has no beginning and no ending and so the power continues to flow. Blessed be.

* Then the prayer sticks can be planted either on a small mound nearby or in the centre of the circle while a communal chant is made.
* You can make ceremonies as elaborate as you wish with dancing or drumming, or a Tibetan singing bowl or bell can be sounded each time an individual plants their prayer stick in the chosen place.

Making and using a prayer tree

Trees bedecked with ribbons or offerings are found worldwide – from fertility trees in India to those growing round or near healing wells in the West Country of England. See also page 185 about having a magick tree in your own garden.

Prayer or feather trees are a variation on this and can vary in size from a large forked staff at shoulder height to a tall, uprooted branch with several smaller branches or an actual growing tree. There is no reason why a living leafy tree cannot be a feather tree. Indeed, the flowing life force will empower the feathers.

* Strip off the foliage from a dead branch or use one that has been lying a while and is quite dry.
* If you are setting a branch permanently to act as a prayer tree, dig a deep hole and fill the base with stones to secure the tree in all weathers. You can also erect a temporary tree for private or collective use.
* On top of a small mound is ideal or any open area where the breezes will catch the feathers, but where the wind will not immediately blow them away.
* Alternatively, you can use your existing magickal tree either at home, in the local park or in a forest.
* If working alone, circle the tree or branch nine times clockwise, nine times anticlockwise and nine times clockwise again, while holding your feather in your receptive hand. You can smudge as you move if you wish.
* Silently endow the feather or feathers with the purpose for which you are going to attach them to the prayer tree.
* Secure the feather/s with a firm cord or thread so that it/they will ripple over a period of days – if the feather/s do detach it does not matter at all.
* For matters that you are eager to change but which are not in your hands, suspend feathers on very thin thread on a tree in a windy place. As you tie the feathers, one for each person or circumstance blocking you, say:

May the winds of change release this power and move matters forward when the time is right.

The extra wind power will stir the energies to work fast.

* For an ongoing matter, attach feathers weekly to the prayer tree and remove any that have decayed.

- You can have feathers on a tree for any purpose: healing, peace, for a missing person or an estranged relative, calling them in love as you add your weekly or monthly feather.
- Put a feather on your tree for a birthday, a milestone in your own or a loved one's life or to mark the days or weeks to an anticipated change or event. Melanie, a sailor's wife in Cornwall, adds a feather every week her partner is away at sea, sending love across the ocean. When he was in active service in the Iraq conflict she added a special pigeon peace feather each week.
- For a communal ritual, you can use a basket of feathers with ties, one for each person present. The basket of feathers is handed round and each person takes one, naming their wish for the occasion.
- Afterwards, they repeat the empowerment silently as each ties his/her feather to the tree.
- You could have a coven prayer tree made of willow, the moon tree, as part of a full moon ritual and use the feathers of any night bird.
- Use a prayer tree as a healing circle or, if you work alone, write the names of people who need healing in a book, and add a feather each week, naming those in need of healing.

Wind magick

The wind, as manifestation of the ancient element of air, features in formal ceremonies and impromptu spells from Scandinavia to Native North America.

The power of the winds has brought universal respect as well as a desire to control them.

In Iroquois myth, Gaob, the lord of the winds, appointed animal guardians of the four winds herds and tethered them, so that the power would not overwhelm the world. He called the bear and tied him with a leash to control the herd of the north winter winds. The moose became protector of the herds of the eastern stormy skies. The panther was tethered to be guardian of the rainy west winds, while the gentle fawn led the herds of the warm south winds out to graze on sunny days.

Witches and women who have recently given birth are said in lands as far apart as Africa and Russia to have the power to raise winds. Celtic Druids and Druidesses strove to master the winds – a spiritual exercise of their own ability to merge with and use the elements creatively. In CE 60, the Roman military governor of Britain

Suetonius Paulinus led two legions into north-west Wales and attacked Anglesey with the aim of wiping out the Druids and Druidesses forever. Tacitus, the Roman historian (circa CE 55–117) described how the Druids lifted their hands to the skies, calling down divine aid. The subsequent terrible storm terrified the Roman soldiers on the opposing bank of the Menai Straits, though eventually the Roman war machine triumphed. He received accounts years later from Roman soldiers who were present at the massacre.

The four winds were given names and personalities in Greek and Roman myth where they were four brothers, sons of Eos or Aurora, the goddess of the dawn. Aeolus or Aiolos was keeper and father of the winds and lived on the floating island of Aiolia. He released the winds on the instructions of the deities.

The north wind

Boreas rules the north wind. He had brown wings, a dragon's tail, a rain-cloud cloak and streaming white hair. He was very tempestuous.

Use the north wind for bringing about endings, to blow away what is no longer needed in your life and for any banishing magick, especially of negative influences, fears or bad habits.

Quality of wind: Fierce, cold

Suggested foci for spell: Branches with dead leaves, strands of wool attached to an old branch or tree that the wind can blow away, if you set them in an open place

Message: I cast away

The east wind

Apheliotes (Eurus in Latin) rules the east wind. He was the youngest of the brothers and was always impatient to be away, flying through the sky, scattering clouds.

Use the east wind for new beginnings, new perspectives, for any changes in direction in your life, for travel and for blowing away inertia or stagnation.

Quality of wind: Intense, stirring

Suggested foci for spell: A kite or balloons, with written messages attached to the string, that can be launched from high places; seeds to be scattered to the winds

Message: I change

The south wind

Notus rules the south wind. He is the most amiable of the winds, filled with sunlight and emitting sparkling light beams in his wake.

Use the south wind for bringing all manner of good things into your life, especially good luck and good news, for growth and expansion of any venture or opportunity, for success and for filling you with power and confidence.

Quality of wind: Warm, uplifting

Foci for spell: Feathers, petals that can catch the wind and be uplifted as you release them

Message: I carry/I seek

The west wind

Zephyrus rules the west wind. He is a gentle wind, married to Flora, the flower goddess, or Iris, goddess of the rainbow (depending on which myth you believe), and fills the sails of boats with breezes when they become becalmed.

Use the west wind to bring fertility into your life, to seek blessings, for healing and for bringing peace and to give impetus or bring existing ventures to fulfilment.

Quality of wind: Moist, gentle

Foci for spell: Bubbles to blow wishes upwards, miniature boats with sails to float gently across a pond or downstream with an empowerment

Message: I forgive/I receive

Finding your wind direction

The wind is named after the direction from which it comes, so a pennant being blown towards the east is being driven by the west wind. You can buy weathercocks quite cheaply or improvise with a long, heavy strip of fabric about 1 m/3 ft long, tied to a tall post in the garden where it can blow freely unhampered by buildings.

Using the power of the winds

* You can use the power of the winds in spellcasting by linking them with the four directions. Remember that inviting wind from all four directions, as opposed to the more usual east, into any spell is really going to get things moving. However, if you are in an impasse or need some urgent action or radical change, call Boreas from the north, Apheliotes in the east, Notus in the south and Zephyrus in the west or the bear, the moose, the fawn and the panther.

* For gentler wind magick, call upon the four angels of the wind, Moriel, Ruhiel, Rujiel and Ben Nez. Go to a hilltop or open, treeless plains. Call them one after the other three times in the given order as you face the direction the wind is coming from. Ask for the change or movement you need in your life and listen to the wind for an answer. Scatter seeds into the wind, that any new venture will take root or opportunities come.

* These angels can also be used in protective magick in times of high winds or when winds are threatened in your area. Call their names in reverse order, starting with Ben Nez, again saying them three times as you face the direction of each wind and ask that people, animals, homes and other property may be protected from the worst of the squalls. Scatter petals into the wind.

* You can use the above spell to calm down a situation that is threatening to get out of hand, perhaps a family quarrel or major workplace dispute.

* If there is something you wish to get rid of in your life, stand in the wind and call it out nine times so the wind carries your words. Afterwards, say:

May this burden/obstacle/restriction/bad luck be carried by the wind and good fortune/joy return with the new wind.

To send spiritual support to people in an area hit by a tornado or whirlwind or if there is really bad weather forecast, the following is as stronger spell than the four-angel one.

* Go to a slope or hillside. Hold a long, wide scarf in a breeze so that it streams out. If there is no breeze, hold the scarf behind you and run down a slope.
* Turn and form the scarf into a bag, knotting the top and saying:

Rest easy within, you winds that blow too fiercely. I call on Zaamiel, angel of whirlwinds, hurricanes, tornadoes and tempests. Let the tempest blow more gently, keep all safe within the eye of the storm, and afterwards may all be restored as it was before. And so I ask your blessing.

* Release the scarf and say:

Winds blow free, blow gloriously, but not tempestuously.

* Tie the scarf tightly round your neck and, on your way down the hill, scatter a few dried lavender heads or dried fennel seeds (you can get this in spice jars in supermarkets or use the dried leaves). These are Zaamiel's special herbs. Say:

I cast your own power back into the wind that the bargain may be sealed.

* You can also use this spell at the time of a major personal crisis or to deflect a potential one.

3

FIRE MAGICK

Fire magick is the most dynamic, exciting and powerful form of elemental magick. Because of this you should only work with fire spells when you are in a positive, calm frame of mind and take extra precautions with the physical flames as they can burn quite fiercely with the dynamic psychic energy being released.

Candles offer an instant and safe form of fire power in a confined space or indoors. See also pages 88–89 for information on fire dishes and ways you can introduce fire to rituals using these and other burners.

The creatures of fire

As you would expect, the magickal creatures of fire are powerful and exotic. See page 507 for information on salamanders or fire lizards.

The phoenix, the bird of fire, is an almost universal symbol that is sacred in Ancient Chinese spirituality and the Middle East, where the Westernised concept arose. In Christianity the phoenix represented the resurrection of Christ.

According to legend, the phoenix burned herself on a funeral pyre every five hundred years. From the ashes, as they turned golden, a new phoenix would be born. She may have once been an exotic form of heron that is now extinct. Phoenix magick is potent for spells of regeneration, healing and renewal.

Dragons are the most powerful of the fire creatures and once may have roamed the earth. Smaller kimono dragons, which can grow to over 1.8 m/6 ft still live in Indonesia, and remind us of their strange beauty. Dragons are a wonderful focus for fire magick since they take physical fire spell power into the spiritual realms where now they exist and bounce it back, filled with energy to enrich our lives.

I have written about phoenix and dragon magick later in the chapter.

The gifts of fire

In myths of different lands, fire was said to burst from the flames of the womb of the earth in the form of volcanoes or to be sent down from the heavens by the gods in lightning strikes or when meteors hit the earth.

Black obsidian is a volcanic glass, a form of magma that is formed when lava hardens so fast that there are no crystalline structures. It is the sacred crystal of Sekhmet, the Egyptian lion-headed fire and solar goddess. Her seven obsidian arrows (in the form of shards of obsidian) can be placed in a circle, pointing outwards to defend and inwards to bring power and success, and, in the modern world, employment. As you position each arrow, use the words:

Arrows fly swift and swift return, Sekhmet.

Pele, the Hawaiian goddess of volcanoes, fire and magick, is the mistress of volcanic lava that in its molten form destroyed Pompeii — a reminder that fire and fire products aren't tame putty to be played with by would-be magicians. She is a very old goddess, pictured sitting in her cave beneath a volcano by the light of a blue flame.

Lava is especially magickal because it involves the fusion of the four elements, the molten lava being the element of water. Lava protects the home from lightning, fire and intruders. At work it will act as an amulet of protection against bad-tempered employers or colleagues and spiteful workplace gossip.

Perun, the Slavic god of thunder and lightning, is said to have sent the gift of bottle-green moldavite, which is very protective and opens doors to other dimensions, in a meteor collision about 15 million years ago in the Moldau River valley in the Czech Republic. An ever-burning fire was dedicated to him and also to Svarog, the sky god, the giver of fire who hammered the sun into shape.

Green olivine crystals, which are found within some meteors and are also cast up in volcanic rock, are likewise gifts of the deities and are considered bringers of good luck and prosperity when used in spells. Make a square with eight olivine crystals to enclose a symbol to be empowered, two to form each side. Olivine crystals are said to be the tears of the Hawaiian volcano goddess Pele.

Legends of very ancient origin abound of heroes and animals that stole fire and brought it to humans. It was apparently hard to believe that such a precious gift would be given willingly by the gods. In Maori legend, the inventor and trickster hero Maui stole fire for the people from the female fire guardian. Maui-Tinihanga, Maui of the Many Devices, a demi-god hero, went to Mahuika, the ogress clan mother, who kept fire in her fingernails. Each time he asked she gave him one of her fingernails of fire. Maui deliberately extinguished the flames and it was not until he demanded the last nail that she created a huge conflagration.

Sacred fire

Humans return the gift of fire to the deities, both by making offerings on their hearth and ritual fires, keeping a perpetual flame burning (as to Perun) and in creating seasonal fires to strengthen the power of the sun as it moves through the year.

Evidence of hearths has been found as far back as 400,000 BCE in Ancient China and so we can only guess the date of the earliest sacred fire ceremonies.

In a number of cultures women have traditionally been the guardians of fires both of the home and as priestesses tending the eternally burning flame of a state, city or country, for example the vestal virgins of Rome.

The family hearth was in many lands the centre of the home, not only for living family members but also to welcome the wise ancestors, especially at the seasonal change points. In Ancient Greece, a bride would take fire from her mother's hearth to keep the goddess Hestia's flame alight and so transfer protection and good fortune to the new hearth. At every feast, food offerings would be cast on to the flames at the beginning and the end as tribute to Hestia.

Gabija, the Lithuanian goddess of the hearth fire, was honoured in a similar fashion by throwing salt on the fire each evening after the main meal. Some older Eastern European people continue this tradition today.

The four major festivals of the eightfold ritual and agricultural year, at the beginning of February, May, August and November, are all fire festivals (see Seasonal magick, pages 438–64). Ritual fires are also kindled on the solstices and equinoxes, as well as at new year, representing the surge of new energy and the cleansing of the old – and to empower the sun on its journey.

Ritual fires were and are sometimes still kindled by friction because it was believed that wood contained burning fire. This mystery of drawing fire out of wood is enshrined in many myths. For example, the West Coast Maidu American Indians tell that the earth began as a ball of fire which gradually cooled so that soil and trees grew on top. However, the roots of trees are still connected to this fiery centre and so fire may be created directly from wood.

Fire spells

* Fire stands in the south of your altar as a red, orange or gold candle and sometimes as directional candles for the four elements, brown or green in the north, yellow or grey in the east and blue or silver in the west or natural beeswax at the four quarters.
* You may also add two altar or god and goddess candles.
* Fire, whether a central fire dish, a bonfire, a cauldron or a huge candle in sand, can become the central focus in spells of change, courage, action, passion or creativity as well as protection.
* Cast or burn loose incense or herbs in a fire to make wishes or to invoke the power represented by the herbs, such as basil for prosperity or dill for protection.
* Throw dead sticks or petals on the fire, naming what you wish to banish from your life.
* Create a circle of fire using tea lights or candles, lighting one after the other clockwise to fill yourself or a gathering of friends or a coven with light and power. Each candle lit represents an empowerment and you can, by lighting one after the other, pass the magick on.
* Fire circles are also very good for casting psychic defence around yourself or for sending the power to the vulnerable.
* For even more instant effect, whirl a large lighted incense stick really fast round yourself as you stand in total darkness, while calling out faster and faster your need or desire. Then make a final spiral over your head bringing the fire downwards and vertically up again, as you release the power. This is wonderful at night if you need a burst of courage for the next day.
* Alternatively, use the swirling stick to write against the night sky in fire your empowerments, your personal magickal names and an affirmation of what you are and what you can achieve.
* Make a fire on a beach on the incoming tide or near water and into the flames

cast small food offerings. Ask for abundance to come into your life or to be sent to a person or place where it is needed or for an urgent request to be granted. Call upon Uriel or Samael, the archangels of fire and transformation, to help you to make your own contribution to bringing that abundance or to empower you to make the changes you are seeking. Archangels will aid us most to help ourselves. Leave the tide to wash away the fire or use water from the water source to douse it and send the power upwards by means of the sudden fusion of fire and water.

* Light a candle and call an unknown lover in the flame. Blow gently three times so the flame flickers but does not go out. The first flicker is to find where your future love is, the second to call telepathically to that love and the third to encircle him or her psychically with the mutual desire to find you. Make these ideas into a personal call. Finally whisper into the flame:

Find the way by land or sea, through the mists and over mountain, across city streets or empty plains. Call to me that I may know the time and place we first shall be together. Blessed be.

Leave the candle to burn through. You can also adapt this spell for an absent lover or one from whom you are estranged.

A fire spell for a problem you cannot overcome, a situation that stops you moving forward or a destructive influence you cannot break

* Tie three long, dried sprigs of lavender or rosemary or long grasses together with three knots along the length left to right.
* Name what you are tangling into each knot (it can be the same words for each) or state the three steps required to be free.
* Set a natural beeswax or white candle in a cauldron or heatproof pot of sand or in a holder on a heavy metal tray.
* Light the candle. Sprinkle three grains of salt in the flame as you name the burden three times.
* Then hold the first knot, working left to right, into the flame so it singes and breaks. Drop the two separated sections on to the tray or into the cauldron, saying:

I walk the path to freedom. Thus the bonds are weakened.

* Blow out the candle, sending the light to the destructive person, situation or influence, asking that there will be enlightenment.
* Throw away or bury the short section that has broken off.
* Repeat the words and actions on the next day for the right-hand knot and throw that section away.
* On the third day burn through the final knot, saying:

I am set free by the power of fire. May all be purified and blessed.

* Sprinkle just one more pinch of salt in the flame and, naming what has hurt or held you and can harm no more, say:

Cleansed and purified. I send blessings to _____.

* Leave the candle to burn through and afterwards bury the final knot even if you threw the others away, saying:

Fire to earth to transformed and so reborn.

Dragon magick

Western and Eastern European and Scandinavian dragons are the true fire dragons. They are primarily guardians of gold, described as the life blood of the earth, and live in caves. The Oriental dragons are mainly air and water dragons, associated with life-giving rain, with winds and storms and with gems and pearls, though there are the fiery kinds as well, as seen in processions (see page 368 in Weather magick).

Dragon magick uses the spiritual power associated with fire-breathing dragons to protect your own particular treasures. These treasures might be tangible ones like your home or your family. Less tangibly, treasure to you might represent speaking the truth or receiving honesty from others, the power to develop your career or healing powers, or the ability to love or gain knowledge. Dragon magick is also a good way of manifesting prosperity in your life, not for its own sake but in order to have the resources to do all the things you want to do – and so that you don't need to worry and can bring happiness to others.

For despite their bad press in Christian times as symbols of the earth mother, dragons are essentially wise and noble. Of course, physical dragons don't exist. By means of visualisation, however, you can build up a connection with the huge energy field of the dragon that exists spiritually, in the same way that love and altruism are real.

Fire dragons are variously described as possessing all or some of the following: eagles' feet, bat-like wings, the front legs of a lion, a reptile or dinosaur's head with a huge mouth and teeth from which smoke and fire pours, huge scales, the horns of an antelope, a soft underbelly and a spade-like snake or lizard-like tail that may begin close to the head.

Smaller fire drakes, found in the myths of France and Germany, don't have wings, but are red and have fiery breath. They live in caves with their great hoards, the riches of the earth.

According to Bulgarian dragon lore, the male dragon is the fiery one and is a benign protector of humans and the crops, in contrast to his watery and less well-disposed sister. In this tradition, dragons have three heads, and wings.

The ruler of the fire dragons is called Fafnir, whose name comes from the Norse and German culture. He was once a dwarf but was transformed into a dragon because of his love of the treasures he created and the metals he forged. He was killed by Sigrid Volsungr or Siegfried who burned himself, licked his fingers and so absorbed the dragon's power to commune with the birds.

This isn't a straightforward legend and has a lot to do with the overcoming of the earlier earth goddess power as typified by the dragon. Therefore, Fafnir shouldn't be thought of as a greedy dwarf who became a dragon to be slain, as in the patriarchal, monk-recorded legends. Rather, Fafnir is lord of the dragons, who guards from the greedy and insensitive the power of the hidden treasures, whether these be of the goddess or your own potential. So if you do include Fafnir in your dragon chants recall his wonderful craftsmanship and how he conserves the minerals of the earth – not a bad lesson for modern times.

Finding dragons

Dragons live deep underground in caverns, usually with many passages and inner caves where the treasure is kept.

* Some areas, like Wales or the Catalan region around Barcelona, have strong fire-dragon traditions.
* Visit places with dragon or drake names, such as Dragon Hill near Uffingham on the Berkshire/Oxfordshire borders, close to the huge chalk horse symbol of the Celtic horse goddess Epona.
* Go also to those spots where there are dragon legends, such as Krakow in Poland where the dragon lived in a cave beneath Wawel Hill under the castle. You can be sure people in times past experienced dragon energies there and so wove the legends. Enter 'dragon' in the regional website of the place you intend to visit.
* Explore dry, rocky, sandy regions, like Almeria in the south east of Spain. Visit also the bush lands of Australia and the Midwest of America and New Mexico, where European and Scandinavian settlers from the Old World carried the dragon mythology and the absorbed energies to join with the indigenous myths.
* Explore the sacred sites of the creatrix rainbow serpent in Australia. In America, Serpent Mound in Ohio, just east of Cincinnati, which was used for worship by the Adena Indians, somewhere between 800 BCE and CE 100, is another perfect dragon location.
* Most deep forests also have their share of dragon legends, especially in Germany. Visit different cavernous or rocky areas and feel for your dragon.
* You may even find friendly fire-dragon energies near seaside caves in sandy coves (watch for tides). Western dragons traditionally live alone except for mating.
* Collect the legends and your own impressions in your Book of Shadows.

Making dragon magick

* Half-close your eyes as you sit outside or near caves or rocks. If the light is bright, you may see the swirling iridescent silver, purple, gold, green and blue of the dragon outline shimmering ahead. Let the image enclose and energise you and breathe slowly and regularly, allowing the warm, shimmering colours to flow in and out of your own energy field, your aura. If you see nothing externally allow the image to build up in your mind and superimpose it in your imagination on the scene.

* You may see an image of the dragon and her fabulous treasures within the cave or see her flying upwards towards the sun. There is no danger in this for she is a spiritual force, experienced through the layers of countless millennia.

* You may feel very warm as though close to a bonfire and see sparks or sunbeams dancing in the air all around.

* When you are ready, close your eyes and gently push away with your hands, palms outwards and upright. Allow the energies to move away, or you may sense them fading spontaneously as the dragon moves on.

* Don't ask for anything. The experience is enough and will help you to move with confidence and attract and spread the abundance you need.

* Be sure to take a bottle of water to drink afterwards and splash on your hairline, brow, throat and wrists or palms to cool you down.

* While you are still there, take time to write in your Book of Shadows. You may have heard words in your mind as you experienced the dragon power or they may come now and, even if you are not normally poetic, the encounter will trigger off rich and vivid descriptions of flying with the dragon, the mysterious smoke-filled air within the cave and the metallic colours of your dragon. If you open your eyes in the night before sleep, the colours may re-form.

* Afterwards is a good time to explore the caves and rocks, if accessible. Even if you are crammed in a tourist party, you can sense your dragon and maybe the special place that you connected with in your visions and see the shimmering silver and purples reflected on the dark walls.

Dragon rituals

After one or two visits to a dragon place, you can try a ritual. I rarely invite dragons into my indoor altar as they are so potent and the energies diffuse and so are best encountered in their natural environment. You can, however, cast a dragon ritual in your garden. Equally, when working with dragon magick, I don't cast a formal circle because dragon energies need lots of space to avoid spiritual overheating.

* Dragon rituals should be carried out no more frequently than bi-monthly though there is nothing to stop you visiting a dragon place and absorbing the power weekly. I have a local dragon cave at Freshwater Bay on the Isle of Wight. When the tide is very low I sometimes sit here and work. Inside the cave is too small an area for spellcasting as the dragon energies need to be free.

* Create chants or drum to tune in with the dragon energies. You can chant spontaneously during a ritual or write one that you use to call your dragon or to connect with a particular dragon site that you visit regularly.

* If you wish, you can use a crystalline dragon's egg in dragon spells as a focus for

power, courage or abundance, and afterwards keep it on your garden altar or in the heart of your home. Light a red candle next to it once a week to keep the dragon power flowing.

* A dragon's egg is a white, opaque, very solid kind of rock crystal that resembles an egg. Alternatively, you can use two matching halves of a stone egg with tiny crystals embedded inside, like a geode. Any agate egg or oval white stone can be substituted.

* If you are lighting incense in the dragon place, use dragon's blood. Use tarragon, the dragon's herb of courage and power, to sprinkle as the earth element. This is also a good offering to leave for your dragon in her place. If there is a suitable spot near the rocks, you can plant a tiny tarragon seedling and add a new one whenever you visit.

* Empower a dragon charm, ring or pendant by setting it in the centre of a spell like the one below. Re-empower it by wearing or carrying it when you visit your dragon place.

* Face south for dragon spells and rituals. East will then be on your left instead of right hand though the actual direction does not change.

* After a dragon spell or ritual, leave an offering of thanks. Dragons love gold, perhaps in the forms of a small earring, or a small carnelian or bright red flowers.

A dragon spell for gold

What gold do you need? Health, a spurt of energy to see a task through, some money for your child's school trip, the courage to take up the career you really want? Or is the gold for a loved one who is struggling, for your sick pet that needs healing or for the people in a war-torn area of the world?

It is your choice, but because dragon power cannot be used very often, think carefully before you make your request and use some of the extra energy you will feel to help someone else who is struggling.

You will need: A flat, raised surface such as a rock to hold your spell materials (or your outdoor altar cleared of everything else); a small dish of tarragon (or parsley or sage) in the north of the rock/outdoor altar; an incense stick in the east – use any spicy incense if you can't get dragon's blood; a small red candle in the south; a bowl of crystal carnelian water in the west; a larger bowl of water to the south and a larger bowl of soil to the north, both positioned on the ground some way from where you are working to keep the spiritual energies cool and grounded; a dragon's egg, a white, egg-shaped stone or an agate egg in the centre of the rock/altar to symbolise your spell focus (alternatively use red flowers).

Timing: Tuesday is a good dragon day; as bright as possible light-wise

* Light the candle of the south, while facing south and say:

> *I call upon you, wondrous golden dragon, guardian of all treasures, not in greed, but in need.*
> *I kindle your flame and would welcome your shimmering presence.*

* Light the incense from the candle and say:

> *I call upon you, wondrous golden dragon, not in greed, but in need. I kindle your fragrance.*

* Holding the egg or flowers in your receptive hand, and the incense in your power hand, draw the outline of a dragon in smoke. Make this as large as you can, reaching above and below, and all round yourself, without moving your feet, so that the smoke surrounds you.
* Say:

> *I call upon you, wondrous golden dragon, that I may draw on your power not in greed,*
> *but in need. I kindle your image and your shimmering presence.*

* Return the incense to its holder and the egg or flowers to the centre of the rock.
* Focus on the area round yourself and try to picture the shimmering iridescent colours filling in the dragon outline and flowing within your own aura. You may start to feel warmth.
* Now you are going to try to extend your own connection with the dragon power.
* Pick up the dish of tarragon and, starting in the south, create with your footsteps an imagined larger outline of your dragon so the head is to the south and the tail in the north.
* Scatter the tarragon as you walk to ground the dragon power, saying:

> *So grows your fire, not to harm but to protect and bring abundance. I kindle your herbs*
> *with your shimmering presence.*

* Replace the herb dish and continue to walk around your dragon with spiralling footsteps, drumming, chanting or singing and calling to the power of the dragon to bring the gold.
* When you see the lights getting brighter and feel the warmth increasing, blow out the candle, saying:

> *I seek gold and I pledge to share my gift with those also in need.*

- Drop to the ground and sit motionless with your eyes closed and your arms outstretched like dragon wings and receive your gold. Wait until you feel the warmth receding and the dragon leaving.
- Speak your own thanks and state how you will return the gift you now know is within you.
- Clear up quietly. The spell is done.

Phoenix magick

In the Western world, the phoenix concept was adopted by mediaeval alchemists and the resurrected glorious phoenix was the symbol of alchemy's ultimate aim of turning base metal into gold. The bird is described as having brilliant gold, red and purple feathers and being the size of a huge eagle. In Western tradition there is only one phoenix. She is female and signifies immortality, joy, creativity, infinite possibility and total energy and purpose.

In Ancient Egypt the blue phoenix or Benu bird was the bird of the sun god Ra who perched on the first mound of earth on the morning of creation and symbolised the rebirth of the sun each morning.

In China and Japan the appearance of the phoenix in a dream or vision foretold the coming of a great emperor or sage. Images of the phoenix were carried or worn to ensure long life and health. In China the male phoenix, Feng Huang, the vermillion bird made of flames, is symbol of the yang positive energy associated with the sun. The female is the yin or receptive principle, called Hou-ou, bird of the moon.

The phoenix in the Orient is either the enemy or lover of the dragon, but they are never indifferent. To the Japanese, the phoenix symbolised the empress and so signifies fidelity as well as fire, the sun, justice and obedience. The dragon is the creature of the emperor. The Oriental phoenix has the head and comb of a cockerel, the back of a swallow and the tail of a peacock.

Phoenix spells

You can carry out phoenix spells for any regeneration, rebirth or new beginnings; also for rekindling love, optimism or reviving an ailing relationship or business. For like the dragon, the phoenix is the creature of gold, both spiritual and material. Use the phoenix when things are really dire or when you have a burning dream, but are scared or prevented from following that path. Call her too to overcome grief or pain.

- Get up early just before it is light. You may be lying awake worrying or thinking, and in this case get up and stir the phoenix energies. If not, set your alarm for a morning when you will have plenty of time.
- Outdoors, light a small ritual fire or use four sticks of sun incense in any or all of the following fragrances: chamomile, frankincense, marigold, orange and rosemary.
- Name as you do this what is dead or soon to die in your life or what you have lost and you fear cannot be revived. This could be finances, a relationship, health or a career reversal.

- Sit by the fire or light a candle and write your call to the phoenix to sing or chant. These words must be your own.
- There is no guarantee that your phoenix will come, though she usually does if your need is urgent.
- When the ashes are cool, scoop some of them into a gold-coloured metal bowl.
- Drop gold-coloured crystal chippings or small gold-coloured petals into the ashes, naming the gold you seek.
- Face the rising light and raise your arms like tall wings, curved at the top over the bowl.
- Speak your words of the phoenix. These may be three or four lines repeated. Make sure you can memorise them by the time the ashes are ready. This will focus your mind.
- Make your own private call for new life, new hope, and new health. Sing softly to her. She won't care if you are out of tune, but sing your heart out.
- Sing as you face the growing light with your arms stretched upwards until they ache and then sing some more until the light is strong.
- You may hear in your mind the beating of her wings, whether you picture the Oriental or Westernised phoenix or your own fire bird. You may see shimmers of light or darting sunbeams and you will feel her warmth and maybe the brush of her feathers. Rest your arms and let her inspire you.
- It is said that we see the phoenix only once in actuality and some people never do, but she still works her magick and over time you will be able to sense her presence more easily.
- If you don't feel her, scatter the ashes and crystals to the wind and ask that she will hear you. Within a few days you will see a sign, usually an unusual bird, and things will slowly start to get better.
- Only use phoenix magick every few months or in a crisis.

4

FLOWING AND STILL WATER MAGICK

Pure water is vital for life. For this reason sources of pure water, whether a fountain, a lake, billabong, river or waterfall, have been accorded sacred significance. Water is associated with the waters of the womb of the earth mother because of its life-sustaining powers.

Legends have grown up of water goddesses, faeries and water spirits who must be given offerings in order to grant wishes, magickal dreams or healing. For example, the Gwragedd Annwyn, the beautiful, Welsh, fair-haired faerie women who live in underwater palaces in lakes close to the Black Mountains, are reputed to be kind to children, those who have no money and to mothers. Their singing can be heard on still nights and in times past pure silver was dropped in the lake to ask for their blessings and the safe delivery of infants. They are close kin to the Tylwyth teg water women (see page 511).

Waters from sacred wells and streams were used both for healing and to carry offerings and petitions to the earth mother. Holy wells are still visited for healing waters, though now they are under the protection of the Virgin Mary or the female Christian saints. Those with male protectors usually have female links. For example, Madron well near Penzance in Cornwall is named after a seemingly shadowy Celtic saint. However, Madrona is the old Celtic pagan name for the mother goddess. (The Madrones, matrons to the Romans, were the three mothers of abundance.)

Because water sources were regarded as flowing from the womb of the mother goddess, the deities of fountains, wells, rivers and streams were once invariably female, localised aspects of the generic earth goddess.

The power of water

Ancient Egypt embraced as central to its spirituality the chaotic power of the annual flood of the Nile. This brought fertility to the land in the form of the rich black soil left on either side of the river when the waters receded. Protective fertility goddesses, such as Tauret the hippopotamus goddess who guarded households and ensured safe childbirth, and Heket or Heqet the frog-headed fertility and creatrix goddess, were among the earliest deities.

Water is the alter ego of the sun or fire, personalised as Ra the sun god. It was believed that the universe, including the sky, was surrounded by water and so Ra sailed his sun boat across the waters of the sky from dawn to dusk. At night Ra sailed in the night boat through the Duat, the waters of the womb of the sky mother Nut to fight the chaos demon Apep before emerging triumphant at his daily rebirth.

The sun represented order and time, as the rising and setting of the sun marked the parameters of day and night and the passing of the year. But water was equally vital to sustain life, especially with the extremes of heat in the Middle East. The Nile was chaos, but also the fertilising power that is still responsible for the fertility of the strips of land around it.

So water as a force can swirl seemingly chaotically in our lives. This will carry us to new places and attitudes, and at others times to stillness and depth like the lake, bringing healing and tranquillity. What is more, feelings and intuitions as represented by water are as vital as the ordered power of the sun. But even in the stillest lake there must be movement, an in-flow and out-flow, or stagnation results.

At the time of the flood, offerings were made to Hapy the Nile god that he would send a good flood. Too fierce and the irrigation ditches and villages would be washed away; too weak and there would be an insufficient depth of silt when the water levels dropped.

When fire predominated in the dry season, the beautiful water goddesses, Satis, lady of the waterfalls, with her gazelle headdress, and her mother, Anukis, poured cooling waters on the parched earth to ensure full grain stores.

Water magick

In both psychological and magickal terms, the quantities of the elements in a ritual must be correct. Too little water will leave the ritual stranded on the mental, intellectual level; too much focus on the earth, and the ritual will fail to get off the ground; too fiery and mystical and the ritual will fail to answer real needs and intentions. Too much water in a ritual and the beautiful emotive words and graceful actions overwhelm the other aspects and the magickal mix doesn't occur (a bit like jelly that refuses to set).

Drumming is a powerful way of raising energies and can be used to increase water power in your life, whether for love, healing, making a smooth transition in any new area of life, for a relationship or fertility issue or to become more intuitive. For a special ritual you can drum at the quarters to open them (see also Sound magick, page 295). Take inspiration from the different beats in nature, such as the human heartbeat, which is a microcosmic or miniature form of the beat of the earth. Birds have a much more fluttery heartbeat that is closer to air. The beat of fire is the ceremonial dance and drum rhythm associated with Native North America. Water is more harmonious and flowing, and each beat merges into the next.

A ritual using the power of water

Carry out this ritual in an open space, a park or a campsite in the early morning, a beach or a forest clearing. If you live in the middle of the town, it's not always easy to find space and solitude, but you can always use a small drum or tambour (even a child's drum) and drum softly. You can tap out the quarters very quietly but no less powerfully whether in the back garden or even indoors.

You don't have to be an expert drummer. Let your hands and your feelings convey the different elemental energies by the way you sound the drum. If you haven't yet acquired a drum or a tambour, you can often buy them cheaply from ethnic stores where the profits go directly to the workers or at garage sales.

You will need: A drum or tambour. If you have three willing friends you can set them in three of the quarters and work with water yourself. Have a little practice as a group in advance so that the four sounds merge, adding one sound on top of the other. Once water is added, the others can merge into the background but remain ever present. If you have to work on your own, it is still great fun to move round the directions in turn.

A stick for drawing a sign in the sand or soil or some small stones, glass nuggets or shells for creating the sign on the grass:

Water

Timing: Early morning or, if you prefer, dusk (the time of water)

Though this is water-based ritual and so water is going to be the predominant element, decide in advance on the proportion of water you need in your life at the time of the ritual. Compare this with the existing inflow of the other elements. Do you require a flood to carry forward a new idea or wash away what is overwhelming you, whether it be debt, sickness or despair? Would a gentler, steady flow be better for the gradual and continuing inflow of love, health or prosperity?

Do you want a smaller but still significant amount of water to sustain you if another element is feeling too powerful in your life but can't be dismissed because of circumstances: logic (air), material concerns (earth) or anger or pressures either of your own or someone else's (fire)?

- Draw your water sign to symbolise Akhet in the centre of your intended circle of sound. Akhet was the time in Ancient Egypt of the flood or inundation in early July when water predominated (see also Seasonal magick for more on the Egyptian seasons, page 439).

- Starting in the north (even if you normally work from the east), begin the circle of sound by drumming open the quarter of earth and carrying the circle purely by sound towards the east. You can use approximations of direction. Earth sound is a steady pulse. Listen to your heartbeat – that is earth.

- As you drum facing north, for a minute or two focus on your watery magickal purpose and add the earth stability and practical steps that must be taken. Draw up the earth power from your feet. You will sense instinctively when you have absorbed enough earth.

- When you are ready move to the east, focus still on your watery aim. Drum more lightly now, faster and regularly to build up the circle power and add the focus and lightness of air in your drumbeats. Continue for a minute or so allowing the sound circle to grow to the south. You will know when you have absorbed enough air as the natural stirring of breeze round you will start to feel cold.

* When you are ready, move to the south. Fire drumming is powerful and intense but also sensuous. Think of a snake charmer or a tall flame wrapping itself around a post that forms the centre of a bonfire. Continue for a minute or so, adding inspiration, illumination and passion to the ritual. You will know when you have enough fire as you may start to feel a bit over-excited or hot.

* Finally, switch to the all-important water. Think about the kind of water you are adding, a soft gentle flow that gradually deepens in intensity and speed, a bubbling stream that bounces along, a bore of water racing up a river? Is your drumming intense or is it gradual? Don't analyse, but let your hands and drum make the water sound you require. You will need to drum for longer than at the other elements and this sound will join up with the circle in the north. Gradually lighten the beat and intensity.

* At this point move into the centre and clockwise round the water symbol. Drum your water ever more intensely and faster again so even your bubbling stream speeds up and leaps over the stony river bed. Then when you feel a wall of water rising round you, with three final separate drum beats, absorb the water power into your life.

* If you hate drumming or are stuck in an upstairs apartment, you can sing your quarters, using words and rhythm to create the feeling of the elements.

* A sound circle will disperse. Drum or sing steadily and slowly to bring yourself down to earth until the sounds fade into silence.

* Rub out or dismantle your Akhet symbol for you no longer need it.

* You can use the drumming technique for bringing other elements to the fore in your life, drawing the appropriate elemental glyph in the ground (see pages 31–35).

Using water magick

Water stands in the west of the altar. The qualities within this water can be varied according to the kind of spell you are casting. You can substitute different crystal waters (see page 136), for example carnelian water in a spell for courage and self-confidence or amethyst water for the healing of addictions. You can also use sun water, moon water, storm water, sacred water with salt (see pages 126–31) to empower the spell in different ways. The water is vital to get things flowing and the type of water sets the direction.

Some people believe that you should never use salt water on the ground outdoors because it harms plant life. There are plenty of substitutes and I certainly keep it to a token amount and would advise using sacred salt water only on unplanted soil or sand rather than directly on growing vegetation.

* Sparkling mineral water is good for energising spells and still mineral water for harmony and in healing spells.

* Rainwater (with a drop of flower essence if the rain is very acidic) collected from a bowl on a low roof or a picnic bench can be use in love or inner radiance spells, or in gentle banishing.

* When working outdoors, cleanse your magickal area before a spell or ritual with a large deep bowl of tap water on which you have made the sign of the cross

three times. You can use either the equal-armed Christian or the diagonal earth mother form (as on hot cross buns).

* Sprinkle the water using a bunch of twigs that you have tied together firmly by the ends with twine, so making a mini besom.
* Dip the twigs in the bowl of water (on the ground in the centre) as you walk in spirals round the area. You can create a blessing chant as you work. You can also choose a small leafy branch to asperge a smaller area.
* Asperge the boundaries of your home along fences, walls and gates. In an apartment use a small bowl and small, fresh sprig of greenery to scatter water drops along window ledges and thresholds. To avoid damaging paintwork, use only the tiniest amount of water.
* Use water protectively by scattering water droplets horizontally left to right across your threshold. Then stand within the barrier facing outwards. With your raised power hand palm vertical and outwardly splayed, say:

You shall not cross this water with malice in your heart. You shall not disturb nor threaten. Turn away, do not stay.

* Before going away for a weekend or holiday, set in place the water barrier at the front and back doors.
* If you have to leave your car in a deserted place or high-crime area, it is reassuring to scatter a protective square of water around it. Take a small bottle of water and walk round clockwise. You can then, as you are leaving the car after locking up, make the splayed hand gesture facing outwards while standing by the driver's door. Such rituals can be carried out subtly so that people just think you are walking round the car checking the locks and that you are a careless drinker, spilling your drink.
* Use sparkling water to open your main chakras (the heart, throat, brow and hairline/crown, moving upwards) so you exude confidence and charisma in your daily encounters.
* Use still water and move downwards to calm or close down energies when you need protection.

Flowing waters

These include rivers, streams, fountains and waterfalls.

Use flowing water magick for any rituals of improvement, for positive change, for the increase of money, love, success or healing, to bring into reality travel or house- and job-moves and to wash away what you no longer need in your life.

Rivers and streams

Rivers throughout northern and western Europe, the Mediterranean and in Asia were usually dedicated to goddesses. For example, the Seine in France was under the guardianship of Sequana, and the Boyne in Ireland of Boanna or Boanne. To Hindus, the Ganges in India, named after the water goddess Ganga, daughter of the mountain god Himavan or Himalaya, is the embodiment of the goddess Ganga Ma or Mother Ganges herself. Daily offerings of fruit and flowers are cast into the river and at dawn people face the east on her banks and pray to Mother Ganges. Bathing in the water washes away all sin.

But any stream or river can be used for water magick, even in the most urban setting. Water gardens at stately homes may provide a variety of small running streams and bridges, while a small garden can support a mini stream powered by a pump connecting a couple of tiny ponds.

River and stream magick will carry a small venture forward so that it grows and prospers until it reaches the sea.

The most basic river and stream rituals involve casting a symbol of your need plus an offering such as a small piece of silver like an earring, a silver-coloured coin or a few white flowers. You can also cast dying or dead flowers to signify taking away what is no longer wanted.

Waterfalls

Whether you use a holiday to visit one of the spectacular falls like Niagara on the borders of Canada and America, the numerous smaller roadside or hillside falls in Wales, Scotland or the Sierra Nevada foothills in southern Spain, the waterfall is a reminder of the waters of the earth mother's womb pouring forth in a torrent.

St Nectan's Glen and Waterfall, between Boscastle and Tintagel in Cornwall, set in a deep forest, is renowned for its faerie sightings. At the foot of the falls, in caverns, are shrines to the mother goddess, called locally 'the lady of the waterfall'. Around the caverns are cairns, piles of stones that have been left with prayers. The trees are hung with ribbons and there are crystals in every niche.

Nectan is the name of the Irish water deity who was married to Boanne, the mother goddess after whom the river Boyne is named. Close to the last day of October, at the beginning of the Celtic winter, there is a torchlight procession to light candles in the former chapel, now once more a shrine to the goddess.

We know from legends that Nectan's sisters dwelled near the waterfall at one time, so there may have been an ancient priestess order that served the lady of the waterfall and became entwined in the Christian version.

Waterfall magick is very fast moving and will clear most stagnation, inertia or indecision, or carry away something that is frightening or disempowering in any area of your life.

If there is a path or bridge over the top of the waterfall, cast your symbol from it, and then go down to the pool and splash yourself with spray to absorb the blessing of the water. Tie biodegradable ribbons to over-hanging trees or begin a stone pile in thanks. Next time you return you will find your pile has been added to with other wishes and petitions.

Fountains

Fountains, whether a mini water feature in your garden pond or a spectacular cascade in a town square, supply a constant source of energy, enthusiasm, health, long life and joy. Small indoor water features are a very positive natural source of energy even if you live in the centre of town.

The Trevoli Fountain in Rome has become immortalised as the ultimate wish magick fountain, especially for love and for granting a wish to return with your lover in the future in even better circumstances.

Brittany is famed for magickal fountains and white-clad female faeries, the Corrigans, who in legend gathered around the fountains at night. In the forest of Broceliande near Rennes is La Fontaine de Jouvance, the fountain of youth, a natural water flow where even today healing and long life is sought and offerings are left around the natural pool that has formed just downstream from the bridge.

At the Fountain of Barenton, also in the forest, the appointed guardian, in earlier legends a female, could by sprinkling water on the stone slab, called the step of Merlin, conjure up storms.

Fountains are bubbling and cyclical, with the water constantly being recycled, though the more natural ones, like the fountain of Jouvance do have an inward and outward flow. Fountain magick is good for wishes that will need a lot of personal effort to bring to reality, such as becoming a singer; matters that require continuing input, such as a chronic illness or overcoming depression; a regular inflow of money or ideas; a long course of study or a relationship in which the couple spend a lot of time apart.

Set or cast your symbol, such as a crystal or coin, into the base of the fountain and make your wish. You can renew it regularly. Leave flowers round the outside of the fountain.

Joining the waters, a spell to bring about a desired change of location or career

This is a flowing water spell. These are faster acting than still water ones and so can be cast for a need in the immediate future, especially if matters are slow moving. The larger and faster flowing the water source, the faster and more powerful the results will be.

If you really can't get to a flowing water source, use a running tap, preferably outdoors. This is also an effective confidence-building spell if you are scared of the change even though you really want it. Try it also for an urgent infusion of money or resources.

You will need: A bottle of tap water; a willow twig or any twig from a tree that grows near water or your wand; a very small water crystal like a fluorite, an amethyst or alternatively clear quartz to endow the spell with extra life force if you are feeling tired.

Timing: Before noon during a waxing moon if possible but whenever the need arises

* The day before the spell, soak your crystal in the bottle of water for eight hours. Leave it in the bottle.
* When you are ready to begin, stand next to the point where the water is moving fastest.
* Hold the bottle in your receptive hand and the wand or twig in your power hand.
* Though this is a fast flowing spell, you should take your time and watch the water flowing until you feel connected with the sound and the rhythm. Merging with your water source is the main key to water spell success.
* Repeat in rhythm with the sound and movement of the water:

I flow. The water is flowing, flowing and going, flowing and growing, flowing and flowing.
I flow.

✴ When you feel connected, circle the twig or wand three times over the bottle saying:

Lady of the flowing waters (name a goddess only if you wish), carry me as is right to be.
I surrender to the flowing waters.

✴ Place your wand or twig on the side of the bank and undo the bottle.
✴ Hold the bottle high over the flow, tip it slowly and continuously into the river and repeat:

I flow. The water is flowing, flowing and going, flowing and growing, flowing and flowing.
I flow.

✴ Do this until the bottle is empty and the crystal (your offering) in the bottle has also flowed into the water.
✴ If you are using a twig, cast that also into the water with a secret wish or fear connected with the change. Otherwise, cast in a few small leaves or petals as an offering. You can adapt this spell if using a tap by holding the twig under the flow and then planting it after the bottle is empty. In this case remove the crystal from the bottle before the spell and place it in a small dish of water on your altar. Leave it there for a moon cycle from the day of the spell.
✴ Repeat the spell after a week if things seem slow moving or whenever your personal impetus weakens.

Still waters

Still waters include lakes, ponds, billabongs, wells and canals, and bowls of water. Use still waters for healing, for fertility, for making wishes, for calling and deepening love and commitments, for receiving psychic insights and for protection of all kinds.

Sacred wells

For hundreds and thousands of years, settlements have sprung up wherever there is a well, and so well magick is extra potent.

The Maya regarded wells as sacred to the rain god Chac or Tlaloc (as he was called in the Toltec and later Aztec tradition) – he who makes things grow. A cenote was a natural well formed by the collapse of subterranean limestone caverns. A particular red algae turned the well, known as the well of sacrifice, the colour of blood. The two most famous sacred cenotes are in Chichen Itza, sacred city of the

Maya and Toltecs in Central America. The city was abandoned by the Maya around CE 900 and rebuilt by the Toltecs a century later.

In western and northern Europe and Mediterranean lands, many sacred and healing wells, which were considered the entrance to the womb of the mother, were reassigned to Christian female saints. According to lore, the female saint would have performed a spectacular miracle on that spot to explain why the well or a spring suddenly appeared (regardless of the fact that the well had been there for hundreds or thousands of years before the saint was around). This encouraged locals to transfer their allegiance from the original well spirit or goddess, though the healing properties of the well remained the same.

The triple goddess wells, once sacred to Brigid, were Christianised as Saint Brigit or Bride wells and you can be sure a place with the name Bridewell has one of these Brigid wells, though it maybe disused and overgrown. The Virgin Mary, not surprisingly, became guardian of the ancient mother wells.

The Christianised wells of St Anne or Anna, grandmother of Christ, became known as Grandmother Wells and offered healing for childhood ailments, for infertility, for the medical problems of older women and to bring about easy childbirth. Her predecessor was Denu or Anu, mother goddess in the Irish Celtic tradition.

In Eastern and Western Europe and the Mediterranean, women through to the 18th century would walk clockwise three times round fertility pools and wells, washing their abdomens in the healing waters, often under the guidance of a local woman, who was custodian of the well. This role was invariably handed down through the female line of the family.

In recent times there has been a great revival of fertility ceremonies and to my knowledge some successes against all the odds.

On 25 November, the feast day of St Catherine, the fourth-century patron saint of young women, young unmarried women would pray at her chapels and sacred wells, such as the one in the now ruined abbey grounds at Cerne Abbas in Dorset. Young girls would turn round three times clockwise and ask St Catherine for a husband, making the sign of the cross on their foreheads with the water. This love ritual can be practised at a Catherine well at any time.

Well rituals will bring love, healing, fertility and marriage, will grant wishes and will sometimes give visions of love.

Following the ancient tradition, cast your offering into the well with your wish. If a matter is long standing, dip a ribbon in the water and hang it to a nearby tree to wither or for the energies to be to be released.

Lakes and pools

In the Chinese tradition, still waters are reflectors of the ever-changing heavens and attract the energy of the universe, sun, moon and stars and the clouds reflected in the surface. In the Classical tradition lakes were called Diana's mirror, as she rode in her full moon form across the skies.

Round bridges form a semicircle that is reflected in the water as a complete circle, the symbol of heaven and a sign of unity.

There are many lady of the lake Arthurian legends in Welsh, Cornish and Breton folklore. One of the most important roles of the Arthurian lady of the lake is as guardian of the sacred sword Excalibur.

In some versions the lady of the lake was a faerie woman, but in an older tradition she was one of the ancient goddesses of life, death and rebirth. Although the lake of Vivian or Vivien, the Breton name for the lake lady, has been identified in the forest of Broceliande, a Cornish Arthurian legend describes Merlin riding with Arthur into Dozmary pool on Bodmin Moor in Cornwall where he pulled Excalibur from a floating stone. After Arthur's death the faithful knight Bedivere returned it to the lady of the lake by throwing it into the lake, where it will remain until Arthur comes again.

Subterranean lakes have a special mystique because of their stillness, which seems to suggest that they extend endlessly into primal darkness. The underground Lake Kov-Ata in Bakharden near Ashgabat in Turkmenistan is located deep in a cave in the mountains. The warm emerald waters have for centuries been attributed powerful healing and magickal properties. One legend tells that the lake was discovered when two young lovers fleeing from their families' anger, found themselves trapped by rocks. They prayed for help. The mountain opened and steps led to the magickal lake. Flying monsters drove off the angry parents and the lovers were able to escape to freedom. Tourists today still bathe in the waters and a number have experienced healing.

Lakes, pools, ponds and indeed canals are good for any wish magick that will take a while to come to fruition, for peace, reconciliation, for keeping secrets, for developing inner stillness and for being a positive influence on someone who has perhaps got into trouble or has lost their way in life; they are also good for revealing potential and undeveloped talents.

Casting stones to create ripples is a very common form of still water magick. The image is of good results or even good fortune extending further and further.

A still water spell to begin a small venture, project or business in the hope it will grow

Casting a single stone into a still pond will cause ripples on a physical level that can be directed to draw magickal power from the mystical level. The desired results should then grow and spread slowly through your life. This is an excellent spell for networking, fame or popularity, for attracting new customers to a business or for anything to do with communication, writing and travel plans. In the Slavic tradition, flowers were cast into water in honour of Kupula, goddess of water, magick and herb craft, when petitions were made to her.

You can name any water deity you feel kin to or you can honour the essence of the water as you make your offering as part of the exchange of energies and the promises you make to the water if your wish is granted.

You will need: A clear quartz crystal or white stone as round as possible and about the size of a medium coin; a few flowers or flowering herbs – you can use the meanings in the chapters on flowers (see page 162) and herbs (see page 176) to choose an offering related to your wish; a still body of water.

Timing: As light rises over the water during the morning when the water is still and everything is quiet

* Hold the white stone in cupped hands and say:

Though you are small, yet shall you grow and your ripples spread ever wider to bring expansion.

* Picture the successful outcome, the increased clients, the expansion of your creative venture developing into a full-blown business or lots of people coming to see your shows.
* Hold the stone in the hand you usually throw with and say:

I charge this stone with power to bring success to me in this venture.

* Cast the stone slowly and deliberately as far out as possible and watch the ripples spread, saying:

And so the power flows invisibly to actuality. I trust all shall be well.

* Float very gently your offerings on the water and say:

I'll give thanks and will use the blessings I receive for the good of others as well as myself. I seal the bargain with the power of still water. Blessings be on all.

* As you watch the results unfold, you could do something to help water fowl, to clean up polluted lakes or to support a water-based charity for clean water in other countries.
* If the venture is very long term, repeat the spell monthly for six months.

Banishing with water

Water, both flowing and still, can be used for banishing by carrying away or quenching what is causing unhappiness (see also Sea magick, pages 358–62). Casting away dark-coloured symbols or dead petals or overripe fruit is a powerful psychological as well as psychic statement.

A banishing or protective water spell for when you can't get to open-air water

This spell can be used to remove any unwelcome intrusions in your life, whether they be noisy neighbours, relatives who cause trouble in your relationship, an illness that is affecting your lifestyle or financial problems that are casting a shadow over your existence. It can also be cast to shield you from spite, malice or gossip or even psychic attack. It is quite a strong spell but a very common one of which there are numerous versions.

You will need: A dark brown beeswax or a deep purple wax candle; a small white candle; a deep ceramic or metal bowl of water.

Timing: Towards the close of a day, a week or a month

* Light your dark candle and say:

I face the dark times / influences / dangers in the knowledge they are soon to end.

✳ Speak into the flame and softly. With your words, pour into the melting waxes your fears, frustrations, etc. Then say:

Now they are within the flame and burn in my life but for a second more. Fade now and come not again to trouble me.

✳ Plunge the candle into the water so that it hisses.
✳ Light your white candle and say:

Yet still I burn, free from their shadow and I shall burn ever more brightly until radiance enters my life again.

✳ Pick up the dark candle and say:

Go in peace.

You can dispose of this after the spell.
✳ Tip out the water that you used to douse the candle into a container and rinse the bowl with fresh water to remove any floating wax.
✳ As you do so, say:

Cleansed of all harm and darkness, filled with promise, show me now what my future shall be.

✳ Float a few pinches of dried culinary herbs such as rosemary or chives on the surface of the fresh water and interpret the images that form.
✳ Write about them in your Book of Shadows until the white candle has burned down.

5

SEA MAGICK

(T)he sea has always been central to the lives of fishermen and travellers for trade, exploration and conquest. So too has the need to seek the blessings of the sea in the personified form of sea deities and sea mothers, because the power of the ocean is so unpredictable and can be destructive as well as life sustaining. This was shown by the devastation of the recent tsunami in South-east Asia.

Every land has its own version of the Great Flood and in myth and actuality the wrath of the sea has wiped out whole civilisations. Plato, in around 360 BCE, wrote of how Atlantis, described as a paradise on earth, was submerged by Zeus with a huge tidal wave. In the space of a day and a night, most of the race of demi-gods who inhabited it and their highly evolved civilisation disappeared beneath the waves. Historically we know that tidal waves around 1,400 BCE also devastated the fabulously wealthy sea-going Minoan civilisation to whom even the Ancient Greeks were once forced to pay tribute.

The sea is still a primary source of food for many people and in indigenous societies there is a strong awareness that the sea can bring abundance or withhold its gifts. In more recent times humans have, by over-fishing and polluting the oceans, upset this natural balance.

Fish and mammal bones are returned to the rivers and the sea by the Inuit people of the Arctic Circle and other societies that rely on fish as the main source of food. This is both an ecologically sound practice as minerals are thereby being recycled, and a ritual act of respect so that the sea life will be reborn in a continuing cycle. To the Inuit, the sea has its own animate power and their sea mother Sedna is the main focus of their reverence, though they have other deities such as Aningan or Igaluk, the moon man, who is a great hunter and can be seen standing in front of his igloo (see Moon magick, page 428).

The sea mothers

The first ocean deities were called sea mothers, for the sea was considered the womb from which all life came, a fact confirmed by modern biologists. Of course, there were sea gods, but in this chapter will focus on the mothers and their magickal creatures.

The first of a catch is still thrown back as an offering to the sea mother, even where the reason and the mythology have become obscured by time.

Offerings have also been made throughout the ages to sea goddesses (and later less frequently to the sea gods) to ask for the safe return of sailors and fisher folk to shore. The wives of sailors would collect sea water in a flask or bottle when their husbands set sail. When the boat was expected to begin the homeward voyage they would pour the water back into the sea, saying:

I return what is yours, return mine to me.

The following are my favourite sea mothers and are ones you may wish to use in your sea spells. However, almost every mythology has its sea mother, some of which date back thousands of years and were once the primal creating goddesses.

Sedna

Sedna is a very ancient fertility mother, called the Old Woman Who Lived Under the Sea. She is given different names throughout the Arctic, including Nerivik in Alaska and Arnarquagssag in Greenland. She is goddess of the ocean and all sea animals. In the most common version of the myth, Sedna was a beautiful Inuit girl who fell in love with a handsome hunter who sang to her in her hut. He offered her necklaces of ivory and a tent covered with the finest furs if she went to live with him in the land of birds.

He lured her into his waiting canoe and abducted her, revealing his true form as Kokksaut, the bird phantom. Her father, Angusta, who was searching the oceans for his lost daughter, found her weeping alone on an ice flow. He took her in his canoe but Kokksaut pursued them and when Angusta refused to hand back his daughter, Kokksaut changed into the evil bird form and created a terrible storm.

The waves demanded the sacrifice of Sedna. Angusta become afraid that he had so offended the sea and spirits of the air that he would be killed, and he cast Sedna into the waves.

When Sedna tried to cling to the boat, her father seized an ivory axe and cut off her fingers. The girl sank into the water and her fingers became seals. Three times she tried to reach the kayak but her father hacked at her wounded hands until she was lost beneath the waters. Her knuckles became walruses and whales.

When the people do not catch seals or other sea creatures, the shaman dives in astral or soul form to the bottom of the sea to entreat Sedna to set the sea animals loose. There the dark, gigantic Sedna listens to magickal chants of the shaman and tells him or her either that the people must move to another place to seek the sea creatures or that she will send shoals to the current hunting grounds. The shaman will in return comb the tangled hair of Sedna since she cannot do this herself with her damaged hands.

Mama Cocha or mother sea

Originally worshipped by the Incas, Mama Cocha is the Peruvian whale goddess. She has been revered through the ages by the peoples living along the South American Pacific Coast, though she is feared by inland dwellers. The whale was worshipped as a manifestation of her power with ceremonies in her honour. In different areas, particular fish species were sacred totem creatures and might not be eaten.

The archetypal lords or clan leaders of all the different sea mammals and fish were the servants of Mama Cocha. They lived in the upper heavens and each offered their own species to humans; Mama Cocha then released the sea mammals and fish at her will.

Stella Maris

The name Mari has been used for sea goddesses in different lands all of whom are described in a similar way, in a blue robe, fringed with pearly foam, and a pearl necklace.

For many centuries, because of the importance of the stars in navigation, there were a number of goddesses who took the title of Stella Maris or Star of the Sea.

The first Stella Maris was Isis, the Ancient Egyptian mother goddess. Isis was given this name when her worship spread to Rome, though in Egypt she was associated with Sirius the Dog Star whose annual rising heralded the fertilising Nile flood.

With the coming of Christianity, the Virgin Mary became Stella Maris. Images of the Virgin crowned in stars are found in many Mediterranean coastal towns and villages and as far west as the Atlantic coast of Brittany.

The goddess Venus in her Evening Star aspect was also called Stella Maris in Italy.

Even today on Ascension Day the Doge of Venice carries out a ceremony (a relic of the sacred marriage, in seafaring communities, between the sea and the people) in which a golden wedding ring is cast into the waters. This ceremony was originally performed in honour of Venus.

Sea goddesses

Because water is a feminine element, the goddesses have retained their place as empathic deities concerned with the lives of human kind and the sea creatures.

Benten or Benzai-ten

Benten is the Japanese sea goddess.

She is described as being very beautiful and rides a dragon while playing a harp-like instrument, for she is also the goddess of music and dancing. Alternatively, she swims through the water with her retinue of white sea snakes – another form she can take.

Benten is eight armed. Six of her hands clasp a sword, a jewel, a bow, an arrow, a wheel and a key. The other two are clasped in prayer. Legend tells how she came to earth to save the children from an evil dragon. The island of Enoshima rose from the sea so that she could walk across it on her journey. She is called one of the seven fortunate or lucky deities for she brings prosperity to her devotees who come to her water-side shrines to make offerings.

Originally her worship came from India and travelled with the spread of Buddhism to Japan in the sixth century. Her symbol is the white serpent, and snake skins are carried in her honour in wallets or purses to attract prosperity even today.

Cliodna

Cliodna of the Golden Hair was daughter of Manannan, Celtic sea god and lord of the Isle of Man, but was a powerful sea goddess in her own right. She was also Queen of the Land of Promise over the waves, another realm of the Celtic otherworld in which there was perpetual peace and harmony. When she was downsized with the coming of Christianity, to a faerie queen, myth tells she took mortal lovers to faerieland. She loved young mortal Ciabhan so much that she left the otherworld to live with him. However, while he was hunting, her father sent a faerie minstrel to enchant her and carried her back in a magickal sleep. She is seen on seashores either as a huge wave or a seabird seeking her lost love.

As sea queen, she still rules over every ninth wave; she is said to heal the sick with her magickal rainbow birds.

Tide magick

Tides are caused by the gravitational pull of the moon and the sun, with the moon having the greater influence. The Bay of Fundy between Nova Scotia and New Brunswick in Canada experiences the greatest differences between high and low tides and north-west Australia also has great tidal variations.

Sea tides are potent for all kinds of magick. Tidal rivers and estuaries also offer a context and energy force for sea spells. Large lakes likewise experience very small tidal ranges and may be used for slack tide magick at any time (see page 360).

All you need for successful sea spells is a local tide table for wherever you are working. Some tides do come in incredibly fast so check with locals.

Even if you live a long way from the sea, try to visit the ocean at least twice a year. For not only is the sea the source of restorative powers in the sea breezes, the salt tang and the movement of the waves, but tide magick offers an instant force to carry your spells with great impetus and in rhythm with the pulse of nature. Any beach will hold sufficient material for spells.

Spring tides refer to the movement of the water to unusually high and low levels, not the season. They occur twice monthly, during the weeks of the new and full moon. During these periods the sun, moon and earth are aligned, so creating terrific energy surges reflected in the sea. These two weeks each month are extra potent for sea magick.

There are four tides a day, two high and two low, plus the slack tides between each when the direction of the currents are reversing.

Working with the tides

For all sea magick you should make an offering to the essence of the sea, whatever you call him or her. You can just use lord/lady ocean or father/mother sea.

This symbolically represents your part of the bargain, but you may, if the sea grants a special wish, decide to help an endangered sea species or to campaign for clean seas.

Gold-coloured money, an aquamarine, a gold earring or small pearl, are traditionally offered. You can also offer a white shell or stone.

The sea has her moods like the weather and you can work with these for different kinds of magick, as well as the variations of ebbs and flows, the high, low and slack tides.

A calm sea

Whether incoming or outgoing, a calm sea is ideal for harmony and peace-making spells; for stability in your life, finances or career; to bring and maintain love and happiness; for family matters, children and pets, safe travel and happy holidays.

A stormy sea

Whether incoming or outgoing, this is the sea of changes and movement, for spells for justice; a sudden rush of confidence or determination; for taking a stand against bullies and for overcoming obstacles; also for making a huge or sudden impact in a particular area of your life.

Incoming tide

The incoming tides are powerful for all attracting magick, for restoring or bringing good luck and for travel and prosperity.

The higher the tide you work with, the more immediate and dramatic will be the results. Choose a higher tide for a spell just before an examination, an operation or medical intervention, a competition or a court case, a job or promotion interview, when you are seeking a love commitment, need a large or urgent sum of money or to sell or find a house quickly.

The lower level of tide is effective for attracting a new or undiscovered love that will grow slowly but steadily, for maintaining love and fidelity over the years, for the gradual increase of prosperity, health, or fertility; also for the development of a creative venture or self-employment from small beginnings and for those situations where you know the right time is a necessary factor in waiting for an improvement or new beginnings.

* Make your offering of a coin or crystal to the sea by casting it on to the seventh wave (or ninth if you are working with Cliodna). The seventh wave is lucky for all forms of sea magick.
* Scratch on a round stone with a pointed pebble what it is you want to attract, whether a relationship, a new job or even a new approach to a problem. Throw both stones as hard as you can together, one from each hand (the pointed one in your power hand), calling out:

So may it be, mother sea, as you decree.

* Alternatively, write your wish with a stick in the sand so the sea will cover it as the tide comes in. Enclose your wish in a clockwise circle.
* Another spell involves building a sandcastle to represent your wishes. Write your name in stones or shells in front of it or with the letters encircling it, for an affirmation of power, determination or independence.
* Say:

*I build my castle for _____. Sea, carry my wishes and fill them with vitality,
that I may build my castle in actuality.*

* You could also dig a channel from a rock pool left by the previous tide or make a deep hole in the sand, so that the sea will rush in. This will bring a sudden burst of creativity, energy, will power or inspiration, or further a wish to travel or bring new opportunities that you need.
* Plant a stick in the centre of the rock pool or hole and say:

I make my mark. I mark my identity. Come sea, carry me to where / what I most would be.

* Stand in the inrush of water and feel the energies rising through you. Raise your hands to draw energy likewise from the sky and then stretch them out to take in the power surrounding you.
* When the hole or pool is covered, leave the sea to do its work.
* Another option is to find a strand of seaweed and tie in it three knots. Name the person you would like to spend your life with as you tie each knot and say:

Sea surge, ocean surge, waves rise high and with it let love flow passionately, deeply and eternally.

* Cast the seaweed into the waves and call the name of your lover three times:

Come to me, be with me, stay with me.

* Name your love once more to seal the spell.

The slack tide or tide turn

This short period called the slack tide may last an hour or more, and is a time of magickal balance. It occurs between high and low and low and high tides as they prepare to turn.

During the slack tide there is no real current flow and so you can gently launch your desires especially for longer-term results to be carried when the sea is ready, either in or out. Slack tides will balance emotions, people or priorities that are pulling you in opposite directions or restore balance to your home and life after a period of instability. They will also help banish extreme mood swings or cravings.

The slack tides are also an effective force for replacement magick. This follows the banishment of regrets (for what has been lost or should be released) with something to be gained, removes bad luck and attracts good fortune in its place, loosens the ties of a bad relationship and at the same time attracts a readiness for new love or removes debt by calling money-making opportunities into your life.

Which slack tide you use depends on the emphasis of your spell, whether you have a lot to clear in your life before moving forward (high slack will carry out) or if you are ready to move forward but still have lingering doubts, guilt, fears or the final obstacles to clear (low slack to carry in what is new).

In effect it really doesn't matter that much and the slack tide that is closest to the time you need to work will be fine because of the inherent balancing nature of this tide state.

Finally, slack tides aid spells for seeking the return on a subsequent incoming tide of what has been lost or a person who has gone away. Launch the call on the high slack to go out and the call will echo psychically and surge in again after the resulting low slack, like a swing-boat movement. This will carry your message telepathically over great distances.

* While the sea is poised on the point of change, sit on the shore and focus on what you want to shed and what you want to replace it with. You will need a bag of dark and light shells or small dark and light stones. For each aspect of a situation or fear you wish to banish, drop a dark stone or shell into the water, naming what now must go in peace. Follow this by a white stone or shell for a step on the new pathway or a wish or empowerment. When you have finished balancing losses with gains or have no more shells, say:

What is lost and what is gained are equal. The past can be left in the past without bitterness or regrets. I will walk forward when I am ready into the promises of tomorrow. So shall it be.

* Another slack-tide spell involves walking in clockwise circles on the edge of the water to focus on your determination to make a major decision or a change in the very near future. Speak a chant aloud or in your mind, such as:

*Tide turn, carry _____ to fulfilment/bring me the power to _____
with the surge of the sea.*

Take with you a small tribute for the sea and a symbol of what you are asking for. When you feel ready, call out the words three more times and, as you stand in the shallows, cast your tribute on the seventh wave. Then on the next seventh wave, cast the symbol of what you desire (a piece of ripe fruit for fertility, a coin for wealth, flowers for love, a toy boat for travel, a door key for a new home, an old car key for a new car, or the name of your loved one carved on a stone if you seek consummation of your love or to strengthen fidelity in marriage).

* Recall an absent or faithless lover if you want him or her back by collecting the water of the slack tide in a bottle with a lid. You can also use the spell to send protection to a friend or family member who is overseas or to call telepathically someone you have lost touch with to contact you. As you scoop up the water, say:

*Lady ocean, mother sea,
I take of yours not thoughtlessly.
But as a sign of whom I lack.
I ask your help to bring him/her back.*

Put the lid on the bottle and shake it nine times, calling the name of the absent person and then adding any personal message. Take the lid off and wade out a little way if safe or tip the water from a harbour wall, saying:

*Lady ocean, mother sea,
I return what is yours, send _____ back to me.*

The outgoing/ebb tide

Use the ebb tide for banishing magick, whether for ill health, financial or career problems, a destructive relationship or bad luck or for reducing any negativity, spite or malice in your life by washing it away.

You can also launch on the outgoing tide excess weight, smoking that is ruining your health, debts, anxiety, overwhelming shyness or unnecessary guilt. Or you can use this tide to put a distance between you and someone who will not leave you alone, such as an interfering neighbour.

* Wade out a little way if the tide is not too fierce or stand at the water's edge and cast dying flowers, leaves, crumbled driftwood or overripe fruit. For an important matter set a tiny lighted beeswax candle on a wide piece of driftwood and cast this into the water.
* Say:

I let go of _____ once and forever. May it not return.

* If a problem is very long standing or you have a difficult person you need to ease gradually from your life, work on the first or one of the early days of the week of the new moon so you can take advantage of the spring tides. You can find these out from a diary or the weather section of the newspaper or *Old Moore's Almanac*. This is the period when tides are most extreme, especially high or low.
* Light a small lamp on the shore.
* Work on the evening ebb tide and float your dying leaves or petals or crumble dead driftwood, and say:

I put this space between us in gentleness and in peace. Go now and find happiness in other places where other eyes will smile for you. Leave me free from your thrall that I may grow and go forward on the path that is right for me.

* Put out the light and leave the shore without looking back.
* Repeat the spell on the first ebb tide of the full moon week or an early day during that week and for the third time the next month during the following new moon week's early ebb tide. Each time cast fewer petals into the water.
* On the final full moon early ebb, cast nothing and leave your lantern alight.

Sea creatures as power icons

In the chapters on animal and bird magick, I suggest spiritually absorbing the strengths of different creatures and adopting their archetypal or idealised forms as spirit guardians. The sea has a number of powerful warm-blooded mammals whose forms go back into antiquity and who have a mythology all of their own. They offer water qualities of imagination, empathy, protection, ancient wisdom, healing and spirituality, but in a powerful, constantly moving form that symbolises the immensity and sheer force of a crashing sea as well as its gentler moods.

The whale and dolphin are huge, highly evolved creatures that signify the creative/destructive duality of the sea itself. They are revered yet hunted, and increasingly in polluted seas poisoned or injured by fishing nets of sophisticated fishing vessels. Sea creatures will always be challenging power icons, especially the fiercer whales, but ones that are life-changing and always for the better.

Dolphins

Dolphins are the healing, protective face of the oceans and offer gentleness even if the sea is at her wildest.

These are the most magickal of all sea creatures. A number of the ancient sea goddesses adopted this most intelligent and sensitive of creatures for their icon, including Aphrodite, the Greek goddess of love and the Egyptian Isis in her later role in Rome as Stella Maris, star and goddess of the sea.

Dolphins have throughout history been lifesavers of humans at sea. The Greek historian Herodotus recounted how a dolphin saved the harpist Arion after Corinthian sailors had thrown him overboard from the ship on which he was travelling. The dolphin carried Arion to Taenarus, his destination. There are numerous testified modern stories of dolphins aiding people in trouble at sea or guiding vessels through dangerous waters.

For example, between 1888 and 1912, a rare white Risso's dolphin that was called Pelorus Jack safely guided steamers through the treacherous waters of Pelorus Sound, waters off South Island, New Zealand.

Dolphins also act as healers; swimming with dolphins is very therapeutic for any form of depressive condition or disorders triggered by stress. Dolphins are especially beneficial to autistic children and those with cerebral palsy and other forms of brain damage, and there is a great deal of ongoing research to uncover the full potential of dolphin healing. You can read more of this if you are interested in my *Psychic Power of Animals* (see Further reading, page 513).

Use dolphin energies to heal yourself or to develop your own healing powers, to enhance your musical talents, for imagination, for wise knowledge and whenever you need gentle protection or rescuing from a difficult situation on land or sea.

Whales

Whales are the largest of the sea mammals. In Maori myth, two of the sea gods take the form of whales and, it is said, can still occasionally be seen along the eastern coast of New Zealand's South Island, the island which, in legend, they created.

According to early Chinese mythology, Yu-kiang, a huge whale with mortal hands and feet, was lord of the sea. When angered by human misdemeanour or disrespectfulness towards the sea and its creatures, he would become a huge bird who created storms.

In the Bible the prophet Jonah, who was thrown overboard a ship by the crew in a storm because they feared he had angered God, was swallowed by a whale. The whale safely conveyed him to dry land after three days.

Use whale energies for any huge undertaking in your personal life; when you encounter prejudice, injustice or abuse; for the fierceness to defend yourself and any vulnerable family members; for the power to get creative ventures off the ground; for the strength to change the prevailing tide of your life; and for bringing harmony through communicating with others — for whales, like dolphins, make wondrous sounds.

Seals and sea lions

Seals and sea lions are different species, but share spiritual qualities. They are able to live on land and water but are able to move faster and more gracefully in water. This makes them creatures that can inhabit two dimensions and therefore as an icon they can assist us to bring imaginative, creative water qualities into the everyday world. However, the seal cannot function in one dimension alone, a reminder not to neglect our own spiritual aspects.

Hebridean and Gallic tales tell of the Selkies, the seal people who were sometimes lured ashore and would then marry their earthly lover and sometimes have a half-mortal child. In several seal legends the husband locked away the sealskin so his bride would forget the sea. The wife, though, could only stay a year and a day on land, and became ever more lifeless. Only by retrieving the skin and diving back into the waters, could the seal woman survive.

The male Selkie fared better in myth and would return to the waters, usually after the first child was born. His partner on land would then light a candle in the window to tell her lover she was missing him and he would return for a while.

In legend the seal people are likewise famed for their singing, though earthly seal sound is a matter of taste.

In northern Canada among the Tlingit Indians, it is recounted how the hunter Natsihlane healed the son of the clan chief of the sea lions who had been wounded by a harpoon. Natsihlane had been abandoned by his jealous brother-in-law on a shore far from home. In one version of the legend, in return for the help, the sea lion chief restored Natsihlane to his homeland and he was given the power to create live fish by carving cedar forms.

Use seal energies if you are under pressure or live a frantic life, to stay in touch with your spiritual world, to bring out your psychic awareness, to balance two very different priorities or lifestyles and to make your life more meaningful personally and creatively.

Using sea creatures in nature

There are many ways in which you can bring the magickal energies of sea creatures into your life. Some of these involve actually seeing them first hand, preferably in their natural environment.

* Dolphins, seals and whales can be seen swimming freely round many coast lines and often there are whale-, seal- or dolphin-watch boat trips from ports or fishing towns. From the Farne Islands off Northumberland in England for seal

watching to the Marina Del Rey area near Los Angeles where you can pick up a catamaran to go off shore for whales, you can take advantage or these trips with experienced boat people who know where to take you to interact with curious creatures who may swim up to the boat. Some commercial ferries pass close to sea-life hot spots. The Portsmouth to Bilbao P & O ferry passes through the Bay of Biscay where you can sometimes see a hundred or more dolphins and whales pass close to the boat. South-west Wales also has its share of dolphins that come close to the coast. You can internalise a complete spell and release the power as you point and exclaim like the rest of the tourists when the creatures swim near.

* Seal and sea lion conservancies exist worldwide. There is an excellent one I have visited near Gweek in Cornwall where seals and sea lions can be seen living happily, and there are plenty of picnic tables at which to sit as you focus and weave your magick or you can circle the pool areas where they swim. The healthy animals, abandoned as pups, are returned to the sea.

* Use holiday times to visit warmer areas where there are known to be regular resident schools of whales or shoals of dolphins. You may get to swim naturally with curious dolphins or you can sit on the shore and weave a beach spell as they dip and leap before your eyes.

* Some dolphinariums are very ecologically sound and some may offer the opportunity to swim with the dolphins.

* Beware of the concrete prisons where some sea animals are kept, and encourage others to visit those sanctuaries where endangered species or weak sea animals do interact lovingly with their carers. Some do have release programmes. Discourage those places where the creatures are not cared for properly by passing information on via the Internet in a factual, non-confrontational way and by supporting sea-life charities.

* Campaign peacefully with the spoken and written word, and campaign for the protection of dolphins, whales and seals from unnecessary slaughter and cruelty. I sometimes find it hard to remember that many people do still live by and rely on hunting seals and whales and that this accords with the nature of the sea. Nature is red in tooth and claw, but never deliberately cruel for pleasure or sport, unlike some humans.

Using the sea energies within

The power of the sea creatures can also come to you through visualisation and using the powers of your imagination.

* Listen to dolphin music by the light of a blue or turquoise candle, holding in each hand an aquamarine or jade crystal. Merge with the dolphin energies. Weave words and pictures in your mind of them swimming free to bring the dolphin or whale energies into your life or to heal you.

* Take the experience also into your bathroom, adding seaweed essence or bath salts (there are some very fragrant natural products around) and pushing away in the pools of light any disharmony. Place several small candles round the bath to shine on the water.

* Empower sea crystals like aquamarine, ocean jasper and jade by sprinkling them with water in which you have mixed three pinches of sea salt. Say:

Be as protection to me, (name your sea creature), be as power to me and be as healing that I may swim through the waves with you even as I walk the concrete streets.

When you hold the crystal in the everyday world you can absorb the power and the healing you invoked.

* Book a session in a floatation tank where you float in semi-darkness in warm saline water. Floatation tanks may be found in a number of alternative health centres, health clubs or spas. The tanks are very safe even for non-swimmers because the saline water is so concentrated that even if you fall asleep (which many people do) you cannot sink. Ask that your dolphin or whale music be piped through into the tank room and, as you lie motionless, merge with the energies of your special creature. You need say no words, nor even try to visualise. The connection will happen and will cause a spontaneous shift upwards in consciousness that will make you sensitised to colours, sounds and psychic impressions for at least a week afterwards. If you can manage a monthly floatation session, the effects will accumulate and you will float through life with the harmony, grace and the strength of the glorious mammals of the goddesses.

* Finally, go to any seashore or a large inland lake and call upon Manakiel, angel of all aquatic animals and fish who protects dolphins, whales, seals and all tropical and coldwater fish. Sit facing the water and picture Manakiel riding across the waters on your favourite sea creature, dressed in green-blue robes and carrying a huge seashell in which he can hear the call of any distressed sea creatures. Ask Manakiel to lead you into the subterranean realms of the sea creatures and ride with him across the waters or dive deep to talk to the clan father or mother of the dolphins, whales or seals.

WEATHER MAGICK

Weather magick, unlike that based on regular and predictable natural cycles such as the moon, the sun and the seasons, draws strength from less controlled but very dynamic forces. For this reason weather magick tends to be spontaneous, its timing fixed by a five-minute rainbow in the sky or a sudden downpour. Weather forecasts can help to some extent, especially with longer periods of rain or snow. It has long been known that animals, birds, insects and even plants know when there is bad weather expected.

The scarlet pimpernel flower is called the farmer's weather glass because it closes its petals before rain, as does the daisy and clover (with its leaves). The common spider will only weave webs if fine weather is going to continue. Rain is foretold when frogs croak loudly, cows won't go into the fields but gather under a hedge, and fish swim closer to the surface.

Almost all cultures have their weather deities. Rain is as essential as sunshine for the crops to grow and to provide drinking water to supplement water from wells. Storms could cause damage to dwellings, destroy crops, animals or people and so, although they were welcomed for bringing rain, they were also feared as the anger of the gods.

In the Andean mountains, it was believed from early times that the weather deities lived on the peaks. Offerings were made in high places by the Inca and pre-Incan peoples and these deities are still revered by local people, even where Christianity holds sway.

The Andean weather god was known as Tunupa to the Aymara peoples of Bolivia and in Peru was called Illapa by the Inca. He was supreme lord not only of rain, but of snow, hail and storms, in a region where there are extremes of weather. Pachamama the earth mother, was mother of the weather gods and they became her consorts. Offerings to Tunupa encouraged the flowing of those energies necessary to harmonise social relationships as well as calling the rains.

In Africa where drought is a constant threat, the rain gods of different peoples were usually associated with the creating god, for example Mukuru, the supreme deity of the Herero Bushmen of Namibia. He is a caring deity sending rain and also protecting the old and the sick.

Dragons and weather magick

In the chapter on fire magick you encountered the all-powerful dragons of fire that come mainly from the Eastern and Western European traditions.

Chinese dragons are said to have a 4,000-year birth cycle and do not grow their wings to fly until the last thousand years. They are described as having bearded lion's-mane-like faces, 81 or more scales on their back (in multiples of nine, their sacred number) and five huge claws. Japanese dragons only have three claws.

Chinese dragons are made up of the parts of many creatures, including two antlers like horns on their heads. They are depicted in blue, black, white or red and often carry a pearl in their mouth or between their claws. The pearl symbolises wisdom, the power of healing, fertility and the moon.

Their mating and birthing cycles can cause extremes of weather, whirlwinds, hurricanes and storms that last for many hours, especially when the male dragon stirs up the energies of the newborn dragon (a mere 1,000 years old) as it emerges from its jewel-like egg.

Clouds, mists and fog were believed to be formed from dragon breath and rain was thought to fall as they fought. Rain also was caused if their claws caught in a cloud as they roamed across the skies. If the fighting became too fierce, a storm occurred. Certain powerful dragons could regulate the rainfall to ensure a good harvest and they are still recalled in dragon processions like those held on the Chinese New Year.

Chinese and Japanese dragons are also associated with waters, such as lakes, rivers and the ocean. The four Japanese dragon kings, who control the four seas, are given offerings if there is too much or little rain since they, like the Chinese dragons, are believed to have the power to control the weather.

The call of the air dragons

You can call upon air dragons in the spring or whenever you need positive change or fresh energies in your life. You can also invoke their strength when rain is needed, either in a particular area of the country or world or when you need rain in your life after a stagnant, arid period (in terms of relationships, work or creativity). Oriental weather dragons are also potent for any form of healing. Their healing powers were found as small pearls after rain, and red sage is said to grow where dragons rested on the earth.

They assist any artistic or creative venture and will wash away or stir the winds to carry off anything that is no longer making you happy or has run its course (see also Air magick, pages 328–31). Call the weather dragons whenever you are feeling stifled, whether by physical overcrowding or possessiveness.

Dragons love strings of bells or the Tibetan pairs of bells (mini cymbals you can clash together to stir the powers). Alternatively, buy a rain stick (long wooden tubes containing beads or seeds with spikes inside to create the rhythm). You can buy these in all sizes in any ethnic craft store or on the Internet, and can also use them for rain magick. Write your own dragon call if mine does not feel right for you.

* Find an open space away from trees. The centre of a lawn in your garden is fine, but you can create your dragon call in different places in order to sense different dragon energies.

* In time you can internalise the process and call for space in a crowded train. I sometimes visualise the call ritual if I am overloaded with luggage, as I usually am on work trips, to get a seat on a train.
* Tie long scarves to your wrists and one round your neck that will swirl as you move. You may even find scarves with a dragon design.
* Picture your dragons, swirling blues and yellows, rising and swooping like Chinese kites on the breeze.
* To begin, shake your rain stick three times, make three sounds with your Tibetan bells, shake your string of bells three times or clap loudly three times, to stir the air.
* Call out:

Dragons of the skies, rise.
Dragons of the skies, rise.
Dragons of the skies, rise, if so is right to be.

* Still holding your instrument or, if you are not using one, clap as you move round the area in spirals. You can modify the movements, scarves, etc. if people are around, but try to find a quiet time and place to get the full effect at least once.
* Call as you move and play or clap:

Dragons, rise.
From earth to skies,
Dragons share with me,
your pearls of immortality,
that I may be free,
Dragons of the skies.

* Continue moving faster, shaking or clapping and calling louder, until you feel the air dragon strength, vitality and creativity stirring within you.
* When you feel filled with confidence and optimism, on the final word 'free', give a final single loud shake of your rain stick, bells or a last clap.
* Sit down wherever you are and shake your hands with the scarves attached to release any excess dragon power.
* Quietly thank the dragons and leave a single small mother of pearl or pearl button or earring as an offering to be found by someone to whom it would give pleasure.
* When you get home hang the scarves near an open window to absorb any breeze and wear one whenever you need creativity or space.
* Repeat the dragon call whenever stagnation returns.

Rain magick

Almost every culture has its ancient rain deities and rain spells because rain is as vital as the sun to make the crops grow. Green jasper was often used in Native North America in rain-making ceremonies, for example the Hopi Indian buffalo and snake dances, during which they prayed to the Great Spirit to send the rain.

Until comparatively recently in parts of Russia and the surrounding countries, rain-makers would climb trees in times of drought. One would hammer on a metal kettle or small cask to imitate thunder; one would knock two flaming brands together to imitate lightning; while the third, the rain-maker supreme, sprinkled water from a vessel with a bunch of twigs, while singing his magickal chants.

Use rain magick for bringing new energies into your life, for washing away what you no longer want whether it be sorrow, debt, a bad habit or the effects of an old relationship. Use it also for attracting abundance into your life.

Rain deities

In hot lands, rain is essential to prevent drought. For this reason, among a number of African nations the rain god was linked with the creator god and was of the highest rank. The names of these creator or rain gods vary according to the people, but their supremacy and the importance of appeasing them is the same throughout sub-Saharan Africa. Though some have become linked with the Christian god, they are still regarded as important protectors in their own right. For example Domfe is deity of rain, water and wind among the Karumba people, and ceremonies still call upon his powers to bring the rains at the appointed season.

Mother of rain

The Huichol Indian rain goddess is associated with the divine serpent and is herself considered an embodiment of the rain. In this tradition, millions of tiny serpents are said to fall from the clouds that are burst by magickal salamanders. The serpents protect the crops from rats.

Ua-Roa

Also called Uanui (hail) and Ua Nganga (rainstorm), Ua-Roa (long rain) is the Maori god of rain. His son is Hau Matingi, the god of mists or fog. Each of these weather conditions was interpreted as a message from the god who ruled its states. So a long rain might suggest long-term favour from Ua Roa to the people, while mists would indicate confusion to be resolved.

Zeus

Father of the Greek gods, lord of justice and defender of all who were helpless, Zeus was also god of rain. In this role he was called the cloud gatherer and ensured the rains would fertilise the crops and the fruit trees. The role of supreme god as rain god reflected the importance of rain in the heat of Greece. In common with the storm gods of other cultures, Zeus hurled thunderbolts at those who offended him.

A rainy day spell to bring money into or back into your life

You will need: A money-attracting plant such as basil, rosemary or a small bay in a pot or a pot of roses still growing; a bowl for rain water; a green jasper, fluorite or jade crystal.

Timing: A showery day rather than a day of torrential rain

* When it begins to rain set the bowl outdoors on the ground to collect the water.
* Return indoors to fetch the plant and crystal and set them in a triangle (the symbol of increase) on the ground, with the bowl at the apex.
* As rain falls on to the plant, cup your hands round the pot and say nine times:

Rain, rain, bring growth, I ask, to nature and my life.

* Stand for a minute cradling the plant pot, endowing it with positive energies as you picture the plant growing and money coming into your life from unexpected sources or from situations or people you had forgotten or dismissed as unprofitable. It's worth getting wet, as the rain does stimulate all kinds of spontaneous good ideas.
* Return the pot to the ground.
* Dip the crystal into the bowl of rainwater three times and say:

Be for me prosperity, abundance and fertility.

* Push the wet crystal into the earth round the plant and repeat three times:

Rain, rain, bring growth, I ask, to nature and my life.

* Leave the pot and the bowl in the rain.
* Bring the plant indoors when the rain has stopped or plant it in the earth.
* Water the plant daily with the rainwater (if it is dry weather use tap water in which you have soaked green jasper, jade or fluorite for two hours). Repeat as you water it:

Be for me prosperity, abundance and fertility.

* As the plant grows, so your finances and money-making opportunities should steadily improve.

Rainbow magick

Rainbows occur when it rains and the sun shines at the same time and when the light from the sun shines through rain drops, which create prisms, splitting light into a spectrum of colours.

Rainbows are considered incredibly lucky and in almost all cultures have magickal associations with the granting of wishes and also with prosperity. The crock of gold at the end of the rainbow belongs to the fairie folk and if you can find it before the rainbow fades, it is yours.

Rainbow magick is so fleeting you may have to act very fast. However, this gentle magick will restore hope, bring healing and happiness and fulfil any secret dreams or ambitions. Therefore it is worth dropping everything, slipping out of your office for a minute or two or finding a safe place to stop the car when a rainbow appears in the sky. Double rainbows, though rare, are twice as fortunate.

Rainbows, which are frequent in New Zealand, were used as a vital source of divine counsel. A low rainbow directly ahead would indicate that a projected journey might be difficult. A high-arched rainbow promised favour in any enterprise and one forming a circle or a double rainbow assured total success and happiness.

Rainbows are seen as bridges between the heavens and the earth. Bifrost, the rainbow bridge in Norse tradition, was the bridge over which the gods travelled between the realms of the gods (Asgard) and mortals (Midgard).

In Australian Aboriginal myth, the rainbow serpent, the mother of all, sacrificed herself to bring forth creation. After a while she became tired and the birthing process stopped. She asked the kingfishers, one of the first tribes to come forth, to shoot an arrow at her head to allow the rest of creation to be freed. As her rainbow scales flew into the air to become the colourful lorikeet tribe, the reflection of the colours became the rainbow in the sky.

In the biblical tradition the rainbow was set in the sky as God's pledge that there would never again be separation of man from God, and it became also a token of reconciliation.

Iris, angel of the rainbow

Iris is one of the few identifiable female angels. Once called a goddess in Ancient Greek mythology she has retained the role she was assigned then as the messenger between the heavens and the earth (and in Greek tradition the underworld), always bringing good news, peace and consolation.

In the angelic tradition, Iris has rainbow wings and carries a purple and yellow iris and a golden lily. She comforts bereaved husbands who traditionally plant an iris on their wives' graves and also sorrowing sons and daughters who have lost a mother.

Her candle colour is a two- or three-coloured candle or a pink one, her incense is jasmine, lavender or rose and her crystals are rainbow quartz, rainbow obsidian, opal aura and cobalt aura. For more on Iris and other female angels see my book *Touched by Angels* (Further reading, page 513).

A rainbow ritual to make a wish come true

The colours in a naturally occurring rainbow, converging into white, offer an instant colour lift for all your chakras or energy centres even if all you have time to do is stand and breathe in the rainbow light from an open window five floors up.

You will need: Carry with you, when possible, seven tiny different rainbow-coloured crystals in a white fabric or velvet bag. These could be kept in your bag, in the glove compartment of your car or on a window ledge at home or at work.

Timing: When you see a rainbow

* Spread out your seven crystals facing the rainbow, forming them into an arch. If possible, sit down on earth or grass with them on the ground.
* Touch each crystal in turn and name the seven individual powers they possess (see below for crystal suggestions and powers).
* Hold up each crystal towards the rainbow and again name the separate powers.
* Set each down after you have held it.
* Finally, with all seven crystals in your outstretched and raised palms, repeat your dearest wish seven times in your mind.
* Wait for the rainbow to fade and return the crystals to their bag.
* In the evening, hold each crystal again in turn, starting with red and ending with violet, and repeat the wish in your mind for each.
* Leave them in a horseshoe shape where they will catch the first light of the next day and carry with you one, beginning with red and ending with violet, on each of the following seven days as a talisman.
* By the eighth day an unexpected small boost to further your wish will usually come your way.
* Of course you won't be able to work on every rainbow, but whenever possible try to tune into the sky colours just by naming the individual colours and powers to make you feel refreshed.

Rainbow crystals

Red

Power: Courage

Suggested crystals: Jasper, garnet, red tiger's eye

Orange

Power: Joy

Suggested crystals: Amber, aragonite, carnelian

Yellow

Power: Will power

Suggested crystals: Citrine, honey or yellow calcite, lemon chrysoprase

Green
Power: Love

Suggested crystals: Aventurine, jade, olivine/peridot

Blue
Power: Idealism/justice

Suggested crystals: Blue lace agate, chalcedony, lapis lazuli

Indigo (a blue purple)
Power: Wisdom

Suggested crystals: Bornite (peacock eye), sodalite, titanium aura

Violet
Power: Enlightenment

Suggested crystals: Amethyst, fluorite, sugilite

Alternatively, substitute the seven chakra crystals (see page 268).

I can sing a rainbow

Sometimes you won't have your crystals with you or it's just not the place or time to get them out. If you still want to carry out a spell or empowerment, however, you can sing or even hum the rainbow.

Each colour represents a particular sound vibration, forming seven notes of the eight-note scale. You can either sing the seven colours and then go down the scale again or add white to take you up to the next C (doh), white being the synthesis of the colours.

* Sing the colours three times up and down the scale, then sing the seven powers (see above) three times using the same note formation up and down the scale and finally the colours up and down three more times. The power of white is harmony.

* Remember to reverse the order for the descent, so upwards would be red, orange, yellow, green, blue, indigo, violet (plus optional white), then (optional white again), violet, indigo, blue, green, yellow, orange, red. The same applies with the power names.

* Practise a few times beforehand so that the lists become automatic.

- Sing more and more powerfully or hum the tune and sing the words in your mind with greater speed and intensity.
- Let the sounds flow and then on the last three sets reduce the power and intensity so that the final descending colour chant ends in silence.
- Cup your hands over your mouth, whisper the wish and gently push it towards the rainbow.
- When stressed or when success seems far away, visualise the rainbow and sing the colours once more.

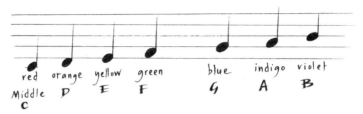

Storm magick

Storm magick is instantaneous, dramatic and needs very little input on your part. It feels more like holding on to a galloping horse. It is a cleansing power, bringing illumination to dark corners, blind spots, old fears, empty threats, illusions and creative blocks.

Storms will also empower you to speak out against injustices and being paid far less than you are worth and will remove self-doubt and underachievement. They also offer instant energy, power, confidence and courage for the spellcaster.

Storms seen over water are especially potent for bringing prosperity and success.

In the Maori tradition, like rainbows, storms were used as omens. Each of the villages had sacred heights, whether the peak of a mountain or sacred mound, where the movement of storms was interpreted. If lightning flashed vertically towards the home village, this was seen as inauspicious for the people living there and so ceremonies had to be held to propitiate the gods. Lightning flashing away from the village indicated that the tribe was protected. Sheet lightning indicated war or problems stemming from human rather than divine error, perhaps the breaking of *tapu*, a taboo or prohibition.

The magickal creature of the storm is the thunderbird.

Thunderbirds

A gigantic form of the eagle and a feature of many totem poles, thunderbirds are most usually associated with Amerindian tradition. To many of the peoples, the thunderbird is the bringer of rain which spills from a lake on its back as it flies. Its flashing eyes create lightning and its vast eagle-like wings cause thunder.

The thunderbird was chief of all the birds of the upper world and was in constant battle with the land animals led by the trickster raven.

Thunder is very common as spring turns to summer and this was the time when the thunderbird moves from the winter to the summer side of his house.

Japan also has a thunderbird that resembles a giant rook and is, like the eagle, a solar bird. It creates thunder and lightning and guards the approaches to the heavens.

The thunder/storm gods

Thunder gods in most cultures have proactive energies that are good for both women and men to express assertively but not aggressively or over-emotionally what they wish to achieve or change. They offer a focus for fast-tracking your career.

Perun

The Slavic god of thunder and lightning, Perun (or Piórun in Polish) is dark-haired with a beard of gold and carries a huge axe or mace. His sacred tree, like that of the majority of the thunder gods, is the oak. Oaks are often struck by lightning and so were said to offer protection to homes against storms. Twigs from oaks that have already been struck are highly prized as domestic talismans kept close to the hearth. Rocks and trees struck by lightning are considered blessed because they contain his sacred fire. Arrows were fired into oak trees in Perun's honour at the beginning of the hunt and to ask his blessings.

Raiden

The Japanese god of thunder and lightning, Raiden is portrayed as fierce and red with sharp claw-like hands. He carries a huge drum and when he beats it, those on earth hear the thunder and know he is angry.

Lei-King or Lei-Kung

Chinese lord of thunder and also justice, Lei-King is described as having a blue skin, wings and claws and would hurl thunderbolts upon the unrighteous who had escaped earthly justice.

Thor

Thor (or Thunor in the Anglo Saxon) is the principal and physically largest of the Germanic thunder gods. He controls the clouds, the lightning and the rains as well as justice and the crops. The wheels of Thor's gigantic wagon cause thunder as they roll across the sky. He probably preceded Odin or Woden the all father mythologically, though he is called Odin's son. Thor is a mountain-top dweller, hurling thunderbolts and lightning flashes against the unrighteous, both frost giants and humans.

Thor, however, was linked not mainly to destructive storms, but to summer tempests believed to cause the crops to grow. There are many mountains and high rocky crags in Germany and Scandinavia containing the old name Donar (another ancient name he used) or Thor/Thunor. One example is Thuneresberg, in Westphalia, close to Warburg.

Thor's magickal hammer Mjollnir aimed true and returned to his hand. When he threw it in the ongoing battles against the frost giants, sparks flew that caused lightning.

A storm spell for power

Be careful not to stand near trees or to carry anything metal during a storm. You can cast this spell anywhere, even from an open back door or window.

You will need: A shiny, grey haematite crystal, a fire and storm crystal or a black one like obsidian; a bowl of tap water.

Timing: When you see the first lightning

* Set the bowl of water on the ground. Stand facing the storm and hold your crystal in your receptive hand.
* Raise your arms above your head, hands closed, and then hold out both hands at waist height towards the storm. Your power hand should be totally flat, palm uppermost, your receptive hand still closed around the crystal. Say:

> *Fill me with your might, Storm of Mightiness (add the name of a Thunder god if you wish).*
> *I flinch not from the power but would embrace it.*

* Drop the crystal into the bowl with a splash and turn both hands vertically, palms facing inward towards you (the reverse of the protective splayed hand gesture). Say:

> *I welcome your courage and your strength that I may be/do likewise.*

* Picture the thunder and lightning stirring within you and filling you with determination and certainty that you can succeed.
* Then raise the bowl and say:

> *Lightning flash and thunder roll, fill this bowl likewise with enduring strength and purpose.*
> *Blessings be.*

* Leave the bowl out in the storm, but remove the crystal and take it indoors. Let the crystal dry naturally and carry it as a talisman in the coming days.
* After the storm, bottle the water and use a few drops in your bath to fill you with confidence. If you want to drink the water after the ritual, put cling film over the bowl for the duration of the ritual if the rain is acidic. This is an alternative way of making storm water (see also page 130).

The power of snow and ice

With the changes in climate, occasional snow has reached even warm areas such as the Costa del Sol in Spain and Majorca. In more northerly regions of the world, snow and ice can feature for up to six months of the year.

Snow magick is good for melting away anger, quarrels, opposition and prejudice. Try it also in identity, personal power and confidence spells in which you stamp wishes or your own independence and power as footprints in the snow.

In Sweden children and adults alike make snow lights to position outside their homes. A snow light is a very large snowball with a hollow centre and open top (or sometimes a little snow house) in which candles or tea lights can be lit after dark. Even houses with tiny front gardens have them in winter. They attract good luck to the home and act as a source of household protection, not only against the harmful effects of bad weather but against burglary and psychic attack.

Norse mythology tells how creation came about through the fusion of ice and snow from the foggy realm of Nifleheim in the north with fire from the realm of fire, called Muspelheim, in the south.

The Germanic snow and ice deities

Hulda or Mother Holle

In the Norse tradition, snow is said to fall when the old earth goddess Hulda or Mother Holle, or Frau Holle in the myths of Germany and the Netherlands, shakes her bed and the feathers from the eiderdown fly. It is said that Holland is named after her because her name means 'in the lower regions or levels'.

Holle, the queen of the winter months was married to Holler or Uller the Norse god of snow, ice and frost. He ruled for five months as the alter ego of Odin and is god of archery, hunting and skiing.

The Celtic snow and ice goddesses

In the chapter on animal magick I describe the Scottish Cailleach Bhuer – the Blue Hag. She roamed the Highlands during the winter, breaking the ice-covered pools with her holly staff and ensuring the wild cattle had enough straw and food for the winter. She would occasionally knock at a crofter's door and ask to warm herself by the fire. If the residents granted her request their food stores and cattle feed would replenish themselves. But those who turned her away would soon find the larder empty.

Brighid, the triple or three-aspected goddess, would on Oimelc, the feast of ewe's milk at the beginning of February, melt the snows with her white wand so that the first shoots might come through the earth.

From Celtic Christianity come legends of how on St Bridget's (Bride's) day, 2 February, the saint's lamb fought against and defeated the dragon of the old hag of winter, Cailleach. This was originally the battle between winter and spring that was transformed into the battle of the lamb of God against sin. In mystery plays in parts of Scotland the theme is still played out. Bridget is, of course, the Christianised form of the pagan goddess Brigid or Brighid.

Japanese snow goddess legends

The lady or goddess of the snow, Yuki-Onna, was also the death goddess because of the many people who perished in snowy places in times past. Her long, white hair merges with the snow and only part of her body which is clothed in white can be seen as she merges into the snowy landscape. Her attendants, the snow women were once mortal but died in the snow. Various legends tell of these women seducing travellers who had sheltered from the snow in huts, and were found frozen to death in the morning.

Snow and ice magick

Though you can use ice from your freezer or the supermarket in rituals to melt frozen feelings, mend quarrels or break an impasse or blockage, if you can work with real snow even for a short period, you will really experience its power. With air fares so cheap, even people in warmer climes that rarely see snow might like to visit a snowy place and try snow magick.

* Begin by naming the purpose of the spell over ice or snow that you have marked or collected in a heatproof bowl. Warm the bowl over a night light or in a pan over a low light on a stove or leave it to melt naturally, saying nine times as you begin:

Ice/snow go, life flow, bring to me (name the area of your life you wish to transform or the relationship you wish to mend).

During the spell you can stir the ice regularly anticlockwise to melt and clockwise to get the new energies moving. Cast the melted ice or snow in running water to increase the power even more or pour it on a growing plant, for example a rose bush, to mend a quarrel or mint to get money flowing into your life.

* For a long-term venture, use the water for planting bulbs.
* Write in snow the name of a person to whom you wish to be reconciled, scoop up the snow and leave it in a bowl to melt, surrounded by pink candles.
* Catch hailstones in a fireproof dish and, adding a little cold water, heat them gently or allow them to melt naturally. In Viking lore hail was called the cosmic seed because it held the potential for new life. This is a good pre-conception ritual if you want a baby or an effective ritual for any venture you wish to grow.
* Lie wrapped warmly in snow and spreading out your arms and legs make a snow angel outline. If you prefer, draw a circle around yourself as you stand. In either case, write with a stick in the circle or on the angel, for example:

I exist/I am free/I will succeed.

Walk round and round the outline clockwise, leaving layers of footprints. You have made your mark.

* If the snow is long lasting, make a snow light or a circle of them. Sometimes people make a small circle of snowballs and then build them up to form a circular wall of snowballs so that you have a space on the ground in the middle of the wall for a tea light or small candle in a holder.

* Inside, set a small night light. After dark, light the candle and make a wish. You can use a new light and repeat the wish each night while the snow lasts (or up to nine consecutive nights).
* You can make other lights for other members of the family and allow them to make wishes or maybe make a circle of lights, one for each family member, including those absent for whom you can make a blessing as you light the candle.

7

CRYSTAL MAGICK

Crystals are both a natural focus and a source of energy for spells. This is because they contain concentrated energies from their long formation in the earth, heated by volcanic fire, washed over by water and shaped by air.

What is more, after the spell they carry within them the absorbed accumulated powers, protection or healing. This can be released gradually into your life or the life of the person for whom you cast the spell when the crystal is carried or set at home or in a work space.

Historically, crystals have been used for magick as well as healing. In Ancient Egypt, turquoise was the sacred stone of Hathor the fertility and mother goddess who nourished the gods, pharaohs and ordinary people alike. Tiny turquoise phallic symbols were set on Hathor's domestic altars to bring a child and magickal words were spoken over them to invoke the blessings of Mother Hathor.

Turquoise was likewise used to make protective amulets of the scarab beetle, symbol of young Khepri, god of dawn. These were carried by the living as a charm for new beginnings and fertility and were placed within the heart cavity on the mummy to ensure rebirth. Chants and spells were recited over each crystal amulet placed on the mummy, and the scarab was often heart-shaped and given wings. The hair of the sun god Ra was made of turquoise and so represented earthly power and authority.

The Romans engraved lions, archers, heroes or warrior gods on carnelian and red jasper to give themselves courage in battle.

Crystals and astrology

The Chaldeans, who lived in Mesopotamia in 4,000 BCE and studied the stars for divinatory purposes, believed that certain planets were linked to crystals which were said to reflect their energies and characteristics.

The Greek philosopher Plato claimed that stars and planets converted decayed and decaying material into gem stones. Planetary associations are still associated with crystals, especially in the form of birthstones.

Therefore it was believed a crystal should be engraved or empowered when the sun was in its own zodiacal sign (see list later in the chapter). Of course this is not always possible, but you can empower a crystal you use regularly, during its sun sign period and this power will remain in it throughout the year. Equally, moonstones (like topaz) become more powerful as the moon waxes, achieving maximum strength on the full moon, making this a potent time for moonstone magick.

In Scandinavia, Denmark and the lands in which the Anglo-Saxon influence was strong, including Germany and the UK, spindles with clear quartz crystal whorls, the circular spindle tops, were used in spinning thread. Magickal spells and incantations were chanted so that the thread would be filled with magick to protect the warriors and voyagers as they wore garments sewn with the crystal-infused thread. Amber, called the tears of the fertility goddess Freyja, was also set in spindles to ensure a prosperous journey. Jet spindles were chosen to endow protection and safe return, as Viking voyagers sailed huge distances across tumultuous seas. Frigga, the Viking mother goddess, Frige in the Anglo Saxon tradition, was patroness of spinning and her crystal spindle may be seen in the stars close to Orion's Belt.

You can also wear or carry your own birthstone (see page 401) whenever you need to make a mark in the world or if you feel challenged or uncertain.

Choosing a crystal for spells and rituals

In the following section I have written about crystals that are particularly effective in spells and rituals. However, you can use any crystal for magick and sometimes you may sense that a particular crystal would be effective in a spell.

Colour is of significance – check the colour meanings on pages 258–65.

The type of crystal can also be a guide. Any quartz crystal is an energiser and promoter of change, ranging from the dazzling instantly active clear crystal quartz to the rutilated quartz, filled with golden or brown needles that releases its and your potential more slowly.

Jaspers are natural strengtheners and can be used in rituals for success, courage or power as well as protection rituals.

Agates are balancers of energies, to infuse spell energies with harmony and calm.

Often by holding a crystal and allowing its energies to pass via the sensitive chakras or energy centres in your palms, you can tell its purpose. For example, the gleaming golden brown tiger's eye exudes abundance and courage, even if its external wealth-invoking appearance is ignored.

In any crystal, the brighter and more intense the shade, the more powerful and active the energies.

Opaque red jasper is packed with power. Opaque stones are those that even when highly polished do not reflect light.

Clear or transparent sparkling crystals like yellow citrine are natural joy-bringers, while transparent stones such as the gentle healing paler forms of rose quartz allow positive energies to filter more slowly. Hold the two and you will feel the difference.

Translucent, gleaming stones that you can't see through, reflect and magnify your own inner gifts, such as creamy soft moonstone that enhances intuitive awareness and helps you to reconnect with natural energy cycles.

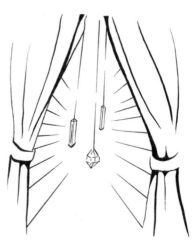

On page 514 I suggest some crystal books and there are countless sites on the Internet with crystal pictures and information. Stones can also be bought on the Internet.

Using crystals in spells and rituals

See pages 136–37 for information about making crystal waters for different purposes and page 147 for empowering crystals as talismans or charms. I have also suggested throughout the book a number of spells in which a crystal acts as the focus.

❋ An empowered crystal can signify any quality you need in your life or can attract good luck, health, love or happiness. Speak the purpose as you hold the crystal in your cupped hands saying:

> *Be for me / bring to me / protect me from* _____ *(name the strength or luck you need nine times).*

❋ You can alternatively write the purpose nine times in incense smoke.
❋ Make a crystal mini altar at work, outdoors or at home with four key crystals: smokey quartz or another dark crystal like tiger's eye or tourmaline in the north/earth/winter/midnight direction; citrine or lemon chrysoprase in the east/air/spring/dawn direction; red jasper or carnelian in the south/fire/summer/noon direction, and fluorite or jade in the west/water/autumn/dusk direction.
❋ In order to balance yourself, touch each crystal in turn, absorbing the powers of the direction it has taken on. Alternatively, use the four elemental strengths to empower a symbol you set in the centre by circling each crystal in turn over the symbol and calling upon the elemental strengths each represents. Shake the four crystals together in your cupped hands to raise the power and scatter them to release it.
❋ If you are at work, you can carry out the crystal spell entirely in your mind. Name and visualise the central symbol or use another crystal that is related to the need.
❋ Pointed crystals can be used pointing outwards to repel harm, or, using four, two pointing outwards and two inwards in a square to alternately draw back what you need, like a new job, a lover or money. Point them inwards to absorb strength, protection or healing.
❋ Gentler crystal points like amethyst also send healing powers to improve the atmosphere and darker ones like smoke quartz will help to lower your psychological profile and filter negativity. On a desk at work or pointed outwards on window ledges at home, dark crystals will keep you safe from all forms of harm.
❋ A clear quartz point, the good fairie wish crystal, will give a rush of energy that purifies and brings light. This can be pointed in the direction of what or who it is you seek to enter your life.
❋ Cleanse crystal points regularly by passing a pendulum nine times anticlockwise over them and nine times clockwise to re-empower. Plunge your pendulum in water in between, and afterwards allow the natural light to dry it.

* Use pointed clear quartz as a magick wand in places where you can't get out your wooden wand. No one will take any notice of you apparently circling a quartz point absent mindedly as you think. In this case, use the quartz pointing outwards over a document or the printout of an important e-mail while asking for what you really need.

* Use a smoky quartz point to circle as you talk on the phone to someone potentially confrontational, or touch one in your pocket as you wait for a late-night taxi or train, pointing outwards to repel unwelcome intrusion into your space.

* Put crystals that relate to your life (see list on the next page) in a bag and, last thing at night or first thing in the morning if you don't have to leave too early, choose one that will be of help to you during the day to come. You can also pick one before a trip or journey.

* Light a white or natural beeswax candle, pass the chosen crystal nine times clockwise round it and say nine times:

Empower, protect, guide and strengthen me this day/this trip that safe and victorious I may return.

* Carry the chosen crystal in a special purse until you come home and then set it close to greenery for 24 hours to be cleansed and restored.

* If you are experiencing a turbulent period or you are suffering from anxiety, panic attacks or stress related to a frantic lifestyle, carry a pair of balancing crystals. Choose an active empowering one such as a carnelian or yellow jasper and a softer balancing crystal such as a blue calcite or a banded agate. Hold them in each hand or have them in pockets or opposite sides of the desk (the power crystal on the side of the hand you write with), especially if a barrage of conflicting opinions or demands is flying your way.

* Set them also on two sides of a room at home to avoid quarrels between strong personalities among the family or flatmates. If you wish, place receptive crystals in the north and west and active ones in the east and south to preserve unity and calm during a potentially difficult family gathering.

* For protection and courage, paint on an appropriate stone your power animal or bird with a thin brush and acrylic paint. Alternatively, write over the crystal in incense smoke the name of the animal.

* Make three clockwise circles of salt round the crystal, saying:

Protect me in dark places and dark times, from danger and from stranger and bring light and joy into my life.

* You can also empower the different crystals with power creatures (see pages 215–20) for family members. If they are sceptical, set the crystal under their bed to protect and empower them while they sleep. In this way you are combining the strength of the creature with the inherent power of the crystal.

* You can add crystalline or stone energies to virtually any spell simply by leaving a relevant crystal at the centre of your cast circle or by making a physical circle round the symbol with small relevant crystals as you begin the spell.

* You can also add suitable crystals to charm bags of any kind for extra effectiveness (see page 139).

Crystals for magick

The following crystals are easily obtainable and relatively inexpensive. You only need small ones. If you prefer you can restrict yourself to one of each colour.

You may wish to have separate crystals for magick and for healing. Certainly it is useful to keep a set of your favourite magickal crystals in a drawstring bag so you can pick one to empower yourself for a particular event. If you aren't sure which crystal to use for a spell symbol, let your mind go blank and pick one from the bag. I have given for each crystal basic associations so you can build a crystal spell or empower a crystal simply by burning the relevant incense, candle colour, etc. next to the crystal and saying whatever feels right to endow the crystal with the necessary qualities to be amplified by its own innate strengths.

Use also any fresh herbs, tree leaves or flowers listed under the herbs, oils and incenses. I have sometimes given a second element for a crystal where it draws strengths from more than one.

You may choose to write empowerments for each crystal as I have done. I have also suggested for each its protective function and different kinds of spellcasting for which it is effective. If you want to know more about different crystals, I have listed more than 150 crystals with many different properties for animals, children, the workplace and healing, as well as for divination and magick, in my *Illustrated Dictionary of Healing Crystals* (see Further reading, page 514). I have listed crystals that have the same name, such as agate, according to their colour as each colour has very different properties.

Amazonite

Composition: Feldspar

Colours: Blue green or turquoise, to darker greens with white lines, opaque

Zodiac sign: Gemini, the heavenly twins (22 May–21 June)

Element: Earth

Planet: Jupiter

Candle colour: Turquoise

Herbs, incenses and oils: Basil, bergamot, fennel, mint and patchouli

Magickal: Protects against others taking advantage of you, whether in the home or work; attracts customers and new orders to a business.

Use amazonite in all money spells, to bring good luck and when gambling or speculating.

Empowerment/affirmation: *I have the right to expect fair treatment and consideration from others*

Amber

Composition: Organic gem made from fossilised resin from coniferous trees that exited about 30 million years ago

Colours: Translucent, yellow or golden orange, sometimes brown, often containing fossilised insects or tiny plants

Zodiac sign: Leo, the lion (23 July–23 August)

Planet: Sun

Element: Fire

Candle colour: Gold

Herbs, incenses and oils: Bay, frankincense, marigolds, saffron, St John's wort

Magickal: Protects against physical harm, mental hostility and psychic attack. Use it in love magick to call a twin soul; also in all goddess rituals.

For fertility, wrap a rounded amber and pointed jet crystal in a red cloth bag, tied with three red knots and place beneath the mattress during lovemaking.

Empowerment/affirmation: *I am filled with the radiance of the sun*

Amethyst

Composition: Quartz, with very large crystals

Colours: From pale lilac and lavender to deep purple, translucent, semi-transparent and transparent, also purple and white

Zodiac sign: Aquarius, the water carrier (21 January–18 February)

Planet: Jupiter

Element: Air

Candle colour: Dark blue/purple

Herbs, incenses and oils: Chamomile, lavender, patchouli, rose, sweetgrass (smudge)

Magickal: Removes negative earth energies that may make a house feel cold or unfriendly; good placed on a computer table to avoid excessive strain on eyes and mind; effective in any healing spell

Place under a pillow to drive away nightmares and psychic attack; use in spells to reduce the power of addictions of any kind.

Empowerment/affirmation: *I am in control of my body and like myself as I am*

Angelite

Composition: Sulphate/anhydrite, opaque and veined with wings, but smooth when polished. It is celestite that has been compressed for millions of years.

Colours: Pale or mid to celestial blue lilac or violet. It can also be white or grey violet.

Zodiac sign: Aquarius, the water carrier (21 January–18 February)

Planet: Uranus

Element: Air

Candle colour: Pale blue

Herbs, oils and incenses: Cedarwood, chamomile, lemon verbena, rosewood, vanilla

Magickal: Protects against angry people at work or home and calms them; also defensive against prejudice or intolerance of your way of life. Use it in all angel and archangel spells and for calling absent family members or friends who have lost contact or are estranged or cold towards you.

Empowerment/affirmation: *I turn anger into love*

Aquamarine

Composition: Beryl

Colours: Clear light blue or blue-green, the colour of a calm sea; occasionally a watery green

Zodiac sign: Pisces, the fish (19 February–20 March)

Planet: Neptune

Element: Water

Candle colour: Turquoise

Herbs, oils and incenses: Eucalyptus, kelp (seaweed), myrrh, tea tree, vanilla

Magickal: Ensures safety when you travel, especially overseas or on a boat; for justice spells to resolve legal matters favourably and usually amicably. Use in all sea rituals. Cast a tiny aquamarine enclosed in a shell tied with twine on to the seventh wave for a really important wish or to call a loved one home or into your heart.

Empowerment/affirmation: *I open my heart with love and forgiveness*

Aventurine

Composition: Oxide, quartz, containing mica that can sometimes give aventurine a metallic, iridescent glint

Colours: Light to darker green, often a soft mid-green, blue, opaque; also red, peach and blue

Zodiac sign: Gemini, the heavenly twins (22 May–21 June)

Planet: Mercury

Element: Earth

Candle colour: Mint green or silver

Herbs, oils and incenses: Bay, oakmoss, parsley, patchouli, sagebrush

Magickal: Protects against money losses, accidents and psychic intrusion; known as the gambler's stone, the luckiest of all stones in games of chance and competitions, it is often placed in charm bags for good fortune and money.

Empowerment/affirmation: *I attract good fortune into my life*

Banded agate

Composition: Oxide, cryptocrystalline quartz, chalcedony

Colours: There are a vast number of agates with curved bands of colour. Browns and fawns of all shades are very common. Some take their names from the place a particular variety was discovered, e.g. banded pink Botswana agate

Zodiac sign: Libra, the scales (23 September–23 October)

Planet: Mercury

Element: Air/earth

Candle colour: Dark yellow or fawn

Herbs, oils and incenses: Anise, ferns, lemongrass, sagebrush, sweetgrass

Magickal: Protects against excesses of any kind; also to prevent you absorbing the sorrows and negativity of others into your energy field; good for stability to take examinations or tests and interviews without panic; also for steady financial increase or good investments for the future.

Empowerment/affirmation: *I walk through life at my own pace and to my chosen destination*

Blue calcite

Composition: Calcium carbonate, either polished smooth or as water ice

Colours: From pale to mid-blue, sometimes with white veins; semi-transparent to translucent

Zodiac sign: Cancer, the crab (22 June–22 July)

Planet: The moon

Element: Water

Candle colour: Silver

Herbs, oils and incenses: Ambergris (artificial for environmental reasons), jasmine, mimosa, rose, violet, yarrow

Magickal: Deters crime, if placed on inner window ledges and near doors or valuable equipment; use it in rituals to connect with water spirits and as offerings to water deities; heals quarrels and discourages factions or cliques; also to give you creative dreams to provide solutions to dilemmas while you sleep.

Empowerment/affirmation: *I put aside divisions and dissent*

Blue lace agate

Composition: Agate

Colours: Usually pale powdery blue, sometimes brighter periwinkle blue with white lace threads through; opaque

Zodiacal sign: Aquarius, the water carrier (21 January–18 February)

Planet: Neptune

Element: Water/air

Candle colour: Pale blue

Herbs, oils and incenses: Fern, star anise, vervain, vetivert, yarrow

Magickal: The stone of the peacemaker. Make blue lace agate water for kind words and avoiding confrontations at family gatherings; use also to protect against and calm irritability.

Use in spells when you need to communicate something important at home or work; also for sea or air rituals and to cleanse pollution.

Empowerment/affirmation: *I speak the truth that is in my heart, but with gentleness*

Carnelian/cornelian

Composition: Chalcedony

Colours: Translucent orange to red, also occasionally yellow or brown

Zodiac sign: Leo, the lion (23 July–23 August)

Planet: Sun

Candle colour: Orange

Element: Fire

Herbs, incenses and oils: Copal, frankincense, juniper, orange, rue

Magickal: Protective against fire, storm and malevolence of all kinds, also acts as a shield from attempted psychic intrusion into your thoughts; guards against accident, especially related to building or DIY and kitchen mishaps.

Good for all love and sex rites, especially in rekindling passion that has faded in an otherwise loving relationship. Place a carnelian under each corner of the mattress. For spells and in charm bags for courage, self-confidence, creativity and independence. Fire magick is more effective if you circle a red candle with carnelians.

Empowerment/affirmation: *I am as courageous as a lion/lioness*

Chrysoprase

Composition: Chalcedony (quartz) with nickel

Colours: Apple green, opaque, can vary through lighter greens, also lemon

Zodiac sign: Taurus, the bull (21 April–21 May). In mediaeval times chrysoprase was engraved with the image of a bull to give strength and protection to the wearer.

Planet: Venus

Element: Earth

Candle colour: Mint or apple green

Herbs, oils and incenses: Apple blossom, lemon balm, rose, vervain, vetivert

Magickal: Protects against stagnation; use in rituals to bring fresh energies into your life and home by opening all the windows and doors at home and afterwards placing a chrysoprase near the front and back or patio doors. This and other chrysoprase spells will attract abundance, love, health, happiness and enthusiasm. At work, chrysoprase is excellent for beginning a new job, a new venture or project.

Empowerment/affirmation: *I open myself to love and to opportunity*

Citrine

Composition: Quartz

Colours: Yellow, from pale to golden, honey or dark orange; always sparkling

Zodiacal sign: Gemini, the heavenly twins (22 May–21 June)

Planet: Mercury

Element: Air

Candle colour: Lemon yellow

Herbs, oils and incenses: Almond, bergamot, lemon verbena, lily of the valley, papyrus

Magickal: Citrine will drive away fear and danger, and protect against negative people, atmospheres and unfriendly ghosts. It also helps us to feel less alone when we are far from home.

Excellent for rituals of prosperity, you can charge a citrine with energies of abundance by burning a yellow candle next to your citrine at dawn. Blow out the candle and send the wish to the lightening sky; keep the crystal in your purse; also for spells for new beginnings, travel and optimism.

Empowerment/affirmation: *I attract abundance into my life*

Clear crystal quartz

Composition: Silicon dioxide, crystalline

Colours: Clear, glassy, sparkles in the sun. Other quartzes are listed separately

Zodiac sign: Leo, the lion (23 July–23 August)

Planet: Sun

Element: Air/fire

Candle colour: Gold

Herbs, oils and incenses: Bay, frankincense, orange, rosemary, St John's wort

Magickal: Clear crystal quartz will absorb any negativity and transform it into rays of healing and positive feelings. It will also act as a channel for angelic powers and spirit guides; use for any empowering or energising purpose or in healing magick.

Empowerment/affirmation: *Each day is a new beginning*

Haematite

Composition: Iron oxide, a very heavy stone

Colours: Brilliant silvery black, steel grey metallic, also dark red or reddish brown, with a red streak

Zodiac sign: Aries, the ram (21 March–20 April)

Planet: Mars

Element: Fire

Candle colour: Silver

Herbs, incenses and oils: Dragon's blood, ginger, juniper, parsley, saffron

Magickal: Known sometimes as the lawyer's stone, haematite will help with all legal wrangles or matters of injustice and is especially good for neighbourhood or boundary disputes. Bury hematite at the corners of your land or in pots at the four corners of your house to keep out all forms of malice, to guard against fire and reflect negativity back to the sender. Haematite is good to counter fears of flying and to prevent jet lag.

Empowerment/affirmation: *I draw my own boundaries*

Jade

Composition: Jadeite and nephrite/silicates

Colours: Transparent to opaque, from pale through to dark green

Zodiac Sign: Pisces, the fish (19 February–20 March)

Planet: Venus/Neptune

Element: Water

Candle colour: All shades of green

Herbs, incenses and oils: Chamomile, lavender, mugwort, patchouli, rose

Magickal: Jade is protective for babies, children and women, especially when pregnant or as new mothers, and young lovers; good for gentle love and fidelity spells; for health and for healing and for animal welfare.

Empowerment/Affirmation: *Life and health flow within me*

Jet

Composition: Organic fossilised wood that has been turned into a dense form of coal and, like amber, is of great antiquity

Colours: Black or occasionally very dark brown, opaque but glassy

Zodiac zign: Capricorn, the goat (22 December–20 January)

Planet: Saturn

Element: Earth

Candle colour: Very dark purple or black

Herbs, incenses and oils: Cedar, cypress, ivy, hyssop, myrrh

Magickal: In home and business, jet will help to stabilise finances and to take practical steps to overcome debt problems; eases grief of all kinds; good for property matters. Place one at home or work facing the outer door to keep negative people and vibes at bay.

Though a mother goddess stone, jet often represents the god energies in witchcraft. Use it in spells for the safe return of loved ones and for leaving the past behind; also for psychic invisibility.

Empowerment/affirmation: *My ancestors live within me and fill me with their wisdom*

Lapis lazula/lazuli

Composition: Silicate of sodium calcium and aluminium, with some sulphur

Colours: Opaque, rich medium to royal blue, violet blue and azure even greenish blue, sometimes mixed blues, with flecks of iron pyrites, fool's gold; the gold looks like stars

Zodiac sign: Libra, the scales (23 September–23 October)

Planet: Jupiter

Element: Air

Candle colour: Royal blue

Herbs, oils and incenses: Black cohosh, lemon, sandalwood, sweetgrass, thyme

Magickal: Protects against the fears and dangers of the night; against betrayal and psychic and emotional vampires; use for star and night magick, for promotion, house moves, for leadership opportunities, for female power rituals (it is the stone of the Egyptian sky mother Nut) and to unite the family.

Empowerment/affirmation: *I speak the truth without hesitation and without fear or to seek favour*

Malachite

Composition: Copper carbonate

Colours: Emerald to grass green with black or occasionally pale green stripes, bands, swirls or marbling; opaque

Zodiacal sign: Aquarius, the water carrier (21 January–18 February)

Planet: Uranus

Element: Earth

Candle colour: Emerald green

Herbs, oils and incenses: Cedar, fennel, parsley, pine, sage

Magickal: The best crystal for cleansing and protecting workspaces against all the pollution and toxicity of noise, from over-bright fluorescent lighting and harmful rays emitted by electrical equipment. Place near a computer or phone to filter out negative communication and potentially harmful energies.

Keep near white goods at home in the kitchen and by televisions and home PCs; also for protection if travelling by air or on congested motorways; and for increased business success.

Empowerment/affirmation: *I will not absorb the negativity of others or my own self-doubt*

Moonstone

Composition: Feldspar

Colours: Translucent white, cream, peach, pink, grey and less commonly blue, all with an iridescent shimmer

Zodiac sign: Cancer, the crab (22 June–22 July)

Planet: Moon

Element: Water

Candle colour: Silver

Herbs, incenses and oils: Jasmine, lemon, mimosa, myrrh, poppy

Magickal: Moonstones protect travellers, especially those who travel at night and on or over the sea. Frequent travellers should keep one in the glove box of a car for safe night driving and as protection against road rage; also potent against psychic attack and all supernatural malevolence.

Use in moon magick and for wish magick and fertility spells. Leave on the bedroom window ledge from the crescent to full moon in an egg shell; prick it with a silver pin on the night of the full moon to signify conception and cover the eggshell and crystal until the next crescent moon. Repeat if necessary.

Empowerment/affirmation: *Wishes can come true if I believe they will*

Moss agate

Composition: Oxide, chalcedony (quartz), smoother and more translucent than tree agate

Colours: Colourless with profusion of deep green tendrils inside of hornblende that may make it appear green, also pale blue or a deeper green with pale blue or white inclusions; translucent to opaque

Zodiac sign: Virgo, the maiden (24 August–22 September)

Planet: Earth

Element: Earth

Candle colour: Moss or olive green

Herbs, incenses and oils: Ferns, fennel, lemon balm, oakmoss, patchouli

Magickal: Called the gardener's crystal, moss agate soothes panics and fears of the unknown; it brings gradual increase in any attracting spells, whether for money, love, health, promotion or happiness; a good offering for nature spirits and essences, especially earth-based ones; also for animal and plant spells.

Empowerment/affirmation: *I draw strength and harmony from the natural world*

Obsidian

Composition: Volcanic glass/magma, formed when lava hardens so fast that no crystalline structures are created.

The kind that is called Apache tears is sufficiently transparent that you can see light through it. Most obsidian is opaque, though shining in the polished form in which we usually buy it. The more opaque the obsidian, the more concentrated its powers

Colours: Black, dark smoky grey as Apache tears, mahogany brown (see also snowflake obsidian)

Zodiac sign: Scorpio, the scorpion (24 October–22 November)

Planet: Pluto/Saturn

Element: Fire/earth

Candle colour: Burgundy

Herbs, oils and incenses: Basil, mint, parsley, pine, sandalwood

Magickal: Very protective both from negative people and from psychic or psychological attack. A traveller's stone, especially by night.

Use seven opaque obsidian arrows pointed outwards and recite what you need to return to or come into your life, then turn them inwards to allow it to flow in; good for employment spells and also to drive away those who would wish you harm.

Use Apache tears in smudging rituals and to carry with you on spiritual journeys to ancient sites, etc. Apache tears is an amulet against sorrow, especially if you have experienced a lot.

Empowerment/affirmation: *Tomorrow really is another day* (Apache tears); *I will not squander energy on useless regrets but focus on what can be achieved* (black obsidian)

Purple fluorite

Composition: Halide/fluorspar

Colours: Purple, lavender, blue (as Blue John from Derbyshire, UK); fluorite is found in green, colourless, its purest form red and orange, transparent or semi-transparent and is usually very gentle in its shades

Zodiac sign: Pisces, the fish (19 February–20 March)

Planet: Neptune

Element: Water

Candle colour: Lilac

Herbs, oils and incenses: Apple blossom, chamomile, clary sage, rosewood, sweet pea

Magickal: Reduces hyperactivity and over-concern with work; will bring peace into the home and workplace and calm pets; use in study spells and whenever you will be questioned whether legally or in a job interview or presentation to stay calm and focused; good for angel, spirit guide and archangel work and any water-inspired rituals.

Empowerment/affirmation: *I need not fear, for my guides and angels watch over me*

Red jasper

Composition: Chalcedony quartz

Colours: From a brick red through orange to a brownish red hue. Red includes poppy jasper and brecciated or mottled jasper. Some poppy jaspers have a bull's eye pattern in grey, brown or yellow. Other jaspers are listed separately

Zodiac sign: Aries, the ram (21.March–20 April)

Planet: Mars

Element: Fire

Candle colour: Red and burgundy

Herbs, incenses and oils: Cedar wood, dragon's blood, fennel, ginger, mint

Magickal: The stone of the warrior, red jasper offers defence against physical threats and from psychic attack; protects against accidents and bad luck and will return any negative energies to the sender.

Use in spells to increase passion; for success, overcoming obstacles and for courage and confidence; also for any fire rituals.

Empowerment/affirmation: *I reach out to and welcome life's experiences*

Rose quartz

Composition: Quartz

Colours: Transparent or sometimes translucent pink, from pale to bright. The paler shades are transparent

Zodiac sign: Taurus, the bull (21 April–21 May)

Planet: Venus

Element: Earth

Candle colour: Pink

Herbs, incenses and oils: Apple blossom, feverfew, geranium, lilac, mugwort, strawberry, vervain, ylang ylang

Magickal: Drives away nightmares and deters bullying, helps to heal and prevent abuse of any kind; use in rituals to attract gentle love and romance or to call a lover when the crystal is empowered by the crescent moon; for family harmony, for reconciliation and to reduce addictive behaviour, especially food disorders associated with a poor self-image; also for fertility magick.

Empowerment/affirmation: *I will be as kind to myself as I am to others*

Rutilated quartz

Composition: Quartz with golden rutiles inside that are sometimes called the hair of Venus

Colours: Clear to occasionally smoky quartz with golden yellow to brownish red needles inside that can form patterns and stars within the crystal

Zodiac sign: Leo, the lion (23 July–23 August)

Planet: The sun

Element: Earth/fire

Candle colour: Gold

Herbs, incenses and oils: Basil, frankincense, garlic, neroli, nutmeg, orange

Magickal: Protects all who live or work in or near town centres; counters prejudice in the workplace; use for spells of prosperity and developing latent creativity and hidden talents, also to bring out new talents later in life and for any spells concerning people from their fifties upwards to find fulfilment and new opportunities.

Empowerment/affirmation: *I can see beyond the superficial to the deeper meaning*

Smoky quartz

Composition: Quartz (also called cairngorm)

Colours: Translucent, tinted smoky brown or dark grey by natural radiation

Zodiac sign: Capricorn, the goat (22 December–20 January)

Planet: Saturn

Element: Earth

Candle colour: Indigo

Herbs incense and oils: Carnation, ivy, mimosa, mullein, patchouli

Magickal: Protects the home and work premises. It guards vehicles from theft, mechanical breakdown and the driver against road rage; use it for channelling the wisdom of earth spirits at old sites; also in spells when things seem bad to find the light at the end of the tunnel; hold it up to sunlight or candlelight and call for better times.

Empowerment/affirmation: *There is always light beyond the darkness*

Snowflake obsidian

Composition: Volcanic glass/magma in which a few grey feldspar inclusions appear as the obsidian begin to crystallise

Colours: Black with white spots or small white flower shapes; opaque

Zodiac sign: Capricorn, the goat (22 December–20 January)

Planet: Saturn

Element: Earth

Candle colour: White

Herbs, oils and incenses: Hyacinth, lemongrass, lemon verbena, sweet tobacco, yarrow

Magickal: Protects against guilt at having personal negative emotions and allows you to express these creatively and instigate positive change; good in animal healing spells, especially for horses; add to a charm bag to mix protection with luck; helps you to discover the truth about a person or situation; also for closing doors on the past.

Empowerment/affirmation: *I walk towards my future with confidence*

Sodalite

Composition: Lattice silicate

Colours: Deep blue with white flecks of calcite that can sometimes be quite large. The whiter the stone, the more active its properties. Occasionally indigo

Zodiac sign: Cancer, the crab (22 June–22 July)

Planet: Moon

Element: Air

Candle colour: Indigo

Herbs, incenses and oils: Hyssop, lavender, mugwort, rosewood, violet

Magickal: Overcomes fears of flying and protects all travellers; good for justice spells or house moves that involve relocation, or after a loss; also for any matters and rituals concerning older women or wise women. Amethyst has similar properties for older women's magick.

Empowerment/affirmation: *The best years are yet to come and I welcome their wisdom*

Tiger's eye

Composition: Oxide, quartz, brown and gold striped

Colours: Honey or golden brown bands; chatoyant, reflecting light in wavy bands so the crystal gleams translucently

Zodiac sign: Leo, the lion (23 July–23 August)

Planet: The sun

Element: Earth/fire

Candle colour: Gold

Herbs, oils and incenses: Bay, blessed thistle, neroli, spearmint, sunflower

Magickal: Traditionally protective against the evil eye or in the modern world against verbal or psychic attack or emotional blackmail by someone in a position of power; a stone of courage, it attracts prosperity in spells or charm bags and encourages a positive response to and by officialdom; keep a tiger's eye in a money pot to which you add a coin every day. Keep the pot in a warm place to bring a steady inflow of resources into your life.

Empowerment/affirmation: *My efforts will bring results if I persist*

Tree agate

Composition: Oxide, quartz; quite coarse and knobbly even when polished

Colours: White with green, tree-like inclusions or veins (see also moss agate which is very similar in mineralogical terms but looks and feels different); opaque

Zodiac sign: Gemini, the heavenly twins (22 May–21 June)

Planet: Mercury/earth

Element: Earth/air

Candle colour: White

Herbs, oils and incenses: Apple, cedar, cherry blossom, peach, pine

Magickal: Protective for air and car travel and for preserving family links; use in spells for increasing influence through networking and the gradual expansion of business; for all family spells and for tree magick of all kinds.

Empowerment/affirmation: *I make connection with others who share my path*

Turquoise

Composition: Phosphate of aluminium with copper and traces of iron

Colours: Opaque, light blue/blue-green

Zodiac sign: Sagittarius, the archer (23 November–21 December)

Planet: Jupiter

Element: Air/fire

Candle colour: Bright blue

Herbs, incenses and oils: Carnation, honeysuckle, lemon, lemongrass, mistletoe, sandalwood

Magickal: Protects animals and birds from being stolen or straying; stops horses and people from stumbling; keeps travellers safe; guards against financial, professional or personal misfortune and malpractice by others.

Use for all spells for power, leadership, earthly success, connection with ancient wisdom; for travel, to discover truth and to overcome any organisation or individual who holds power over you and is seeking to silence or intimidate you.

Empowerment/affirmation: *I do not fear power in myself or others*

Yellow jasper

Composition: Chalcedony quartz

Colours: Single-coloured yellow, often mustard or burnished colour through to sandy beige, brown, also mottled; opaque

Zodiac sign: Capricorn, the goat (22 December–20 January)

Planet: Saturn/earth

Element: Earth

Candle colour: Sandy yellow

Herbs, oils and incenses: Chamomile, fennel, hops, Melissa (lemon balm), patchouli

Magickal: Protects against spiteful neighbours and work colleagues. Place near your workspace to stop others gossiping in your absence; good for all earth magick and as an offering to earth spirits and guardians; use also in spells for any home or property matters, to learn or improve practical skills and to rebuild after a setback.

Empowerment/affirmation: *I am accountable to myself and my own principles*

Birth crystals

Empower your own birth crystal on your birthday and at significant periods during your life.

There are a number of different stones given in different traditions to correspond with the zodiac signs. The discrepancies come because over thousands of years and in different cultures the month stones, as they were then called, varied both according to those most available in different parts of the world and because of spiritual and religious associations. Zodiacal birthstones as such were not introduced until the early 18th century.

The lists I give combine several of the traditions where there is agreement, as well as more modern associations made by jewellers.

I have listed a crystal and the more traditional precious stone for each sign, as you may decide to buy yourself your birth gem to wear as jewellery or ask for one for a birthday, Christmas or anniversary.

Aries, the ram (21 March–20 April)
Crystal: Clear crystal quartz
Precious stone: Diamond

Taurus, the bull (21 April–21 May)
Crystal: Rose quartz
Precious stone: Emerald

Gemini, the heavenly twins (22 May–21 June)
Crystal: Citrine
Precious stone: White sapphire

Cancer, the crab (22 June–22 July)
Crystal: Moonstone
Precious stone: Pearl

Leo, the lion (23 July–23 August)
Crystal: Carnelian
Precious stone: Golden topaz

Virgo, the maiden (24 August–22 September)
Crystal: Jade
Precious stone: Blue sapphire

Libra, the scales (23 September–23 October)
Crystal: Lapis lazuli
Precious stone: Opal

Scorpio, the scorpion (24 October–22 November)

Crystal: Obsidian

Precious stone: Black pearl

Sagittarius, the archer (23 November–21 December)

Crystal: Turquoise

Precious stone: Blue zircon

Capricorn, the goat (22 December–20 January)

Crystal: Garnet

Precious stone: Ruby

Aquarius, the water carrier (21 January–18 February)

Crystal: Amethyst

Precious stone: Clear spinel

Pisces, the fish (19 February–20 March)

Crystal: Heliotrope

Precious stone: Golden beryl

PART 7

MAGICK OF THE SPHERES AND SEASONS

INTRODUCTION

We are all sanctified by the power of the earth and the skies and can draw strength from the turning of the cosmic wheels of sun and moon and also the seasonal cycles of the earth.

Many of us, myself included, sometimes feel that it is the hamster wheel we ride or the Big Wheel at a funfair that whirls us round too fast and then deposits us on the ground with a bump.

Each day turns into night, the moon revolves through the skies on her monthly course. The sun moves through the year and we also, willingly or unwillingly, aware or unnoticing, travel through youth to maturity and hopefully wisdom, like the moon – and then rely on our particular belief system to understand rebirth or immortality.

Rituals to tune into the ebbs and flows and rhythms of the natural world, to celebrate the sowing of seeds and the harvest, are relevant even in the centre of a city. Tangible symbols can be empowered by words and actions whether the burning of last year's corn dolly on a country bonfire or a child depositing a can of baked beans on the harvest table. Ritual, the repetition of words and actions to mark an event or to give and receive energy in mutual exchange, helps us to take advantage of the high points of moon, sun and seasons and to relax with the inevitable downturn rather than struggling to flow against the psychic and psychological tide.

This section contains a great deal of traditional knowledge and ritual, but also applies the concepts to the everyday world where most of us live much of our lives. Whether you have five minutes or five hours, a small table or a whole beach or forest to work in, the natural cycles empower, harmonise and protect. You can make every day sacred by becoming aware of the movement of the sun and moon through the skies and also change gear smoothly as you dance or spiral, rather than crank or crash, through the seasons.

SUN MAGICK

The sun was one of the earliest deities to be worshipped, along with the moon, because of its life- and light-giving powers. Its apparent disappearance at night and its lowness in the sky and the shortness of daylight led to rituals to ask the blessings of this mighty deity without whom there was nothing.

This reverence for the power of the sun existed both in hot lands and those where return of the sun after the long winter was long awaited and welcomed. Indeed, among hunting societies whose way of life has remained unchanged through the years, like Baiwe in Lapland, the sun mother still forms a focus for ceremony and invocation for warmth and fertility. She is invoked by lost hunters to find the way home.

In societies where the changing agricultural seasons became central to a stable and settled way of life and people lived close to the land, for example the Celts, sun mothers also appear. Aine was one of the sun mothers of the Celts, linked with fertility and healing, she was the goddess of cattle and corn, and the cycles of the solar and lunar year, for she was also a moon goddess. The top of her sacred hill in Munster, in Ireland, like that of the hill of her sun sister Grainne in Leinster, was the scene for torchlight processions and bonfires at the summer solstice and the first grain harvest at the beginning of August. These ceremonies have persisted as folk customs.

Sun gods tend to be more prevalent in warrior societies like the Aztecs or more structured societies such as in Ancient Greece and Rome. In this chapter I have described both traditional sun magick and a modern way of celebrating the passage of each day that fits easily with city life and the demands of the working day.

The sun and creation

Sun deities of both sexes were frequently regarded as creators or closely involved in creation, associated with creators or the sun itself that was set in the sky at the dawn of creation.

According to Genesis I, God said, 'Let there be light' on the second day of Creation and then on the fourth he created the 'sun to rule the day and the moon to rule the night'.

According to a generic Australian Aborigine creation myth, the sun mother was sent to earth to awaken all the spirits or potentials for life. As her rays illuminated their dark sleeping places they emerged into the sunshine and were shaped by her.

The sun mother then created two children, the god of the morning star and his sister the moon who themselves had two children who became the ancestors of all humans.

In the Navajo tradition, First Man and First Woman made the sun from a huge disk of turquoise and set it in the sky to bring light to the world. They also formed the moon from a glistening white crystal (see page 424 for more details).

According to Chinese legend, there were once ten suns. The sun mother Heng O took her children the ten suns each morning to the eastern Valley of Light and set nine of the suns in a huge mulberry tree. The chosen sun child would travel across the sky to the mountain Yen-Tzu in the west. But one day the ten suns decided it would be fun all to be in the sky at the same time. Because this made the earth too hot, their father sent his archer to frighten them. By mistake nine were shot with magickal arrows and so there is only one, who mourns for his brothers at the times of the eclipse.

Sun mothers

As the sun mother tradition is the oldest I will describe that first. Sun mothers tend to be remarkably homely and involved in their creation.

Sun mothers appear in hot and cold lands alike. In another Australian Aboriginal legend from the Wotjobaluk tribe of Victoria, Australia, the sun mother carries a bark torch through the skies each day and returns to the west each evening to feed her waiting child.

In Lapland among the Sami reindeer hunters, because the warmth comes so late in the year, sun-rings made of grass are woven in honour of the sun mother Baiwe. On the summer solstice, to welcome the return of the light, butter is smeared on doorposts to attract abundance to the home. The mother of the home creates a sun porridge, rich in dairy foods. After this has been eaten, the father asks Baiwe's bright sunlight to endow the reindeer with plentiful milk and the people with rich meat.

In the folk customs of Lithuania, Estonia and Latvia, the solar goddess Saule, queen of the heavens and earth, dressed and crowned with gold, is still, in folk tradition, said to drive her shining chariot across the skies and to walk among the people to bless the growing fields. In winter, on the feast of St Lucia, the saint and once the goddess of the returning  light on 13 December, Saule pauses to dance with her daughters, the planets, in defiance of the darker days. Throughout the year, Saule scolds her lazy husband Menulis the moon, who will not keep up with her and disappears for three days each month.

In the Basque region of northern Spain, the sun is still revered in folklore as grandmother sun. Her worship has been transferred to the Virgin Mary who is associated with mother Mari, the storm goddess in whose wise bosom grandmother sun sleeps at night.

The Japanese sun goddess Amaterasu Omigami was the chief deity or kami. She is compassionate and wise. However, because Amaterasu is all-seeing and all-knowing, occasionally the behaviour of humanity makes her temporarily despair and return to her sun cave, causing an eclipse.

Sun gods

Solar gods tend to be less personal that the sun mothers and sit above the human world or gallop across it in their gleaming chariots or, in the case of the Ancient Egyptian Ra, sail across the skies in a sun boat.

Helios was the Ancient Greek sun god, called Sol by the Romans. He was regarded as an embodiment of the sun and wore a golden helmet from which the sun's rays radiated. He ascended the heavens in a chariot drawn by winged snow-white horses to give light and in the evening descended into the ocean. Homer wrote:

Drawn in his swift chariot, he sheds light on gods and men alike; the formidable flash of his eyes pierces his golden helmet, sparkling rays glint from his breast and his brilliant helmet gives forth a dazzling splendour. His body is draped in shining gauze, whipped by the wind. His 350 cattle, the white and golden or red clouds, trail after him as gold and red clouds at sunrise and sunset.

His successor, who existed alongside Helios, was the young golden god Apollo, most handsome of the gods and the ideal representation of a young emperor, cultured, wise but also warlike.

Apollo, twin brother of Artemis, the moon goddess, made the fruits of the earth ripen and at Delos and Delphi where he slew Python, symbol of the old mother goddess religion, the first crops were dedicated to him. The Ancient Greeks rededicated the shrine and oracular powers at Delphi to Apollo who became god of prophecy as well as music, poetry, archery, healing and divination. This gave the sun a far wider role than Helios, being the source of culture and intellectual and spiritual power.

But the most intriguing sun god of the Roman Empire was Mithras, called Sol Invicta, the unconquered or unconquerable sun. His worship originated in Persia almost 4,000 years ago and spread throughout much of the known world, especially with the Roman armies who regarded him as their personal deity. The sun itself was called the eye of Mithras and in legend he was born around the midwinter solstice in a cave (see page 462). His deeper worship involved secret ceremonies of dedication and he became one of the most significant deities of the mystery religions.

The sun gods of the Middle East

Shamash was the principal sun god of the Assyrians and Babylonians and the great judge of the universe, because his light penetrated into every corner.

In Ancient Egypt the sun was the ordered, stable force necessary to counter the chaotic forces of water as represented by the Nile flood that would otherwise overwhelm civilisation and wash the seeds away. Ra the Egyptian sun god, as this icon of stability and the power represented in the pharaoh to maintain order, was the ultimate solar deity who brought light out of the primal darkness.

Some myths claim Ra was the first deity to be worshipped and that his origins are lost in prehistory. In some myths the first shining cosmic egg, floating on the primal waters of Nu, contained Ra, and his birth set time in motion and caused dry land to emerge form the waters of Nu.

Over the centuries he became linked with other major creator deities, Ptah and as Atum Ra and Amun Ra. Over time too his role as father of the gods became undisputed and he was said to have created himself, a fact that did not stop him entering the womb of the sky mother who in earliest myth may have been a form of the original Nu that existed at the beginning of time.

Ra was portrayed as the sun at its full power and is depicted by the symbol of the sun and also in his solar boat. Ra is shown variously as a man or a hawk-headed man, crowned with the sun disk and sacred Uraeus serpent with his usa, a dog-headed, forked rod of power.

The Maya, the Aztecs and the sun

Because Central America has only two seasons, wet and dry, the sun is as vital as in the Middle East to ensure growth of the corn.

To the Maya, Yucatan, the sun god was known as Kinich Ahau, lord of the face of the sun. He was linked with the fire bird or Arara and was also called Kinich-Kakmo (sun bird).

The sun god ruled the north. Myths recount that the Maya came from the sun. Because the sun rose in the east, so the hero gods came from the ascending light, bringing culture, law and art, writing, architecture, mathematics, ceremonies and astronomy.

Kinich Ahau took the form of a macaw by day and a jaguar at night to fight the fierce nightly battle in the underworld, akin to Ra's nightly battle with the chaos serpent Apep.

Kinich Ahau is also linked to Toltec and Aztec solar mythology and in these cultures the sun god was instrumental in the creation and destruction of the five different worlds, their suns and all who lived within them.

According to the Toltec and the Aztec myths the first four suns were each made of a single element, earth, air, fire and water. Because of this they were not powerful enough to enlighten the people and so they and their worlds were destroyed. This total destruction occurred because life could not exist without the sun. The fifth sun was created from all the elements mixed together and was given life by the sacrifice of the god Nanquatzin or Nanauzin who leaped into the fires of the fifth sun as it was being created. He became the sun and as a result some quite nasty sacrifices were required of humans in the Aztec tradition to honour this original sacrifice and ensure the sun would continue to shine (very different from the nurturing sun mothers of other lands).

The eagle symbolised the sun by day. During the night when it disappeared from view and crossed the Mictlan, the underworld, it became the jaguar, the largest and most feared creature who lost part of his flesh in the nocturnal battle.

In the Aztec world too, those who died what was considered a good death in battle sacrifice or childbirth accompanied the sun on his daily passage.

As among the Maya, the macaw was also significant to the Aztecs as a solar power creature. Twin macaws symbolised the sun's passage, a red one the sun in the sky in the day and a black the unseen sun crossing the underworld.

As god of the solar light, Nanquatzin made the fruits of the earth ripen.

Drawing down the power of the sun goddess or god

In witchcraft there is a popular ceremony known as 'drawing down the moon' in which the high priestess takes into herself the power and wisdom of the moon. In some traditions the power of the sun is called down by the high priest at the beginning of the esbat or monthly celebration and on other major seasonal ceremonies into the priestess. There is another ceremony where sun power is called down into the priest by the high priestess or into herself, especially at seasonal solar change points such as the equinoxes or solstices (see Seasonal magick, pages 438–41).

However, in both cases, whether you work alone as a witch or in a coven or practise less formally, you can at any time of the day or year call into yourself the strength, fertility and joy of your chosen sun god or goddess. See pages 410–11 for personal sun invocations.

At dawn: Draw down the powers of the rising sun for a new beginning or for a fresh approach or for optimism or inspiration

At noon: Plug into the inrush of pure life and light force for a make or break situation or to spur yourself on if you are tired or dispirited – or for sudden illumination

At dusk: The sun consoles, heals and harmonises disparate demands or people and draws gentle abundance to you

Drawing down the visible sun

In Ancient Egypt, there was a period when the sun, called the Aten, was worshipped as the only deity. The Aten was depicted not through statues but as an image of the solar disk with rays emanating from it that ended as ankhs, the key-like symbol of immortality.

The sun's patron on earth was King Akhenaton (the glory of the Aten), who changed his name from the family name Amenhotep IV (meaning Amun or Amen is at peace). He ruled for a relatively short time, 1,352–1,336 BCE, 16 years, yet his actions gained him the name of the heretic king and his name was removed from many of his monuments after his death.

His message was that without the sun there is no life and that we all receive our own inner radiance from the undifferentiated source. He also left the legacy of a wonderful 'Hymn to the Great Aten', traditionally recited each morning facing the sunrise. It can be very empowering to create your very own chant of praise to the Sun as the life giver and sustainer.

Whether you get or choose the opportunity to draw down the sun in an Ancient Egyptian temple or work in your local park, the garden or on the beach in brilliant sunshine or as the sun rises blood red over a snowy landscape, the first step is to write your own solar chant of power.

You may wish to create a poem in your Book of Shadows to recite at special sun drawing-down ceremonies or when you incorporate this into a solar festival celebration. For inspiration there are many sites on the Internet that include the 'Hymn to the Aten'.

Alternatively, you can speak spontaneously on different occasions when you draw down the sun. Record your words as the basis for different sun chants, at dawn, noon, sunset and midnight (see below for channelling the sun at midnight). Chants may also vary according to the solar deity focus you prefer or your need for specific strengths in your life. The Ancient Egyptians believed that by speaking the words to the sun we became the sun spiritually and in power terms.

Incorporate into the chant any deity names that seem appropriate or the sun itself as the focus. Express what you love about the sun, based on your own life experiences. List sun images, animals and birds that you associate with the sun, and herbs and flowers that seem appropriate. See pages 405–7 for some suggestions. State also why you need the sun in your life and all the positive attributes it has for growth, warmth and fertility.

Beginning the sun ceremony

Choose the time of day that is best for your purpose. Clear conditions are ideal though of course you cannot look directly at the sun at any time. Eventually you will be able to visualise the orb. Though Sunday is the special day of the sun, you can choose any day that feels right.

Decide on the kind of sun energy you want to focus on for this particular ceremony, a loving sun mother to bring joy, abundance and a sense of well-being, an aesthetic sun god for spiritual and mental clarity and focused creativity or a warrior to empower you and give you the courage of purpose. You don't have to pick a god or goddess from a particular culture but can picture your own or use the sun itself as your focus of light, life and health-bringing powers. You can adapt your chant accordingly or use one that refers to these attributes.

* Occasionally, just draw down the sun or recite your chant as a way of giving thanks for life or to send the sun to those who need it spiritually or in actuality.
* Find your sun place where at particular times of year the sun casts radiating beams or dancing rays. You may have to wait for just the right conditions for your first sun encounter.
* Mediterranean and oceanic tropical sunrises can be spectacular and can be appreciated while on holiday. Personally, I still recall the pelicans flying in a line across the sun at Marina del Rey near Los Angeles at sunset. Though I was with an organised party on a break from my work, those few minutes of solitary sunset connection provided a very deep healing experience.
* It may help to hold a clear crystal sphere or rainbow quartz (any with fractures inside will reflect rainbows).
* Set on the ground, on a rock or on your outdoor altar a dish of any gold jewellery, golden crystals, gold-coloured coins, flowers and fruit to be empowered by the sun.
* Next to it place a glass bowl of sparkling mineral water. Afterwards the water will be charged with the power of the sun and you can use it in baths or to splash on pulse points.
* Raise your arms high and wide, palms uppermost and set your feet quite widely apart.

* Speak your words aloud, unless there are too many people around.
* Then wait until you feel the light beginning to enter you.
* Now move your arms so they are extended horizontally either side of your body with your palms still uppermost to absorb the light. At this point breathe in the golden light through your nose, slowly and gently, and exhale the darkness through your mouth.
* As you continue breathing, visualise the light spreading to every part of your body from your toes right to the tips of you fingers and the crown of your head.
* Allow the light to extend now beyond your body, forming a shield of golden rays all around you and above you so that you are enclosed in a shimmering sphere.
* Gradually move your arms and hands so they cross at about waist height. Repeat this in succession and in the rhythm that is right for you, raising, extending and enfolding yourself with light as if you were splashing it over yourself.
* When you feel that you are completely filled with the radiance, cease to breathe in gold deliberately. Stand with your arms still raised, close together in front of your body with elbows bent.
* Say slowly and with confidence three times:

I am filled with the light of the sun. I am pure light.

* Allow the energies to flow between your body, the pool of light and the golden sphere.
* Kneel or reach down and splash a few drops of the newly made sun water on your hairline, brow, throat and wrist pulse points, saying:

The sun enters my spirit, enriches my mind, transforms my words and warms my heart.
Blessings be.

* Listen and you may hear a message from the sun mother or father.
* If you face opposition or spite, shake your fingers and see golden sparks emanate from your fingertips like miniature sun rays.
* Extend your arms in a circle over your head so you create a psychic protective force field of sparks all around you that will gently repel any malice.
* Make a sign, perhaps touching the place between and just above your eyes that is regarded as the third psychic eye, the brow chakra, a spiritual energy point. Or you may prefer to touch your heart or make a circle in the palm of your hand.
* As you do so, say:

When I touch my brow/heart, I will invoke the power of the sun within me.

* Look upwards and picture the sun mother or father or a whirling, spinning solar disc and gradually allow the radiance and the goddess to fade, knowing that you can recall the sun into your life any time you are in need, just by making your psychic sign.
* Spend the rest of the day or at least part of it in the sunshine and the next day do something amazingly brave or dynamic to make the most of your new power.

Drawing down the sun at midnight

Drawing down the sun at midnight is a different technique and is best practised after you are familiar with drawing down the visible sun.

Should you live or be holidaying in regions where it is light at midnight, this can be a fabulous natural phenomenon and you can use the method described earlier.

But even in the depths of winter anywhere in the world you can draw down the power of the midnight sun.

It is effective for any powerful healing or banishment, to resist bullies or to connect you with the power of nature and to receive her wisdom on a deep inner level. Use the sun at midnight also for times when you have to wait for your talents to be recognised or if you need to keep a low profile or secrets and so must temporarily step into the background.

During the night, the sun is shining on the other side of the world, or as the ancients believed travelling through the womb of the earth or sky mother, or battling the forces of darkness.

You can use this method to draw power for change and renewal on a partial or, if you are lucky enough, total solar eclipse.

* Create for yourself a special 'sun at midnight' chant, calling on the dark sun to fill you with inner fire and light. Focus on the time spent travelling through the womb of the mother and on fighting your own particular enemies, whether a person who is unkind but you feel unable to leave or addictions or crippling worries or chronic illness.
* Stand outdoors in total darkness. If your garden has streetlights shining into it, focus on a dark corner.
* Call the sun and picture a dark sphere ahead of you in the sky, just lighter than the dark sky.
* Stand with your hands by your side. This time breathe in darkness and imagine pure light leaving your body and strengthening the visualised sun.
* As you continue, see as with an eclipse, the solar rays beginning to shoot from behind the dark sphere and gradually spreading to cover the sphere, which becomes lighter and lighter.
* Now raise your arms and visualise sparks of fire emanating from your fingertips. Chant:

I am pure light, I am radiance. I am the dark sun no more. The sun at midnight is as brilliant as noon. Light surround and enfold me. Darkness is no more.

* This is quite tiring and you may hold the vision only for half a minute at first.
* Relax and sit down, allowing the courage of the night-time battle won to fill you with quiet confidence for the next day.
* If you wish, light an incense stick in frankincense or chamomile, fragrances of the sun, and let any pain, sorrow or fear rise to the skies.
* Occasionally carry out this ceremony just before dawn so that the natural light will follow soon after your vision. This is especially wonderful when seen over the sea.

* In time the sun at midnight will have messages for you. If you are not too tired, light a candle and turn over tarot cards, cast runes or gaze deep into a crystal sphere held over the light, for this is the time when even the least confident of us can receive prophecy.

Living by the sun, making every day sacred

The Ancient Egyptian priests and priestesses had four daily ceremonies to make offerings and to purify the altar and the deity statue. These were held at the four day/night tides, dawn, noon, sunset/dusk and midnight.

Occasionally, on holiday or during a free weekend, mark the four solar change points of the day and night with a mini ritual or celebration. I have suggested appropriate herbs, etc. for each of the four marker times.

If you are in the countryside, try to live by natural light. When it gets dark, burn a candle and sleep when it is burned through or sit in the darkness.

In this way you will become more aware of the light ebbs and flows, unaffected by 24-hour lighting. Your body and mind will move into harmony with the external light patterns. A few days of this will generally cure insomnia.

The times of dawn and dusk vary according to the time of year and so except at the equinoxes (equal day and equal night) the time frame between the four periods won't be regular. Experiment with your four rituals within 24 hours at different times of the year. Note down in your Book of Shadows the different feelings the light patterns create according to whether dawn and dusk are early or late in the day.

Around midsummer, dawn is very early and dusk is very late. The days of greatest time contrasts are the midwinter solstice (around 21 December in the northern hemisphere) and the midsummer solstice (around 21 June in the northern hemisphere). (These dates move round by six months in the southern hemisphere.) The solstices plus the equinoxes (around 21 March and 22 September) are very potent as a framework for solar day and night rituals within a 24-hour period. You could divide your main equinox or solstice rite into four separate parts, as many Druids do on the summer solstice and its eve.

Even if you can't get the actual solstice or equinox days off work, the nearest weekend will have similar energies and the effect is out of all proportion to the effort, even if you do spend celebrate them round your outdoor altar at home rather than at a sacred site or shore.

Everyday solar magick

Such ceremonies are a vital source of solar power. However, if you live by the sun in your daily life you can make every day count, even work days or otherwise unremarkable ones. Too often with a frantic schedule, whole weeks can pass unnoticed and we can feel we are not connecting with life on a meaningful level. By focusing on the four sun periods of the day (dawn, noon, dusk or sunset and midnight) it is possible to make every day sacred.

If you spend much of the day at home, for example with young children or because you are unwell, the four daily change points offer a clear structure and help you to regulate your own energy flows to avoid exhaustion.

Of course you may not want to stay up until midnight or rise with the dawn – this is unrealistic given teething children, late-night chores, commuting or the needs of a partner for sleep. Therefore on ordinary days substitute the time you get up as dawn. (Night workers can greet the dawn as they go home or reverse the process and begin the dawn activities at dusk, that is when they start their working day. Neither is ideal, but with lots of visualisation, it is possible to create a pattern that is right for you.)

Below I give a shortened version of the associations for each of the four times of day, though these are of course identical to the associations of the elements (see page 31 for full list). Use these to weave your own spells.

As the four solar points (dawn, noon, dusk and midnight) correspond with the four directions on the magick circle, over the day you will open all four quarters. When you are ready for sleep, close the energies or sleep protected within the created psychic circle.

Some people create a chant for each time period. However, you may prefer to be spontaneous to meet the differing daily challenges.

Decide in advance who is/are to be the guardian(s) of your four directions each day – the four archangels, particular deities associated with each direction (see pages 31–37), plus any you have added.

Would a particular nature essence be of help, a sturdy practical dwarf in the north or maybe a giant to defend you? Perhaps there is someone in your personal world, living or an ancestor, who represents the qualities you seek as you start or end the day. Often you will just call them guardians or wise ones of the east, etc.

Of course you won't be able or want to carry out mini rituals every day, but when you do have time try at least to hold each of the crystals at its appropriate time, face that direction, connect with what is going on outside the window (and go out if at all possible, even for a minute or two) and focus on the different energies. I have found this takes less time than making and drinking an extra cup of coffee that I don't really want – and is far less hyping.

I have also listed for each day tide the kind of magick you can carry out in general spellcasting using the particular time of the day as additional power.

Dawn

This is the beginning of the day (either dawn or when you wake) and a chance to change things if you want to, if only by your own new approach. It is also the time to ask for energy and health. Dawn marks the start of the day that you hoped for or worried about (maybe all night). Now you can empower yourself to tackle opportunity or difficulty and win through.

Direction: East

Ruling season: Spring

Element: Earth

Colours: Yellow and grey

Archangel: Raphael, the healer archangel and travellers' guide

Crystals: Amethyst, clear crystal quartz, citrine, diamond, lapis lazuli, sodalite,

sugilite, sapphire, turquoise

Herbs and incenses: Acacia, agrimony, almond, anise, benzoin, bergamot, borage, caraway, clover, dill, elecampane, eyebright, fennel, fenugreek, lavender, lemongrass, lemon verbena, lily of the valley, linden, marjoram, meadowsweet, mulberry, nag champa, palm, papyrus flower, peppermint, sage, star anise

Sacred substance: Incense

Qualities: Logic, clear focus, an enquiring and analytical mind, the ability to communicate clearly, concentration, versatility, adaptability, quest for truth, commercial and technological acumen, healing powers through channelling higher energies

General foci you can use dawn magick for in spellcasting:
* Travel
* Initiating a project or new beginnings in any aspect of your life
* Creating hope
* Stirring up positive energies at a time when life is going badly
* Improving health
* Improving career prospects
* Bringing good fortune
* Improving financial matters
* Bringing new love and trust

Working with dawn energies

What wakes me? The mobile phone alarm, the cat, the baby? Nothing and then there is an ensuing panic? How would I like to wake and how can I make that happen more often?

What is of significance when I do wake? Getting up in a frantic dash to get everyone out of the house, moments gazing at a glorious sunrise, birds singing, noticing new growth in the garden or on an indoor plant, icicles on the window, silvery mist? How, given the constraints of real life, can it become more harmonious for me and others?

Greeting the dawn

* Get up five or ten minutes earlier and go out into the garden, on the balcony or to your outdoor altar, warmly wrapped if it is cold. If you need to greet the dawn in your indoor place, use a fruit incense stick (there is no time for charcoal).
* Notice the light quality and what you feel. Suspend the worries of the day for a moment. They will wait for you or better still they may go away.
* Is the moon still in the sky? If so, face in that direction and bid it farewell.
* Greet the dawn even if the day ahead is not that promising.
* Take an incense stick if you have time and/or an air crystal.

- Facing east or the direction of the rising sun, welcome your chosen guardians of the east into your day by lighting incense or raising your crystal in your cupped hands.
- If it is still dark when you get up in the winter, and whether you are working indoors or out, light a candle and then the incense from the candle. You can use a natural or white colour that you can then continue to use for the other day markers.
- Blow the candle out after each mini ritual, and by midnight when you light it, the candle will be packed with energies. It may last two or three days.
- Having greeted just the east, cast a complete circle clockwise, large enough to enclose you and your altar if you are working from it by stepping it east to east, barefoot if possible.
- For day-time solar magick start in the dawn or east position even if you usually cast circles from the north. Carry your crystal and your incense if you lit it (the crystal in the power hand) as you make the circle.
- When you return to the east, face the light and state any new beginnings and new opportunities of the day or maybe a new approach you need. Also state one purpose for your day ahead, however small.
- Leave any incense to burn as you get ready, but take your crystal with you as a reminder.

Noon

When you get to work, set your dawn crystal in approximate east in your workspace. If you work right through lunch generally, try to give yourself at least 15 minutes out of the workspace and preferably outdoors. This can either be at noon precisely or when you take your lunch break.

This is the time of full power, confidence and creativity, a time to draw energy to you to launch yourself into the afternoon.

Direction: South

Ruling season: Summer

Element: Fire

Colours: Red and orange; gold

Archangel: Michael, archangel of the sun and light and the warrior angel

Crystals: Amber, bloodstone, boji stones, carnelian, garnet, hematite, lava, mookaite, iron pyrites, obsidian, red jasper, ruby, sunstone, topaz

Herbs and incenses: Allspice, angelica, basil, bay, cactus, carnation, cedarwood, chamomile, chrysanthemum, cinnamon, cloves, copal, dragon's blood, frankincense, galangal, garlic, juniper, lime, marigold, nutmeg, olive, orange, pennyroyal, rosemary, snapdragon, sunflower, tangerine, thistle holy, thistle milk, witch hazel

Sacred substance: Candle

Qualities: Fertility in all aspects of life, creativity, light-bringing power, passion, joy, initiating, transformation, courage, mysticism, clairvoyance, prophecy (also a power of midnight)

General foci you can use noon magick for in spellcasting:
* Creating a sudden burst of power, confidence, strength or passion
* Bringing a fast infusion of money, promotion or career success or for a successful house move
* Sending absent healing for serious or acute conditions

Working with noon energies

What have you achieved this morning? Was it as you hoped? Do you feel powerful, exhausted or frustrated? This is another change point and so time to change your own mood and re-focus if you can't change that of others.

Magick is all about making positive change within ourselves and so being able to influence others and events. What is your aim for the rest of the day? How can it be achieved? Who can help and who might hinder?

You can make lunch part of the ritual by having it immediately afterwards or, if your blood sugar is low, have it before so that you are in the mood for a mini spell.
* If you are at home, you can light a candle outdoors if possible, but at work use a fire crystal such as amber, carnelian or red jasper.
* Face south and greet your chosen guardians of that direction by lighting the candle and/or holding your noon crystal in cupped hands. If using a candle this would be the same one you burned at dawn if it was dark.
* Fill a small bowl or cup with sun water (see page 127 for making it). You can carry it in a mineral water bottle or substitute sparkling mineral water.
* Still facing south, dip your crystal in the water and anoint the centre of your hair line, saying:

Above me the light.

* Now dip the crystal in the water again and anoint the centre of your brow, saying:

Within me the radiance.

* Dip it a third time and anoint the centre of your throat round your Adam's apple, saying:

That I may speak wisely.

* Dip your crystal a final time into the sun water and anoint first your left and then your right wrist pulse points, saying:

The truth in my heart.

* You have now opened your four higher chakras or energy centres to full power but also so that you don't have to compromise your natural integrity and kindness.
* Walk round a complete circle clockwise beginning in the south while carrying

your noon crystal. If there are lots of people around, you can visualise doing this as you stand in the centre facing south.

* When you return to the south, face the light and state what power you need for the afternoon ahead and any creative opportunities there may be – or the need for courage and confidence.
* If you lit a candle, blow it out and reaffirm your own confidence and creativity.
* Set your crystal in the south position on your workspace. You now have completed half the crystal circle.
* Try to spend a few minutes in the fresh air before getting on with the day.

Dusk

'Never let the sun go down on anger,' my late mother used to say. This is the daily message of dusk.

What is gained and what is lost all merge into the approaching darkness and we can drain away resentment, regrets and guilt for what was not completed, words spoken unwisely and opportunities missed so they don't come home with us to sour the evening.

You may go home long after dusk has fallen in winter or before dusk in summer, but the energies represented are the same – of balance. Even if you work from home or are at home with children, marking this point will help you to relax into any unavoidable unfinished work or chores and acts as a mini recharging of your batteries. Of course, it is not easy if you have to collect hungry children from an after-school activity or face a long commute followed by the need to prepare a meal as soon as you get home.

Nevertheless, try to make five or ten minutes, if necessary after you have given the family some food and settled them down or before leaving work as you are tidying up, especially if the workplace is quiet. If you are doing your dusk ritual at home or on the way home (maybe you cross a park), take the first two crystals with you. These five minutes really do improve the quality of the time you then spend at home or with the family, though I know all too well how hard it is.

Alternatively breathe in the sunset through a window at work or home and settle to your dusk mini ritual when you get home or after the children are in bed.

Direction: West

Ruling season: Autumn

Element: Water

Colours: Blue, from dark inky or grey blue, to brilliant Mediterranean turquoise; and silver

Archangel: Gabriel, archangel of the moon, who represents the fruits of the harvest

Crystals: Aquamarine, blue and pink chalcedony calcite, jade, moonstone, fluorite, ocean or orbicular jasper, opal, pearl, tourmaline

Herbs and incenses: Apple blossom, apricot, balm of Gilead, camellia, catnip, coconut, coltsfoot, cowslip, cyclamen, eucalyptus, feverfew, hyacinth, iris, jasmine, lemon, lemon balm, lilac, lily, lotus, lucky hand, myrrh, orchid, passionflower, peach, strawberry, sandalwood, sweet pea, tansy, thyme, valerian, vanilla, violet, yarrow

Sacred substance: Water

Qualities: Intuition, empathy, sympathy, healing powers, inner harmony, peacemaking, unconscious wisdom, divinatory powers especially connected with water scrying; the ability to merge and interconnect with nature, the cycles of the seasons and the life cycle

General foci you can use dusk magick for in spellcasting:
* Letting go of the regrets of the day or of your life
* Completing unfinished tasks or issues
* Reducing pain and illness
* Reducing debt
* Bringing love in maturity
* Bringing justice and just reward

Working with dusk energies

What can be taken from the day? What should be left behind? Is there anyone you wish to phone, talk to or mail to mend fences? Or would you sooner sleep on matters?

Is there a loved one or friend you want to offer encouragement to or to reconnect with on the way home? Do you want to catch up with family news when you get home – or would you prefer your five minutes to yourself first? Maybe if family pressures are constant you could incorporate the children in a quiet five-minute dusk rite.

* If you are at home, relight the dawn/noon candle. If at work or on the way home, cup in your hands the crystal of dusk to focus instead.
* Wherever you are, fill a bowl (or a cup if easier) this time with moon water (see page 129) or still mineral water. Set the bowl on a table, the ground outdoors or your altar.
* Face the west and, holding your dusk crystal, greet the guardians you have chosen for the west.
* Place the index finger of your receptive hand in the water and name what you wish to leave behind from the day.
* Then dip the crystal in the water and state what you would like to take from the day, or if it was a truly awful day, say:

Let all be set to rest.

* Beginning in the west, walk a complete circle clockwise holding your dusk crystal and then set the crystal in the west.

* Put the dawn and noon crystals in place before you begin, if they are not already there. Three-quarters of the crystal circle is in place now and you can see the day connecting.
* Blow out any candle and tip the water away on the ground if outdoors or under a running tap, saying:

Go from me, flow from me. Leave only harmony.

Midnight

This is sometimes called the time of the dark sun, for you can imagine the sun shining on the other side of the world through a hole in the darkness (see the Ra legend, page 406, and the ritual to see the sun at midnight, page 411).

This is the time of healing (10pm is the healing hour), for accepting what cannot be changed, for harmony and for forgiving yourself for what you didn't get done during the day. It is also good for banishing free-floating worries or mental shopping lists.

Direction: North

Ruling season: Winter

Element: Earth

Colours: Green, brown

Archangel: Uriel, the archangel of transformation

Crystals: Amazonite, aventurine, banded brown agate, emerald, fossils, jet, malachite, moss agate, petrified wood, rose quartz, rutilated quartz, smoky quartz, tiger's eye, tree agate, all yellow-brown and mottled jaspers like Dalmatian jasper, all stones with holes in the centre

Herbs and incenses: Bistort, cypress, fern, geranium, heather, hibiscus, honesty, honeysuckle, knotweed, magnolia, mugwort, oak moss, oats, oleander, primrose, patchouli, primrose, sagebrush, sorrel (wood), sweetgrass, tulip, vervain, vetivert

Sacred substance: Salt

Qualities: Stability, common sense, practical abilities, caretaking of the earth, protectiveness, upholding of tradition, love of beauty, patience, perseverance, generosity, acceptance of others, nurturance

General foci you can use midnight magick for in spellcasting:
* Overcoming grief and sorrow and healing chronic pain
* Contacting wise ancestors
* Bindings and banishing of all kinds and forgiveness

Working with midnight energies

If you work at bedtime, this will ease the transition from the day. Even if you are tired, this closing ritual will enable you to sleep easier rather than falling exhausted straight from chores or sitting at the computer and then lying awake worrying about tomorrow.

After the ritual you can place the circle of crystals round your bed for protection. You only need to cleanse these crystals occasionally (smudge over them once a month at the end of the last day or the beginning of the new month before the morning ritual) as they are accumulating power daily.

* Before bed, indoors or out if it is warm enough, relight the candle you used earlier or if you didn't burn one at dusk, light it now.
* Set before it your crystal of midnight.
* Facing the north, greet your chosen guardians and then drop a few grains of salt in the candle flame, naming what keeps you awake and asking for healing for anyone who needs it.
* Walk round a circle clockwise from north to north, carrying your midnight crystal and set it in its place to make up the four crystals of your miniature circle. This can be on your altar or wherever you are working.
* Now face the four directions anticlockwise in turn, thanking your guardians and asking them to keep you safe while you sleep. You can picture the circle energies fading or leave them as a protective psychic field for you will be renewing them the next morning.
* Blow out the candle and make a wish.

The sun in magick

The following associations can be used in spellcasting or when calling down the power of the sun.

Element: Fire

Colour: Gold

Day of the week: Sunday

Metal: Gold

Animals and birds: Eagle, hawk, jaguar (the dark sun), lion, macaw, raven, salmon, stag, sometimes the bear

Crystals: Amber, carnelian, diamond, clear crystal quartz spheres and rainbow quartz, tiger's eye, topaz

Herbs, incenses and oils: Chamomile, cinnamon, cloves, frankincense, olive, rosemary, saffron, St John's wort

Flowers: Any yellow or golden ones, but especially sunflowers, marigolds and golden carnations

Trees: Bay, birch, laurel, palm

Archangel: Michael

Use sun magick for: Personal fulfilment and ambition, power and success. It will help to increase the flow of the life force, enabling you to assert or strengthen your identity and individuality. Use the sun for innovation of all kinds and new beginnings. It is potent also for energy, joy, health, prosperity, spiritual awareness and self-confidence. It will bring wealth and prosperity where there is poverty and failure and will help to break a run of bad luck. The sun is for all matters concerning fathers.

2

MOON MAGICK

Moon magick is another very early form of ritual. The cycles of the moon have long been linked with the cycles of female fertility and the life cycle of humans, from birth through maturity to age, death and then rebirth.

Among the earliest mother goddess icons is the goddess of Laussel who was found in the entrance to an Ice Age cave in the Dordogne region in central France. She dates from around 23,000 BCE and is important because she is the first representation of the earth mother as a lunar deity. She holds in her right hand a bison horn, shaped like the crescent moon. The horn is divided by 13 marks probably representing the 13 moons in a lunar year. Her other hand is positioned over her womb.

There is a natural association between the earth mother and the moon since the moon month coincided with the female reproductive cycle. The full moon became linked to the moon mother and was considered the ideal time for conception. In an unbroken cycle, the moon mother gave birth to her moon daughter every month, having become old and died with the disappearance of the waning crescent. The three days of darkness are the gestation period before the rebirth on the crescent and the three-day deity disappearance occurs in a number of resurrection myths of gods and goddesses and, of course, in the Christian Easter.

The first indication of the triple moon goddess appeared as a trinity of huge carved lunar stone goddesses found in a cave at the Abri du Roc aux Sorciers at Angles-sur-l'Anglin, dating from between 13,000 and 11,000 BCE.

Once the hunter-gatherer way of life gave way to agriculture, the moon goddess's fertility became identified with the fecundity of the earth. When it was realised that the tides rose and fell with the moon, the concept was applied to agriculture. In planting and reaping, the waxing moon was said to increase all growth and ripening while the waning moon decreases the speed of growth and richness of fruit. This principle is still recognised by gardeners today.

In time the belief developed that persisted until the teachings of Plato in Ancient Greece, that, after life, souls were taken to the moon to be re-absorbed and reborn like the new moon or to travel via the moon to the sun to be restored as the spirits of newborns.

Living by the moon

The first calendars were lunar ones, calculating time from full moon to full moon. Among hunter gatherer societies, simple markings on rock or bone would indicate particular full moons to anticipate the coming of the herds after the long winter or the migration of the flocks of geese. We have indications of this from the moon calendar names of later hunter gatherer societies in native North America, though research from footprints in 2005 has suggested the first people inhabited the Americas many thousands of years before it was previously thought. The September/October full moon is called nut time, a recognition that the moon heralded the time when nuts could be more readily gathered to store for the winter. At the same time, migratory flocks of geese would be passing overhead.

Agricultural societies, such as the Celts and those of Native North America, marked the agricultural year by the moons and in both hunting- and agrarian-based societies carried out full moon rituals to encourage abundance.

On Silbury Hill in Wiltshire, the tallest prehistoric monument in Europe and one of the world's largest manmade mounds, was started around 2,600 BCE. Here offerings were made to the Celtic sun goddess Sulis at the beginning of August and the full moon shining in the water of the moat round the hill was said to represent the mother's milk and promised a rich harvest.

There is nothing to stop you marking the full moons for the 12 months ahead in your diary (usually 13 moons, the goddess number) and naming them after events in your life or your local natural conditions. This can make every full moon celebration subtly different. I have written about this in my *Practical Guide to Witchcraft and Magick Spells* (see Further reading, page 516).

A dedication to the moon mother

Before I write more of moon energies and myths, I include this simple ceremony for connecting with the mystery and fertility of the full moon as people have done for thousands of years.

This is an alternative or can be part of the drawing down the moon ceremony (see page 429). Both men and women can gain wisdom and strength or consolation from the moon mother by using this dedication.

This is centred on the idea of the triple or three-personed goddess, who is common to a number of cultures in representing the three phases of the moon. In the Ancient Greek and Roman tradition, for example, Diana is the maiden or waxing moon (who can also be the moon mother), Selene is the moon mother and Hecate is the wise mother. For this reason, though based on the full power of the mother and of the moon, the other phases and goddesses of the triplicate also appear in this month-long ceremony.

You will need: A large clear crystal bowl, either an open fruit bowl or, if you can find one, the kind once used for goldfish. The latter are called witch bowls and were traditionally used for sea scrying when water was collected, often on the full moon, and shells were dropped in the water to create sounds and patterns.

Three moonstones or three small white shells, one for each of the three main phases of the moon.

Clear water from any source or seawater if you are near a beach. (Seawater, and shells, are considered especially sacred to Levanah, the moon mother who controls the tides; see page 427.)

Timing: When the full moon or near full moon is bright and the night is clear

❋ Set your moonstones or shells in a row on the ground or on your outdoor altar so that the light of the moon shines upon them. You can work indoors but the ceremony is fabulous on a clear night (particularly on snow) so wrap up warmly if necessary and go outside where possible.

❋ Half-fill your bowl with water and, holding it between your hands as you face the moon, move the bowl around until the water is filled with moonlight.

❋ If you are very lucky and the moon is in the right position, the reflection of the moon herself may be caught in the water.

❋ Speak to the moon mother in your own words, asking her to enter and bless your life and help you to live more harmoniously. You can use one of the moon god/goddess names if you wish or work with the lunar disk, picturing her in any way that feels right for you and calling her 'lady' or 'mother' moon.

❋ Sit down on the ground with the bowl in front of you and pick up the first moonstone or shell. Drop it gently in the water, saying:

First the maiden.

❋ Drop the second moonstone or shell into the water and add:

Then the mother.

❋ Drop the third moonstone into the water and say:

And last and greatest, the wise woman. Maiden, mother, wise grandmother, walk with me and teach me your ways and your wisdom.

❋ Gaze into the moonlit bowl and hear words or see images come into your mind from the kind voice of the moon mother whose night it is.

❋ Close your eyes, open them, blink and you may see or sense in the water the images of daughter, mother and grandmother and know you are blessed.

❋ Leave the water overnight to gather moonlight. If you used sea water, remove the three crystals or shells and tip it away either back into the waves or down any running water source. Do not pour seawater on to planted ground.

❋ If you are using fresh water, you can remove the moonstones or shells, bottle it and use it as your moon water for the coming month (see page 129).

❋ When you see the crescent moon, refill your bowl with fresh or seawater and cast all three moonstones or shells in one at a time, making three wishes or the same wish three times and then listening for the maiden's enthusiastic message.

* Remove the crystals and leave them to dry naturally.
* Tip this water away under a flowing water source or on the ground.
* Finally, on an early day during the last week of the waning moon (see below and check a moon diary or newspaper), around days 22 to 25 in the cycle, refill the bowl with fresh or seawater.
* Drop the three moonstones or shells one after the other into the water, naming regret or something you wish to discard.
* Ask the wise grandmother to take these sorrows from your life and reabsorb the energies for rebirth. As before, tip the water away and this time dry the moonstones or shells carefully on a soft cloth. Because the moon rises about midnight and sets around midday the next day, unless you are up late you won't see her, but she will be there.
* Repeat the ritual, starting on the full moon, at any time when you need to bring your life back together.

Mythology of the moon

In legend, the moon was seen as the home of the goddess or as the goddess herself and like the sun was among the first things to be created.

The creation of the moon

The Navajo legend tells of the creation of the sun and moon. The first people emerged from the underworld to live on the surface of the earth. But the earth was dark and cold and so First Man and First Woman fashioned two disks from glowing crystal quartz to form the sun and moon so that there would be light by both day and night.

First the sun disk was adorned with a mask of blue turquoise with red coral around its edge and it offered warmth as well as light. First Man and First Woman next attached eagle and lark feathers to the sun so that its light and heat would be cast to all four corners of the earth. The sun disk was fixed in the eastern sky with lightning darts. First Man and First Woman paused to admire the great beauty they had created for the day and then turned to the night.

The moon disk was decorated with clear shimmering crystals and pearl white shells and, like the sun, was fixed high in the sky. But to the sorrow of the first people, their creations were static and lifeless.

Two wise old men offered their spirits to the disks that they might live and move forever. First Man and First Woman then marked out the daily path of the sun by fixing twelve eagle feathers at equal points. At dawn, the sun began to move across the sky, warming and illuminating all in the blackness beneath. At dusk, the sun returned tired from his journey, and the moon, also adorned with eagle feathers, began his course.

However, Wind Boy, who thought it unfair that the moon should have to travel so far by night alone, blew his strong breezes so that the moon might glide effortlessly across the darkened heavens. However, the moon's eagle feathers blew across his face, temporarily blinding him and so to this day the moon follows an irregular passage across the night sky.

The Chinese moons

Chinese tradition tells how once there were 12 moons, one for each month of the year. Their mother Heng O, who was also mother of the ten suns (see page 405), washed her 12 moon children in a lake at the western edge of the world and each travelled for their month's journey to the east where the sun children waited.

In one version the divine archer Yi killed nine of the sun children and was punished by their father (whom he also killed) by being made mortal. Yi then married Heng O, who agreed to spare her life and those of the moon children, if she became his wife. But he tricked her and killed 11 of the moon children as well. She stole from him the herb of immortality and fled with her youngest child to the skies where Yi could not follow her. Here she took the form of the toad who can still be seen in the moon and who is a symbol of prosperity and good luck in China. In some versions all the moon children were saved and they went to the physical moon from which each still flies his moon chariot on his appointed month high across the sky so that Yi cannot harm him.

Moon goddesses

Every society has its moon deities. The majority of moon deities are goddesses, but there is also a strong tradition of moon gods who are often consorts of the sun goddesses. Moon and sun are brother and sister or consorts, like the Norse Mani, the moon god, and his sister Sunna who race through the heavens in their shining chariots. The alchemical King Sol (sun) and Queen Luna (moon) came together to produce the Divine Hermaphrodite who held the secret to and substance of the elusive philosopher's stone that could turn base metals into gold and grant immortality.

Al-lat

The Arabian full moon goddess, Al-lat was once the prevailing goddess over shrines which are now prohibited to women. She was represented in ancient times by an immense uncut block of white granite in the village of At Ta'if near Mecca.

Al-Uzza

The greatest Arabian crescent moon goddess, Al-Uzza was considered to be enshrined in the black stone of Mecca, the Ka'aba, where she was served by her priestesses.

Today the stone is served by men who are called Beni Shaybah (the sons of the old woman). Her sacred grove of acacia trees stood just south of Mecca.

Andraste

A British Celtic moon goddess, Andraste was worshipped by Queen Boadicea. Her sacred animal was the hare and she is associated with the waxing moon and the spring equinox.

Aphrodite

The Greek moon goddess, Aphrodite was also the goddess of fertility and love. She was also called Marianna, the ocean, and so was a form of Stella Maris, star of the sea and the goddess who guides sailors. She was a powerful enchantress and mistress of illusion.

Ariadne (Crete)

Another form of the Cretan moon goddess Britomaris, often portrayed with snakes in her hands. These represent her oracular priestesses who prophesied in her name, especially on the night of the full moon. Ariadne means 'high fruitful mother'.

Artemis

Goddess of the hunt as well as the moon, Artemis was known under different names from Neolithic times.

Described as the twin sister of the young Graeco-Roman sun god Apollo, she travelled the night sky in a silver chariot pulled by white stags, shooting silver shafts of moonlight and subjecting even the great sea god Poseidon to her sway as she controlled the tides. The poet and historian Robert Graves believed she inspired men to poetry and women to magick.

Blodeuwedd, Blodwin, Blancheflor

The Welsh maiden aspect of the triple goddess, Blodeuwedd was accompanied by Rhiannon as the mother and Cerridwen as Wise Woman.

Goddess of May Day, of the moon and the blossoming earth, her bird was the owl. She was made of flowers as bride for the young sun god Llew and followed the sun king through the wheel of the year.

Bomu Rambi

A West African moon goddess, Bomu Rambi is associated with wisdom. She brings comfort, especially to mothers, and heals all sorrow. Her followers wear crescent moon necklaces.

Britomaris (Crete)

Originally a Cretan moon goddess, Britomaris was adopted by the Greek invaders, since she offered protection to all who crossed the seas. She was sometimes called Dictynna.

Cerridwen

This Welsh mother goddess and crone moon goddess was especially associated with Druidic initiation. Keeper of the cauldron of inspiration, a mistress of shape shifting and a prophetic goddess, she was also a white sow goddess as she represented aspects of the destroying mother who brings about death as well as rebirth.

Diana

The ultimate moon goddess, Diana had a daughter Aradia who brought the wisdom of magick to humankind. As the Graeco-Roman hunter goddess associated with Artemis, she became the official goddess of the witches as early as 500 BCE in Italy. Though a maiden goddess she is also worshipped as goddess of all aspects. Her own triple image, Diana Triformis, has been found on coins throughout the Roman Empire up to the 4th century CE.

Hecate

Ancient Greek goddess and one of the earliest deities, the phase of the waning and dark of the moon belongs to Hecate. She is also called goddess of the side of the moon that is not visible from earth. Hecate is the goddess of the underworld and uses her torch to guide others through the darkness.

Hecate is goddess also of the crossroads where offerings were left for her at midnight, especially at triple crossroads, the intersection of past, present and future. She was regarded as the goddess of rebirth, secrets and dreams as well as of sailors (part of her role as controller of the tides) and mistress of enchantment. In the British Museum in London is a triple Hecate statuette of three women with linked hands facing in three different directions.

Isis

The most significant goddess for lunar magick, the Ancient Egyptian Isis was goddess of the moon and sea and mistress of magick and enchantment. She was often depicted wearing a crown that represented the full moon held within the crescents of the waxing and waning moons.

In modern magick, Isis was immortalised as lady of lunar enchantment by the 20th-century occultist Dion Fortune in her novels. In the modern world too, Isis is a central figure in goddess-focused spirituality, such as the Fellowship of Isis, which has members worldwide.

Levanah

The Chaldean moon goddess associated with the first day of the waning moon, Levanah rules the tides and is also a mother goddess form.

Lucina

The Ancient Greek and Roman moon goddess, Lucina represents the maiden aspect as part of the triple goddess with Diana as the full moon goddess and Hecate the wise one. (See also Selene.) Her name means 'she who brings the light'.

Luna

The Roman goddess who gives us the word 'lunar'. Her name means 'the moon that rules the months'. She orders the passage of the moon through the year and her special time is the first day of the waning moon. She is also associated with Selene and Diana in her full moon aspects.

Rhiannon

Welsh goddess of the underworld and a moon goddess, Rhiannon is associated with white horses. She is a goddess of fertility as well as of death, and a bringer of prophetic dreams.

Selene

The phase of the full moon is attributed to Selene. Twin sister of Helios the older Greek sun god, she rose from the sea in her chariot drawn by white horses at night and rode high in the sky on the full moon.

Selene was also a prolific mother, producing Pandia, goddess of brightness, Ersa, goddess of the dew, and Nemea, the mountain goddess. By the mortal Endymion she had 50 daughters, each it is said symbolising one of the lunar months between the ancient Olympic games.

A goddess of marriage, married women and mothers, she is also mistress of enchantment and magickal ritual. Not surprisingly, Selene is invoked for fertility, at the time of the full moon by women eager to conceive.

Selene was known as Luna to the Romans.

Moon gods

Alako

A Romany moon god, Alako was worshipped until the 19th century and some of the rituals have survived. Tiny stone idols depicted Alako with a quill in his right hand and a sword in his left. Children and marriages were carried out under his auspices, even if more conventional religious ceremonies also took place. When a Romany died, Alako took his soul back to the moon. He was worshipped also at the full moon.

Aningan

The Inuit moon god, Aningan was the moon brother of Seqinek, the sun girl. They were also called Akycha and Igaluk. He is a great hunter who can be seen standing in front of his igloo. He has a sledge loaded with seal skins and his team of spotted dogs occasionally chases its prey down to earth where the dogs are seen as shooting stars. Their path around the heavens was seen as a perpetual race in which the moon, at first close to his sister the sun, lost ground until she finally overtook him at the end of his cycle, which explains why the moon can be seen during the day.

Chandra

The ancient Hindu god of the moon, Chandra has the hare as his symbol.

Candi is the female counterpart of Chandra, and lunar god and goddess presided over the moon on alternate months.

Khonsu or Knensu

The Ancient Egyptian moon deity, Khonsu is depicted in human form with a crescent moon supporting the full moon disk or as a mummified youth holding a crook, a flail and a sceptre, crowned by both crescent and full moons. He was associated with pregnancy and invoked for driving away malevolent spirits. His name means 'he who crosses the sky'.

Khonsu was son of Amun the creator god and Mut the vulture goddess of rebirth. Khonsu was the alter ego of the sky god Horus, and was sometimes linked with Thoth, the other major lunar deity of Ancient Egypt.

Myesyats

The Slavic moon god, Myesyats represented the three stages of the life cycle. He was first worshipped as a young man until he reached maturity at the full moon. With the waning phase, Myesyats passed through old age and died with the old moon, being reborn three days later. As he was the restorer of life and health, parents would pray to him to take away their children's illnesses and family sorrows.

Drawing down the full moon

The full moon has always been regarded as the most important night in magick and gradually became dedicated to Diana, though Aradia may also be invoked.

It was chosen for the monthly Esbat or coven meeting for the practical reason that in pre-electricity days it was a time when not only witches but ordinary village people would meet and dance and carry out empowerments for the success of the crops on which the community depended. Indeed it would seem from various mediaeval prohibitive church edicts that priests and people still carried on the old folk magick on the full moon as well as seasonal celebrations without any division into coven/non-coven moots (meetings). Often the seasonal celebrations would be moved to a period when the moon would be bright.

The full moon is the time when the moon energies are not only most powerful but also most accessible for magick. The moon at this phase is believed to endow humans, plants and animals with a particularly potent form of the life force. This energy can be channelled into spellcasting at this time and, more specifically by drawing down the moon energy, into the spellcaster, the high priestess or indeed anyone standing below the moon who wishes to be empowered.

This can be regarded as lighting the divine spark within us all and, whatever your religion, is a positive and natural rather than supernatural experience. There is not a great tradition of drawing down moon god power but there is no reason why men and women cannot try what is a subtly different approach.

Drawing down the moon is a ritual you can carry out as effectively alone as with friends or your coven, but it can be inspiring to work with collective energies.
There are many methods. All you need is you and the moon to weave your own. This is my favourite:

* Stand in full moonlight looking up at the moon. If this is your first time, I'd recommend a night when the moon is shining brightly. When you are more experienced, you can visualise the brilliant moon rays even if it is very cloudy.
* If more than one person is present, stand in a circle with enough space between you to spin round separately.
* Raise your arms above your head, palms uppermost and slightly curved (some people hold them flat).
* Call the moon mother into your life and your heart with a chant. You can, if working with others, devise a simple repetitive group chant in advance.
* The chant I use is:

> *Draw down the moon, draw down the power,*
> *mother great one at this hour.*
> *Draw down the moon, draw down the moon,*

Selene, (Sell-ee-nee), Diana, Isis, Hecate, (Hekartay or Heck at- ay), Cerridwen, mothers of the moon
Mothers of the moon, come to me,
come within me, be with me,
be of me, stay with me,
stay within, that we may be as one,
at this moment and forever,
mothers of the moon.

* You can adapt this for more than one person.
* Turn round in small moonwise (anticlockwise) circles making a larger moonwise circle as you spin and chant. This works whether you are alone or with others.
* Circle your arms as you move in front of you, over and round your body, chanting faster and moving faster until you become dizzy. Let the movements and words flow and don't worry if they change as you become more enchanted.
* Finally call out:

Be within me, come to me now and for eternity, mothers of the moon.

* Sink to the ground, look up, and the physical moon will come rushing towards you. This is a purely physiological effect but is the most effective psychic method I know for bringing together the experience on all levels.
* You may spontaneously speak or sing aloud or hear words channelled from the moon mother or see images of light and moonbeams circling round you.
* If you wish, you can now use the absorbed rush of power and inspiration to direct a wish or send healing by pointing with both hands fingers outstretched in the direction from which fulfilment will come or towards which healing will be sent.
* Alternatively, point your fingers inwards to fill yourself with power. Your fingertips may sparkle either in actuality or within your mind.
* When you are ready, gaze into a selenite sphere (these are translucent and often have a satin-like shimmering band across them). Alternatively, use a completely clear crystal sphere or small glass globe. You need only use a small sphere or if you prefer hold any moon crystal to the moonlight. Images will enter your mind or the crystal that will inspire you and maybe explain what has been puzzling you in the everyday world. If you don't have a crystal, you can also use a plain glass bowl of moon-filled water to gaze in as your focus.
* If working with others, pass the sphere or crystal round so that each person can speak a few words or describe images.
* Unless the weather is bad, remain in the moonlight, singing, dreaming or working with your tarot cards or perhaps using the light of a candle to supplement the moonlight to create a chant to the mothers in your Book of Shadows.
* Keep a page for these full-moon musings. Over the months you may receive a great deal of personal insight and begin to retrieve information from the collective well of wisdom or even recall past worlds and other moons.

Moon associations for magick

These are the general associations given for moon work but there are variations in different traditions.

Element: Water

Colour: Silver or white

Day of the week: Monday

Metal: Silver

Crystals: Opal (unpolished green or pink ones are very cheap), moonstone, mother of pearl, pearl, selenite, white or pearly sea shells, especially double ones

Animals/birds: Bat, heron, moth, owl, snake, wolf

Herbs incenses and oils: Jasmine, lemon, lemon balm, lotus, mimosa, myrrh, poppy, wintergreen

Flowers: Any with small white flowers or which are especially fragrant at night

Trees: Alder, eucalyptus, mimosa, willow

Archangel: Gabriel

Use moon magick for: Spells concerning the home and family matters, especially the mother, children and animals. Its prime focus is fertility, and it rules over all the ebbs and flows of the human body, mind and psyche. The moon will provide protection, especially while travelling, and will aid psychic development, clairvoyance and meaningful dreams. It is potent for all sea and gardening rituals and for herb magick and healing — as well as for keeping secrets.

The phases of the moon in magick

The different phases of the moon offer differing energies that can help not only the timing of a spell, but add power to strengthen a wish (waxing) or can or banish sorrow or bad luck (waning).

The full moon is the most powerful force of all for change and for action. You can follow the different moon phases in the weather section of the paper or a diary. But what you see in the sky and what you feel are always your best guides to using moon energies in spellcasting.

The best way to follow the monthly journey of the moon is to watch her in the sky, not just for one month but for several. Each day in your Book of Shadows write just a line or two on the way you feel and over the months you may detect a pattern that explains hitherto seemingly random mood patterns and energy flows. Even in town you can use buildings as markers and will note slight variations in position on ensuing months, because of the moon's irregular path.

Men as well as women are affected by the moon, emotionally and perhaps also physically. If we can tune in with the ebbs and flows then we become more harmonious and able to use natural energy surges as the moon waxes and not try to force ourselves more than necessary or to take risks when the moon is waning.

There are many ways of dividing the moon cycle. In magick there are three main divisions: the waxing or increasing period, the time of the full moon and the waning period. The waxing period is usually calculated from the crescent moon to the night before the full moon. The time of the full moon is calculated as anything from the second the moon becomes full (by purists), the day of the full moon and the period until the next day or even the week of the full moon. The waning period extends until the moon disappears from the sky. The intervening two and a half to three days are called the dark of the moon and while this generally is not used for magick, it is a powerful period for divination and meditation and for allowing the seeds of the future to grow.

The triple divisions accord with the maiden, mother and wise woman mythology.

There are also more subtle divisions and these I will describe as well so you can decide the best way of relating to the energies.

Other practitioners have the dual waxing and waning periods with the full moon in the centre as the waxing reaches a climax of power.

The new moon

Days 1, 2 and 3

The new moon (or dark moon) rises at dawn and sets at dusk. Because the sun and moon are in the same part of the sky, the sunlight obscures the moon in the day. At night the moon is on the other side of the earth with the sun and you will see nothing.

Use for formulating new plans, assessing what has gone before and for keeping secrets. A time when you stand poised for the new month and so can allow ideas to germinate.

Day 1 is good for meditation and for attuning the energies of mind, body and soul with the natural lunar cycles; also for finding what was lost during the previous month.

Some months you may glimpse the crescent moon on day 3, in which case you can merge the two energies of the new and crescent.

The waxing moon

This is from when the crescent first appears in the sky to the day the full moon rises. The light increases from right to left during this period. The closer to the full moon, the more intense the energies and the larger the moon disk.

Use the waxing moon for:
* Making a new beginning
* Working towards a longer-term goal
* Improving health
* Gradually increasing prosperity
* Attracting good luck
* Enhancing fertility
* Finding friendship, new love and romance
* Hunting for a job
* Making plans for the future
* Increasing psychic awareness

The crescent moon

Days 4–7

The crescent moon rises mid-morning and sets some time after sunset. The moon can be seen on a clear day from moonrise to moonset.

Use for new beginnings, to set plans in motion, for matters concerning animals and small children and for optimism and for new love. Turn over a gold-, a silver- and a copper-coloured coin on the evening when the crescent first appears while facing the crescent moon so that money will flow into your life during the month.

The first quarter or waxing (increasing) moon

Days 8–11

The moon rises about noon and sets about midnight. The moon can be seen from rise to set.

Use for improved health, good luck, courage and finances. Day 8 is very good for healing. Day 10 is special for visions and spiritual insights.

The gibbous moon (bulging, almost full moon)

Days 12–14

The gibbous moon rises in the middle of the afternoon and sets before dawn the next day. She can be seen soon after rising and then until she sets. She is easily recognisable by the bulge on one side.

Use for increased power or increasing commitment in love, also for patience, for the relief of long-standing illnesses and problems and for physically planting what grows mainly above ground.

Days 13 and 14 are good for all purification and cleansing rites (a bit like weeding a garden to allow new flowers to grow or spring cleaning).

The full moon

Strictly speaking, the moon is only full at the second it rises; thereafter it wanes. In practice, however, the moon is considered to be full from moon rise to moon set on the night of the full moon. The hours immediately around that period and also, to a lesser extent, the following day can also be counted part of the full-moon period. The day of the full moon is the day of full power, but also of instability, as – astrologically – the moon is in opposition (or in the opposite side of the sky) to the sun.

Use the full moon for:
* Fulfilling an immediate need
* Boosting power or courage immediately
* Changing career or location
* Travelling
* Protecting psychically
* Healing acute medical conditions
* Raising a large sum of money needed urgently
* Consummating love

- Making a permanent love commitment
- Ensuring fidelity, especially in a relationship that is looking shaky
- Bringing about justice
- Fulfilling ambition
- Gaining promotion

Days following the full moon

Day 15–17

The full moon rises at sunset and sets at sunrise so you can have a brief period when both sun and full moon are in the sky together, which creates amazing energy. Use these days to initiate sudden or dramatic change, for a surge of power, the consummation of love, for healing, for prophecy, for all matters concerning women and also motherhood, for conception and for granting small miracles, for artistic and creative success and all legal matters.

Day 15 is like day 1 of the new moon, another good attunement day with the energies of the moon cycle and good for meditation as well as channelling wisdom from the moon mother or Gabriel, archangel of the moon (for full moon angels and the other lunar angels see my *Touched by Angels* in Further reading).

The waning (or decreasing) moon

The moon decreases from right to left until, finally, the crescent disappears from the left. About two and a half days later the crescent reappears on the right. Waning moon magick should not be thought of as dark or negative but rather a process of bidding farewell to what is no longer wanted or helpful.

Use the waning moon for:
- Removing pain and sickness
- Removing obstacles to success and happiness
- Lessening negative influences
- Reducing the hold of addictions and compulsions
- Banishing negative thoughts, grief, guilt, anxiety and destructive anger
- Banishing the envy and malice of others
- Ending relationships gently

The disseminating moon (the waning or decreasing full moon)

Days 18–21

The full moon is shrinking and rises now in the mid-evening, setting in the middle of the next morning, being visible for much of the time.

Use the decreasing full moon for protection of home, self and loved ones, for banishing bad habits, phobias and fears, for ending a long-standing destructive or abusive relationship, for relieving acute pain and fighting viruses and for leaving behind the past that holds us back from happiness.

The waning half moon or last-quarter moon

Days 22–25

This moon rises about midnight and sets around midday the next day. She is visible for the whole time she is in the sky.

Use for protection while travelling, especially at night, from fears that wake us in the night, from phantoms and nightmares, for reducing major debts, for concerns about older people, for mending quarrels and for avoiding intrusion of privacy, for peaceful divorce and for relieving stress.

Day 23 is an important time for healing and day 25 for all women's petitions and needs.

The balsamic or waning crescent moon

Days 26–28 and day 29 where relevant

The balsamic moon rises before dawn (after the midnight of its day) and sets at mid-afternoon of the following day. She is best seen in the eastern sky in the dawn and very early morning.

Use the waning crescent for quiet sleep if you are an insomniac, for peace of mind if you have been anxious or depressed, for protection from crime and harm, for the easing of addictions, for saying goodbye finally and for finding what is lost or has been stolen – also the dark of the moon for the latter.

The moon void of course

This is not apparent in the sky, but is a brief time when spells tend to be less effective and, in everyday life, meetings or projects tend to get stuck and travel plans can go haywire.

The void of course occurs as the moon leaves one astrological sign and travels to another. The moon spends about two and a half days each month in each zodiac sign. The void of course can last from a few minutes to almost a day.

You can check in any almanac like *Old Moore's* or, increasingly, horoscope pages in newspapers will alert you to this and the times. In an almanac it will be marked as v/c or even VOC next to the moon symbol and the time this begins. The next entry will tell you the time the moon enters the new zodiac sign, marking the ending of the 'void of course' period. If you need to do spells at the 'void of course' time, add extra incense, fresh flowers or herbs to counter the effect.

Using the moon for magick

Best of all, moon magick is practised outdoors beneath the moon. You can use your existing outdoor or indoor nature altar for moon magick, adding appropriate moon herbs, etc. However, for a special spell or ritual, you might like to collect a small box of moon tools for your moon workings. These you can keep wrapped in a white, natural fabric cloth in the box when not in use.

Making a moon altar

* Outdoors, use a rock or a table and on it either set a silver tray or make a circle with white stones, shells or clear glass nuggets. Thirteen stones for the 13 moons is most symbolic unless you are really superstitious, in which case use nine (for the three by three of the triple moon goddess).

* Set the stone circle anticlockwise if following moon lore or keep to the normal clockwise direction if you prefer. I don't associate anticlockwise with anything negative, though I do use it for unwinding a circle and for drawing out pain in healing.

* If you are using an indoor altar, place a white or natural beeswax candle at the four main direction points. If you decide to work outdoors, you can use small, glass, enclosed white night lights that will not blow out in the wind or you can rely on the moonlight.

* In the centre of the altar place a dish of moon water (in beach rituals you can collect sea water, the water ruled by the moon).

* Circle this bowl with moonstones or white shells (13 or nine), creating an inner circle.

* Position a moon incense (see page 431) to the right of the dish of water as you face west, still within the moonstone inner circle.

* You will also need a metal or ceramic oil burner with a night light underneath it to the left of the water bowl within the middle circle as you face west.

* You can, if you wish, enclose just the bowl in a third, even smaller circle of three small white stones, shells or moonstones, thus giving one circle for each phase of the moon.

* The bowl of water will act as the medium for raising the power.

* If you have a willow wand (or a pointed willow twig), lay this directly in front of the bowl with the tip facing west (outside the innermost circle if you make one).

Spells with a moon altar

You will need: Your moon altar or, for spontaneous spells, a bowl for water; moon or still mineral water; an oil burner with a small night light; a small willow twig or wand; a small clear drinking glass; a white, natural beeswax or silver candle (optional).

Timing: On a significant moon phase for your spell (see pages 431–35)

* You will always face west, the approximate direction of the rising moon for moon magick.

* Light the candles if you are using them, calling on the moon goddess associated with a particular moon phase or just calling her 'lady moon'.

* If you haven't made the three triple circles of crystals and stones because you are working spontaneously, walk anticlockwise three times round the circle beginning in the west, saying softly just once:

Maiden, mother and crone, inspire, empower and protect.

* You can, of course, still do this if the three circles of crystals or shells are in place on the altar in order to define the area in which you will be working. I like to do this.
* You don't need to open the quarters of a moon altar.
* Pick up the bowl of water and blow softly and slowly three times into the water, speaking the following words between each breath:

Lady of the moon, bless this water and this intention (name the purpose of the spell).

* Return the bowl to the rock or altar. If working on the ground you can kneel or sit.
* Circle your willow wand moonwise (anticlockwise) over the water nine times, then nine times clockwise and nine times anticlockwise, saying just once:

I charge this water with the inspiration of the maiden, the power of the mother and the protection of the wise grandmother. I ask for the fulfilment of my intention, if right it is to be.

* Name the wish or purpose of the spell once more and state the number of moons or phases you want to pass before you seek fulfilment.
* Put down the wand and raise the bowl once more to the moonlight. If the moon is not shining because of clouds or if it is too early for the moon, lift the bowl skywards anyway and say either:

Light of lady enter here and charged may this water be with light.
or:
Power of the yet unseen moon, enter here and charged be this water with your hidden radiance.

* Pour a little of the water using a small clear glass into the oil-burner bowl and light the night light beneath it.
* Pick up the bowl again and splash a little on your four higher energy centres (hairline, brow, and throat and wrist pulses) in silence and then gaze into the water.
* If necessary, light a white, natural beeswax or silver candle so light falls on the bowl and allow the images of light and darkness to suggest pictures in your mind. Divination is an important part of moon magick whatever the moon phase.
* When steam begins to rise, the power of the spell is being released into the cosmos. Blow out the oil-burner candle while there is a little water left in the oil-burner bowl. When it is cool, tip this, followed by the rest of the water from the large bowl, on to the ground, saying:

Return to the earth and be transformed as growth and new life.
Blessings be.

* Write in your Book of Shadows any wisdom you received from the moon goddesses through your divination.

3

SEASONAL MAGICK

Seasonal celebrations are as old as time itself, prompted not by calendars but by the changes in light, warmth, rainfall and the natural growth cycle. They also occurred at the appearance of the herds with their young and for a particularly bright star such as Sirius, whose annual rising heralded the Nile flood and the Season of Akhet or Inundation.

Once moon times were calculated, as marks on bone, wood or stone, people could anticipate the coming of the rainy season or when the reindeer herds might be returning. Once the seasons could be predicted, the celebrations were used to ask the deities for good hunting or fertile crop growth. In this way people became part of the turning of the year and by their ritual recognition of the change points could help in turning the wheel of the seasons.

Indeed, among the Inuit of the North American continent the Inuit deity Tekkeitserktok, god of the earth, is offered sacrifices in the autumn, the main time for reindeer or caribou hunting.

Once the hunter gatherer way of life had been replaced in more temperate regions by the farmers of the Neolithic period, the ritual year became inextricably linked with the annual sowing and reaping cycle. The father of the hunt, who was lord of the winter, and the mistress of the animals, who was lady of the summer, were succeeded by grain goddesses and gods. The gods were regarded also as the spirit within the grain and sacrificed their lives annually for the fertility of the soil with the harvesting of the crops.

Seasonal patterns

How the year and its rituals are divided is influenced by the nature of the land and weather patterns. Some lands do not have the four seasons that form natural marker points. For example, in Ancient Egypt there were only three seasons: Akhet, Peret and Shemu.

Akhet was the time of the flood and water from July to October/November. At the festival of Hapy, the Nile water god, the people asked that the flood might be not too deep, yet still fertilise the land. Peret was the time of growth, sun and water mixed, honoured by Ra the sun god and also vegetation gods such as Osiris and Geb. This lasted from October/November to March. Last came the time of harvest, the dry season when Ra the sun god predominated and also Min the fertility god and Isis in her role as grain mother. This lasted from March/April to July and was called Shemu.

In contrast, one of the most important rituals in the Aboriginal ceremonial year was the annual coming of the rains, a sacred sex ceremony in honour of Kunapipi, the earth mother and Jarapiri, the male form of the rainbow snake in Northern Australia. It was held just before the monsoons were due to begin and so not only heralded but it was believed brought about the welcome end of the dry season.

In northern areas of Scandinavia, America and Canada, it may still be snowing and icy on May Day. The Swedish people, for example, still have the equivalent of the maypole dancing and flower goddess celebrations round their midsummer tree on the midsummer solstice around 21 June. This became Christianised as midsummer on 24 June.

In the Old Norse world where hunting remained an important way of life – and still does, even in cities – there were only two seasons, *sumar* (summer) and *vetr* (winter). The Norse winter began on 14 October and summer began on 13 April until Christianisation in the 11th century.

The Celts also had two seasons whose beginnings were marked by the greatest of the fire festivals. Samhain, the beginning of the Celtic new year, around 31 October, was the time when animals were slaughtered for the winter food and breeding animals were put into barns. It was the time of the ancestors when they too returned to the warmth of the family hearth, as the dimensions parted on the new year. Their release into the fields with their young on Beltane, the beginning of the Celtic summer, around our May Day, was also the major fertility festival for people, cattle and grain, and another marker point when faeries roamed everywhere.

The seasonal wheel of the year

In this chapter, I work around the traditional wheel of the year used in Wicca and Neo-paganism. The four solar festivals, the quarter days that divide the wheel, fall on the solstices and the equinoxes. These provide astronomical marker points of the high and lows and stable points of cosmic and earth energies, in spite of their variation by a day or two caused by the tilt of the earth. They must have been significant because builders of passages, graves and stone circles from the 4th millennia BCE aligned entrances and marker stones with the rising and setting of the sun on these days.

But in terms of magick and ritual, the cross-quarter days, midway between each of these solar festivals, the four annual great fire festivals, form the major rites in the Wiccan and Neo-pagan calendar. In Japan the traditional lunar calendar uses the cross-quarter days as markers for the seasons so that, for example, the first day of spring, called Risshun, fell on the first cross-quarter day of the year on 3 or 4 February. Once this festival marked the beginning of the new year.

In modern Druidry, witchcraft, Neo-paganism and personal forms of spirituality, these eight change points, occurring every six weeks, have become the focal point for magickal celebrations, both personally for tapping into the prevailing energies and symbolically, as in earlier times, to assist the wheel to turn. Wherever you live in the world you may find it helpful to work with the magickal eightfold wheel of the year (moved round six months for the southern hemisphere). However, you can just as easily adapt the wheel to your own climate, using the weather conditions and plants to mark out your own journey through the year.

The deities of the wheel

Some people get very confused by the mythological circle of the wheel of the year – and with good reason because there are two separate factors/myth cycles in operation that sometimes overlap. The light/darkness cycle is represented by an ongoing battle for supremacy between two brothers, a light and a dark twin, called in the Celtic tradition Lugh or Llew (the Welsh form) and Gornwy. They are not strictly twins since they were born six months apart, though they are often called this since each is the alter ego of the other.

In an even older tree myth saga they are the oak king (the light brother) who ruled from midwinter to midsummer and the holly king whose reign was from midsummer to midwinter. In Christianity these two were mirrored in Christ who was born at midwinter and John the Baptist, his cousin, who was born around the midsummer solstice and whose name was adopted for the Christian midsummer (St John's Day on 24 June).

Neither of these times was bad, for the dark quiet times, when the land lies fallow and people are also supposed to rest more, are as essential as the bright, active times.

There is also the god/goddess progression through the year, with each taking predominance at different festivals or coming together as in a sacred dance. This cycle mirrors the agricultural year and also the older hunter traditions when the god of winter died at the start of the hunting season, still around the autumn equinox in many lands. Occasionally the two cycles overlap, for example at Lughnassadh at the beginning of August when Lugh or Llew as sun king and barley king is cut down in the last sheaf of grain at the first harvest.

In the annual celebrations of Europe and Scandinavia, women from the village or town, or, in earlier times, the priestesses, would represent the goddess in her different forms. For it was believed that she was present in spirit and might be seen leading the processions, by those with clairvoyant sight, children or virgins.

The goddess also appears in different aspects as the maiden, the mother and the wise old grandmother of winter, linking us with the moon goddess, and often the four cross-quarter days are attributed to lunar influences, as for example Lughnassadh at Silbury Hill talking place when the harvest full moon shone on the water (see page 455).

Moving through the year

It is not always possible to celebrate a seasonal festival on its day(s) because of work or travel commitments. Wherever you are though, do try to take a few minutes to acknowledge the change points in your own life, however hectic it may be. You can celebrate at the weekend or on the next free day afterwards and by this time the energies will be settled. For the powers of the new season start to build up in the days before it and remain strong for at least a week afterward.

The cross days are traditionally three days from sunset to sunset when the Celtic and other ancient days began. I have allowed the same three-day period for the solar festivals, though the eve and the day itself are the most potent. Purists who try to keep to a strict six-week pattern use the day upon which the sun enters 15 degrees of Scorpio for Samhain (end of October/beginning of November), 15 degrees of Aquarius for Oimelc (end of January/beginning of February) 15 degrees of Taurus for Beltane (end of April/beginning of May) and 15 degrees of Leo for Lughnassadh (end of July/beginning of August). Again, consult an ephemeris.

In yet another tradition, the festivals are celebrated at the first full moon of the four star sign periods. Or you can adapt them to Christianised festivals, such as Christmas instead of the midwinter solstice and Easter instead of Ostara and bring fresh energies to the commercial festivals. You can of course move your Christmas and Easter to the older dates (Easter Sunday is the first Sunday after the first full moon after the spring equinox) especially if you have to divide family celebrations with a partner who does not live with you or you want your own nature-based celebrations after maybe a tense family get-together on the recognised days.

For each festival I have given the associations as well as the background and suggested magickal spells and activities from which you can weave your own seasonal celebrations, whether alone or with others.

Imbolc or Oimelc, the return of light

Significance: Imbolc means 'in the belly of the mother' and Oimelc, the feast of 'ewes' milk', the rising of the light and the stirring of new hope. The first festival of spring often when the land is still frozen, it is a reminder that new life stirs within the earth.

Duration: A cross-quarter day. The festival lasts from sunset on 31 January until sunset on 2 February.

Mythological energies: This is a maiden goddess festival, but the god is present as her young suitor and in some traditions the first mating takes place, though conception does not occur until the spring equinox.

The dark brother still holds sway but the young god of light is growing in power as he is nursed by the goddess in her mother aspect.

Focus: New ideas; for the promise that winter, whether actual winter or misfortune or stagnation, will end; for planning the future and for putting out the first shoots of new love and the growth or regrowth of trust; and for any projects that start in a small way

Symbols: Milk, honey, seeds, early budding flowers and greenery, also straw to weave crosses in honour of St Bridget/Brighid the triple goddess

Animal: Serpent

Tree: Willow – with her willow wand, the goddess melts the snows of winter

Incenses, flowers and herbs: Angelica, basil, benzoin, celandine, crocus, heather, myrrh, snowdrops, violets

Candle colours: Blue, green, pale pink, pastels, white

Crystals: Dark gemstones such as the garnet and bloodstone, but also amethysts and rose quartz and gentle moonstones for the stirring of fertility and awakening feelings

Element: Fire/earth

Direction: North-east

Deity forms: The maiden goddess Brighid, the Virgin Mary, any maiden goddess or goddesses of the returning light

Agricultural significance: This was the all-important time when sheep and cattle had their young and so fresh milk and dairy products were available to the community; for the young and very old this could mean the difference between life and death. It also marked the very early stirrings of life with the first flowers and when the land might be soft enough to plough.

Mythological and magickal significance: Though it is the time of the maiden, the other two aspects of the goddess also overshadow her, the newly delivered mother of the sun king whose milk is mirrored by the milk of the ewes who gave this festival its name of Oimelc. Also present is the crone of winter whom the god/tribal chief embraced and thus transformed into the maiden goddess of spring.

The Celtic festival was dedicated to the maiden goddess Brighid who became Christianised as the fifth-century Irish St Bridget or St Bride (from which we get the modern term for a woman about to be married).

On Bride's Eve, until Victorian times in Celtic lands, on 31 January or the night after, a bride's bed would be made.

This was created from a sheaf of corn, sometimes with corn preserved from the last cut down at the first harvest at Lughnassadh/Lammas (the end of July), and would be decorated with ribbons in honour of the earth goddess/St Bride. It would also be adorned with any early spring flowers.

The bed was made in front of the fire of the tribal hall or later of the main farmhouse in the area, and at dusk the inhabitants would shout:

Bride (Bridget), come in, your bed is ready.

The symbolic bride maiden would leave her cows and a cauldron at the door, bringing in peace, fertility and plenty.

The women of the household poured milk and honey over the bride bed. The men folk were summoned and, having paid a coin, a flower posy, or a kiss, would enter the circle of firelight and ask for help with their craft or agriculture and make a wish on the bride bed.

In Rome, on 15 February, the love and fertility festival Lupercalia was dedicated to Lupa, the goddess she-wolf who suckled Romulus and Remus, the twins who founded Rome. Love and sex rites by young unmarried girls and men were performed in the grotto of the she-wolf to bring fertility to animals, land and people. This festival gave rise to modern Valentine's day customs.

At dusk on 31 January in the pagan calendar and midnight on 1 February at the Christianised Candlemas, torches, candles and sacred bonfires were lit to attract the sun. There was also a procession clockwise around the frozen fields with blazing torches led, it was said in pre-Christian times, by the maiden goddess herself or a huge corn maiden pulled on a cart made from the last sheaf cut from the previous harvest. This was believed to contain the spirit of the corn mother Brighid who brought back life to the land on this night.

This was a festival of healing of the land as well as people and animals. Eight candles were placed in a circle in water and lit so that the light rose from the water of the goddess, the unity of fire and water. This was a festival of milk also, milk being as sacred to the Celts as communion wine is to Christians, for it is the milk of the mother.

Imbolc spells and rituals

❋ On 31 January after dark, make a tiny straw bed (you can use a small pack of animals' straw from a pet store). Place in it a small doll wrapped in white to represent Brighid, and next to it set a small jug of milk in which you have stirred three drops of honey, making a wish for abundance for you or someone else.

❋ Surround the bed and jug with the first greenery or buds of spring. Place round it symbols of the blessings you would like in your life, whether tiny charms related to your craft (a pen, a small piece of wood or a computer jump drive) or connected with your home. Add a coin asking that your home and those you love will not be short of money. Leave until 2 February at sunset near the family hearth or a source of warmth and each evening add another coin.

❋ On either 31 January after dark or early the next morning, walk around your external boundaries with a small, lighted smudge or one of the Oimelc incense sticks. Waken the energies with a simple chant spoken three times, one after the other, such as:

Light return. Maiden, melt the snows and melt the hearts of all who cannot love or accept blessings. Bless me and bring the new beginning I desire/need.

* Finish by setting the incense in a deep pot to burn away and pour a little fresh milk on to the earth in the centre of the open area, repeating the chant once more.
* If you live in an apartment, you can smudge indoors and tip the milk into another jug to be used for drinks or cereal.
* After dusk on the night of 1 February, place night lights safely at every window of your home to welcome Brighid/St Bridget into your home. Light first a single white candle in the centre of your home from which you will light the window night lights, and ask any family member or friend coming (you could have a Candlemas party) to light a small candle from the central flame. As they do so, they should name someone who needs healing or strength. If alone, light one small candle or tea light each hour or half-hour until bedtime, naming someone for each and creating a circle round the central flame.
* Following the old tradition you can invite friends or family round for a candle-making session and they can take the results home. Candlemas candles protect against fire, storm and accidents, and against sore throats.

Alban Eiler, Ostara or spring equinox

Significance: Alban Eiler means in Gaelic the light of the earth that returns after the winter. Ostara was the Norse goddess of spring and the festival is one for planting the seeds of what was planned at the earlier festival.

Duration: A quarter day. This lasts from sunset for three days around 21 March according to the astronomical calendar.

Mythological energies: The maiden goddess opens the doors of spring and mates with the young virile triumphal god of light (in earlier times the lord of the hunt) to conceive the child of light who will be born on the midwinter solstice the following December.

The light and dark brothers fight, and the light twin kills his brother, so henceforward the days will be longer than the nights. The actual astronomical equinox is the point of battle when it was feared the fight could go either way. The dark twin descends to the underworld or the womb of the mother, like the seeds planted in the earth, to await rebirth.

Focus: A more powerful version of Imbolc, to put the new beginnings and hopes into action and to develop new relationships to a deeper level; also a festival of fertility and positive life changes, initiating creative ventures, travel, house moves, clearing what is no longer needed in your life (a psychological and lifestyle spring clean); anything to do with pregnancy, babies, children, mothers and healing or easing of chronic conditions and ecological awareness

Symbols: Eggs, especially painted ones, feathers, spring flowers or leaves, a sprouting pot of seeds, pottery rabbits and birds, anything made of dough or clay

Animal: Hare

Tree: Birch

Incenses, flowers and herbs: Celandine, cinquefoil, crocus, daffodil, honeysuckle, hyacinth, lemon, primroses, sage, tansy, thyme, violets (also Oimelc)

Candle colours: Yellow and green

Crystals: Sparkling yellow crystals, such as citrine, the strengthening stone, yellow beryl, the energiser, or yellow rutilated quartz with streaks of gold, the regenerator, for your spring talisman; also jade and moss agate

Element: Air

Direction: East

Deity forms: The Virgin Mary to whom Gabriel appeared telling her she would bear Christ; Ostara, Oestre, all dawn and spring goddesses

Agricultural significance: Life returns, more young animals are born, crops are sown, flowers appear and the greenery returns to the trees; most significantly with 12 hours of daylight, hens began to lay again after the winter and fresh food returns

Mythological and magickal significance: Ostara is Viking goddess of the moon and spring, the maiden aspect of Frigg the mother goddess; she was named Eostar and Eostre in the Anglo Saxon tradition, giving us the modern names for Easter and oestrogen. Her magickal hare became the Easter rabbit.

In the Greek tradition, Kore or Persephone the grain maiden comes back from the underworld and so her mother Demeter rejoices and the land can be fertile once more.

The maiden goddess conceives a child. This links with the Christian annunciation of the Blessed Virgin Mary, on 25 March, the day that the angel Gabriel told Mary she was to bear a son. It is also close to the UK's Mothering Sunday.

This is the time of the resurrection of light and, indeed, in some cultures, the rebirth of the sun god/barley king or his return from the underworld, as with the Christian resurrection.

On the spring equinox morning the sun dances in the water at sunrise, an association transferred to angels on Easter morning.

The first eggs were painted and placed on the shrines of Ostara, later dedicated to the Virgin Mary in Germany, Eastern and Western Europe, parts of the Mediterranean, Russia and in Mexico and South America. In Poland it is said that Mary painted eggs in bright colours to delight her infant and so Polish mothers continue the custom.

Special dough cakes sweetened with cinnamon, dried fruit or other spices were marked with a diagonal cross and eaten on the first day of spring to absorb the powers of the earth mother. These became hot cross buns, which in the UK were hung from ceilings of churches in sea-faring communities to offer protection from drowning.

Bonfires were lit and the corn dolly from the previous year or an effigy of straw was burned and was scattered on the fields. In Christian times the Judas man was burned on the Easter fires and all lights were extinguished on Easter eve after dark, to be relit at midnight to symbolise the return of light (a parallel with the midwinter festival).

Ostara spells and rituals

* Visit sacred waters or a clear river or pond on equinox morn and witness the light dancing. Cast a tiny equinox crystal or white stone in the water and, as it splashes, make a wish for the next six months. You will be rewarded by a momentary image that will help you to plan your future path. If you don't have time when you get up on equinox morning, fill a bowl with sparkling mineral water or bubbling from a tap and cast three equinox crystals in one after the other, saying just once:

> *The maiden is now fertile by the light. Enter me likewise with inspiration and the growth of creativity.*

* Dry one of the crystals and carry it as your equinox talisman, having held it towards the light.
* When you come home, take the others and allow them to dry naturally. Keep them in a purse for whenever you need their inspiration on two key days ahead. When the first special occasion arises, carry one of the crystals with you during the day to release the light energies of the spring and optimism. Use the second crystal as a talisman on another important occasion, and so on.
* Leave rain or tap water in the light from dawn until noon (put it out overnight, unless you rise in time for dawn). At noon or whenever you can in the light of day, plant seeds or small seedlings, if necessary under glass, to symbolise hopes for the future. Name the growth you seek or the light or love you wish to return to your life. Water with the equinox water, saying:

> *I sow the seeds of hope. I walk the path towards the light and so I need fear nothing. Life will get better with each dawn. These plants/seeds are the promise.*

* If they do not thrive, plant new seeds or small seedlings until they do.
* At sunset, dig a tiny equinox crystal (jade or moss agate) into the soil at each corner of the plants, saying:

> *So shall light grow and like these plants my wishes shall with care bear fruit.*

* Water regularly and repeat the empowerment.
* The night before, for equinox breakfast or the first free Sunday morning afterwards, use vegetable dye to paint eggs with flowers, mother goddess spirals, birds and bees.
* Leave them overnight (refrigerated if necessary) and on equinox morning set them on the breakfast table in a basket of spring flowers.

* Serve also warmed hot cross buns or cinnamon buns (make your own the day before if you have time, decorated with dough symbols of abundance). Ask any family members or friends you invite to breakfast to make a wish and to name what particular talent they will develop in the six months ahead.
* Give small chocolate eggs to friends or anyone who needs cheering. Repeat at Easter if you wish.
* For increasing fertility, in any area of your life or if you are hoping to conceive a child, prick an egg and take out all the white and yellow. Pass the shell through a candle flame or a small fire as the equinox dawns or the first Sunday afterwards.
* Then carefully cut the shell in half and leave it open for the sun or light to shine on it. On the first night of the crescent moon after the spring equinox, split the shell and place a tiny moonstone in one half, leaving it on the window ledge until the full moon. Then prick the moonstone very gently with a silver pin and leave pin and moonstone out on the night of the full moon. Thereafter, close the egg and wrap up egg, pin and moonstone until the moon leaves the sky. Then you should bury them and repeat the ritual monthly. This can help not only for conceiving babies but also for re-establishing the natural rhythms of your life to bring any new venture to birth.
* Spring clean your home and with it your psyche. Shed any clutter, open windows, and then fill a bucket with warm water and ten drops of lemon juice or lemon essential oil. Scrub any uncarpeted areas and make a second mix to wipe surfaces and window ledges, saying the old cleansing rhyme:

> *One brings love,*
> *Two guards from danger,*
> *Three and four from foe or stranger,*
> *Five takes bad luck clean away,*
> *Six good fortune alone does stay,*
> *Seven, eight and nine new hopes tomorrow,*
> *Three by three, thus be gone sorrow.*

* Scatter lavender heads on carpets and vacuum in alternate anticlockwise and clockwise circles, saying:

> *Dust to dust*
> *away you must.*
> *Health, prosperity, joy to bring,*
> *be gone sorrow, welcome spring.*

* Finally, sweep paths and yards and scrub doorsteps with a salt and pepper protective mix added to your favourite cleanser. Say:

> *Welcome, spring. You are very welcome. Winter, farewell.*

* Tip water away down outside drains.
* Now, while magickally charged, go for a walk in the fresh air.

* When you return or on the next free day, answer any correspondence that is piling up. Deal with unavoidable issues. Change your routine so that you rise earlier and can enjoy the growing light, perhaps to walk to work or to sit in the spring sunshine on your balcony or in your garden. Initiate those projects you always meant to start by clearing out the clutter of old commitments or activities that you no longer enjoy.

Beltane or Beltaine/Beltain/May time

Significance: The time of the kindling of fires sacred to the god Bel or Belinus and the goddess Bellissima in the Gallic traditions. The ultimate fertility festival and the all-important marker of summer in the old traditions; for the uniting of earth and sky and for the unbridled life force

Duration: A major cross-quarter day. This lasts from sunset on 30 April to sunset on 2 May.

Mythological energies: The marriage of the goddess of flowers and the god (here the god of vegetation, the green man or Jack o' the Green) aspect. The last appearance of the maiden. The god moves forward to take his place as equal, giving up his wild ways and his lifetime in the forest. He marries her in the woodland wedding and crowns her with flowers, promising one day a crown of gold.

The light god becomes ever stronger as light and warmth increase and the two myths merge for a while.

Focus: Fertility, whether for conceiving a child or bringing a business matter to fruition, for passion and deepening love, for developing a creative project, improving health and increasing energy, optimism and self-confidence; for abundance in every way and for generosity; for giving up bad habits or moving on to the next stage of life or commitment (good for taming your Jack or Jill of the Green)

Symbols: Fresh greenery and blossom, especially hawthorn (indoors only on 1 May), any flowers that are native to your region, dew gathered in a dropper on May morning. Traditionally girls would bathe their faces in it for enhanced beauty and radiance. You can substitute pure spring water left for a moon and sun cycle in a crystal or glass container, beginning at sunset on 30 April; also ribbons, staffs or staves decorated with flowers and ribbons

Animal: Cow

Tree: Hawthorn

Incenses: flowers and herbs: Almond, angelica, ash, bluebells, cowslip, frankincense, hawthorn, lilac, marigolds and roses for love; also any flower or light floral fragrance

Candle colours: Dark green, scarlet and silver
Crystals: Amber, clear crystal quartz, golden tiger's eye, sparkling citrine, topaz

Element: Fire/earth

Direction: South-east

Deity forms: Fire gods such as Belenus/Bel, all the flower goddesses (see page 158). Jack of the Green and the green man (see page 32).

Agricultural significance: The beginning of the Celtic summer when those cattle that have survived the winter in barns were once more released into the fields and driven between twin fires for cleansing. The major theme of this festival was the interlinked fertility of the fields, the animals and the people. A good time for women to become pregnant so they would produce their children at the beginning of February, giving them time to nurse them before returning to the fields. Also the beginning of better weather and food supplies.

Mythological and magickal significance: Also known as May eve, May Day, and Walpurgis night, Beltane celebrates the coming of the summer in the Celtic calendar and the flowering of life.

The goddess is manifested as the May Queen, Maia, the Greek goddess of spring who gives her name to the month and Flora, the goddess of flowers whose love and fertility festival was celebrated in Ancient Rome as Floralia from sunset on 28 April until May Day. Young people would collect baskets of flowers and children make tiny Flora images of flowers on 1 May.

The Celtic maiden flower goddess Blodeuwedd was created from nine flowers: primrose, broom, meadowsweet, cockle, bean, nettle, hawthorn, oak and chestnut blossom on 1 May, by the magicians Math and Gwydion, to be the wife of Llew, the Welsh sun god.

In Germany, the Netherlands and Scandinavia, the goddess of this festival, Walpurgis or Walpurga was Christianised as St Walpurga, sister of Saints Willibald and Wunnibald who went as missionaries, it is said, from England to Germany in the 8th century.

The bridegroom, in his form as Jack o' the Green or Robin Hood, leads the procession to his woodland wedding to the May Queen of Morris dancers, like him dressed in foliage, bearing horns or darkened with soot. The maypole symbolised the sun god fertilising the womb of the earth mother so the fields would be fruitful.

Druidesses and Druids kindled twin fires with nine sacred woods, using a wooden spindle. The fires were kindled by friction from the nine sacred woods: willow, hazel, alder, birch, ash, yew, elm, rowan and oak. Divinations were made from images seen in the flames, especially concerning the fate of the harvest, and sacrifices were offered to ensure a good harvest.

Young men and women would hold hands and leap the fires to make themselves fertile, the height they jumped signifying the height the corn would grow. They made love in the woods after collecting the sacred hawthorn blossoms and on May morning danced around the maypole signifying the world tree, thus uniting earth and sky energies and increasing the fertility of the earth.

Tales of the wicker man and in early times a person in a huge wicker cage shaped like a grain king, are associated with this festival. A victim, usually willing and of noble birth, was sacrificed on behalf of the land. The victim may have been chosen from 13 candidates. Each took a piece of cake from a bag. The sacrifice was the one who picked the charred portion of the Beltane cake.

This is a time of great faerie activity, especially around standing stones and stone circles. Sacred wells are also very potent on 1 May both for healing and fertility. Traditionally, the ritual should be finished by sunrise but any May morning energies will work as well.

Beltane spells and rituals

* Fill small baskets with garden flowers or greenery for your mother, sisters, daughters or friends with a message of love spoken as you create each one. Leave one the doorstep of anyone who is sick or lonely, to spread the abundance of the season.

* Rise at dawn on May morning and wash your face in water in which you have added drops of the morning dew (you can collect it with an eye dropper for the pure life force and for peak potency in any aspect of your life). You can substitute pure spring water left for a moon and sun cycle in a crystal or glass container, beginning at sunset on 30 April and wash your face in the water at noon.

* Visit a sacred well in accordance with tradition and walk round it three times sunwise (clockwise), drinking the water if possible and asking for healing for yourself or loved ones; tie a ribbon to a nearby tree. You can do this on the nearest free day.

* Decorate a tree or branches in your garden or in woodland with flowers and ribbons. Let your feet direct you to spiral round it clockwise and anticlockwise, allowing your feet to trace and amplify the energies of the earth. With friends, family or coven you can make a spiral dance round the tree in a step and tread movement and stamp your energies into the earth.

* Alone or with others, create a May chant, based on 12 names of flowers that grow in your region and for each flower add a wish or empowerment for each month for the year ahead. Afterwards, scatter petals in the air to release the May energies.

* On May eve make a small fire and burn as many of the sacred woods used traditionally on the Beltane fires as you can easily obtain. Alternatively use one or more tree types local to your area. Look in the flames for images to predict the month ahead. Invite friends and family and have a meat or meat-substitute barbecue to celebrate the fertility of the herds.

* When the fire is burned though, scatter a few of the ashes to the four winds from a hilltop, sending your wishes for the future with them.

- If you can't have a fire, light twin pillar candles in a metal bowl or bucket of sand, one for the goddess and the second for the god energies, asking as you light each flame, the second from the first, for fertility and creativity where most needed. Burn 12 flower petals (they can be from the same flower), six in each candle alternately.
- In the god-assigned candle, name creative or work-based ventures where you need success and the sacrifices you will make to achieve each. In your goddess candle ask for love and fertility in your personal or spiritual life and for each name fears or obstacles you will remove to attain each.
- Leave the candles to burn through and look for images in the area around the flames.

Alban Heruin, Litha or the summer solstice

Significance: Alban Heruin means in Gaelic 'the light of the shore' and is the height of the light year and so the festival of power and triumph. The light shines on the fields and, as promised, the queen shall be crowned with the gold of the sun.

Duration: A major quarter day. This lasts for three days from sunset around 21 June according to the astronomical calendar. The solstice day is the most important.

Mythological energies: The god takes his place as the equal of the goddess, as man and woman, no longer boy and girl, and they are crowned formally with the crown of gold (or silver if she is associated with the moon) – she was crowned with flowers at the Beltane woodland wedding.

The god reaches his full power and maturity, but knows that after the festival he will begin to lose this vitality. Even at the height of joy is an awareness that even he is subject to the powers of the changing seasons.

In the light god cycle, the dark twin is reborn, but cannot yet challenge the light god though the power is starting to drain from him. In some myths they do fight but the dark brother backs off, having made the first small wound in his glorious brother. This will, however, prove fatal.

Focus: Power, joy and courage, male potency, success, marriage, fertility of all kinds, especially for older women, happiness, strength, energy, self-confidence, identity, health, wealth and career; also for maximising opportunities, seizing chances and enjoying the present and present love and success

Symbols: Brightly-coloured flowers; oak boughs; golden fern pollen that is said to reveal buried treasure wherever it falls; scarlet, orange and yellow ribbons; gold-coloured coins and any gold jewellery that can be empowered at the festival; any golden fruit or vegetables

Animal: Bear

Tree: Oak

Incenses, flower and herbs: Chamomile, dill, elder, fennel, lavender, frankincense, lemon verbena, marigolds, orange, rosemary, sage, sagebrush, St John's wort, vervain, any golden, red or orange flowers

Candle colours: Red, orange, gold

Crystals: Brilliant red or orange crystals, stones of the sun, such as amber, carnelian or red jasper, sun stone; also sparkling crystal quartz spheres

Element: Fire

Direction: South

Deity forms: All sun gods and goddesses; the legendary Arthur, as a god not a mortal king

Agricultural significance: The long days and warm weather are vital as young animals grow strong and crops begin to ripen; but there is awareness that the summer solstice does mark the longest day of the year and that henceforth, though imperceptibly, darkness increases; so time for the growth of the crops and the stable conditions for the young animals are limited. Therefore it is a time also for sun rituals.

Mythological and magickal significance: The sun god is crowned by the goddess and she by him.

This is the sacred marriage of the earth and sky or the land/king and the goddess/priestess in which the goddess, or her representative, in later times a married woman of rank from the local settlement, casts the wedding bouquet made of brilliantly coloured flowers and fragrant flowering herbs on a hilltop fire to add her power to the sun.

In Poland and Eastern European countries, unmarried girls would wear wreaths of flowers for the celebrations and then in the afternoon cast them into a river, for would-be suitors to claim. As at the midwinter solstice, strength is offered to the sun in rituals. Fire wheels were rolled from the tops of hills and flaming tar barrels and torches hurled into the air. In Hungary, pigs were driven between flaming wheels to purify them and make them fertile.

Women who wanted to get pregnant would walk naked in a garden at midnight and pick the golden herb of midsummer, St John's wort, originally on the solstice eve and in Christian times on the eve of St John, 23 June. Young girls would pick the same kind of herb, having fasted all day, to place beneath their pillow to dream of a future or present love that would last.

On midsummer's eve in the Basque region of northern Spain and also in Eastern Europe, sun vigils were held and still are in folk custom to see the sun goddess touch the mountain tops and dance at dawn. The watchers would then bathe in streams in the magickal midsummer waters that are still in many cultures believed to have healing and empowering properties.

Stonehenge is oriented to mark the sunrise and moonrise at the summer and winter solstices. Druidic ceremonies are held at dawn and noon on the summer solstice at sacred circles such as Stonehenge, and some groups and individuals keep a vigil from sunset on the previous evening. At sunset on the summer solstice at Stonehenge, another significant ritual point, the heel (sun) stone outside the circles, casts a shadow on the altar stone, thus marking the beginning of the dying of the year.

In the ancient Germanic tradition, on the solstice eve and later on St John's eve, mountain- and cliff-top fires were lit. Similar festivals persist still, not only in the original lands but in places such as America where European ancestors settled.

Litha spells and rituals

* On the eve of the summer solstice, watch the sun go down and burn in a candle, herbs, grasses or wool and any negative thoughts, injustices, feelings or worries that hold you back from happiness and fulfilment. Sunset on solstice eve is a very strong outgoing solar tide.
* Use this evening for burying any old charms and amulets that no longer work and making or setting out new ones you have bought to be empowered at dawn tomorrow.
* Blow out the candle and sleep. If the weather is fine you can sleep in your back garden and wait for the coming of the dawn. Check your sunrise times for you will need to be ready early. Best is an unrestricted view, a hilltop, a beach or an old stone circle where others may gather with you to celebrate.
* Wait in the darkness for the light to return, and set before you on a dish anything you wish to be empowered: charms, crystals, coins for prosperity or herbs for health.
* Raise your arms as the sun rises and recite your special hymn to the sun (see Sun magick, page 409) or call out nine times slowly and ever louder on a rising note the Druidic call Awen (Aaah-oo-wen), which like the Buddhist *AUM* is a sacred sound that called creation and the sun into being. Lower your arms between each call and let the sound fade away before calling the next Awen.
* If you are by the sea, my favourite place on the summer solstice, carry your dish of items to be empowered as you walk through the pathway of light in the sea towards the sun. This combines earth as the sand beneath your feet, the fire of the sun, the rippling sunlight air and the water of the sea, so creating the magickal fifth element in which anything is possible.
* At noon, light a small fire or burn a candle. Surround it with flowers and your dish of charms. Sprinkle sage into the flame to symbolise the riches of the day and the potential you have in your life.
* Finally, watch the sun go down to complete your 24-hour vigil and send love and healing into the darkness for any from whom you are estranged.
* End by casting golden flower petals or herbs into the air from a hill, a handful at a time, making empowerments for courage and achievement to the winds. Where they land and take root represents, in the old traditions, places of buried treasure or in this case new or buried talents you can develop to realise your potential.
* Make your solstice water, the most potent sun water of the year, by leaving water in a gold-coloured dish surrounded by gold-coloured flowers from dusk on the solstice eve until noon on the longest day. This is especially healing and

empowering and you can keep it in clear glass or gold-coloured bottles to drink or add to bath water to give you energy and confidence.

* If you don't have a chance to celebrate, set flowers and sun crystals and use sun oils (frankincense, rosemary, orange or sage) or burn them as incense or sagebrush smudge to bring the sun power into your home or workplace.

Lughnassadh/Lammas

Significance: The first grain harvest and the funeral games of Lugh the sun god or, in an earlier tradition, the funeral games of the earth mother Talitiu, foster mother of Lugh and one of the three Celtic mothers. She was said to have died preparing the fields. A festival of bread, for justice and willing sacrifice.

Duration: A cross-quarter day. This lasts from sunset on 31 July until sunset on 2 August.

Mythological energies: The god enters, renews or sometimes makes for the first time the sacred contract with the goddess in the Celtic form of Eriu/Nass. In this he promises to defend and die for the land, a ceremony undertaken by the king or leader and the priestess or goddess.

The sun/grain god transfers his remaining light and warmth to her for the continuing growth of the crops. He willingly sacrifices himself for the growth of the rest of the crops and ensures the continuing fertility of the land, entering the grain as the living spirit. Eriu was the Irish earth and sovereign goddess.

In one of the magickal transformations from maiden/mother/crone, Eriu was pictured as a hag who was thus made lovely by the golden light of the sun.

This is where the myths divide, for in the god/goddess cycle above the god dies and descends to the underworld, back into her womb, to be reborn on the midwinter celebration.

But, of course, the final battle with the dark twin cannot take place until the autumn equinox six weeks later when he wins the battle for the light.

Some practitioners fix the sacrifice of the god as the autumn equinox, the second harvest or see the barley god as fatally wounded but lingering until the second harvest is home, allowing the dark twin to deliver the death blow in the autumn.

But the two myths don't have to coincide. In the straightforward light/darkness saga the light brother grows weaker as his dark brother grows in strength but his dark twin cannot yet challenge him and win.

Focus: Justice, human rights, freedom from abuse of any kind; for partnerships, both personal and legal or business; for signing contracts or property matters; promotion and career advancement and the regularising of personal finances; for journeys to see friends and family or on business, and the renewal of promises and fidelity. With corn and corn dollies, a feature of the time, fertility is also favoured, perhaps preparing for future ventures or getting healthy in order to have a child

Symbols: Any straw object such as a corn dolly, a corn knot or a straw hat, decorated with harvest flowers such as poppies or cornflowers, containers of mixed cereals, dried grasses, stones with natural holes; bread and dough

Animal: Stag

Tree: Alder

Incense, flower and herbs: Cedarwood, cinnamon, fenugreek, ginger, heather, myrtle, poppies, sunflowers, any dark yellow, deep blue or brown-gold flowers

Candle colours: Golden brown or dark yellow

Crystals: Amber, fossilised woods, rutilated quartz, tiger's eye; brown, yellow or sandy jasper, all brown stones

Element: Earth

Direction: South-west

Deity forms: All grain and sacrifice gods, earth mothers

Agricultural significance: The first grain harvest and especially the corn (which came to the UK about CE 1,500) were of vital importance to the people and indicative of the success of later crops and fruits. Traditionally, soldiers would return to help with the harvest. Because of the dry roads it was a time for travelling. Druidesses and Druids and Viking courts would arbitrate in disputes; also the time for making and renewing, when temporary marriages were made for a year and a day.

Mythological and magickal significance: Lugh/Llew, after the sacred marriage is renewed and the transfer of his power to the crops, must seal the bargain by willingly being cut as the last sheaf of corn; everyone hurls sickles at the same time so none will know who killed the god. He returns to the womb of the mother.

Bread was made from this sheaf to be offered to the earth mother. From this also was fashioned a corn mother or in earlier times barley or wheat mothers. It decorated with the scarlet ribbons of Cerridwen, the Celtic mother goddess or in Scandinavia the red ribbons of Frigg, the mother.

The dolly would be hung over the hearth of the main homestead to bring health, abundance and protection to the whole settlement throughout winter.

Corn knots and dolls were made from other corn that was cut on this day to be hung in barns and smaller homes through the long winter. It would be returned to the fields as ashes on the spring equinox the following year.

In the Christian tradition, the festival was called loaf mass or Lammas and a loaf baked from the first harvested sheaf was offered on the altar. On 15 August, at the feast of the Assumption of the Virgin Mary into heaven, a bannock was made from bread and milk to be broken by the father and given to the family.

On Lughnassadh, hilltop processions and bonfires were held. The tops of hills were associated with the mother goddess, such as the Irish Aine. Young girls would, when the moon was bright, hold a ring up to the moon and through the hole see the golden-haired corn mother leading her processions. Lughnassadh fires still burn in parts of the world where there is Celtic ancestry.

In the Classical world, the festival of bread was dedicated to corn goddesses such as Demeter in the Greek tradition, the Roman Ceres and Juno the Roman mother goddess. All are aware that the goddess is now alone and that the success of the harvest is now in the hands of the mother.

Lughnassadh spells and rituals

* Making corn animals and dollies is a skilled craft and one you may have the opportunity to learn at a craft fair or workshop as it is becoming popular again. However, we can all using dried corn or dried grasses to create corn knots, animals and corn mother figures (a featureless head, arms, body and legs) tied with red and blue thread on this day. Hang them in the home through the winter to bring protection and burn them on the first Monday after Twelfth Night or on the spring equinox fires.

* Alternatively, decorate a display of dried grasses with red ribbons and twine, the largest knot tied three times for luck. The three knots also recall the triple goddess, the first to call the power of the corn maiden, the second the corn mother and the third the wise woman who as the goddess Eriu was made young again by the sunlight Llew the sun god gave her at Lughnassadh.

* If you want to make a corn king, you can burn him at Lughnassadh and scatter the ashes in your garden or on indoor plants to bring abundance to the home during the winter.

* If justice has not been done, burn an ear of corn or dried grass in a big orange candle set in sand, naming a matter and saying:

> *By the father and the mother, justice shall be done in due course.*
> *This I know and this will sustain me.*

* Alternatively, if you feel you have been unjustly treated and cannot put matters right, knot dried grasses, one for each injustice, and cast them on the waters or bury them, planting late-flowering seeds or autumn flowers. If the matter has caused family estrangement, contact them shortly afterwards to try to sort matters out.

* Make bread with milk on Lughnassadh eve. As you stir the mix in turn with friends and family or alone, make wishes for abundance and the harvest you wish to reap during the coming months. At dawn, give a few crumbs to the wild birds. Enjoy the rest for breakfast or share it on a picnic with friends and family.

Alban Elued or autumnal equinox

Significance: Alban Elued means in Gaelic 'light on the water' and so the sun is moving away over the water to shine on the Isles of the Blest, leaving the world with encroaching darkness. It is a festival of discarding what is rotten like overripe fruit and storing what will last for use through the winter – not just material but spiritual resources.

Duration: A quarter day. This lasts for three days from sunset around 22 September.

Mythological energies: The god is in the underworld, the womb of the mother awaiting rebirth and while the goddess mourns for her love she must prepare for the harvest over which she presides. But she is tired herself and getting heavier with the light child. Some myths blame Llew the Welsh god of light's faithless wife Blodeuwedd or Arthur's Queen Guinevere for transferring their attention to the dark twin who destroys the light brother and impregnates the goddess. But even these treachery myths reflect the need for the new dark twin to be born at the summer solstice so the wheel continues to turn.

In this strange legend, Blodeuwedd is instrumental in bringing about the death of Llew at the hands of Gornwy and the dark magickian. Llew becomes an eagle whose physical deterioration progresses as pigs, icons of Cerridwen, mother of regeneration, eat the rotting flesh as it falls to the ground. Llew will not be released from the form of the eagle until his rebirth at the midwinter solstice.

In the light cycle, the dark brother challenges and kills the light brother who returns to the earth/the womb and the two legends temporarily merge again.

Focus: Abundance, the fruition of long-term goals, for mending quarrels and forgiving yourself for past mistakes, for reaping the benefits of earlier efforts, for assessing gain and loss, for family relationships and friendships and for material security for the months ahead.

Symbols: Copper-coloured, yellow or orange leaves, willow boughs, harvest fruits such as apples, berries, nuts; copper or bronze coins and pottery geese

Animal: Salmon

Tree: Apple

Incenses, flower and herbs: Ferns, geranium, myrrh, pine, sandalwood, Solomon's seal; Michaelmas daisies and all small petalled purple and blue flowers

Candle colours: Blue for the autumn rain and green for the earth mother

Crystals: Soft blue crystals, such as blue lace agate, blue beryl, chalcedony or azurite, also rose quartz and all calcites

Element: Water

Direction: West

Deity forms: All river and freshwater deities, also the mistresses of the animals and lords of the hunt

Agricultural significance: The gathering of the second or green harvest of fruit, nuts and vegetables, as well as the final grain harvest; the storing of resources for the winter and barter for goods not available or scarce. Feasts of abundance and the offering of the finest of the harvest to the deities was a practical as well as magickal gesture, part of the bargain between humans and deities. Rotten fruit and vegetables were, where possible, fed to animals or discarded. Barley wine was brewed from the earlier crop.

Mythological and magickal significance: The thanksgiving for the abundance of the harvest and in Christian times the harvest festival and supper.

In traditional pagan celebrations a priestess and later a woman representing the goddess would carry a wheat sheaf, fruit and vegetables and distribute them to the people. A priest or man, representing the slain god, given the name of John Barleycorn, would offer ale, made from the fermented barley cut down at Lughnassadh.

In Ancient Greece, the rites of the Greater Eleusinian mysteries took place at this time in honour of Kore/Persephone and her mother Demeter.

Michaelmas, the day of St Michael, the archangel of the sun, was celebrated on 29 September with a feast centred on geese. Since St Michael was patron saint of high places and replaced the pagan sun deities, he was an apt symbol for the last days of the summer sun. Goose fairs were held and workers in the fields were often paid with slaughtered geese.

Some Druidesses and Druids climb to the top of a hill at sunset on the autumn equinox day to say farewell to the horned god, lord of animals as he departs for the lands of winter.

The autumn equinox in many lands in the northern hemisphere still signals the beginning of the hunting seasons, and in Scandinavia huntsmen still leave the entrails of slain animals on rocks in the forest as a relic of the ancient offering of the first animals.

Alban Elued spells and rituals

* Prepare a feast of fruit and vegetables, game meat, duck, goose or meat substitute, bread, cider and barley wine or fruit cup and warming soups and hold an outdoor equinox party.
* Bless a dish of cakes and a large goblet of fruit juice/wine/beer in the name of the mother and father of abundance and ask for protection throughout the winter for all present.
* Make offerings to the land and the earth mother and the spirit of the corn of wine/juice and bread by dropping a little of each on the ground.
* Then pass round a dish of small fruit cakes, each person making a wish for abundance for a person or place that needs it.
* Next pass the communal cup, asking each person in turn before they drink to send individual blessings to people and places, naming with thanks someone who has been kind to them during the past year.
* Ask everyone to bring along small personal treasures or household items (not junk) they no longer use or maybe never used, in the style of the Native North American giveaway. Let everyone take what they want and donate the rest to a car boot sale or charity shop to pass on abundance.
* Stand where autumn leaves are falling and catch one for each precious thing you want to carry forward to the winter. Collect them together in your crane bag. Pick up other leaves for each thing you must let go. Put those also in your crane bag.
* Before dusk, climb to the top of a hill to say goodbye to the sun and release all your leaves, so all are carried, gains and losses, to be transformed by the cosmos.

Samhain, the Celtic new year

Significance: This is the time of the wise ancestors and the parting of the dimensions between past, present and future, when the goddess herself descends into the underworld for three days and nights; a festival for acceptance and surrender of fear.

Duration: A major cross-quarter day. This runs from sunset on 31 October until sunset on 2 November

Mythological energies: The goddess descends into the underworld to visit her lost love, the sun king, and the world is in mourning. Meanwhile in her absence, beings of timelessness rule, like naughty children when the teacher leaves the room for a while. Spirits and faeries roam free and other ancestors come to visit families.

The dark brother rejoices at his supremacy and is growing in power. In some myths he takes the throne alongside the goddess who, in tune with the seasons, must also embrace the darkness and accept loss.

Focus: Remembering the family ancestors; for looking both backwards to the past and into the future; for protection, both psychic and physical; for overcoming fears of inner as well as outer darkness; for laying to rest old ghosts in our minds; for marking the natural transition between one stage of life and the next.

Symbols: Apples, pumpkins, nuts, autumn leaves (mingled with evergreens as a promise that life continues), salt, scary masks, fantastic costumes, lanterns

Animal: Raven

Tree: Silver fir

Incenses, flower and herbs: Cypress, dittany, ferns, garlic, nutmeg, sage, thyme, pine; also large white flowers, rose petals; rose fragrances, spices

Candle colour: Orange, purple

Crystals: Deep blue, purple, brown and black, for example lapis lazuli, sodalite, dark amethysts, smoky quartz, deep brown jasper, jet, obsidian (Apache tears)

Element: Air/fire

Direction: North-west

Deity forms: The crone goddesses, the gods and goddesses of winter, snow and ice

Agricultural significance: The time when the herds came down from the hills and family members returned to the homestead for the winter. The animals that were to be kept during the winter were driven though fires so that they might be cleansed of disease and parasites and others were slaughtered with reverence and salted to be preserved for food.

Mythological and magickal significance: Samhain means summer's end and the acceptance that the nights would get longer and the weather colder. At this time of no time, the family spirits returned shivering to seek warmth at the family hearth and the faeries were on the move to their winter quarters.

For those with courage it was a time to look back into the past, to past lives and worlds and forward to the future. For this reason it was a popular festival for love divination.

The Cailleach, the crone goddess of the Celtic world, moves to the fore at this festival. She is the winter sun which shines from All Hallows to Beltane eve and Grainne or Dia Greine, the Celtic sun goddess, ruled the rest of the year. They are mother and daughter in a revolving cycle.

The fires of Ireland were in pre-Christian times extinguished at sunset on Samhain. A fire was kindled by the Arch Druid/ess, on the hill of Tlachtga in Ireland and every great family carried home torches to rekindle their hearth fires which thereafter were kept burning. St Patrick challenged the Druids with his own fires that it is said burned brighter than theirs and Hallowe'en fires do still feature in Celtic lands and among those with Celtic ancestors. The fires are said to guide loved ones home through the darkness on this psychically unpredictable night of the year.

In parts of Scotland, youths would take fire and run around field boundaries to protect creatures and homes from malevolent faeries and spirits who might also be abroad.

Pumpkins or Jack o' lanterns, grinning faces with candles inside, were set at windows to keep away malevolent spirits. It is said that if you stand at a crossroads on Samhain eve the wind will tell you all you need to know for the coming year. Young girls right through to modern times would follow the Druidic custom of bobbing for apples in a barrel of water. When they had succeeded in grasping the apple between their teeth they would set it under their pillow and dream of their true love. (See my *Complete Book of Spells* for a whole section on traditional love divination in Further reading, page 516.)

Samhain spells and rituals

* Place a clove of garlic on a west-facing window of a room in which you are sitting or on the west side of your outdoor altar. Say:

> *May only good enter here.*

* Light protective incense like pine, rose or sage and ask your special guardian angel to stay with you and protect you from anything that might frighten you.
* Light a purple candle and hold photographs or mementos of deceased family members. Alternatively, focus on a distant ancestor or a spiritual ancestor to whose culture you are attracted. He or she may be a spirit guide.
* Gaze into the candle flame or hold a smoky quartz or Apache tears to the candlelight and ask that you may be shown in the flame or in the crystal something from the past what will guide you in the present.
* Relax and half-close your eyes, blinking when necessary.
* You may see in the crystal or flame or in your mind's vision, your beloved great grandmother smiling and hear her wise comforting words. Alternatively, you may sense her presence or see, hear or feel a gentle breeze and be given a picture of a past world.
* This is the night of the year when it is easiest to make contact with past dimensions and encounter those who can guide you to wise choices in the future. What you may encounter may be your own evolved soul that can access the

wisdom of other times and places. Nothing can harm you, for you are not calling up spirits, merely images and, with personal relatives, family love that never dies.

⁕ When you are ready to end the experience, thank whomever you connected with, saying:

Go in peace and blessings on your own paths of wisdom.

⁕ Blow out the candle and in the darkness you may see, as though etched in light, the possible pathway ahead if you choose to take it.
⁕ Smudge the room or round yourself and your outdoor altar.
⁕ Alternatively, set a lighted pumpkin or an orange candle at a window facing the road or on your outdoor altar to protect loved ones wherever they are. Sit behind the pumpkin so you face the light. Name each person and say:

May they be blessed and protected.

⁕ For each person drop a little sage or thyme into the flame. Try to name a few people you are angry with or from whom you have become estranged. Don't forget to include yourself.
⁕ Let the candle burn from dusk until midnight on Hallowe'en or until the light goes out. Then scatter the herbs outdoors, saying:

May all be blessed and protected.

Alban Arthuran or the midwinter solstice

Significance: Alban Arthuran means in Gaelic the light of Arthur and refers to the rebirth of Arthur as the divine child called the Mabon; the festival of the restoration of the power of the sun and the sun gods and the almost imperceptible return of the light and, with it, hope

Duration: A major quarter day. This lasts from sunset around 21 December for three days.

Mythological energies: The sun god is reborn after the fear that the world will be overwhelmed by darkness on the shortest day. The crone goddess or sometimes the three mothers act as midwife. In some legends the maiden goddess Brighid acts as midwife.

The light twin returns and the dark twin knows his power is on the wane. He watches jealously as the attention is paid to his new brother.

Focus: For the rebirth of light and hope, for domestic happiness and security, family togetherness and for financial security; for older family members, for long-term money plans, for healing chronic pain or easing chronic sickness, for increasing inner vision and psychic powers, for accepting what has been and cannot be changed but letting go of the old guilt, sorrow or pointless anger and jealousy as typified by the dark twin's resentment

Symbols: Evergreen boughs, especially pine or fir; small logs of wood, especially oak, pine and ash; holly and ivy; gold coins and jewellery; silver and gold ribbons and baubles; tiny wrapped presents to be opened on the solstice or at Christmas

Animal: Bull

Tree: Holly

Incenses, flowers and herbs: Bay, cedar, feverfew, frankincense and myrrh mixed, holly, juniper, pine, rosemary, sage and all spices; poinsettias, scarlet and white flowers; rosemary

Candle colours: White, scarlet, gold, purple for what is being left behind

Crystals: Amazonite, aventurine for luck, bloodstone, malachite, garnet, snow quartz

Element: Fire/air

Direction: North

Deity forms: All sun kings, sun goddesses and mother and crone goddesses

Agricultural significance: There was a natural fear about food supplies not lasting the rest of the winter, especially if the weeks ahead were hard. The sun had reached the lowest point in the sky. After the midwinter solstice when the physical and psychic crisis point was passed people held feasts as a magickal gesture to attract abundance. They hung lights from evergreen branches to encourage the trees and vegetation to sprout green again and to give power to the sun.

Mythological and magickal significance: In many traditions, the midwinter solstice was the time the goddess gave birth to the sun. In Ancient Egypt earlier myths identified this as the time the sky goddess Nut gave birth to Ra, the sun god and father of every pharaoh. (Ra impregnated the wife of the existing monarch thus creating a virgin birth since the child did not have an earthly father.)

The Egyptian mother goddess Isis also gave birth to Horus, the young sky god on this night, secretly in a cave. As with the infant Jesus, Horus had to be hidden because the reigning king, his uncle Set, like Herod, would have killed him. Images of Isis holding the infant are believed to have inspired many of the Black Madonna statues.

The Anglo Saxons named 25 December the day of the infant, and Christmas eve was the night of the mothers or Modraniht after the shadowy guardians of the hearth and home, the midwife goddesses who protected women in childbirth and their infants.

Mithras the Persian sun god was likewise born in a cave. The timing of Jesus' birth was moved to overlay the earlier pagan celebrations.

In ancient southern Europe, the midwinter solstice was called Brumalia, the return of the unconquerable sun.

In rituals in many different lands on midwinter night, all lights are extinguished at dusk and the crone goddess or the person representing her invites those present to walk into the darkness with her, an act of pure surrender and faith that light will return. In passage graves throughout the world, such as Newgrange in Ireland, people waited for the first shaft of light on the solstice morning to illuminate the inner shrine. Then the lanterns are relit from a single flint.

In Ireland today a candle is left burning in a window on Christmas Eve to guide the Virgin Mary on her way.

Alban Arthuran spells and rituals

* As the solstice night draws in, light a dark purple candle. Extinguish all other lights and, if possible, sit outdoors so all that is visible is the flame of the dark candle.
* Say softly:

  I will walk into the darkness with you, wise grandmother, in trust that light will return.

* Listen to the night and if you are afraid of the dark, picture the kind grandmother beside you enfolding you in a cloak of stars.
* Do nothing, say nothing. Just wait and let the tide of the old sun carry away what must go: the illusions, the excuses, the inertia. Wait for a tomorrow that only you can make.
* It's not a sad time, it's just like tidying up your desk on the last day of school.
* When you are ready, light a white candle from the dark one and say goodbye to the grandmother who, like wise Hecate in the Ancient Greek world, carried the torch through the underworld to find the lost Persephone.
* Look into the white candle flame, not in triumph, for the wind may flicker the flame. Say:

  The dark times are ended and light returns.

* Begin to light a circle of tea lights, the first from the white candle and then one from the other. For each, name someone who is away for Christmas or who is sick, and when all the tea lights are aglow, look at the circle of lights you have created and call the names of all those you love – or, if you are alone, call new people into your life.
* If you are working with friends or families, they can, in turn, light their candles from the solstice candle, making wishes for the future. If the weather is bad, you can carry out the ritual indoors, but blot out all light except for the candles.

PART 8

MAGICK OF THE NATURE SPIRITS

INTRODUCTION

Nature is empowered and made lovely by the energies of the spiritual beings that oversee and care for the planet. The blueprint of the natural world is developed by those spirits. They work with the powers of the earth, the sky, fire and the waters and harmonise those disparate forces into an integrated whole.

Each nature spirit form, angel, deva, elemental, faerie and nature essence has a place in this dynamic process of creation, growth, fruition, decay and rebirth and depends on the other nature spirit forms to work in synchronicity. In this way the first creation is replicated countless times in small but significant ways so that the wheel of the year can continue to turn harmoniously and creatively.

We can tap into this process so that we become personally empowered and harmonised.

Through rituals to connect with these positive spiritual forces, our personal life cycle moves into alignment with the wider wheel of nature, which then enriches our daily lives. Angels enter the world of nature from higher realms and enable us to see the potential beauty of nature at her most ideal. For example, Zuphlas, the angel of the forests, may be experienced in any woodland, however scruffy, but connects you with the energies of the most beautiful forest ever imaginable. Nature angels open us to possibilities both in nature and in our own lives that make us aspire beyond the actual to the ideal.

Devas are frequently described as huge, shining, higher nature essences who make sure the blueprint of nature is carried out and that the first creation is replicated daily. They have in recent years moved closer to mortals to warn us of the effects of pollution and of squandering the earth's resources. An individual deva controls for example the development of woodland, not the ideal heavenly forest revealed by the angels, but the actual woodland. It progresses from the seed through to the evolution of the mightiest trees, their growth and ultimate dying and then making sure the new trees from their seeds are ready to replace them.

The elementals are the dynamic forces that drive nature – earth, air, water, fire, the engine room that generates the physical growth and dynamic life force. Through spells the elementals can fill us with the different strengths we need in our lives and help us to keep the energies fresh and flowing in home and workplace.

The nature spirits are those who care for specific trees and flowers and, jointly with others of their kind, keep lakes filled with water and able to support fish, plants and wildlife. They offer easy connection with humans, allowing us to work directly with them to resolve personal dilemmas by calling on the healing powers of the water spirits or the protection of the earth element, house elves. In this section there is a great deal of information about these beings, whose presence represents nature at her most vital, and I suggest a number of ways you can work with these wondrous spirits.

Finally, there are the faeries. The word 'fairy' or 'faerie' comes from the ancient French *faes*, derived from the Latin *fata* or fate, and was first used around the 13th or 14th centuries to describe winged ethereal spirit beings who had been central for centuries in the oral folk tradition of many lands.

The best-known fairies were those of the faerie courts of Ireland and Scotland, called the *sidhe* or *sith*. They are portrayed as a beautiful and noble race who are as tall as humans or even more statuesque and resemble them. The *sidhe* of Ireland, according to folklore accounts of the 1800s and early 1900s, lived in subterranean faerie palaces of gold and crystal and are endowed with youth, beauty, joy and great musical abilities. Finarra or Fin Bheara, who ruled the faeries of the west of Ireland, was perhaps their most noted king, loved hurling and was never beaten by a mortal at chess. His queen Oonagh has been described in true Victorian style by Lady Wilde, who collected accounts of faerie folklore in Ireland, as having:

> *Golden hair sweeping to the ground, clad in silver gossamer glittering as if with diamonds that were actually dew drops.*

So, go out into the countryside in different weathers and feel the spirits of nature in all her different forms all round you, and share momentarily their world and their wisdom.

ANGEL MAGICK

Angels are spiritual essences and messengers from higher realms. They are described in all major religions, but increasingly have been incorporated into the spiritual beliefs and practices of those who have no formal religion, but who have a reverence for life and seek to connect with their own more spiritual nature.

In this chapter we will work with the angels who are associated with the natural world and draw these higher forms of energy into our lives. Nature angels work to make the planet more beautiful and fruitful and, as pollution and destruction have been wreaked by careless humans on mother earth, so angelic contact has become more prevalent to get us back on course.

Nature angels also assist individuals in their daily lives in many ways. In return for these blessings we are required to do something positive and practical in the area of nature ruled by the helping angel in order to preserve cosmic balance.

Nature angels represent nature at its most ideal, even though their efforts may be manifest in places made ugly by human waste and neglect. So when, for example, we invoke Zuphlas, the angel of the forests, in any wooded area, even in a scruffy urban park, we can experience momentarily and be enriched by the energies of the most beautiful forest ever imaginable.

Seeing sky angels

We have all driven towards a magnificent sunset where the clouds appear painted gold and scarlet, pink and purple, against a blue sky. You may have been sitting at the end of the day in your garden or on a hilltop on holiday and noticed angelic formations in the clouds, complete with wings, a face, a halo and flowing robes. Or you may have seen on a sunny day a sudden pillar of light breaking into rays that form an angelic image against the canvas of a clear sky. I once followed such a formation for about half an hour as I drove across the downs that form the backbone of the Isle of Wight's landscape.

A trick of the light? Or a way of suddenly connecting with these higher forms of nature through the channel of our physical eyes?

Certain places in the natural world have become associated with angelic visitations and sightings, sometimes over many years. Angelic cloud pictures are different in quality and intensity from other cloud images.

Sky angels cannot be explained away purely as meteorological phenomena because they are far clearer than ordinary cloud images and fade quite suddenly and dramatically. They may be seen by a number of people at the same time and may flood the whole sky with momentary brilliance.

I have collected a number of accounts of angels in the clouds, like the one experienced by Sally, whom I met her in Glasgow at a healing festival where I was giving a talk. She was describing a place we both loved, the Grey Mare's Tail, above Moffat in the Scottish lowlands, where there is a waterfall and a tiny hidden loch on the top of a hill, accessible only by steep footpath. She told me, 'My marriage had ended, my career as an office manager was going nowhere and I was back living in rented accommodation.

'On impulse I drove from Glasgow to Moffat in pouring rain not even knowing if I could still find the path I had last visited in my teens with my late father. When I arrived the clouds parted, leaving blue sky and the sun came out.

'After a steep climb I spent the afternoon by the loch just sitting, my mind unable to deal with the reality that I had been betrayed by the man I loved, had lost everything and was too old ever to have children of my own.

'Before I knew it the sun was getting low in the sky and I scrambled up, angry with myself for wasting the day, not even comforted by the beauty and stillness. Then a hawk seemed to swoop down across the sun and the sky was flooded with brightness.

'There, unmistakably in the sky, was an angel, huge with outstretched wings, tipped with gold, a halo from which rays of light were radiating, and scarlet and pink robes. Most importantly, I was suddenly filled with joy and certainty that all would be well and I positively raced down the steep track.

'The next day I applied for a college course to train as a children's nurse, which is what I had always wanted to do but had dismissed as impractical at my age. Four years later I qualified. I haven't met a new partner and it has been a financial struggle, but I have remained inspired by my angel through all the hard times.'

Magick from the angels of nature or within Sally, whose mind created the angel image to inspire her?

Throughout history, people have been equally inspired by angels in the clouds. St Brynach, for example, an Irish-born Celtic monk used to climb the Hill of the Angels, set above Nevern near Tenby in south-west Wales, to talk to the angels who appeared in cloud formation above the hill at sunrise and sunset.

Finding cloud angels

* If you want to see cloud angels but their appearance eludes you, watch the sky at different times, at sunrise or sunset, on hot days when the light is brilliant, when scarlet-tipped clouds float across a clear sky, after rain or as storm clouds gather as the sun still shines or when the sun breaks through and there is a rainbow.
* Go to hilltops or open plains or, if you are driving, stop the car in a safe place and get out. Whatever you were hurrying for will probably wait. Maybe you'll decide you didn't need to dash to the superstore or to the drinks party with people you hardly know after all.
* Try also when you are flying in a plane and you are looking down through the clouds.
* Focus on an area of radiance ahead and allow your eyes to take in the scene; as

when you were a child, allow cloud pictures to form, not necessarily angels, without analysing them.

* Still your mind by breathing gently and regularly. On the out-breaths blow away, through your mouth, imaginary bubbles of doubts and worries. Above all, give yourself time to let experiences form (much harder than learning formal meditation techniques but a thousand times more effective). Merge with the stillness of the day or evening (even if there is a motorway roaring along a short distance away).

* If you wait, you may see an angel in the clouds and at such moments you will be flooded with peace and sometimes answers to questions that are troubling you.

* State your wish softly three times and blow it through your fingertips three times towards the angelic figure, while imagining that you are holding a dandelion clock.

* If you see or feel nothing, keep looking at the clouds and ask that you may be given a sign. A white feather may float down, a common angelic symbol. An unusual bird or butterfly may suddenly appear. There may be a breeze or a shower of light rain from a clear sky.

* Within a few days you should see your angel in the sky when least expected.

* Note down when you see cloud angels, the dates, times and the circumstances. Post your experiences on the Internet. I always welcome them on my site and others may contact you who have experienced similar blessings.

* Psychological, spiritual, meteorological? We are very quick in the modern world to rationalise and dismiss and so close our minds to the wonders perceived by our ancestors and used for transmitting wisdom.

Making an angel altar

This is a variation of your basic existing outdoor altar (see page 74) so I will give the original form as a reminder.

An angel altar, whether in your garden or created on a rock in your favourite outdoor place, is a focus for attracting natural power of the highest kind to enrich the place and empower and protect you. After an angel ritual you can leave the angelic substances on the altar for a day or two and this will help to make your space sacred.

You can, if inclement weather prevents you carrying out angel rituals in the open air, use the same format indoors with a small cauldron or deep dish to contain what you would normally pour on the ground. This offerings dish is set on the floor to the north of the angel altar. Indoors, be sure to surround the altar with plenty of greenery.

* Place on the altar, in the north, your special small pillar stone that represents the earth element, the strength, stability, the abundance and permanence of the earth. Find such a stone on one of your natural adventures or use a small amethyst geode or even a crystal angel statue.

* Directly in front of this on the altar (as you move inwards) is the dish of earth, your earth elemental substance. On an angel altar substitute a dish of the relevant dried or chopped fresh herbs, flower petals or dried flower heads (see pages 473–78 for the alternatives according to your chosen angel).

* In the east is your feather (itself a symbol of angels if it is white). This represents the air element, the movement needed to activate your rituals, the freshness of the life force and the positive changes in accordance with the cycles of your life or the seasons.
* Directly in front of this as you move inwards is your smudge stick or sage, pine, cedar or rosemary incense (or maybe a mix) as your air substance. For the angel altar, use the incense or smudge fragrance of the nature angel you are invoking (see next page).
* In the south you have your twig wand and in front of it your natural beeswax candle or small lamp as your fire substance. This represents the fire element, the inspiration and power inherent in nature to bring life and creation and burn away the dead or the redundant aspects of your life.
* Substitute for the usual candle, one of the colour associated with the relevant nature angel. You can buy an array of naturally dyed beeswax candles or make your own (see Insect magick, page 242). Alternatively, use another pure wax candle that has colour all the way through (not dipped).
* Finally in the west you already have a sea shell and in front of it your small bowl of rainwater, sea water or still mineral water to which a pinch of sea salt has been added. Water adds the healing powers and the energy so that good things can flow into your life and the bad can drain away.
* For the water, substitute angel water. This is made by adding to rain or still mineral water a smooth, round, polished angel crystal such as angelite, celestite, amethyst, blue lace agate, blue or pink chalcedony or rose quartz, or the crystal of the nature angel being invoked. Leave the crystal in the water for at least eight hours, preferably from first light or when you wake until just before the rituals.
* In the centre on your slate or flat stone or unglazed pottery dish, set the crystal dedicated to your nature angel once you have removed it from the water. For example Ariel, archangel of nature, would have a moss or tree agate. Here also set a symbol of your chosen angel.
* As you work with the nature angels over the months ahead find a personal symbol for each. These can be carried as a charm when you need the power of a nature angel, as well as being used in rituals. This could be something natural or a small crystal or ceramic angel or a power icon or charm that you link with the angel.

Substitutions

If you cannot get any of the specific angel substances or are carrying out a general ritual to bring the power of nature angels generally into your world, use the following substitutes:

* Dried lavender heads, rose petals or rosemary for the herbs (earth)
* Sage, pine or cedar incense or smudge (air)
* A natural undyed beeswax or white candle (fire)
* Water in which one of the angel crystals listed above or a clear quartz crystal has been soaked (water)

The archangels and angels of nature

A number of angels oversee the natural world. You can draw their energies into your life both spontaneously in the open air, or in the places I suggest for each, using the angel symbols as a focus. You can also use your angel altar for indoor or outdoor rituals at those times when you need to feel close to nature but can't go off into the countryside to find a special place.

Then after the ritual or time in the angel place, you can take your empowered angel symbol with you, calling through it the power of the most beautiful forests, seashores or open moorland into your office, an airless train or plane or apartment. The symbols I have listed are only suggestions. Have a special small purse or drawstring bag in a natural fabric for carrying them with you and between rituals keep them wrapped separately where you keep your magickal artefacts.

Ariel

Archangel of nature and nature spirits, Ariel is the supreme archangel or higher angel over all nature, the waters of the heavens and the earth, of animals, birds, fish and nature essences and spirits such as faeries and elves. You can invoke him for any magickal purpose connected with nature if there is not a relevant angel.

His name means lion of god. Picture Ariel with long silver hair, surrounded by yellow light and with eyes that have been called violet. His cloak is described as radiant white and becomes all the colours of the rainbows as it gets nearer the ground.

Colour: Violet or any shade of purple

Incenses: Lemon, lemon verbena, moss, musk, any fruit incenses

Herbs: Garlic, sage, tarragon

Crystals: All earth jaspers and agates, such as leopardskin, Dalmatian jasper, snakeskin agate, moss agate, tree agate

Call on Ariel for: Clean water and land everywhere, protecting animals against bad farming or living conditions and cruelty, bringing back a love of nature and natural beauty to despoiled or neglected places, to care for your pets, for healing the ozone layer; also any general nature ritual

Personally call him for developing psychic, healing and prophetic abilities, for clearing away what is stagnant and destructive in your life and for healing unfairness or abuse; also for finding a new home or improving your present one.

Where to go to connect with him: In wooded glens or glades or by streams where nature spirits reside; in hidden spots in popular locations; at large open animal or bird conservancies or wildlife reserves where animals live in natural habitats; at recognised beauty spots even if these are litter-strewn; anywhere grassy where you take your dog for a walk or go horse riding or where there is wildlife such as rabbits or wild birds

Suggested symbols of connection: A particularly beautiful feather, a lion or faerie icon

Catharel

Angel of gardens, parks, town squares and smallholdings, Catharel is the angel of anywhere where nature is tamed and orderly, whether the ornamental gardens of a stately home, a botanical garden, a Zen garden (see page 194), a city park or square or a private garden.

Picture him as a working angel with a spade and rake, dressed in soft muted greens and with a pale green halo, so that he merges with the garden and can only be seen hazily in bright sunlight.

Colour: Brown

Incenses: Carnation, lavender, lilac, lily of the valley

Herbs: Cumin, fenugreek, meadowsweet

Crystals: Amber, jade, orange or yellow aragonite

Call upon Catharel for: Bringing the countryside to the town in the form of beautiful gardens; for safe parks and town squares without vandalism or crime; for encouraging a slower pace of life in tune with nature and the seasons; for the creation of safe playgrounds and playing fields for children and for teaching the young about nature

Personally call on Catharel for the restoration of good luck in your life after a reversal, for helping you to create a beautiful garden, no matter how small, for encouraging rest and leisure into a busy life, for happy holidays and for a contented family life and settled home.

Where to connect with him: In a beautiful garden, in any open recreational space or in a quiet corner of the local park

Suggested symbols of connection: Any small potted flower or herb or mixed edible seeds such as sunflower, pumpkin and sesame in a twist of brown paper or a drawstring bag

Orifiel

Angel of the wilderness, Orifiel is the angel or archangel of wild places and remote areas, whether deserts or deep dark forests, wild shores or snowy wastes. He is invoked for reclaiming and restoring land as countryside, whether from the sea or when it has been allowed to go to waste or be spoiled.

Picture Orifiel as ever-changing, sometimes like mountain peaks at sunset, sometimes like deep dark forests, sometimes like the deep blue of lakes, but always with his wings like rainbows with swirling colours.

Colour: Deep green

Incenses: Fern, lemongrass, patchouli, sweet grass

Herbs: Chives, fennel, rosemary

Crystals: Azurite, chrysocolla, laboradite, sodalite, turquoise

Call on Orifiel for: Protection of those who live or work in the wilderness; those who go camping or backpacking, walking or holidaymaking in wild places; also for protecting the ecology, the flora and fauna of undisturbed places and for creating new quiet habitats and country parks for humans, plants and creatures alike; for overcoming problems of overcrowding in cities

Personally call him to overcome any seemingly insurmountable obstacles, for finding peace and stillness in a frantic life or when you cannot rest, for any travel plans or for restoring direction in life when you feel lost.

Where to go to connect with him: Deep country, camping grounds, wildlife gardens anywhere and also uncultivated areas of your own garden; country parks, gardens of ruined abbeys and castles

Suggested symbols of connection: A tiny compass, small dried wildflowers tied with natural twine (replace when they crumble)

Phul

Angel of the lakes, wells and still waters, Phul is the guardian of all pools, lakes, reservoirs, canals, wells and garden ponds, especially by moonlight as he is also an angel of the moon. He protects holy healing wells and places where animals drink such as waterholes.

Picture him as silvery blue almost transparent, usually standing motionless, with moonbeams illuminating his halo and silvery wings.

Colour: Any blue or silver

Incenses: Coconut, jasmine, myrrh, poppy

Herbs: Cloves, coriander, lemon balm

Crystals: All fluorites, moonstone, selenite

Call upon Phul for: Clear and clean waters everywhere that all may bathe and drink safely wherever they are in the world, for preserving the water holes and pools of wild animals, for peace and for the cessation of wars, and occupations which cause the innocent to suffer for years afterwards

Personally call Phul for the restoration of love and trust, for healing of all kinds, for harmony in your life and the mending of quarrels.

Where to go to connect with him: By a lake, a well, a pool, a canal or pond, especially in moonlight or early on misty mornings

Suggested symbols of connection: Anything silver

Rahab

Angel of the sea, Rahab is also the angel of all salt marshes and salty inland waters; he protects all sea creatures and fights constantly against polluted oceans and oil spills from tankers; he also protects sailors, ferry operators and their passengers and fishermen.

Picture Rahab in deep blues and greens with a trident, striding over the white foamed waves with his billowing white wings like sails.

Colour: Turquoise or red

Incenses: Anise, copal, dragon's blood, kelp

Herbs: Agrimony, cinnamon, ginger

Crystals: Aqua aura, aquamarine, aventurine, ocean or orbicular jasper

Call upon Rahab for: Safety at sea; for protection from tidal waves, tsunamis, high tides, especially on flat lands, erosion and from pollution of the oceans.

Personally call Rahab to protect you while travelling by water and from fears of water, from bullying of all kinds, from excessive emotions, violence, addictions and obsessions and from sudden misfortune and to recover what has been lost or stolen, whether on land or sea.

Where to connect with him: On the sea shore, on salt marshes or inland seas

Suggested symbols for connection: Shells of all kinds, dried kelp or seaweed

Rampel

Angel of the mountains and the high places, Rampel is the guardian of hills and mountains, from rocky inaccessible peaks to gentle flower-covered hillside. He also watches over all who climb, ski, walk on or live on or near hills and mountains, endeavouring to prevent landslides and avalanches in winter.

Picture Rampel as very tall and slender; his wings are perpetually shrouded in silver mist and he wears deep purple.

Colour: Dark blue or indigo

Incenses: Frankincense, heather, hibiscus, hyacinth

Herbs: Hyssop, marjoram, sagebrush

Crystals: Blue chalcedony, clear crystal quartz, lapis lazuli, malachite, sugilite

Call on Rampel for: Cleansing air pollution, radiation and mobile phone mast emissions; for wise leadership among nations; for protecting those who climb or fly. especially to potential danger spots; for all journeys by whatever means; for keeping alive mountain communities, people, flora and fauna

Personally call on Rampel for overcoming fears of flying, to achieve dreams and ambitions, for success in career or creativity or for moving far away.

Where to connect with him: On mountains, in the hills, on top of tall towers or while in a plane looking out of the window

Suggested symbols of connection: A tiny model plane, a pure white feather

Rismuch

Angel of agriculture and cultivated farm or grazing land, Rismuch is the friend of farmers and food producers, of the harvest and of harvest grains, vegetables and fruits, as well as the animals who graze.

Picture him in every shade of brown, with tawny wings and halo, carrying a scythe and a hoe as symbols that he is conserver of the land and the crops.

Colour: Natural beeswax or pale yellow

Incenses: Chamomile, mimosa, rosewood, sandalwood

Herbs: Dill, parsley, yarrow

Crystals: Banded agate, brown jasper, fossils, flint, yellow jasper

Call upon Rismuch for: Good harvests, especially in lands where there is famine; for the wise use of land resources; for fertility of the land and the crops; for protection against drought, disease in animals and chemical pollution of food; and for the end of poverty in cities as well as the countryside

Personally call Rismuch for fertility in your life whether the birth of a child or the success of a project or business venture, for abundance and prosperity, for justice and for a long life; also the reduction of debt.

Where to go to connect with him: Footpaths and green ways through agricultural land, farm parks, agricultural museums and unploughed fields left to grass

Suggested symbols of connection: A small corn dolly or corn animal; a plaited ring of dried grasses tied with red ribbon

Trsiel

Angel of the rivers and running waters, Trsiel is the angel of rivers large and small, of all running water and also estuaries where the river enters the sea; he also controls floods and works to prevent flowing water sources drying up or becoming polluted.

Picture him in many shades of green, holding a golden oar and with a halo of sparkling rainbow water drops.

Colour: Pink or pale blue

Incenses: Bergamot, lily, lotus, rose

Herbs: Blessed thistle, catnip, peppermint

Crystal: Blue calcite, pearls, pink chalcedony, rose quartz, any tourmaline

Call upon Trsiel for: Clean rivers where fish and water life survives, to regulate the rainfall and river flow so there is neither drought nor flood, for safety from drowning for all who sail or fish in or swim in rivers; also for fair trade between the people of different lands

Personally call Trsiel so that new energies and opportunities may flow into your life, for love and friendship, for safety from accident and road rage on regular short-distance travel and for protection from spite, gossip, bullying and negative feelings or attack from others.

Where to go to connect with him: River banks, streams, estuaries, especially as the tide comes in

Suggested symbols for connection: A dish of blue and green glass nuggets, a pearl necklace or bracelet

Zuphlas

Angel of the forests and of trees, Zuphlas is also the angel of groves and woodlands, arboretums, urban copses and vast tracts of wooded countryside; he works for the conservation of rainforests and for the planting of new forests in industrialised areas and on the edges of cities.

Picture him in pine green with his golden axe, over his head a halo entwined with laurel and pine (in some accounts), his wings wreathed in leaves and carrying a staff from which are sprouting small branches, leaves and blossoms.

Colour: Soft moss green or autumnal orange

Incenses: Apple or orange blossom, cedar, eucalyptus, pine, tea tree

Herbs: Basil, bay, thyme

Crystals: Green jasper, jet, petrified wood, rutilated quartz, tree agate

Call on Zuphlas for: The preservation of trees, for protecting the rainforests, for the revival of ancient forest land and the re-introduction of native species; for the creation of forests on the edges of towns and for building playgrounds of natural wood for children

Personally call him for your own spiritual growth, for strength, the return of health, for faithfulness in love, for valuing traditions and the healthy growth of children.

Where to go to connect with him: All forests, woodlands or an arboretum; beneath any tree

Suggested symbols of connection: A perfect pine cone, a small carved wooden statue of a woodland animal

Angelic rituals

Angelic rituals are not like conventional spells. You don't build up the power and then release it into the cosmos or channel it into herbs or crystals (see spellcasting on pages 26–39).

Rather the power is already present in the angelic connection. As you call the angelic name and carry out the actions with the angelic substances, angel blessings are automatically channelled into you and your chosen purpose for the ritual. They will continue to flow gently and steadily into your life or the chosen place over the days and weeks ahead.

* You can connect with each angel by going to one of his places with one of his symbols (see lists on previous pages). If appropriate, take the items necessary to set up a small altar (see making a crane or magick bag on page 71).
* Alternatively, work with the symbols listed for each angel and use your hands and voice to draw down the blessings.
* At home, adapt your outdoor altar to an angel altar (see page 471) and visualise the place you are asking the angel to heal or help.
* Angel rituals have a dual focus. If you are working for an ecological purpose – for example, invoking Rahab angel of the sea to help minimise damage caused to marine life and the fishing industry by an oil slick – as a bonus, blessings will also enter your personal life in the most appropriate way. In this example, any bad luck you may have recently suffered would be reversed – or if you haven't had any, the continuation of present good fortune would be assured.
* However, if you have a pressing personal need, for example if someone is making you unhappy at work or in the neighbourhood by means of spite, gossip or bullying, then it's hard to focus on fair trade or clean rivers until you feel happier. In this case you could ask Trsiel, angel of flowing water, to help you. As a bonus, the ecological issues will also be given strength quite spontaneously. I will describe two actual rituals as a templates around which you can create your own.

A Rampel, anti-mobile-phone-mast ritual

Heather lives in a small development of new houses on the outskirts of a village in a hilly area of Northern England. She has two small children. Recently a large mobile phone company has erected a huge mast near the village. Heather is worried because she has read a great deal about the adverse effects of mobile phones and radiation on children. This ecologically based ritual is specific to this particular problem, but you can use this format and work with whichever angel you choose and his symbols to weave your own ritual for your ecological or personal needs.

You will need: Three pure white feathers, symbols of Rampel; a malachite crystal that is effective against radiation and technological pollution; a sagebrush smudge stick; Rampel's herb.

Timing: Ideally early morning so that the sun is rising over the mast; a still day will mean that the malachite crystal is particularly effective.

The ritual is carried out at the top of one of the local hills, with the mast visible in the distance

* Put the smudge in a deep jar with a little sand in the bottom and the feathers in

a deep narrow jar. Set the containers side by side with the malachite between them. The line of items then forms a horizontal to the vertical mast in the distance.

* Light the smudge and hold it in your power hand.
* Take the crystal in the other hand.
* Stand facing the mast and the sun, then, in silence, turn to greet the four directions with your smudge. Then facing the mast again, raise the smudge to the sky and then down to the earth (see page 109).
* Holding the smudge at a 60-degree angle from the vertical, pointing upwards, say nine times:

Rampel, Rampel, Rampel, Rampel, Rampel, Rampel, Rampel, Rampel, Rampel, you who love the high places, protect I ask the young from this threat of harm imposed upon the landscape without our will.

* Make nine anticlockwise spirals towards the mast, saying:

Remove the danger.

* Make nine clockwise spirals, saying:

Restore all as before.

* Then bury the crystal at the top of the hillside and release the feathers into the air, repeating Rampel's name nine times more.
* Extinguish the smudge by holding it downwards in the sand in the container and walk down the hill slowly.
* By saying angelic names, you are invoking or calling their power and protection into your life. It does not matter if you are uncertain how to pronounce their names, because in different countries the pronunciation of an obscure name will differ anyway.

Some weeks after the ritual, I heard that the local authority had taken a stand against the company because of the strength of local pressure and they were forced to remove the mast at least for the foreseeable future. As a personal bonus Heather won a place on the local council so she can monitor the situation from within.

A personal Phul angel altar ritual for mending a quarrel

Paul had lost contact with his father as result of a major quarrel. Instead of joining the family engineering firm after college as Paul had promised, he wanted to work abroad with a charity in Africa for a year, setting up a computer system at a university to create a database of antidotes for poisonous snake bites for the region. This meant his father had to postpone his own travel plans in order to train someone new.

This is a reconciliation ritual, specific to Paul's problem, but you can follow the format for a reconciliation ritual of your own.

You will need: A stone (for earth); a dish of coriander seeds; a feather (air); myrrh incense stick (Phul's fragrance); a twig wand; a blue-dyed beeswax candle; a sea shell; water in which a green fluorite crystal had been soaked for eight hours; a round, flat, wooden altar plate; the same green fluorite crystal; a silver heart (to represent love that Paul believed still existed within his father).

Timing: Sunset, a good time for reconciliation rituals

* Position the following items on the altar: in the north, the stone and dish of coriander seeds; in the east, the feather and in front of it the myrrh incense stick in a holder; in the south, the twig wand and the blue dyed beeswax candle; in the west, the sea shell and the water in which the crystal had been soaked.
* In the centre of the altar, on the altar plate, place the green fluorite crystal and the silver heart.
* Light the incense stick and, beginning in the north, create a complete clockwise circle of smoke at waist height round the angel altar and working space. This should extend about 90 cm/3 feet all round the altar.
* As you do this, name Phul nine times and say:

I cast this circle for peace, love and reconciliation.

* Return the incense to its holder and take the dish of coriander seeds. Beginning in the north, make a complete clockwise circle of seeds round the central plate containing the crystal and the heart. As you scatter the seeds, name Phul three times and say:

I call upon the healing earth to heal this bitterness and ill-feeling.

* Return the coriander to its place and taking the incense once more, begin in the east and make a complete clockwise circle of smoke about 2.5 cm/1 in above the seed circle.
* As you do so, say the name of Phul three times, followed by:

May the winds of change bring a new softer attitude that my father and I may speak again together.

* Return the incense to its place.
* Next light the candle and, beginning in the south, make a complete clockwise circle of light round the altar plate (with the candle in its holder upright so it does not drip wax).
* As you do so, call on Phul three times more, saying:

May the sun flame on a new day and bring warmth once more to my family.

* Return the candle to its place on the altar.
* Finally, beginning in the west, take the water bowl and make a complete circle of water drops round the altar plate over the seeds. Call on Phul three times and say:

May the waters of love and kindliness flow once more between my father and me
and bring healing.

✴ Return the water to its place and pass the altar plate with the crystal and silver heart over the four elemental substances in turn without speaking, beginning in the north over the dish of seeds and moving clockwise.
✴ Return the plate to the centre and say:

Gentle Phul, I ask for healing of this quarrel and I pledge _____ (name what
you will do towards one of Phul's causes in return for the personal blessing).

✴ Blow out the candle very slowly and softly and say:

Love and light.

✴ Close the circle by making an anticlockwise circle of smoke beginning and ending in the north, saying:

Though the circle is closed, may the love remain unbroken.

✴ Leave the incense to burn through in its place on the altar and pour the remaining coriander seeds from the dish and the rest of the water on to the earth.
✴ To end the rite, say:

Blessings be.

✴ After you have cleared up, put the heart and crystal in a small purse and set it next to a picture of the estranged person.
✴ Relight the candle each night for three nights, putting the crystal and heart on top of the purse in front of it.
✴ Call on Phul nine times to bring reconciliation. Each night blow out the candle, slowly and gently, sending love and light in the name of Phul.
✴ On the fourth night (including the night of the original ritual) leave the candle to burn through.

Paul contacted his father on the fifth day and they agreed to meet. Paul took the crystal and heart with him in the purse as a talisman. His father is still not happy but has agreed Paul should go for six months and see how things progress. Paul has promised to cover for his father at the end of the year at the latest, so his father can have his own trip if the replacement cannot be left in charge by then. Paul also arranged to spend a week digging wells in Africa before his contract began, in thanks to Phul.

2

DEVA MAGICK

Whereas angels enter the world of nature from their own realms to beautify the earth so it moves closer to the heavenly realms, devas are always present within the natural world. Their role is to manifest the spiritual blueprint of creation into actuality and constantly to renew the original work of creation by ensuring the cycle of birth, growth, destruction and new growth is unbroken.

As pollution and destruction of the earth's resources has spread, so devas have increasingly made their presence known to sensitive humans to warn us and to guide us back to living in harmony with the natural cycles.

Who are the devas?

The word 'deva' comes from the Sanskrit language, and means 'a being of brilliant light'. Devas may occasionally be perceived as huge opalescent beings set against brilliant sunlight or, because they adapt to the environment, as a wise face etched in rock, as a gigantic shadow at an ancient stone circle, as sparkling, dancing, swirling figures shedding moonbeams as the full moon rides high over a shoreline or as cascading flowers of every hue and fragrance as the wind blows the blossoms in the spring. More often you will just sense the presence and feel a surge of energy as though you are plugged into the life force, and hear words that seem to come from all round you but at the same time echo as your own inner wise voice.

A healer in the north of Sweden told me the following story about the creation of devas.

Devas were in God's own blueprint intended to become nature spirits, and were quite small and brown. As the sixth day was ending and God said, 'Creation is finished', He noticed that the devas whom He wanted to bless were missing. He became angry at their lateness.

Then God looked with his all-seeing eyes and realised that the small brown devas kept stopping to mend broken flowers, to struggle to lift heavy trees that had not taken root, to help the animals to give birth to the first young and to help the birds build their nests. They were planting seeds that had fallen by the wayside that were already sprouting into wonderful fruit trees, vegetables and flowers.

God's heart was filled with love for them. He told them they should henceforth be the shining ones, tall in stature and able to take their chosen form at will. Because they had helped the weak and the vulnerable, they would be rewarded by becoming the overseers of nature and so would possess bodies of pearl and opalescent light for evermore.

Devas are credited with great powers in the skies, water and earth: exploding star clusters, regulating the tides, making forests grow and the huge mountains shift and change imperceptibly over thousands of years, creating perfume in flowers and infusing herbs with healing properties for modern ills. Devas ensure that the original creation is replicated over the millennia and species of flora and fauna adapted to new climates and needs. It may even be that a crop circle is a message from the corn devas for us to stop damaging mother earth.

Devas love music and singing and can sometimes communicate through the sounds of nature such as water flowing over pebbles or the wind in trees.

They are also associated with the four elements (earth, air, fire and water) and rule over the elemental beings. In Wicca and ceremonial magick, devas are called lords of the watchtower, and represent the four quarters of the ritual circle. Indeed, they use the energy of the elemental spirits (see pages 490–92) to bring their creations into life.

The power of devas

Devas do not cause major natural disruptions such as earthquakes, tidal waves and hurricanes, which are geological phenomena. Though these are upsurges of nature, and though they can cause great destruction, they are ecologically necessary to release pressures within nature herself.

Nevertheless, human-induced factors such as global warming do upset the balance of nature and make it harder for devas to limit and control the harmful effects of the necessary and spontaneous global destructive processes. Nature isn't sweet and gentle, but powerful and, in human terms, even with modern measuring devices, still unpredictable. The devas aren't cosy guardians who spend their days painting flowers.

One way to connect with devas is by asking the question, 'How can I be of help to the earth and its creatures?' and by showing reverence for the natural world, practically as well as in ritual.

Deva rituals are important to help to empower and energise nature, as our ancestors knew and as indigenous people with unchanged lifestyles close to nature are still aware. Each individual can make a difference for we are all part of the interconnected life web, and when we offer power or healing from our own innate power source, then we are empowering the turning of the world.

Earth chakras and devas

One of the most vital roles of devas is to keep the earth chakra sites open so that they can take energy from the skies, and so that energy can flow throughout the earth causing growth and health in all who walk upon it or swim in its waters.

Many of the most sacred sites of the world are located on these vortices or centres of earth energy or chakras. These vortices are among the most powerful places to experience deva energy and healing. Our ancestors knew where the power centres were and so channelled the energy into their sacred constructions or carried out rituals on the untouched land.

These earth power locations are similar to the chakras or energy centres that humans have in their bodies. Contact with these earth energy chakras is a good way of energising our own system. I have written more of chakras in my book *Chakra Power* (see Further reading, page 514).

The following places are some of the major and minor earth chakra points (some are recognised earth chakra centres; at others I have personally experienced deva power):

* the Pyramids at Gaza in Cairo in Egypt
* Mount Sinai in Israel
* Mount Kilimanjaro in Africa
* the Serpent Mound, in Ohio, just east of Cincinnati
* Moose Mountain Wheel, the oldest existing stone medicine wheel, in south eastern Saskatchewan
* Sedona in Arizona
* Montserrat near Barcelona
* the caves of Nerja in Andalusia in Spain
* the labyrinth in Chartres Cathedral in France
* Findhorn in Morayshire in north-east Scotland where the devas created a fabulous garden with huge flowers and vegetables out of barren earth
* New Grange passage grave in County Meath in Ireland
* Avebury Stones, Stonehenge and Glastonbury in England
* Wawel Hill in Krakow in Poland
* the Zagorsk monastery complex near Moscow
* Uluru (Ayers Rock) in Australia, called in Aboriginal tradition 'the navel of the world'
* Mount Fujiyama in Japan
* the shinto shrine of Ise in southern Honshu in Japan
* the Forbidden City in Beijing, China.

In these places you will feel pure deva power and healing at its most intense and magickal.

Finding earth chakra sites for deva contact

Just as the energy centres in the human body are linked by countless energy channels, so devic energy can be experienced at any ancient site, standing stone, dolmen, holy well or hill with mythological associations such as the Goddess Hill at Silbury near Avebury, at turf or stone outdoor labyrinths that are common throughout Scandinavia, England, Germany, the Netherlands and the Baltic. Go also to lakes set in mountains or in the middle of a plain, anywhere where earth and sky energies naturally fuse.

By visiting these places and making offerings, tuning into the energies and sending our individual power, we can help to keep the chakras and energy channels of the earth unblocked and the energies flowing – and as a bonus the pure energies flow more freely through our own psychic energy system.

A personal deva place of power

You may already have found your deva place, perhaps instinctively selecting it as your special magickal sanctuary to which you travel periodically to carry out your most sacred natural magick (see page 69). If not, continue to search for this personally powerful place.

* Choose an area of wild outstanding beauty or one where there are legends of serpents, dragons or giants. People may describe these mythical beings to explain the power surge of the deva, which they tune into spontaneously at the site, but may not understand.
* Use holidays in different locations and the added relaxation factor to tune into devas at old sites and beautiful wild place or tropical gardens. Each deva will amplify and convey the essence of the place, exotic, untamed or of deep sanctity. Often thyme will grow profusely near the spot.

The deva connection rite

You will need: A clear crystal pendulum (optional).

Timing: Work at a transition time – dawn, dusk, the full moon night or during the day at the beginning or end of the moon cycle (see page 431 for details, or consult a moon diary or the weather page of the local newspaper). Major festivals like the longest day (around 21 June), the shortest day (around 21 December) or the equinoxes are good because on these days the barriers between the dimensions are more fluid. The first and last day of the month are also potent.

* Walk around the place until your feel as though you are on a carousel. If you have a pendulum, the closer you get to the earth power spot, the more it will spiral and swirl as if caught in a whirlpool. You may sense a tugging downwards as though you are being pulled by gravity, like in Alice in Wonderland's rabbit hole or the star gates at a major vortex.
* This is the place of the guardian deva. You may begin to see a swirling form.
* Close your eyes and connect with the deva energy. You will know when you are linking because you will feel the carousel slowing or you may feel steadied and supported as if the deva is holding you steady in the eye of a storm.
* Open your eyes and you may momentarily see the deva or may be aware of a face or figure as though against brilliant light or as huge brown shadows or swirling mists (particularly near old stones). Through the deva you can momentarily see the place in other ages, for these places are also time portals.
* Find a quiet place to sit down. Sing softly or speak in a rhythmic chant a greeting to the deva of the place (see page 298 for creating chants).
* Then listen. The deva may communicate through the sounds of nature, such as water flowing over pebbles or the wind in trees or you may hear soft, slow words almost as a whisper.

- Look ahead at the central rock, the centre of the lake or the peak of the mountain and you may momentarily see in speeded up motion the structure of the place, the seeds taking root, the blossoms forming on the trees, crystals forming and rock being worn away into earth or a dead butterfly crumbling and returning to the soil to start the new cycle.
- This vision will help you to feel, not just know about intellectually and understand, a little of the wider cycle of growth and decay both of a single flower and the universe.
- Bury a small crystal or one of the treasures from your crane bag (see page 71) near the deva's power centre to strengthen the place and to keep the energies flowing.
- Finally, ask how you may be of help and the answer will come quite unexpectedly in the next day or two.

Such rituals are wonderful in major places of power, so try at least every two months to spend just a day at an ancient site or place of beauty. As a bonus of your connection with the deva at these major earth centres, you will feel a huge infusion of power that will last weeks or months. You can also fill your treasures and crystals with power if you set them on the ground.

Channelling the deva power and protection spell

You can also carry out specific regular devic energising and protective rituals at your local special place. Often it's not possible to use fire or incense but you can still use your altar formation as outlined here. You don't even need an actual altar if you can't find a suitable stone, but can set the elements at the edges of the visualised circle and any offerings on a natural fabric cloth in the centre.

You will need: A small stone (earth); a feather (air); a gold-coloured coin or small piece of gold-coloured jewellery like an earring (fire); a silver-coloured coin or small piece of silver-covered jewellery (water); your wand; two or three of your natural treasures from your crane bag or a favourite crystal; your pendulum to find the precise centre of power

After the first ritual you will automatically be able to identify the centre of power. The full energy will extend at least five adult paces in every direction from the central point and thereafter will weaken but not disappear for least another five outward steps from the power base. This will give you plenty of room to cast your circle.

Timing: Any transition of the day, week or month or a seasonal change

- Begin with a compass reading or use approximate directions to mark the four quarters with four sticks or stones from the site. The perimeter of this imagined circle will be about ten paces outwards from the central point.
- Set out the elemental symbols just inside the visualised perimeter, the stone in the north, feather in the east, gold in the south and silver in the west.
- Cast the circle clockwise, beginning in the north so that the elemental artefacts are just inside.
- Hold your wand in your extended arm pointing downwards at about a 60-degree angle from the vertical (your arm should be just below waist height). Say:

*I cast this circle in the place of the devas, asking their blessings, their power and
their protection upon this ritual and this land.*

* Though you are working with the deva of the specific place, you will also call on
the devas of the different directions and their elemental powers.
* Move to the perimeter of the circle and face the north, looking outwards.
Holding the stone between your cupped hands (to make your palm chakra or
energy centre connection), say:

*You devas of the earth, you who make the soil fertile, the flowers and trees grow
strong and beautiful, I greet you.*

* Put the stone down. Move to the east, again on the perimeter looking outwards.
Hold the feather between your cupped hands and say:

*You devas of the air, who form the clouds, create the winds, direct the stars and guide
the heavenly planets on their courses, I greet you.*

* Set the feather down and go to the southern perimeter. Facing outwards, hold
the gold between your cupped hands and say:

*You devas of the fire, who assist the sun to move across the sky on its daily and yearly journey,
who sustain with life corn and animals and humankind alike, I greet you.*

* Return the gold and move to the western perimeter facing outwards. Hold the
silver and say:

*You devas of the west who order the tides, fill the mighty rivers with the rainfall
and act as monthly midwife to the moon, I greet you.*

* Return to the centre and stand so that your wand is pointing directly downwards
over your treasures/crystals, about 2.5 cm/1 in above them.
* Face north and say:

Protect the earth, protect with the earth.

* Face east and point upwards with the wand, saying:

Empower the skies, empower with the skies.

* Now face south and point with your wand directly southwards and say:

Give life to the sun, give life from the sun.

* Finally, face west, point westwards with your wand and say

Heal the moon, heal with the moon.

* Return to the northern perimeter of your circle and walk round within the circle clockwise nine times, swirling your wand in large circles vertically in front of you, repeating faster and faster:

Protect, empower, give life and heal.

* Stamp quite deliberately as you move to connect with the devic energies of the place.
* Then reverse and go nine times anticlockwise, repeating the chant and then nine times clockwise, chanting again and swirling the wand.
* End by returning to the centre, facing north, raising your wand to the skies and bringing it in a slashing movement down to the earth, then behind you to your right and forward again, calling:

Devas all, be blessed and bring blessings.

* Now starting in the west, face outwards, holding your wand ahead and say:

I thank you, devas of the water, hail and farewell.

* If appropriate, bury the silver in that spot.
* Return to the south and close that direction using the same words but addressing the devas of the south. Bury the gold in this spot if you can.
* At the east repeat the farewell to the devas of the east and set the feather free if possible.
* Finally, at the north, thank the devas of that direction and if possible leave the stone standing.
* If you can't bury, release or leave the symbols, take them with you and bury, release or leave them in the four directions in an appropriate place as offerings to the devas.
* Now standing in the centre, turn in all four directions, beginning in the west, and say for each:

May the circle of power and protection be uncast but its blessings remain.

* Sit a few minutes in the centre on the ground allowing the energies to flow back into the earth.
* This is a good basic ritual to be carried out regularly, but you can modify the words to ask for any specific blessings.

3

ELEMENTAL MAGICK

Elementals are the forces behind each act of creation and destruction. They conduct the life force through nature. Each of the four elements (earth, air, fire and water) is manifest through the essences of the individual elements. They translate the blueprints of the nature devas into the actual flowers, trees or crystals. Elementals give the seeds the power to grow and the energy to flourish as mature trees. They continue to energise the cycle of growth, maturity and decay through the scattering of new seeds until the eventual bark decays, the tree dies and is replaced; in the case of a yew tree this can take up to two thousand years.

Elementals don't exist permanently as separate entities from their element. Nor do they have distinct species or personal characteristics in the same way as for example a gnome, the archetypal earth nature spirit, does. However, they can appear as wavy, flickering, flame-like figures, as swirling shimmers of water rising from a waterfall, as darting flashes of light in the air or as wispy mist rising over the land. People fleeing from forest fires have described how animated flames seem to curl like huge fingers to snatch at them.

When an elemental has finished its task, which could last anything from a few minutes to a thousand years or more, they return to their own element in undifferentiated form. They can change size and appearance while they are animated, but remain as part of the same element. What is more they cannot after the first creation brought the elements into being, be created or destroyed.

The elemental beings are, therefore, the bridge of power between the material and spiritual plane.

The powers of the elementals

There are magickal beings that typify the elemental energies in a more stable form and are energised by them. These include the gnomes of the earth, the sylphs of the air, the salamanders or djinns of the fire and the undines of the water (see Faerie magick, pages 501–12).

In this chapter we will work with the elemental spirits as manifest in nature herself and through magickal ritual.

Elemental magick is the most dynamic and powerful of all, manifest in the everyday world through nature at her most magnificent and unpredictable. It can be experienced in storms and thunderbolts, waterfalls, rough seas, bonfires, wild craggy mountain sides with tiny pieces of stone perpetually slipping down the slopes, rocky shorelines, clay cliffs constantly eroding and shimmering deserts.

Magicians, especially in mediaeval times, worked a lot with elemental spirits, trying to bind them for their ritual purposes. Some wizards got themselves into very bad psychological and psychic situations by setting themselves above the elementals and ordering them around. They summoned elemental spirits as servants and in doing so made them into independent tulpas or thought forms, rather than working with them within nature itself.

Of course, as you can imagine, a fire tulpa was very powerful in a spell, but however much protection you may use psychically, such a concentrated form of energy is hard to banish or to bid farewell, especially since it cannot be destroyed and as a tulpa has its own free will.

There are a number of very old magick books and a few modern irresponsible ones that give such rituals. I would seriously advise, no matter how extensive your magickal development, against creating elemental thought forms, especially collectively with coven members or friends, unless you are very careful.

What is more, elemental energies are neutral and can be used for good or ill. In nature herself, a forest fire can clear an area of dead woodland, but an out-of-control conflagration destroys homes, habitats, animals, birds and people. The tragic effects of the December 2004 tsunami in South-east Asia were caused by natural phenomena and demonstrate the power of water – we shouldn't deal with water or any other elementals lightly. Above all, it is really important not to work with the elementals when you are feeling angry or negative as your thoughts can be amplified by the elemental powers and you may unwittingly unleash powerful negative feelings. So dig the garden, thump pillows or complain until you feel calmer.

Earth elementals

At their most powerful, earth elementals are manifest in earth tremors, as earth lights, in crop circles, leaves on a tree shaken by the wind, rock falls, avalanches, snow and hail blizzards or within the centre of enclosed groves of trees. They are also concentrated in passages within caves, in railway and canal tunnels and in underground mines where they may be perceived as mine spirits. Feel them at stone circles and near ley lines, especially on the festivals, where they can use the powerful and unstable forces of the parting dimensions to take temporary form. At such times they may be seen as dancing lights or figures round stone circles.

UFO sightings are very common over stone circles, such as Arbor Low in Derbyshire where more than forty ley lines converge and at seasonal change points, especially on the summer solstice, the time of the union of sun (fire) and earth power. Some people attribute this extra-terrestrial activity to the appearance of elementals as whirling metallic disks or at least that UFO sightings are made possible by the release of elemental power at times of intense natural force.

Earth elemental energy may also be manifest in animal power, the bull, the bear, the buffalo/bison, and the badger, and also in snakes, spiders, moths and bees.

Air elementals

At their most powerful, these are manifest as the sudden tossing of a pile of leaves, as high winds, storms, sandstorms, dust clouds, whirlwinds, hurricanes, tornadoes, rainbows, comets and shooting stars. You can experience air elementals if you are standing on the deck of a ship in a high wind; see their patterns in the clouds outside the cabin of an aircraft during turbulence; and witness them on swing bridges and in all high, open places, especially in unsettled weather.

They are also expressed through the power and flight of the eagle, hawk and birds of prey, in swooping flocks of birds, as butterflies and as the mythical Native North American thunderbird.

Fire elementals

These are the most dramatic of the elementals and appear in all kinds of fire, from hearth fires, wood burning stoves, barbecues, and garden chimeneas to bonfires, especially those at festivals, forest fires, in deserts and on huge expanses of sand in the shimmering heat. They express their force in volcanoes, eclipses, hilltop beacons, near lighthouses, at firework displays, in children's sparklers, in torches, fire dishes; and in addition during heat waves, lightning and meteor showers.

Their energy may be manifest in the animal kingdom as the stag, lion or lizard; as fireflies and dragonflies; as dragons and as the legendary golden phoenix (symbol of transformation and rebirth, which burned itself on a funeral pyre every 500 years, only to rise again golden from the ashes).

Water elementals

These are manifest in rough seas, flowing rivers, mill streams and fast-flowing watercourses, as will o' the wisps over marshland, in waterfalls, in bubbles and foam, in water spouts, geysers, hot streams and pools, near water holes and wells that are still used regularly, on busy inland waterways used for leisure or commerce and near estuaries especially at tide turn; in any water on the night of the full moon; also in Jacuzzis, whirlpool baths and flumes at swimming pools.

They appear in the animal kingdom as frogs, dolphins, whales, seals, walruses, all fish – especially the salmon – as sea horses, crabs and all crustaceans.

Using the power of the elementals to clear negative earth energies

Elementals are essential to the movement of energy through the earth. But sometimes energy lines get blocked because of human pollution such as motorway construction, phone-mast erection, or mine working that has been abandoned though the resources are not naturally exhausted. Other causes include major housing developments especially in direct line with sacred sites (and so on natural earth power lines not intended for dwellings). Sometimes housing or workplaces are created from old business premises or institutions such as mental hospitals, prisons or warehouses. These can carry negative feelings from earlier inhabitants that likewise sour and slow the flow of energies through the new homes and offices. These negative earth energies are sometimes called geopathic stress.

If you live or work in a place of negative earth energies then the building or certain rooms may feel cold or seem dark even in summer. Plants will not thrive and animals refuse to settle. Children may become fractious there or have nightmares if the blocked psychic streams are below a bedroom. You may feel tired or suffer a series of minor illnesses and accidents in common with others who live or work there or there may be a lot of quarrels seemingly triggered by no logical causes. Stress-related illnesses are common among workers in such establishments.

There are numerous ways of removing these negative energies and I have written more about this in my book *Psychic Protection Lifts the Spirit* (see Further reading, page 516). One of the best methods is to set amethyst geodes (tiny crystals in rock) around the area and wash them regularly. However, an elemental ritual is very effective and very fast-acting, so this can be repeated every month or so if you feel the negativity returning.

Because you won't be at a spot of natural elemental power, you can use elemental spirit substances to transfer elemental energies to a problem area, large or small. You can also use the same ritual near the centre of your home to revitalise the energies to restore good luck and happiness if you have had a run of misfortune.

A spell to remove negative energies from a place or to bring an infusion of good luck

You will need: A natural living earth substance containing earth elemental power. The safest is a crystal (amethyst, calcite or rose quartz) which should be rough-edged and unpolished, or a rock containing glints of quartz.

A natural living air substance, either a smudge stick in sagebrush or cedar or a natural herbal or floral incense burned on a charcoal block on an open fireproof dish with a heatproof lip for carrying (see page 100). This is one occasion when an incense stick is not so suitable, though you can use one if you can't get the other kind (try sage or pine).

A flame for fire, such as a very squat candle on a flat fireproof dish (one with a spike to secure the candle is a good idea). Make sure the dish is the kind that can be carried or has a heat-resistant handle.

Water from a bubbling tap or sparkling mineral water shaken well before pouring it into in a glass bowl.

A pendulum (optional).

Timing: A peak of energy such as noon, the day or night of the full moon. Alternatively, a windy and rainy day.

The essence is speed and combining the elemental forces to stir up the stagnant earth energies and clear blockages.

* Go to your outdoor altar if it is a matter of restoring good luck to the home or a business.
* Alternatively, work in the centre of the room where the stagnant or negative energy feels most prevalent. You can use a pendulum to identify this centre (it may extend at least three or four paces in every direction). If you have a blocked energy stream, it may be like a wavy band about five or six adult paces wide across the whole room. This stream will extend from external wall to external wall. Again, work in the most central place in the most central room affected by the stream.

* The floors above and below will be affected in the same places so work in the lowest room and the cleansing will occur downwards towards the blockage. The negative energies from above will gradually disperse over the following hours once the prime source of negativity has been cleared.
* You are going to use the earth and water as the balancers and the air and fire as the energy movers.
* Light the incense before the ritual so the charcoal is white and hot when you begin. Alternatively, light the smudge so it flares and then when it dies down place it upright in a heatproof container. Ventilate the room well and keep children and pets out of the way.
* Arrange the four elemental substances in a tight square in the centre of the affected area on a low table. Each should be no more than about 2.5 cm/1 in from the next, with the earth in the north and so on.
* Draw protection round yourself as the elemental energies, even channelled through natural substances, can be powerful. Four guardian gatekeeper crystals, one in each corner is, I think, more effective for this kind of ritual than circle casting as it does not cramp the elemental energies, but nevertheless ensures that they are benign. However, some people do prefer a circle. Jet, black tourmaline or any brown agates are good gatekeepers, as is smoky or rutilated quartz.
* Facing north, request the assistance of the elementals (don't summon or demand) and that they will enter their own elemental substance, for the duration of the ritual.
* Light the candle and with the crystal in your receptive hand and the candle in the other, face north.
* Proceed to lift and move the candle and crystal in front of you, crossing your hands at about face height, to establish a slow regular movement of the two elements (keeping the candle at a safe distance).
* As you do so, say nine times:

> *Earth and fire, rock and flame, earth and fire, rock and flame, release stagnation.*

* Return the candle and crystal to their places and put the first of the incense on the charcoal or blow on the smudge to create a steady stream of smoke (relight if necessary).
* Taking the water bowl in your receptive hand and the incense or smudge in the power hand, proceed to lift them in front of you, as with the candle and crystal.
* Cross your hands as you hold them at about face height, in a regular rhythm. Say nine times:

> *Water, air, flowing fragrance, water, air, flowing fragrance, release stagnation.*

* Return the water bowl and incense or smudge to their places. With your hands spiralling upwards and downwards in front of your face above your head, down as far as your waist height, in serpentine movements, move in three clockwise, then three anticlockwise, then three clockwise circles. As you move, say faster while moving faster:

Elementals all, free stagnation. So shall it be.

❋ On the final words, blow out the candle as hard as you can, raise your hands above your head and swing them back on either side of your body and forwards again, saying:

Henceforward shall this place be free.

Or if you were working for good luck:

Good luck be mine.

❋ Thank the elementals and request that they return to their own places.
❋ No matter how bad the weather, take the four elemental substances outside immediately.
❋ Tip the water over the incense or smudge so it hisses and over the crystal to cleanse it. Then tip the rest away. Generally you don't douse smudge or incense as part of a ritual, but in this case it will rapidly remove any free-floating elemental energy that might buzz around. But if you prefer, have some sand or earth nearby for the same purpose.
❋ Dispose of the candle and incense or smudge in an outdoor bin or if it is a beeswax candle you can bury it. Leave the bowl and crystal outside for 24 hours so that any lingering elemental power can return to its undifferentiated state.
❋ Leave the gatekeeper crystals in place also for 24 hours and then wash and put them to dry in natural light.

Drawing elemental power from within nature

The elemental powers have non-tangible or psychological/psychic powers that can be attracted into your life by calling on the physical or tangible powers of the relevant elemental force (see next page). The process occurs by transference during contact with the physical form of the element that contains the essence of the elemental spirit.

The best places to connect with the different elements are listed on pages 31–37. You may feel that some of these locations are a little out of reach, but wherever you live you can find a spot where each elemental power is potent. For example, you might not often be able to connect with fire in the desert or on shimmering sand on the seashore. You can, however, find a stretch of baked earth, abandoned builders' sand (or buy a bag from the local DIY store), a child's sand box in a playground or in your garden.

Holidays and weekends away offer an opportunity to explore the elementals in their more exotic settings. You can then recall the miles of pure white sand in shimmering heat when working in the sand box in the garden. Since elementals can be affected by human thoughts, imagining an exciting elemental location will transfer the full potency of the elementals to a localised setting.

The following are the non-tangible or mental qualities you can absorb from the elementals, and also the areas of your life they can affect positively.

Earth

Qualities: Stability, common sense, practical abilities, caretaking of the earth, protectiveness, upholding of tradition, love of beauty, patience, perseverance, generosity, acceptance of others, nurturance

Areas of power: Abundance and prosperity, fertility, finance, law and order, institutions, authority, motherhood, the physical body, food, home and family, animals, the land, agriculture, horticulture, environmentalism

Air

Qualities: Logic, clear focus, an enquiring and analytical mind, the ability to communicate clearly, concentration, versatility, adaptability, the quest for truth, commercial and technological acumen, healing powers

Areas of power: New beginnings, change, health and healing, teaching, travel, house or career moves, knowledge, examinations, the media, science, ideas, ideals, money-spinning

Fire

Qualities: Fertility in all aspects of life, creativity, light-bringing, power, passion, joy, initiation, transformation, courage, mysticism, clairvoyance, prophecy, spirituality

Areas of power: Ambition, achievement, illumination, inspiration, all creative and artistic ventures, poetry, art, sculpture, writing, music, dance, religion and spirituality, innovation, sexuality, the destruction of what is no longer needed, binding and banishing, protection, psychic powers (especially higher ones such as channelling)

Water

Qualities: Intuition, empathy, sympathy, healing with crystals and herbs, inner harmony, peace-making, unconscious wisdom, divinatory powers (especially those connected with water), ability to merge and interconnect with nature, the cycles of the seasons, the life cycle

Areas of power: Lovers, love, relationships, friendship, dreams, the cycle of birth, death and rebirth, purification rites, healing, the use of the powers of nature, water and sea magick, moon magick, travel by sea

Six steps to absorbing elemental strength

1 Experience the elements from the inside

For earth, walk barefoot on sand, soil or grass, press your hands against trees, trudge through snow or piles of leaves; sit on the earth or grass and allow the elemental strength to flow upwards through your feet and perineum.

For air, walk against the wind, run downhill, fly a kite, visit a fragrant rose garden, look up at the stars and breathe slowly and deeply so you breathe in time with nature.

For fire, walk in sunlight at different times of day and in different seasons, use holidays to experience hot as well as more temperate places or vice versa, light a bonfire or sit by an open fire in the dark and watch the fire faeries.

For water, paddle in a flowing stream; watch a waterfall, run through the rain, feel the foam as you wade into the sea, swim in a pool illuminated by lights, splash in a Jacuzzi or whirlpool bath.

2 Merge with the powers

Banish conscious thoughts and analysis and become part of the wind that blows, the sudden fierce rain shower or hail that lashes you as you run for shelter. Watch a storm and, as when you were a child, count the seconds between the thunder claps. Freewheel down a hill on your bicycle, paddle upstream, roll down a grassy slope, or skate over ice.

The secret is to connect physically rather than to meditate on nature. Dive into life and play as you did when you were a child. Roll in the snow and make snow angels with your outstretched arms and on a beach bury your feet in sand.

3 Exchange tangible, physical energies with the elementals

Pretend you are playing catch and extend your receptive hand towards the sun to receive fire power, and then push power out of your body with the other hand back towards the sun. Establish a rhythm and you will feel your own power building up within you.

Then you can gradually slow the game down until it stops naturally. You can do the same in a swimming pool or Jacuzzi, pushing water away and then scooping it towards you.

Push your hands, palms upright and outwards on a windy day to make the two-way air connection.

For earth, scoop up sand or soft soil with one hand and make a castle with the other, so that you establish a natural spontaneous rhythm.

4 Greet the elementals in nature

Using your experiences of the elements, create four elemental chants that you will use to make contact with each of the elements. Chants really are very easy to devise (see page 298). They don't need to rhyme, to be complex or to use thee and thou. They are just a personal declaration of the joy and the wonder of nature as expressed through and in the four elements. You can incorporate these elemental chants into other rituals when you need to raise power and combine the four where appropriate.

5 The non-tangible or psychic/psychological energy exchange

Kneel, sit or stand so you are surrounded by the elemental power and ask quite simply and quietly for the physical strength to be transferred into the psychological power in the area of life where it is required. You don't need to raise or release power for it is all around you and within you.

Then offer what you can, however small, to put energy back into the specific element from which you are taking it. Helping wild birds or building a bat box would be a suitable air offering, or you could do something on a more intellectual level.

6 Ending the elemental encounter

Don't be in too much of a hurry to end the ritual. Slow, gradual withdrawal where you consciously separate yourself from the elements will ensure that the energy is focused and not excessive or enervating.

Thank the element and press down with hands and feet on the ground or point your fingers downwards if you are standing and let the excess energy drain away.

Then slowly walk away from the place, without looking backwards.

Don't switch on your mobile phone yet (of course you switched it off before the ritual!). The world will wait and, though your new found power is humming away like a well-tuned engine, take time to settle back into yourself before climbing that emotional mountain or fighting the office dragon.

4

FAERIE MAGICK

Faeries are the most commonly reported form of nature essences. They have been described either as opalescent beings that live in faerie courts or as tiny winged ethereal creatures that fly around magickal glades especially near water.

Faeries can be friendly to mortals and bring good luck and prosperity to those they favour. However they can also, like nature herself, be cruel and unpredictable. There are tales from the folklore of many lands of young men or women, especially young brides and mothers, being spirited away to faerieland by the queen or king. They would be returned years later (seemingly only an hour or two in fey time) to find all their family old or even long dead. However, faeries are just one form of the natural essences that embody elemental energies in more permanent forms. Fey creatures have been reported in lands as diverse as England — especially Sussex and Cornwall, Scotland, Ireland, the Isle of Man — Scandinavia, France, Germany, Eastern Europe, Russia, Japan, America, Australia and Africa.

Indeed, in lands where nature still predominates, nature essences are accepted as part of the everyday world and are asked for protection and help. In Sweden, it is common among the general population to prepare a special porridge sweetened with honey, for the house elves on Christmas Eve to ensure luck remains with the home. At harvest time in Eastern and Western Europe until comparatively recently a few apples and sheaves of corn would be left unpicked as a tribute to the little people.

Modern experiences

With increasing industrialisation and the increased use of transport, we no longer walk huge distances through open countryside or sleep at night on hillsides. Faerie and nature-spirit sightings are much rarer in the modern world. However, children still report seeing faeries and nature essences and some can clearly recall early childhood experiences even when they are teenagers. Anna, who is now 15 and lives in Sundsvall in northern Sweden, used to talk regularly to the gnomes living by the local stream, when she was about five years old. She told me there were two couples and the men had long white beards and pointed red hats. One of the male gnomes was older; both wore green clothes. Their wives also had green dresses and there were two small gnome children with them. One day a local boy asked Anna who she was talking to. She said it was to the little people, and he told her she was crazy. Anna says that after that she never talked to them again, though she still saw them.

Faeries can even turn up in the centre of a town. Libby lives in Liverpool and, though now in her forties, can remember playing with faeries when she was young, in her terraced home. She would make a bed every night in her chest of drawers for one particular faerie. Libby says the faeries were very tiny and very pretty and, above all, fun.

Once at school in the playground some children wouldn't let Libby join in their game. She felt very left out, so lay down at the side of the playground so that her face was in the grass. She could see the faeries in the blades of grass but only, she said, if she put her face right down.

The hidden world of the fey

Pan is the god of the nature spirits and is sometimes associated with Puck who is the mischievous and quite malevolent faerie in Shakespeare's *Midsummer Night's Dream*. Pan is described as half-man and half-goat and is attended by fauns who have horns, the hooves of a goat and a short tail, similar to Greek satyrs. In modern Italy, fauns are the faeries who guard fields and forests.

Pan plays upon his magickal pipes made of elder wood to call the nature spirits and also (like the elf king of legend) to cause mortals to dance until they drop (see also the Celtic Cernunnos, the horned god, on page 211).

Though you may not want to follow the sound of faerie music, there are a number of ways you can identify faerie places.

* An obvious indication of the faerie colonies once said to inhabit every hillside, are names such as Puck Pool or Faerie Hill.
* Old burial mounds, sacred sites and the paths between them are where you will most easily sense their energies and at twilight see the darting figures you may at first think are rabbits in the grass.
* Dawn or just before sunset are good times for fey encounters, as is midnight. Some nature essences, like dwarves, cannot come out in sunlight.
* Faeries can be seen dancing in faerie rings, the circles of inedible mushrooms or toadstools, usually red with white spots, that feature in all the best faerie stories. They grow naturally in grassy places in Eastern and Western Europe, Britain, Scandinavia and North America and may spring up after rain.
* Faeries are likely to inhabit any place where faerie flowers grow in profusion. These include bluebells, cowslips, ferns, foxgloves, harebells, lady's smock, lily of the valley, primroses, thistles, thyme, and flowering yellow St John's wort; also clover or shamrocks in Ireland. A four-leafed clover will give you the power to see the fey people at any time. Any flower with bells or flower petals or leaves like cups are fey flowers, as are plants growing alongside water.
* The space between two oaks traditionally offers an entrance to faerieland. Anywhere that has faerie trees, which include the elder, hawthorn and willow, or where the three magickal trees oak, ash and thorn grow together is also a potential site for seeing faeries.

* On Fridays, the day of Frigg, the Viking mother goddess and protector of faeries, magickal beings hold sway. For this reason you should not cut your hair or nails on a Friday or it is said the faeries will use the clippings to play tricks on you.
* The old agricultural festivals are also occasions when faerie activity reaches a height and so they may be more readily visible; notably Walpurgisnacht, Beltane or May eve on 30 April, midsummer eve (23 June), the true summer solstice whose eve is around 20 June and, most significantly, Hallowe'en.

Elemental nature beings

A popular view that still persists in countries of Celtic origin is that faeries are fallen angels driven out of heaven with Lucifer, but not sufficiently evil to be cast into hell. A faerie's station in life was determined by where he or she was cast down on to the earth. For example, those who fell in water became undines or water nymphs.

The 16th-century alchemist Paracelsus, who is credited with great medical and magickal expertise, identified the four personified forms of the elemental forces (the first to appear for each element in the list below), but if you identify with one of the other spirits of the element, then work with that. I tend to prefer to work with fire faeries rather than Paracelsus' elemental salamanders that seem less related to humans.

Earth nature spirits

A large number of nature spirits belong to the earth, though some may have wings. The earth spirits are listed below, starting with the main earth elemental spirit, the gnome.

Gnomes

Originating in northern Europe and Scandinavia, these ancient dwarf-like creatures are said to live mainly underground or in deep forests for a thousand years. Some live in the forest. They vary in size from 60 to 90 cm/2 to 3 feet and resemble garden gnome statues, though they are generally browner and more gnarled.

They are ruled by Gob whose throne is covered with crystals, silver and gold. He is guardian of miners and of the nature spirits who live or work in the earth, for example dwarves and mine spirits.

Earth elementals are also ruled by Galadriel, made famous in Tolkien's *Lord of the Rings*, the original faerie godmother.

Gnomes care for the earth, the minerals and metals, the roots of plants and for forest animals and birds.

Dwarves

Dwarves are associated with Germany, Scandinavia and Switzerland. Male, small, wrinkled and grey-bearded even when young, they mine for and jealously guard gems and minerals. Famed for forging magickal weapons, they avoid sunlight for fear of being turned to stone.

Duegar are malicious French and northern English dwarves who guard the ancient faerie paths and can be malevolent to travellers; dressed in lamb and mole skin, they are blamed for removing signposts.

Dryads

Dryads are female tree nymphs, so named in Ancient Greece, and are associated especially with willow (the tree of the moon), oak and ash. Hamadryads remain within the same tree, especially oak trees and die if it is cut down. Hamadryadniks are Eastern European tree spirits, akin to hamadryads who disguise themselves as foliage, but, unusually for tree spirits, they leave their homes during daylight.

Mine spirits

Knockers are dwarf-like Cornish mine faeries and Coblynau the Welsh equivalent. They are left tributes of food and drink by miners and in return warn of danger by tapping sounds. In the Andes, the Tio or earth spirits are under the care of our lady of the mineshaft, a name for the Virgin Mary whose worship replaced the old earth goddess.

Leprechauns

Irish faerie shoemakers, dressed in green with tricorn hats, leprechauns are solitary because they guard ancient treasure, which they hide in crocks that can be revealed but rarely captured. The elusive end of the rainbow invariably shines over one of these hiding places.

Dark or earth elves

Found in troops in Western Europe, especially Germany, Netherlands and Scandinavia, dark or earth elves live in underworld realms and are skilled metalworkers. They are also expert spinners even, according to Grimm's faerie story, spinning straw into gold.

Mound elves, a sub-group of the dark elves, can be helpful or malicious according to whim. They live above ground near ancient burial mounds or in dark forests like the Black Forest.

Korrs or Korreds are male Breton elves with huge heads and spiky hair who guard ancient stones and stone circles in Brittany; believed to have created the sacred sites, they frighten away those who would desecrate the stones.

Light elves are air spirits.

Pixies

Small, dark, winged Cornish elves, pixies are said to have once been Picts who have continued to diminish in size. In Cornwall there are said to be two kinds of pixies: those who live on land and those who make their homes close to the sea between the high and low water marks of the tide. Said to be no larger than a human hand, but shape shifters who can increase or decrease their size, they are tricksters, stealing horses at night to ride them across the moor, twisting and tangling their manes. Pixies also lead humans in circles using the powers of illusion to create and cause paths to disappear, calling down patches of mist alternated by dazzling sunshine, creating lights at night to indicate houses that are not there and making marshland appear solid.

Lessons we can learn from contact with earth spirits and gifts they bring us: Protection of ourselves, our homes and of all animals and plants; herbal and crystal wisdom; security; prosperity; good luck; patience and perseverance; practical skills

Earth places: Caves; ancient sites, such as burial mounds and stone circles; forests and forest clearings; faerie rings; farm buildings and houses especially with wood-burning stoves or open hearths; gardens

A house spirit spell to welcome/ attract household essences to bring good fortune, health and prosperity to your home

Every land has its house elves or gnomes.

The *tomte, hustomte* or *nisse* of Scandinavia, the Netherlands and Germany is described as a small, elderly man spirit who lives in houses, often in the store cupboard or in stables, barns or grain stores on farms. He wears grey, and a red knitted cap, sometimes having a white beard. If offended, he will leave the home, taking good luck with him.

In Scotland, and England, they are called brownies (*bwbach* or *bwca* in Wales) because of their brown skins and clothing, and come out at night. You may occasionally see one out of the corner of your eye early on a dark morning or if you are working late at night in the home.

In Poland, Domowije is the grandfather house spirit and keeps peace in return for nightly bread and cheese or sweetened porridge. He lives on the threshold under the door or under the stove.

In Russia, house elves called *domovoi* (the feminine form is *domovikha*), dwell in apartments as well as rural homes and help with household tasks. Dolya, a tiny old lady who brings good luck, lives behind the stove. Dolya manifests herself either as a grey-haired old woman or a young beautiful woman at the birth of a child.

In Ireland and Scotland and parts of America, Australia, New Zealand and South Africa to which people from Celtic lands travelled as colonists, some fortunate homes have a *bean-tighe*, a faerie housekeeper. She guards children, especially during the night, cares for family animals and sweeps the hearth. She also helps with household chores and supplements the mother's work if she is tired.

Even if you do not accept the concept of house elves literally, you can work with the benign, protective and luck-bringing powers they represent.

You will need: A dark place in your home that will remain undisturbed, whether a hearth, a cosy corner, a shelf or an alcove close to the stove or an outbuilding. Floorboards or tiles are better than carpet for house elf sanctuaries.

A small table or stool; a wooden or pottery offerings bowl (fey people are not keen on metal, especially iron, except as tools); very tiny crystal chippings as offerings (these are available from most crystal stores or on the Internet, or substitute glass nuggets in silver and gold or bright colours); a small ceramic or wooden pot with a lid; nuts and seeds for birds or crumbled bread (small fat balls when the baby birds are first flying as nuts and seeds are bad for them); a small icon such as a pottery gnome or dwarf or even a small troll (ugly but benign) to focus the energies of the house elf corner; a cosy rug or blanket to make it welcoming; a small beeswax candle in a natural colour; a small natural fabric drawstring bag.

Timing: Fridays before bed and when you get up the next morning, as both Friday and Saturday are good earth spirit days

* On the first Friday, before bed set your house spirit icon in place and light the beeswax candle.
* Speaking into the flame and looking through it to a dark area, ask that your home may be blessed by the presence of kindly earth spirits and that they will bring health, prosperity, good luck and protection to your home.
* Set the offerings dish to the left of the candle and the pot with the lid on the right.
* Into the offerings dish put a handful of crystal chippings or a glass nugget and say:

> *Wealth as a gift, not as payment, kind spirits, I leave this for you. I ask that you may draw on your store of treasures to bring me likewise blessings.*

* Next into the pot scatter a few seeds or some nuts or put in a tiny fat ball, saying:

> *Food I offer as gift, not payment. May I be likewise blessed with abundance in my home.*

* Finally, hold your hands a comfortable distance above the candle flame, palms down and say:

> *Protect, kind spirits, I ask, my home and family pets and goods from harm. I offer you my shelter and respect in return as gift and not as payment.*

* Blow out the candle and you may hear a rustling or feel scurrying movements round you. You aren't suddenly invaded by mice but by house elves either entering your premises for the first time or making themselves known.
* Put the lid on the pot and go quietly away for they do not like being disturbed.
* In the morning, tip the seeds, nuts or bread outdoors for the birds and put the chippings or nuggets in the drawstring bag, which you should hide close by the house elf place.
* Repeat every fourth Friday if you can or if you are going away leave the offerings early. Ask the house elves to protect the premises while you are away. Include a few coriander or cumin seeds in the seed mix as these are protective against thieves. Put these out for the birds on your return.
* On subsequent Fridays leave the candle to burn through in a safe container and write 'Blessings be' in the melted beeswax with a small twig. Burn or bury the wax outdoors or in a large planted pot of earth.

* When the drawstring bag is filled, hide it around your home with that Friday's wax talisman, which you will save overnight as protection and to start a new bag. Replace the hidden first bag when you have filled a second and return the contents with a sprinkling of dried thyme or rosemary to the earth.
* If you have received special luck, leave out a bowl of porridge sweetened with honey or rice pudding likewise sweetened. Elves eat only the essence of the food so you can feed it to an animal or leave to dry and add to a bird mix.

Air nature spirits

The air spirits are listed below, starting with the main air elemental spirit, the sylph.

Sylphs

Sylphs are the winged air spirits who live for hundreds of years and can, it is said, attain an immortal soul through good deeds. They reside on mountain tops and their ruler, Paralda, lives on the highest mountain of earth.

Sylphs may assume human form for short periods of time and vary in size from as large as a human to much smaller, like a tiny bird or large butterfly; they are most usually seen in the wind.

Sylphs carry new seeds for germination and oversee cross-pollination of species as well as ensuring that the insect, butterfly and moth world continues to flourish and remain in balance.

Light elves

These winged creatures have elven kings and queens who possess great magickal and prophetic ability and live in courts like faeries. The light or air elves are associated with forest glades, faerie circles and woodlands and are much more ethereal than their earthier cousins, the lower dark elves. But in Germany the erl or elf king is greatly feared by mortals.

In England the term 'elves' is used especially for small faerie mischievous boys, while in Scotland faerieland is called Elfhame and elves are synonymous with faeries of human proportions. Though elves are gifted musicians, they have the unfortunate habit of making mortals dance until they drop.

Sprites

Sprites frequently assume the form of birds. Hyter sprites are from East Anglia but are also found in Spain and Mexico; they live in flocks or groups.

Folletti

These are Spanish and Mexican faeries who shape shift into butterflies and travel on the wind, sometimes causing dust clouds.

Gans

Mountain spirits of the Apache Indian nation, gans are invoked in dance, song and night-time rituals for safe journeys and good weather, especially in mountainous regions.

Tengu

These Japanese winged woodland faeries carry fans made of feathers; they may change into woodland animals, but have little contact with mortals.

Jimaninos/jimaninas

These winged nature spirits live in Mexico and Central America, but probably originated from Spain, rather than being indigenous.

They are said to resemble well-fed small children and are most visible on El Dia del Muerte, the Mexican days of the dead on 1 and 2 November, when departed children are remembered.

Lessons we can learn from contact with air spirits and gifts they bring us: Clear focus, the ability to communicate clearly, improved memory, concentration, versatility, health, advantageous risk-taking and speculation, new beginnings, travel, the granting of wishes

Air places: Mountain tops, hills, towers, the sky, pyramids, open plains, tall buildings, balconies, roof gardens, in clouds, on the wind, open windows upstairs in a home

An air spirit bubble spell

Air magick is associated with wishes and you can send wishes into the air in the form of bubbles. These rise high and can carry the wishes to the air spirits who will transform dreams and desires into actuality. You can choose any wish, not only in those areas ruled by air.

You will need: A bubble blower and bubbles. You can use a child's bubble-blowing set or make environmentally friendly bubbles with a pure liquid soap and distilled water. Alternatively, make a bubble blower out of any circle such as twisted wire or even the end of a straw dipped into the bubble mix. For a giant bubble wand for big wishes, twirl a coat hanger into a perfect circle, bending the hook to make a handle and taping it so that it isn't too sharp to hold. Making your own solution enables you to empower it.

Timing: Bubbles blow best on a cloudy day or after rain when it is not too cold. Wednesday and Thursday are the special air spirit days

* Make your bubble solution. Use 3 parts of an environmentally friendly liquid soap, washing-up liquid or baby shampoo, 7–10 parts of distilled water (some people recommend very warm water but I use cold) and 1 part of glycerine.

Glycerine is not essential but gives lovely rainbow-coloured bubbles.

* You can make more or less mixture, according to the size of your bubble blower and the number of bubbles you want to blow. It's a good idea to make plenty as you will repeat the spell weekly for a month and the mixture can be stored in lidded containers.
* Put the ingredients into a bowl, mix gently with a whisk or spoon, saying softly over and over again:

You spirits of the air, sprites and sylphs and rainbow butterfly folletti, aid my wish that it may travel to the skies and be transformed.

* When the mixture is bubbly, shake it ten times, naming your wish ten times.
* Put the bubbles in a sealed container and, as late on Wednesday afternoon as possible, go to a hilly place or open an upstairs window.
* Holding the bubbles and blower, recite the mixing chant three times and name your wish three times. If you are using a commercial bubble set, this stage is very important to empower the mix.
* Blow the first bubble and as it floats away, say:

Wish fly free, go from my thoughts to reality.

* Continue blowing and wishing (more than one wish if you like) until you feel you have blown enough bubbles. Thank the spirits of the air.
* If you really want to connect with the spell, practise blowing bubbles with your hands beforehand. Put the bubble mix in an open, flat container, dip your hands in it, lock your thumbs and slowly make a circle with your joined hands. Gently blow. This is totally magickal once you master it and was taught to me by a friend's child.
* Repeat the spell weekly for four weeks in total, if possible on a Wednesday and if possible in the same location.

Fire spirits

These are the least common nature spirits and are very volatile. As with pure fire elementals, you should only work with fire spirits when you feel positive. The fire spirits are listed below, starting with the main fire elemental spirit, the salamander.

Salamanders

These are the lizard people who come from the desert places of the Middle East. They have been described as fire lizards, about 30 cm/1 foot or more in length or as elongated wand-like beings in the shape of flames.

Though salamanders mainly live in volcanoes or lakes of fire, they also appear in ritual fires made of wood, in furnaces and forges, in forest fires and hot sandy places in shimmering heat when they resemble golden lizards.

Their ruler is a flaming being called Djin, a glorious flame-like creature with flashing ruby eyes, who is never still.

Salamanders do occasionally manifest as beautiful dancing females with lizard-like eyes and flaming hair, and have been associated with desert mirages.

Their work, like that of other fire spirits, is to make transformation possible, so that decomposition is followed by regeneration and that light and warmth flow to make plants and creatures grow.

Djinn or Jinns

In Islamic tradition, Jinns live on earth in a parallel universe and so are invisible. They were created, it is said, before mortals from smokeless fire.

Originating in the Middle East, the Jinn are shape-shifting creatures and are best known as genies in the stories of Aladdin.

Kept in bottles or oil lamps to be summoned by their masters, who were either potentates or master magicians, they were dangerous servants, able to travel almost with the speed of light, but bringing destruction to any who tried to abuse their power. Often they would only grant a limited number of wishes that needed to be phrased carefully, as the genie would bring what was asked for literally. This is definitely not a magickal avenue to pursue.

Because of their shape-shifting abilities, Djinn have been linked in recent years with some extra-terrestrial encounters, explicable as meetings with these spirits in one of their stranger manifestations

They will appear rarely in oil lamps and oil-based candle flames.

Fire faeries

These are by far the most common and friendly of the unpredictable fire spirits and may be seen in any open fire or hearth, around bonfires, in cauldrons, in fires lit on sandy beaches and in the modern world round barbecues, chimeneas and fire dishes. They also prefer beeswax candles and especially like fossil fuels such as barbecue coals. I suggest you work with them rather than the other fire spirits unless you are very experienced in magick. You may also see fire faeries as fireflies.

Lessons we can learn from contact with fire spirits and gifts they bring us: Fertility in all aspects of life, creativity, power, passion, joy, transformation, courage, mysticism, clairvoyance, prophecy, spirituality, ambition, achievement, illumination, removing what we no longer need from our life

Fire places: Bonfires, deserts, furnaces, hearths, volcanoes, sacred festival fires, hilltop beacons, all conflagrations, solar eclipses, sunrises and sunsets, lightning, cauldrons, fire dishes, chimeneas, barbecues

A fire spirit spell for power, courage or to make a major change

Though this is a personal spell, you can carry it out with any number of people for individual or collective purposes as long as they each have three twigs and some dried thyme.

You will need: An outdoor fire source on which you can burn small pieces of wood; dried thyme (the protective nature spirit herb) in a dish; three sticks or twigs (long enough to hold in the fire for a moment without burning yourself; put them away from the fire to collect when you are ready). If you have more than one person present, a drummer can help to build up the power (or play drum music well away from the fire).

Timing: After dark and best of all on one of the seasonal festivals, but any Tuesday or Sunday is fire spirit day

* Make an outdoor fire (a bonfire or a fire in a chimenea or large cauldron or fire dish, see page 88).
* Light the fire and wait until you see the sparks flying. Before long you may notice the fire faeries not only in the sparks but dancing round the fire — and, if it is a big fire, maybe an elongated figure, a salamander and fireflies or little dancing balls of light.
* Begin to circle the fire clockwise with your dish of thyme and chant continuously as you throw thyme on the fire:

> *Spirits of the fire, come only in good intent; dance with me, make me flame,*
> *for I seek power / courage / change only with good intent.*

* When the thyme is gone, slow yourself so you can feel the power throbbing in a controlled way within you.
* Taking your first piece of wood, name the power you need and hold it in the fire carefully until it begins to smoulder.
* At this point cast the stick into the fire and say:

> *Fuel to fire, flame to flame, give I ask, what I do name. (Name your need again.)*

* Circle the fire three more times clockwise, repeating continuously:

> *Fuel to fire, flame to flame, give I ask, what I do name. (Name your need each time.)*

* Repeat the process for the other two pieces of wood and when you have circled the fire for the last time, stop.
* Leap into the air or clap and stamp and call:

> *Salamanders, djinn, fire faeries, genies all, grant me this _____ (name your need),*
> *and bring all to fruition.*

* At the Beltane, May eve festival, people would leap over the twin fires — the height they jumped indicating the height the corn would grow. However, I would strongly discourage you from jumping over fires.
* If working with other people, you can co-ordinate the casting of wood and chanting to reach a powerful climax.
* Now circle slowly anticlockwise round the fire, bidding the fire faeries farewell and giving thanks for their power and good intent.
* Do not fuel the fire source any more but let it die down naturally.
* Sprinkle the ashes when cool on the garden or cast a token few on any open space to bring fertility in every way into your life.

Water spirits

Water is another well-populated element for nature spirits. Water spirits are very easy to work with and mostly good-tempered. The water spirits are listed below, starting with the main water elemental spirit, the undines.

Undines

These elemental spirits of water, who originated in the Aegean Sea, live in coral caves under the ocean, on the shores of lakes and the banks of rivers, in estuaries or on marshlands. They shimmer with all the colours of water in sunlight and are so insubstantial they can rarely be seen, except clairvoyantly or as a rainbow within a waterfall or fountain.

The ruler of the undines is a being called Necksa.

They work to conserve water creatures, the sea itself and its plant life.

Mer people

Mer people are invariably regarded as beautiful, with human heads and bodies to the waist, and a fish tail below the waist. Sailors throughout the ages have brought back tales of beautiful sea women with mesmeric voices, sitting on rocks combing their long golden hair.

Usually Mer people are helpful, saving drowning sailors and guiding ships away from rocks, though occasionally they can be malevolent.

Fossegrim

These Norwegian water faeries disappear into mist where their feet should be. Guardians of waterfalls and fjords, they play exquisite harp music and have mesmeric voices, which can enchant mortals. They are able to change rapidly from male to female.

Kappa

These are malevolent water spirits in Japan who attack swimmers and fisher folk in remote lakes and rivers.

Kul

An Inuit water spirit, the kul helps fishermen to find the shoals and protects them. He can be unpredictable, reflecting the wildness of the Arctic seas, and so is offered the first fish of the season.

Naiads

The naiads preside over rivers, streams, brooks, springs, fountains, lakes, ponds, wells and marshes. They can also be associated with trees, especially those close to water.

Selkies

The seal maidens or selkies of Scotland, Ireland and North American shores assume mortal form on land and were sometimes captured by or agreed to marry a human husband. After a while they would wish to return to their own world, but they could only go back if they still had their sealskins. Male selkies are ugly and create storms to deter seal hunters.

Tylwyth teg

Known as the fair family in Wales and also bendith y mammau (mothers' blessing), the tylwyth teg live either beneath lakes, on faerie islands or underground in beautiful palaces. They are kind to children, those who have no money and to mothers. Occasionally they were known to marry mortals, but the unions did not last.

Well spirits

These are most commonly described as beautiful women in white. For example, the Breton corrigans are seen close to wells, fountains and sacred springs. Corrigans are said to be former pagan priestesses who refused to convert to Christianity; as a punishment they become hideous hags by day and hide themselves away.

Well spirits are traditionally invoked for female fertility and healing. Some, like the spirit of the Faerie's Pin Well, in Selby in Yorkshire, so named after the custom of young women dropping bent pins, made of gold or silver, would give suppliants a dream of a future bridegroom.

Lessons we can learn from contact with water spirits and gifts they can bring us: Intuition, peace, unconscious wisdom, the ability to merge and interconnect with nature in all its forms, female fertility, love, increase in every way, reconciliation and forgiveness, healing and healing powers, the ability to let go of the past

Water places: The ocean, rivers, lakes, pools, sacred wells and streams, marshland, bridges, flood plains

A water spirit spell for forgiveness

Whether you need to forgive someone for an injustice that can't be put right, to mend a quarrel or to forgive yourself for a stupid mistake that cost you dearly, water spirits are wonderfully healing and will carry away sorrow, anger or regrets.

This is an updated version of an earlier spell that I have used for years. Since linking it with the water spirits it has become doubly effective.

You will need: A bridge over flowing water (the setting does not matter); five white flowers; a small bottle of still mineral water; a cheap silver-coloured earring or ring or a silver or a small aquamarine, jade, tourmaline or fluorite crystal

Timing: Towards sunset but while still light. A Monday or Friday is good for water spirit work

✱ Stand on the bridge facing upstream.

✱ Say:

> *Spirits of the water, kindly naiads and undines, carry from me this burden,*
> *wash away this sorrow (name it). So do I give you tribute.*

❈ Drop your first flower in the water and go to the other side of the bridge to watch it flow through and off downstream. Say:

> *Water under the bridge, the gain and the loss, the pain and the joy are now one and the*
> *same and hurt is no more.*

❈ Repeat the action and words until all five flowers are gone.
❈ Return to face upstream and pour a few drops of water into the river or streams, saying:

> *What cannot be now brought back or saved, I let go in peace and in forgiveness.*

❈ Drink a little of the water and say:

> *What still remains is precious and brings healing.*

❈ Repeat until the water is gone.
❈ Cast the crystal, ring or earring into the water as thanks. Go and either enjoy your new sense of freedom or take steps to mend the quarrel.

FURTHER READING

Alchemy
Holyard, E J, *Alchemy*, 1990, Dover Publications
Jung, Carl Gustav, *Alchemical Studies*, 1983, Princetown University Press

Amulets and talismans
Gonzalez-Wipler, Migene, *Complete Guide to Amulets and Talismans*, 1991, Llewellyn
Thomas, Willam, and Pavitt, Kate, *The Book of Talismans, Amulets and Zodiacal Gems*, 1998, Kessinger

Angels, faeries and nature spirits
Bloom, William, *Working with Angels, Faeries and Nature Spirits*, 1998, Piatkus
Burnham, Sophie, *A Book of Angels*, 1990, Ballantine
Eason, Cassandra, *Touched by Angels*, 2005, Foulsham/Quantum
Newcomb, Jacky, *An Angel Treasury*, 2005, Element

Animal powers
Eason, Cassandra, *Psychic Power of Animals*, 2003, Piatkus
Andrews, Ted, *Animal Speak*, 1994, Llewellyn

Annual almanacs
Llewellyn's Almanac, Llewellyn
Llewellyn's Pocket Planner and Ephemeris, Llewellyn
Old Moore's Almanack, Foulsham
Tybol Astrological Almanac, 27 Heversham Avenue, Fulwood, Preston PR2 9TD
Witch's Almanack, Foulsham/Quantum

Candle magick and candle-making
Bruce, Marie, *Candleburning Rituals*, 2001, Foulsham
Buckland, Ray, *Advanced Candle Magic*, 1996, Llewellyn, St Paul, Minnesota
Eason, Cassandra, *Candle Power*, 1999, Blandford
Guy, Gary V, *Easy-to-make Candles*, 1980, Dover Publications
Heath, Maya, *Ceridwen's Handbook of Incense, Oils and Candles: Being a Guide to the Magical and Spiritual Uses of Oils, Incense, Candles and the Like*, 1996, Words of Wisdom International Inc
Innes, Miranda, *The Book of Candles*, 1991, Dorling Kindersley

Larkin, Chris, *The Book of Candlemaking: Creating Scent, Beauty and Light*, 1998, Sterling Publications, New York

Pajeon, Kala and Pajeon, Ketz, *The Candle Magic Workbook*, 1991, Citadel Carol, New York

Celtic spirituality

Anderson, Rosemarie, *Celtic Oracles*, 1999, Piatkus

Eason, Cassandra, *The Modern Day Druidess*, 2004, Piatkus

Ellis-Berresford, Peter, *The Druids*, 1994, Constable Robinson

Green, Miranda, *Dictionary of Celtic Myth and Legend*, 1992, Thames & Hudson

Matthews, Caitlín and John, *The Encyclopaedia of Celtic Wisdom*, 1994, Element

Nichols, Ross, *The Book of Druidry*, 1990, Aquarian/Thorsons

Chakras

Dale, Cyndi, *New Chakra Healing, The Revolutionary 32-Center Energy System*, 1996, Llewellyn

Eason, Cassandra, *Chakra Power*, 2002, Foulsham/Quantum

Karagulla, Shafica, and Van Gelder Kunz, Dora, *Chakras and the Human Energy Field*, 1994, Theosophical University Press

Colour healing and magick

Buckland, Ray, *Practical Color Magic*, 1996, Llewellyn, St Paul, Minnesota

Klotsche, Charles, *Color Medicine: The Secrets of Color/Vibrational Healing*, 1993, Light Technology Publications

Sun, Howard and Dorothy, *Colour Your Life*, Piatkus, 1999

Crystals

Bourgault, Luc, *The American Indian Secrets of Crystal Healing*, 1997, Foulsham/Quantum

Cunningham, Scott, *Encyclopaedia of Crystal, Gem and Metal Magic*, 1991, Llewellyn, St Paul, Minnesota

Eason, Cassandra, *Crystal Healing*, 2002, Foulsham

Eason, Cassandra, *The Illustrated Dictionary of Healing Crystals*, 2004, Collins and Brown

Eason, Cassandra, *Crystals Talk to the Woman Within*, 2000, Foulsham/Quantum

Dowsing and Earth energies

Bailey, Arthur, *Anyone Can Dowse for Better Health*, 1999, Foulsham/Quantum

Eason, Cassandra, *The Complete Guide to Labyrinths*, 2004, Crossing Press, Ten Speed, US

Eason, Cassandra, *Pendulum Power/the Art of the Pendulum*, 2004, Piatkus, Red Wheel Weiser, US

Lonegren, Sig, *Spiritual Dowsing*, 1986, Gothic Images

Flower remedies

Barnard, Julian, *A Guide to the Bach Flower Remedies*, 1992, C W Daniel & Co

Harvey, Clare G, and Cochrane, Amanda, *The Encyclopaedia of Flower Remedies*, 1995, Thorsons/HarperCollins

Korte, Andreas, *Orchids, Gemstones and the Healing Energies*, 1993, Bauer Verlag

Flowers, trees and plants

Graves, Robert, *The White Goddess*, 1988, Faber and Faber (in my opinion the best book on the tree alphabet and tree lore)

Tompkins and Bird, *The Secret Life of Plants*, 1974, Avon Books, New York

Goddesses

Budapest, Z, *The Holy Book of Women's Mysteries*, 1990, Harper Row, New York

Eason, Cassandra, *Complete Guide to Women's Wisdom*, Piatkus, 2002

Farrar, Janet and Stewart, *The Witches' Goddess, The Feminine Principle of Divinity*, 1987, Phoenix Publishing Inc, New York

Gadon, Elinor, *The Once and Future Goddess*, 1990, Aquarian/Thorsons

Starhawk, *The Spiral Dance*, 1999, Harper Row, San Francisco

Healing

Brennan, Barbara Ann, *Hands of Light: A Guide to Healing Through the Human Energy Field*, 1987, Bantam Publishers

Eden, Donna, *Energy Medicine*, 1999, Piatkus

Herbalism

Cunningham, Scott, *The Encyclopaedia of Herbs*, 1997, Llewellyn, St Paul, Minnesota

Lipp, Frank J, *Herbalism*, 1996, Macmillan

Rodway, Marie, *A Wiccan Herbal*, 1997, Foulsham/Quantum

Incenses and oils

Cunningham, Scott, *The Complete Book of Oils, Incenses and Brews*, 1991, Llewellyn, St Paul, Minnesota

Dunwich, Gerena, *The Wicca Garden, A Witch's Guide to Magical and Enchanted Herbs and Plants*, 1996, Citadel, Carol, New York

Eason, Cassandra, *Smudging and Incense Burning Guide*, 2002, Foulsham/Quantum

Radford, Joan, *The Complete Book of Family Aromatherapy* , 1993, Foulsham/Quantum

Native Americans

Meadows, Kenneth, *Earth Medicine*, 1996, Element

Page, James Lynn, *Native American Magic*, 2002, Foulsham/Quantum

Wallace, Black Elk, and Lyon, William, Black Elk, *The Sacred Ways of a Lakota*, 1990, Harper and Row, New York

Psychic phenomena

Eason, Cassandra, *Discover Your Past Lives*, 1995, Foulsham/Quantum

Sheldrake, Rupert, *Dogs that Know When Their Owners Are Coming Home and Other Unexplained Powers of Animals: An Investigation*, 1999, Crown Publishing

Psychic protection

Eason, Cassandra, *Psychic Protection Lifts the Spirit*, 2000, Foulsham/Quantum
Fortune, Dion, *Psychic Self-Defence*, 1988, Aquarian

Seasonal magick, old festivals and mythology

Budge, Wallis, trans., *Book of the Dead*, 1995, Gramercy Books
Cooper, J C, *Aquarian Dictionary of Festivals*, 1990, Aquarian/Thorsons
Green, Marian, *A Calendar of Festivals*, 1991, Element
Stewart, Bob, *Where Is St George? Pagan Imagery in English Folksong*, 1988, Blandford
Walker, Barbara, *The Woman's Encyclopaedia of Myths and Secrets*, 1983, Pandora
Willis, Roy, *World Mythology*, 1993, Piatkus

Shamanism

Castenada, Carlos, *Journey to Ixtlan*, 1972, Penguin
Devereux, Paul, *Shamanism and the Mystery Lines*, 2000, Foulsham/Quantum
Rutherford, Leo, *Your Shamanic Path*, 2001, Piatkus
Wahoo, Dhyani, *Voices of Our Ancestors*, 1987, Shambhala

Theosophy

Blavatsky, Helena, *The Key to Theosophy*, 1991, Theosophical University Press
Blavatsky, Helena, *The Secret Doctrine: The Synthesis of Science, Religion and Philosophy*, 1992, Theosophical University Press

Western magical tradition and the Golden Dawn

Gilbert, R S, *Revelations of the Golden Dawn*, 1997, Foulsham/Quantum
Matthews, Caitlín and John, *The Western Way: A Practical Guide to the Western Mystical Tradition*, 1986, Arkana
Regardie, Israel, *The Golden Dawn: A Complete Course in Practical Ceremonial Magic*, 1989, Llewellyn, St Paul, Minnesota

Witchcraft and magick

Bruce, Marie, *Everyday Spells for a Teenage Witch*, 2004, Foulsham/Quantum
Bruce, Marie, *How to Create a Magical Home*, 2004, Foulsham/Quantum
Bruce, Marie, *Magical Beasts*, 2003, Foulsham/Quantum
Buckland, Raymond, *Buckland's Complete Guide to Witchcraft*, 1997, Llewellyn
Cunningham, Scott, *Living Wicca, A Guide for the Solitary Practitioner*, 1994, Llewellyn
Eason, Cassandra, *Cassandra Eason's Complete Book of Spells*, 2004, Foulsham/Quantum
Eason, Cassandra, *A Complete Guide to Divination*, 2002, Piatkus
Eason, Cassandra, *The Complete Guide to Magic and Ritual*, 1999, Piatkus
Eason, Cassandra, *Every Woman a Witch*, 1996, Foulsham/Quantum
Eason, Cassandra, *Fragrant Magic*, 2003, Foulsham/Quantum
Eason, Cassandra, *Magic Spells for a Happy Life*, 2003, Foulsham/Quantum
Eason, Cassandra, *The Practical Guide to Witchcraft and Magick Spells*, 2001, Foulsham/Quantum
Farrar, Janet and Stewart, *A Witches' Bible*, 1985, Phoenix Publishing Inc., New York
Fortune, Dion, *Applied Magick*, 2000, Samuel Weiser, New York

Fortune, Dion, *Moon Magick* (fiction), 1985, Aquarian
Fortune, Dion, *The Sea Priestess* (fiction), 2000, Samuel Weiser, New York
Gardner, Gerald, *Gardener's Book of Shadows*, 2000, Star Rising Publications
Steele, Tony, *Water Witches*, 1998, Capall Bann Publishing
Valiente, Doreen, *The Charge of the Goddess*, 2000, Hexagon Publications
Valiente, Doreen, *Natural Magic*, 1985, Phoenix Publishing Inc, New York

Witchcraft history
Adler, Margot, *Drawing Down the Moon*, 1997, Penguin, USA
Briggs, Robin, *Witches and Neighbours, The Social and Cultural Context of European Witchcraft*, 1996, HarperCollins
Crowley, Vivienne, *Wicca, The Old Religion in the New Age*, 1989, Aquarian/Thorsons
Guiley, Rosemary Ellen, *The Encyclopaedia of Witches and Witchcraft*, 1989, Facts on File, New York
Murray, Margaret, *The God of the Witches*, 1992, Oxford University Press

Cassandra Eason's website can be found at: www.cassandraeason.co.uk.

INDEX